Egon Ronay's

2006

Guide to the Best

RESTAURANTS

AND

GASTROPUBS

in the UK

Publisher: Egon Ronay Organisation Ltd
Editor-in-chief: Egon Ronay
Editor: David Sinclair
Operations Director: Anneli Cartwright
Legal Adviser: Dante Campailla
Research Base: Nigel Jones
Front Cover: John Dunne
Sales: Derek Searle Associates
Distributed by Macmillan Distribution (MDL)

First published in the United Kingdom
by the Egon Ronay Organisation Limited 2005

Copyright © Egon Ronay Organisation Limited 2005

Egon Ronay Organisation Limited
37 Walton Street
London SW3 2HT

ISBN 0-900624-28-0

Printed and bound in Great Britain by Polestar Wheatons Limited, Exeter

Contents

The gastropub phenomenon

By Egon Ronay

PROUD as we justly are of this country's considerable number of internationally outstanding restaurants, this achievement of culinary excellence, which has taken place gradually, pales into insignificance against the puzzling phenomenon of the sudden emergence of hundreds – yes, there are literally hundreds – of excellent gastropubs (in addition to long established pub-restaurants).

The word 'gastropub' itself is not an ideal one, in contrast to the products of the establishments to which it is applied, and one would be tempted to replace it with 'British bistro', were it not for the fact that the gastropub is such a thoroughly British insititution, and that in a number of ways it is much more appealing than French bistros. So let it be.

In attempting, over the course of many months, to assess the dramatic rise of the gastropub (how we arrived at the number of 300 is explained in the page *About This Guide*, together with our coverage of some 230 top-rated restaurants), I have been intrigued by one fundamental question: Where have all these good, often outstanding cooks been hiding all this time? I say cooks, rather than chefs, partly because they are thoroughly British, with rare and distinguished exceptions, even to the extent of some having given a new lease of life to what is called 'traditional British cooking', and partly because the dexterity and good taste of a great number are less all-encompassing than they

The question is, where have all these good, often oustanding cooks been hiding all this time?

5

are among those running large kitchens. But the skill of many certainly equals the best in French bistros. Anyway, the word 'chef' is *cuisinier* in France, except for the one in charge. The foreign though faint knocking on the British kitchen door is of a Thai character and the theory that Indian is the conquering trend of British diet is certainly not borne out by gastropubs. As for the rapid rise of the genre, there is no obvious explanation for the puzzle except an accelerated spread of word of mouth.

Listen to just a few typical motifs I have selected at random from the gastropub symphony, quoting verbatim from the our anonymous inspectors' hundreds of reports:

'Lobster ravioli with gossamer-thin pasta with foamy shellfish broth and crunchy, tender young fennel; courgette flowers stuffed with ricotta and lightly fried mint; peach tarte Tatin; chargrilled sirloin of grass-fed Aberdeen Angus with a sauce of Pinot Noir and butter; irresistible raspberry crème brûlée; beautifully flavoured Morecambe Bay brown shrimps in light puff pastry with shellfish stock; seared scallops with a salad of cucumbers and fresh cockles in ginger dressing; cold marinade of whitebait with coriander and chillies; sea bass with sautéd garlic shrimps; pot-roast beef with oregano and olives; Lancashire hot-pot mixed with red cabbage, topped with slightly crispy potato crust'.... the list could fill pages.

Amazingly, these delights are created mostly in kitchens a fifth or even a tenth of the size of those in grand restaurants, yet frequently producing food that achieves the same standards.

Not that you will always find these temptations on the menu. In almost all gastropubs blackboards are not only constantly used but are also often changed during the meal, partly because of the capacity of the kitchen, and also because this is a handy way of determining how well some dishes are received. So try to have yourself placed so that

Kitchens a fifth or even a tenth the of size of grand restautants can produce the same standards

the blackboard (and sometimes there will be more than one of them) remains in your sight. But all this is only half the story. The great importance and the greatest difference from French bistros – which strike you as soon as you cross the threshold – lie in the immediate friendliness and heartiness of the welcome, often by the family of the proprietor (it is part of the charm that you cannot always tell the difference). The informality is so much more natural than the underlying artificiality of the determined *lack* of dress code and old-fashioned formality almost de rigueur nowadays at the Claridges level, and which is somewhat jarring.

So your first visit to a gastropub makes you feel like a regular and you forget, and happily fit into, surroundings that are sometimes basic. Then there are often young, easygoing staff, rarely without a smile even when rushed off their feet, even if there might occasionally be a certain lack of formal serving skills. The sometimes long intervals between courses are clearly caused by cramped kitchens and overburdened cooks. Anyway, while you wait, expertly selected and mostly well-kept draught beer is universally available.

Obviously, French bistros and their staff could learn a very great deal from our gastropubs; and so could some of our traditional restaurants. In addition, your bill will be much smaller in gastropubs, not only because prices are generally low (perhaps £12-£13 for a two-course lunch) but also because no one will mind if you order just one dish. And the portions can be huge.

In the midst of all this, though, I perceive a latent danger. The increasing popularity of gastropubs is likely to attract people who used not to eat out, and also to draw in regulars more frequently. One can only hope a resulting but ultimately counter-productive temptation to raise prices will be resisted. In fact, many gastropub prices are even now dangerously near restaurant prices. The other temptation is

The great importance lies in the immediate friendliness and heartiness of the welcome

to compensate for any fall in alcohol consumption at the bar by increasing food prices or, indeed, by foolishly accommodating more diners at the expense of the atmospheric bar space, risking a gradual change in the attractive gastropub character.

Wine prices in gastropubs are modest compared with the unintelligently runaway pricing of lists in most restaurants proper. Many gastropubs serve surprisingly good wines by the glass at between £3 and £3.50, although it has to be said that some do charge too much. There is merit, too, in friendly wine lists of manageable size and, for most customers, of less embarrassing complexity. Such short lists need real know-how or savvy advice, resulting in a higher overall quality. Some even serve all the wines on their lists also by the glass.

Another attractive aspect is that the great majority of gastropubs take pride in local produce which they actively and laudably promote. For example, The Three Fishes in Mitton, Lancashire, not only lists all its thirty-three producers of local food by name and map location on the back of its menus, but also displays their pictures on the walls and even names some dishes after them. Naturally, game is a constant item, much of it locally shot, some, of course, not restricted by the calendar. Cheeses almost always include something local – for instance Kidderton goat's cheese, Burland Green organic 'Brie' (both from Cheshire) and Kirkham's (from Lancashire), Swaledale, Lincolnshire Poacher (made with unpasteurised milk) and many just 'from a local farm'.

Even with local food consciousness and unexpectedly satisfying, mainly British cooking added to the atmosphere of a British pub, there would still be something vital lacking. For it is the heartfelt friendliness, warmth and informality that complete the picture and that have turned gastropubs into the unstoppable success story they have become.

The great majority of gastropubs take pride in local produce, which they actively promote

About This Guide

THE TWO main constituents of this guide are restaurants and gastropubs. They are listed in a single index in alphabetical order, but they are differentiated on the maps by a different symbol as they are, indeed, of a distinctly different character. That of gastropubs, their considerable and fast-growing significance and their uniquely British character, are detailed in the chapter *The Gastropub Phenomenon*.

Our search for good gastropubs covered the whole of the UK and involved great efforts to arrive at a reasonably comprehensive picture. Not only did we wade through all conceivable sources of information, but we also consulted widely, particularly the hoteliers and restaurateurs all over the country in whose judgement we have confidence and some food writers, asking for their tips, which they gave generously and speedily. We are very grateful to them.

This initial research was carried out by true experts, our professional, full-time inspectors (months before they started on their actual inspections), most of whom have been working for this organisation, on and off, for some twenty-five years. We arrived at what we think was an incomparably well-informed list of some 430 gastropubs. All these we then anonymously inspected by means of trial meals, which resulted in the rejection for the purposes of this Guide of 129. (According to our very strict and decades-old practice, our inspectors paid their bills and then introduced themselves to the proprietor or another responsible person to obtain information such as days of closure, prices and so on.)

Many people envy our inspectors' job, but the cry for help from one of them – *A Food Inspector's Lament* – following these pages gives a more realistic impression.

As we progressed and the differences between gastropubs crystallised, it was natural to apply our long-standing system of rating. However, because the very nature of 'restaurants' and 'gastropubs' is so different, to avoid any confusion we introduced a slight change in the meaning of our stars by printing them in colour for gastropubs and in black for restaurants. As always, our stars are awarded for the quality of the cooking, irrespective of all other factors.

It is important to point out that when a gastropub is featured in the Guide at all, even without a star, this means its cooking is very good. One star will indicate that its food really stands out even among the 'very good' ones, while the award of two stars – and there are only a handful – means that the food is truly exceptional.

As there will be a growing number of pubs calling themselves gastropubs when they really are not, we have also introduced a somewhat arbitrary but necessary dividing line. We use the designation 'gastropub' if the pub serves food and keeps draught (not just bottled) beer. (The latter also happens to preserve the 'pub' atmosphere, if only because there has to be a bar counter in order to serve draught beer.) It is a side-issue, but near to our hearts, that this formula will undoubtedly also please those restaurant customers who would not consider it a sin to order beer instead of wine with their food.

Apart from the overall index, there are additional indexes: for starred gastropubs and starred restaurants. We have also chosen a Gastropub of the Year and a Restaurant of the Year.

Changes in gastropubs, not just in ownership but in quality of cooking, can easily occur, so we would be grateful if readers could make use of the Comment pages, at the end of this Guide, for their own recommendations or detailed criticisms, with emphasis on the cooking. Such valuable remarks will be kept in confidence and borne in mind for our continuing researches.

A Food Inspector's Lament

Spare a thought for the bloke in the
   corner,
With the newspaper, notebook and pen.
He put away four courses at
   lunchtime
And this evening he's at it again.

Before the black pudding
   (with scallops)
Came velouté of butternut squash,
'Compliments of the kitchen', how
   charming,
(And *velouté* makes soup awfully
   posh!).

And afterwards, sea bass 'n' pesto
Risotto and shaved Parmesan, too,
With buckets of oil and balsamic,
What happened to old-fashioned
   stew?

Then they wheeled in the organic
   duckling,
A slow-cooked confit....on mash!
Why's it always spud-u-might-not
   like,
A question of style – or just cash?

The sauces were drizzled and dribbled,
Foaming waves soaked the
   Gressingham fat.
My Donald should have worn
   a sou'wester
Or stayed in, in weather like that.

Mediterranean madness now grips us
Its stranglehold on the increase,
Though for the price of a goat's'
   cheese tarte Tatin
You could fly EasyJet down to Nice.

And despite all this healthy indulgence,
I find I get portlier yet.
In reply to your question, I answer,
'Well it must have been something
   I ate'.

Even cool, refreshing gelati
Are now made with mustard instead.
Or spinach and minced minestrone,
Mr. Walls must be glad that
   he's dead.

Designer wines, too are, *de rigueur*,
New World white or Monrovian red.
I once drank a Rioja from Romford
And spent most of the next day in
   bed.

For an inspector's life isn't all roses
When the fish isn't brill (like the
   pun?),
And when chef comes in search of his
   bouquet
Sometimes you wish for a brickbat,
   or gun.

I've got chorizo up to my shoulders,
Aïoli coming out of my ears.
What I'd give for a tikka massala,
Mushy peas and a couple of beers.

But at least we've still got sticky toffee
And crumble to clog up our veins,
Eton Mess, clotted cream and
   crème brûlée
And a triple by-pass for our pains.

But it's not the cream sauces and
   foie gras,
Or the portions that make you
   feel ill.
What prompts a restorative brandy
Is when they arrive with the bill.

Ten pounds for a bottle of water?
A fiver for house vin de pays?
Mr. Rothschild, not the wine but
   the banker,
Must be helping them stash it away.

But when I own up to my occupation
I'm asked how on earth I get
   through it,
"All that twice-a day-tasting and
   tippling?"
Yes it's tough, but someone's got to
   do it.

So spare a thought for the bloke in
   the corner
With the heart attack lying in wait,
And if he seems a bit down in the
   mouth, well,
He's got rather a lot on his plate.

Egon Ronay's star ratings

Restaurants

Three stars ★★★

Gordon Ramsay, London
Hibiscus, Ludlow
Tom Aikens, London
Waterside Inn, Bray-on-Thames

Two stars ★★

LONDON
Aubergine
Capital
Le Gavroche
Gordon Ramsay at Claridge's
The Ledbury
Morgan M
Orrery
Pétrus
Rasoi Vineet Bhatia
Richard Corrigan at Lindsay House
The Square

ENGLAND
Bath Priory, Bath
Bohemia, Channel Islands
Box Tree, Ilkley
Le Champignon Sauvage, Cheltenham
Chewton Glen, New Milton
Fat Duck, Bray-on-Thames
Fischer's Baslow Hall, Baslow
Gidleigh Park, Chagford
Gilpin Lodge, Windermere
Jessica's, Birmingham
Le Manoir aux Quat' Saisons, Great Milton
Midsummer House, Cambridge
New Angel, Dartmouth
Winteringham Fields, Winteringham

SCOTLAND
Andrew Fairlie at Gleneagles, Auchterarder
Martin Wishart, Edinburgh

WALES
Tyddyn Llan, Llandrillo
Ynyshir Hall, Eglwysfach

NORTHERN IRELAND
Oriel, Gilford

One star ★

LONDON
1 Lombard Street
Allium
Assaggi
Aurora
Chez Bruce
China Tang, The Dorchester
Chutney Mary
Club Gascon
The Connaught, Angela Hartnett
Embassy
Fifteen
Foliage, Mandarin Oriental
Glasshouse
Greenhouse
Hakkasan
The Ivy
Locanda Locatelli
Mirabelle
Mosimann's Private Dining Club
L'Oranger
Painted Heron
Real Greek
Redmond's
Rhodes Twenty Four
The Ritz
River Café
Roussillon
Royal China
Salloos
The Savoy Grill
Shanghai Blues
Sketch, Lecture Room
St. John
Tamarind
La Trompette
Umu
Le Vacherin
The Wolseley
W'Sens

ENGLAND
36 on the Quay, Emsworth
Alba, St. Ives
Allium, Fairford
Anthony's, Leeds
Arkle Restaurant, Chester Grosvenor, Chester
Barnsley House, Barnsley
Café Bleu, Newark
Castle Hotel, Taunton
Chapter One, Farnborough

One star ★

ENGLAND
Charlton House, Shepton Mallet
Chesil Rectory, Winchester
Devonshire Arms, Bolton Abbey
Drakes on the Pond, Abinger Hammer
Drake's Restaurant, Ripley
Edmunds Restaurant, Henley-in-Arden
L'Enclume, Cartmel
Establishment, Manchester
Fisherman's Lodge, Newcastle Upon Tyne
George, Isle of Wight
Gingerman, Brighton
Hambleton Hall, Hambleton
Harry's Place, Great Gonerby
Hart's, Nottingham
Holbeck Ghyll, Windermere
Horn of Plenty, Tavistock
Jersey Pottery Garden Restaurant, Channel Islands
Jonathan's At The Angel, Burford
JSW, Petersfield
Longueville Manor, Channel Islands
Lucknam Park, The Park Restaurant, Colerne
Mallory Court, Bishop's Tachbrook
McCoys at the Baltic, Gateshead
McCoys Bistro, Staddlebridge
Melton's Restaurant, York
Morston Hall, Morston
Mr Underhill's, Ludlow
Northcote Manor, Blackburn
Ockenden Manor, Cuckfield
Old Vicarage, Ridgeway
One Paston Place, Brighton
L'Ortolan, Shinfield
Le Poussin at Whitley Ridge, Brockenhurst
The Quay, Ilfracombe
Read's, Faversham
Restaurant Sat Bains, Nottingham
Ripley's, St. Merryn
Rish, York
The Samling, Windermere
Seaham Hall, The White Room, Seaham
Sharrow Bay, Ullswater
Simpson's, Birmingham
Souffle Restaurant, Bearsted
St. Ervan Manor, St. Ervan
St. Petroc's Bistro, Padstow
Strawberry Tree, Milton Ernest

One star ★

ENGLAND
Thackeray's, Tunbridge Wells
Vineyard at Stockcross, Stockcross
Waldo's at Cliveden, Taplow
West House, Biddenden
Whatley Manor, The Dining Room, Easton Grey
Wing Wah, Birmingham

SCOTLAND
Abstract, Glenmoriston Town House Hotel, Inverness
Ballachulish House, Ballachulish
Braidwoods, Dalry
Champany Inn, Linlithgow
Inverlochy Castle, Fort William
Kinnaird, Dunkeld
Monachyle Mhor, Balquhidder
Number One, Edinburgh
Plumed Horse, Crossmichael
Sangster's, Elie
Summer Isles Hotel, Achiltibuie
Three Chimneys, Colbost

WALES
Churton's Wine & Food Bar, Rossett
Crown at Whitebrook, Whitebrook
Le Gallois, Cardiff
Old Rectory Country House, Llansanffraid Glan Conwy
Plas Bodegroes, Pwllheli

NORTHERN IRELAND
Roscoff, Belfast

Gastropubs

Two stars ★★

LONDON
The Alma
Guinea Grill
The House
The Salusbury

ENGLAND
Black Boys Inn, Hurley
Bull's Head. Ashford in the Water
The Star, Harome
Three Fishes, Mitton
The Waterdine, Llanfair Waterdine
Yorke Arms, Ramsgill-in-Nidderdale

One star ★

LONDON
Anchor & Hope
Anglesea Arms
Bollo House
Builders Arms
Cat & Mutton
The Cow
Cumberland Arms
Drapers Arms
The Eagle
Fox & Hounds
Fox Dining Room
The Garrison
Golborne Grove
The Havelock Tavern
Junction Tavern
Lots Road Pub & Dining Room
The Northgate
The Palmerston
The Peasant
The Swan
The Wells
White Horse
White Swan & Dining Rooms
William IV

ENGLAND
I Up at the Mad Moose Arms, Norwich
Arundell Arms, Lifton
The Bell Inn, Horndon-on-the-Hill
Benton's Brasserie, Nottingham
Bramhall's at The Crown Inn, Marston Montgomery
The Bridge, Manchester
The Cabinet, Reed
Chequers Inn, Froggatt
Crab at Chieveley, Chieveley
The Crabmill, Preston Bagot
Cricketers, Clavering
Crooked Billet, Stoke Row
Crown Hotel, Exford
Dartmoor Inn, Lydford
Drewe Arms, Broadhembury
The Falcon, Fotheringhay
Fisherman's Retreat, Shuttleworth
Fox & Hounds, Knossington
Fox and Goose, Fressingfield
Foxcote Inn, Little Barrow
General Tarleton Inn, Ferrensby
The George, Stamford
George & Dragon, Rowde
Goose at Britwell Salome
Green Dragon, Haddenham
The Greyhound, Stockbridge
The Greyhound, Rotherfield Peppard
Hand and Flowers, Marlow
Hare Restaurant, Hungerford
Harrow at Little Bedwyn, Little Bedwyn
Helyar Arms, East Coker

One star ★

ENGLAND
Hillside, Hertford
Hind's Head, Bray-on-Thames
Jackson Stops Inn, Stretton
King of Prussia, Farnham Royal
King's Arms, Fernhurst
Kings Arms, Strete
King's Head, Aston Cantlow
King's Head Inn, Bledington
Kings Head, Bawburgh
Mason's Arms, Knowstone
The Millbank, Mill Bank
Museum Inn, Farnham
Nobody Inn, Doddiscombsleigh
Old Boat, Alrewas
Old Butchers', Stow-On-The-Wold
Old Bridge Hotel, Huntingdon
Old Passage Inn, Arlingham
Olive Branch, Clipsham
Pear Tree, Whitley
The Pheasant, Keyston
Pheasant Inn, Higher Burwardsley
Red Lion Inn, Stathern
Rising Sun, St. Mawes
The Sandpiper, Leyburn
Snooty Fox, Lowick
The Star, Lidgate
Star Inn, Sulgrave
Sun Inn, Dedham
The Swan, Stafford
Swan Inn, Monks Eleigh
Sweet Olive at Chequers Inn, Aston Tirrold
Three Acres, Roydhouse
Three Horseshoes, Madingley
Three Lions, Stuckton
Trouble House, Cherington
Victory Inn, St. Mawes
The Wheatsheaf, High Ongar
White Horse, Brancaster Staithe
Wildebeest Arms, Stoke Holy Cross

SCOTLAND
Sorn Inn, Sorn

WALES
Felin Fach Griffin, Felin Fach
The Foxhunter, Nantyderry
The Talkhouse, Pontdolgoch
Walnut Tree Inn, Llandewi Skirrid
White Swan, Llanfrynach
Y Polyn, Capel Dewi

A new, exciting category joins our annually honoured 'Restaurant of the Year'

GASTROPUB OF THE YEAR 2006

THE STAR
HAROME (North Yorkshire)

Thatched roof, story-book charm, instant and infectious happiness in the bar, dreams of moving house to be nearer the captivating, cosy dining-room – all compete for stardom with chef/proprietor Andrew Pern's traditionally English yet admirably original creations, every morsel bursting with flavour. The smiling efficiency of omnipresent Jacqueline Pern and the young cooks even extends to their wonderful, very English delicatessen. This place is a quintessentially British gastropub without competition in any country.

□□□□□□

RESTAURANT OF THE YEAR 2006

CHINA TANG
THE DORCHESTER (London)

At this dazzling establishment, the level of luxury and attention to detail is obsessional. The whole staff's only concern is your happiness, from the patient bookings to the acme of courtesy at the table. Luxurious table-settings with expensive glasses; beautiful paintings of huge yet graceful fish; miraculous, scintillating décor everywhere, including the bar...even the washrooms. The succinct menu is shrewdly user-friendly, the dim-sums large, and the cooking excels, with a promise of future perfection. An overwhelming experience.

London

EC3   **MAP** 7 E2

1 Lombard Street ★

1 Lombard Street, London, EC3V 9AA
Tel. 020 7929 6611 Fax 020 7929 6622
e-mail info@1lombardstreet.com

THE FINE cooking of Herbert Berger more than matches the sophistication and elegance of this combination of bar-brasserie and grand gastronomic restaurant. Essentially classical French in approach, the cuisine pays full attention to the simplicity of regional styles yet still manages to add some notable innovations.

Berger's handling of fish is particularly outstanding, as shown in his langoustines with shellfish velouté and sauté of John Dory, or roast turbot on the bone, complemented by woodland mushroom and herb ragout with Pinot Noir jus. His deft touch with textures and combinations is nowhere better demonstrated than in the gratin of crayfish with artichokes and spinach purée.

Equally impressive, though, is a meat dish such as rack of lamb with truffled potatoes, or suprème and fricassee of black leg chicken with cream of morels and vin jaune.

No disappointment, either, in game consommé intensely flavoured and enhanced by wild mushrooms and truffles, or its duck version with ravioli of duck confit, nor yet in desserts that combine the classic and the novel, from pear poached in Sauternes, served with a brandy-snap, to a pyramid of bitter Ecuadorean chocolate with almond milk granité, the soufflé of the day, or bilberry sorbet with chocolate sauce and vanilla syrup.

The wines are chosen carefully and with flair and are surprisingly reasonably priced. Those costing less than £30 a bottle have more maturity than most.

Their pride: Seared sea bass with Provençal vegetables, basil mash and saffron jus
Inexpensive wines: Château Timberlay 2002, £18.50; Muscadet sur lie 2003, £18

Proprietor: Jessen & Co.
Last orders for dinner: 10 pm
Closed: Saturday and Sunday
Closed for holidays: Bank Holidays
Set lunch: from £34
Set dinner: from £45
Wheelchair access

SW3   MAP 7 C4

Admiral Codrington

GASTROPUB

17 Mossop Street, London SW3 2LY
Tel. 020 7581 0005 Fax 020 7589 2452
e-mail: admiralcodrington@longshotplc.com

IN A NARROW Chelsea street, the Admiral Cod still looks at first sight like the 1960s drinking pub then infamous for Hooray Henrys at play, often to the sound of breaking glass. It's all more relaxed and certainly quieter now, even if the front bar has changed little in forty years, with bare wood floors and hunting prints on the walls to make the occasional cavalry subaltern feel at ease. The bar menu (lunchtime only) offers a happy mix of comfort food and some modern takes on Mediterranean flavours, Lincolnshire sausages or farmhouse pork pie and pickles happily co-habiting with crispy fried squid, rocket salad and saffron aïoli.

The real action is found in the chic brasserie-style restaurant, a banquette running the full length of one wall, the roof opening to the sky in fine weather. Sharp-suited estate agents, 'ladies who lunch', pretty Sloanettes and their escorts at dinner, all are drawn to the bistro cooking, which is a distinct cut above the average.

The fish specials of the day, such as roasted silver bream with steamed broccoli, stand out, as do little things like excellent breads. The pasta is home-made and delicate, a delicious base for assorted wild mushrooms, or there is the ravioli of St. Maure's goat's cheese from the Loire with confit of red pepper. Leave room for the home-made passion fruit cheesecake and its sorbet.

Thirty fine wines by the glass run the gamut from keenly priced South African house selections to fine burgundy and port. Considerate service is a real plus. There is a beer garden in which you can enjoy a peaceful pint of well-kept real ale.

Speciality food: The Admiral's Cod
Draught beers: Badger, Bombardier
Average wine price by the glass: £5

Licensees: Michael Bailey, Alexander Langlands-Pearse
Last orders for dinner: 11pm
Open every day
Main courses: from £12.95
Private dining: 10-25
Beer garden
Children welcome
Wheelchair access

SW1   MAP 7 D4

Allium ★

Dolphin Square, Chichester Street, London SW1V 3LX
Tel. 020 7798 6888 Fax 020 7798 5685
e-mail: info@allium.co.uk

MIDNIGHT blue walls and comfortable armchairs at tables laid with classical white napery create a striking ambience in this restaurant at the centre of the Dolphin Square complex.

Allium is in the mainstream of modern European cooking, under the direction of executive chef/patron Anton Edelmann and an exceptional restaurant manager, Marco Di Meglio. The mainly Italian front-of-house team perfectly balance deft professionalism and natural warmth. You are really made to feel at home here.

Head chef Peter Woods offers a diverse range of dishes. Start with a classic parfait of foie gras and chicken liver, or excellent black ink linguine with crab and maize velouté. A fish course could be monkfish wrapped in Ardennes ham with broad bean purée and red wine reduction, then slow-roasted loin of lamb, braised neck and dauphinoise potato, or excellent roast partridge with sautéd red and green cabbage and haggis spätzle. Peter has a sound sense of restraint, knowing instinctively what works on the plate.

There is a superior board of prime cheeses in top condition and some indulgent desserts. The fig tart shows exemplary pastrywork, the flavour of the fig enhanced by almond paste, or try an intriguing alternative of caramelised apples on egg bread with calvados cream.

The wine list avoids showy expensive bottles in favour of real quality and genuine value for money, from fine South African Chardonnay and distinctive Saumur Champigny by the glass to especially fine burgundy.

Their pride: Seared sea bass, sautéd squid, tomato fondue and fennel salad
Inexpensive wines: Colombelle de France Vin de Pays des Côtes de Gascogne 2003, £16.50; Fleurie 2002, £15

Proprietor: Sodexho Restaurants
Last orders for dinner: 10.15 pm
Closed: Saturday lunch, Sunday dinner, Monday
Set lunch: from £18.50
Set dinner: from £29.50
Private dining: up to 70
Accommodation: 145 rooms
Wheelchair access

SW18   MAP 8 B3

The Alma ★★

GASTROPUB

499 Old York Road, London SW18 1TF
Tel. 020 8870 2537 Fax 020 8488 6603
e-mail: drinks@thealma.co.uk

THIS green-glazed corner gastropub opposite Wandsworth Station owes its success partly to its excellent value for money, but mainly to the top quality of its products, cooked to perfection.

To ensure such quality, Charles and Linda Gotto, who also own The Ship nearby, have been running their own farm in Dorking, Surrey, since 1996, producing beef, lamb, pork and eggs.

The menu is supplemented by a couple of daily specials, drawing its inspirations primarily from the Mediterranean. Among simple starters, including several creative salads, roasted root vegetable soup has a good consistency and flavour and is served with warm and crusty home-made bread.

Main courses are more elaborate. Top-quality sea bass is baked to perfection with a warm salad of oriental noodles mixed with leaf spinach, baby tomatoes, slices of onion and chopped aubergine and red pepper perfectly accompanying the delicate flavour.

Beef, matured for at least five weeks, is grilled to perfection and arrives succulent, tender, full of flavour and served with chive horse-radish butter or green peppercorn sauce and pommes frites.

There are few puddings but there is a good selection of delicious icecreams and sorbets. The wine list offers interesting choices, well described and reasonably priced, starting at £10.40 a bottle.

Speciality food: Beef rib chop, peppercorn sauce, fried potatoes
Draught beers: Youngs Special Premium Ale, Youngs Ramrod Strong Ale
Average wine price by the glass: £3.50

Licensees: Linda Gotto, Stewart Day & Eric Niemard
Last orders for dinner: 10.30pm (Sunday 10pm)
Open every day
Closed for holidays: 25 December
Main courses: from £8.50
Private dining: 20-50
Children welcome
Wheelchair access

N1   MAP 7 E1

Almeida

30 Almeida Street, London N1 1AD
Tel. 020 7354 4777 Fax 020 7354 2777
e-mail: almeida-reservations@conran-restaurants.co.uk

IT IS worth having a drink in the sunken bar of this smart French brasserie, which relies to a large extent for its custom on the Almeida theatregoers, before you venture into the restaurant. It is here that the theatre influence is most in evidence, with black and white photographs of surreal and humorous images against a backdrop of warm burgundy-coloured walls.

In contrast, the restaurant has a simple, contemporary design soft colour schemes with hanging lanterns creating pockets of warmth over booth tables, while the emphasis is very much on the food.

A bistro-style menu contains starters such as oysters, impressive charcuterie, and a grilled herring and warm potato salad, served with a delicious, intensely flavoured mustard sauce. Fish is cooked simply. Sea bass, for example, is wrapped in paper before being put into the oven, preserving its delicate flavour. The steamed vegetables that come with it are the perfect accompaniment

Competent sauces accompany classic meat dishes such as filet de boeuf au poivre or selle d' agneau à la provençale.

Round the meal off in French style with the appetising cheeses and, if you can manage it, a delicious gratin de fruits rouges.

An extensive, predominantly French wine list offers good value for money.

Their pride: Coq au Vin
Inexpensive wines: Anjou Les Pierres Girard Domaine de la Bergerie 2002, £24; Saint-Chinian Rosé Château Creissan (France) 2004, £19.50

Proprietor: Conran Restaurants Ltd.
Last orders for dinner: 11 pm
Open every day
Closed for holidays: 24-27 December (dinner), 1 & 2 January (dinner)
Set lunch: from £14.50
Set dinner: from £14.50 (pre or post theatre)
Private dining: up to 20
Al fresco dining
Wheelchair access

SW1   MAP 7 C3

Amaya

Halkin Arcade, Motcomb Street, London SW1X 8JT
Tel. 020 7823 1166 Fax 020 7259 6464
e-mail: amaya@realindianfood.com

TUCKED away in a Belgravia arcade, Amaya is a relatively new glass-fronted, contemporary restaurant that offers Indian dining at its most up to date. With a smart cocktail bar leading to wooden tables lit by spotlights, the restaurant specialises in grilled or roasted marinated meats, poultry and fish, the chefs working at open cooking stations in full view of the diners.

Skillet-griddled spiced clam cakes are prepared in authentic Goan style, which means that the taste of lightly cooked clams is vivid, while the spicing with coriander and cumin is assertive but not too fiery. Alternatives could be chargrilled marinated lamb chops or slow-roasted leg of lamb with garam massala. Fish dishes include fresh grouper with fenugreek leaf and turmeric, or else flavoured with mustard, chilli and peanut.

Another speciality is biryani cooking, one example being Hyderabi chicken, which is particularly good – moist, accurately cooked, subtly spiced and mixed with perfect rice. The recommended accompaniment for biryanis is the slow-grilled, spiced aubergine.

When it comes to desserts, the marriage of eastern and western influences is evident in such dishes as grilled spiced mango with passion fruit fool.

The wine selection has been arranged with great care, strong in the very best champagne (Billecart-Salmon), but also in Italian wines and some less common Australian bottles, such as the bush vine Grenache from Yalumba. The staff, led by a manager in Sikh attire, are charming.

Their pride: Seafood platter: tandoori tiger prawn, king scallop, oysters
Inexpensive wines: Verdicchio Classico Casal di Serra 2003, £18.55; Lérane Rouge Vin de Pays d'Oc 2004, £17.05

Proprietors: Masala World, Ranjit Mathrani, Namita Panjabi, Camellia Panjabi
Last orders for dinner: 11 pm
Open every day
Set lunch: from £14
Set dinner: from £26
Private dining: up to 14
Wheelchair access

SE1   MAP 7 E3

Anchor & Hope ★

GASTROPUB

36 The Cut, London SE1 8LP
Tel. 020 7928 9898 Fax 020 7928 4595

INFORMALITY is the keynote in this busy pub just a stone's throw from the Old Vic theatre. You sit at plain wooden tables and you might be asked to share with other customers as you wait on a first-come, first-served basis. But any wait is well worth it for the fairly simple yet imaginative food that emerges from the kitchen of talented chef Jonathan Jones.

The crusty brown bread sets the tone for what is to follow: a hearty pumpkin soup, more like a thick broth, the flavour of pumpkin dominant but enhanced by other vegetables and very accurate seasoning. Or start with skate, potato and green sauce, or Spanish ham, salsify, quince and walnuts.

A juicy home-made burger with fresh chips and Béarnaise follows, or oxtail and mash. For fish-lovers, plump grilled Dover sole and brown shrimps are a great combination, while an alternative for vegetarians could be Berkswell cheese gratin.

Jones's imaginative streak shows itself in dishes such as a roast partridge and choucroute, the succulent Yorkshire bird moistened with light cooking juices and served with a positively but subtly flavoured choucroute that contains slices of warm Montbelliard sausage from Lyons.

Puddings include an excellent chocolate tart and the list of some 35 wines shows how it should be done – fine drinking at kind prices, from Verdicchio dei Castelli di Jesi, a white of character in bottle, carafe or glass, to a fine Bandol rouge. Good espresso ends a delightful, inexpensive meal.

Speciality food: Slow-cooked stuffed duck, turnips and peas
Draught beers: Kirin, Red Stripe
Wine by the glass: £2.50

Licensees: Robert Shaw, Jonathan Jones, Harry Lester
Last orders for dinner: 10.30 pm
Closed: Sunday, Monday lunch
Closed for holidays: Bank Holidays, Christmas
Main courses: from £10
Al fresco dining
Wheelchair access

W6   **MAP 8** A2

Anglesea Arms ★

35 Wingate Road, London W6 OUR
Tel. 020 8749 1291 Fax 020 8749 1254

IN A residential road on the borders of Hammersmith, this is a well-known pub justly renowned for its exceptional food. And a pub it certainly is: simplicity pervades the unvarnished bar; *Guardian*-reading local government workers prudently sip house wine while smartly dressed-down ladies order food for lunch on the front patio. The 'restaurant' beside the kitchen hatch is endearingly Spartan – schoolroom tables, cottage chairs – and very airy because of its four skylight windows.

All ambition is funnelled into the cooking, which steers a confident middle course between the best of pub food (braised lamb shank) and sophisticated restaurant dishes of refined textures and subtle flavours, as in the impressive boudin of duck confit accompanied by a beautifully defined carrot purée.

Irish oysters are available in season and class is equally obvious in roasted skate wing with Puy lentils and spinach, or in a supreme, rarely seen brasserie dish, grilled ox-tongue with mash and perfectly seasoned spring greens. Sensibly, there are just two puddings of the day, perhaps rich St. Emilion au chocolat or the home comfort of apple crumble with ginger ice-cream.

The nicest surprise was the bill: three courses from the blackboard carte, a glass of excellent Shiraz (a snip at £3.35) and a double espresso, all for £27.30. The set lunch at £12.95 (three courses) is great value.

Gentle prices also mark the fine (Bibendum) wine, list with 10 kindly priced selections by the glass.

Speciality food: Duck and foie gras terrine, Irish oysters
Draught beers: Adnams Broadside, Enterprise IPA
Average wine price by the glass: £4.50

Licensees: Jill O'Sullivan and Connie Kaler
Last orders for dinner: Tues to Saturday 10.30 pm,
Sunday and Monday 10 pm
Open every day
Set lunch: from £9.95
Main courses: from £12.50
Al fresco dining
Children welcome
Wheelchair access

E2   MAP 8 C2

Approach Tavern

GASTROPUB

47 Approach Road, London E2 9LY
Tel. 020 8980 2321 Fax 020 8981 6888

ENTRY to this lively Bethnal Green pub is through a tented beer garden with wooden benches, a very pleasant and relaxing place to sit in the summer, weather permitting. Otherwise, you can eat in the rather dark room inside, where the fireplace and wooden panelling create a baronial atmosphere.

The blackboard menu changes every day, offering familiar dishes but usually with a little creative touch. Fried crab cakes arrive with a delicious mango mayonnaise, while grilled swordfish comes with very lightly fried potato wedges and a refreshing Greek salad.

Marinated lamb kebabs, beautifully grilled, moist inside and full of flavour, arrive on the spit and are served with minted yoghurt and tabbouleh. Simplicity is the motto: fresh ingredients, precise cooking, attractive presentation, no fancy sauces.

Vegetarian options include beanburger with chips or risotto of feta cheese, mint and plum tomato.

There are also imaginative desserts such as apricot and almond frangipane or apple caramel with granny cake.

The wine list, also on a blackboard, is adequate and includes about a dozen wines by the glass, including an excellent Pinot Blanc d' Alsace Réserve, Cave de Türckheim 2002, at £3.40, or else £13 per bottle.

Speciality food: Marinated lamb kebabs with minted yoghurt and tabbouleh salad
Draught beers: London Pride, Discovery
Average wine price by the glass: £3

Licensees: Gabriel Early and Johanna Nyrander
Last orders for dinner: 10 pm
Closed: Sunday evening
Closed for holidays: 25 December, 1 January
Main courses: from £8
Al fresco dining
Beer garden
Children welcome
Wheelchair access

Assaggi ★

39 Chepstow Place, London W2 4TS
Tel. 020 7792 5501 Fax 0870 051 2923

'TASTINGS', as Assaggi would be in English, consists of ten or so tables that are usually booked a month or more ahead by a young and loudly enthusiastic clientele. There is nothing in its sparse interior to deaden the sound of animated chatter, but it is the obvious enjoyment of those within that leads you to this discreet little restaurant over a pub, hidden as it is down an alley, marked with a tiny sign.

Paola and Thomas take care of the service, which is perfectly pitched between serious enthusiasm and casual ease, while chef Nino presents a variety of light, easygoing Italian dishes on his regularly changing carte.

Nino's Sardinian origins are much in evidence, with many of his ingredients arriving directly from home, including the wafer-like carta da musica bread which is presented on arrival. His petto di anitra (duck breast) is developed from a traditional recipe that involves cooking for four days.

In general, though, the accent is on simplicity and a purity of style that relies on the rich, natural flavours of excellent raw materials. Seafood ravioli is a good example of this approach, which continues with high-quality meats and fish simply pointed up by, perhaps, some grilled shallots or a few wild mushrooms. Fresh buttered vegetables are an effective garnish.

The list of desserts is given verbally, so pay careful attention before making your choice. The lemon tart has an excellent creamy filling. Espresso coffee is, of course, dark and strong.

Their pride: Tagliolini erbe
Inexpensive wines: Nuragus di Cagliari 2003, £18.95; Monica di Sardegna 2003, £17.95

Proprietor: Pietro Fraccari
Last orders for dinner: 11 pm
Closed: Sunday
Closed for holidays: 2 weeks Christmas
Main courses: from £19.90

SW6   MAP 7 B4

The Atlas

GASTROPUB

16 Seagrave Road, Fulham, London SW6 1RX
Tel. 020 7385 9129 Fax 020 7386 9113
e-mail: theatlas@btconnect.com

DOWN a quiet street off Lillie Road and the sky-blotting mass of Earls Court Exhibition centre, The Atlas is an unusual mix of the traditional 'local' and the modern gastropub. Step into the main bar and you walk back fifty years: bare wood floors, big tables and fine old panelling.

At lunchtime, the Fulham regulars enjoy well-kept real ales, as their fathers did before them when this was very much a working man's district. There is a charming beer garden, the ideal spot for whiling away a springtime afternoon, and there is a large upstairs room for special dinners and functions.

Modern cooking with a certain Mediterranean feel features on the blackboard menu, which changes daily and is slightly modified for dinner. A basket of excellent crusty bread and little dishes of olive oil and coarse sea salt arrive while you wait for your meal and read a complimentary newspaper. High-quality ingredients and the skill of the kitchen team result in lunchtime choices such as butternut squash soup, loin of pork in grilled bruschetta bread, with piquant tomato and chilli relish, and a risotto of courgette marjoram, mascarpone and Parmesan.

In the evening, the place buzzes with the sound of the young and successful: traders from the City, professionals from legal London, chefs and partners on their night off. Come early to be sure of a table and enjoy the great dish here, halibut fillet pan-roasted with couscous and home-made mayonnaise. As for the puddings, the hazelnut and chocolate cake is streets ahead of most gastropub offerings. Staff are relaxed, warm and efficient.

Speciality food: Mediterranean
Draught beers: Adnams Broadside, Caledonian Deuchars IPA
Average wine price by the glass: £3.50

Licencees: George and Richard Manners
Last orders for dinner: 10.30 pm (Sunday 10 pm)
Open every day
Closed for holidays: Easter, Christmas
Main courses: from £9
Private dining: 20-40
Beer garden
Children welcome until 7 pm
Wheelchair access

SW10   MAP 7 B4

Aubergine ★★

11 Park Walk, London SW10 0AJ
Tel. 020 7352 3449 Fax 020 7351 1770
e-mail: auberginerestaurant@yahoo.co.uk

ALTHOUGH situated in one of the less popular reaches of Chelsea, and with an ambience that is pleasing but unexceptional, this is a restaurant to attract seekers of seriously good cooking. Chef William Drabble is a stickler for sourcing the finest ingredients, such as fish from Dorset and meat from Cumbria, and he has a particular talent for the preparation and reduction of stock for sauces.

A starter of poached lobster tail on cauliflower purée, with sliced white truffles in a wine-flavoured stock thickened with a little cream, makes a perfect marriage of texture and taste. Another tempting choice might be boned quail poached in a wine jus with black truffles, accompanied by sautéd veal sweetbreads and foie gras – a delicious combination.

Fish is ordered early each morning and there is a good selection. John Dory, the skin impeccably seared and the flesh firm and not overcooked, was served with sliced button mushrooms and dried mushrooms marinated in a light stock. The addition of lightly fried mussels coated in herbs and breadcrumbs completed a truly memorable dish. Of the desserts, banana soufflé is light yet intensely flavoured and comes with an unusual toffee sauce.

The welcome from manager Thierry Tomasin is Gallic and warm, the service efficiently attentive without being unctuous. The set lunch menu – three courses with a half-bottle of good wine and still mineral water, coffee and petits fours – is a bargain.

Their pride: Quail salad, sweetbreads, foie gras, truffle dressing
Inexpensive wines: Bourgogne Rouge Domaine Charlopin Parizot 2002, £20; Côtes du Luberon Verget 2002, £19.50

Proprietor: London and Henleys Restaurant 2 Limited
Last orders for dinner: 11 pm
Closed: Saturday lunch, Sunday
Closed for holidays: Bank Hols, Christmas–New Year
Set lunch: from £34
Set dinner: from £60
Wheelchair access

EC2   MAP 7 F2

Aurora ★

**Great Eastern Hotel, Liverpool Street, London EC2M 7QN
Tel. 020 7618 7000 Fax 020 7618 5035**

ONE OF the strongest runners in the Conran stable, this ambitious restaurant is well on the way to achieving the class of the Orrery, having already overtaken another stablemate, Le Pont de la Tour. Situated in the Great Eastern Hotel, Aurora is a magnet for young City traders, who luxuriate in the refined, high-quality cooking of Allan Pickett.

The sophistication and skill of the kitchen are immediately clear in starters such as escabèche of lobster with watercress and an apple and shellfish dressing, or roasted langoustines served with crispy pig's trotter, or the flavoursome duck and beetroot broth.

Main courses are no less impressive, even the straightforward roasted organic salmon with a salad of cucumber and mustard seed and purée of black olives. Braised shin of veal, its succulence guaranteed by long, slow cooking, has a marjoram jus and is accompanied by an excellent pomme mousseline. Breast of cornfed chicken is poached and roasted and served in jus gras with risotto of girolles.

Nor do the desserts disappoint, with stars such as pain perdu, which is a sort of French equivalent of bread and butter pudding, with orchard fruits, and an equally fine chocolate fondant.

The cheeseboard offers up to 30 choices and the wine list features a serious collection of classics at high prices, though there is also a reasonable number of half-bottles, including a leading Chianti Classico and a good Spanish Tempranilla.

Their pride: Dorset crab and melon salad, shellfish dressing
Inexpensive wines: Bogle Vineyard Chenin Blanc 2003, £28; Costières de Nîmes Château Bourges du Gres 2002, £26

**Proprietor: Conran/Wyndham
Last orders for dinner: 10 pm
Closed: Saturday and Sunday
Closed for holidays: 2 weeks Christmas-New Year
Set lunch: from £28
Set dinner: from £50
Accommodation: 267 rooms**
Wheelchair access

The Belvedere

Holland House, Holland Park (Abbotsbury Road), London W8 6LU
Tel. 020 7602 1238 Fax 020 7610 4382
e-mail: sales@whitestarline.org.uk

FOR A romantic atmosphere, this is hard to beat with its cool green setting, Art Deco style and background of gentle piano music. The menu, too, seems familiar and relaxing, featuring the likes of cream of pea soup, calf's liver with sage, rib-eye of beef. grilled salmon, veal cutlet with morel jus and lemon sole.

As you might expect from a member of the Marco-Pierre White set, the cooking of these staples is very sound and based on good fresh ingredients. But it does not end there. There is a varied range of pasta and risottos – veal Bolognese and capellini of crab, for example – and there are also some interesting experiments with modern Asian cooking, such as the Big Thai Fish Sandwich, served with fries.

The daily specials, which might include a terrine de l'océan, can sometimes be rather disappointing, but the overall high standards are obvious in finely flavoured kipper pâté or in rib of Aberdeen Angus beef that is served rare with well-risen Yorkshire pudding, pot-roasted potato and fresh, accurately timed French beans.

Desserts, too, are strong, with excellent sherry trifle, blackberry soufflé and terrine of dark chocolate and digestive biscuits. The quality even extends to the espresso coffee.

The wine list maintains a good balance in that the classic regions of Europe sit alongside a representative selection of interesting bottles from the southern hemisphere.

Their pride: Scallops and roasted chicken wings, potato purée, bean and shallot salad, Madeira butter
Inexpensive wines: Sauvignon de Touraine P. Buisse (France) 2003, £17; Vasse Felix Cabernet Merlot Margaret River (Australia) 2001, £28

Proprietor: Jimmy Lahoud
Last orders for dinner: 10 pm
Closed: Sunday dinner
Closed for holidays: 26 December and 1 January
Set lunch: from £14.95
Set dinner: from £14.95
Private dining: 10-60
Al fresco dining
Limited wheelchair access

SW3   MAP 7 C4

Bibendum

**Michelin House, 81 Fulham Road, London SW3 6RD
Tel. 020 7581 5817 Fax 020 7823 7985
e-mail: manager@bibendum.co.uk**

THIS, of course, must be counted among London landmarks, since it is situated in the eye-catching Art Deco Michelin Building that dominates the fashionable end of the Fulham Road. It is also something of an institution, opened in 1987 as the temple of a simple approach to food based on the best ingredients treated in lively Mediterranean style. It quickly attracted a sophisticated international clientele and its success inspired many another new London restaurant.

Still true to its origins, Bibendum has inevitably lost some of the excitement of its early years, but chef Matthew Harris's changing menus are simple, generous and as competent and enjoyable as they ever were.

Among the always reliable starters are soupe de poissons with rouille, oeufs en meurette and millefeuille of tender sweetbreads served with Jerusalem artichokes and fresh trompettes de la mort mushrooms. Standing out as main courses are roasted Bresse chicken with cream and morels, grilled calf's liver and deliciously fresh hake fillet with an anchoïade crust.

Plum and almond tart with Jersey cream is an excellent pudding, especially when matched with a fine dessert wine such as Côteaux du Layon, Beaulieu, from Anjou.

The ambience and service remain engaging, even if the meal – and particularly the wine – is very fully priced, and people are here as much for a great evening as for the food itself.

Their pride: Poulet de Bresse à l'estragon
Inexpensive wines: Iona Sauvignon Blanc (South Africa) 2004, £27.50; Côtes du Rhône Vieilles Vignes 2002, £24.50

**Proprietors: Sir Terence Conran, Simon Hopkinson, Michael Hamlyn, Graham Williams
Last orders for dinner: 11.30 pm
Open every day
Closed for holidays: Christmas
Set lunch: from £28.50
Main courses: from £16.50**
Wheelchair access

W4   MAP 8 A3

Bollo House ★

GASTROPUB

13-15 Bollo Lane, London W4 5LR
Tel. 020 8994 6037
e-mail: thebollohouse@btconnect.com

WHITE painted walls and soft background music give this corner pub close to Chiswick Park tube station a relaxing feel.

The good-quality food, reasonably priced and ordered from the bar, is attractively presented and the menu is predominantly British with some influences from Italy and Asia.

Starters include home-made soup, a plate of charcuterie and an interesting selection of pasta dishes and salads. A thick piece of buffalo mozzarella is surrounded by rocket and impeccably cooked roast peppers and grilled aubergines, a symphony of Mediterranean flavours.

Examples of the main courses are seared tuna, of perfect texture, marinated in soy sauce, honey and ginger and served with al dente courgette spaghetti, grilled spring onion and red chilli. The impeccably roasted lamb is full of flavour and arrives both pink and juicy, served with sweet potatoes, roast tomatoes and mint sauce.

There is a limited choice of desserts featuring the likes of tiramisù and apple crumble, and a good selection of cheeses.

A short but well-chosen and excellent-value wine list has prices starting at £10.50 and most bottles are less than £20. Syrah Les Montarels, Languedoc 2003, at £14 a bottle, is a well-balanced, refreshing wine. A glass of Monbazillac, Domaine de l' Ancienne Cure 2001, at £4.30, rounds off the meal nicely.

Speciality food: Roasted Elwyn farm lamb with sweet potato, roast tomatoes and mint sauce
Draught beers: Abbot Ale, Greenes IPA
Average wine price by the glass: £3.25

Licensee: Mark Iwaniak
Last orders for dinner: 10.15 pm
Open every day
Set lunch: from £6
Main courses: from £6.50
Beer garden
Children welcome
Wheelchair access

Brackenbury

129-131 Brackenbury Road, London W6 OBQ
Tel. 020 8748 0107 Fax 020 8748 6159
e-mail: lisa@thebrackenbury.fsnet.co.uk

LOCATED in a quiet residential road between Hammersmith and Shepherd's Bush, this is a popular and successful neighbourhood restaurant, under new ownership since 2003, which simply offers excellent ingredients well cooked and plainly presented. In its two cosy rooms, and at the few tables outside, there is no place for pretension or culinary faddism.

The set lunch is attractively priced and might feature a creamy soup of Jerusalem artichoke and almond, finely seasoned and complemented by good wholemeal bread, perhaps followed by a crisp-skinned Orkney sea trout with taglierini and spinach.

From the simple carte, which is available at lunch and dinner, a signature dish is lamb rump with braised red cabbage and Puy lentil jus, though fish is given equal prominence, with pan-fried skate wing and beurre noisette or roasted monkfish saltimbocca with sage and ham.

Alternatives might be a starter of ham hock terrine with piccalilli, then Gruyère omelette with home-made chips, or wild mushroom risotto with mascarpone.

The short wine list shows an eye for both quality and value in selections from Europe and the New World. Service is informal and friendly, but also quick and responsive, as welcoming to chance callers as it is to regular customers.

Their pride: Rib-eye steak, home-made chips, Béarnaise sauce
Inexpensive wines: Le Marquis Grenache Syrah 2003, £12; Soave Alpha Zeta 2003, £12.50

Proprietor: Lisa Inglis
Last orders for dinner: 10.45 pm
Closed: Saturday lunch, Sunday dinner
Closed for holidays: Christmas, 1 January, Bank Hols
Set lunch: from £12.50
Al fresco dining
Wheelchair access

SW13   MAP 8 A3

The Bridge

GASTROPUB

204 Castelnau, Barnes, London SW13 9DW
Tel. 020 8563 9811 Fax 020 8748 9421
e-mail: thebridgeinbarnes@btinternet.com

THE LOGO on the olive-green frontage is apt: Pub & Dining Room. The Bridge, named after its location just on the south side of Hammersmith Bridge, is a smart addition to the superior pub scene in affluent Barnes. All tastes and thirsts are catered for. The front bar has a traditional feel, without being either staid or trendy, comfort the key.

At the end of a stressed time in town, alight from the 209 bus and relax with a cocktail at the horseshoe bar counter, which is made of solid oak. The lounge bar has warm claret walls, low deep sofas, and sturdy wooden tables, where you can sup excellent ale, do the crossword, or eat a snack. The Bridge beefburger, with Emmental cheese and tomato chutney, matched by a glass of Australian Shiraz, is a great favourite of Barnes locals, who span the generations from retired university professors and doctors to media types, City traders and secretaries on their way home.

Children are welcome in the slightly more formal restaurant, which opens on to the decked terrace and leafy little garden. The menu has an attractive spread of cuisines, ingredients are fresh and the cooking generally sound. Lunch choices are simpler: chilli crab and cod cakes before, say, pappardelle with wild mushrooms and Parmesan.

At night, the fresh fish special is often a winner, as is something like braised neck of lamb with parsnips and red wine jus. Forty deftly chosen wines by the bottle, strong in Australians and South Africans, reflect the homelands of the staff, who are unfailingly warm and motivated.

Speciality food: Fresh of the Bay (fish) Special
Draught beers: Ruddles, Wells Bombardier
Average wine price by the glass: £3.90

Licensees: Mark Rivington, Margie Souter
Last orders dinner: 10.30 pm
Open every day
Main courses: from £11
Beer garden
Children welcome
Wheelchair access

SW3   MAP 7 C4

Builders Arms ★

GASTROPUB

13 Britten Street, London SW3 3TY
Tel. 020 7349 9040
e-mail: buildersarms@geronimo-inns.co.uk

TUCKED away in a quiet residential Chelsea street, this attractive Georgian building is only a couple of minutes' walk from the buzz of King's Road. In the evenings and at weekends (especially Sunday lunchtime) a predominantly young local clientele come for the convivial atmosphere, delicious food and excellent value for money. Weekday lunches attract older customers.

The open fireplace, comfy leather sofas, casual bookshelves and surrealistic Dali-like oil paintings create a homely, Bohemian atmosphere.

The short carte, modern European in style, is supplemented by a blackboard selection in which the emphasis is on simplicity.

Starters include home-made soups, salads, savoury tarts and pasta. Red onion tarte Tatin, for example, arrives with perfectly cooked pastry and a refreshing rocket salad topped with shaved Parmesan; risotto arrives precisely cooked al dente.

Main courses might be crisp fried haddock with home-made chips, mushy peas and tartare sauce, or lamb steak, moist and pink, with sautéd spinach, cabbage, new potatoes and rosemary jus.

Desserts such as black grape panna cotta or apple crumble with vanilla ice-cream are equally successful.

Wines, also by the glass include Chardonnay de l' Ardèche 2003 at £14.80 and Malbec Bodega Norton (Argentina) 2004 at £13.

Speciality food: Lamb steak with sautéd spinach, cabbage, new potatoes and rosemary jus
Draught beers: Adnams, London Pride
Average wine price by the glass: £3.50

Licensee: Simon Harris
Last orders for dinner: 10.15 pm
Open every day
Closed for holidays: 25 December, 1 January
Main courses: from £10
Al fresco dining
Children welcome before 9 pm
Wheelchair access

SW3   MAP 7 C3

Capital ★ ★

22-26 Basil Street, London SW3 1AT
Tel. 020 7591 1202 Fax 020 7225 0011
e-mail: restaurant@capitalhotel.co.uk

A WEALTHY international clientele is justifiably attracted to this hotel restaurant that rises above the simply excellent into the realm of the exceptional. In a setting that recalls the Paris of Coco Chanel – sycamore panelled walls, cornflower blue chairs, flock curtains – Eric Chavot's distinguished French cuisine needs no extravagant descriptions on the menu: the excitement is all in the taste.

The flavours of a seemingly simple smoked haddock risotto are extraordinarily vivid yet refined, the risotto perfectly cooked, the herbs and seasonings exactly right. Another outstanding dish is the pan-fried halibut, served with choucroute that features the more gently flavoured Morteau sausage to create a harmonious medley of tastes.

More grand-mère than grand hotel, one might say, are the rustic flavours of Eric's daube of beef with lardons and other garnitures, yet he is equally at home with adventurous pairings such as roast venison and osso bucco, accompanied by creamed cabbage and boulangère potatoes flavoured with bacon.

The cheeses – including wonderful Roquefort and Morbier – and the desserts are also exceptional. The blackberry clafoutis would be irresistible, were it not for the alternatives of chocolate moelleux with lime and ginger sorbet, or banana tarte Tatin with green tea ice-cream, and perhaps a glass of Passito di Pantelleria. An uncompromising wine list is notable for the depth of vintages of great claret and burgundy, but there is lots of fine alternative drinking from the New World, too.

Their pride: Pan-fried langoustine with slow-cooked pork belly
Inexpensive wines: Levin Sauvignon Blanc 2004, £31; Côtes du Ventoux Domaine de Frondèche 2003, £32

Proprietor: David Levin
Last orders for dinner: 11 pm
Open every day
Set lunch: from £29.50
Set dinner: from £55
Private dining: up to 24
Accommodation: 49 rooms and 10 apartments
Wheelchair access

E8   MAP 8 C2

Cat & Mutton ★

GASTROPUB

76 Broadway Market, London E8 4QJ
Tel. 020 7254 5599
e-mail: info@seamless.uk.com

THIS gastropub has been transformed out of all recognition from a 'local', with the cooks working in the large, impeccably clean, open-plan kitchen, giving a reassuring and civilised feel.

The exposed brickwork, comfortable leather armchairs and sofas, wooden tables, school chairs and large windows, and the pop or Latino background music, create a convivial atmosphere.

The place is very busy, especially at Sunday lunchtime when many people come for the traditional roast. Quality ingredients, attractive presentation and simple but precise preparation and fresh accompanying salads are the secrets of its success.

The sensibly short blackboard menu features simple dishes such as home-made soups, salads, fishcakes or sausages, alongside a couple of more elaborate ones.

Gravadlax comes beautifully presented, served with dill-flavoured new potatoes, rucula and a delicious mustard cream sauce that contains chopped apples, onions and capers. Blue fin tuna, seared to perfection, arrives brown outside and pink inside, together with excellent steamed pak choi and rice noodles inside a lemongrass and coriander broth – a light, beautifully balanced dish.

The meal finishes on equally high notes with desserts such as chocolate tart with raspberry sauce or a sublime tiramisù.

There is also a good selection of cheeses from Neal's Yard.

Speciality food: Seared blue fin tuna with rice noodles, pak choi and lemongrass and coriander broth
Draught beers: Red Stripe, Pilsner Urquell
Average wine price by the glass: £4

Licensee: Kevin Cooper
Last orders for dinner: 10 pm
Closed: Monday daytime
Set dinner: from £12.50
Main courses: from £13
Al fresco dining
Children welcome
Wheelchair access

EC4   **MAP 7** E2

The Chancery

9 Cursitor Street, London EC4A 1LL
Tel. 020 7831 4000 Fax 020 7831 4002
e-mail: reservation@thechancery.co.uk

THERE is a great deal to like about the food in this intimate City restaurant, tucked away among office blocks near Chancery Lane. Nor is it merely a popular lunch venue for lawyers and business executives. In the evening, poised South American staff add a touch of exoticism that helps to create the perfect ambience for a romantic dinner.

Andrew Thompson's cooking is precise, accurate and attractive in texture and presentation. As a pre-starter, try his mildly flavoured velouté of pumpkin with Parmesan shavings. Caramelised ricotta cannelloni, served with confit tomatoes and basil, offers a very good combination of tastes and may be a wiser choice than one alternative, the odd but fashionable coupling of seared scallops with braised oxtail.

As a main course, grilled fillet of beef is cooked medium-rare and served with the short rib (braised for six hours), then simply and effectively garnished with sweet potato purée and spinach. Or there is braised pork cheek, sauerkraut and lardons. Vegetarians, meanwhile, might well be tempted by the baked cheese soufflé with roasted cherry vine tomatoes in aged balsamic vinegar.

Best of the desserts – which cover various fruit-based Tatins and brûleés – is probably chocolate fondant pudding with cappuccino foam. That goes down well with a glass of Muscat de Rivesaltes, and there are other glass selections including a rarely seen Nebbiolo from South Africa. The main list is broad in scope from both classic and New World sources, all fairly priced.

Their pride: Trio of pork, cauliflower-purée, Calvados apples
Inexpensive wines: Bordeaux Sauvignon blanc Cave Bel Air 2003, £14.50; Montepulciano d'Abruzzo Colle Morino 2002, £14.50

Proprietors: Zak Jones and Andrew Thompson
Last orders for dinner: 10.30 pm
Closed: Saturday and Sunday
Closed for holidays: 22-31 December
Set dinner: from £32
Wheelchair access

Chelsea Ram

GASTROPUB

32 Burnaby Street, London SW10 0PL
Tel. 020 7581 4008

BUILT as a public house in the 1800s, the Ram has had a varied history. Today it is a sand-coloured prominent building in a quiet residential road in a district known locally as World's End, close to Stamford Bridge, home to Chelsea Football Club.

Beneath its round-topped windows, trestle tables are neatly arranged on the pavement outside. Inside, there is the feel of a good old traditional pub with its grandly proportioned rooms, tall ceilings, large L-shaped bar counter, painted wood panelling and sturdy furnishings.

The place is popular with locals, especially in the evenings, so it is prudent to book to be sure of a table.

Starters include crispy risotto balls with sauce vierge or celeriac linguine with avocado salsa.

For the main course, a local favourite is salmon or haddock fish-cakes, but you might prefer to go for the wild boar sausages with cider jus or one of the daily specials such as chargrilled chicken with smooth mashed potato incorporating diced spring onions and served in a light and creamy dill sauce.

Puddings include passion fruit cheesecake and sorbet, or a svelte mousse duet of raspberry and mango with summer berries. There is an English cheeseboard.

No fewer than 30 wines are offered by the glass.

Speciality food: Salmon and dill fishcake
Draught beers: Youngs Bitter, Youngs Special
Average wine price by the glass: £3.60

Licensee: Henry Cripps
Last orders for dinner: 10 pm (Sunday 9.30 pm)
Open every day
Main courses: from £7.75
Private dining: up to 20
Al fresco dining
Children welcome
Limited wheelchair access

W2   MAP 7 B3

The Chepstow

GASTROPUB

39 Chepstow Place, London W2 4TS
Tel. 020 7229 0323
e-mail: chepstow@massivepub.com

IN THE heart of Notting Hill, The Chepstow has a separate bar area for aperitifs or cocktails. The dining area, beyond the bar, was refurbished two years ago in chic urban style, clean lines with no frills or clutter, plain furniture and polished wood floors.

This is essentially a table-service establishment where, starting at noon, brunch is served every day until 3 pm, and until 4 pm on Sundays, when you can relax with a full English breakfast; omelette with sautéd mushrooms and semi-dried tomatoes, or eggs Benedict – poached with bacon and served on ciabatta with hollandaise.

For starters there might be Thai fishcakes with cucumber noodles, merguez sausages with chive mayonnaise and fried cabbage, or a soft roasted pepper stuffed with couscous and warmed goat's cheese accompanied by rocket – a successful combination.

For an adventurous main course, try the black ink linguine with squid, garlic and chilli. Otherwise, opt for a grilled rib-eye steak with asparagus, dauphinoise potatoes and red wine jus, or the generous home-made beefburger infused with garlic and topped with chargrilled bacon and a thin slice of melted cheese.

Desserts include a smooth passion fruit crème brûlée and bread and butter pudding.

There are more than 20 wines by the glass.

Speciality food: Butternut squash and goat's cheese risotto
Draught beers: John Smith, Hoegaarden
Average wine price by the glass: £4.20

Licensee: Ian Samways
Last orders for dinner: 10 pm (Sunday 9.30 pm)
Open every day
Main courses: from £8.50
Private dining: 20-60
Al fresco dining
Children welcome
Wheelchair access

SW17   MAP 8 B3

Chez Bruce ★

2 Bellevue Road, London SW17 7EG
Tel. 020 8672 0114 Fax 020 8767 6684
e-mail: chezbruce2@aol.com

A DESERVEDLY busy restaurant on two floors, the upper level with fine views of Wandsworth Common, Chez Bruce draws affluent customers from the leafy parts of London south of the river. And quite right. Bruce Poole's very assured cooking is wide-ranging in inspiration but with a fondness for Burgundian, Savoyard, Provençal and Italian dishes that gives it regional character and individuality – Elizabeth David brought up to date, if you like.

The daily changing menu of some eight starters and eight main courses could begin with a richly flavoured foie gras and chicken liver parfait, with toasted brioche, followed by an impressive dish of red mullet and squid, the interplay of flavours of the two fish both successful and contrasting. Aubergine pastille is a fine accompaniment. Equally exceptional is loin of venison cooked pink, garnished with excellent game sausage, red cabbage and sauce poivrade.

There are also some satisfying cuisine bourgeoise options, such as daube de boeuf à la bourguinonne, or Châteaubriand with Béarnaise sauce and chips. Persillade of plaice is combined with scallop mousseline, vermouth sauce and shrimps. The Midi is also reflected in bream fillet with artichokes barigoule and brandade ravioli.

Tempting desserts include Valrhona chocolate mousse, served with pistachio anglaise and florentines, and caramelised apple millefeuille with calvados and sultanas. The fully priced wine list is broad in scope and high in quality, especially in Burgundy and the Rhône. Admirably, there is a choice of 30 wines by the glass.

Their pride: Duck magret with pithiviers Savoyard
Inexpensive wines: Côtes du Rhône Domaine Charvin 2000, £28; Grüner Veltliner Smaragd Domaine Wachau, 2003 £27.50

Proprietors: Bruce Poole and Nigel Platts-Martin
Last orders for dinner: 10.30 pm (Sunday 10 pm)
Open every day
Closed for holidays: 25 & 26 December and 1 January
Set lunch: from £23.50
Set dinner: from £35
Private dining room: 12-22
Wheelchair access

W1   **MAP 7** C3

China Tang, The Dorchester ★

Dorchester Hotel, Park Lane, London W1A 2HJ
Tel. 020 7629 9988 Fax 020 7629 9595
e-mail: reservations@chinatanglondon.co.uk

THE Dorchester keeps improving the quality and variety of its catering. It triumphs with the hypnotically beautiful China Tang, opened in September 2005. It must be the envy of every caterer with its artistic décor, cleverly interlocking party rooms, the exceptionally courteous reservation service (generally missing in London) and an amazingly efficient waiting staff of eastern restraint, friendly and patiently helpful. Even the wash-rooms are unusually luxurious.

But the silver chopsticks – silver because in the emperors' times they showed stains if contaminated with poison – are unusable in their slipperiness, so we had to stab shamelessly.

The Cantonese food has its highlights, such as beef in black beans or one or two large dim-sum (the latter served in the dazzling bar should, too, you just want a snack). Yet our highlight was a non-Chinese rose apple cake. Some other items will undoubtedly have been further refined. Prices are surprisingly restrained.

David Tang is a scintillating personality with China Clubs in Hong Kong, Beijing and Singapore, and he even advises prestigious establishments in Shanghai, London and Canada. He is worth meeting if you can catch him mid-flight.

Also, try the huge, elegant and comfortable Promenade – it was previously The Lounge – an all-purpose eatery for anything from sandwiches to full meals (or one of twenty-four teas).

Their pride: Steamed scallops in black bean
Inexpensive wines: Pinot Blanc Mise du Printemps 2004, £30; Knappstein Clare Valley (Austrialia) 2004, £25

Proprietor: David Tang
Last orders for dinner: midnight
Open every day
Closed for holidays: 25 December
Main courses: from £15
Private dining: 12-30
Accommodation: 196 rooms
Wheelchair access

SW10   MAP 7 B5

Chutney Mary ★

535 King's Road, London SW10 0SZ
Tel. 020 7351 3113 Fax 020 7351 7694
e-mail: info@realindianfood.com

TRANSPORT your taste-buds through a dazzling array of regional cuisines and culinary styles at this stunning Indian restaurant, once thought unmissably trendy and still attracting a wide range of customers. Chef Rubinath, from his roots in south-east India, has worked throughout the Sub-continent, his wide experience no better demonstrated than in his curry tasting platter.

In addition to creamy lamb korma, this dish offers a lively spiced Bangalore sauce on prawn, Goan green chicken, and aubergine massala. Excellent for those who like to pick and share (there is a full tasting menu, too), although the price – £20 plus service for the miniature portions and without any side-dishes – might seem to be a little exaggerated even by London standards.

Overall, prime, home-sourced ingredients are much in evidence, though they receive cross-cultural treatment. Gressingham duck comes with cinnamon, coconut and black pepper, Devon lamb korma with Himalayan screwpine flower.

Presentation is colourful and sometimes idiosyncratic. Tokri chaat, for example – advertised as 'street food' and offering a veritable cornucopia of flavours – spills in self-consciously artistic fashion out of a rather clumsily made basket of fried straw potatoes.

There is no doubt about the authenticity of the flavours, yet the impression is that they are sometimes understated. According to chef Rubinath, however, this apparent restraint is a sign of the dominant trend in modern Indian cooking.

Their pride: Lamb Rack Ghazala
Inexpensive wines: De Gras Sauvignon Blanc Colchagua Valley (Chile) 2004, £17.25; Lérane Rouge Grenache/Syrah Vin de Pays d'Oc 2004, £16.25

Proprietor: Masala World
Last orders for dinner: 11.30 pm (Sunday 10.30 pm)
Open every day
Set lunch: from £16.50
Main courses: from £15.35
Private dining: 12-30
Wheelchair access

Clarke's

122-124 Kensington Church Street, London W8 4BH
Tel. 020 7221 9225 Fax 020 7229 4564
e-mail: restaurant@sallyclarke.com

A PROTEGEE of Alice Waters of the Chez Panisse restaurant in Berkeley, California, Sally Clarke opened her restrained, calm Kensington restaurant in 1984, dedicated to providing meals based on naturally produced meat, fish, fruit and vegetables. The business has since expanded, incorporating a now-famous bakery and a fine food shop selling notable English cheeses and the best olive oils and wines from Italy and California, but the restaurant remains as steady in quality as it always was.

Changing daily, the food on the limited-choice dinner menu looks simple, but the impression is deceptive. Between conception and realisation, the dishes acquire a special quality as a result of the thoughtful combination of flavours.

Fresh goat's cheese crostini came with a salad of nectarines, cob nuts, thyme and bitter leaves in balsamic vinegar. Roasted fillet of Cornish cod might be served with gherkins and capers and accompanied by fennel and leek fritters. Crisp potato pancake and basil mayonnaise are matched with breast of cornfed chicken.

At lunchtime, the choice is wider and features trusted staples such as Gloucester Old Spot pork chop, while on Saturdays, a fine brunch menu majors on old favourites like eggs Benedict and Lincolnshire sausages but also includes an innovative kedgeree of smoked haddock with spiced Basmati rice and a poached egg.

The wine list is an expert selection from among the best of Italy, France and California.

Their pride: Fresh crab salad with dill flat bread, sprouting grains and crème fraîche dressing
Inexpensive wines: Les Fumées Blanches Sauvignon 2003, £15; Palacio de Otaz Crianza Navalla 2000, £17.50

Proprietor: Sally Clarke
Last orders for dinner: 10 pm
Closed: Sunday
Closed for holidays: Christmas-New Year
Main courses: from £14
Private dining: 20-60
Limited wheelchair access

EC1   MAP 7 E2

Club Gascon ★

57 West Smithfield, London EC1A 9DS
Tel. 020 7796 0600 Fax 020 7796 0601
e-mail: info@clubgascon.com

BOOKING is absolutely essential at what must be among the most distinctively stylish establishments on the gastronomic circuit, in terms of both the décor of the fairly small dining-room (just 50 covers) and, above all, the originality of some of the dishes on offer. Pascal Aussignac promises the traditional food of South-West France, and a whole section of the monthly changing menu is devoted to foie gras. Typical piperade, cassoulet and country dishes are regularly present, but what really makes this place special is the daring innovation that will surprise and delight the taste-buds of even the most hardened epicurean.

The sombre colours, mirrored walls and black-garbed staff might convey the impression that you are attending some kind of ritual, where the unexpected lies just around the corner, and this helps to prepare you for the eccentricities of the menu.

South-Western in character they may be, but what would they say in Pascal's homeland about such things as suckling pig and andouillette with mustard ice-cream – though it works very well – or equally successful cappuccino of black pudding, lobster and asparagus, or rabbit with calamari and chorizo?

There is a relatively small selection of almost jokily named desserts, such as Choco Bar and Juicy Grapes, although here again flavours are strong and the decorative effect is stunning. The wine list is a compendium of exclusively French South-West bottles, with a fair selection of glasses (including an excellent, full-bodied red Gaillac) and half-bottles.

Their pride: Duck foie gras Gascon
Inexpensive wines: Jurançon-Clos Lapeyre, J.B. Larrieu 2002, £24; Bergerse-Château Moulin, Magie D'Automne 2002, £22

Proprietors: Vincent Labeyrie and Pascal Aussignac
Last orders for dinner: Monday to Thursday 10 pm, Friday and Saturday 10.30 pm
Closed: Saturday lunch, Sunday
Closed for holidays: 25 Dec-5 Jan, Bank Holidays
Set lunch: from £38
Set dinner: from £38
Limited wheelchair access

EC1   **MAP 7** E2

Coach & Horses

GASTROPUB

26-28 Ray Street, London EC1R 3DJ
Tel. 020 7278 8990 Fax: 020 7278 1478
e-mail: info@thecoachandhorses.com

THIS might look like a traditional, unpretentious, no-nonsense pub, with bare boards and tables simply adorned with pot plants, yet it is very much a foodie destination, not least because it shares its executive chef, Juliet Peston, with Alistair Little.

The menus are short, just four choices at each stage, but notable for clear, assertive flavours in well-conceived combinations such as roasted Bleasedale partridge with Jerusalem artichoke wrapped in thyme and bacon and accompanied by chunky leeks sweated with trompette mushrooms. Baked brill is served with endive, shallot purée and spinach, daube of Scottish beef intelligently matched with carrots and parsley dumplings.

Start, perhaps, with moist, succulent chargrilled quail, which is interestingly partnered by tabbouleh flavoured with pomegranate and fresh coriander, and finish with chocolate tart baked to order, or else ginger cake with quince and crème fraîche.

There is a blackboard bar menu that features Scotch egg, black pudding hash with fried egg, charcuterie and grilled ox tongue sandwich in excellent bread. Everything is home-made

The wine list offers a couple of dozen reds and a similar number of whites from various parts of the world and always gives the grape variety along with a fittingly unpretentious tasting note. There are about 10 selections by the glass, not counting dessert wines, ports and 10 Madeiras, and lovers of single malt whiskies are very well catered for.

Speciality food: Gloucester Old Spot trotter stuffed with morcilla and fennel seeds, mash and greens
Draught beers: Timothy Taylor Landlord, Fullers London Pride
Average wine price by the glass: £4

Licensee: Giles Webster
Last orders for dinner: 10 pm
Open every day
Closed for holidays: 24 December-2 January, Easter
Main courses: from £9.95
Al fresco dining
Limited wheelchair access

SW3   **MAP 7** C4

Le Colombier

145 Dovehouse Street, Chelsea Square, London SW3 6LB
Tel. 020 7351 1155 Fax 020 7351 5124

ONCE a pub, this convivial and traditional French brasserie, tucked just behind the Royal Marsden Hospital, is loved by its Chelsea clientele, who find it a relaxing place that suits most occasions and represents good value for money.

The tables in the cosy dining-room are well appointed, but so close together that you can overhear the conversations of other diners nearby. For those who prefer more privacy and air, there is an attractive terrace in the summer.

The menu offers a wide choice of traditional French dishes such as foie gras, snails in garlic sauce, sole meunière, chicken with tarragon sauce, sweetbreads with morels, crème brûlée and crêpes Suzette. Ingredients are fresh, the meat is very tender, cooking times are accurate and sauces are simple but competent, if slightly on the rich side.

A salad of sliced seared tuna, cooked beautifully rare, is garnished with fresh chicory and topped with a generous quantity of oregano-flavoured vinaigrette. Thick, appetising steaks are served with Béarnaise or green peppercorn sauce and excellent pommes frites.

The nine-page wine list, which includes two useful pages of half-bottles, is almost entirely French and represents a good selection and good value. One could start, for example, with half a bottle of Riesling d' Alsace, Trimbach, at £11.50, then continue with a refreshing half-bottle of Chinon at £12. There are nine wines by the glass and French bottled beer is also available.

Their pride: Grilled veal chop with herbs
Inexpensive wines: Le Colombier Château Brown (Graves) 2001, £23.90; Chablis Alain Geoffrey 2003, £22.90

Proprietor: Didier Garnier
Last orders for dinner: 10.30 pm (Sunday 10 pm)
Open every day
Set lunch: from £14.50
Main courses: from £13
Private dining: 10-30
Al fresco dining
Wheelchair access

W1   MAP 7 C3

The Connaught, Angela Hartnett ★

Carlos Place, London W1K 2AL
Tel. 020 7592 1222 Fax 020 7592 1223
e-mail: reservations@angelahartnett.com

GORDON RAMSAY has transformed eating at The Connaught into a more contemporary experience, from the décor to the service. Gone are the waiters with morning-coats and the jacket and tie requirement for men. Modern paintings and attractive flower arrangements have lightened the atmosphere at the old Restaurant (now called Menu), but mahogany panelling, silver trolleys and crisp pressed linen preserve part of the old tradition. The Grill has kept its name but has also lightened its décor.

Angela Hartnett, who had an Italian grandmother, draws her inspiration mainly from the Mediterranean, relying for her flavours on fresh produce of the highest quality rather than on elaborate sauces. Fresh Italian bread arrives with exquisite olive oil. Pasta always features among starters; risotto is cooked to perfection and is the highlight of any meal here.

Main courses make full use of fish, vegetables and herbs. John Dory is simply roasted and served with a warm salad of summer vegetables, globe artichoke purée and hazelnut vinaigrette. Breast of duck arrives pink and moist and with roast foie gras, port-glazed turnips and candied red onions, giving it a pleasing, slightly sweetish flavour. Panna cotta of rhubarb with port jelly, white chocolate and raspberry sorbet mixes textures and flavours.

The reasonably priced set lunch menu is less elaborate and does not always reach the same culinary heights, but is nevertheless perfectly satisfactory.

Their pride: Pressed foie gras, Joselito ham, new season truffle, with white peach chutney
Inexpensive wines: Vermentino di Sargedna Funtana Irada, Andrea Marchi £30; Côteaux du Languedoc Les Secrets Château de Lascaus 2000, £28

Proprietor: Gordon Ramsay Holdings Ltd.
Last orders for dinner: 11 pm
Open every day
Set lunch: from £30
Set dinner: from £55
Private dining: 8-50
Wheelchair access

W2   MAP 7 B2

The Cow ★

89 Westbourne Park Road, London W2 5DN
Tel. 020 7221 5400/020 7221 0021 Fax 020 7727 8687
e-mail: thecow@thecow.freeserve.co.uk

THE COW is renowned for its seafood platter, a gargantuan feast of crab, clams, shrimps, whelks, winkles and, of course, the other ingredient the place is famous for – oysters.

You see them almost as soon as you step inside, a glass cabinet full of ice and three to four types of oysters – Irish Rocks, Fines Claires and Falmouth Rocks all year, and Irish Natives when there is an R in the month.

The less fatty Fines Claires taste splendid with granary bread, French butter, a pint of Guinness or a glass of crisp Saumur blanc. Or, if oysters are not for you, just order a pint of prawns.

Specials change daily, and include dishes such as an excellent summer vegetable risotto of broad beans and runner beans enriched with lightly melted Parmesan.

For meat eaters there are fine plump sausages with home-made mashed potato, or grilled leg of lamb with red wine sauce, while, if you fancy a touch of the exotic, there is sesame crusted tuna with spinach and wasabi dressing. Home-made ice-creams, in particular the vanilla tinged with caramel, make a fine end to the meal.

The upstairs dining-room specialises in the great fish of the sea, perhaps roast turbot and artichokes with mashed potato au beurre, or poached sea trout with salad of new potatoes. The fish is super-fresh, the cooking accurate and the accompaniments and sauces are discreet.

Speciality food: The Cow seafood platter
Draught beers: Fullers London Pride, Sharps Doom Bar
Average wine price by the glass: £3.50

Licensees: Tom Conran and Bajram Berisha
Last orders for dinner: 10.30 pm
Open every day
Closed for holidays: 3 days at Christmas
Main courses: from £12
Private dining: 10-40
Al fresco dining
Children welcome

SW3   MAP 7 C4

Cross Keys

1 Lawrence Street, London SW3 5NB
Tel. 020 7349 9111 Fax 020 7349 9333
e-mail: cross.keys@fsmail.net

IN AN elegant side-road road off Cheyne walk, just yards from the Thames, the Cross Keys has a handsome frontage emblazoned with two giant carved white swans, a fox and huge crossed keys and illuminated by carriage lanterns.

Inside this old hostelry are flagstone floors, open brick fireplaces, gilded mirrors and assorted grand ornaments that all create an individual, baroque style in the spacious bar – take a peek at the first-floor gallery and its amazing suspended light fitting.

To the rear is the bright restaurant with its full-width glass atrium ceiling. This is more conventionally furnished, with wooden tables and pew-style bench seating, the open-plan kitchen working at one end. Service is relaxed, helpful and comfortably attentive.

A tabletop miniature blackboard lists daily specials – perhaps mushroom soup; tortellini with asparagus sauce; poached egg, spinach and mushroom tart, or salmon fishcake with rocket salad and tartare sauce. The main menu has starters like full-flavoured gazpacho Andalou with flaked crabmeat and croutons, or chicken liver, foie gras and cognac parfait. To follow, perhaps, a Yakitori rib-eye steak with Asian greens, or roasted sea bream with peas and broad beans, or roasted pork belly in a light calvados jus.

Puddings continue to impress: crème brûlée with a madeleine and chocolate sauce, or caramelised lemon tart on pain sucré.

Weekends bring a fixed-price menu (two or three courses) of ample choice.

Speciality food: Modern European
Draught beers: Courage Best, Courage Directors
Average wine price by the glass: £3.75

Licensees: Carmel Azzopardi, Rudi Weller and Michael Bertorelli
Last orders for dinner: 10.45 pm (Sunday 9.45 pm)
Open every day
Closed for holidays: Bank Holidays
Set lunch: from £14.50 (Saturday and Sunday)
Main courses: from £12.50
Private dining: 15-40
Children welcome in restaurant
Limited wheelchair access

E3   MAP 8 C2

The Crown

GASTROPUB

223 Grove Road, London E3 5SN
Tel. 020 8981 9998 Fax 020 8983 2336
e-mail: crown@singhboulton.co.uk

OVERLOOKING Victoria Park, this gastropub strives to serve organic food and beer and generally adopts eco-friendly policies. Wild salmon is not served 'because it is an endangered species'; all shellfish comes from Scandinavia and Iceland, and oysters come from the west of Scotland, because these waters are not over-fished.

The menu changes twice a day and might include, for example, carrot, coriander and coconut soup, salmon fishcakes, salad or crisp belly of pork with squash gratin and piquant sauce.

Chilled melon and mint soup is made from melon, water-mint, a little sugar and a touch of Saussignac wine, a refreshing starter that illustrates the virtues of simplicity.

Roast trout is beautifully moist and served with delicious pommes lyonnaise, a ragout of leeks and a very competent beurre blanc sauce. Excellent ingredients and good presentation.

As well as a range of organic beers, there is an excellent wine list, which includes an Assyrtico Tsantali from Greece at £3.90 for a standard glass, or a Côteaux de Tricastin at £4.30. Larger glasses are available, as is good wine advice.

Last but not least, a jug of tap water is often suggested as an alternative to mineral water, refreshing in more ways than one.

Speciality food: Roast organic salmon fillet, saffron potatoes, wilted spinach and aïoli
Draught beers: Shoreditch Organic Stout, St. Peter's Organic Best Bitter
Average wine price by the glass: £4.40

Licensee: John Smart
Last orders for dinner: 10.30 pm
Closed: Monday lunch
Closed for holidays: 25 December
Main courses: from £10
Private dining: 15-26
Al fresco dining
Children welcome
Wheelchair access

W14   MAP 7 A4

Cumberland Arms ★

29 North End Road, London W14 8SZ
Tel. 020 7371 6806 Fax 020 7371 6848
e-mail: thecumberlandarmspub@btconnect.com

A DISTINCTIVE blue-painted pub, with beautifully maintained flower boxes, near the Olympia end of the North End Road, the Cumberland specialises in Mediterranean cuisine that is much appreciated by discerning local residents.

Food naturally takes centre stage in the simple bar and eating area behind a balustrade to the rear. The blackboard menu, on duplicated sheets, changes twice daily; the intelligently selective choices – six starters, half a dozen mains, just a couple of desserts – speaking volumes of a serious culinary approach.

The warmth of the south is vividly recalled in a fine baked goat's cheese bruschetta served with a caponata of Sicilian aubergine, tomato relish, pine-nuts, sultanas and basil. And the same theme continues with excellent grilled Italian sausages accompanied by potato and beetroot gratin, an original, harmonious combination. Alternatives might be marlin steak and black olive tapenade or smoked haddock poached in aromatics.

The chocolate and almond cake is a must for lovers of rich desserts, and a savoury mountain Gorgonzola served with grilled bread, shaved apple and mixed leaves is a strong choice.

The approach to wine is a model for a gastropub: both the dozen whites and reds by the glass and the impressive bottle selection have been listed to match the distinctive Mediterranean cooking. Service is always friendly, professional and swift. Breads and dip come at once and the meal is well paced.

Speciality food: Mediterranean cuisine
Draught beers: Fullers London Pride, Deuchars IPA
Average wine price by the glass: £3

Licensees: James Gill, Richard and George Manners
Last orders for dinner: 10.30 pm
Open every day
Closed for holidays: Easter and Christmas
Main courses: from £9
Al fresco dining
Children welcome before 7 pm
Wheelchair access

Drapers Arms ★

44 Barnsbury Street, London N1 1ER
Tel. 020 7619 0348 Fax 020 7619 0413

THIS Georgian building boasts a spacious ground floor and, at the back, a lovely terrace. You can choose to eat, from the same menu, on the ground floor or (in the evening and for Sunday lunch) in more comfortable dining-room upstairs, where you quickly get a feel of the quality that is to follow by the arrival of excellent warm walnut and raisin bread with a small bowl of an exquisitely light, lemony hummus.

Starters on the extensive, quite ambitious menu include good home-made soups and unusual salads, while main courses, even when trying to cater for simpler palates, have a creative touch. Fish and chips, for example, might involve deep-fried plaice, pea purée and crème fraîche tartare sauce.

Tuna tartare with wasabi and lime pickled cucumber is a very refreshing starter, with balanced flavours and textures. Shoulder of lamb is roasted slowly and arrives tender, moist and full of flavour, together with carrots, capers and soft herbs to balance the richness of the meat.

A popular main course is scallops, beautifully served in their shells with creamed fennel, baby onions en croûte and truffle mash. Desserts include the likes of panna cotta and chocolate cake.

An extensive wine list covers most regions and styles, with many bottles at under £20 and a selection of about 20 reasonably priced wines by the glass.

Speciality food: Deep-fried plaice and chips, pea purée, crème fraîche tartare
Draught beers: Old Speckled Hen, Courage Best Bitter
Average wine price by the glass: £4

Licensees: Paul McElhinney and Mark Emberton
Last orders for dinner: 10 pm
Open every day
Closed for holidays: Christmas
Main courses: from £9.50
Private dining: up to 45
Beer garden
Children welcome (after 8 pm must be dining)
Wheelchair access

EC1   **MAP 7** E2

The Eagle ★

GASTROPUB

159 Farringdon Road, London EC1R 3AL
Tel. 020 7837 1353

LIKE most great successes, The Eagle – which is, of course, the original gastropub – is a simple, charming place where the smell of careful cooking wafts across the room from a tiny cooking range behind the bar, such as you would find in a trattoria in Northern Italy or a tapas bar in Spain.

There is no formal menu, just the day's specials on blackboards, likely to change completely between lunch and dinner.

Tapas could range from smoked mackerel pâté to Serrano ham and tortilla Española. This is genuine modern European cooking, unfussy, steady and delicious.

Herbs are used judiciously in penne with tomato, marjoram and Parmesan, and again in a pot-roast of topside of beef flavoured with oregano and olives, these savoury, herbal notes in fine harmony with the casserole cooking juices. As a change from meat there might also be riboleta, a summer bean stew.

Usually there is just a single dessert, which might be Portuguese custard tart, but there is always the splendid Manchego, Iberia's best ewe's milk cheese, with slices of apple and toast.

Warm flavours of the south also pervade the wine choice and include a fine Syrah/Grenache blend from Costières de Nîmes. Excellent strong coffee is made in a traditional Italian Vesuvius metal pot.

Speciality food: Bife-Ana (marinated rump steak sandwich)
Draught beers: Eagle IPA, Charles Wells Bombardier
Average wine price by the glass: £3

Licensee: Michael Belben
Last orders for dinner: 10.30 pm
Closed: Sunday evening
Closed for holidays: 24-26 Dec, 1 Jan, Bank Hols
Main courses: from £7
Al fresco dining
Children welcome
Wheelchair access

W5   MAP 8 A3

Ealing Park Tavern

GASTROPUB

222 South Ealing Road, London W5 4RL
Tel. 020 8758 1879 Fax 020 8560 5269

A GREAT cavernous tavern, its round tower reminiscent of some horror film-set in Transylvania, this pub overlooks South Ealing Park. Until 2002, it was nothing more than a local boozer, but since then, Nicholas Sharpe has built up a sound reputation for classic bistro cooking backed up by a good range of real ales.

Vestiges of the old place are there in the main bar, with its dark, well-worn wood floors, but the food action is subtly sectioned off through an archway that leads to an ante-room with a zinc bar counter. There are a few tables for diners here, but more in the main dining-room, where you can see the chef and his team at work in the kitchen.

Dishes majoring on Mediterranean flavours are the heart of the changing blackboard menu. Typical starters are asparagus and cannellini bean soup, or duck liver pâté with pickled cucumber, or goat's cheese and ratatouille tart, the latter featuring exemplary light pastry and exactly the right flavours.

Pan-roasted halibut was very fresh and nicely cooked, the crushed new potatoes a better accompaniment than the over-generous portion of shaven fennel, its strong flavours tending to eclipse that of the fish. Other choices include marinated lamb steak with couscous salad and risotto of chicken and woodland mushrooms.

Sharpe is as passionate about wines as he is about his food. The selection by the glass ranges from a Dr Bürklin Wolf Riesling Trocken, great with the halibut, to a Couly Dutheil Chinon, ideal with the lamb.

Speciality food: Classic bistro cooking
Draught beers: Timothy Taylor, Grand Union
Average wine price by the glass: £3.75

Licensee: Nicholas Sharpe
Last orders for dinner: 10.30 pm
Closed: Monday lunch
Closed for holidays: 25 and 26 December
Main courses: from £9
Beer garden
Children welcome
Wheelchair access

SW18 MAP 8 B3

Earl Spencer

GASTROPUB

260-262 Merton Road, Southfields, London SW18 5JL
Tel. 020 8870 9244 Fax 020 8877 2828
e-mail: theearlspencer@hotmail.com

ON THE rather soulless A217 Merton road through Southfields, the Earl Spencer is a godsend. Once merely an undistinguished roadhouse, it was taken in hand by Jonathan Cox (ex-Havelock Tavern) in August 2002 and is a now a destination bistro-pub for South Londoners, with its terrace/beer garden and its simple, comfortable bar. The Hook Norton bitter here is so good that any drinker wedded to wine should try it as a natural partner to the honest, gutsy cooking of Mark Robinson, a colleague of Jonathan's from the Havelock.

Mark is keen on baking and smoking (fish, that is), so don't miss his splendid breads and in particular his half-pint of oak and beech smoked Atlantic prawns with aïoli.

There are plenty of pure flavours, such as duck, beetroot and summer vegetable soup, the medley of tastes well balanced and given a lift by horse-radish crème fraîche. Slow-cooked lamb shoulder was moist and succulent, not too fatty. The bavette (skirt) steak is also a winner, nicely tender after marinating for four days. Puddings include coconut and banana fritters – rich and sweet, but light and digestible – with passion fruit sauce. There are fine sorbets and ice-creams and a duo of superior mature Cheddar and Dunsyre blue cheeses.

The wine selection is laudable for range, quality and value. Ten by the glass include Griollo Lamura (£3.10), a dry Sicilian white of real presence. There is a spacious function room upstairs, where regional wine and food dinners are popular events.

Speciality food: Home-baked breads; home-smoked prawns
Draught beers: Shepherd Neame Spitfire, Hook Norton Best
Average wine price by the glass: £2.90

Licensees: Peter Richnell and Jonathan Cox
Last orders for dinner: 10 pm
Closed for holidays: 5 days at Christmas
Main courses: from £10
Private dining: 35-70
Beer garden
Children welcome
Wheelchair access

WC1   MAP 7 E1

The Easton

GASTROPUB

22 Easton Street, London WC1X 0DS
Tel. 020 7278 7608

THREE years ago, the two pioneering Australian owners boldly changed this pub's name and refurbished the whole place, at the same time identifying their priority as imaginative, well-prepared food.

A two-minute walk from the Royal Mail Mount Pleasant depot, it is in the style of the new wave of gastropub – clutter-free, with wooden floor, open fire, upholstered chairs and wooden tables.

Friday nights are frantically busy, so then the kitchen serves only tapas. A blackboard menu does not list first courses as such, but a salad of tasty buffalo mozzarella with vine tomatoes, kalamata olives and basil could be ordered as a lighter dish.

For main dishes some Antipodean influence is brought to bear in emu sausages with champ, cauro nero (black cabbage) and pancetta gravy, or chargrilled ostrich steak. Try the roasted lamb rump with couscous and harissa, or the smoked paprika chicken schnitzel thinly coated in a breadcrumb crust with a chickpea, artichoke and feta salad.

Roast cod with herb and lentil salad and basil aïoli, or risotto with scallops, roast tomato, saffron and chilli, may also feature.

There is usually only one pudding offered. One example is the soft apple tarte Tatin with its paper-thin, caramelised, buttery pastry, accompanied by delightful clotted cream ice-cream.

Sundays see only traditional roast dishes served.

Speciality food: Roasted lamb rump with couscous
Draught beers: John Smith, Red Stripe
Average wine price by the glass: £3.50

Licensees: Andrew Veevers and Jeremy Sutton
Last orders for dinner: 9.45 pm (Sunday 9.30 pm)
Closed: Saturday lunch, tapas only Friday night
Closed for holidays: 1 week Christmas
Main courses: from £8.95
Al fresco dining
Children welcome before 7 pm
Limited wheelchair access

SW1   MAP 7 C4

The Ebury, Ground Floor   *GASTROPUB*

11 Pimlico Road, London SW1W 8NA
Tel. 020 7730 6784 Fax 020 7730 6149
e-mail: info@theebury.co.uk

ON THE fringes of Chelsea and Belgravia, The Ebury's bar and brasserie is on the cusp of the restaurant category yet just makes it as a pub serving draught real ale.

It is a case of first come, first served and, as the place is packed early in the evening, particularly later in the week, it pays to arrive in good time in order to get a table.

This is upmarket brasserie-style food with quite stiff prices to match – a starter of Cornish crab is £16.50. Better value are the competently prepared lamb's sweetbreads, which are tender and well trimmed, accompanied by green beans, shallots and sherry vinaigrette. This full garnishing tendency can spill over into too many flavours in one dish: witness the ceviche of salmon and both mackerel and hand-dived scallops.

Yet, overall, the cooking is consistent and enjoyable. A good main course is the chicken breast, potato and onion cake, with baby artichoke salad and fresh girolles.

Desserts are a strong point, from an innovatively conceived Valrhona milk chocolate tart through champagne poached peach with raspberry jelly to panna cotta with fresh strawberries.

The 60-strong brasserie wine list, with 12 choices by the glass, is a fine compilation. It ranges from good growers' champagnes and Morgon from a top producer to very interesting whites from a wide variety of sources: Galicia, Alto Adige, Western Australia, and New Zealand.

Speciality food: Confit pork belly sandwich on Poilâne bread
Draught beers: Fullers London Pride, Leffe
Average wine price by the glass: £4

Licensee: Hannah Bass
Last orders for dinner: 10.30 pm
Open every day
Main courses: from £15
Private dining: 20-65
Children welcome
Wheelchair access

Embassy ★

29 Old Burlington Street, London W1S 3AN
Tel. 020 7851 0956 Fax 020 7734 3224
e-mail: restaurant@embassylondon.com

ONE OF the best values in town is the superb three-course menu du jour at this long, sleek restaurant near Savile Row. In what looks at first sight like an archetypal venue for executives with generous expense-accounts, the surprise is the rare distinction of the cooking and the relatively modest prices.

Executive chef and partner Gary Hollihead and head chef Mark Grogan will offer such delights as a ballottine of chicken and foie gras with a salad of tender green beans, shallots and girolles, or butternut squash soup, or carpaccio of beef fillet with a poached egg and truffle dressing. Perfectly seasoned roast monkfish is accompanied by sweet and sour aubergine and mussels in a very subtle mouclade of saffron and lightly curried spices.

The quality continues with dessert, perhaps a tart of lemon and mascarpone rendered unforgettable by the addition of figs that have been marinated in tarragon syrup.

Then there is carte, which deals in luxuries such as rock oysters and caviar or lobster ravioli, buttered baby spinach and shellfish vinaigrette jus, with to follow robust roasted belly of pork, glacé carrots and parsley mash. And to finish, you might have white chocolate cheesecake with mandarin sorbet or chocolate banana fondant and peanut brittle ice-cream.

The wine list initially looks rather limited, but the actual selection cannot be faulted for quality and interest, the wines by the glass being particularly good. Service by the gently mannered staff is discreet, effective and reassuring.

Their pride: Lobster tagliatelle Americaine, tomato and shallots
Inexpensive wines: Flagstone cellarhand 'The Spinnaker' (South Africa) 2003, £19.50; Primitivo di Puglia Castellani 2004, £17.50

Proprietors: Mark Fuller and Garry Hollihead
Last orders for dinner: 11.30 pm
Closed: Lunch Saturday, Sunday and Monday
Closed for holidays: Bank Holidays
Set lunch/dinner: £19.50 Tuesday-Friday
Al fresco dining

W1   MAP 7 D2

The Endurance   **GASTROPUB**

90 Berwick Street, Soho, London W1F 0QB
Tel. 020 7437 2944 Fax 020 7287 5248

IN THE heart of Soho, The Endurance is a deceptively simple pub: a single bar for eating and drinking, dark highly polished floor, modest natural wood tables and a spotless counter. Only lunch is served every day, seven days a week, usefully to 4 pm, so there is no food in the evening.

The choice of dishes on the oft-changing menu is short, but there is more than enough to trigger the gastric juices. Nibble quality fresh breads with a dip of virgin olive oil and balsamic as you decide what to eat. Starters range from fine smoked salmon on bruschetta through home-made hummus with flat bread, to chicken liver pâté served with sweet chilli and fig jam on toast.

Main courses have a pleasing, imaginative simplicity – maybe a Thai green curry with aromatic rice, grilled swordfish with steamed couscous, the meaty Endurance burger with a mango relish, or a chicken Caesar salad with avocado and crispy bacon.

Roast beef or pork at Sunday lunch is rightly popular: the loin of pork tastes freshly cooked, with moist flavoursome meat and crisp crackling. The apple pie, more like an open strudel, tastes as if it comes from a good Soho pâtisserie.

The wine list is similarly selective, but full of interest and sound judgment. Of seven choices by the glass, there is a pure-fruited River Edge Sauvignon from South Africa and a smooth organic Merlot; by the bottle, a good Rioja Crianza and an excellent Moutard Grande Cuvée from a champagne producer who still uses the rare Arbanne grape.

Speciality food: Grilled swordfish with steamed couscous
Draught beers: Fullers London Pride, Deuchars IPA
Average wine price by the glass: £3

Licensee: Alan Lyndon Drew
Last orders for lunch: 4 pm
Open every day
Closed for holidays: 25 and 26 December
Main courses: from £10
Beer garden (June to September)
Children welcome
Wheelchair access

SW3   **MAP 7** C4

The Enterprise

GASTROPUB

35 Walton Street, London SW3 2HU
Tel. 020 7584 3148 Fax 020 7584 2516
e-mail: enterprise@christophersgrill.com

A CORNER pub that has converted to semi-restaurant status in such an up-market neighbourhood can surely only be one more seriously trendy haven for the super-rich. Not a bit of it. Welcome to utter normality and an easygoing atmosphere reminiscent of a Parisian brasserie, with its paper tablecloths, bare boards and even a discreetly placed television set over one corner of the bar.

Will Woods's young service team adopt a welcoming, no-nonsense approach which is capable and attentive. It's all as comfortable and accessible as Australian chef Shaun Arrantz's offerings from his tiny, open-plan kitchen where he and his team concoct a fresh and uncomplicated selection of favourites (plus the odd surprise) on a regularly changing carte augmented by daily specials.

Salads abound (classic Caesar; caramelised onions with Muscat sultanas and Parmesan; pumpkin, pine-nuts and goat's cheese), or how about straightforward wild mushroom soup, a mixture of salami with prosciutto and melon, or else more exotic risotto of crayfish tails with tarragon for starters?

Mediterranean influence is apparent, with a welcome freshness and simplicity of style and presentation exploiting natural flavours to the full in, for example, breast of cornfed chicken with green olive tapenade pasta, chargrilled tuna with cucumber, tomato and mint sauce, or a handsome dish of prime, tender veal set on a pair of juicy, balsamic-braised field mushrooms and served with crunchy baby leeks and firm, buttery new potatoes. Old favourites such as bread and butter pudding, cheesecake and a particularly rich, gooey chocolate tart offer a satisfying finish.

Speciality food: Mediterranean influence
Draught beers: Grolsch, Guinness
Average wine price by the glass: £3.95

Licensee: Will Woods
Last orders for dinner: 10.30 pm (Sunday 10 pm)
Open every day
Closed for holidays: Christmas
Main courses: from £9.50
Children welcome
Limited wheelchair access

W1   MAP 7 D2

L'Escargot, Picasso Room

**48 Greek Street, London W1D 4EF
Tel. 020 7439 7474 Fax 020 7437 0790**

LIKE a rock star who goes back to producing a return-to-basics, acoustic album towards the end of a long and successful career, it seems that Marco-Pierre White has sought to retrace his roots at this quintessentially Gallic landmark on the gastronomic skyline.

The Master may not be personally in charge of the kitchen, but he must surely have more than a hand in its operation and output, and between him and head chef Jeff Galvin, L'Escargot continues to produce solid, dependable classics such as its duck consommé, foie gras terrine, fillets of red mullet with a tian of aubergines and tomato, magret de canard, poached beef and the obligatory snails, sauté à la bourguignonne with a chausson of spinach.

Crab lasagne was an excellent starter, the delicious crab meat between thin layers of pasta set in a velouté of wild mushrooms. Other choices might be paupiettes of salmon with caviar, or the subtle cauliflower soup with scallops and truffle. To follow, the chicken breast en cocotte was tender and moist, its creamy albufera sauce honest and enjoyable and packed with broad beans and slices of bacon. As an alternative, there was fillet of lamb with Provençal vegetables and a herb jus, or else the superb pigeon dish with ravioli of wild mushrooms and a fumet of ceps.

A good tarte fine of apples with crème normande, or blackberry soufflé with green apple sorbet, epitomise the trustworthy nature of a meal of notably even quality throughout.

Their pride: Challan duck
Inexpensive wines: Lacroix Blanc Sauvignon Blanc/Grenache Vin de l'Aude 2003, £15; Lacroix Rouge Cabernet Sauvignon/Grenache/Merlot 2003, £15

**Proprietors: Jimmy Lahoud and Marco-Pierre White
Last orders for dinner: 11 pm
Closed: Saturday lunchtime; Sunday, Monday
Closed for holidays: August, Christmas
Set lunch: from £20.50
Set dinner: from £42
Private dining: up to 60**

SW7   MAP 7 B4

L'Etranger

36 Gloucester Road, London SW7 4QT
Tel. 020 7584 1118 Fax 020 7584 8886
e-mail: etranger@etranger.co.uk

THE DECOR is modern and minimalist in style, mostly in shades of grey and black, at this Asian-influenced French restaurant named after the classic novel by Albert Camus to reflect the Algerian origins of its owner, Ibi Issolah.

Head chef Jérome Tauvron is a veteran of the kitchens of Alain Ducasse, Pierre Gagniaire and Michel Guérard, but he also has a profound interest in eastern cooking, which shows itself in such dishes as prawn soup with water mimosa and laksa leaves, or Thai chicken soufflé with coconut milk and holly basil, or flash fried fillet of Kobe beef with wild white and green asparagus and summer truffles, or monkfish tabanyaki with shizo leaves.

The more Gallic contributions include tartare of Charollais beef, a beautifully constructed terrine de lapin en gelée and roasted veal chop with truffle mash and mushroom cream. Vegetarians have their own menu. Among desserts, the trio of fig, green tea and liquorice crèmes brûlées stands out. The three individual crèmes come in little square pots along with a small bowl of macerated strawberries garnished by fresh coriander and a vanilla pod, all neatly arranged Japanese-style on a platter.

The wine list covers some 600 bins and is packed with interest in an impressive geographical spread. There is a good number of half-bottles spread through its pages, but for those for whom a half-bottle is just not quite enough, each of the two dozen or so wines offered by the glass is also available in 50cl pichets.

The restaurant has its own cocktail bar, Opal, in the basement.

Their pride: Eel with foie gras, steamed vegetables and seaweed
Inexpensive wines: Viognier "Le pied de Samson" George Vernay 2002, £39; Les Terraces de l'Ermita Palacios 2002, £39

Proprietor: Ibi Issolah
Last orders for dinner: 11pm
Closed: Sunday
Closed for holidays: 25 December
Set lunch: from £14.50
Main courses: from £7.50
Private dining: up to 20
Wheelchair access

N1   MAP 7 F1

Fifteen ★

13 Westland Place, London N1 7LP
Tel. 0871 330 1515 Fax 020 7251 2749

BE AWARE that Jamie Oliver's colourful restaurant, which aims to help unemployed youngsters by turning them into potential star chefs, is booked weeks ahead for dinner and several days ahead for lunch. Once you do get in, you will understand why.

From the start, there is so much that appeals: scallop sashimi cured in Japanese lime with Asian herbs, or buffalo mozzarella marinated in crème fraîche, then on to, say, a skilled rendition of ravioli of wild rabbit with mascarpone, lemon, thyme and a chanterelle sauce, or quite excellent potato gnocchi with beet leaves, served in a well-married creamy Castelmagno and walnut sauce.

Fish-lovers will be drawn to roast turbot with late-picked, lightly cooked radicchio, or West Mersea sea bass with stem artichoke trifolato. Outstanding meat dishes include chargrilled marinated leg of lamb with spice-rubbed squash, fresh herbs and Italian spinach – though perhaps the salsa of balsamic vinegar is not really necessary with such good lamb.

For dessert, bitter-sweet chocolate tart with date and banana ice-cream produces a superb combination of flavours and the pastry is feather-light.

Overall, ingredients are first-class and the vivid flavours of the mainly Mediterranean cuisine are skilfully brought out by clearly well-trained chefs. Friendly and natural young front-of-house staff are swift and efficient, and the two Australian sommeliers show both great knowledge and the talent to communicate it.

Their pride: Scallop crudo
Inexpensive wines: Basa Blanco (Spain) 2004, £22; Porcupine Ridge Syrah (South Africa) 2004, £25

Proprietor: Fifteen Foundation
Last orders for dinner: 9.45 pm
Closed: Sunday dinner
Closed for holidays: Christmas, 31 December
Set lunch: from £25
Set dinner: from £60
Limited wheelchair access

Fino

33 Charlotte Street, London W1T IRR
Tel. 020 7813 8010 Fax 020 7813 8011
e-mail: info@finorestaurant.com

NO STRANGERS to the hospitality business, brothers Sam and Eddie Hart combine respect and passion for all things Spanish with a keen eye for a market niche waiting to be filled, and Fino fulfils all these criteria. Smartly contemporary and comfortably airy despite its basement setting, the restaurant manages to be both authentic and sophisticated.

The familiar appeal of Spanish country cooking has been cleverly refined to provide a sort of Iberian gastronomic excursion. Tapas tasters are followed by, say, morcilla and white beans, rump of lamb with prune sauce, or crisp pork belly, so that a pre-dinner bite becomes a substantial meal of strong, uncompromising flavours that still manage to display a certain finesse.

Simplicity is very much a keyword, and the toasted tomato bread, pepper croquetas and straightforward seafood from la plancha sum up the typically unfussy appeal. There is obvious enthusiasm for producing authentic food, and with a good deal of style.

In general, the food is hearty but not heavy and even deep-fried items – including squid that really does taste as if it has recently come from the sea – are reassuringly grease-free, and there is a thoroughly enjoyable sparkle about the simple and well-chosen fresh ingredients.

Fino it most certainly is, very far from the cliché image that has attached itself to Spanish restaurants.

Their pride: Suckling pig
Inexpensive wines: Lagar de Cervera Albariño Rias Baixas 2003, £24; Urbina Crianza Rioja 2000, £25

Proprietors: Sam and Eddie Hart
Last orders for dinner: 10.30 pm
Closed: Sunday
Closed for holidays: Bank Holidays
Set lunch: from £17.95
Set dinner: from £28
Wheelchair access

SW19   MAP 8 A4

Fire Stables

GASTROPUB

27-29 Church Road, London SW19 5DQ
Tel. 020 8946 3197 Fax 020 8946 1101
e-mail: thefirestables@thespiritgroup.com

NAMED after its original use as a stable for the horses that used to pull the local fire engines, this Wimbledon village establishment has a vibrant dining-room at the back with open-plan design, bare walls and wooden floors, but it is rather noisy. Those who prefer peace and quiet can choose to eat in the comfortable, rustic bar area where tables are available on a first-come-first-served basis.

The daily changing menu draws its inspirations primarily from the Mediterranean, with some Asian ideas thrown in. Starters such as home-made soup, pâté and salads are attractively presented and competently prepared. A tasty sweet potato, lemongrass and fresh coriander soup has intense flavours harmoniously balanced.

More elaborate main courses may include supreme of chicken with saffron and chorizo risotto or rack of lamb with dauphinoise potatoes and peperonata. Duck breast arrives beautifully pink and full of flavour; fillet of salmon is pan-fried and served with crispy lettuce, garlic, ginger and a pungent soya-based oriental sauce.

Desserts are a speciality and consistently enjoyable: two grilled peach halves are topped by mango ice-cream of faultless texture and flavour; greengage tart is equally successful, perfectly baked and served with crème fraîche.

The wine list is strong on the New World, with the wines grouped by style. A glass of the luscious Golden Miranda Botritus from Australia, sipped sitting on one of the comfortable leather sofas in the bar area, is the perfect finish to the meal.

Speciality food: The Fire Stables lamb burger, served with big chips and salad
Draught beers: Affligem Blonde, London Pride
Average wine price by the glass: £4

Licensees: Cathy-Sue Hope and Lisa Phillips
Last orders for dinner: 10.30 pm (Sunday 10 pm)
Open every day
Set lunch: from £12.50
Set dinner: from £19.50
Children welcome
Wheelchair access

Foliage ★

**Mandarin Oriental, 66 Knightsbridge, London SW1X 7LA
Tel. 020 7201 3723 Fax 020 7201 3811**

SLEEKLY made-over and renamed, this venerable Knightsbridge dining-room, overlooking Rotten Row, is now one of the best hotel restaurants in town. Chef Chris Staines is not afraid to try out new ideas, but he does so with an impeccable sense of balance and harmony, and a sure mastery of flavours.

His talent is shown to real advantage in the three-course menu du jour at lunch, which might begin with roasted foie gras served on a caramelised pineapple tarte Tatin, and continue with fillet of beef roasted medium-rare and served with open cannelloni of braised oxtail, white onion soubise and sauce Gevrey Chambertin, and a garnish of pleurote mushrooms and spinach.

The selection of wines by the glass is just as thoughtful as the cooking. An Austrian 2003 Grüner Veltlinger of real presence goes well with the foie gras, while a Côteaux du Tricastin from the Rhône, light on tannin but rich in pure Grenache fruit, is an ideal lunchtime red for the beef.

At dinner, the carte might feature poached Scottish lobster, crab fondue with oven-roasted tomato, or Limousin veal under a herb crust with cauliflower risotto and truffle jus. Among the tempting desserts is Tahitian chocolate mousse with orange yoghurt ice-cream. Excellent petits fours and espresso to finish. In addition, there is a tasting menu of five courses.

The wine list is extensive and the prices are fair considering the location, with several excellent bottles under £30.

Their pride: Duo of foie gras, caramelised endive tarte Tatin, vinaigrette of leeks
Inexpensive wines: Château Tour des Gendres 2003, £19.50; Château de Las Caux 2002, £19.50

**Proprietor: Mandarin Oriental Hyde Park (Part of the Mandarin Oriental Hotel Group)
Last orders for dinner: 10.30 pm (Sunday 10 pm)
Open every day
Closed for holidays: 25-26 Dec (dinner only), 1 Jan
Set lunch: from £25
Set dinner: from £50
Accommodation: 200 rooms**
Wheelchair access

EC2 MAP 7 F2

The Fox Dining Room ★ *GASTROPUB*

28 Paul Street, London EC2A 4LB
Tel. 020 7729 5708

GASTRONOMIC treasures abound behind the understated brown ceramic exterior and old etched windows of The Fox, which lies between Old Street and Moorgate Underground stations and is a popular place, so it pays to book for anything more than a bar snack.

The ground floor houses an endearing bar with ceiling fans, wall lights, swept wooden floor, simple furnishings and a central circular servery. Upstairs, the candlelit dining-room leads to a sizeable open-air terrace complete with shrubbery.

Bar meals might consist of lighter offerings such as marinated rump steak sandwich, the renowned hot salt beef sandwich, or perhaps poached wild sea trout.

The daily set menu of two or three courses, with choices in each sector, is served both in the bar and the dining-room. Starters include duck consommé, tasty razor clams with melted butter and flat parsley, or chicken livers on toast.

For main courses try onglet with roasties and Béarnaise sauce or the precisely roasted (pink) leg of lamb with its lightly salted outer crust and supremely tender meat.

Temptation remains strong with sublime puddings such as white peach and almond tart with crushed almonds (served hot), raspberry mess, or gooseberry polenta cake.

Most of the 22 listed wines are available by the glass.

Speciality food: Hot salt beef sandwich on rye
Draught beers: Charles Wells Bombardier, Stella Artois
Average wine price by the glass: £3.25

Licensee: Michael Belben
Last orders for dinner: 10 pm
Closed: Saturday and Sunday
Closed for holidays: Bank Holidays
Set lunch: from £15
Set dinner: from £15
Private dining: up to 35
Al fresco dining
Children welcome
Wheelchair access

SW11   MAP 8 B3

Fox and Hounds ★

66 Latchmere Road, Battersea, London SW11 2JU
Tel. 020 7924 5483 Fax 020 7738 2678
e-mail: foxandhoundsbattersea@btopenworld.com

BETWEEN Battersea and Clapham Common, this pub is not only a genuine 'local' but also a food stop of strong regional character, where the Portuguese chef does wonders with the vivid flavours of southern Europe.

From the daily changing blackboard menu, you could start with Jerusalem artichoke soup with thyme and olive oil, then perhaps *espetadas*, Portuguese skewered lamb served with borlotti beans, tomatoes and mint yoghurt. Simple and quite excellent is the griddled pork chop with polenta, or go for the chicken 'fiorentina' casserole with rosemary and fennel roast potatoes.

Fish-eaters are catered for with, for example, the aromatically flavoured poached haddock, or there is rib-eye steak with sweet potato and celery gratin. The attractive French cheese plate features Pont l'Evêque and Bleu d'Auvergne, and the puddings, which include strawberry tart and an almond and chocolate cake, more than pass muster.

As an extra boon to all this good food, the atmosphere is still that of a traditional pub, complete with Battersea regulars downing the excellent Deuchars and Harveys Bitter. The place is simple, with bare wood floors, a patio and a beer garden.

The wine list is as exceptional as the food, a dozen wines by the glass ideal for quality and variety. Among the bottles is Seghesio Old Vines Zinfandel from Sonoma and Kim Crawford Pinot Noir from Marlborough.

Speciality food: Mediterranean
Draught beers: Deuchars, Harveys
Average wine price by the glass: £3.60

Licensees: Dennis Reus and Richard Manners
Last orders for dinner: 10.30 pm
Closed: Monday-Thursday lunch
Closed for holidays: 24 December-1 January
Main courses: from £10.50
Beer garden
Children welcome before 7 pm
Wheelchair access

SE1   MAP 7 F3

The Garrison ★

99–100 Bermondsey Street, London SE1 3XB
Tel. 020 7089 9355 Fax 020 7407 1084
e-mail: info@thegarrison.co.uk

NOTABLE for its dark green ceramic tile exterior, The Garrison, which was formerly The Honest Cabbage, sits on a corner site just a short stroll from London Bridge station, in the regeneration area of Southwark.

It offers food that is inventive without being over-ambitious and, interestingly, breakfast is served every day, featuring the likes of omelettes and smoked haddock, poached egg and hollandaise.

For lunch, you might start with mackerel escabèche, saffron and olives, French onion soup with Gruyère crouton, or a daily special such as linguine with shell-on succulent clams enlivened by red chilli and chives, which can also be ordered as a main course, as can some other starters.

Main courses tempt with the likes of roast wild trout with Parma ham, sage and mushroom polenta in a red wine jus, or pork belly with crisply roasted casing and supremely tender, moist meat, served with a delicate and smooth potato purée.

Lighter dishes at lunchtime include a roast beef sandwich with tomato, horse-radish and chips.

In the pudding sector, fusion cooking is manifested in a thinly crunchy oriental roll filled with banana and dark chocolate and served with a caramel sauce, or you might opt for the lemon tart or apple crumble.

Speciality food: Pork belly with smoked bacon and endive
Draught beers: Star Opramen, Adnams
Average wine price by the glass: £4.20

Licensees: Adam White and Clive Watson
Last orders for dinner: 10 pm (Sunday 9.30 pm)
Open every day
Closed for holidays: 25 & 26 December, 1 January
Main courses: from £10.40
Private dining: up to 30
Children welcome at weekends
Wheelchair access

W1   MAP 7 C3

Le Gavroche ★★

43 Upper Brook Street, London W1K 7QR
Tel. 020 7499 1826 Fax 020 7491 4387
e-mail bookings@le-gavroche.co.uk

RESTAURANTS come and go, tastes for food and ambience change, but Le Gavroche continues to delight. Michel Roux took over from his father, Albert, as chef/patron in 1991 and with a team headed by chef de cuisine Nicolas Laridan, he combines his family's high standards with his own enthusiasm for innovation.

The amuse-bouches, a portion of lobster bouillabaise in aspic and tiny tarts of foie gras terrine on a bed of celeriac in mayonnaise, were delicious. So was the marbled terrine of meats and pâté, the mixed flavours and textures topped by slices of white truffle with a vinegar, herb and mustard sauce.

Equally good was poached monkfish in a saffron sauce with a wine and cream base and bacon-flavoured button mushrooms. Puff pastry apple tart with an apricot glaze and vanilla ice-cream lived up to expectations.

Alternatives could have been chicken mousse with Roquefort and nuts, leg of larded and marinated lamb served with chestnuts, and a stunning cheeseboard. A half-bottle of good wine, including Chorey les Beaunes 2001, coffee and petits-fours, make the £46 lunch price an absolute bargain.

The à la carte dishes, and the Menu Exceptionnel (seven courses at £86) ranged from lobster mousse with caviar and champagne butter sauce to hot foie gras with crispy duck pancake flavoured with cinnamon. The formidable wine list covers all tastes and pockets from a 1998 Bergerac de Raz at £16.50 to an 1849 Château d'Yquem at £18,800.

Their pride: Escalope de foie gras chaud et pastilla à la cannelle
Inexpensive wines: Pinot Blanc Leon Beyer 2003, £20; St. Emilion Château Vieux Sarpe 2001, £42

Proprietor: Le Gavroche Ltd
Last orders for dinner: 11 pm
Closed: Saturday lunch, Sunday
Closed for holidays: 25 Dec, 1 Jan, Bank holidays
Set lunch: from £46
Set dinner: from £86

Glasshouse ★

14 Station Parade, Kew, London TW9 3PZ
Tel. 020 8940 6777 Fax 020 8940 3833
e-mail: info@glasshouserestaurant.co.uk

A MINUTE'S walk from Kew Gardens railway station, this glass fronted restaurant is especially agreeable at lunchtimes or on balmy mid-summer evenings. Tables are quite closely packed and there are sometimes noticeable waits as the amiable staff strive to meet the discerning customers' needs in quite a small space. The patient will be rewarded by modern cooking showing a good balance of flavours with a lightness of touch. Lunch and dinner menus change daily and choosing from the eight starters and eight main courses is an absorbing exercise.

Grilled Glenarm salmon was finely cooked and served with Dorset crab, Waldorf salad and walnut crostini. Alternatives were a warm salad of wood pigeon or a superior leek and potato soup with pecorino and croutons. Black pudding, served with caramelised endive, sauce soubise and a poached egg, is particularly good.

Vegetarians are looked after in the sauté of ceps with pumpkin and creamed white polenta. And that staple of bourgeoise cuisine, blanquette of chicken, is given a modern treatment with wild mushrooms, truffled mashed potato, onions and lardons. If you like rich flavours, try the Longhorn beef and foie gras haché with a fried duck's egg, or for simple fresh fish, monkfish brochette, scallops and prawns with saffron linguine and aïoli – excellent.

The cheeses are from the best sources, and desserts do not fail, as in a hot chocolate fondant with crème anglaise or creamed rice pudding with rhubarb and ginger compote. The serious wine list from round the world is especially strong in burgundy and Rhône. Some prices are high, but so is the quality.

Their pride: Slow-roasted pork belly, apple tarte, choucroute
Inexpensive wines: Bergerac La Combe de Grinou 2003, £15; Côtes du Ventoux Sud Absolu Latitude 44 2003, £15

Proprietors: Nigel Platts-Martin and Bruce Poole
Last orders: 10.30 pm (Sunday 10 pm)
Open every day
Closed for holidays: Christmas and 1 January
Set lunch: from £23.50
Set dinner: from £35
Limited wheelchair access

W10   MAP 7 A2

Golborne Grove ★

GASTROPUB

36 Golborne Road, London W10 5PR
Tel. 020 8960 6260 Fax 020 8960 6961

BY THE iron bridge in Golborne Road, a cultural melting-pot in North Kensington, this gastropub, which changed ownership and its name some three years ago, is a winner.

Handwritten menus change twice a day and, as in all good places, choosing what to eat is a delightful process: nibble on marinated olives with quality breads, then kick off perhaps with chargrilled sardines and tomato brochetta.

The broccoli and spinach soup, ladled with care from the stockpot, had finely defined flavours of each vegetable, all of which were delicate and positive.

The diversity of choice is illustrated by such things as Argentinian rib-eye steak, pan-fried red sea bream and smoked halibut and spring onion risotto. The fish is admirably bright and fresh.

The veal saltimbocca was cooked accurately to order, the medley of veal and ham flavours just right, moistened with natural juices and nicely accompanied by sweet potato hash and mangetout.

There is a sensibly short choice of puddings, maybe tiramisù and crème brûlée, or the excellent white chocolate cheesecake.

Wines by the glass are a skilled selection of fresh, fruity reds and whites, showing a penchant for bold New World flavours.

Speciality food: Red sea bream with saffron risotto
Draught beers: Fullers London Pride, Budweiser
Average wine price by the glass: £3.15

Licensee: Z. Radojevic
Last orders for dinner: 10.30 pm
Open every day
Closed for holidays: 2 days Christmas
Set lunch: from £13
Main courses: from £9
Private dining: 15- 40
Al fresco dining
Children welcome
Wheelchair access

Gordon Ramsay at Claridge's ★★

Brook Street, London W1A 2JQ
Tel. 020 7499 0099 Fax 020 7499 3099

THIS glorious Art Deco restaurant is glamorous and sophisticated yet it has a relaxed atmosphere, and lunch – especially at the weekend, when the choice of dishes is wider – is remarkable value, so long as you select the wine carefully.

Many people wonder whether Gordon Ramsay has overexpanded, perhaps compromising standards of cooking at his restaurants. The answer lies in his commitment to perfection, as well as in his ability to discover chefs who have the talent to become real artists. As his Claridge's operation shows, Marc Sergeant is one of Gordon Ramsay's success stories.

A pea and mint veloute, topped with a little olive oil, makes a light and appetising amuse-bouche. Poached duck egg with broccoli purée, goat's cheese and truffle might be an unlikely combination of textures and flavours, but it works brilliantly.

Rump of lamb is another triumph: tender and full of flavour, cooked pink, its richness is skilfully balanced by a fricassee of broad beans, celeriac and shitake mushrooms and an exquisite shallot sauce.

A perfect dessert is assiette of peach – a small peach crumble, moist and with perfect texture; a roasted slice on Amaretto cream, and a small jar of peach jelly with rose petal granité.

There are no house wines and you have to be astute to find a relative bargain, such as a fine Albarino from Galicia at £29.

Their pride: Blue fin tuna two ways: carpaccio with pickled white radish, seared and marinated with sesame seed and soy dressing **Inexpensive wines:** Chenin Blanc/Sauvignon Blanc Jean Daneel 2004, £29; Chinon Vielles Vignes Michel Page 2002, £32

Proprietor: Gordon Ramsay Holdings Ltd
Last orders for dinner: 11 pm
Open every day
Set lunch: from £30
Set dinner: from £60
Private dining: 8-60
Wheelchair access

SW3   MAP 7 C4

Gordon Ramsay ★★★

68-69 Royal Hospital Road, London SW3 4HP
Tel. 020 7352 4441 Fax 020 7352 3334
e-mail: royalhospitalroad@gordonramsay.com

GORDON RAMSAY'S flagship restaurant displays rare perfection and refinement. The room has a warm, sophisticated feel, with beautiful flower arrangements and Venetian glass ornaments. The service is polished and knowledgeable. Above all, the cooking, under the direction of executive chef Mark Askew, is better than ever, and if some inconsistencies may have been noticeable in the past, they have now disappeared.

An amuse-bouche of potato salad and chopped marinated salmon, blended with a mild horse-radish cream and topped with a delicate Sauternes flavoured jelly and caviar, is a splendid start and is typical of the chef's genius.

Two round pieces of roasted saddle of rabbit are served with a fricassee of wild mushrooms, artichokes and spinach, while two pink rabbit ribs sit on celeriac purée and a spoon-shaped biscuit is stuffed with grain mustard and a tarragon sauce of perfect consistency and flavour. This is a visual and a culinary masterpiece.

Fish and shellfish dishes abound and are sensational. A fillet of line-caught turbot, roasted to perfection to bring out its freshness, is served on a bed of spinach, accompanied by asparagus, baby morels, water melon cubes and an exquisitely delicate citrus jus. The same magic appears in desserts such as a delicious lime parfait with a mouth-watering melon sorbet encased in white chocolate, or a bitter chocolate cylinder with coffee granité and ginger mousse. The raving could be endless.

Their pride: Ravioli of lobster poached in light bisque and lemon grass and chervil velouté
Inexpensive wines: Château Bauduc Bordeaux blanc sec 2004, £18; Saint-Chinian Domaine Rimbert 2003, £22

Proprietor: Gordon Ramsay
Last orders for dinner: 10.45 pm
Closed: Saturday and Sunday
Closed for holidays: 2 weeks Christmas and New Year
Set lunch: from £40
Set dinner: from £70

SW1   MAP 7 D3

Goring Hotel Restaurant

17 Beeston Place, London SW1W 0JW
Tel. 020 7396 9000 Fax 020 7834 4393
e-mail: reception@goringhotel.co.uk

THIS restaurant, run by the fourth generation of the same family, is a time capsule of the 1960s. Just fifty yards from Buckingham Palace, here you will discover strait-laced service, an eagle-eyed management presence, and morning coats and Ascot hats on royal garden party days. Some elderly regulars claim that not only have standards been rigidly maintained, but also that any new embellishments are strictly in the style of an elegant dining-room at a gentleman's club – admitting ladies, of course. The spacious and comfortable bar is perfect for a pre-prandial chat that no one can overhear.

You visit this place for unadorned and untitivated poached fillet of Cornish haddock, steak-and-kidney pie, breast of Norfolk duck, grilled calf's liver and Scottish Châteaubriand with Béarnaise sauce. These may be prefaced by glazed Scottish lobster omelette or deep-fried whitebait with tartare sauce.

The excellence of raw materials takes precedence, unlike some of the productions of modern fusion cuisine or over-eager young chefs that deliver confusing assemblies on your plate. Vegetarians are paid more than scant respect with wild mushroom and leek tart with asparagus sauce and new potatoes, or 'twice baked' Cerney Ash goat's cheese soufflé with celeriac sauce – their very sounds are tempting.

Waitresses and waiters glide by with the cheese tray laden with a respectable choice, or a sweet trolley of gâteaux and fruit salads. Perhaps here good old British puddings would be more in style. Some excellent choices are offered on the adroitly assembled wine list.

Their pride: Grilled calf's liver with sweet-cured Suffolk bacon
Inexpensive wines: Côtes du Luberon Château Val Joanis rosé 2004, £25; Fleurie Château de Raousset 2003, £28

Proprietor: Jeremy Goring
Last orders for dinner: 10 pm
Closed: Saturday lunch
Set lunch: from £29.75
Set dinner: from £40
Private dining: up to 50
Accommodation: 71 rooms
Wheelchair access

W9   MAP 7 A2

Grand Union

GASTROPUB

45 Woodfield Road, London W9 2BA
Tel. 020 7286 1886 Fax 020 7286 6446
e-mail: grand.union@ukonline.co.uk

RIGHT beside the Grand Union Canal on the borders of the Harrow Road and Westbourne Park, this pub's great feature is the beer garden and terrace above the waterway. Weather permitting, most people choose to eat here rather than in the main bar. Food is served all day, and you give your order at the upstairs bar.

The speciality here is a range of reasonably priced home-made pies, which are full of flavour under crisp, properly cooked pastry. They include a traditional chicken, asparagus and leek pie, cod and salmon pie and a new addition, pork and chorizo.

The main menu offers more modern dishes with the usual Asian and Mediterranean touches: Thai pumpkin soup with red chilli (not too fiery), Thai fish cakes, or the very popular platter of smoked salmon, guacamole, hummus and Turkish bread – all fresh and good.

More substantial options might include beefburger with mint raita or lamb shank with mustard mash. There is always a vegetarian option, such as risotto of roast butternut squash, aubergines and courgettes.

Finish with rich desserts such as sticky toffee or banoffi pudding, the flavour of fresh banana coming through well, all set on a digestive biscuit base. Eight decent wines by the glass feature a fine Chilean Cabernet Casa de Piedra.

Speciality food: Home-made pies
Draught beers: Adnams Broadside, Marston Pedigree
Average wine price by the glass: £3.30

Licensee: Louise Lawler
Last orders for dinner: 10 pm
Open every day
Main courses: from £8.50
Beer garden

W1   MAP 7 C3

Greenhouse ★

27a Hay's Mews, Mayfair, London W1J 5NY
Tel. 020 7499 3331 Fax 020 7499 5368
e-mail: reservations@greenhouse.co.uk

THE REFURBISHED Greenhouse sets itself very high standards, and these are certainly achieved in terms of the wine list, one of the most interesting in London. Not content with offering the French and Italian classics, it also provides an admirable selection from the New World, from less well-known regions of Spain and even from Switzerland. The question is whether such excellence can be matched by the cooking.

The starters and the main courses on the carte are innovative, though perhaps sometimes with a tendency to try too hard to be different, as in the steamed turbot dish that comes with fricassee of seabeef and periwinkles. Scottish langoustines are a good starter, or there is pheasant and chestnut soup with pheasant quenelle and black trompettes.

An amuse-bouche of creamy white Lebanese cheese and what tasted like olive oil with spices was pleasant enough. Panna cotta of cauliflower with a velouté of cauliflower, which is served as a pre-appetiser, was very attractively presented and also refined and light in texture.

Main courses include, in season, grouse, roasted to perfection and served pink with foie gras and jus, or there is seared fillet of beef with slow-cooked short rib of beef, an excellent dish of well-defined flavours, though the accompanying ice-cream of orange marmalade and horse-radish was perhaps, again, an eccentric mixture. For dessert, the prune soufflé was faultless.

Their pride: Pan-seared foie gras with espresso syrup and Amaretto foam
Inexpensive wines: Laurent Brusset Gigondas Montmirail (France) 2000, £50; Sybille Kuntz Riesling Dreistern Mosel 2001, £50

Proprietor: Marlon Abela Restaurant Corp. (MARC)
Last orders for dinner: 10.45 pm
Closed: Sunday, Saturday lunch
Closed for holidays: Bank Holidays
Set lunch: from £28
Set dinner: from £60
Private dining: 6-10
Wheelchair access

SW11   MAP 7 C5

Greyhound at Battersea   `GASTROPUB`

136 Battersea High Street, London SW11 3JR
Tel. 020 7978 7021 Fax 020 7978 0599
e-mail: eat@thegreyhoundatbattersea.co.uk

THE GREYHOUND, in Battersea High Street, looks like a perfectly traditional, handsome pub that has had some money spent on it. Closer inspection, though, suggests that it is quite outside the mainstream of London pubs known for their food and drink chalked on a blackboard. Whether in the bistro-style dining-room, hung with French posters, or at overspill tables in the front bar, the feel is very much that of a restaurant. The food offered is exclusively from set-price menus, the wine list is encyclopaedic and expensive. It's all the brainchild of Australian sommelier Mark Van der Goot, who wants to provide a 'fine dining experience' in an informal setting.

Yet the Greyhound just about makes it as a pub: excellent Brakspear bitter is available and a young couple who arrived just too late for lunch were encouraged to take a consoling drink in the bar. Another party of local residents came in just for the ale and to read the papers.

The front-of-house and kitchen teams are young, enthusiastic and international. Head chef Tomislav Martinovic, who is Croatian, cooks in competent modern style, exemplified by Sunday lunch. Chicken rillette with cornichons was a light and flavourful starter, while Argentinian sirloin served in a shallot sauce was tender, well aged. The dinner menu moves into higher gear with Herdwick mutton loin and baby artichoke, or Scottish halibut, asparagus and quail's egg.

The 20 wines by the glass are real discoveries and the range of North American and Southern Hemisphere Pinot Noir is excellent.

Speciality food: Herdwick mutton loin
Draught beers: Brakspear Bitter, Leffe
Average wine price by the glass: £4

Licensee: Mark Van der Goot
Last orders for dinner: 9.30pm
Closed: Sunday evening, all day Monday;
Closed for holidays: Bank Holidays
Set lunch: from £12
Set dinner: from £26
Private dining: 8-25
Beer garden
Children welcome for Sunday lunch
Wheelchair access

W6   MAP 8 A3

The Grove

GASTROPUB

83 Hammersmith Grove, London W6 0NQ
Tel. 020 8748 2966 Fax 020 8741 4093

THE aim of this gastropub is to provide modern European cuisine with a strong Mediterranean influence and an organic thrust that does not cost a fortune.

From the open-plan bar and eating areas one can see the chefs at work in the equally open-plan kitchen with ingredients that are universally fresh.

A good start is the leek tart, the pastry crisp and fully cooked, the diced fresh leek and vegetable base topped with a slice of goat's cheese and two warmed cherry tomatoes. Vivid Mediterranean flavours are realised in crabmeat and lemon risotto or chargrilled merguez sausages with couscous and red pepper salad.

Complemented by garlic mash and an innovative caraway sauce, the pan-roasted guinea fowl has the fresh-cooked flavour of an excellent bird. It is also a fine idea to steam broccoli.

Other choices include a chargrilled loin of marlin with pine kernels or pan-roasted neck of lamb with rosemary and crushed new potatoes.

Puddings are a strength. Try the pear and apple crumble or the home-made white chocolate cheesecake.

Pure-flavoured wines in fine condition include an aromatic Sauvignon and a rich Cabernet from the Cape.

Speciality food: Modern European cuisine, strong Mediterranean influence and organic thrust
Draught beers: John Smith, Kronenbourg
Average wine price by the glass: £3.50

Licensee: Susana Fernandez
Last orders for dinner: 11 pm
Open every day
Closed for holidays: 25 and 26 December, 1 January
Set lunch: from £13
Main courses: from £13
Private dining: up to 24
Al fresco dining
Children welcome

W1 MAP 7 C3

Guinea Grill ★★

GASTROPUB

30 Bruton Place, London W1J 6NL
Tel. 020 7499 1210 Fax 020 7491 1442
e-mail: guinea@youngs.co.uk

TUCKED away in a Mayfair back street, in a former stable behind an olde-worlde pub, The Guinea Grill offers the best of traditional British fare.

Head chef Ewan has been there for nine years and believes British cooking achieves the best results by using top-quality ingredients interfered with as little as possible. Oysters, smoked salmon or fresh asparagus shine with their freshness alone. Steaks, made from Aberdeen Angus beef, dry-aged for twenty-eight days, are unbeatable: a thick piece of sirloin, for example, is perfectly grilled, brown outside, pink inside and exceptionally tender, juicy and full of flavour. Fried or mashed potatoes and, perhaps, some green vegetables are all that is needed to balance the richness of the meat.

Such is the expertise of the chefs at making exquisite savoury pies that they have been crowned three times National Steak and Kidney Pie Champions and even won the Steak Pie of the Century Award in 2000. Their magic with pastry shows equally in desserts, such as a delicious lemon tart

The wine list is particularly strong on clarets and offers excellent value, England being represented by Three Choirs Phoenix 2002 from Gloucestershire at £15.50.

Sommelier Farid has been here for 15 years and his memory is legendary. He is reputed not only to remember guests who have not been back for several years, but even the wine they chose.

Speciality food: Angus sirloin steak with Béarnaise sauce
Draught beers: Youngs Bitter, Youngs Special Premium Ale
Average wine price by the glass: £5.50

Licensee: Carl Smith
Last orders for dinner: 11 pm
Closed: Saturday lunch, Sunday
Closed for holidays: Christmas and Bank Holidays
Main courses: from £11.50
Private dining: 8-28
Children over 10 welcome

E14   MAP 8 C2

The Gun

GASTROPUB

27 Coldharbour, Docklands, London E14 9NS
Tel. 0207 515 5222 Fax 0207 515 4407
e-mail: info@thegundocklands.com

THERE is one remaining vestige of old-fashioned humanity in Docklands and it is The Gun. It is fun, lively and cosmopolitan and, unlike much of what surrounds it, it has history. Legend has it that Nelson used to have secret trysts with Emma Hamilton here, which makes one wonder whether the food was as good as it is now.

They might not have had recourse to the potted duck with pear chutney, or a ballottine of (raw) salmon with onion relish and crème fraîche as potential starters, followed by a choice of smoked haddock and garden pea risotto with Parmesan foam, or grilled whole sea bass with vanilla and Chardonnay dressing, or supremely moist and tender rump of lamb with samphire and wild asparagus, or pork loin with chanterelles.

There is the occasional foray into what the illustrious admiral might have called Frenchie fodder, but overall the home-produced fare in the dining-room, plus an enticing array of bar snacks, remains defiantly English.

Even the oft-borrowed 'Mediterranean slant' is kept steadfastly at bay and good, honest, homespun flavours predominate, with a minimum of fussy presentation and a maximum of respect for top-quality raw materials.

To finish, some particularly well-made desserts include a cracking nougat glacé with citrus fruits.

Speciality food: Modern British with French influences
Draught beers: Adnams Broadside, Youngs Ordinary
Average wine price by the glass: £3.10

Licensee: Tim Rawlins
Last orders for dinner: 10.30 pm
Open every day
Closed for holidays: 25 and 26 December, 1 January
Main courses: from £13
Private dining: 4-12
Beer garden
Children welcome
Wheelchair access

W1   **MAP 7** D2

Hakkasan ★

8 Hanway Place, London W1T 1HD
Tel. 020 7927 7000 Fax 020 7907 1889
e-mail: reservation@hakkasan.com

BEHIND a distinctly modish profile, this is a serious Chinese restaurant with excellent food and quite outstanding service. It is always busy, yet the staff, under constant pressure, are ready to meet every request – if you want a particular sauce that is not part of a dish, it comes at once.

At lunchtimes the dim-sum are impressive for their quality and originality, ranging from Assam bay cuttlefish to blue swimmer crab rolls and Chinese chive dumpling. At dinner, tong fong sha soft-shell crab is a model of what this delicacy should be, while salt and pepper squid is a splendid example of freshness, tender texture and precise cooking.

Among main courses, roasted silver cod with champagne and Chinese honey is a signature dish, while steamed sea bass and braised whole abalone with Hokkaido scallop are also strong choices. Equally sure is stir-fried Szechuan duck breast served with oyster mushroom and Chinese mustard, the duck admirably cooked, the sauce spicy and piquant.

Desserts are more European in character, as in lemon tart, fig clafoutis and Bailey's crème brûlée. The wine selection covers some of the world's best.

Hakkasan is very much a rendezvous for well-heeled, fashionable young people, a fact reflected in the prices of the more recherché fish dishes and many of the wines.

Their pride: Peking duck
Inexpensive wines: Estate Dry Riesling Wittman 2003, £30; 'Areti' Biblia Chora (Greece) 2003, £32

Proprietor: Alan Yau
Last orders for dinner: Monday-Wednesday 11.30 pm, Thursday-Saturday 12.30 am
Open every day
Closed for holidays: Dinner 24, 25 Dec, lunch 1 Jan
Main courses: from £12.50
Wheelchair access

SE1   MAP 7 F4

The Hartley

GASTROPUB

64 Tower Bridge Road, London SE1 4TR
Tel./Fax 020 7394 7023
e-mail: enquiries@thehartley.com

THE HARTLEY is on a busy London street a few minutes from Bermondsey market. It is named after the famous jam-maker whose premises opposite were the site of fruit deliveries from Kent. Inside the red brick Victorian building is a spacious room with old oak flooring and music playing quietly. Service by a young team is notably friendly and easygoing and chefs can be seen at their work in the open-fronted kitchen.

The lunchtime menu is light, the evening dishes rather more extensive, supplemented by a blackboard of daily specials. On Saturdays, brunch starts at 11am and the popular Sunday roasts are served until 9pm.

Among the starters are a smoothly textured chilled gazpacho with a distinct pimento flavour, served with a crunchy crouton, and chicken salad with pancetta and avocado.

Main dishes worth trying include beef and Guinness pie – very generously portioned, tender diced beef in a rich, flavoursome sauce topped with flaky pastry and served with mashed potato and nicely firm cabbage.

Specials might be seared swordfish with niçoise salad or roast baby chicken with pancetta and tomato salsa. Alternatively, go for the salmon and smoked salmon fishcakes or perhaps beefburger with large chips cooked in duck fat. Vegetarians may opt for the vegetable risotto. For dessert, try the tangy lime mousse brûlée, with a thin caramelised lid, or the chocolate fondant.

Speciality food: Braised pig's head and scallops
Draught beers: Boddingtons, Guinness
Average wine price by the glass: £4.50

Licensee: David Jackson
Last orders for dinner: 10pm
Open every day
Closed for holidays: 25 and 26 December
Main courses: from £9
Private dining: 10-80
Children welcome

W14   MAP 7 A3

Havelock Tavern ★

GASTROPUB

57 Masbro Road, London W14 OLS
Tel. 0207 603 5374

SLOANE SQUARE goes west. In a once anonymous back street behind Olympia (now at the heart of a gentrified quarter of West London) is this great food pub that does things entirely on its own terms.

You cannot book, so in the evening you will have to fight for a table unless you arrive at seven-sharp (though single diners are welcome at the counter), and payment is by cash or cheque only. Every corner is packed, round the bar, in the 'dining area' at the rear, at six tables on the patio.

And there can be times when you must wait for your food, but the wait is worth it. Chef/owner Johnny Haughton (now in his eleventh year) and his kitchen team consistently cook some of the very best pub food in London. Pan-roasted fillet of cod, topped with the crispest skin and delicately seasoned with black pepper, was fresh and beautifully cooked, served with perfect chips and home-made tartare sauce. Just as memorable was roast chump of lamb, warm and light pink, framed by golden fat, ideally matched with boulangère potatoes and green beans.

The menu changes daily at both lunch and dinner. For lighter appetites, spiced red lentil soup with yoghurt and coriander or spring vegetable risotto are sure-fire choices. No short cuts in the puddings, either: try warm apple and treacle tart.

A dozen exciting, gently priced wines by the glass include a rich Shiraz from Santa Barbara and a mineral-fresh Soave. Brakspear ales on draught.

Speciality food: Oysters and langoustines (as available)
Draught beers: Brakspear Pride, Brakspear Pedigree
Average wine price by the glass: £3

Licensees: Peter Richnell and Jonathan Haughton
Last orders for dinner: 10 pm
Open every day
Main courses: from £10
Beer garden
Children welcome
Wheelchair access

NW3 MAP 8 B2

The Hill

GASTROPUB

94 Haverstock Hill, London NW3 2BD
Tel. 020 7267 0033

FOR many years a favourite bar among Belsize Park locals, this pub has now been made-over and renamed The Hill. The dining area is pleasantly sectioned off from the main bar with proper table settings on natural wood surfaces. The smiling staff take your order accurately and deliver it speedily.

The blackboard menu is typical brasserie food in modern European style. Regionally sourced ingredients are emphasised as in six native oysters with shallot vinegar. A summer tart with roasted peppers, bocconcini and basil is another good starter, and there is a soup every evening.

Main courses continue the regional theme: a fine chargrilled Scottish rib-eye was firm yet tender, accurately cooked pink and enhanced with a Merlot jus. There is a daily changing pasta dish or perhaps a salmon fillet with lemon and caper potato cake. Vegetarians are not forgotten with dishes such as melted goat's cheese with Puy lentils, spinach and rocket.

There are good puddings, too, such as the colourful Dame Rouge, consisting of chocolate ice-cream, strawberries and coulis, or the cassis cheesecake, which is light and ideally coupled with apricot compote.

The wine selection is a model of its kind with some 30 offerings. A dozen by the glass include excellent Provençal rosé, fresh Pinot Grigio from Trentino and Muscat de Frontignan. The drinking side of the pub remains very much a 'local', happily dispelling any sense of The Hill being too twee and trendy.

Speciality food: Regionally sourced ingredients
Draught beers: Fullers, Budvar
Average wine price by the glass: £4

Licensee: Kevin Simpson
Last orders for dinner: 10.30 pm (Sunday 9 pm)
Open every day
Closed for holidays: 25 December, 1 January
Main courses: from £11.95
Private dining: up to 20
Beer garden
Children welcome before 6 pm

The House ★★

GASTROPUB

63-69 Canonbury Road, London N1 2DG
Tel. 020 7704 7410 Fax 020 7704 9388
e-mail: info@inthehouse.biz

ON A tree-lined street in the outskirts of Islington you will find a red brick corner building that houses one of the best gastropubs in London. Friendly, welcoming staff, comfortable leather sofas round a brick fireplace, the cream colours on the walls, white linen on the well-spaced tables, and the small but spotlessly clean open-plan kitchen make one feel immediately relaxed. French windows lead to a small terrace, ideal for summer, and bring a lot of natural light into the dining-room.

The food shows a light and sophisticated touch and draws its inspiration from all over the world, especially the Mediterranean and Asia. A creative carte is supplemented by daily blackboard specials.

Starters include seared scallops; beef carpaccio with capers and a refreshing salad of tomatoes; French beans and grilled haloumi cheese. Sashimi of yellow tuna is presented with exotic leaves and flowers of different colours – a delight to the eye as well as the palate.

Main courses are equally exciting. Salmon is grilled to perfection and accompanied by crayfish tails of exquisite flavour, crushed new potatoes and a fresh green salad. Vegetarians are catered for with unusual, tasty dishes such as a spinach and tomato dhal served with a spiced feta samosa.

The meal finishes on the same high note with desserts such as a delicious banana Tatin served with home-made vanilla ice-cream.

Speciality food: Sashimi of yellow tuna, yuzu and pickled ginger
Draught beers: Hoegaarden, Adnams
Average wine price by the glass: £4.50

Licensee: Barnaby Meredith
Last orders for dinner: midnight
Closed: Monday lunch
Set lunch: from £14.95
Main courses: from £13.50
Private dining: up to 30
Beer garden
Children welcome
Wheelchair access

Hunan

51 Pimlico Road, London SW1W 8NE
Tel. 020 7730 5712 Fax 020 7730 8265
e-mail: hunan.peng@btopenworld.com

THIS fixture of the Pimlico/Belgravia restaurant scene has been owned and run by the same family for some twenty-five years and three generations now work in the business. The intimate room, fronted by green shrubs and plants, has a simple and warm *en famille* atmosphere and they like to make up a meal for you, which could include regional specialities such as pan-fried spicy frogs' legs, equally spicy braised chicken with aubergine, or prawns in chilli sauce.

If fiery dishes are not your preference, there are plenty of more gently flavoured offerings: crispy aromatic duck with pancakes, quick-fried chicken with mangetout, or steamed whole sea bass in toasted sesame oil dressing. Ingredients taste fresh and cooked to order.

But the specialities of south-western China are the real stars of the menu. Sesame seeded king prawns are enhanced by a Hunan sauce which, in this case, is not too fiery. Good quality fillet of beef is similarly well handled, accompanied by finely sliced root ginger and fresh spring onions, the steamed rice accurately cooked and seasoned, the spicy aubergine exactly that, crispy and flavoursome. To finish, an old faithful of Chinese restaurants, glazed toffee-apple, is a very good example of its kind.

The wine list, selected by the son of the house, is a thoughtful compilation of fine things at sensible prices, including excellent Barolo from Prunotto and especially Ridge's superb old vines Geyserville Zinfandel 1999 from Sonoma, which is a perfect red to accompany spicy food.

Their pride: Belly pork with Chinese herb crust, garlic vinaigrette
Inexpensive wines: Semillon Cuvée des Conti Château Tour des Gendres 2003, £16; Tavel Rosé Domaine de la Mordorée 2004, £19

Proprietor: Yung-Shuan Peng
Last orders for dinner: 11 pm
Closed: Sunday
Closed for holidays: Bank Holidays, Christmas
Set lunch: from £28.80
Set dinner from: £32.80
Private dining: 6-25

Inn the Park

St. James's Park, London SW1A 2BJ
Tel. 020 7451 9999 Fax 020 7451 9998
e-mail: info@innthepark.co.uk

REPLACING the old cafeteria in St. James's Park, this gastro-café has been unobtrusively designed, with extensive use of natural wood, to harmonise with the beauty of the park, across which it presents lovely views to Horseguards and Whitehall.

The naturalness of the setting is reflected in the cooking, which uses organic produce wherever possible in seasonally changing menus. Suckling pig was tender and succulent, with good crisp crackling, and came on champ with the freshest apple sauce and the clearest of roasting juices.

Cornish crab with light mayonnaise and drizzling of excellent olive oil, served on toasted country bread, bursts with flavour yet is an ideally digestible starter, popular with the politicians and lobbyists who cross the park for lunch here. Both the grilled wild halibut with tomato hollandaise and the fish pie also look to be good choices.

For those who love the nursery puddings of their childhood and early schooldays, there are jam roly-poly and custard and steamed treacle sponge. Somewhat lighter is a pavlova with refreshing strawberries, blackberries and blackcurrants. The espresso coffee is very good.

Service by very informally dressed waiters, some with pony-tails, is disarmingly friendly and the selective wine list, with reasonable prices, features choices from the best growers round the world.

Their pride: Cornish crab on toast
Inexpensive wines: Sauvignon Blanc Colchagua Valley (Chile) 2004, £14.50; Rooks Lane (Australia) 2004, £15

Proprietor: Oliver Peyton
Last orders for dinner: 10 pm
Open every day
Closed for holidays: 25 and 26 December
Main courses: from £13.50
Al fresco dining
Wheelchair access

WC2   MAP 7 D2

The Ivy ★

1 West Street, London WC2H 9NQ
Tel. 020 7836 4751 Fax 020 7240 9333

THOSE who try hardest to visit this restaurant often do so for the wrong reasons: because it is frequented by celebrities. So it is supposed to be a place for rubbernecking. This is absurd, for although it is perhaps the most notoriously difficult restaurant in which to get a table – unless you book weeks ahead and then only if you are lucky – it is a very good one indeed and sought out equally for that reason alone.

Once inside, you are hit by what is music to any trencherman's ears: the joyful noise heard in all restaurants packed with customers who find happiness in the enjoyment of good food they can get their teeth into.

Another unmistakable sign of quality is the speed of waiters and headwaiters, darting in and out with trays held high. Relax and concentrate on the vast menu.

Perhaps first a duck and watercress salad, lovely crisped pieces in a nicely flavoured Chinese-type sauce with a very well-dressed salad – or try a lighter dish, the prettily presented plum tomato and basil galette.

Otherwise, after a superb truffled white bean soup with foie gras tortellini, focus on the elusive mutton: a Black Face mutton and turnip pie with a surprisingly light crust.

Then again, if you are particularly hungry, do not overlook the impressively portioned (and priced) Glen Fyne rib steak, well hung, juicy and well marbled.

Their pride: Salmon fishcake, sautéd spinach and sorrel sauce
Inexpensive wines: Monte Verde Sauvignon Blanc (Argentina) 2004, £15; Syrah Domaine Massamier La Mignarde (France) 2003, £15

Proprietor: Richard Caring
Last orders for dinner: midnight
Open every day
Closed for holidays: Christmas and August Bank Hol
Set lunch: from £21.50
Private dining: 25-60
Limited wheelchair access

NW5   MAP 8 B2

Junction Tavern ★

101 Fortess Road, London NW5 1AG
Tel. 020 7485 9400 Fax 020 7485 9401

THIS lively corner pub is an oasis in the gastronomic desert of Kentish Town. A wood-panelled bar invokes a traditional pub atmosphere whereas the dining-room, with its dark red walls, high ceiling and well-spaced tables, is a more relaxed place.

A sensibly short menu offers simple starters such as gazpacho with pimento relish alongside more ambitious fresh scallops, seared to perfection, topped with finely chopped pork crackling and served with a delicious pea purée. This a dish you might expect in a top restaurant, rather than a pub, and it clearly shows the freshness and quality of the ingredients as well as the skills of the chefs.

The same attributes are evident in fresh swordfish, beautifully grilled and served with braised Puy lentils and a mild paste of anchovies and olives. Poussin is simply roasted and arrives juicy and full of flavour, accompanied by a refreshing green bean, bacon and new potato salad. The chef's creativity extends to the desserts, which might include baked ginger cheesecake with rhubarb compote, or a chocolate frangelico cake with organic hazelnut ice-cream.

The wine list is not exceptional, but good value can be had by ordering Viognier Domaine de la Ferrandière 2004 at £14.50, or Côtes du Rhône Darriaud 2002 at £15.50.

Food from the same menu can be ordered in the conservatory at the rear and there is also an attractive beer garden.

Speciality food: Seared scallops, pea purée, pork crackling
Draught beers: Deuchars IPA, plus two guest ales
Average wine price by the glass: £3.50

Licensees: Chris Leech and Jacky Kitching
Last orders for dinner: 10.30 pm (Sunday 9.30 pm)
Open every day
Closed for holidays: 24-26 December, 1 January
Main courses: from £9.50
Beer garden
Children welcome in dining area
Limited wheelchair access

NW1   MAP 8 B2

The Lansdowne

GASTROPUB

90 Gloucester Avenue, London NW1 8HX
Tel. 020 7483 0409
e-mail: thelansdowne@hotmail.co.uk

POPULAR with young locals from Primrose Hill, the Lansdowne offers a spacious pub area with a bustling atmosphere on the ground floor, where diners can choose from a blackboard menu, as well as a dining-room of greater comfort (open for dinner only) on the first floor. The dining-room has dark colour schemes, a jazz soundtrack and, with its discreet lighting, a romantic atmosphere.

Unusual starters are red pepper soup with Greek yoghurt, or grilled sardines with fennel, apricot and pine-nut breadcrumbs. Main courses include such dishes as roast hake with mashed potato, braised fennel and garlic and paprika dressing; and roast chicken risotto with lemon and ricotta of a pleasant savoury flavour.

To finish, there is a large selection of unusual home-made desserts, ice-creams, sorbets and cheeses.

An excellent, sensibly priced wine list caters for most tastes, with a short description given on every wine. There are five whites, five reds and one rosé available by the glass. Château Les Crostes 2004, at £16.90 per bottle, is a very refreshing, dry rosé from Provence that goes with practically anything.

Organic beers and ciders are also on offer.

Speciality food: Chicken liver pappardelle, pancetta and sage
Draught beers: Star Opramen, Carling Black Label
Average wine price by the glass: £4.25

Licensees: Amanda Pritchett and Sandy Marshall
Last orders for dinner: 10 pm
Closed: Monday (until 5 pm)
Closed for holidays: Christmas
Set dinner: from £25
Main courses: from £12.50
Private dining: up to 60
Al fresco dining
Children welcome during day and in restaurant
Wheelchair access

W11   MAP 7 A2

The Ledbury ★★

127 Ledbury Road, London W11 2AQ
Tel. 020 7792 9090 Fax 020 7792 9191
e-mail: info@theledbury.com

EVEN with the magic lent to Notting Hill Gate by the film starring Hugh Grant and Julia Roberts, this seems an unlikely location for one of the capital's best restaurants. It opened in spring of 2005, its creators filling the same roles at the brilliant Square in Mayfair.

Chef/patron Brett Graham, a 26-year-old Australian, indulges in a veritable orgy of creation impossible to rank, in which lasagne with rabbit and girolles and London's best soufflés immediately spring to mind. But it goes on: raw tuna with avocado gazpacho; superb, paper-thin slices of duck breast with foie gras partnered, surprisingly yet successfully, by a light slice of peach tart.

An enthusiastic mention, too, is due to an exceptional beignet of frog's legs with watercress mayonnaise and to a rarity, toothsome confit of leg of guinea fowl with girolles.

Chicory crème brûlée, with fine coffee ice-cream, is unsurpassed for lightness and memorable flavour – though that is perhaps unfair to the excellent parfait of peach kernel with poached peach sorbet.

These delights are served partly in a room of minimalist, but far from cold, black-and-white décor surrounding diplomatically spaced tables and partly on a brand new, atmospheric terrace under giant umbrellas and suddenly conjured-up vegetation.

The icing on the cake is the admirable skill of the young staff.

Their pride: Lasagne of rabbit and girolles, velouté of thyme
Inexpensive wines: Saint-Veran Domaine de la Croix Senaillet 2003, £27.50; Côte de Brouilly Château Thivin 2003, £27.50

Proprietor: Bridgwater Entertainment Ltd
Last orders for dinner: 11 pm
Open every day
Closed for holidays: 2 days at Christmas
Set lunch: from £19.50
Set dinner: from £39.50
Wheelchair access

W1   MAP 7 C2

Locanda Locatelli ★

8 Seymour Street, London W1H 7JZ
Tel. 020 7935 9088 Fax 020 7935 1149
email: info@locandalocatelli.com

AS TYPICALLY Italian as the row of Vespas lining the pavement outside, this elegantly smart restaurant near Marble Arch provides a home-from-home for expatriates in search of the real thing, including many from the Italian embassy.

Always on hand (when kitchen duties permit), *il padrone*, Giorgio Locatelli, also provides more than a note of animated authenticity with his long, Latin locks and an air of excitable bonhomie as he marshals his ultra-professional team.

No stranger to London's Italian restaurant scene, Giorgio knows exactly what is required, both the atmosphere to be created and, above all, his native food at this chic rendezvous decorated in soft browns and beiges that has almost a 1960s feel about it.

The food, though, despite its defiantly traditional origins in which charcuterie and a range of more unusual pastas feature strongly, is firmly up-to-date in its presentation and the colourful dishes are packed with strong, natural flavours.

Ceps and radicchio marry well with beautifully gamey venison and the goat's cheese and truffle gnocchi are exquisite.

A delicious assortment of home-made breads – almost a meal in itself – deserves a special mention, as do the mouth-watering desserts, too often something of an afterthought in many Italian restaurants. Millefeuilles of maraschino with a toffee ice-cream provide a perfect finish.

Their pride: Rabbit with polenta
Inexpensive wines:: Verdicchio Lyricus Colonnara 2003, £12; Nero d'Avola Sangiovese Angelo 2000, £12

Proprietor: Giorgio Locatelli
Last orders for dinner: Monday to Thursday 10:30 pm, Friday and Saturday 11 pm, Sunday 10 pm
Open every day
Closed for holidays: Christmas and Bank Holidays
Main courses: from £14
Wheelchair access

SW10   MAP 7 B5

Lots Road Pub & Dining Room ★

114 Lots Road, London SW10 0RJ
Tel. 020 7352 6645
e-mail: lotsroad@thespiritgroup.com

THIS is an up-market pub/restaurant two minutes' walk from Chelsea Harbour and offering a sensibly composed menu of five starters, ten main courses and five desserts. Most tastes are catered for, with choices ranging from hamburger and chips or Toulouse sausage with mashed potato and onion gravy, to more creative and elaborate ones with some Asian influences, such as the use of vegetables like choy sum and lemongrass, and sweet and savoury combinations.

A mixed seafood risotto (containing diced clams, mussels, salmon and parsley) was made to order – a twenty-minute wait – and arrived beautifully moist and with a perfect al dente texture. A honey roasted duck breast cut in thick slices, cooked pink, juicy and full of flavour, came with lemongrass, choy sum and caramelised oranges. A more conventional, main course is pork chops, grilled to perfection, with sweet potato rösti and glazed pineapple.

There is a small but interesting selection of cheeses and the desserts include the likes of Rocky Road (chocolate with cherries, marshmallows, peanuts and raisins) and apple tarte Tatin with cappuccino ice-cream. The coffee is excellent and there is also delicious fresh mint tea.

The wine list is eclectic and sensibly priced, with the emphasis on Italy and the New World, and there is a good selection of about a dozen wines by the glass.

Speciality food: Sticky toffee pudding
Draught beers: Stella, Hoegaarden
Average wine price by the glass: £5.75

Licensees: Letitia Creevy/Spirit Group
Last orders for dinner: 10.30 pm
Open every day
Main courses: from £7
Children welcome
Wheelchair access

W2   MAP 7 B2

Mandalay

444 Edgware Road, London W2 1EG
Tel. 020 7258 3696
e-mail: picton@mandalayway.com

WHERE in London can you eat really well for less than £20 a head, including wine and everything else? Sadly, the list is too short for comfort, but Mandalay must come very near the top.

From the outside this looks like any ordinary café at the north end of the busy Edgware Road, close to Maida Vale. However, over the years this simply decorated restaurant has succeeded in putting Burmese cuisine on the London map.

The sheer quality of the home-made cooking and the amazing value for money mean that the place is packed every night and advance booking is essential.

Burmese cuisine is a hybrid of Chinese, Thai and Indian. The use of lemongrass, tamarind, coconut and tropical fruit means that flavours are intense and aromatic, but not pungent.

Large, firmly textured king prawns are beautifully lifted by lemon-grass sauce. Other notable dishes include perfectly fried mixed fritters as a starter, served with a choice of soya, chilli or tamarind sauce; coconut noodles with chicken, and delicious aubergines with potatoes.

Finish with seaweed-based gara gara jelly (an acquired taste) if you are adventurous, or with a soupy, coconut-flavoured tapioca if you prefer a more soothing dessert.

The wine list offers extraordinary value for money, with a list of nine adequate wines all priced at £8.90.

Their pride: Lemongrass king prawns
Inexpensive wines: Syrah Rosé Vin de Pays d'Oc £8.90; Chardonnay (Chile) £8.90

Proprietor: Altaf Ally
Last orders for dinner: 10.30 pm
Closed: Sunday
Closed for holidays: Bank Holidays
Set lunch: from £5.90
Main courses: from £5
Accommodation: 18 rooms
Limited wheelchair access

W2   MAP 7 B3

Mandarin Kitchen

14-15 Queensway, London W2 3RX
Tel. 020 7727 9012 Fax 020 7727 9468

THE HEYDAY of this well-known Chinese restaurant was during the 1990s, but it still draws legions of customers throughout a long day, attracted as much as anything by the straightforward treatments of good shellfish at prices that will not break the bank.

Roasted baby squid with garlic and chilli, or the steamed razor clams that are available seasonally, are popular choices, as is a starter of scallops in black bean sauce. Lobster features heavily on the menu, with a series of familiar Cantonese sauces, and fish such as sea bass, turbot and monkfish are usually available at market prices, often best when they are simply cooked.

Chinese regular customers will often opt for the whole braised abalone in oyster sauce, or else eel with pork and mushrooms. As for meat and poultry, there is, of course, a selection of stir-fried chicken dishes, the conventional Cantonese duck, and you will even find veal chop, served with black pepper sauce. Particularly noteworthy in all cases are the fine steamed rice and pak choi.

British favourites among Cantonese desserts, such as toffee apple and banana, are presented, but it is probably worth being a little adventurous and choosing something like red bean pancake.

The wine list offers good value throughout a careful selection. Service is jolly and friendly.

Their pride: Lobster noodle
Inexpensive wines: Le Saumon Sauvignon (France) 2004, £13.50; Mont-Auriol Merlot (France) 2003, £15.50

Proprietor: Stephen Cheung
Last orders for dinner: 11.15 pm
Open every day
Set lunch: from £10.90
Main courses: from £5.90
Wheelchair access

SW8   MAP 7 D5

Masons Arms

GASTROPUB

169 Battersea Park Road, London SW8 4BT
Tel. 020 7622 2007 Fax 020 7622 4662
e-mail: themasonsarms@ukonline.co.uk

AT WHAT you might call the railway end of Battersea Park Road, not far from the Dogs' Home, the Masons Arms might look like a typical drinker's haunt, but it is in fact a genuine gastropub.

For those just in the mood for a light snack, choose side-plates of chicken liver, pancetta and balsamic pâté with Turkish bread. Otherwise kick off with, say, spicy black bean tartlet and Greek yoghurt, or Thai fishcake with mango salsa and chilli dip. The house quartet of salads features one based on wok-fried squid with olives, capers, potatoes and poached egg.

A substantial platter to share has baba ghanoush (aubergines with tahina), hummus, guacamole, tabbouleh, alubia beans and Turkish bread as a taste-tour of the Mediterranean.

One perennially good dish is the roast rump of beef, pink and juicy, served with big chips, salad and red wine jus.

The range of main courses continues from the risotto of roasted pumpkin, spinach and shitake mushrooms, through chicken bhuna with basmati rice, to lamb chops marinated in mustard and soy sauce and served with feta cheese and olive and herb salad.

A couple of old faithfuls for dessert – sticky toffee pudding and banoffi pie – or a fair cheese selection of English goat's cheese, Stilton and mature Cheddar.

Wines by the glass have some fine Chilean choices from cooler vineyards and there is an excellent Miramar merlot.

Speciality food: Roast rump of beef with chips and salad
Draught beers: Adnams, Marston Pedigree
Average wine price by the glass: £3

Licensee: Mark Jackson
Last orders for dinner: 10 pm
Open every day
Main courses: from £9.25
Al fresco dining
Children welcome before 7 pm
Wheelchair access

W1   MAP 7 C3

Maze

10-13 Grosvenor Square, London W1K 6JP
Tel. 020 7107 0000 Fax 020 7107 0001
e-mail: maze@gordonramsay.com

THE instant success of Gordon Ramsay's latest innovation shows his marketing skills as he has now targeted another important sector of the market by offering a more casual dining experience. A relaxing, welcoming atmosphere is created by the eye-catching modern design by American David Rockwell and the rhythms of the background pop music.

The bar, where one can dine, leads to a maze of secluded dining areas where unusual, sometimes eccentric, dishes are offered in tasting portions, some also available in full portions. Foie gras and truffles feature prominently among the intricate descriptions. Results are consistently appealing, at least to the eye, and some to the palate, too.

A salad of violet artichoke and fresh truffle, topped with lettuce and truffle mayonnaise, is harmonious and refreshing, while risotto of peas, broad beans, wood sorrel and grated truffle creates an explosion of flavours, perfectly balanced. Scottish lobster with white radish, asparagus, and marinated beetroot with Sairass cheese, could do with a little more flavour; roasted scallops were slightly on the rubbery side, and the delicious Cornish crab mayonnaise with avocado was topped by icy sweet corn sorbet.

Main courses such as wild trout with confit lime, peas and caper purée, or beef with foie gras, snail and garlic, are consistently enjoyable. Eccentricity is reflected in some desserts; lemon thyme marinated peach with basil sorbet, strawberries and pepper jelly ends the meal on a high note.

Their pride: Risotto of carnaroli with peas, broad beans, wood sorrel and grated truffle
Inexpensive wines: Gewürztraminer Bollenberg Château d'Orschwihr 2003, £30; Château les Ormes le Pez 1997, £29

Proprietor: Gordon Ramsay Holdings Ltd
Last orders for dinner: 11 pm
Open every day
Main courses: from £7.50
Private dining: 6-10
Wheelchair access

TWICKENHAM   MAP 8 A3

McClements

2 Whitton Road, Twickenham, London TW1 1BJ
Tel. 020 8744 9610 Fax 020 8744 9598

THERE is something rather reassuring about the food at what is the flagship restaurant of John McClements's small local catering empire. There is no resort to gimmickry or artiness. The guiding principle is naturally contrived combinations of fine ingredients, which are presented quite straightforwardly. This is a place that deserves to be better known.

McClements and his chef have put together an attractive menu, which, although based on tradition, nevertheless contains a few surprises – the seasonal grouse choucroute, for example, or the vegetarian carrot jelly salad with confit tomatoes, baked round carrots, pickled yellow carrots and tomato consommé foam.

Otherwise, there is no shortage of classic choices: lobster, foie gras, quail, duck, venison, sweetbreads and chunky fish, all of which come in a variety of forms, all of them prepared in ways showing admirable restraint.

Of particular note is the wonderful selection of matured French farmhouse cheeses.

Their pride: Langoustine with pig's trotter, pickled vegetables
Inexpensive wine: Gigondas Clos du Joncuas 1998, £24

Proprietor: John McClements
Last orders for dinner: 10.30 pm
Closed: Sunday and Monday
Closed for holidays: 2 weeks from 26 December
Set lunch: from £25
Set dinner: from £38
Private dining: up to 20
Wheelchair access

WI   MAP 7 C3

Mirabelle ★

56 Curzon Street, London W1Y 8DL
Tel. 020 7499 4636 Fax 020 7499 5449
e-mail: sales@whitestarline.org.uk

TAKEN OVER and modernised by Marco Pierre White a few years ago, the Mirabelle has kept its beautiful Art Deco design and, though perhaps not as vibrant as before, it still radiates a certain glamour, making it a suitable place for a celebration. It is worth having a drink at the impressive bar, with its atmosphere of an ocean liner, before moving to the dark parquet flooring, brown leather banquettes, elegantly set tables and extravagant flower displays of the dining-room.

The never-changing classic French menu looks as if it had been written fifty years ago. This is one of the few places where you can still find dishes such as eggs Benedict, omelette Arnold Bennett, coulibiac de saumon or daube à l' ancienne. In addition, starters like raw marinated salmon salad, terrine de foie gras and a well-balanced aspic of oysters with watercress in a champagne jelly are attractively presented and thoroughly enjoyable.

Mediterranean flavours are recalled with main courses of grilled sole with citrus fruits, fennel and olive oil, and a superb veal chop, seasoned with herbs, grilled to perfection and served pink in its own jus. Desserts like tarte Tatin à la vanille and a refreshing gelée of fresh fruits in rosé wine, served with a raspberry syrup, cannot be faulted.

The wine list features the best producers, especially from France, and there is a useful selection of half-bottles. Dessert wines include no fewer than fifty vintages of Château d' Yquem, dating back to a bottle of the 1847 vintage at £30,000.

Their pride: Aspic of oysters and watercress, champagne jelly
Inexpensive wines: Touraine Sauvignon P. Buisse 2003, £21; Château Leboux Pic St. Loup 2000, £18

Proprietors: Jimmy Lahoud and Marco-Pierre White
Last orders for dinner: 11.30 pm
Open every day
Closed for holidays: 26 December, 1 January
Set lunch: from £17.50
Private dining: up to 48
Al fresco dining at lunch

Morgan M ★★

489 Liverpool Road, Islington, London N7 8NS
Tel. 020 7609 3560 Fax 020 8292 5699
e-mail: info@morganm.com

THIS is a very fine restaurant, simple and informal, with natural wood floors, yet elegantly appointed with classic table settings and pastel green colour schemes, the windows discreetly frosted and etched with the monogram of Morgan Meunier, its remarkable chef/patron.

Morgan, who comes from the Champagne country, previously cooked with Marc Meneau at L'Esperance in Vézelay and, with such a background, he is obviously a master of classical cooking technique. What mark him out, though, are his intelligence and his imaginative and thoroughly modern approach.

Mildly flavoured pumpkin soup acquires intensity with the addition of rosemary, and is further enhanced by an accompaniment of a light wild mushroom beignet. Roast leg of red partridge achieves an exceptional medley of flavours with braised red cabbage, a crouton of its liver and the confident addition of traditional bread sauce.

There is no shortage of other outstanding dishes to choose from, among them fillet of Dover sole meunière, which is accompanied by pancetta, poêlée of girolles and trompettes.

The wine list relies on an excellent, mostly classic and regional French selection, featuring particularly good vintages of Margaux cru bourgeois and Hermitage. Prices are very fair.

Service is attentive, natural and warm.

Their pride: Dark chocolate moelleux
Inexpensive wines: Bourgogne Pinot Noir Henri de Villamont 2001, £24; Muscadet Rémy Luneau 2002, £23

Proprietor: Morgan Meunier
Last orders for dinner: 9 pm
Closed: Sun dinner, Mon, Tues, Sat lunch
Closed for holidays: Christmas
Set lunch: from £19.50
Set dinner: from £32
Private dining: up to 12
Limited wheelchair access

EC1   MAP 7 E2

Moro

34-36 Exmouth Market, London EC1R 4QE
Tel. 020 7833 8336 Fax 020 7833 9338
e-mail: info@moro.co.uk

IN CLERKENWELL, close to Sadler's Wells, this is very much a straightforward, fairly priced restaurant where you are served honest, hearty North African and Spanish food in a very informal setting and in brisk but unhurried style. Not surprisingly, it fills up early, so booking is recommended.

The ingredients are paramount, often wood-roasted or charcoal grilled. In the first category, one excellent choice is pork, served with chestnuts, pancetta and savoy cabbage. The same treatment produces fine brill with sesame sauce, while the charcoal grill delivers good Spanish lamb.

Starters are no less robust. Pumpkin soup is flavoured with sesame and cinnamon, or there is excellent calf's liver with herb salad and cumin yoghurt, or else Cecina beef, oak smoked, which is served with beetroot salad and almond sauce.

Sherry trifle features, perhaps inevitably, among the desserts, but less creamy alternatives might be raisin ice-cream or a tart of chocolate and apricot.

The wine list has a serious selection of exceptional sherries, which includes Lustau old soleras and the supreme single-vineyard 'Innocente' fino. Often unusual Spanish wines share the honours with moderately priced bottles from Italy and Portugal.

Their pride: Crab Brik
Inexpensive wines: Dominio Espinal Yecla Blanco (Spain) 2004, £13.50; Torre de Barreda (Spain) 2002, £14.60]

Proprietors: Sam and Sam Clark, Mary Sainsbury
Last orders for dinner: 10.30 pm
Closed: Sunday
Closed for holidays: Christmas, Bank Holidays
Main courses: from £13
Private dining: up to 80 (Sunday)
Al fresco dining
Wheelchair access

Mosimann's Private Dining Club ★

11B West Halkin Street, Belgrave Square, London SW1X 8JL
Tel. 020 7235 9625 Fax 020 7245 6354
e-mail: dining@mosimann.com

ONE OF the greats of the British gastronomic scene for decades, Anton Mosimann is now at the height of his powers, which cover not only cooking (though he no longer does much personally) but also design (their Christmas dècors are unsurpassed), and powerful public relations – based always on real content.

On his concise menu, look out for dishes marked with the red 'M', his striking logo. Risotto ai funghi is striking for its concentrated wild-mushroom flavour and perfect consistency. The chicken liver parfait is intriguingly flavoured and almost worth having for the remarkable 'pistachio brioche' alone.

The rather pedestrian menu entry of 'Rendez-vous of Steamed Seafood' does not in any way convey the sophisticated taste of this light fish soup, its constituents from the day's market. And what a delight to find shoulder of mutton. Alternatives might be veal kidneys in mustard sauce or perhaps steak tartare Belfry.

The heavenly bread and butter pudding should not be missed, even if you feel you cannot manage a dessert. In a dazzling break with tradition, it is served cold and is so refined that it becomes almost ethereal.

The wine list is outstanding, comprising some ten vintages of Château Pétrus from 1983 back to 1945 (£750 to £12,300), but it does include some reasonably priced bottles.

Their pride: Risotto ai funghi
Inexpensive wines: Mosimann's Bourgogne Chardonnay 2001, £25; Château Calon St. Emilion 2001, £32

Proprietor: Anton Mosimann
Last orders for dinner: 10.30 pm
Closed: Sunday, Saturday lunch
Closed for holidays: Christmas
Set lunch: from £18.50
Set dinner: from £55
Private dining: up to 50
Wheelchair access

SW1   MAP 7 C3

Nahm

Halkin Hotel, 5 Halkin Street, London SW1X 7DJ
Tel. 020 7333 1234 Fax 020 7333 1100

THERE IS a vibrant buzz about this fashionable hotel restaurant a few yards from Hyde Park Corner, to which Thailophiles flock with the aim of recapturing the culinary spirit of memorable holidays. The stylish setting may be a far cry from the eating-houses of Phuket and Bangkok, but the kitchen's faithful interpretation of some of the country's regional specialities goes a long way towards recapturing at least some of that distant magic.

Coriander, ginger and lemongrass abound, of course, and the curry dishes are excellent – pungent and powerful as one would expect. The 'western' elements, though enjoyable in their way, can leave you a bit puzzled as to their inclusion. The likes of fried chicken livers, crispy pork skin and grilled trout could not be plainer (or less seasoned) in comparison with the fragrant curry that accompanies them.

A dish of partridge in a light sweet and sour sauce was excellent and the rustic curries full of a variety of vegetables appear to be the fiery genuine article. Such authenticity is perfectly laudable and the results are rich in native savours, even if some of the ingredients are subject to European influence.

Service is friendly and helpful, and this is a great place to go for a bowl of something spicy with their wonderful sticky rice. The glamorous trappings seem rather unnecessary, however – not to mention the heavy price-tag.

Their pride: Deep royal sea bream with three flavoured sauces
Inexpensive wines: Mud House Sauvignon Blanc (New Zealand) 2003, £28; Casa Lapostolle Merlot (Chile) 2003, £25

Proprietors: Halkin Hotel, Como Hotel Holdings
Last orders for dinner: 10.45 pm
Closed: Saturday and Sunday lunch
Closed for holidays: 24 and 25 Dec, Bank Holidays
Set lunch: from £26
Set dinner: from £49.50
Private dining: 5-50
Accommodation: 41 rooms
Wheelchair access

W1   **MAP 7** D3

Nobu Berkeley

15 Berkeley Street, London W1J 8DY
Tel. 020 7290 9222 Fax 020 7290 9223
e-mail: nobuberkeley@noburestaurants.com

THE controversial fusion cooking, combining delicate Japanese with spicy Peruvian flavours, with a few European ideas thrown in, has been a worldwide hit for Nobu Matsuhisa, a Japanese sushi chef who opened the first of his worldwide chain of restaurants in Beverly Hills in 1987.

And his latest London venture has been an instant success – it is full every night.

The 200-seat restaurant and sushi bar upstairs is simplicity in typical Japanese style, the menu catering for all by offering new and old, raw and cooked, spicy and non-spicy dishes.

Toro (belly of tuna), seared and served with yuzu miso and Jalapeño sauce, Nobu's popular spicy salsa, and the hotter crispy pork belly with spicy miso are popular. Nobu's signature dish, black cod with miso, is a must: the fish is marinated for three days and then caramelised to create a delicate, slightly sweet flavour. This is a very seductive dish.

For those not used to the taste of raw fish, a 'new style sashimi' option is offered in which the fish is cooked for a few seconds before being served with a delicate dressing made from soy sauce, olive oil and lemon. Rock shrimp tempura is served with a delicious ponzu dip, made from soy sauce and vinegar.

A platter of fresh tropical fruits or an excellent green tea sorbet provide a refreshing end to the meal.

Their pride: Black cod with miso
Inexpensive wines: Armador Carmenère (Chile) 2002, £24; Côtes de Fronsac Château la Vieille Croix 1999, £26

Proprietors: Nobuyuki Matsuhisa and Robert de Niro
Last orders for dinner: 12.15 am
Closed: Sunday, lunchtime
Closed for holidays: Bank Holidays
Set dinner: from £70
Main courses: from £25
Wheelchair access

The Northgate ★

GASTROPUB

113 Southgate Road, London N1 3JS
Tel. 020 7359 7392 Fax 020 7359 7393
e-mail: thenorthgate@hppubs.co.uk

EVEN in Islington, which is blessed with fine gastropubs, The Northgate stands out for its quality and excellent value for money.

You may eat in the bright bar area at the front or in the more secluded, dimly lit dining-room at the rear, where you can watch the chefs at work in the open-plan kitchen.

A blackboard menu features home-made soups, salads, pasta, steak sandwiches and a few speciality fusion dishes, brilliantly conceived and executed by the accomplished Australian chef.

Tiger prawns, for example, arrive firm in an intensely flavoured but impeccably balanced hot and sour broth that contains coconut milk, chopped celery and fresh coriander leaves.

Fillet of salmon, pan-fried to perfection to achieve a crispy skin and juicy flesh, is served with parsnips, sweet potatoes, pumpkin, baby pak choi and a delicious lemon and lime beurre blanc.

Desserts are equally impressive: a coconut panna cotta of perfect consistency is cleverly lifted by the sharpness of lime syrup and fresh raspberries, while a chocolate mousse of faultless texture and flavour is balanced by clotted cream and fresh strawberries.

Wine prices range from £12.50 to about £20. A wide selection by the glass includes three dessert wines, a superb example of which is the Australian Botrytis Semillon Riverina 2003.

Speciality food: Pan-fried salmon on roasted root vegetables, baby pak choi, lemon and lime beurre blanc
Draught beers: Deuchars IPA, London Pride
Average wine price by the glass: £4.25

Licensees: Adam Pearson and Sam Haacke
Last orders for dinner: 10.30 pm (Sunday 9.30 pm)
Open every day
Closed for holidays: 24 December, 1 January
Main courses: from £9.50
Beer garden
Children welcome in restaurant
Wheelchair access

SW1   MAP 7 C3

Noura Brasserie

16 Hobart Place, London SW1W OHH
Tel. 020 7235 9444 Fax 020 7235 9244
e-mail: noura@noura.co.uk

LEBANESE cooking has long been popular in Paris, encouraged to a large extent by the Antoun brothers, Nader and Jean-Paul, so it is not surprising that their leading London venture should have a worldly, relaxed atmosphere that seems genuinely Parisian.

At the same time, however, the welcome and the service owe everything to the Lebanese tradition of civilised hospitality. This is a place where you will be looked after as a guest, rather than just another customer.

The food is excellent, a distinct cut above what many people will have experienced with chicken or lamb on skewers. As in any Lebanese restaurant the range is wide and the choices sometimes tricky, but waiters are on hand to offer advice and to warn you if you risk ordering too much.

Cold mezzes range from excellent hummus and tabbouleh (a fine mix of parsley, crushed wheat, olive oil) to shankleesh aged cheese with thyme and lamb tartare with garlic purée and onion. As for hot mezzes, try mana'eesh sesame and herb pizza or the pastry parcels of baked spinach.

After *la grande bouffe*, a medium-sweet Lebanese coffee is a great reviver. There is an interesting selection of Lebanese and French wines.

Their pride: Lamb and chicken chawarma
Inexpensive wines: Château Musar Cuvée Réservée £26; Château Kefraya blanc de blancs £30

Proprietor: Nader Bou Antoun
Last orders for dinner: 11.30 pm
Open every day
Set lunch: from £14.50
Set dinner: from £25
Main courses: from £12.50
Wheelchair access

SW1   MAP 7 D3

L'Oranger ★

5 St James's Street, London SW1A 1EF
Tel. 020 7839 3774 Fax 0207 7839 4330
e-mail: oranger.restaurant@fsmail.net

AT THE bottom of St James's Street, where the Overtons seafood emporium once was, you will find a very different restaurant that has long regarded itself as a beacon of French cuisine in London. It has not always quite achieved its ambitions, but today it is at the top of its form, offering a variety of first-rate dishes rich in the flavours of the Mediterranean.

Rack of Provençal lamb, cooked pink, of course, is served in a style typical of the Midi, with no fewer than three variations on the theme of aubergine. Beef fillet is also given southern treatment, accompanied by bone-marrow cooked in the Provençal manner and simple fondant potato.

Starters such as Spanish ham with pancetta, or artichoke ravioli, show an admirable balance of texture and flavour, of richness and subtlety. Desserts are appropriately refined, a little salted butter, for instance, modifying the sweetness of apple Tatin, an almond biscuit, vanilla cream and caramel ice-cream.

The good wines are expensive, but if you scan the list with care, you will come across the odd bargain (relatively speaking) such as a mature Médoc and a splendid Muscadet.

Service is formal in the old French way, rather too much so at times. The team could relax a little without the slightest loss of professionalism.

Their pride: Fillet of beef with toast of crispy bone marrow à la provençale
Inexpensive wines: Muscadet sur lie de Sèvre et Maine Clos du Ferre, Domaine David 2002, £18; Premières Côtes de Bordeaux Château Farizeau 1996, £28

Proprietor: London & Henley Restaurants Three Ltd
Last orders for dinner: 11 pm
Closed: Saturday lunch, Sunday
Closed for holidays: Christmas
Set lunch: from £25
Set dinner: from £40
Private dining: 6-32
Al fresco dining

W1   MAP 7 C2

Orrery ★ ★

55 Marylebone High Street, London W1U 5RB
Tel. 020 7616 8000 Fax 020 7616 8080
e-mail: orreryreservations@conran-restaurants.co.uk

ORRERY is far and away the best restaurant in the Conran group for restful atmosphere, peerless service and exceptional cooking. Overlooking the fine trees of Marylebone churchyard, in a surreal moment you might imagine yourself in the South of France. This impression is reinforced by the young French staff, who serve you with style. In a word, it is a grown-up restaurant with nothing to prove. No celebrity-watching here, just discerning customers who are looking for a great dinner.

The centrepiece is the six-course Menu Gourmand, showing André Garrett's culinary flair and sure sense of flavour combinations. His dishes may seem fussy, but while they are certainly intricate there is rarely anything superfluous on the plate.

Velouté of white onion is a restorative amuse-bouche, served with sautéd frog's legs of delicacy and savour. Pan-fried escalope of foie gras on a crouton of ginger bread excels, the marinade of beetroot refreshing the palate enough to appreciate an end-taste of sherry vinegar reduction, a triumphant medley of flavours.

Line-caught sea bass tasted as it used to taste and Somerset lamb was beautifully prepared, roasted saddle cooked pink, with mint and basil purée, the shank braised with baby vegetables.

Great cheeses include a Corsican brebis with red peppers, and the millefeuille of milk chocolate with praline ice-cream and almond shake is admirably light. The wine list is famously pricey, but there is always a bargain to be found.

Their pride: Limousin veal – roast loin, sweetbread, blanquette
Inexpensive wines: Tokaji Mandolas Dry Furmint Oremus (Hungary) 2002, £22; Minervois la Livinière Carignanissime Clos Centeilles 2002, £27.50

Proprietor: Sir Terence Conran
Last orders for dinner: 11 pm
Open every day
Closed for holidays: Christmas
Set lunch: from £25
Set dinner: from £55
Al fresco dining
Wheelchair access

SW10   MAP 7 B5

Painted Heron ★

112 Cheyne Walk, London SW10 ODJ
Tel. 020 7351 5232 Fax 020 7351 5313
e-mail: management@thepaintedheron.com

AT THE western end of Cheyne Walk, almost hidden on its corner site, this fine Indian restaurant overlooks the Thames and the houseboats at Battersea Bridge. Everything is modern, elegant, uncluttered, from the blond wooden floors and contemporary art that lines the white walls of the restaurant to the descriptions of the dishes, which are in plain English.

The inventive cuisine is distinctly far above the mainstream UK tandoori/curry house, yielding bold, rich flavours and interesting spicing. Even the chutneys and poppadums are superior.

Lunchtime is a good opportunity to try the great-value platters, such as lamb in a splendidly rich black lentil curry, accompanied by little dishes of yellow lentils, raita, perfect saffron rice and exquisite potato and onion flavoured with cumin.

Evenings can begin with spiced crab meat in light, steamed Nepalese dumplings, served on elegant, deep, silver tasting spoons with a subtly spiced 'Thuppa broth'. Another fine starter is the rabbit leg tikka with chickpea flour and fenugreek, or try the banana and beetroot koftas (fritters) with spiced yoghurt and tamarind chutney.

Guinea fowl breast and spinach curried in North Indian style is a fine main course, the fowl moist and succulent, the spinach very fresh, the spicing assertive but not fiery. For fish-lovers there are monkfish tails, grilled on the tandoor, with mint, green chillies and garlic mayonnaise, or king scallops in hot and sour Goan curry.

Their pride: Guinea fowl and spinach North Indian curry
Inexpensive wines: Little's Semillon Chardonnay 2003/4, £17; Labeye Grenache Syrah (Languedoc) 2001/2, £17

Proprietor: Charles Hill
Last orders for dinner: 10.30 pm
Closed: Saturday lunch
Closed for holidays: 1 week Christmas
Set lunch: from £9
Main courses: from £15
Al fresco dining
Wheelchair access

SE22   MAP 8 C3

The Palmerston ★

GASTROPUB

91 Lordship Lane, East Dulwich, London SE22 8EP
Tel. 020 8693 1629 Fax 020 8693 9662
e-mail: thepalmerston@tiscali.co.uk

AMONG the kebab takeaways and pizza places of Lordship Lane, The Palmerston at first seems like a local with an unpretentious pub ethos and atmosphere, but glance across to tables in the attractive panelled dining-room and you spy couples devouring excellent looking and aromatic smoked haddock risotto.

This is seriously good cooking that would grace the table of a fine restaurant, modern European with an emphasis on southern flavours. The class of the food shows at once with a starter of ravioli of pumpkin with pine-nuts and sage.

Move on to splendidly robust yet refined braised veal cheeks in white wine, admirably partnered by polenta and sugar snap peas.

Dishes catching the eye range from soupe de poissons to Cantabrian anchovy and French bean salad, or, as a touch of indulgence, foie gras marinated in Sauternes.

Good main courses extend from grilled wood pigeon with shallots, thyme and balsamic vinegar to a simple fillet of plaice with herb crumbs and lime mayonnaise.

Of the fine desserts, the passion fruit bavarois is classically light and 'wobbly', the freshness of the fruit flavours vivid.

The list of 50 wines, 12 by the glass, do the cooking justice: the Chilean Sauvignon Blanc from Valdiovesco is spot-on, the Tinto di Toro a heart-warming Castilian red.

Speciality food: Smoked haddock risotto
Draught beers: Fullers London Pride, Greene King IPA
Average wine price by the glass: £4

Licensee: Reg Buckley
Last orders for dinner: 10 pm
Closed: Sunday evening
Closed for holidays: 25 and 26 December
Set lunch: from £10
Main courses: from £12
Children welcome during day
Wheelchair access

EC1   MAP 7 E2

The Peasant ★

GASTROPUB

240 St. John Street, Clerkenwell, London EC1V 4PH
Tel. 020 7336 7726 Fax 020 7490 1089
e-mail: eat@thepeasant.co.uk

AT THE Clerkenwell end of St. John Street, on the way to the Angel, The Peasant has huge character. The downstairs main bar is a true Victorian gin palace, with the massive original oak bar counter taking pride of place.

It is also quirky and 'alternative', with posters of leftist icons of the 1960s and 1970s: Chairman Mao, Che Guevara and, just for good measure, Iggy Pop and Crazyhead. The taped music runs the scale from Satchmo and Ella to Jimmy Hendrix and hard rock.

Upstairs is a proper restaurant, also Victorian, but jazzy with bold, primary, almost psychedelic colours, and a good deal of plush and velveteen. An alcove leads to a bijou glass extension.

The cooking is assured, imaginative, modern European, superior to that of the average gastropub. The bar menu is full of interest and true flavours in Spanish rillettes, spicy deep-fried whitebait, or mackerel with marrow caponata and grilled leek; a perfectly cooked medium-rare steak sandwich; the caramelised pancakes with passion fruit curd richly delicious.

The restaurant is in a higher gear, with tataki beef on fermented soy cream and shitake mushrooms, and the Tallegio and pecorino cheeses with mostado di Cremona is a must for Italophiles.

Excellent wines include the best Forrester Chenin Blanc from the Cape and the best Australian Crittenden Pinot Noir from Victoria. There are also exceptional Belgian bottled beers such as Orval and Chimay Blanc, made by Trappist monks.

Speciality food: Smoked paprika pork fillet
Draught beers: Charles Wells Bombardier, Archers
Average wine price by the glass: £4

Licensee: Gregory Wright
Last orders for dinner: 10.45 pm
Open every day
Closed for holidays: 24 December-3 January
Main courses: from £10
Private dining: up to 70
Children welcome
Wheelchair access

SW1   MAP 7 C3

Pétrus ★★

The Berkeley, Wilton Place, London SW1X 7RL
Tel. 020 7235 1200 Fax 020 7235 1266
e-mail: petrus@marcuswareing.com

PETRUS at the Berkeley Hotel does not have the feel of a hallowed shrine of gastronomy, still less of one of those now increasingly fashionable food laboratories. That, however, does not mean that the cuisine lacks anything in talent and imagination.

Take a terrine of tête de veau, for example. Normally it is a rugged, lusty dish, but in the kitchen at Pétrus it is recreated with elegance and refinement, though losing nothing of its flavour in the process. Another terrine well worth trying is the pressed Anjou rabbit, with foie gras and wild mushrooms.

In less talented hands, complexity can be a problem, but here compositions such as bacon, minted couscous and ravioli of pea and broad bean with sea trout are entirely successful. Of equally impressive quality is the beautifully presented chicken tournedos with sherry sauce and a stuffing of rosemary and thyme.

Cheeses are as exceptional as the cooking and the magnificence of the desserts is exemplified by the uncommon and contrasting flavours of peanut parfait with Valrhona chocolate mousse.

The cellar is an expensive collection of classic wines, especially Bordeaux, with many vintages of Château Pétrus, including the legendary 1947 (Belgian bottling) at £6,500 a bottle. Yet the list also has some very good values from the Loire, Alsace and Provence. Excellent espresso and splendid petits fours, such as banana macaroon and chocolate Vienna sablé.

Their pride: Pork belly cooked for twenty-four hours, asparagus and mooli with mustard dressing
Inexpensive wines: Meerlust Rubicon (Stellenbosch) 2000, £45; Chablis Premier Cru Montée de Tonnerre, Domaine du Chardonnay 2002, £42;

Proprietors: Marcus Wareing at the Berkeley Limited
Last orders for dinner: 11 pm
Closed: Saturday lunch, Sunday
Closed for holidays: 1 week at Christmas
Set lunch: from £30
Set dinner: from £60
Private dining: 12-16
Wheelchair access

W4   MAP 8 A3

The Pilot

GASTROPUB

56 Wellesley Road, Chiswick, London W4 4BZ
Tel. 020 8994 0828 Fax 020 8994 2785
e-mail: the.pilot@london-gastros.co.uk

IN A residential street close to the Chiswick flyover, yet surprisingly quiet, The Pilot does not do modish décor. The bar and dining area have an unstuffy, endearing quality. One look at the blackboard menu and the chefs working below lifts the spirits – this is good gastropub cooking in Mediterranean style with the odd nod to Asia.

Gazpacho soup was cool and wholesome, and the starter platter for two was a light snack tour of the Mediterranean: tabbouleh, guacamole, hummus, feta, Milanese salami and Turkish bread.

Baked chicken supreme is one of the tastiest dishes, stuffed with pancetta and Gorgonzola cheese and accompanied by celeriac and Asian squash. Chargrilled chicken, chorizo and jalopeño burgers are popular, as are the salmon or swordfish steaks. A very good vegetarian option is shitake and spinach risotto rissoles stuffed with provolone cheese.

For desserts, there are just two or three choices: a sticky toffee pudding with caramel sauce, a refreshing plate of kiwi, passion fruit and strawberry sorbets, and a selection of cheeses from round the world with quince jelly.

The selection of 25 wines, 10 by the glass, is interesting: the pick of the bunch at fair prices are Laroche Rosé de la Chevalière 2004, from Languedoc, and Clavijo Rioja Reserva from the great 1999 vintage.

Speciality food: Salmon and swordfish steaks
Draught beer: London Pride, Carling
Average wine price by the glass: £3.50

Licensee: Malcolm McLoughlin
Last orders for dinner: 9.50pm
Open every day
Main courses: from £9.50
Private dining: up to 35
Beer garden
Children welcome before 7pm
Wheelchair access

SE1   MAP 7 F3

Le Pont de la Tour

Butlers Wharf, 36d Shad Thames, London SE1 2YE
Tel. 020 7403 8403 Fax 020 7940 1835

JUST east of Tower Bridge, this luxurious yet unfussy restaurant overlooking the Thames is full of light until dusk. It is always busy and the pressure seems sometimes to tell on the staff, who though charming and warm, are not invariably at hand as you wait to be seated. Once at your table, service improves, a drink, bread and the menu quickly forthcoming.

The cooking remains rooted in the French provincial tradition, but the dishes here are probably the simplest in the Conran group.

Typical starters are West Mersea oysters and langoustines with mayonnaise, or velouté of parsley root and gammon, a good soup that requires skill and time to prepare and that exhibits vivid country flavours. The variety of breads is excellent.

Among the main courses, attractive choices could be Icelandic cod served with mashed potato, tomato and basil dressing, or the Châteaubriand with Béarnaise source, or else Loch Duest salmon with shaved fennel salad.

However, it can happen that an entrecôte steak ordered medium rare arrives too well done – a pity because accompanying caramelised carrot, al dente kale and sweet new potatoes more than passed muster. By the way, the crème brûlée for dessert, could be chilled a little less.

The cheeses are above average and kept in good condition.

Their pride: Whole turbot for two
Inexpensive wines: Circus Viognier Vin de Pays d'Oc 2004, £16.50; Circus Syrah Vin de Pays d'Oc 2002, £16.50

Proprietor: Sir Terence Conran
Last orders for dinner: 11.30 pm
Open every day
Closed for holidays: 25-26 December, 1 January
Set lunch: from £22.50
Set dinner: from £42
Private dining: 10-20
Al fresco dining: 70 covers
Wheelchair access

NW1   MAP 7 D2

Queen's Head & Artichoke   `GASTROPUB`

30-32 Albany Street, London NW1 4EA
Tel. 020 7916 6206
e-mail: info@theartichoke.net

THIS Victorian pub has a lively bar on the ground floor and an extensive tapas menu that includes dishes such as hummus, meatballs, excellent tortillas and spicy sweet potato couscous.

These are also available in the quieter, more formal dining-room upstairs, where a grand piano, a marble fireplace, antique clocks, black and cream colour schemes and a low ceiling create a cosy, romantic atmosphere.

Good home-made bread, served with extra virgin olive oil, creates high expectations which can be met, for example, by a starter of cucumber and mint soup, served chilled and topped with flaked almonds. Follow this with leg of free range lamb seasoned with rosemary, roasted and served with a successful combination of rosemary, black-eyed beans, broccoli and mint sauce.

It is best to avoid complicated dishes, though a starter of seared scallops, black pudding, shallots and port, for instance, does have soundly prepared components. Cod marinated in cumin, coriander and lime, with saffron chickpeas, chorizo and ruby chard, has too many flavours fighting, with the chorizo sadly winning the battle.

Finish with walnut pie served with cinnamon ice-cream. Excellent Manchego cheese is served with oatcakes, grapes and quince jelly.

The wine list is well chosen, particularly strong on Italy, Spain and southern France, with about 10 wines available by the glass.

Speciality food: Cucumber and mint soup with flaked almonds
Draught beers: Ushers, Pedigree
Average wine price by the glass: £3.25

Licensee: Michael Kittos
Last orders for dinner: 10.15 pm
Open every day
Closed for holidays: 25 and 26 December
Main courses: from £9
Private dining: 25-50
Beer garden
Children welcome
Wheelchair access

SW3   MAP 7 C4

Racine

239 Brompton Road, London SW3 2EP
Tel. 020 7584 4477 Fax 020 7584 0077

THE WORD 'racine' means 'root', and for some years now there has been a movement in France dedicated to the promotion of what is known as 'roots cuisine', the sort of food traditionally served in neighbourhood restaurants throughout the country: filet au poivre, or tête de veau, saucisse lyonnaise, soupe de poissons, gratin Dauphinois and so on. That same movement appears to be alive and well in Brompton Road.

Racine is authentically French, or at least successfully creates the illusion that you might be eating in St. Germain or Marseilles. It takes a passing double-decker bus or black cab to remind you of where you really are.

To some extent, an illusion is what it all is. How many authentic French restaurants would be serving smoked Norfolk eel, for instance? But that doesn't matter. The food is fresh and honest, and there are plenty of grand classics on offer to maintain a real Gallic atmosphere, as well as prix fixe menus for both lunch and dinner.

And if one of the owners happens to be an Englishman called Henry Harris, his partner, Eric Garnier, is the genuine article and leads a service team that any restaurant in his homeland would be proud of.

Thankfully, there are still thousands of 'Racines' to be found in France – and England could certainly do with few more. In the meantime, instead of booking a seat on Eurostar, why not head for Brompton Road?

Their pride: Veal entrecôte, creamed spinach and foie gras
Inexpensive wines: Château de Terrefort 2003, £14; Sauvignon Beauvignac 2004, £15

Proprietors: Eric Garnier and Henry Harris
Last orders for dinner: 10.30 pm
Open every day
Closed for holidays: 25 December
Set lunch: from £15.50
Set dinner: from £15.50

SW3   MAP 7 C4

Rasoi Vineet Bhatia ★ ★

10 Lincoln Street, London SW3 2TS
Tel. 020 7225 1881 Fax 020 7581 0220
e-mail: rasoi.vineet@btconnect.com

AFTER a decade or so of involvement with some of the stars of Indian fine dining in London, Vineet Bhatia has struck out on his own with Rasoi, determined to give free rein to his passion and imagination.

His menus are based to a large extent on personal favourites, sometimes complemented by western influences, as witness the addition of pre-starters such as spiced pea soup and pre-desserts like home-made yoghurt flavoured with rose petals.

Overall, strong but never oppressive flavouring remains the basis of the cooking, with many dishes arranged thematically in order to encourage customers to enjoy a wide range of compatible tastes. The pièce de résistance is the nine-course tasting menu, already popular with regulars but perhaps a little daunting for some.

There is an excellent assortment of desserts and your coffee is accompanied by home-made chocolates in neat little two-tier glass dishes sent specially from Singapore, just one example of the attention to detail which is another of the striking features at Rasoi.

Try lunchtime to be sure of getting a table, or else book well ahead for dinner. Could it be that Rasoi is already the best Indian restaurant in London?

Their pride: Ginger and chilli lobster.
Inexpensive wines: Lugana Reveglia (Italy) 2003, £18; Merlot Santa Puerto (Chile) 2004, £22

Proprietors: Mr. Vineet Bhatia, Mrs. Rashima Bhatia
Last orders for dinner: 10.30 pm
Closed: Saturday lunch, Sunday
Closed for holidays: Bank Hols, Christmas-New Year
Set lunch: from £19
Set dinner: from £58
Private dining: 8-18
Al fresco dining

N1   MAP 7 F1

Real Greek ★

14-15 Hoxton Market, London N1 6HG
Tel. 020 7739 8212 Fax 020 7739 4910
e-mail: hoxton@therealgreek.com

THIS lively meze bar and restaurant, with some tables outdoors in a pleasant square, is an ideal spot for a good night out with friends or, equally, for a romantic tête-à-tête. The place used to be a pub, and it remains reassuringly bare-boards informal, but the leisurely service and animated, noisy clientele combine with the food to create an ambience that is 'real Greek'.

Familiar favourites such as moussaka, dolmades, taramosalata and tzatziki are all available, but the menu moves into higher gear with the likes of grilled rabbit with roasted peppers and peaches, or monkfish tail in vine leaves served with fennel. There are also cockles with herbs, marrow filo pie with basil and feta cheese and beetroot with yoghurt and walnuts.

Best to start with meze, bite-sized and full of flavours that are both eastern and European in character.

The presentation of the dishes displays more than a touch of finesse, but the real attraction is a taste explosion that might well prompt you to book the first available flight to Heraklion – or, of course, simply another table at the Real Greek.

Advice is provided to help you accompany your choice of food with the right wine and there is some excellent value among lesser known Greek bottles.

Their pride: Izmir-style dumplings served with trahana
Inexpensive wines: Ritinitis Nobilis Gaia Wines Koutsi (Greece), £18.75; Xerolithia Creta Olympias (Crete) 2003, £13.50

Proprietors: Theodore Kyriakou and Paloma Campbell
Last orders for dinner: 10.30 pm
Closed: Sunday
Main courses: from £8
Private dining: 8-20
Al fresco dining
Wheelchair access

SW14   MAP 8 A3

Redmond's ★

170 Upper Richmond Road W, East Sheen, London SW14 8AW
Tel. 020 8878 1922
e-mail pippa@redmonds.org.uk

THIS has been labelled the ideal neighbourhood restaurant, yet it is a great deal more than that. Redmond Hayward's cooking is laden with class, his creative ideas always successful because he has an unfailing sense of which flavours really work together and is not beguiled by imagination for its own sake. A pity that more chefs do not follow the example of this fine culinary craftsman.

The sunny flavours of southern France and northern Italy are often choices on the daily changing menu. Typical starters are Jerusalem artichoke and black truffle soup; brandade of home-salted cod, the perennial pride of the restaurant, and aubergine and goat's cheese parfait with aged balsamic vinegar.

The plate of duck hors d'oeuvres was a triumph, the flavours mounting subtly but with increased intensity through smoked duck breast, parfait and ballottine to the rich crescendo of seared foie gras, freshened by an ideal beetroot and ginger salad.

Pan-roasted sea bass was cooked with pin-point accuracy and featured an inspired accompaniment of parsley and crème fraîche potato cake, girolles and fish velouté. Other temptations might be braised oxtail with parsnip and walnut purée, or roasted wild duck breast with black truffle risotto.

The beautifully kept British cheeses feature a very fine Wigmore's ewe's cheese and a first-rate Cotherstone. The chestnut and orange tart with prune and armagnac parfait shows a superb medley of compatible flavours, very much the Redmond touch.

Their pride: Open ravioli of Jerusalem artichokes and mushrooms with gremolata, shaved Parmesan and truffle oil
Inexpensive wines: Cheverny Blanc Domaine du Salvard 2004, £17.25; Briego Joven Roble Ribera del Duero 2003, £20

Proprietors: Redmond and Pippa Hayward
Last orders for dinner: 10 pm
Closed: Sunday dinner, lunch Monday-Saturday
Closed for holidays: 3 days Christmas, Bank Holidays
Set lunch: £18:50
Set dinner: early menu from £12.50, normal menu from £27.50
Wheelchair access

EC2 MAP 7 F2

Rhodes Twenty Four ★

Tower 42, 25 Old Broad Street, London EC2N 1HQ
Tel. 020 7877 7703 Fax 020 7877 7788
e-mail: reservations@rhodes24.co.uk

IN THESE security-conscious days, you need a computer check and an entry card before you are allowed to enter the express lift that takes you to this smart, stylish restaurant offering amazing vistas across the City to Docklands and places as far as Alexandra Palace and Epping Forest.

The foundation of Gary Rhodes's culinary principles is the use of the best possible ingredients, and these you will find here in abundance in dishes such as oxtail cottage pie, lamb loin with creamy smoked bacon and runner beans, or sea trout confit.

Typical of the quality and imagination of the cooking is an Irish stew consommé bursting with the pure flavour of lamb. It comes with a little saucepan of diced potato, carrot, shallot and cabbage which you are encouraged to put into the consommé and is served with a braised lamb toast and rillette.

Desserts are just as memorable, especially the bread and butter pudding, and the excellent wine list contains a clutch of fine things at less than £30 a bottle.

Service is swift and watchful, which is how it should be in a City restaurant where time is at a premium and the clientele consists mainly of grandees from the worlds of finance and industry, along with a sprinkling of potential business stars of the future.

Their pride: New season's lamb with broad beans, fresh minced chilli and mutton hash
Inexpensive wines: Les Vigneaux Vin de Pays d'Oc 2004, £17; Domaine Montrose Vin de Pays d'Oc 2003, £19.50

Proprietors: Restaurant Associates with Gary Rhodes
Last orders for dinner: 9 pm
Closed: Saturday, Sunday
Closed for holidays: Bank Hols, Christmas, New Year
Main courses: from £11.60
Wheelchair access

W1   MAP 7 D2

Richard Corrigan at Lindsay House ★ ★

21 Romilly Street, London W1D 5AF
Tel. 020 7439 0450 Fax 020 7437 7349
e-mail: richardcorrigan@lindsayhouse.co.uk

BARE WOODEN floors, period sash windows, fine rugs, a single gilded mirror and elegant table settings add a wealth of character to the first-floor dining-room of this townhouse in Soho, where the rich and sophisticated cooking of Richard Corrigan is entirely at home.

On the menus, dishes are described with disarming simplicity and directness, giving no hint of the coming impact of flavours that are consistently superb. The first clue comes with an excellent amuse-bouche, which might be shredded mackerel and herb quenelle with a beignet of Cashel Blue cheese.

Refinement and attention to detail are evident throughout the meal. An essentially country dish of pressed rabbit terrine with ceps is transformed into something special. Tender caramelised veal sweetbreads burst with flavour and go perfectly with their accompaniment of Jerusalem artichoke and cauliflower beignet.

Imagination comes successfully into play with a dish of grilled red mullet served with shellfish juices and Parma ham ravioli, and again in Irish beef fillet, which is poached in its own consommé and accompanied by tortellini of foie gras.

A six-course tasting menu following the seasons is a good way to become familiar with the outstanding nature of the cooking, shown in adventurous combinations such as scallops with pork belly and spiced carrot. The desserts can be exquisite, with such things as a seasonal apple pudding with pumpkin on a base made from calvados, cream and eggs instead of sponge.

Their pride: Caramelised veal sweetbreads, cauliflower beignet
Inexpensive wines: Sangiovese Villa Vieja Mendoza 2003, £21; Côtes de Saint Mont Les Vignes Retrouvées 2003, £22

Proprietor: Richard Corrigan
Last orders for dinner: 11 pm
Closed: Sunday, Saturday lunch
Closed for holidays: 24 & 25 December, Bank Hols
Set lunch: from £25
Set dinner: from £48
Private dining: 6-32

W1   MAP 7 D3

The Ritz ★

150 Piccadilly, London W1J 9BR
Tel. 020 7493 8181 Fax 020 7493 2687
e-mail: enquiries@theritzlondon.com

THERE is no grander hotel restaurant in London than this dramatic Louis XV dining-room overlooking Green Park, which, having delivered something of a chequered performance in recent years, has one again become the place to go for the haute cuisine to match the surroundings.

Classical and yet not afraid to encompass some of the best of modern trends, the cooking is flawless, from the first-rate breads (especially the tomato and black olive one and the crusty pain rustique) to marvellous desserts such as rosewater and ginger sorbet or the traditional vanilla soufflé 'Rothschild' and the classic crêpes Suzette.

For a tasting experience you will never forget, try the lobster bisque, with armagnac and fresh lobster, rich and smooth. If soup is not the thing on the day, you might choose the superb terrine of goose liver with pistachio and peach wine jelly. To follow that, perhaps, halibut or turbot in Sauternes sauce with asparagus, morel mushrooms and broad beans.

At lunchtime, plats du jour known as The Ritz Classics might be such things as Lancashire hot-pot, rack of lamb or boiled brisket and tongue.

The wine list and the service are everything you would look for in such a magnificent setting. Service, as you might expect, is by waiters in tail-coats.

Their pride: Poached fricassee of lobster
Inexpensive wines: Ritz Chablis Joseph Drouhin 2004, £36; Ritz Claret St. Emilion Private Reserve 2001, £36

Proprietor: The Ritz Hotel London Limited
Last orders for dinner: 10.30 pm
Open every day
Set lunch: from £45
Set dinner: from £45
Private dining: 12-50
Al fresco dining: at lunchtime
Accommodation: 133 rooms
Wheelchair access

SW13   MAP 8 A3

Riva

169 Church Road, Barnes, London SW13 9HR
Tel./Fax 020 8748 0434

THIS is a highly individual Italian restaurant almost hidden away in a fairly anonymous row of shops, and very much a magnet to which those who know it are attracted time and time again.

The food reflects the character of the Veneto and the Italian lakes, with starters such as culatello ham, which comes from the Po region, or prosciutto of goose, or fish soup flavoured with saffron.

Luganega sausage, leeks and red wine are combined in a very good risotto, while a ragû of hare comes with tagliolini.

There are always 'special' dishes, which might feature fish such as sea bass or turbot, or else roast meat, among which Scottish lamb is splendidly flavoured, served with roast potatoes and given the interesting accompaniments of pecorino and peperonata.

Also noteworthy is the pan-fried calf's liver, not to mention the zabaglione, a favourite Italian dessert that seems to be becoming rather more difficult to find in restaurants these days.

Service by a young team is swift and engaging and owner Andrea Riva is a constant presence whose style and charisma attract a loyal clientele that includes actors, publishers, critics, film stars and politicians

Their pride: Maialino al finocchietto (roast piglet and fennel)
Inexpensive wines: Rubesco Lungarotti 2001, £22; Verdicchio Casal di Serra 2004, £22

Proprietor: Andrea Riva
Last orders for dinner: 10.30 pm
Closed: Saturday lunch
Closed for holidays: Christmas, Easter, Bank Holidays, last 2 weeks August
Main courses: from £11.50
Wheelchair access

W6   MAP 7 A4

River Café ★

Thames Wharf, Rainville Road, London W6 9HA
Tel. 020 7386 4200 Fax 020 7386 4201
e-mail: info@rivercafe.co.uk

IN ITS seventeenth year, the River Café is as busy as ever and remains a magnet for the very different worlds of radical chic and corporate suits. Ruth Rogers and her partner Rose Gray are still active overseers in the kitchen and they are not bashful about their worth – prices are undeniably stiff in this sleek 'café'.

The best Tuscan cooking north of the Alps is the name of the game here. Perfect risotto con funghi arrives a reassuring twenty minutes after being ordered, the Scottish girolles beautifully flavoured, the dish given added depth of flavour by chicken stock, a touch of heady vermouth and very real Parmesan. The very best raw materials are used, as in chargrilled pink Yorkshire lamb or turbot roasted with anchovies, marjoram and cherry tomatoes.

Desserts are simple, as in Italy, and on display. As a cheese course, try the *degustazione* of four regional Italian cheeses, such as the pecorino aged under Le Marche grape pressings and served with Selvapiana honey.

There is a great Italian wine list that includes some outstanding Tuscans, properly aged – a rare thing in Italy nowadays. Isole e Olena's Ceparello 1990 (£120) catches the eye, but there are plenty of good wines in the £17 to £30 price band.

The young floor team are welcoming, helpful and knowledgeable, too. In every respect, the River Café becomes more grown-up with the years yet never loses its freshness. Bravissimo.

Their pride: Turbot baked in salt with balsamic and chard
Inexpensive wines: Pinot Grigio Livio Felluga 2004, £34; Dolcetto D'Alba Vajra Aldo 2004, £23.50

Proprietors: Ruth Rogers and Rose Gray
Last orders for dinner: 10 pm
Closed: Sunday dinner
Closed for holidays: Christmas, New Year, Bank Hols
Main courses: from £27
Al fresco dining
Wheelchair access

SW1   MAP 7 C4

Roussillon ★

16 St. Barnabas Street, London SW1W 8PE
Tel. 020 7730 5550 Fax 020 77824 8617

IN THIS bright, elegant and civilised restaurant off Pimlico Road, you feel a sense of well-being the instant you cross the threshold as an outstanding staff of alert young men and women combine natural charm with highly professional focus. You never have to ask twice for anything here; the service seems effortless.

Its ambience is quietly convivial and cosmopolitan; the spacious room in stylish stone-grey offers tulips on each immaculate table, and there is a bold art de vivre painting of a Mediterranean lunch scene to remind us of the Roussillon, that lovely corner of France.

The modern French cooking is precise, consistently accomplished, subtly flavoured and delicately textured. Breads, Normandy butter, and appetisers such as the crayfish, cucumber and ginger brochette, or potato gnocchi with truffles are first-rate.

Fish is a great strength, as in perfectly grilled native scallops with roasted quince; or maybe Dublin Bay prawns with sautéd ceps and light chicken jus. For the best, try the fillet of John Dory with black pepper roasted autumn roots and veal stock.

Highland venison with caramelised pumpkin, William's pear and truffle is a speciality and a soft juicy Languedoc Pinot Noir drinks beautifully with it. Cheeses are well kept and feature great Rocamadour chèvre and a rich Chambertin. For dessert, the warm vanilla millefeuille with caramel velouté is excellent, as are the roasted black figs with French toast.

Their pride: Wild sea bass on crunchy skin with ham and sage tempura and green peas à la française
Inexpensive wines: Côtes du Roussillon Villages 2002, £14.50; Domaine des Lauriers (France) 2003, £18

Proprietors: James Palmer and Alexis Gauthier
Last orders for dinner: 10.30 pm
Closed: Sunday
Closed for holidays: 28 August-5 September
Set lunch: from £30
Set dinner: from £45
Private dinning: 12-25
Limited wheelchair access

Royal China ★

13 Queensway, London W2 4QJ
Tel. 020 7221 2535 Fax 020 7792 5752
e-mail: royalchina@btconnect.com

JUST A few paces from the Queensway Underground station and Kensington Gardens, this deservedly popular Chinese restaurant is a place of dim-sum delights such as steamed crab or pork and shrimp in sweet chilli sauce.

That is not all, however. Lunchtime specials like abalone served with pork in a fine broth, or Dover sole fillet with noodles and veg-etables, mean that the place fills up very quickly. One fish dish, steamed bass, is rightly famous, and there is also lobster that can be steamed or else baked and accompanied by various Cantonese and Mandarin sauces.

Meat and poultry dishes are no less finely made, ranging from duck with sweet and sour sauce to roast chicken flavoured with beans, and stewed pork belly.

As a final palate-cleanser, you could try the almond bean curd with mixed fruits or the chilled mango pudding. Another excellent choice is a lightly baked egg and milk tart.

The décor of black lacquered walls with golden birds is pleasing and the staff are quick and attentive. The house white wine has been chosen to set off the food admirably

Their pride: Lobster noodles
Inexpensive wines: Baron du Pont Chardonnay 2003, £15; Baron du Pont Merlot 2003, £15

Proprietor: Pearl Investment Ltd
Last orders for dinner: 11 pm
Open every day
Closed for holidays: 24-26 December
Set dinner: from £28
Main courses: from £7
Private dining: 5-40
Limited wheelchair access

SW1   MAP 7 C3

Salloos ★

62-64 Kinnerton Street, London SW1X 8ER
Tel. 020 7235 4444

AT THIS fine Pakistani restaurant close to the Berkeley Hotel in Belgravia, chef Abdul Aziz has been preparing some of the most delicious Mughlai dishes in London for more than twenty years. He and his team built a formidable reputation in Lahore, the Lyons of Pakistan, and their meticulous care and highly exacting standards have ensured an extraordinary consistency over the years.

Only fresh chicken and the most tender English lamb are used. The spices are fresh and each dish is cooked to order exactly to its recipe. At Salloos, there is no part-roasting beforehand to shorten the waiting time for the tandoori dishes. Be patient.

The restaurant is comfortable and traditional with well-spaced tables, the décor quietly elegant in white, the walls hung with good pictures. Qureshi, the maître d'hôtel, offers you a drink immediately and brings the lightest of spiced poppadums. Mulligatawny soup, that emblem of the British Raj, is as good as you will find anywhere, with its well-defined flavours of lentils, finely chopped chicken and spices.

The tandoori charcoal barbecues and grills are the centrepiece. No colouring is added and you are advised to eat them separately to appreciate their flavour fully.

Two strong recommendations: chicken shish kebab, the mildly marinated chicken barbecued with tomato, onions and capsicum, is a great starter, and the tandoori lamb chops, the renowned Salloos speciality, are as succulent and memorable today as they were in the early 1990s.

Their pride: Marinated tandoori lamb chops
Inexpensive wines: Semillon Chardonnay (Australia) 2004, £19.50; Shiraz Merlot (Australia) 2004, £19.50

Proprietor: Muhammad Salahuddin
Last orders for dinner: 11.15 pm
Closed: Sunday
Closed for holidays: Christmas and Bank Holidays
Set lunch: from £16
Main courses: from £12.90

NW6   MAP 7 A1

The Salusbury ★★

GASTROPUB

50-52 Salusbury Road, London NW6 6NN
Tel. 020 7328 3286
e-mail: info@thesalusbury.com

IT IS worth making the journey to this now smart and fashionable part of Kilburn simply to eat here. It is not the place for a quiet conversation, unless you come on a weekday lunchtime, or for a romantic dinner. If anything, the Bohemian atmosphere of the bar is more intimate. The dining-room, simply decorated with mirrors and portraits, is packed every night (booking is essential), noise levels are high and you might have to share a table.

The real reason for coming, however, is to enjoy the true flavours of Mediterranean cuisine, brought to excellence in the open-plan kitchen by the Italian chef and his team. Top-quality ingredients, attractive presentation, precise cooking and imaginative use of vegetables and herbs combine to achieve consistently remarkable quality.

The daily changing menu includes unusual starters such as delicious courgette flowers, stuffed with ricotta and mint and lightly fried; good home-made soups and several authentic Italian pasta dishes, including a triumphant asparagus risotto. Among the main courses, oven-cooked sea bass wrapped in paper with courgettes, tomatoes and spring onions is a speciality; a huge grilled veal chop is moist and full of flavour, and the braised shank of lamb with lemon and thyme is tender and succulent.

Desserts are equally fine, whether a peach tarte Tatin with superb vanilla ice-cream or an equally irresistible raspberry crème brûlée. An interesting and sensibly priced wine list includes Coldora 2003, a clean and refreshing unoaked Chardonnay from Italy, at £3.40 a glass.

Speciality food: Bucatini with Cornish crab and green peppers
Draught beers: Adnams, Hoegaarden
Average wine price by the glass: £3.50

Licensees: Robert Claassen and Nick Mash
Last orders for dinner: 10.15 pm (Sunday 10 pm)
Closed: Monday lunch
Closed for holidays: 25-26 December
Main courses: from £11
Al fresco dining
Children welcome before 7 pm

WC2   MAP 7 D3

The Savoy Grill ★

The Savoy, Strand, London WC2R 0EU
Tel. 020 7592 1600 Fax 020 7592 1601
e-mail: savoygrill@marcuswareing.com

WHILE much publicity has been given to Marcus Wareing's changes at the Savoy Grill, the room does not seem to have changed basically, except for its light wood panelling and subdued lighting. Churchill and other historic personalities ate regularly at their own tables and today the place is still imbued with the atmosphere of a favourite venue of the rich and powerful. Service is appropriately old-school, attentive but now less stiff than in previous years.

The menus strike a sensible balance between the traditional and the modern. The kitchen team have sure hands in, for instance, accurately cooked brown crab risotto and fines herbes, or deftly prepared calf's sweetbreads, though the accompaniment of pancetta and onion marmalade could conceivably overwhelm their delicacy. Sauté of rabbit leg with fine linguine, peas, girolles and fèves, is a modern combination, that works.

The classic rack of Cornish lamb, cooked pink, is of top quality, coupled with richly flavoured confit of its shoulder – very much a signature dish. The customs of a former age are reflected in smoked salmon and gravadlax carved from fish on the trolley, and there are old faithfuls such as steak and kidney pudding. Summer berries with pastis sabayon is an intriguing dessert.

The wine list is stoutly classic with predictably great bottles of claret and white burgundy – pricey, of course, but with affordable good drinking by the glass. As at the Connaught and Claridges, you can dine at the Chef's Table overlooking the kitchen.

Their pride: Baked pithivier of quail breast and forest mushrooms, crispy quails' legs with walnuts, Madeira sauce
Inexpensive wines: Chablis Premierer Cru Montmains, Domaine Tremblay 2003, £40; Médoc Château Latour 1998, £40

> **Proprietor: Marcus Wareing at the Savoy Grill Ltd.**
> **Last orders for dinner: 11 pm**
> **Open every day**
> **Set lunch: from £30**
> **Set dinner: from £55**
> **Private dining: 16-60**
> Wheelchair access

WC1   MAP 7 D2

Shanghai Blues ★

193-197 High Holborn, London WC1V 7BD
Tel. 020 7404 1668 Fax 020 7404 1448

THIS recently opened venture, with its elegant décor and subdued lighting, is rather different from the usual London restaurant where dim-sum is the star attraction. For a start, there is none of the usual rush and the young staff are charming and eager to help.

And then there is the food. The manager apologised for the delay but, he said, the dumplings were being rolled and prepared to order – their freshness was evident. The standard menu is already extensive, but the Cantonese chef enthusiastically delves into his vast repertoire for specials, such as sea bass and mango roll.

And where else will you find scallop dumplings in gossamer-fine spinach juice pastry laid on carrot shavings so they do not stick to the steaming basket? Such attention to detail and lightness of touch set the place way above much of the opposition.

If you think dim-sum is rather bland, the Shanghai shui jiao rolls in chilli sauce will make you think again. In true Chinese style, the dumplings are served until late afternoon, then they become starters on the even more wide-ranging evening menu.

Seafood is important here, ranging from a dish of mixed seafood with lily bulbs, pai ling oyster mushrooms and sugar snaps, to steamed razor clams with bean sprouts and Chinese olives. For a real feast, there is the wok-fried lobster with Shanghai sea spice and chilli, or try the fried rice served in an omelette casing and opened up like a lotus leaf at your table.

Their pride: Dim-sum and Chinese fish dishes
Inexpensive wines: Goldwater New Dog Sauvignon Blanc (New Zealand) 2004, £20; Costières de Nîmes La Sommelière de Campuget 2002, £22

Proprietors: David Yiu and the Weng Wah Group
Last orders for dinner: 11.30 pm
Open every day
Main courses: from £9
Private dining: up to 28
Wheelchair access

WC2   MAP 7 D3

J. Sheekey

28-32 St Martin's Court, Covent Garden, London WC2N 4AL
Tel. 020 7240 2565 Fax 020 7497 0891
e-mail: reservations@j-sheekey.co.uk

YOU can almost smell the grease-paint at this famous haunt of stage actors and playwrights, with its photographs of West End stars from the 1950s and 1960s.

Apart from the atmosphere, top-quality fish is the draw here, as exemplified by the freshness, flavour and accurate cooking of a fine thick tranche of wild halibut on the bone, with matchstick chips and excellent buttered spinach.

One of the daily specials might be leek and potato soup with a garnish of black truffles, though these might be thought a rather odd accompaniment to what is essentially a homely soup.

Choices such as potted shrimps, plateau de fruits de mer, oysters and lobster mayonnaise look good, and market fish like Rye Bay plaice are winners. In season, roast grouse with bread sauce is available for the traditional game-eater.

Overall, you probably have to select with care to get the best dishes, and no doubt the senior waiters will guide you if you ask them nicely.

The wine list is serious and absorbing, kicking off with well-priced, fresh Sauvignon Blanc from Chile at £15 and rising through the classics of Chablis to a magnificent mature Clos de la Roche 1991, £225.

Their pride: Whole grilled turbot
Inexpensive wines: Sauvignon Les Fumées Blanches 2003, £18.75; Viña Monte Merlot (Chile) 2004, £16.75

Proprietor: Richard Caring
Last orders for dinner: midnight
Open every day
Closed for holidays: 4 days Christmas
Set lunch: from £21.50 (weekends)
Main courses: from £10.75
Wheelchair access

W1   MAP 7 D2

Sketch – Lecture Room ★

9 Conduit Street, London W1S 2XG
Tel. 0870 777 4488 Fax 0870 777 4400
e-mail: info@sketch-uk.com

PROBABLY the most expensive in London, this restaurant is the joint venture of celebrated Parisian chef Pierre Gagnaire and restaurateur Mourad Mazouz. Eye-wateringly steep prices (£45 and up for starters from the carte) target young celebrities. Thus, if you want to experience the ideas of one of France's most interesting culinary minds, the set-price lunch is good value.

Four starters in tasting portions sent out a mixed message. Black rice with mussels and clams in a creamy emulsified sauce was exquisitely flavoured; carpaccio of tuna with sesame seeds and a slice of barely coloured smoked haddock proved excellent, and better than chicken and garlic crumble flavoured with ginger, accompanied by cannelloni of celeriac, while a velouté of parsnip seemed bland.

Roasted veal came in four pink slices of loin, moist and beautifully flavoured, while parsnip and beetroot were well prepared. Another velouté, pumpkin this time, was strangely dilute. An excellent duo of raspberry tart and jelly and a rose mousse completed what was, in the final analysis, overall an above-average meal.

The evening carte contrasts attractiveness with some bizarre combinations. Delicious saddle of lamb poached and roasted in oregano comes with lamb dumpling, dried apricots and figs and garlic roasted lamb cutlets, while Limousin beef fillet is served somewhat strangely in a bitter orange sauce with a carpaccio of cuttlefish.

Their pride: Langoustines addressed four ways: tartare, mousseline, grilled and roasted
Inexpensive wines: St. Estèphe La Secret de Lafon-Rouchet 2000, £34; Domaine du Vieux Chène, Vin de Pays de Vaucluse Cuvée Friande 2002, £21

Proprietors: Pierre Gagnaire and Mourad Mazouz
Last orders for dinner: 10.30 pm
Closed: Saturday lunch, Sunday and Monday
Closed for holidays: 25-26 Dec, 1 Jan and Bank Hols
Set lunch: from £35
Set dinner: tasting menu £90
Main courses: from £48
Private dining: 8-60
Limited wheelchair access

N1   MAP 7 E1

The Social

GASTROPUB

33 Linton Street, Arlington Square, London N1 7DU
Tel. 020 7354 5809 Fax 020 7354 8087

PART of The Social's appeal for its young local customers lies in the quality of its disco music. It is part of the Heavenly Jukebox group, founded in Nottingham, and DJs liven it up at weekends and on special evenings. It is always packed, too, on Sunday afternoons. Located on the corner of a leafy, quiet, Islington square near Regent's Canal, a sign outside shows its earlier pub name, the Hanbury Arms. Inside, wood panelling, leather sofas, a fireplace and candlelit tables create a relaxing setting. Though the music from the bar and dance floor is audible in the dining-room, for most people it is not obtrusive.

The sensibly short, daily changing menu offers simple, reasonably priced dishes, attractively presented and competently prepared. Savoury tarts and pies are a speciality: a leek and spinach tart is baked to perfection and arrives crisp and tasty, served with green beans, wild mushrooms and mixed salad. Chicken, tarragon and leek pie is faultless, light and full of flavour, and arrives with either mash or chips and a mixed salad. Precise cooking also shows in the pasta dishes, though the accompanying sauces and some of the salads may sometimes be a little dull.

Other typical dishes are chicken or steak sandwiches and, on Sundays, roast beef and Yorkshire pudding. There is a selection of cheeses and there are two or three desserts – the chocolate brownie is well made and satisfying. The wine list is limited, but well described and fairly priced. A Sauvignon blanc from Chile at £15.50 is crisp and refreshing. There is an interesting choice of beers and an unusually large selection of whiskies.

Speciality food: Chicken, tarragon and leek pie
Draught beers: Red Stripe, Kirin
Average wine price by the glass: £3.50

Licensee: Bradley Golshahi
Last orders for dinner: 10 pm
Closed: Lunchtime Monday-Friday
Closed for holidays: 25 December
Main courses: from £7.50
Al fresco dining
Children welcome at lunchtime
Limited wheelchair access

W1   MAP 7 D3

The Square ★★

6-10 Bruton Street, London W1J 6PU
Tel. 020 7495 7100 Fax 020 7495 7150
e-mail: info@squarerestaurant.com

FOR ALL the splendours of the food, this remains a delightfully unpretentious restaurant, modern and elegant yet at the same time restful, not least because of the personable and polished, mostly French staff. But what really counts here, of course, is the cooking, a beacon of refined creativity.

Starters often feature pasta with shellfish and crustaceans, as in sautéd langoustines with Parmesan gnocchi, or the superb crab lasagne. Among the main courses, one particular triumph is the saddle of lamb under a herb crust, the meat pink and flavoured with garlic, balsamic vinegar and rosemary.

If fish is your preference, you will probably have tasted nothing better than the roasted Dover sole, served perhaps with truffles, cauliflower purée and caramelised root vegetables.

Desserts are an invitation to indulge yourself, bearing in mind that the soufflés here bid fair to be the best in town, especially the roasted fig soufflé that comes with mascarpone ice-cream. Otherwise, try the trio of flavours in the chocolate assiette.

The cheeses are excellent and so is the cellar, with an impressive selection of champagnes from the best growers, good burgundies and Rhône vintages and affordably priced wines by the glass, such as a fine Riesling Scharzhof Kabinett.

Their pride: Lasagne of crab with shellfish and basil cappuccino
Inexpensive wines: Bourgogne F. Jobard 1999, £29; St. Joseph (Rhône Valley) 2000, £27

Proprietors: Nigel Platts-Martin and Philip Howard
Last orders for dinner: 10.45 pm (Sunday 9.45 pm)
Closed: Saturday and Sunday lunch
Closed for holidays: 24-26 Dec, 1 Jan, Bank Hols lunch
Set lunch: from £25
Set dinner: from £60
Private dining: 8-18
Wheelchair access

EC1   MAP 7 E2

St. John ★

26 St. John Street, London EC1M 4AY
Tel. 020 7251 0848 Fax 020 7251 4090
e-mail: reservations@stjohnrestaurant.com

THIS noisy, bustling, bare-boards eatery is hidden away in a mews within a steak's throw of Smithfield. It is a hive of activity and you will need to book early, though you can drop in for a snack, a glass of wine, or to buy home-made bread from the open-plan bakery.

In the almost stark and certainly simply furnished dining-room, Fergus Henderson and his team have made no serious attempt at interior design, preferring to concentrate on the food, excellent, no-nonsense English cooking served on plain china plates.

No-nonsense English best describes the service as well. You want pea and ham soup? That is what they offer. Mushrooms on toast? This must be the only restaurant that calls a mixture of girolles and other champignons des bois simply 'mushrooms'. You will find brawn, tripe and fennel, grouse, mallard and swede at St. John.

But any thoughts of a canteen are banished when it comes to quality. The very finest ingredients are beautifully handled, with natural flavours enhanced by spot-on seasoning. Cuttlefish cooked in its ink, topped by sliced onion is, perhaps, verging on the exotic, but it is tender and scrummy, and the two generous slices of calf's liver – a test for any hard-pressed kitchen – were pan-fried to succulent perfection.

There are real English puddings, too, such as a light-as-a-feather pear crumble cake with a generous dollop of Jersey cream.

Their pride: Roast bone-marrow and parsley sauce
Inexpensive wines: Bourgogne Aligoté Domaine Larue 2004, £21.20; St. John Vin de Pays d'Oc Grenache/Merlot 2003, £14.50

Proprietors: Fergus Henderson and Trevor Gulliver
Last orders for dinner: 11 pm
Closed: Saturday lunch, Sunday
Closed for holidays: Easter, Christmas, New Year
Main courses: from £13.50
Private dining: up to 18

St. John's

GASTROPUB

91 Junction Road, London N19 5QU
Tel. 020 7272 1587 Fax 020 7281 0059

ON Tufnell Park's Junction Road, close to the Archway Tower, St. John's does not look much from the outside, but step inside to the bar, take a drop of the award-winning Deuchars bitter, note the serious range of good wines, and your spirits lift.

There is a little enclosed garden for al fresco dining, but go into the restaurant at the rear and you get the warm feeling that food and wine matter here.

In line with good gastropub practice, the menu changes twice a day from an open kitchen where you can see the brigade at work. The cuisine is mainstream gastro-brasserie fare with a nice choice of maybe good Serrano ham and celeriac remoulade or an authentic, spicy gazpacho as appropriate summer starters.

Attractive main courses are well conceived without fussiness. Pork chop is partnered by beetroot, apple and fennel, calf's liver by horse-radish crème fraîche.

Fish-lovers could opt for the seared tuna with leeks, lentils and salsa verde, vegetarians for the penne, squash, mushrooms, peas and Parmesan.

Puddings are a strong section, the pineapple tarte Tatin with vanilla ice-cream a winner.

Special offers of fine wine include an especially good Chablis and white burgundy from top growers, also Château Lanessan, Médoc 1985, a steal at £45.

Speciality food: Modern European
Draught beers: Deuchars IPA, Black Sheep
Average wine price by the glass: £3.50

Licensee: Nick Sharp
Last orders for dinner: 11 pm
Closed: Monday lunch
Closed for holidays: 25 and 26 December
Main courses: from £11.50
Beer garden
Children welcome
Wheelchair access

W6   MAP 8 A3

Stonemasons Arms GASTROPUB

54 Cambridge Grove, London W6 OLA
Tel. 020 8748 1397   Fax 020 8748 6086

ON THE CORNER of Cambridge Grove, a couple of minutes' walk from Hammersmith shoppers' multi-storey car park, this is a no–frills pub of bare wooden floors and colourful abstract pictures (some for sale). The rows of sturdy tables in the open-plan bar and restaurant give a hint that it's the good drink and freshly cooked food that draws the crowds of faithful locals and a cross-section of office workers and 'resting' actors.

The Spanish cooking packs a lot of flavour into the cooking, the best and most popular dish being the perfectly chargrilled (pink) rump of beef with wok-fried potatoes, herbs, sauté greens and red wine jus. A fine starter that showcases ingredients from all over is the hors d'oeuvres platter of chorizo, salami, Serrano ham, Greek feta, raita, hummus, babaganoush and Turkish bread. Other Mediterrranean-style winners are goat's cheese bruschetta, lamb and olive burger and the baked cod on potato galette with tapenade.

Desserts are not always so successful, as in a blandly flavoured coconut ice-cream with 'chocolate sauce', which was dry and rather too solid. The thoughtful wine list (30 by the bottle, 10 by the glass) shows a sure eye for quality and value, from a decent vin de pays d'Oc (£2.85 a glass) through delicious Michel Laroche Viognier up to Marlborough, New Zealand, Pinot Noir.

Service by jeans-clad young staff is laid-back, very friendly and helpful, even if there are sometimes small gaps and waits between courses. Drinkers enjoying a pint and a good natter are just as welcome as diners, which is as it should be.

Speciality food: Chargrilled rump of beef, wok-fried potatoes
Draught beers: Adnams, Marston Pedigree
Average wine price by the glass: £3.45

Licensees: Euan Guinness and Matt Jacob
Last orders for dinner: 10 pm
Open every day
Main courses: from £9.25
Private dining: 10-40
Beer garden
Children welcome
Wheelchair access

SW7   MAP 7 C3

Swag and Tails

GASTROPUB

10-11 Fairholt Street, London SW7 1EG
Tel. 020 7584 6926 Fax 020 7581 9935

FIVE minutes' walk from Harrods and Knightsbridge shopping, this is a discreet pub and restaurant with the atmosphere of a genuine local.

But the real action is at the back, down a step into the intimate and appealing restaurant. First impressions are of typical modern brasserie fare with some luxury items: assiette of foie gras, Parma ham and polenta fritters in addition to hummus or rocket salad with smoked salmon.

But it is clear that some dishes show some skill in the kitchen: cod and pea fishcakes really taste of cod, are crisply coated and come served with a good lemon and parsley mayonnaise.

Among the more eye-catching main courses, such as roast fillet of sea trout or seared loin of tuna, are some less flashy dishes cooked with care and a good sense of the flavour combinations. Fine, juicy breaded veal escalope is partnered by caper and pancetta potato salad, also endive and green beans in a lemon and sage butter – imaginative and successful.

There is a classic burger and there are sirloin steak sandwiches or, if you want to go Asian, duck pancakes with spring onions and hoi sin sauce, or tempura king prawns and Thai dip.

Wines by the glass are much above average, ranging from the excellent Australian Shiraz to tempting dessert wines that are fine accompaniments to tartes Tatin and fruit based puddings.

Speciality food: Breaded veal escalope, caper and pancetta potato salad
Draught beers: Charles Wells Bombardier, Adnams
Average wine price by the glass: £4

Licensee: Anne Maria Lennon Boomer-Davies
Last orders for dinner: 10 pm
Closed: Saturday and Sunday
Closed for holidays: 1 week Christmas, Bank Holidays
Main courses: from £11.25
Private dining: up to 70 (weekends)
Children welcome
Wheelchair access

W4   **MAP 8** A3

The Swan ★

GASTROPUB

1 Evershed Walk, 119 Acton Lane, Chiswick, W4 5HH
Tel. 020 8994 8262 Fax 020 8994 9160
e-mail: theswanpub@btconnect.com

THE Swan, on the Chiswick/Acton borders, is unpretentious but full of character. Outside, there is a play area for children and there is a leafy garden in which to enjoy al fresco early dinners.

The pub is a role-model for genuinely excellent and imaginative Mediterranean cuisine. The menu changes twice daily and is an intelligently selective assembly of mouth-watering dishes.

For starters, sample the manifold flavours of baked goat's cheese bruschetta served with a verdura mista of grilled aubergines, courgette, peppers and basil. Another fine option are the antipasti of chicken liver and armagnac purée, spiced black beans with smoked paprika and smoked salmon with herb aïoli.

The Moroccan beef tagine is a great dish, the slow-cooked beef tender and beautifully flavoured with dates and apricots and accompanied by couscous with toasted almonds, sultanas, mint and cucumber yoghurt.

Other choices range from pan-roasted duck breast with sage and red wine to grilled rib-eye steak and braised Puy lentils with bayleaf and nora peppers.

Finish with a plate of Taleggio and Gorgonzola cheeses or the first-rate tiramisù.

The wine list is well chosen for bold flavours, a nutty Garganega from the Veneto or a rich Grenache from Languedoc as whites by the glass, or some fine Italian wines by the bottle.

Speciality food: Moroccan beef tagine
Draught beers: Fullers London Pride, Deuchars IPA
Average wine price by the glass: £4

Licensee: Ailsa Caird
Last orders for dinner: 10.30 pm
Closed: Monday-Friday lunchtime
Closed for holidays: 24 December-1 January
Main courses: from £10
Beer garden
Children welcome before 7 pm

Tamarind ★

20 Queen Street, London W1J 5PR
Tel. 020 7629 3561 Fax 020 7499 5034
e-mail: reservation@tamarindrestaurant.com

ONE MUST definitely rethink preconceived ideas about Indian food at the Tamarind. True, there are plenty of wonderful eastern savours to excite the taste-buds, but here they are produced in a subtle way that makes them almost elusive.

The tandoor oven is still much in evidence, of course, producing such dishes as chicken with paprika and cinnamon, and you will find on the menu the sort of staples common to neighbourhood Indian restaurants – bhuna gosht, biryanis, shammi kebabs, paratha – though at Tamarind they are made with exquisite refinement that sets them apart.

Much of the menu, however, is situated several levels above the ordinary, with first-rate, fresh ingredients prepared in a subdued, delicate manner to bring out the sort of innate qualities that are too often overwhelmed by heavy-handed spicing.

The desserts follow more conventional lines, although the kulfi made with mango rather than pistachio is quite a discovery.

This place is about as far as you can get from the experience of the neighbourhood curry house, except for one thing – irritating piped music that is too loud and seems quite out of character in such refined surroundings.

Their pride: Tandoori grilled lamb chops
Inexpensive wines: Omer Bay Chenin Blanc (South Africa) 2004, £18; Paarl Height Cinsault/Shiraz (South Africa) 2004, £17

Proprietor: Indian Cuisine Ltd.
Last orders for dinner: 11.15 pm
Closed: Saturday lunch
Closed for holidays: Bank Holidays, 25 & 26 Dec, 1 Jan
Set lunch: from £16.95
Set dinner: from £48

SW3   MAP 7 C4

Tom Aikens ★★★

43 Elystan Street, London SW3 3NT
Tel. 020 7584 2003 Fax 020 7584 2001
e-mail: info@tomaikens.co.uk

ONCE in a while, along comes a chef of dazzling originality whose vision is so clear that it enables him to combine a cornucopia of different ingredients into a whole of perfect flavours. In the 1980s and 1990s, John Burton Race was the foremost exponent of this style: now it is almost certainly Tom Aikens who is Britain's most creative chef.

The discreet exterior of his restaurant in a smart Chelsea street hides a treasure-house of gastronomic excitements. They start with breads as good as you will find anywhere and pre-appetisers such as cassoulet of borlotti beans with truffle jus. Innovative starters include brilliantly executed poached cod served tiède with cucumber jelly, avocado mousse and beads of sevruga caviar.

Other temptations range from roasted scallops with crisp pork belly to braised snails with potato ravioli, before, perhaps, roast turbot with choucroute, Morteau sausage and red wine sauce. An outstanding main course is roasted sweetbreads with celeriac milk and fondant, a balanced combination of rich offal and savoury vegetable flavours crowned by the equally grand tastes of lasagne of veal shin bound with chicken mousse.

The 35 choices on the prime-condition cheeseboard, deceptively simple desserts such as delicious coffee and hazelnut cake with coffee mousse and parfait, and the aristocratic wine list, make for an unforgettable meal.

Their pride: Roasted lamb with fennel risotto, anchovy filo tart and roasted garlic
Inexpensive wines: Pacherenc du Vic Bilh sec Vielles Vignes Domaine Berthoumieu 2003, £25; Bourgueil Grand Clos Domaine Yannick Amirault 2002, £32

Proprietor: Tom Aikens
Last orders for dinner: 11 pm
Closed: Saturday and Sunday
Closed for holidays: 2 weeks at Christmas, 2 weeks in August, Bank Holidays
Set lunch: from £29
Set dinner: from £60
Wheelchair access

W4   MAP 8 A3

La Trompette ★

5-7 Devonshire Road, London W4 2EU
Tel. 020 8747 1836 Fax 020 8995 8097
e-mail: reservation@latrompette.com

THIS is a bistro-type restaurant of a comfortable size, uncrowded and with an appealing, shaded pavement terrace. It is simple, without frills, but it exudes professionalism right from the start when the staff solicitously receive you. They are well briefed and knowledgably help with explanations, particularly the sommelier, whose advice is well worth taking.

So that you know you are in for a treat, there is an amuse-bouche of gazpacho which, with toasted almonds, croutons and basil oil, is also on the menu. One of the first courses is a stunning plaice, steamed with scallop mousseline, samphire and buttered cockles, all in a square parcel that even Michel and Alain Roux could be proud of.

Chicken liver and foie gras are made up into an attractively served parfait accompanied by faultless brioche. This can be followed by a breast of duck, pink and well flavoured, its skin crispy, with foie gras, as well as endives and cherries. It would have been difficult for the cod to follow totally the example of the foregoing, nice and fresh as it was. Chips are magnificent, and so they should be to live up to the generous grilled steak and its Béarnaise sauce.

Desserts are good but, again, it would be difficult for them to match the excellence of some of the main courses, except for the hot chocolate pudding, an outstanding example of a sensuously captivating and rich finish at what is (together with the Vacherin restaurant) the pride of Chiswick.

Their pride: Steamed plaice with scallop mousseline, samphire, buttered cockles
Inexpensive wines: Galeria Bical Bairrada (Portugal) 2004, £16; Bonarda Alamos Catena (Argentina) 2003, £18.50

Proprietor: Bruce Poole
Last orders for dinner: 10.15 pm
Open every day
Closed for holidays: 24-26 December, 1 January
Set lunch: from £23.50
Set dinner: from £32.50
Wheelchair access

Umu ★

14-16 Bruton Place, London W1J 6LX
Tel. 020 7499 8881 Fax 020 7016 5120
e-mail: eric@umurestaurant.com

THIS is a serious restaurant, a relative newcomer to the London scene and an unusual one in that although the sashimi chefs are Japanese, and highly skilled in their specialised craft, the director of the restaurant and several staff are French.

Start, perhaps, with the simplest of choices, marinated sardine with grated radish, or, for a real delicacy, sea urchin with sesame tofu. Among the classical tsukuri – that is, without marinades or sauces – hikizukuri is composed of three different fishes from the day's market, which might be red tuna, sea bass and scallop, thickly sliced. The skill with which this raw fish is prepared at Umu is breathtaking.

Perhaps even more challenging is the modern tsukuri, exemplified here by exquisitely flavoured turbot, sliced wafer-thin and served appropriately with sansho vinaigrette. Such preparations are among the best in London. The modern sushi options, with rice, are also to be highly recommended.

Yakimono grilled dishes are an alternative to raw fish. Grilled grouse comes with vegetables and sansho pepper, while lightly cooked tuna is accompanied by faultless miso sauce.

To drink, sake is possibly more appropriate than wine, and there is a choice of no fewer than 40. Ask for advice about which one will go well with your selected food.

Their pride: Sesame tofu, Suppon Jitate
Inexpensive wines: Pouilly Fumé la Demoiselle de Bourgeois 2002, £35; Rias Baixaso Rosal Terras Gauda 2002, £25

Proprietor: The MARC Group
Last orders for dinner: 11 pm
Closed: Sundays
Closed for holidays: Bank Holidays and Christmas
Set lunch: from £22
Set dinner: from £60
Private dining: 6-12
Wheelchair access

W4   MAP 8 A3

Le Vacherin ★

76-77 South Parade, London W4 5LF
Tel. 020 8742 2121 Fax 020 8742 0799

SIMPLE restaurants offering high-quality food at reasonable prices are few and far between in London. So Chiswick residents are very lucky to have the perfect example in their neighbourhood. The value here, at lunchtime in particular, is amazing.

Two bright rooms, unpretentious surroundings. plastic tablecloths and tiled floors, French staff and background *chansons* create a bistro atmosphere. Caribbean chef/proprietor Malcolm John trained with the Savoy Group for six years and was previously head chef at the Brasserie St. Quentin.

He has a sure hand with French provincial dishes like escargots de Bourgogne, tarte au fromage, bourride or cassoulet. The secrets of his success are fresh ingredients, precise cooking, intense flavours, expert saucing and generous portions. The steamed mussels, for example, are served with delicious Provençal sauce.

Lamb kidneys, cooked to perfection, are moist and full of flavour, and served with a faultless mustard sauce. Slow-cooked organic pork belly melts in the mouth, its richness balanced by Puy lentils. The meringue of île flottante has a firmer than usual consistency that combines beautifully with toasted almonds and caramel sauce. Profiteroles au chocolat are served with a refreshing vanilla ice-cream that cuts through the richness of the chocolate.

The all-French wine list is extensive, well compiled and reasonably priced. This is probably the best bistro-type restaurant in London, and an example for the others.

Their pride: Ile flottante
Inexpensive wines: Viognier Bardet Clement (Languedoc) 2004, £15.50; Côtes du Rhône Domaine de l'Enclos, A. Brunel 2002, £16.50

Proprietor: Malcolm John
Last orders for dinner: 10.30 pm
Closed: Monday lunch
Set lunch: from £12.95 (Tuesday-Saturday)
Main courses: from £11.95
Private dining: up to 35
Wheelchair access

SW14   MAP 8 A3

The Victoria

GASTROPUB

10 West Temple Sheen, London SW14 7RT
Tel. 020 8876 4238 Fax 020 8878 3464
e-mail: reservations@thevictoria.net

AN EASY walk from Richmond Park, past the solid mansions of leafy suburbia and the Gothic pile of Temple Sheen church, brings you to this chic, converted pub. Now more like a restaurant with lounge bar, The Victoria none the less has the pubby virtues of well-kept draught Courage bitter, Continental specialist beers and a relaxed atmosphere in the uncluttered bar with its eau-de-nil painted board floors, easy chairs, and affluent locals popping in just for a drink.

The main pull is the airy, contemporary restaurant, which has a conservatory opening on to the garden. Chef Darren Archer changes his menus weekly and he likes to use seasonal British produce: Charollais beef from an Oxfordshire farm, English asparagus, freshwater crayfish and so on. But there is a Continental edge to his cooking, as in lamb's sweetbreads and ceps, lemon sole with samphire and artichokes, risotto primavera.

The one lapse was that an intrinsically fine and meaty steak and Guinness pie seemed to have been heated rather too fiercely. Both the shepherd's pie with French beans and the roast guinea fowl with wild asparagus looked better bets. Darren also has a deft touch with soups and sweet pastry: don't miss his very light chocolate and raspberry tart.

The wines are a great strength here, supplied by a top London independent house, with an excellent Prosecco (£4.95 a glass) and an exceptional Old Vines Red from Stellenbosch (£4.45) – a great partner for Charollais rib-eye steak. The seven bedrooms have flat-screen PCs and broadband internet connection.

Speciality food: Seasonal British produce
Draught beers: Courage, Guinness
Average wine price by the glass: £4.20

Licensee: Mark Chester
Last orders for dinner: 10 pm
Open every day
Main courses: from £12
Al fresco dining
Accommodation: 7 en-suite rooms
Children welcome
Wheelchair access

W'Sens ★

12 Waterloo Place, St. James's, London SW1Y 4AU
Tel. 020 7484 1355 Fax 020 7484 1366
e-mail: reservations@wsens.co.uk

THIS 150-cover glamorous brasserie was opened in December 2004 by twin brothers Jacques and Laurent Pourcel, owners of the three-star Les Jardins des Sens in Montpellier and several other fashionable restaurants round the world.

Its stunning modern design combines bookshelves, a fireplace, Murano glass, leather furniture and strong colours to create a feeling of relaxation enhanced by background pop music.

The bar offers an imaginative light menu while the restaurant menu combines Mediterranean cooking with Asian influences. Warm foie gras is put into a millefeuille and served with apple and lemon confit, the sweet and sour flavour of the fruit beautifully balancing the savoury duck liver.

A roast fillet of turbot is served on a bed of Venere risotto, made from black rice, and served with an emulsion of citrus butter, ethereal pommes soufflées and a green salad – a symphony of textures and flavours.

Fillets of duck breast are marinated in ginger and served moist and pink with a slightly sweet Banyuls sauce and a wasabi-flavoured potato purée, another successful combination. Sashimi of tuna is crusted with bread, seasoned with rosemary and topped with pistachio oil. You can order a mixed platter of desserts but a speciality is W'Sens cappuccino, warm chocolate cream topped with iced espresso granité and whipped cream.

Their pride: Roast fillet of turbot with Venere risotto and an emulsion of citrus butter
Inexpensive wines: Les Vignes de Grangeot Languedoc (red or white) 2003, £15

Proprietors: Olivier Chateau, Jacques & Laurent Pourcel
Last orders for dinner: 11 pm
Closed: Saturday lunch, Sunday
Set lunch: from £18
Set dinner: from £25
Main courses: from £17
Private dining: up to 35
Wheelchair access

EC1   MAP 7 E2

The Well

`GASTROPUB`

180 St. John Street, London EC1V 4JY
Tel. 0207 251 9363
e-mail: drink@downthewell.co.uk

A COMFORTABLE stroll from Barbican Underground station, The Well is named for the Clerkenwell district in which it is situated. Large trestle tables are set out on the pavement and full-length windows are opened wide in summer months. Inside are exposed brick walls, ceiling fans and simple wooden furniture. Pride of place goes to the bar servery, with a blackboard listing speciality cocktails, such as Polish Martini, and bottled beers.

This is a deservedly popular establishment and booking would be sensible. Excellent warmed white and brown crusty bread is accompanied by a dish of olive oil and balsamic vinegar. Fish is sourced daily from Billingsgate, so seek out the blackboard for the day's specials.

Starters might include rock oysters, or a timbale-shaped dish of diced salmon tartare lifted by chopped onion and cornichons, with tiny brown shrimps and a smooth creamed cucumber sauce. Potted confit of rabbit with mustard toasted brioche is another choice.

Apart from daily fish specials, main courses like Périgord sausages with red wine jus,or tender grilled veal cutlet with diced pancetta, firm green beans and a well-made beurre blanc, set the style of dishes on offer.

Indulge in puddings such as the unsweetened dark chocolate tart with its thin, crisp pastry, clotted cream and toasted almonds. Panna cotta with poached peaches and mixed berry compote or crème brûlée might also feature.

Speciality food: Seafood from Billingsgate
Draught beers: Leffe Blonde, Paulander
Average wine price by the glass: £3.45

Proprietor: Tom Martin
Last orders for dinner: 10.15 pm (Sunday 10 pm)
Open every day
Main courses: from £9.95
Private dining: 8-60
Al fresco dining
Children welcome
Limited wheelchair access

NW3 **MAP 8** B2

The Wells ★

30 Well Walk, London NW3 1BX
Tel. 020 7794 3785 Fax 020 7794 6817
e-mail: info@thewellshampstead.co.uk

A FEW minutes from the Heath, amid the steep lanes and elegant streets that make Hampstead so desirable, this 19th-century pub, now sensitively restored, is a very welcome addition to the local restaurant scene.

You can order good bar snacks or a full lunch at a table in view of the chefs labouring behind a glass screen, but their main work is cooking what turns out to be superior gastropub food for the three contemporary dining-rooms above.

There is both quality and good value in set-price meals featuring fresh, top-quality ingredients skilfully cooked. The style is modern European, with fish figuring heavily, as in the salt cod that comes with Jerusalem artichoke soup. Roast halibut with olive oil mash and green beans is a good dish, as is the sea bass.

Among other imaginative but not too complicated dishes are a tart of white onion and field mushroom with light, fresh pastry; wild mushroom risotto and loin of hare with red cabbage.

Simple puddings include a good vanilla crème brûlée served with apricot compote and pear poached in red wine with blackberry sorbet. Fine cheeses come from La Fromagerie and service by a young team is engagingly spontaneous – what it might lack in polish, it makes up for in warmth and is quite appropriate to the surroundings. The wine list is selectively excellent.

Speciality food: Rump of Cornish lamb, pearl barley risotto
Draught beers: Wadworth 6X, Wychwood Hobgoblin
Average wine price by the glass: £3.50

Licensee: Jamie Squire
Last orders for dinner: 10 pm (Sun, Bank Hols 9.30 pm)
Open every day
Closed for holidays: 25 and 26 December, 1 January
Set lunch: from £13.95
Set dinner: from £24.50
Private dining: 10-23 (Monday-Thursday)
Al fresco dining
Limited wheelchair access

SW6   MAP 7 A5

White Horse ★

GASTROPUB

1-3 Parsons Green, London SW6 4UL
Tel. 020 7736 2115 Fax 020 7610 6091
e-mail: whitehorse@btconnect.com

YOUNG traders home from the City and other Fulham locals cram into the White Horse on Parsons Green in the evenings, with the decibel level rising as they throng the bar and spill out on to the terrace. Fight the crowds in the bar or, if you prefer, book a table in the quieter restaurant, where the same dishes are served by well-motivated and efficient staff.

Considering the great turnover, the standard of the food is high, with good, fresh ingredients accurately cooked. The cooking style is an intelligent mix of modern popular seafood starters, such as chilli salt squid, and the flavours of the Mediterranean.

There is a Caprese salad of mozzarella, plum tomatoes, basil and olive oil, or else 'Drunken Risotto', a robust mix of rice, red wine, home-made sausage and beetroot – this may be an acquired taste, but it is good if you like this type of dish.

Some of the best dishes, however, are the simplest: Cornish dressed crab; gutsy pork sausages with beer and red onion gravy; beer-battered haddock and chips, or twenty-one-day aged Aberdeen Angus rib-eye – a winner for flavour and texture.

Fruit tarts or excellent ice-creams are good desserts, and the espresso is authentic. The wine list features 20 exciting choices by the glass from all over the planet. By the bottle, Ridge's old vines Sonoma Zinfandels are world-class reds. The Harveys Sussex bitter is a lovely drop, too.

Speciality food: Slow-roasted lamb with French beans, olives, onions and capers
Draught beers: Harveys Best Bitter, Adnams Broadside
Average wine price by the glass: £4

Licensee: Mark Dorber
Last orders for dinner: 10 pm
Open every day
Closed for holidays: 25 December
Main courses: from £9.25
Al fresco dining
Children welcome before 9 pm
Wheelchair access

EC4   MAP 7 E2

White Swan & Dining-Room ★ *GASTROPUB*

108 Fetter Lane, London EC4A 1ES
Tel. 020 7242 9696
e-mail: info@thewhiteswanlondon.com

ONCE affectionately known as the 'Mucky Duck', the White Swan re-opened in November 2003 after a major refurbishment by its owners. Enter through the rustic ground floor and you can eat quickly and informally from a blackboard menu, but climb the stairs and you will find an elegant dining-room with well-spaced tables, cream walls, white linen tablecloths and comfortable beige banquettes. A ceiling mirror makes this relatively small space look much bigger, and large windows allow in plenty of natural light.

The menu is mainly European, but Asia is represented, too, with such dishes as sashimi of yellow fin tuna. Fresh ingredients, attractive presentation, precise cooking and light, well-balanced sauces are the secrets of its popularity with its mainly business clientele. Not surprisingly, it is extremely busy at lunchtime.

Fresh wholemeal bread augurs well, as do home-made soups such as pumpkin and vanilla topped with balsamic vinegar. Chopped ceps and snails are mixed with peas, carrots and parsnips, sautéd into a fricassee and served with a white wine sauce, a delicious starter. Fresh turbot is roasted to perfection and served with green beans and a caper butter sauce. Desserts include a lemon tart of faultless texture and flavour, served with candied lemon zest. There is a good board of English and French cheeses.

The wine list has more than 150 bottles from round the world, but prices are relatively high. A good selection of wines by the glass includes Recolto di Soave I Capitelli Anselmi at £6.50, which is perfect to round off the meal.

Speciality food: Cep and snail fricassee
Draught beers: Adnams, IPA
Average wine price by the glass: £4.25

Licensee: Tom Martin
Last orders for dinner: 10pm
Closed: Saturday, Sunday
Closed for holidays: Bank Holidays, 25 December
Set lunch: from £20
Main courses: from £9
Private dining: 25-40

NW10   MAP 7 A1

William IV ★

GASTROPUB

786 Harrow Road, London NW10 5JX
Tel. 020 8969 5944 Fax 020 8964 9218
e-mail: williamivnw10@yahoo.co.uk

WHO would have thought it? Way down the Harrow Road towards the West London Cemetery, this solid suburban pub is home to an authentic Spanish restaurant with a delightful walled terrace.

Although there are fresh, delicious tortillas (excellent española of potato and onion), manchego cheese and an olive oil vinaigrette and pimento, and feta cheese croquettes in the tapas range, the food extends far beyond snacks.

Start with berenjeñas aromaticas, a splendidly flavoured salad of rich, spiced aubergine, spring onion and coriander, then go on to calamares romana, tender deep-fried squid, well salted and wrapped in a light tempura-like batter with paprika mayonnaise. Follow this with pollo salteado, which is pan-fried goujons of fresh tarragon chicken, or pato con membrillo, duck with quince, honey, caramelised onions and saffron. Be prepared to wait, though, for everything is cooked to order.

On Sundays, the cooking goes English, with a traditional roast served until 4 pm.

All this is backed up by a list of 30 expertly chosen, mainly Spanish and southern French wines, plus a smattering from the New World

The bar is a comfortable, spacious, panelled room where you can relax easily over a pint of well-kept bitter or a chilled glass of Santiago Sauvignon blanc.

Speciality food: Grilled swordfish with green tomato chutney
Draught beers: Fullers London Pride, Leffe
Average wine price by the glass: £4.50

Licensee: Patrick Morcas
Last orders for dinner: 10.30 pm
Open every day
Closed for holidays: 25 December
Set lunch: from £15 (Sunday only)
Main courses: from £12
Private dining: up to 25
Beer garden
Children welcome
Wheelchair access

W1   MAP 7 D3

The Wolseley ★

160 Piccadilly, London W1J 9EB
Tel. 020 7499 6996 Fax 020 7499 6888

COULD this really be a 'Continental café' in Piccadilly, next to The Ritz? Well, yes, that is exactly what The Wolseley is. You might as well be in Paris, Vienna or Budapest.

Ready on the table you will find superb, oversized, grissini-shaped bread, slightly crusty, light inside and unmatched in London. An unpretentious but rich menu appears instantly. A waiter quickly materialises and rolls off a few recommendations, knowledgeably explained.

The first spoonful of the substantial watercress soup dispels any doubts. A well-made foie gras with a little fig compote, served on slightly toasted brown bread, is just right. Blanquette de veau is a rarity these days, and theirs is superb. And where would you find Wiener Schnitzel, let alone such an authentic one, except in Vienna?

Finish with a sophisticated cheesecake, or real Kaiserschmarren, which are like small pieces of thick pancake – though perhaps they are not really as good as you would find in Salzburg.

A wide variety of after-dinner teas shows you are in professional hands, and this is proved by the general standard of the food.

An unpretentious little wine list is cleverly composed and comes with a well-briefed waiter to help you. There is a good choice of wines by the glass.

Their pride: Wiener Holstein
Inexpensive wines: Condesa de Leganza Crianza 2000, £15.50; Château Haut Rian Semillon/Sauvignon (France) 2004, £15.50

Proprietors: Chris Corbin and Jeremy King
Last orders for dinner: 11.45 pm
Open every day
Closed for holidays: 24 December dinner, 25 December
31 December evening, 1 Jan, August Bank Holiday
Main courses: from £15.50
Wheelchair access

Yauatcha

15 Broadwick Street, London W1F 0DL
Tel. 020 7494 8888 Fax 020 7439 2929
e-mail: mail@yauatcha.com

'WELCOME,' so the translation of Yauatcha goes, 'to Yau's tea-room.' Some tea-room! What we have here is the complete antithesis of every Lyons corner house and ye olde tea shoppe, although maybe you had to queue to get into those, too, once upon a time. If the ground floor pastry shop and tea-room, which you will no doubt have plenty of time to admire, even if you've booked, is more like a set from Star Trek, the restaurant proper, below stairs, gives the impression of eating in a disco, complete with starry ceiling lights. It is almost as noisy, too, the bustle and din reverberating off of plain brick walls at two ends of the square room.

The multi-national staff appear to outnumber the clients, but despite this, an aura of organised chaos reigns throughout. Perhaps that is part of the very nature of restaurants whose main activity centres around that wonderful Chinese snack, dim-sum. Hundreds of half-sized plates and bamboo steam baskets of miniaturised portions require some formidable organisation and half the fun undoubtedly lies in enjoying the higgledy-piggledy arrival of long forgotten dishes.

As dim-sum restaurants go, Yauatcha is very good, but sticking to this style of cookery imposes limitations. Dim-sum is formula food and it is hard for any chef to break the mould. Shumais and har gau, mooli cake, cheung fun and other acknowledged classics, good as they are, can only ever be that without losing their innate quality and integrity. Noodles and stir-fries can give your selection more 'main meal' appeal.

Their pride: Scallop shumai
Inexpensive wines: Alasia Roero Arneis 2004, £21.50; Gary Crittenden Rosato 2004, £26

Proprietor: Alan Yau
Last orders for dinner: 11pm
Open every day
Closed for holidays: 25 and 26 December
Set lunch: from £30
Set dinner: from £40
Wheelchair access

SW1   MAP 7 C3

Zafferano

15 Lowndes Street, London SW1X 9EY
Tel. 020 7235 5800 Fax 020 7235 1971

FROM the smooth service – especially the managerial staff, who remain unflappable, polite and even smiling in the face of some extremely demanding customers (we are, after all, just behind Harvey Nichols) – to the décor and, above all, the food, this is a restaurant that determinedly sets out to be smart...and succeeds.

The approach to the cooking is classically Italian, carried off with finesse and producing results that are entirely enjoyable and rarely show anything but skill and sophistication.

Dishes are simple in both style and presentation, overflowing with natural flavours and imaginatively executed: buffalo mozzarella with aubergines and oregano; veal shank ravioli with saffron; tortellini in brodo; chargrilled tuna with rocket and tomato, and sautéd lobster with chilli and garlic.

Octopus salad is a good light starter, then – from a menu that contains a whole section devoted to grilled meats and fish – sliced lamb cutlet accompanied by potatoes perfumed with thyme and olives offers a taste of Italy that is nothing if not authentic.

The idea of two, three or four courses from the carte, with the appropriate price gradations, makes life easier for everyone and is perfectly adapted to a menu of what is rock-solid, quality Italian cuisine by anyone's standards.

Their pride: Fricasee of lobster medallions with samphire and tomato sauce
Inexpensive wines: Orvieto 2003, £23; Nero d'Avola Villa Tonino 2003, £24

Proprietor: London & Henley Restaurants
Last orders for dinner: 10.45 pm
Open every day
Closed for holidays: Bank Holidays and Christmas
Set lunch: from £25.50
Set dinner: from £29.50
Private dining: 10-20
Wheelchair access

England

ABBERLEY, WORCESTERSHIRE

The Elms

Stockton Road, Abberley, Worcestershire WR6 6AT
Tel. 01299 896 666 Fax 01299 896 804
e-mail: info@theelmshotel.co.uk   **MAP 3** E3

GILBERT White, a pupil of Sir Christopher Wren, designed this handsome Queen Anne property with its impressive setting amid beautiful undulating countryside in the heart of Worcestershire.

The hotel is approached by a sweeping drive. The front entrance overlooks a croquet lawn and an attractive terrace graces the rear of the building. Inside, the best tradition of country house hotels is upheld – large rooms lead off the main hall and are decked out in chintz and dotted about with comfy leather chairs and sofas. Bedrooms have recently been refurbished, as have some of the reception rooms.

A wide range of local groups clearly considers the restaurant to be a spiritual and gastronomic home – suggesting consistent quality and value. Bar food offers a good selection of hot dishes ranging from Welsh rarebit with vine tomato and oregano salad, to confit of Barbary duck, braised red cabbage and port wine sauce, plus various sandwiches. Sirloin steak is exceptionally good, as are the Pont Neuf potatoes that accompany it.

The dinner menu covers a broad spectrum encompassing some modern trends, as in the seared scallops with sweet potato, pineapple, coconut and Asian spiced foam. The cheese selection is entirely British, and many are local. Choose from Elgar Mature – adopted from a 19th-century family recipe – or Old Worcester White Mini Truccle from a nearby farm.

This is an ideal venue for a wedding or private party.

Their pride: Sirloin steak au poivre
Inexpensive wines: Merlot Les Boires (France) 2003, £16.50; Sauvignon Les Boires (France) 2003, £16.50

Proprietor: Von Esson Group
Last orders for dinner: 9.30 pm
Open every day
Set lunch: from £13.50
Set dinner: from £45
Private dining: up to 100
Al fresco dining for bar menu and afternoon tea
Accommodation: 21 rooms
Wheelchair access

ABINGER COMMON, SURREY

Stephan Langton Inn

GASTROPUB

Friday Street, Abinger Common, Nr. Dorking, Surrey RH5 6JR
Tel. 01306 730 775

MAP 2 C4

ASK FOR directions to this pub, hidden away in rural Surrey yet quite near Dorking, as it is well worth finding. The name is taken from an Archbishop of Canterbury (Magna Carta era), who spent his early life in the village. The pub itself is a 19th-century red brick and part-timbered building, with a pretty front courtyard for refreshments and meals in good weather.

Inside, the bar is a simply furnished room with a wooden floor and red-orange walls, and there are two modestly furnished dining-rooms. Food is taken seriously and the menu, printed daily, states: 'All our food is cooked to order, so please be patient.'

Chef/proprietor Jonathon Coomb has devised an appealing menu based on modern English cooking, with Continental influences. Start with ceviche of wild sea bass with samphire, or gazpacho, or unusual tender squid rings with skinned roasted red pepper and rocket salad. Make sure you have some of their wonderful, warm crusty bread.

Main courses might be chargrilled rib-eye of Charollais beef, or duck confit, a moist and plump duck leg with a crispy skin served on fresh spinach leaves and soft chickpeas with chorizo.

The light buttermilk pudding served with poached rhubarb and strawberries and the apricot and almond tart are among their tempting desserts. Chalked up above the bar are some nine wines by the glass and about 25 by the bottle, a careful selection with adventurous and interesting examples.

Speciality food: Hot salt beef and piccalilli
Draught beers: Adnams Bitter, Fullers London Pride
Average wine price by the glass: £3.40

Licensee: Jonathon Coomb
Last orders for dinner: 9.30 pm
Closed: Sunday dinner, Monday
Closed for holidays:1st week of January
Main courses: from £11
Private dining: 30-40
Al fresco dining
Children welcome
Wheelchair access

ABINGER HAMMER, SURREY

Drakes on the Pond ★

Dorking Road, Abinger Hammer, Surrey RH5 6SA
Tel./Fax 01306 731 174

MAP 2 C4

THIS looks like just another roadside restaurant from the outside, but you step inside to a smartly decorated room in pastel yellow, with fresh carnations on classically laid tables. Tracey Honeysett, one of the owning partners, greets customers warmly, and a glass of white wine, chilled just right, and delicious home-baked sultana and walnut bread are a foretaste to an excellent dinner.

Jerusalem artichoke velouté with truffle oil was a pre-appetiser, the taste of artichoke refined but positive, enhanced by judicious use of truffle oil.

The starter of open crab ravioli was a delight, the ravioli light and almost translucent, loosely enveloping fine-sliced fresh white crab meat mixed with avocado and potato salad. This combination and the accompaniments of chilli aïoli and roasted red pepper coulis were impeccably well balanced.

A main course of roasted Croise duck breast with a confit of leg, potato purée, savoy cabbage and Alsace bacon was a delicate dish, the breast medium-rare and served with an appropriate Madeira jus. An alternative would be the best end of Welsh lamb with colcannon potato and a tomato and tarragon reduction.

Desserts range from pistachio crème brûlée and chocolate parfait with orange panna cotta to a quite exemplary apple tarte Tatin with clotted cream and a proper caramel sauce. There is a good wine list covering the world and including some fine half-bottles.

Their pride: Soft-shell crab, tian of fresh white crabmeat and coconut
Inexpensive wines: Brampton Sauvignon Blanc 2003, £19.95; Marques de Cacaras Rioja 2001, £19.50

Proprietors: Tracey Honeysett and John Morris
Last orders for dinner: 9.30 pm
Closed: Sunday and Monday
Closed for holidays: Christmas-New Year, 2 weeks end of August
Set lunch: from £18.50
Main courses: from £21
Limited wheelchair access

ACTON TRUSSEL, STAFFORDSHIRE

Moat House

Lower Penkridge Road, Acton Trussell, Staffs ST17 0RJ
Tel. 01785 712 217 Fax 01785 715 344
e-mail: info@moathouse.co.uk   **MAP 3** E2

REMAINS of a Roman Villa discovered under the church date Acton Trussell to a least the second century. The manor house, built on a mound constructed in Norman times, is Grade II listed and the mound itself is scheduled as an ancient monument.

The Moat House, with 32 bedrooms, boasts a magnificent 14th-century fireplace, which takes pride of place in the bar, and the original timbers testify to the craftsmanship of that period. Popular with locals, the bar is also an ideal stopping place for those passing through by barge on the nearby canal.

A bar menu offers sandwiches between midday and 5pm plus a selection of starters and light salads. Depending on your appetite, fresh crab salad with baby gem, lemon and parsley mayonnaise or Caesar salad with griddled chicken and poached egg, might be a meal in itself.

Otherwise, follow with cod in a soda water batter with chips and mushy peas, or an open sandwich of matured rump steak, red onion chutney with rocket salad and fries.

Puddings might feature a poppyseed parfait with poached rhubarb or a mint brûlée. Special mention should be made of the Conservatory Restaurant, which uses local ingredients and has built up an enviable reputation.

Apart from the carte, a special tasting menu of seven courses, to be followed by coffee and petit fours, will testify to the kitchen's versatility and expertise.

Speciality food: Steaks
Draught beers: Pedigree, Banks
Average wine price by the glass: £3

Licensee: Linda Pickstone
Last orders for dinner: 9.30pm
Open every day
Closed for holidays: 24 and 25 December
Set lunch: from £12
Main courses: from £15
Private dining: up to 45
Al fresco dining
Accommodation: 32 rooms
Children welcome   Wheelchair access

ADDINGHAM, NORTH YORKSHIRE

The Fleece

GASTROPUB

154 Main Street, Addingham, North Yorkshire LS29 0LY
Tel. 01943 830 491

MAP 5 D4

NO WONDER they had to install the heated umbrellas out on the terrace. Chris Monkman's ivy-clad hostelry by the bus stop packs them in, friends and entire families mingling in joyous relaxation where no one remains a stranger for long.

The kitchen brigade and a young front-of-house team provide food and service beyond the expectations of the average village inn. They adhere to exactly the right balance of tradition and innovation.

Local produce and home-spun techniques are combined in their speciality shepherd's, fish and meat and potato pies, for example, along with roasts, sausage and mash, battered fish, braised moorland lamb and comforting puddings. However, there are also antipasti, tapas and more adventurous fish dishes such as an impressive seafood mixed grill with beurre blanc, or simple but effective offerings such as a nicely pan-fried fillet of bream with confit fennel. Lamb and beef are rightly lauded, and an omelette with fat chips comes with much rarer samphire.

The size of the portions will challenge even the most voracious appetite, and the prices definitely won't 'fleece' you, but even so the farmhouse cheeses are hard to resist.

This is a warmly hospitable place with true culinary highlights to surprise even the most demanding tastes.

Speciality food: Slow-braised local lamb and traditional pies
Draught beers: Timothy Taylor Landlord, Black Sheep
Average wine price by the glass: £3.65

Licensee: Chris Monkman
Last orders for dinner: 9.15 pm (Sunday, Bank Hols 8 pm)
Open every day
Main courses: from £7.95
Al fresco dining
Children welcome
Wheelchair access

ALDERWASLEY, DERBYSHIRE

Bear Inn

GASTROPUB

Alderwasley, Nr. Belper, Derbyshire DE56 2RD
Tel. 01629 822 585 Fax 01629 826 676

MAP 3 F2

HIGH in the Derbyshire Dales, on the Wirksworth to Belper road, the Bear Inn is light years away from the modern formula of a gastropub. This is a traditional old hostelry in the best sense, drawing a strong contingent of faithful regulars, be they from the dairy fields around the inn, Derby townsfolk, or young Mancunian couples enjoying a romantic weekend.

In the warren of low-beamed rooms, amid a clutter of stags' heads and bric-a-brac, food is a major draw, and every nook is full, especially on Saturday nights. Squeeze your way to the bar counter and enjoy some very good snacks such as the fresh, breaded whitebait, a regrettably rare dish these days, or else the well-prepared Caesar salad.

If you do manage to get a table, try the Japanese king prawns in sweet chilli sauce; the smoked haddock with lemon and parsley butter or, supremely, slow-cooked lamb in red wine and rosemary sauce – all thoroughly satisfying dishes. The fillet steak, plain or sauced, comes from a good local butcher.

Leave room for banana fritters and maple syrup with a glass of Muscat de Rivesaltes. The staff are all warm and welcoming. They take their lead from Nicki Fletcher-Musgrave, the very model of what a landlord should be. This is tradition at its best.

If you want to stay, one bedroom has a four-poster bed as well as spectacular views over the Dales, and there are good breakfasts.

Speciality food: Slow-cooked lamb, red wine & rosemary sauce
Draught beers: Marston Pedigree, Old Speckled Hen
Average wine price by the glass: £2.90

Licensee: Nicola Fletcher-Musgrave
Last orders for dinner: 9.30 pm
Open every day
Closed for holidays: 25 December
Main courses: from £8.50
Private dining: up to 90
Beer garden
Accommodation: 8 rooms, 2 cottages
Wheelchair access

ALDFORD, CHESHIRE

Grosvenor Arms

GASTROPUB

Chester Road, Aldford, Cheshire CH3 6HJ
Tel. 01244 620 228 Fax 01244 620 247
e-mail: grosvenor.arms@brunningandprice.co.uk   MAP 3 D2

WHEN the gardens of Eaton Hall, six miles south of Chester, are open to the public three times a year, the neighbouring Grosvenor Arms is exceptionally busy at lunchtime, the crowds drawn by the delightful library bar and conservatory opening on to the pub's own immaculate lawns.

While brasserie-style food is served throughout the day, seven days a week, from noon until 10 pm (9 pm on Sunday), there is also a choice of eight imaginatively filled sandwiches for people in a hurry.

The bar menu (there is no formal restaurant as such) changes daily. Of half-a-dozen starters, ham hock terrine with piccalilli, or corned beef hash, are fairly typical, though the tart of goat's cheese, red onion and tomato stands out for its good, fresh and distinctive flavours.

Main courses, of quite traditional choice, range from whole grilled brill with Cheshire new potatoes to braised shoulder of lamb, steak burger or a ploughman's with a laudable choice of mature Cheddar, Cheshire and Shropshire Blue.

Ideal for vegetarians is spinach and ricotta cannelloni with Cashel Blue cheese sauce, a fine dish.

There is a range of six decent desserts, the summer pudding with cream matching the excellent (slightly sparkling) pink Australian Muscat available in half-bottles.

Speciality food: Braised lamb shoulder, redcurrant and rosemary sauce
Draught beers: Deuchars IPA, Robinson Unicorn
Average wine price by the glass: £3

Licensee: Gary Kidd
Last orders for dinner: 10 pm
Open every day
Closed for holidays: 25 December
Main courses: from £10
Beer garden
Children welcome before 7 pm
Wheelchair access

ALREWAS, STAFFORDSHIRE

Old Boat ★

GASTROPUB

Kings Bromley Road, Alrewas, Nr. Burton-upon-Trent DE13 7DB
Tel. 01283 791 468 Fax 01283 792 886
e-mail: info@oldboat.co.uk   **MAP 3** E2

THE Old Boat is aptly named because it stands by a moored barge at a Trent canal lock just off the A38 Burton to Lichfield road. Being so close to the water, it is appropriate that this modern gastropub should concentrate on fish, even if it is far from the sea. The restaurant, just off the lively bar, is attractive, well-lit, with much use made of natural wood.

A blackboard offers up to half-a-dozen fresh fish choices of the day. Pan-fried sea bass fillets, for instance, are expertly cooked, super-fresh and nicely married with roasted tomato and basil and spinach fettuccine.

The chef's hand is just as light with sautéd monkfish and king prawns, neatly coupled with chilli and garlic linguine, or with smoked haddock and pea and Parmesan risotto. Preface this with a fine fresh tomato and red pepper soup.

If fish is not your fancy there is plenty on the printed menu that appeals – a chicken liver and foie gras parfait, chutney and brioche, or a selection of Italian antipasti to start, then perhaps oriental-style duck breast, pak choi, ginger and noodles, or roast pork belly, celeriac mash, peach chutney and seared foie gras.

The orange panna cotta is a suitably light dessert on which to finish a meal marked by class and finesse. Wines are carefully chosen to match the refinement of the cooking. The service is everything it should be.

Speciality food: Fillet of lemon sole with scallops, celeriac and wild mushrooms
Draught beers: Hook Norton Old Hooky, Marston Pedigree
Average wine price by the glass: £3.90

Licensee: Matthew Butler
Last orders for dinner: 9.30 pm
Closed: Sunday evening
Set lunch: from £8.95
Main courses: from £12
Beer garden
Children welcome before 7 pm
Wheelchair access

ALVESTON, WARWICKSHIRE

Baraset Barn

GASTROPUB

**1 Pimlico Lane, Alveston, Nr. Stratford-upon-Avon, Warks CV37 7RF
Tel. 01789 295 510 Fax 01789 292 961**

MAP 3 F4

THIS converted farm building, fronted by an assembly of large deck-terrace and huge summer parasols, is more reminiscent of a Mediterranean or Pacific Coast resort bar than a pub in the heart of England.

The place is hugely popular with people of all ages, in spite of the fact that a chic modern conversion of the beamed restaurant and sleek bar has clearly been designed to attract the younger crowd.

The cuisine is mainstream modern brasserie cooking, the choice quite wide and cannily offered to appeal to all tastes. For the less conservative eater, pan-fried pigeon breast with pancetta and wild mushrooms, or chargrilled polenta cake and tapenade, perhaps. For the more traditionally minded, the Châteaubriand for two is a signature dish.

Meat is generally a very sound choice – organic, well hung and of good quality, as in rib-eye steak, or beef à la bourguignonne, or else the tender veal T-bone steak enlivened by lemon sage and marsala. On the other hand, grilled lobster with saffron aïoli is also a favourite here.

Desserts are the usual brasserie range, including Tatins, sorbets and a good lemon tart.

The wine list is adventurous, wide-ranging and chosen with a shrewd eye for quality and value. For example, the Bourgogne Jurassique is a white burgundy at a reasonable price and the Valdepeñas Crianza is a rich, aged Spanish red and a real bargain.

Speciality food: Châteaubriand for two
Draught beers: Mitchells & Butler Brew XI, Leffe
Average wine price by the glass: £3

Licensee: Nicola Cranley
Last orders for dinner: 9.30 pm
Closed: Sunday evening
Closed for holidays: 25 December
Main courses: from £10.95
Private dining: up to 14
Beer garden
Children welcome
Wheelchair access

ANICK, NORTHUMBERLAND

The Rat

GASTROPUB

Anick, Nr. Hexham, Northumberland NE46 4LN
Tel. 01434 602 814

MAP 5 C2

IT IS A pity that not all rats are as warm and cuddly as this little chap, hidden away in the Northumberland countryside, its beer garden overlooking the green, meandering Tyne valley. After a tenure of fifteen years, the d'Adamos have created a sort of home-from-home full of knick-knacks and general bonhomie where the unsuspecting diner may be roped in for quiz night.

You can choose the more sedate dining-room but half the fun here is joining the regulars in the bar to enjoy Donald d'Adamo's range of blackboard specials. Without adhering to any particular culinary creed, he produces a varied range of dishes in keeping with the spirit of the surroundings, his wife Joan serving them up with cheer and enthusiasm.

Starters, which are also served as bar snacks, are generally old favourites, although they might include fresh mussels in cream sauce or a variety of pastas. The generous main courses, served with home-made chips, encompass fine steaks from the local butcher, crispy duck (with orange sauce, of course), pork fillet with mushrooms and Madeira, and fish such as sea bass or tuna.

More exotic dishes could include something like a chicken stir-fry with black bean sauce. There is a choice of homely puddings, too, including what they say is the stickiest toffee pudding and a crunchy apple and raspberry crumble tart.

Roasts, casseroles and even a chicken khorma feature regularly on the hugely popular Sunday lunchtime buffet, and hats off to Joan and Donald for giving even total strangers the feeling of being welcome guests at their never-ending private party.

Speciality food: Country cooking
Draught beers: Timothy Taylor Landlord, Deuchars IPA
Average wine price by the glass: £2.70

Licensee: Joan d'Adamo
Last orders for dinner: 8.45 pm
Closed: Sunday evening
Main courses: from £9.95
Private dining: 15-25
Beer garden
Children welcome

ARLINGHAM, GLOUCESTERSHIRE

Old Passage Inn ★

GASTROPUB

Passage Road, Arlingham, Gloucestershire GL2 7JR
Tel. 01452 740 547 Fax 01452 741 871
e-mail: oldpassage@ukonline.co.uk   **MAP 1** E1

THIS OLD inn stands on the banks of the Severn at a bend looking across to Newlyn village church and the magnificent Forest of Dean. A pint of excellent local bitter on the terrace triggers thoughts of past travellers about to embark at this historic ferry stage and is enough to give the Old Passage a genuine pub atmosphere.

Yet at heart it is more seafood restaurant than inn, the elegant, light-filled brasserie taking full advantage of those views, the two prominent seawater tanks evidence of a proper fish restaurant.

You have drinks while studying the carte, which offers a fine balance of classic staples – three types of English oysters (Fowey, Helford and Salcombe), lobsters from the tank – and modern specialities such as the chargrilled brill with stir-fried red pepper and ginger.

Head chef Patrick Le Mesurier has a fine touch with anything from the sea: his Provençal fish soup is first-rate, and his poached Cornish hake with spring onion mashed potatoes, fresh peas and broad beans, sauced with fish fumet and white truffle butter, is exceptional. Other mouth-watering choices are escalopes of wild sea trout with sherry vinegar and basil dressing, or turbot with hollandaise. The strawberry and saffron crème brûlée is a very imaginative dessert. Off-season there is a set lunch from £8.50.

The wines are just as distinguished as the cuisine, with fine white burgundies by the bottle, an Australian Chardonnay/Semillon pouring wine, and great dessert wines by glass and half-bottle. Highly professional service by the Moore family and staff. There are three luxury bedrooms.

Speciality food: Fish and seafood
Draught beers: Three Choirs 'Cats Whiskers', Uley Bitter
Average wine price by the glass: £3.10

Licensee: Somerset Moore
Last orders for dinner: 9 pm
Closed: Sunday evening, Monday
Set lunch: from £8.50
Main courses: from £15
Private dining: up to 12
Al fresco dining
Accommodation: 3 rooms
Children welcome
Wheelchair access

ASHBOURNE, DERBYSHIRE

Bramhall's of Ashbourne `GASTROPUB`

6 Buxton Road, Ashbourne, Derbyshire DE6 1EX
Tel. 01335 346 158
e-mail: info@bramhalls.co.uk

MAP 3 E2

THIS is an informal, smart brasserie operation – open seven days a week for breakfast, lunch and dinner. Much use is made of pine in the cosy bar and in the restaurant with its warm terracotta colours and 1930s-style wall lamps. A warm welcome and swift, watchful service are provided by young, well-trained staff.

The brasserie menu shows imagination and flair, with no hint of pretension. The yellow courgette soup is highly enjoyable, the soft natural flavour of the vegetable coming through well, enhanced by excellent bread served with dips of olive oil. For the hungry there is rillette of belly pork with red onion marmalade.

Both Derbyshire beef and fresh fish of the day are the specials that everyone seems to go for – quite rightly. The sirloin steaks are particularly good, and sea fish ranges from fresh sardines to John Dory, all accurately cooked. The span of the cuisine here is illustrated in dishes such as cumin roasted breast of duck served with a stir-fry of pak choi, pepper and mangetout, or a fillet of fresh zander with sweet potato.

Desserts are just as appetising: summer berry brioche pudding, perhaps, or banana and white chocolate marquise garnished with a madeleine.

All this is backed by a compact, thoughtfully chosen wine list: eight selections by the glass, excellent New Zealand Sauvignon and mature Rioja Reserva 1997 (a great vintage) by the bottle. Sparkling wines are also attractive, from keenly priced grower's champagne to the heights of Pol Roger Brut Réserve.

Speciality food: Derbyshire sirloin and fillet steak
Draught beers: Bass, Caffreys
Average wine price by the glass: £3

Proprietors: Timothy and Tracey Bramhall
Last orders for dinner: 9.30 pm
Open every day
Closed for holidays: 25-27 December
Main courses: from £11.95
Accommodation: 10 rooms
Wheelchair access

ASHFORD-IN-THE-WATER, DERBYSHIRE

Bull's Head ★★

GASTROPUB

Church St, Ashford-in-the-Water, Nr. Bakewell, Derbyshire DE45 1QB
Tel. **01629 812 931**
e-mail: **bullshead.ashford@virgin.net**   **MAP 3** E1

THE Bull's Head is a gem set in a pretty stone village, and it
sparkles with all the appeal of a traditional country pub polished
by the excellence of high gastronomic standards. Professional
chef Carl Shaw inherited it from previous generations, so pub-
keeping is in his blood. And happily, that ensures a total lack of
pretension – no restaurant and no bookings; you eat in the small
lounge bar from a menu that changes frequently, sometimes
even while you are looking at it.

Sensibly, there are about four starters, half-a-dozen main courses
and a selection of sandwiches at lunchtime. Starters may be a
tomato and lovage soup with home-made bread or, ringing the
changes, a superb yellow split-pea soup. There may also be a
chicken and pistachio terrine with raspberry vinaigrette.

The sirloin steak was pink and marvellous, ideally partnered by
perfect lyonnaise potatoes. Continuing the beef theme, the steak
and old Stockport ale pie, with braised red cabbage and dripping
roasted potatoes, is a great dish. Other main course options are
rabbit and pear sausages with celeriac mash, and that old classic
of the repertoire, omelette Arnold Bennett, which melds smoked
haddock and cheese memorably.

The blueberry crumble pie with vanilla ice-cream is a must for
dessert, or there are beautifully kept cheeses – Stilton, smoked
Wensleydale, maybe vignotte, served with Scottish oatcakes. The
quality of the wines matches that of the food; the simple vin de
table house red is outstanding and tastes like a very good Rhône.

Speciality food: Steak and Stockport ale pie, dripping-roasted
potatoes
Draught beers: Stockport Bitter, Unicorn
Average wine price by the glass: £2.45

Licensees: Carl and Debbie Shaw
Last orders for dinner: 9 pm
Closed: Thursday evening (winter)
Closed for holidays: 25 December
Main courses: from £9
Beer garden
Children welcome
Wheelchair access

ASTON CANTLOW, WARWICKSHIRE

King's Head ★

GASTROPUB

Bearley Road, Aston Cantlow, Warwickshire B95 6HY
Tel. 01789 488 242 Fax 01789 488 137

MAP 3 E4

STRIKING a fine balance between traditional 'local' and place to eat of serious quality, The King's Head is imaginative but with no trace of chichi. And it is good to see a range of sandwiches served in the bar at lunchtime, an especially fine-looking one filled with rare roast beef.

On the main menu there is plenty to stir the imagination and also trigger the gastric juices. A home-made cream of mushroom soup was faultless for well-judged flavours with what tasted like wild mushrooms to the fore, cream playing second fiddle, a drizzle of olive oil and fine, very fresh bread.

Otherwise, you have choices such as a simple Caesar salad or, for something with more of a flourish, you might try crab, crayfish and avocado tian.

Whole baked lemon sole was admirably fresh, accompanied by a well-wrought chive butter sauce and superior new potatoes, sweet and tender.

The famous dish here is the King's Head Duck Supper, with honey roasted parsnips and plum sauce. Modern options include a pea and broad bean risotto.

The classic desserts are well executed, notably the lemon tart.

There are excellent real ales and the wine list is sensibly priced. The pouring red and white are very good, fruit-rich wines from Berri Estates, Australia.

Speciality food: King's Head Duck Supper
Draught beers: Greene King Abbot Ale, Hook Norton
Average wine price by the glass: £2.90

Licensee: David Bryan
Last orders for dinner: 9.45 pm
Open every day
Set lunch: from £14
Main courses: from £12
Private dining: up to 20
Beer garden
Children welcome
Wheelchair access

ASTON TIRROLD, OXFORDSHIRE

Sweet Olive at Chequers Inn ★

Baker Street, Aston Tirrold, Oxfordshire OX11 9DD
Tel. 01235 851 272

MAP 2 B3

BETWEEN Didcot and Goring, half a mile off the A417, lies the old village of Aston Tirrold, which has the good fortune to have such a fine pub and restaurant.

Pillars in the traditional bar are mounted with wooden wine box ends of famous châteaux and growers. Blackboard menus and a rug-covered, old terracotta-tiled floor complement the authentic atmosphere. The unfussily furnished dining-room, with tongue and groove wood panelling, is quite small, but commendably retains its pub character.

The French-born chef/patron has stamped his Gallic influences on the cuisine and modestly described dishes exceed expectations. Lighter bar snacks are offered, such as organic baguettes filled with home-made gravadlax or crispy duck, or salads in the form Caesar or goat's cheese.

The Mediterranean fish soup is distinguished by its depth of flavour and served with ultra-thin crispy croutons, shredded Gruyère and rouille. Roasted tomato soup with green pesto, or duck and hare terrine, are other alluring possibilities.

Main dishes might include onglet of beef with white wine, Scottish scallops and langoustines with lime butter sauce, or meltingly tender escalope of venison served with humble cabbage lifted to new heights by the simple addition of cream.

Finish with treacle sponge and custard or (when in season) local Victoria plum fool of unique and sublime flavour.

Speciality food: Provençal mussels (steamed, then sautéd)
Draught beers: Deuchars IPA, Hook Norton Hooky
Average wine price by the glass: £3.25

Licensees: Stephane Brun and Olivier Bouet
Last orders for dinner: 9 pm
Closed: Sunday evening (in winter), Wednesday
Closed for holidays: February
Main courses: from £9.95
Beer garden
Children welcome
Wheelchair access

ASWARBY, LINCOLNSHIRE

Tally Ho Inn

GASTROPUB

Aswarby, Sleaford, Lincolnshire NG34 8SA
Tel. 01529 455 205 Fax 01529 455 773
e-mail: enquiries@tally-ho-aswarby.co.uk   **MAP 4** C2

ONCE an estate manager's house, the Tally Ho, on the outskirts of Sleaford, is still owned by the Aswarby estate and looks out on attractive, manicured parkland, the view of which can be enjoyed from the garden's randomly placed trestle tables.

The inn, with a wood-burning stove at one end of the bar and an open fire at the other, has developed a well-deserved reputation, both as a local watering-hole and for its food. It is also popular with overseas visitors, particularly shooting parties and hikers.

The menu choice is expansive rather than excessive and offers good, wholesome food. There is a nod towards current trends in the serving of mustard grain mash with pork, otherwise dishes are straightforward and unpretentious.

Lighter options feature a ploughman's comprised of local pork pie, ham and Lincolnshire Poacher cheese, or various salads and filled baguettes.

Starters might include smoked mackerel and fresh asparagus in a tortilla basket with horse-radish dressing, or perhaps a Greek salad.

The soup of the day, such as potato and chive broth, will be flavoursome and hearty. The steak and kidney pudding should satisfy the biggest appetite.

Desserts range from rhubarb crumble or pineapple fritters to less robust offerings for more delicate tastes.

Speciality food: Dicken's suet pudding
Draught beers: Batemans, Tiger
Average wine price by the glass: £3

Licensees: James and Jo Cartwright
Last orders for dinner: 9.30 pm (Sunday 9 pm)
Open every day
Closed for holidays: 25 December
Main courses: from £5.95
Private dining: 30-40
Beer garden
Accommodation: 6 rooms
Children welcome
Limited wheelchair access

BAGBOROUGH, SOMERSET

Rising Sun

GASTROPUB

Bagborough, Taunton, Somerset TA4 3EF
Tel. 01823 432 575

MAP 1 D3

RAZED to the ground by a devastating fire in 2002, 'The Riser' has been transformed from a centuries-old cider house to a stylish gastropub thanks to tons of new oak, flagstone floors, Art Deco lighting and striking modern art on the walls.

The dining-room, with large antique tables and a baby grand piano, is separated from the bar by a glass screen. A small dining area at the rear is found up a few stairs, and on the first floor a further room with splendid views is ideal for private parties.

It is a striking, if somewhat unexpected environment for some equally striking food. Presentation is modern and highly stylised, with designer crockery and inventive twists.

A starter of lightly spiced duck confit spring rolls, golden, crisp and succulent, is served plated with a shot-glass of home-made chutney. Crunchy beer-battered cod has a geometric tower of thick, hand-cut chips. Bread and butter pudding is accompanied by vanilla ice-cream on a bed of powdered white chocolate.

While the quality of ingredients may not always live up to the quality of presentation, there is much to enjoy on the daily evening menus of about six starters, main courses and desserts. Lunchtimes see a blackboard with a handful of dishes from the evening menu, plus filled baguettes, and there is a reduced fixed-price menu on Sunday offering a couple of locally sourced roasts.

Speciality food: Six-hour belly pork with bubble and squeak and caramelised apples
Draught beers: Butcombe Blonde, Golden Eagle – Cotleigh
Average wine price by the glass: £2.75

Licensee: Rob Rainey
Last orders for dinner: 9 pm
Closed: Sunday evening (food), Monday
Set lunch: from £8.95
Main courses: from £12
Private dining: 12–30
Accommodation: 2 rooms
Children welcome
Wheelchair access

BAMBURGH, NORTHUMBERLAND

Wynding Inn at the Lord Crewe `GASTROPUB`

Front Street, Bamburgh, Northumberland NE69 7BL
Tel. 01668 214 243   Fax 01668 214 273
e-mail: lordcrewebamburgh@tiscali.co.uk   **MAP 5** D1

THIS recently refurbished dining-room attached to a cottagey High Street inn is a model of elegant simplicity with its light oak furnishings and an absence of decoration, and rightly so, since the imposing bulk of the nearby castle provides more than enough of a historical backdrop.

The straightforward menu echoes the uncomplicated style of the surroundings, with a selection of old favourites designed to please a cosmopolitan clientele visiting the local monuments and nearby islands. No surprises among the starters of potted crab and shrimp, chicken liver parfait and home-made soups, although nicely grilled goat's cheese on mâche with a tangy pesto gives a refreshing hint of sunnier climes.

Main courses, too, are designed to please rather than astound, with occasional touches such as a mild chilli salsa topping a fillet of salmon, or the mozzarella and basil used to stuff a chicken breast, providing more inventive alternatives to a plainer roast breast of duck, peppered steak or braised lamb shank.

Desserts are sadly rather limited after an otherwise enjoyable meal, and given the stylish, contemporary setting, it would be nice to see a little more flamboyance emanating from the kitchen.

The restaurant is open only in the evening, but there is a range of lighter bar meals on offer at lunchtime. There is also a good selection of draught beers.

Speciality food: British food with a Mediterranean slant
Draught beers: Bass, Bombardier
Average wine price by the glass: £3.50

Licensee: Marc Eden
Last orders for dinner: 9 pm
Open every day
Closed for holidays: end November to early February
Main courses: from £10.95
Accommodation: 18 rooms
Children over 5 welcome

BANK, HAMPSHIRE

Oak Inn

`GASTROPUB`

**Pinkney Lane, Bank, Nr. Lyndhurst, Hampshire SO43 7FE
Tel. 02380 282 350**

MAP 2 A4

BANK is a hamlet just off the A35 at the very heart of the New Forest and home to this 18th-century white painted inn. Dried hops above the bar create an impression of tradition, as do five locally brewed draught beers, dispensed from old wooden barrels, and a dart board tucked away in one corner.

Closer inspection reveals bar stools created from old milk churns and spears hanging from the low, beamed ceiling. There is an area in the garden for barbecues and in summer a beer festival is celebrated here featuring about forty beers.

In addition to bar snacks, the blackboard menu offers plenty of choice and leans towards seafood with fresh crab and lobster from Selsey or Poole. How about cracked Selsey crab claws to start, or perhaps a lightly peppered chicken liver pâté served in a pot and sealed in butter, or smoked duck breast with a hoi sin sauce?

Main courses may be local sole in lemon butter, or the unmissable pan-fried Test river trout – splendidly fresh and moist, with crispy skin and served on a well-made couscous and red pepper coulis. Cornish cod in beer batter with mushy peas is another temptation, and excellent steaks and pies are always available.

There is a short list of puddings with offerings such as fromage frais cheesecake and soft fruits, or perhaps coconut panna cotta and pineapple compote. Mobile phones are discouraged, which helps to maintain a peaceful atmosphere.

Speciality food: Seafood
Draught beers: Hopback Summer Lightning, Ringwood Bitter
Average wine price by the glass: £3.25

Licensee: Karen Slowen
Last orders for dinner: 9.30 pm
Open every day
Closed for holidays: 25 and 26 December
Main courses: from £10.95
Beer garden
Children welcome before 6 pm
Wheelchair access

BARNGATES, CUMBRIA

Drunken Duck

GASTROPUB

Barngates, Nr. Ambleside, Cumbria LA22 0NG
Tel. 01539 436 347 Fax 01539 436 781
e-mail: info@drunkenduckinn.co.uk   **MAP 5** C3

THIS really is a most glorious spot, with the majestic Lakeland fells rising above Lake Windermere lying hidden in the valley below. And better still, they even have their own brewery. The five-barrel brewhouse distributes to other outlets a range of four beers (named after the pub's pets) as well as supplying the Duck, so at least you won't go thirsty.

You will not go hungry either. The ambitiously varied menu, served in cottagey dining-rooms strung with hop bines, their walls decked with sporting prints and pastoral scenes, offers a wide range of traditionally inspired and more inventive dishes using local seafood and regional produce.

Starters such as niçoise salad with Solway Firth smoked wild salmon, potted Flookborough shrimps, mussels, scallops and grilled oysters tend to stick to a simpler, lighter style, while the larger main course selection is definitely out to impress with a heartier range of dishes.

Despite a conventional bias, there is an inventive twist to, say, roast duck breast with marmalade, parsnip purée and mushroom duxelle; noisettes of Herdwick lamb on garlic mash with leeks, prunes and a redcurrant glaze, or venison fillet with fennel, cherry and vanilla compote, alongside grilled fish or beer-battered cod with some mightily impressive chips.

Desserts include chocolate and hazelnut brownie with iced coffee parfait and tiramisù cream. There are fine farmhouse cheeses.

Speciality food: Cumbrian lamb and fish
Draught beers: Barngates Cracker Ale, Barngates Tag Lag
Average wine price by the glass: £2.95

Licensee: Stephanie Barton
Last orders for dinner: 9 pm
Open every day
Closed for holidays: 25 December
Main courses: from £9.50 (lunch), £13.95 (dinner)
Beer garden
Accommodation: 16 rooms
Children welcome
Wheelchair access

BARNSLEY, GLOUCESTERSHIRE

Barnsley House ★

Barnsley, Nr. Cirencester, Gloucestershire GL7 5EE
Tel. 01285 740 000 Fax 01285 740 900
e-mail: info@barnsleyhouse.com   **MAP 1** F1

AS IF TO echo the rather sparse nature of the interior design in this revamped old Cotswold stone house, simplicity is very much to the fore in the presentation of food that owes more to honest heartiness than fine complexity, and which is certainly none the worse for that.

There is a distinct Italian flavour about much that is on offer, such as mussels in potacchio, pappardelle, brodetto adriatico and spuma di cioccolato – and particularly in the elaborate dish called vincisgrassi, which dates from the 18th century and is composed of Parma ham, porcini and truffles with baked pasta.

Equally, though, the shortish menus, which change more or less every day, might feature on the one hand a simply garnished grilled steak or pork chop and on the other a bouillabaisse – though in reality this was more of an excellent and authentic Mediterranean fish soup – or the more complex braised hare with sage and cabbage.

Garnishing is kept to a strict minimum and, indeed, is probably unnecessary given the robust flavours of the aromatic herbs and vegetables that often come from the property's own garden.

One might argue with the choice of background music, which seems to be mostly frenetic modern jazz, not perhaps the most relaxing of musical styles. That apart, the place is a joy.

Their pride: Vincisgrassi (*see above*)
Inexpensive wines: Domaine Saint Bernard Marsanne Viognier Vin de Pays d'Oc 2003, £21; Salento Primitivo Tenute San Marco 2001, £21.95

Proprietors: Tim Haigh and Rupert Pendered
Last orders for dinner: 9.30 pm (Fri and Sat 10 pm)
Open every day
Set lunch: from £19.50
Set dinner: from £39.50
Private dining: up to 55
Al fresco eating
Accommodation: 10 rooms
Limied wheelchair access

BARNSLEY, GLOUCESTERSHIRE

Village Pub

GASTROPUB

Barnsley, Nr. Cirencester, Gloucestershire GL7 5EF
Tel. 01285 740 421 Fax 01285 740 929
email: info@villagepub.co.uk   **MAP 1** F1

AS A village pub, this is a bit, well, squeaky clean. Faultlessly designed and perfectly functional, it perhaps lacks a little in soul, yet all the elements of Rupert Pendered's other enterprise, his luxury country house hotel across the road, are to be found here. Everything is cosily welcoming: the blink-and-miss-it village, neat garden, designer-rustic interior kitted out in dark furnishings.

The style of the daily changing menu is simple-smart, too, with carrot and tomato soup, farmhouse terrine, or plain grilled steak, as well as now expected cross-culture touches of, say, chicken salad with caramelised carrots, pancetta and French beans, or a little mezze of pepper salad, feta, minted courgette, focaccia and tabbouleh.

There is no denying the inherent quality of some first-class main course ingredients, which are accorded appropriately respectful, straightforward treatment, often using vegetables from their own Barnsley House gardens. Duck breast with beetroot and radishes; chicken breast with celeriac, Jerusalem artichoke and carrots; roasted leg of lamb with wilted endive, olive and anchovies.

There are excellent fish dishes, too, such as a classical poached turbot with beurre blanc or fillet of sea trout with home-grown greens and a broad bean pesto.

As good as the tarts, brûlées and fruit-based desserts are, you might consider instead the range of British farmhouse cheeses.

Speciality food: Modern British cooking
Draught beers: Hook Norton, Wadworth 6X
Average wine price by the glass: £3

Licensees: Rupert Pendered, Tim Haigh
Last orders for dinner: 9.30 pm
Open every day
Main courses: from £12.50
Beer garden
Accommodation: 6 rooms
Children welcome
Wheelchair access

BASLOW, DERBYSHIRE

Fischer's Baslow Hall ★★

Calver Road, Baslow, Derbyshire DE45 1RR
Tel. 01246 583 259 Fax 01246 583 818
e-mail: m.s@fischers-baslowhall.co.uk   **MAP 3** F1

TAKING the direction of Stockport, turn off the Calver Road then follow a chestnut-lined drive to this fine, stone manor house. It looks Elizabethan but is actually Edwardian, with all the space and comforts this implies. What really makes it notable, however, is the dazzling cuisine created by Max Fischer, chef/patron here for some sixteen years.

Dinner can be an unforgettable experience. Amuse-bouches like salmon sushi and tuna with saffron might be followed by mussel and basil soup then firm and creamy pumpkin risotto, before the arrival of the centrpiece, which could be venison, in season, with sweet-and-sour red cabbage and purées of celeriac and parsnip.

Lime and juniper sorbet comes as a palate-cleanser, then there is a particularly fine selection of cheeses and, finally, there are sophisticated desserts like chocolate soufflé tart with chocolate mousse and pumpkin ice-cream.

One of the attractions at Baslow Hall is a sympathetic regard for most budgets, starting with the bargain price for the early-served evening menu du jour, three courses with such dishes as pan-fried sea bream or confit of duck.

The wine list is strong in the best bottles from Australia.

Their pride: New season's Derbyshire lamb
Inexpensive wines: Sauvignon Blanc Wither Hills 2004, £20; Côtes du Rhône Vieilles Vignes 2001, £19.50

Proprietors: Max and Susan Fischer
Last orders for dinner: 9.30 pm
Closed: Sunday dinner, Monday lunch
Closed for holidays: 25 and 26 December
Set lunch: from £20
Set dinner: from £30
Al fresco dining
Private dining: up to 40
Accommodation: 11 rooms
Limited wheelchair access

BASSENTHWAITE LAKE, CUMBRIA

Pheasant Inn

GASTROPUB

Bassenthwaite Lake, Nr. Cockermouth, Cumbria CA13 9YE
Tel. 01768 776 234 Fax 01768 776 002
e-mail: info@the-pheasant.co.uk   **MAP 5** B3

PART pub, part hotel, this graciously weatherbeaten, ancient inn is a monument to Lakeland hospitality. Half-an-hour from the M6, its surrounding fells and forests are a walkers' paradise and after a long day's rambling, its cosily understated luxury behind the rustic, timber-frame façade must beckon like a heart-warming and irresistible siren.

Snug bars and comfortable lounges, where dark woodwork, gleaming copper and china abound, are there to cosset you while a young and conscientious staff respect the formal demands of the house customs while remaining amenable and breezy.

And you are unlikely to find anything too outlandish on the set lunch and dinner menus, though a more rebellious streak does sneak in among an otherwise classically oriented choice.

Melon, Stilton quiche or a well-made chicken liver and brandy pâté with Melba toast may start you off, with a mixed grill of fish, a roast rump of Lakeland lamb or a breast of Gressingham duck to follow. Contemporary trends mean accompaniments such as risotto, crisp pancetta, mashes of various kinds, tapenade and sun-blushed tomatoes.

That said, there is nothing remotely wrong about a silver-served fillet of Old Spot pork on black pudding with spinach and a fruity calvados cream, turned carrots and sauté potatoes.

It would be a shame to see them trying to jump on the modern gastropub bandwagon.

Speciality food: Traditional country inn food
Draught beers: Jennings Cumberland, Youngers
Average wine price by the glass: £3.30

Licensee: Matthew Wylie
Last orders for dinner: 8.30 pm
Open every day
Closed for holidays: 25 December
Set lunch: from £17.50
Set dinner: from £28.95
Private dining: up to 12
Beer garden
Accommodation: 15 rooms
Children over 12 welcome for dinner   Wheelchair access

BATH, SOMERSET

Bath Priory ★★

Weston Road, Bath, Somerset BA1 2XT
Tel. 01225 331 922 Fax 01225 448 276
e-mail: mail@thebathpriory.co.uk   MAP 1 E2

STUFFED with delightfully 'lived-in' period furniture, the walls hung with ornately framed oil and watercolour paintings, Bath Priory resonates gentility and nostalgia for a bygone age. There is nothing remotely old-fashioned about the cooking, though.

As the menu makes clear, the aim here is to present dishes that extract to the full the tastes of even the simplest ingredients. In order to achieve this, the best of raw materials are handled with consummate skill and imagination yet entirely without fuss or pretension. The combinations are well balanced, so that the often innovative mixture of flavours is always intriguing.

Quail breasts are partnered by caramelised onion tart, ceps and a crisp 'tile' of Parmesan, for example. Tender monkfish medallions are given a lobster sauce and the thoughtful accompaniments of creamed potatoes with chives and Chinese leaves.

Desserts are both refined and refreshing. Coffee and petits fours are served in the appropriately graceful surroundings of the lounge to round off a delightful meal.

Set among tranquil and gorgeous gardens close to the Royal Victoria Park, Bath Priory has an atmosphere of genteel house parties and generally gracious living.

Their pride: Pan-roasted wild salmon with stuffed cappelletti of pea purée, pea shoots and citrus foam
Inexpensive wines: Regaleali Bianco Conte Tassa D'Almerita (Sicily) 2002, £20.50; Madiran AC Lafite Ceston 2001, £26.50

Proprietor: Andrew Brownsword
Last orders for dinner: Sunday–Thursday 9.30 pm, Friday and Saturday 10 pm
Open every day
Set lunch: from £20
Set dinner: from £49.50
Private dining: 8-64
Accommodation: 31 rooms
Limited wheelchair access

BAWBURGH, NORFOLK

Kings Head ★

GASTROPUB

**Harts Lane, Bawburgh, Norwich, Norfolk NR9 3LS
Tel. 01603 744 977 Fax 01603 744 990
e-mail: anton@kingshead-bawburgh.co.uk**   **MAP 4** E3

A MODEL for what the country gastropub ought to be, the 17th-century Kings Head is set opposite the lawned banks of the little River Yare, which is shallow enough for children to paddle in it, accompanied by the chorus of a family of irascible ducks.

Inside, natural wood has been lightened and the restaurant has been sensitively modernised, with elegant leather chairs and a view of the kitchen team at work.

As for the food, local ingredients are cooked in a style influenced by ideas from Japan, the Mediterranean and the sea-bed off the Norfolk coast.

From the set lunch menu, perfectly timed, juicy seared scallops are served with a salad of wakame (Japanese spinach), cucumber and fresh cockles in a ginger dressing. Each ingredient in a main dish such as crispy belly pork, chorizo, clams, piquillos pepper and new potatoes is faultlessly prepared, but so many flavours do add up something of an assault on the palate.

There is plenty to attract on both the lunch and dinner cartes: escabèche of whitebait, coriander and chillies; smoked eel, creamy scrambled eggs, watercress and organic rye bread; Suffolk ham; bouillabaisse; rib-eye steak; grilled fresh snapper; strawberry parfait, praline and almond shortbread.

British farmhouse cheeses are another feature, especially the first-rate Lincolnshire Poacher made with unpasteurised milk.

Speciality food: Seared scallops, Japanese wakame, cucumber and cockle salad
Draught beers: Adnams, Wherry
Average wine price by the glass: £3.50

**Licensee: Anton Wimmer
Last orders for dinner: 9.45 pm
Closed: Sunday and Monday evening;
Closed for holidays: 25 December
Set lunch: from £16.50
Main courses: from £13.50
Private dining: up to 26
Beer garden**
Children welcome
Wheelchair access

BEARSTED, KENT

Souffle Restaurant ★

31 The Green, Bearsted, Maidstone, Kent ME14 4DN
Tel. 01622 737 065 Fax 01622 737 065

MAP 2 E3

THEY LOOK after their village greens in Kent and even in this satellite suburb of workaday Maidstone, the greensward, with its ball-chasing dogs and tree-shaded lovers, is well manicured. Nick Evenden's discreet little red brick, picture postcard cottage restaurant forms an integral part of the idyll. Gnarled beams, colourful prints and crisply damask-clothed tables looking out on a flower-decked terrace are the sympathetic backdrop to concise, well-conceived menus that eschew outlandish creativity and ground-breaking innovation.

Alongside the likes of a layered terrine of smoked salmon with anchovy butter, the tortellini of langoustine and salmon with a langoustine bisque, fillet of beef or loin of venison, there is more than a touch of interest from pan-fried coriander risotto with sea scallops, the roasted rump of lamb with Moroccan spices and a Thai-style osso bucco of monkfish.

Light, pungent and creamily sauced ravioli of wild mushroom might be followed by perfectly cooked fresh halibut under a herb and almond crust, simply dressed on some crunchy mangetout and spinach with vermouth sauce.

Throughout a meal of admirably even quality – including desserts such as light lemon tart with crème fraîche ice-cream – nothing interferes with your enjoyment and appreciation of their endeavours, even if one might want to encourage a little more eloquence in the flavouring. The style is as endearing and time-honoured as the surroundings, old school rather than old hat and reliant on sheer quality.

Their pride: Pan-fried scallops with black pudding
Inexpensive wines: Chenin Blanc Klippenkop (South Africa) 2004, £17; Bordeaux Supérieur Château Livey 1998, £19.50

Proprietor: Nick Evenden
Last orders for dinner: 9.30pm
Closed: Monday
Closed for holidays: Boxing Day
Set lunch: from £13.50
Set dinner: from £22.50
Private dining: up to 25
Al fresco dining
Wheelchair access

BEAULIEU, HAMPSHIRE

Montagu Arms Hotel Terrace Restaurant

Palace Lane, Beaulieu, Hampshire SO42 7ZL
Tel. 01590 612 324 Fax 01590 612 188
e-mail: reservations@montaguarms.co.uk   **MAP 2** B5

WITH the celebrated ponies and the motor museum, this grand old lady is a jewel in the glorious New Forest crown. Here you are transported away from ye olde tea shoppes to the more genteel times shown in old photographs adorning the polished panelling. The Terrace offers a particularly restful setting, with bay windows overlooking the gardens, and what seem like acres of elegant dining chairs covered in damask and tapestry.

The background suggests a serious dining experience, and that is exactly what you get. Even a simple terrine on the lighter lunch menu takes on a refined mantle, made from suckling pig and baby leeks, followed by the freshest of monkfish with saffron cream, cockles and vegetables. At dinner, there might be fresh pea and mint soup with lobster; scallops with lentil and coriander sauce; fillet of beef with fresh goat's cheese gnocchi, or organic chicken with watercress sauce and morels.

Desserts are a must, too, with a Hungarian version of good old English trifle offering a more substantial alternative to mousses, a Muscat crème caramel or an ethereal passion fruit soufflé.

Simpler menus are available in Monty's Brasserie and Bar next door. The approach here is relaxed and informal in a village pub setting, but with added interest among the selection of snacks and full meals.

Choose from confit duck and liver terrine, Gorgonzola and walnut risotto, chump of lamb with chorizo cassoulet, or chicken breast with potato pancake and tarragon sauce.

Their pride: Scallops with lentil and coriander sauce
Inexpensive wines: Frontonnais Château Baudare 2002, £20; Finca Carbonell Viura Chardonnay (Spain) 2003, £17

Proprietor: John Leech
Last orders for dinner: 9.30 pm
Open every day
Set lunch: from £22.50
Set dinner: from £39
Private dining: up to 100
Al fresco dining
Accommodation: 23 rooms
Wheelchair access

BIDDENDEN, KENT

West House ★

28 High Street, Biddenden, Kent TN27 8AH
Tel. 01580 291 341 Fax 01580 292 501
e-mail: westhouse@fsmail.net   **MAP 2** E4

IT IS one of the glories of England that there are still restaurants like this to be found. Discreet, almost self-effacing, it offers the sort of cooking that is neither flag-flying English nor adapted French, and still less involved in any sort of fusion. It is simply very good.

In the middle of the medieval High Street in Biddenden, you are welcomed by Graham and Jackie Garrett as if you were arriving for a family meal. Don't expect a phalanx of waiters, or the very fashionable pre-starters and pre-desserts. Just look forward to enjoying your meal as much as, if not more than, you ever have anywhere.

As for the food itself, the dishes are completely reliant on local availability of the best-quality produce, including some superb fish from Rye. The menu – a simple sheet of A4 paper – offers no more than a handful of starters, main courses and puddings from chef Graham, who adores preparing wholly seasonal ingredients in the most natural way imaginable.

Regular features, in addition to the fresh fish, are Romney lamb, local mallard, carpaccio of smoked haddock and slow-cooked belly of pork with black pudding, roasted quince and sage oil.

There are probably very few husband-and-wife proprietors of restaurants at this level, and even fewer with so much reason to be proud of their achievement.

Their pride: Foie gras crème caramel, aged vinegar and raisins
Inexpensive wines: Le Lesc Vin de Pays du Gers 2004, £12.95;
Bodegas Urbina Rioja Crianza 2000, £19.95

Proprietors: Graham and Jackie Garrett
Last orders for dinner: 9.30 pm
Closed: Saturday lunch, Sunday dinner, Monday
Closed for holidays: 2 weeks Aug, 2 weeks Christmas
Set lunch: from £21
Set dinner: from £29.50
Wheelchair access

BIRCHOVER, DERBYSHIRE

Druid Inn

Main Street, Birchover, Nr. Matlock, Derbyshire DE4 2BL
Tel. 01629 650 302

MAP 3 E1

THIS early 17th-century inn is named after the Druids who, according to legend, used to practise their magic on the Rowter Rocks behind the inn. A local pastor, the Reverend Thomas Eyre, was so fascinated by the Druids' rocks that he carved seats in them so that he and his friends could sit and admire the Peak District views.

The inn is now a shrewd mix of traditional Derbyshire country pub and modern brasserie-style food, the latest venture of Sheffield café group Thyme for Food. The bar and little rooms off have a genuine pub atmosphere, serving excellent real ales from local breweries, with some brews reflecting the historical associations of the inn, such as Druid Ale and Reverend Eaton's.

In the bar, the set-price menu features staples such as fishcakes or meat pies with mushy peas, while in the upstairs restaurant – informal yet smartly and contemporarily decorated – the carte takes in ideas from all over. Smoked haddock chowder, for example, or an intriguing and successful bruschetta of asparagus, rocket and deep-fried egg; Portuguese fish stew, and an accurately cooked rump steak burger with thick-cut chips. Vegetarians are offered choices such as the crisp Mediterranean vegetable tart.

Desserts, too, are of a good standard, especially the chocolate marquise. Wines by the glass and bottle are discerningly chosen from the Old and New Worlds and they make an excellent Bellini from a good Prosecco base. The staff both at the bar and in the restaurant anticipate customers' needs, always with a smile.

Speciality food: Rump of lamb with pesto mash
Draught beers: Druids Ale (Leatherbritches), Reverend Eaton's (Shardhow)
Average wine price by the glass: £3.75

Licensee: Adrian Cooling
Last orders for dinner: 9 pm
Open every day
Set lunch: from £12 (Noon–1 pm)
Set dinner: from £12 (6 pm-7 pm)
Main courses: from £10
Private dining: 14-40
Al fresco dining
Children welcome
Wheelchair access

BIRMINGHAM

The Bucklemaker

GASTROPUB

30 Mary Ann Street, St. Paul's Square, Birmingham B3 1RL
Tel. 0121 200 2515 Fax 0121 236 9887

MAP 3 E3

IN A little street flanking St. Paul's Square and not far from the jewellery and diamond trading quarter of Birmingham, The Bucklemaker is an atmospheric cellar bar and restaurant, all exposed brick walls and vaulted arches.

The room is made up of alcoves, ideal for a quiet business lunch or, for those on their own, somewhere to read one of the available newspapers. Tapas are a popular feature, though the choice is wider than you would find in Spain. The usual Mediterranean-style snacks such as braised artichokes, with olive and plum tomato dressing, or sautéed prawns with garlic, are there, of course, but so are smoked salmon with lemon, faggots in red wine and fresh rock oysters when in season.

The set-price menu of two courses plus coffee (£15.95) is fair value for central Birmingham. The ingredients are fresh and the cooking competent. Choices from the prix fixe may be the best option: Mediterranean vegetable tart with Roquefort cheese, say, followed by marinated chicken breast with basil and tarragon. The fully priced specials major on fish and seafood, such as linguine of crab and pan-fried wild salmon with crushed new potatoes. Chips are excellent.

The real asset of The Bucklemaker is the wine list. Delicious wines by the glass range from a pure, fruity South African Chenin Blanc to a very proper French Chardonnay. There is also a good choice of great red classed growth Médoc châteaux, including the superb Palmer 1986 and Ducru-Beaucaillou 1988. Fine aged tawny and vintage ports, too.

Speciality food: Crab linguine with olive oil and balsamic vinegar
Draught beers: Czech Budvar, Tiger Bitter
Average wine price by the glass: £3.45

Proprietor: Nicholas Crudington
Last orders for dinner: 10.30 pm
Closed: Saturday lunch, Sunday dinner
Closed for holidays: 24 Dec-2 Jan, Bank Holidays
Set lunch: from £15.25
Main courses: from £17
Private dining: 8-65
Wheelchair access

BIRMINGHAM

Jessica's ★★

1 Montague Road, Edgbaston, Birmingham B16 9HN
Tel./Fax 0121 455 0999

MAP 3 E3

THE intimate Jessica's is housed in a listed Victorian villa in Edgbaston, and it has first claim to be the best restaurant in the city. Chef/partner Glynn Purnell goes from strength to strength, and his vision of what a dish should be is so vivid that consistently superb combinations of flavours are the result, emulating his mentor Claude Bosi at Hibiscus in Ludlow.

His terrine of foie gras and rabbit is lightened by a sweetcorn purée and the masterstroke, kohlrabi and sweetcorn chilled ravioli, the parcels light and reviving to the palate. This is a dish Tom Aikens would be proud of.

Equally impressive for balanced textures and flavours is perfectly roasted monkfish with lentils, lentil purée and beignets of finely diced pig's trotters, a perfect complement to the 'meaty' fish. The other great dish is the Gressingham duck: the roasted breast with aubergine caviar and tomatoes cooked in orange and thyme, and the confit of leg with salad of white beans and courgettes.

Following the seasons, Glynn's desserts maintain these very high standards of ingredients and congenial flavours – as in a subtly rich white chocolate mousse partnered by poached peach and fresh raspberries, or the turned-out chocolate soufflé with gariguette strawberry sorbet and compote of strawberry.

The appetisers and petits fours are first-rate, the wine list shows both depth and choice. Pascal Cuny and his French team are at once professional and very approachable at front of house.

Their pride: Monkfish, pig's trotter beignets, pineapple, lentils
Inexpensive wines: Sauvignon Daniolle Touraine 2004, £19.95, Cape Gewürztraminer (South Africa) 2003, £25.95

Proprietors: Mr and Mrs K. Stevenson, Glynn Purnell
Last orders for dinner: 10 pm
Closed: Sunday and Monday, Saturday lunch
Closed for holidays: 1 week Christmas, 1 week Easter, 2 weeks end July
Set lunch: from £18.50
Set dinner: from £32.95
Wheelchair access

BIRMINGHAM

Simpson's ★

20 Highfield Road, Edgbaston, Birmingham B15 3DU
Tel. 0121 454 3434 Fax 0121 454 3399
e-mail: info@simpsonsrestaurant.co.uk   **MAP 3** E3

IN A smart part of Edgbaston stands this handsome and spacious Victorian villa, home since late 2004 to Andreas Antona's reborn Simpson's restaurant, formerly in Kenilworth. No expense has been spared to create a luxurious modern ambience that mirrors classical French cuisine brought up to date with a lighter touch.

The conservatory-style restaurant is a delightful, airy room full of natural light, softened by chic blinds in stylish creamy white, a pastel shade repeated in the table settings and marble floor. Service by a young team is impeccable – attentive, professional, approachable and friendly, yet always discreet. The à la carte menu is imaginative: six hot and cold starters, five meat, game and poultry main courses, three fish and shellfish options.

The cooking is certainly worth a one-star rating, but although the speciality duck foie gras was finely accompanied by roast banana, banana purée and pain d'épices, the foie – top quality and nicely seared – needed a further twenty to thirty seconds of cooking to set it. Similarly, the fillet of Aberdeen Angus beef cooked on the bone, served rare and accompanied by haggis and garlic and parsley butter, with chips cooked in duck fat, was excellent; the addition of snails was unnecessary.

Fish dishes are a strong point, as in the fillet of zander, perfectly cooked with a fine scallop, tomato and tarragon hollandaise. Desserts are starworthy – a perfectly risen praline soufflé came after exactly twenty-five minutes, with turron (nougatine) ice-cream. The excellent wines display a good balance of classics and some exciting discoveries from the New World.

Their pride: Foie gras, roast banana, pain d'épices
Inexpensive wines: Riesling F. E. Trimbach 2003, £28; Château Thieuley Réserve 2002, £31

Proprietors: Andreas and Alison Antona
Last orders for dinner: 9.45 pm
Open every day
Closed for holidays: Christmas, New Year, Bank Hols
Set lunch: from £25
Set dinner: from £30
Private dining: 10-20
Al fresco dining
Accommodation: 4 rooms
Wheelchair access

BIRMINGHAM

Wing Wah ★

Unit IA The Wing Yip Centre, 278 Thimble Mill Lane,
Nechells, Birmingham B7 5HD
Tel. 0121 327 7879 Fax 0121 327 7951   **MAP 3** E3

HOUSED in the Wing Yip Chinese supermarket complex, Wing
Wah is a big place but it still fills up quickly at dinner. Both the
Chinese community and European customers from all over the
city are drawn by the exceptional consistency of the cooking.

The evening hot buffet is a strong magnet, with everything from
steaming tureens of braised shark's fin soup and dim-sum to
baked crab with ginger and spring onion or Cantonese-style pork
chops with pineapple. The freshness of ingredients, the accuracy
of the cooking and proper definition of flavours are the keynotes.

Delicate won ton and super pak choi in a soup based on fresh
chicken stock was a promising beginning. The high standards
were maintained in the tender deep-fried squid, nicely salted, and
sizzling fillet of beef Cantonese style, tender and moist, served
with perfect steamed rice and mixed Chinese vegetables.

Seafood generally is also a strong suit, especially steamed sea
bass in various guises, lobster in XO (cognac) chilli sauce, Kung
Po scallops and sautéd king prawn with green peppers.

Crispy apple fritters with vanilla ice-cream might be a well-known
staple of Cantonese restaurants, but it is particularly good here.
Indeed, the strength of Wing Wah is the exemplary standard of
Cantonese old faithfuls.

Their pride: Daily hot buffet
Inexpensive wines: Merlot Palacio della Vega Navarre 2002,
£10.50; Gewürztraminer d'Alsace Turckheim 2003, £12

Proprietor: Tuzhin Ltd.
Last orders for dinner: 10.45pm (Sunday 9.45pm)
Open every day
Set lunch: from £12.60
Set dinner: from £12.60
Main courses: from £8
Wheelchair access

BISHOPS TACHBROOK, WARWICKSHIRE

Mallory Court ★

Harbury Lane, Bishops Tachbrook, Leamington Spa, CV33 9QB
Tel. 01926 330 214 Fax 01926 451 714
e-mail: reception@mallory.co.uk   **MAP 3** F3

EATING in this fine country house between the M40 and Royal Leamington Spa is a very pleasurable 'modern' experience in the best sense.

The set lunches display the same high quality and standard as the evening carte, featuring perhaps excellent crab risotto followed by roast chump of lamb with nicely judged braised red cabbage and tapenade jus.

The carte, as you would expect, is rather more luxurious, the fine ingredients prepared with what might be described as creative respect, as in a lobster salad with avocado and lemon oil or the ballottine of ham hock and foie gras.

Choose from main courses such as mallard in an orange and armagnac sauce or pan-fried sea bass with roasted scallops.

Desserts are particularly good, ranging from a raspberry trio and an apple brûlée to warm chocolate mousse.

The wines, encompassing some of the best of France, Italy and Spain, are not cheap, but there is a good choice by the glass.

Their pride: Salad of foie gras with apples and home-smoked duck breast
Inexpensive wines: Pinot Grigio Ramato Rosé 2004, £21; Bodegas Norton Torrontés (Argentina) 2002, £18.50

Proprietor: Sir Peter Rigby
Last orders for dinner: 9.30 pm
Open every day
Set lunch: from £19.50
Set dinner: from £39.50
Private dining: up to 27
Al fresco dining
Accommodation: 29 rooms
Wheelchair access

BLACKBURN, LANCASHIRE

Northcote Manor ★

Northcote Road, Langho, Blackburn, Lancashire BB6 8BE
Tel. 01254 240 555 Fax 01254 246 568
e-mail: sales@northcotemanor.com   **MAP 5** C5

THERE is a fun, warm, cosy, bluff, unprepossessing and above all genuine welcome waiting for you at this modest 19th-century country (just) house, where the longstanding chef/patron, Nigel Haworth, has undoubtedly made an indelible mark physically and metaphorically.

His menus – including one devoted entirely to the vegetarian cause – reflect an avid evocation of all that is Lancastrian: pig's trotters, Southport shrimp, black pudding, the obligatory hot-pot and so on. Parachuted blindfolded into your seat, you would be in no doubt as to the whereabouts of your landing.

Rich, wholesome, natural flavours are certainly present. The 'spicy red cabbage' was just that, a miniature onion tart garnish was spot-on and the respect for local influences adds undeniable interest, especially in desserts such as the melting ginger parkin or a perfectly light Eccles cake soufflé.

The pity is that the place seems to try to be swishly up-market, offering complicated canapés, foie gras and caviar and wild mushrooms to garnish beef or lamb, treacle-roasted this, truffle jus-ed that.

There is no denying the excellence of the raw materials – plump, tender, almost gamey mallard, richly sauced fillet steaks – which could also be treated in a simpler way as an alternative.

Their pride: Black pudding and buttered pink trout with mustard and nettle sauce
Inexpensive wines: Tempranillo Bodegas Sonsierra (Spain) 2003, £17.50; Chardonnay de l'Ardèche Louis Latour 2002, £18.50

Proprietors: Craig Bancroft and Nigel Haworth
Last orders for dinner: 9.30 pm (Saturday 10 pm)
Open every day
Closed for holidays: 25 Dec, 1 Jan, Bank Holidays
Set lunch: from £20
Set dinner: from £50
Accommodation: 14 rooms
Wheelchair access

BLEDINGTON, OXFORDSHIRE

King's Head Inn ★

GASTROPUB

The Green, Bledington, Nr Kingham, Oxfordshire OX7 6XQ
Tel. 01608 658 365 Fax 01608 658 902
e-mail: kingshead@orr-ewing.com   **MAP 2** A2

THE PRETTIEST of pubs in an idyllic setting, the King's Head stands on Bledington green, approached by a little bridge that passes over a stream running through the village.

The bar exudes warmth and character, from the honey-coloured Cotswold walls and high-backed settles to the locals themselves, who come from every part of the village and beyond: affluent retired couples, a literary gent devouring *The Spectator*, lots of young people, partners having a break, smallholders and farmers.

The landlord, Archie Orr-Ewing, is a leading breeder of Aberdeen Angus cattle and the chef, Charlie Loader, uses the grass-reared beef to excellent effect in his chargrilled sirloin steak with Pinot Noir and butter sauce, available in the bar and restaurant – indeed any dish can had in either setting.

Duck spring roll with the crispest of coatings is a great starter, as is goujons of lemon sole with lemon and chive mayonnaise. Toasted panini at lunchtime rise above the predictable, served with chargrilled vegetables, Gruyère and spicy red pesto. Desserts include twice-baked rice pudding with sugar topping, but be sure to leave room for the fine British cheeses, not missing the Swaledale goat's cheese.

The wines from local independent merchants are first-rate, the choice by the glass including a fine Shiraz from the Barossa and Beaumont des Crayères champagne. The young staff are warm and helpful – in the bar, at breakfast and at reception. There are twelve comfortable and subtly stylish bedrooms.

Speciality food: Fifield Farm Aberdeen Angus beef.
Draught beers: Hook Norton, Wadworth.
Average wine price by the glass: £3.40.

Licensees: Archie and Nicola Orr-Ewing
Last orders for dinner: winter 9 pm, summer 9.30 pm
Open every day
Closed for holidays: 24-26 December
Main courses: from £12
Beer garden
Accommodation: 12 rooms
Children welcome
Wheelchair access

BODIAM, EAST SUSSEX

The Curlew

GASTROPUB

Junction Road, Bodiam, Nr. Robertsbridge, E Sussex TN32 5UY
Tel. **01580 861 394**
e-mail: **enquiries@thecurlewatbodiam.co.uk**   **MAP 2** E4

SOMETHING of a landmark on the Sussex restaurant scene, this attractive little crossroads restaurant-pub has known quite a few illustrious owners. Since joining the latest owning partnership, Simon Lazenby has been keen to ensure the perpetuation of the tradition. He and young chef Robert Leeper continually upgrade and enlarge their seasonally changing menus, constantly seeking new ideas to expand culinary boundaries while maintaining a firm foothold in time-honoured values.

Independent of any one particular gastronomic creed, their restaurant menu (there are plenty of lighter bar meals available, too) crosses just about every known frontier from the Italian influence of, say, sun-dried tomato and mozzarella risotto to Spanish-style warm salad of squid and chorizo. Or there might be Japanese duck with bean-sprout salad or else a lobster and salmon sausage on wilted spinach with a wispy, delicately spiced tandoori foam.

More familiar fare includes fine, extra-matured steaks, succulent lamb rump with haggis mash and buttered salsify and the dishes based on locally caught fish, which are something of a hallmark.

This is fine dining with ambitious standards, but the atmosphere – whether in the classically smart dining-room, its exposed beams swathed in dried hops, in the still nicely pubby front bar with its range of draught beers, or out in the ornamental gardens – is kept on an affable, easygoing footing that suits both restaurant and bar diners. A little fine-tuning still to do, perhaps, on one or two dishes, but they love their work and it shows.

Speciality food: Roasted snapper, lemon and lime potato cake
Draught beers: Badger Best, Fursty Ferret
Average wine price by the glass: £3.25

Licensee: Simon Lazenby
Last orders for dinner: 9 pm
Open every day
Set lunch: from £15.95
Set dinner: from £15.95
Private dining: 16-30
Beer garden
Children welcome
Wheelchair access

BOLTON ABBEY, NORTH YORKSHIRE

Devonshire Arms ★

Bolton Abbey, Nr. Skipton, North Yorkshire BD23 6AJ
Tel. 01756 710 441 Fax 01756 710 564
e-mail: reservations@thedevonshirearms.co.uk   **MAP 5** D4

THE state-of-the art kitchen at this imposing, attractive country house hotel produces quite short, daily changing menus based on prime classic ingredients – cornfed poultry, game in season, the freshest of line-caught fish and local meats. The cooking and garnishing of these follow traditional lines, with just a nod to 'modernity' in things such as the now almost obligatory black pudding, accompanying ravioli, 'foam' sauces and caramelised trimmings. Overall, the food is reassuringly conventional, always deliciously made and well presented.

You might start with a rich terrine, a croustillant of langoustines with celeriac, or the more complex miniature loin of rabbit with cannelloni of osso bucco, sweetcorn purée and vanilla jus. Then on to something like roasted and braised lamb with a shallot purée, or sweetbreads and kidneys with Sauternes and truffle jus, or a selection of top-quality fish.

If the main dishes tend towards lightness and economical use of their main ingredients, your selection is amply complemented by the regular appearance of additional items, from the generous amuse-bouches and a pre-starter to pre-dessert and home-made sweet delicacies with coffee. These welcome and well-chosen intervals add interest and variety and help transform your dinner into a true occasion.

Despite the grandiose nature of the wine list, which appears in two volumes, there are some generously priced bottles available.

Their pride: Poached bresse pigeon, calf's sweetbreads
Inexpensive wines: Le Volte (Italy) 2002, £24.50; Gravitas Sauvignon Blanc (New Zealand) 2003, £29.50

Proprietors: Duke and Duchess of Devonshire
Last orders for dinner: 9 pm for 9.30 pm
Closed: Mondays
Closed for holidays: 24-26 December
Set lunch: from £33
Set dinner: from £58
Private dining: up to 30
Accommodation: 40 rooms
Wheelchair access

BRAFIELD, NORTHAMPTONSHIRE

Red Lion

GASTROPUB

**36 Bridle Path, Brafield-on-the-Green, Northants NN7 1BP
Tel: 01604 890 707 Fax 01604 899 115**

MAP 4 B4

ONE glimpse of the gleaming, late-model German automobiles in the car park and the 'suits' gathered round the bar signals that this is a favourite venue for executives attracted by the stylish, capacious and well-spaced tables in the brasserie. A few miles out of Northampton towards Bedford, this smart pub in the centre of the village is a completely modern brasserie, a formula common to several new pub food operations south of Watford Gap.

This is an ideal place for little power lunches, without pretension. Indeed, the Red Lion is not too chichi thanks to the charming owner, Laura Croxford, who provides good traditional food with a modern twist. The draught beers include the excellent local brew (Charles Wells Bombadier) and there is something to suit every taste and appetite.

Under 'Sandwiches and Something More', hot seafood and prawns are served in a spinach tortilla wrap; the steak sandwich is on toasted ciabatta, or there is a fine ploughman's with home-made pork pie, ham and Neal's Yard cheeses. These are probably the soundest choices on the menu, which can be exotic, as in a hot Moroccan chicken salad, aromatic duck cakes with Vietnamese salad, or pan-roasted breast of guinea fowl.

Traditionalists might go for the calf's liver with garden sage mash or the battered hake, hand-cut chips and home-made tartare sauce. Carefully chosen wines by glass and bottle are strong in fresh selections from the southern hemisphere. Service is swift and welcoming – all well-suited to the largely business clientele, especially at lunchtime.

Speciality food: Cornfed chicken breast with couscous
Draught beers: Charles Wells Bombadier, Fullers London Pride
Average wine price by the glass: £3.80

**Licensee: Laura Croxford
Last orders for dinner: 9.30 pm
Open every day
Main courses: from £12
Beer garden**
Children welcome
Wheelchair access

BRANCASTER STAITHE, NORFOLK

White Horse ★

GASTROPUB

Main Road, Brancaster Staithe, Norfolk PE31 8BY
Tel. 01485 210 262 Fax 01485 210 930
email: reception@whitehorsebrancaster.co.uk   MAP 4 E2

THE HUB of this unfussy yet stylish restaurant is a glass-enclosed extension, with well-spaced pine tables, opening on to a decked terrace for lunchtime eating and a fine view over to the moored boats in the Norfolk marshes.

Every dish is priced individually on the carte, but make a beeline for the daily menu, which is effectively the chef's special choice. The cream of lettuce soup is a delight, nothing watery about it, finely defined flavours of cos lettuce, perfectly seasoned and with a splendid garnish of steamed lettuce and tomato.

Whole grilled local plaice with caper butter is first-rate, cooked with pin-point precision, slipping off the bone in bite-sized, firm flakes – not easy with plaice. Or go for the pan-fried Norfolk pork fillet with fondant potatoes and girolle jus.

If you just want a snack, take it in the bar (lunchtimes only). There is a good choice of fresh sandwiches and lighter options such as gazpacho, dressed Cromer crab with lime crème fraîche, or spiced griddled Norfolk chicken.

Back in the restaurant, the desserts, like the room, are simple, stylish and excellent: lemon tart with citrus cream, maybe, or hot chocolate brownies, chocolate sauce and vanilla cream. The Norfolk cheeses are really worth trying, too.

There is a fine wine list. The Pinot Grigio by the glass is a real cut above the crowd, like the White Horse itself.

Speciality food: Grilled whole plaice with caper butter
Draught beers: Adnams, Woodforde Wherry
Average wine price by the glass: £3.25

Licensee: Kevin Nobes
Last orders for dinner: 9 pm
Open every day
Main courses: from £14
Al fresco dining at lunch
Accommodation: 15 rooms
Children welcome
Wheelchair access

BRANSCOMBE, DEVON

Masons Arms GASTROPUB

Branscombe Village, Devon EX12 3DJ
Tel. 01297 680 300 Fax 01297 680 500
e-mail: reception@masonsarms.co.uk   **MAP 1** D4

ABOUT half-a-mile inland from one of the most celebrated coastal paths you will find The Masons Arms, with its distinctive thatched umbrellas. A pint of locally brewed Branoc on the terrace is one of summer's rewards, the sound of a babbling brook drowned only by the call of seagulls.

Blackened beams and wood panelling add atmosphere both in the bar and in the more formal dining-rooms beyond, and in winter a spit roast takes place over an open fire in the inglenook of the bar. New owners Carol and Colin Slaney plan to refurbish many areas of this well-known inn, but they are determined to maintain the reputation built up over decades by the previous owners for above-average pub food.

Lunchtime snacks of sandwiches and panini are joined by a broad menu of old favourites such as cod and chips and steamed steak and kidney pudding. But look closely and you will find some less usual and very rewarding choices – a wonderfully vivid green spinach and Branscombe crab soup, for example.

Blackboard specials are worth exploring, too – hot smoked mackerel, trout and salmon salad; spinach, mushroom and chestnut lasagne, or slow-roasted belly of pork. Puddings are sound, and there is an excellent cheeseboard boasting the West Country's finest. Evenings are more serious, with a fixed-price three-course menu. A comprehensive wine list offers plenty of quality drinking.

Speciality food: Steak and kidney pudding
Draught beers: Branoc (Branscombe Vale Brewery), Otter Bitter
Average wine price by the glass: £2.50

Licensees: Carol and Colin Slaney
Last orders for dinner: 9 pm
Open every day
Set dinner: from £25
Private dining: 16-40
Al fresco dining
Accommodation: 20 rooms
Children over 14 welcome in restaurant
Wheelchair access

BRANSGORE, DORSET

Three Tuns

GASTROPUB

Ringwood Road, Bransgore, Nr. Christchurch, Dorset BH23 8JH
Tel. 01425 672 232
e-mail: three.tunsinn@btinternet.com   **MAP 1** F4

JUST off the A35, four miles north of Christchurch, the Three Tuns, dating from the 17th century, is something of a landmark with its thatched roof, white painted brickwork and flowers. Inside there are open fireplaces, beams and flagstoned floors. Meals are served in all rooms, but the restaurant is more formally set and there is plenty of space for comfort.

On summer Sunday afternoons, barbecues on the terrace offer Aberdeen Angus rib-eye steak, or perhaps fish or meat kebabs.

At lunchtime, sandwiches and panini are available, with tempting fillings like buffalo mozzarella, home-made pesto and tomato, or ploughman's of ham or cheese with home-made bread. Alternatively there are dishes of crab and avocado salad with peeled and diced tomato and cucumber, moules marinières and Greek or Caesar salad.

If you fancy pasta, try the fiochetti with Gorgonzola, tomatoes and basil. Or you might prefer medallions of Balmoral venison with peppercorns in a light port jus and served with a vividly coloured mashed potato enlivened by red peppers. Pork Goa with basmati rice could be another option.

Puddings offer choices such as lemon cheesecake with lemon compote, strawberry and vanilla crème brûlée, or pavé (literally, a cobblestone) au chocolat, which is a smooth chocolate mousse on a crunchy, nutty base.

Speciality food: Local produce
Draught beers: Ringwood Best, Deuchars IPA
Average wine price by the glass: £3

Licensee: Peter Jenkins
Last orders for dinner: 9.15 pm
Open every day
Main courses: from £9
Private dining: 10-20
Beer garden
Children welcome in restaurant and garden
Wheelchair access

BRASSINGTON, DERBYSHIRE

Olde Gate Inn

GASTROPUB

Well Street, Brassington, Derbyshire DE4 4HJ
Tel. 01629 540 448
e-mail: thegateinn@supanet.com   **MAP 3** F2

AN unspoilt Derbyshire village street boasts an equally captivating little stone pub (circa 1606) apparently untouched by the 21st century. A cheery coal fire burns in an old cast-iron grate, horse brasses and tiled floors gleam, tankards hang from the beams. Customers range from older people taking a leisurely drive to walkers trekking in the Peak District.

At lunchtime the food choice is simple but everything is of good quality: sandwiches made with carved-off-the-bone honey-roast ham, with genuinely rare roast beef or with Scottish smoked salmon. Cromer crab salad is fresh, mainly composed of white crabmeat, served with tomato, red pepper, new potatoes and a decent mayonnaise. Roast leg of lamb is nicely sweet in flavour, tender and moist, with real gravy and proper mashed potato. Other lunchtime options are salami baguettes, leek and bacon quiche, chilli con carne, lasagne and garlic bread.

Dinner moves up a gear, showing modern influences. Typical are the monkfish kebabs marinated in olive oil, a lamb steak with rosemary, and the always popular speciality Great Grimsby plate, a ragout of cod and prawns. Puddings offer the usual fruit tarts and crumbles, sticky toffee pudding, ice-creams and sorbets.

Drink is carefully chosen and well cared for. The Pedigree bitter is beautifully kept, there is fine draught cider and the wines by the glass are in the modern fresh and fruity style – a very good non-oaked Chardonnay, for example. Service has few frills, but is friendly, helpful and quick, entirely appropriate to this charming traditional pub.

Speciality food: Beef in beer with horse-radish dumplings
Draught beers: Marston Pedigree, Guinness
Average wine price by the glass: £3.20

Licensee: Paul Burlinson
Last orders for dinner: Tuesday to Thurs 8.45 pm, Friday and Saturday 9 pm
Closed: Monday, Sunday evening (food)
Closed for holidays: 25 December (food)
Main courses: from £7.50
Private dining: up to 20
Beer garden
Children over 10 welcome
Wheelchair access

BRAY, BERKSHIRE

Fat Duck ★★

1 High Street, Bray, Berkshire SL6 2AQ
Tel. 01628 580 333 Fax 01628 776 188

MAP 2 C3

HESTON BLUMENTHAL may say that his methods have not changed, but there has definitely been an all-round development and further improvement. So the place is now nearing perfection, achieved when all items – even the traditional ones – are given the final touch of his amazingly inventive palate.

As soon as you enter, you will be charmed by the warm and relaxed atmosphere, enhanced by the ceiling beams, the straw and golden colours of abstract paintings and the friendliness and enthusiasm of young, well-trained French waiters.

The surprising harmony of an amuse-bouche of mustard ice-cream with red cabbage gazpacho is the first indication that the chef knows what he is doing. Then a raw oyster, topped with a delicate passion fruit jelly, horse-radish cream and lavender, creates a mouth-watering and balanced symphony of flavours. But this is surpassed by a starter of two crab-flavoured biscuits encasing a thick piece of cold, evenly roasted foie gras with a light oyster vinaigrette.

Main courses are down-to-earth by comparison, with dishes such as an ethereal poached turbot or a beautifully cooked best end of lamb, served with potato gratin, lamb shoulder confit and a jellied lamb consommé. After three perhaps gimmicky pre-desserts, you can end as eccentrically as you started, perhaps with macerated 'mara des bois' strawberries served with pistachio flavoured scrambled eggs and a purée of black olives and leather essence. You need to book at least six weeks ahead.

Their pride: Crab biscuit, roast foie gras and oyster vinaigrette
Inexpensive wines: Sylvaner Vieilles Vignes Domaine Ostertag 2003, £30; Crozes-Hermitage Vieilles Vignes Domaine du Murinais 2003, £31

Proprietor: Heston Blumenthal
Last orders for dinner: 9.30 pm
Closed: Sunday dinner, Monday
Closed for holidays: Christmas
Set lunch: from £37.50
Set dinner: from £67.50

BRAY, BERKSHIRE

Hind's Head ★

GASTROPUB

High Street, Bray, Berkshire SL6 2AB
Tel. 01628 626 151 Fax 01628 623 394

MAP 2 C3

BRAY is one of the prettiest villages in Southern England. Walking from the (free) village car park down the High Street, your eyes are drawn to this handsome late 17th-century inn, its cream frontage set off by russet and gold roof tiles that glint in the sun. In the beautiful panelled bar where, incidentally, Prince Philip held his stag party, little has changed physically since the 1690s. Today's customers, however, are young men in monogrammed polo shirts, designer-dressed women and American visitors.

Heston Blumenthal's new venture here aims to provide the sort of traditional British cooking that is in (almost) complete contrast to his 'laboratory-based' cuisine down the road at the Fat Duck. You can eat exactly the same food in the bar or in the charmingly informal, beamed dining-room, nicely lightened by white walls.

Chef Dominic Chapman certainly does the business, delivering star-standard British dishes. The 'Six Cereals' bread is delicious, the ham and pea soup, lacking nothing in traditional flavour, comes with a froth of peas on top. Oxtail pudding is a fine variant on the braised beef staple and is enhanced by the gutsy flavour of ox kidneys. The treacle tart with milk ice-cream is magic, the pastry and treacle feather-light, the ice-cream refreshing and not too sweet. Fish-lovers should certainly try the lemon sole with brown shrimps.

Superior hot or cold sandwiches are available at lunchtime on weekdays and there are excellent wines by the glass and bottle. Fast, effective service is provided by a smart young team led by Susan Proctor.

Speciality food: Traditional British cooking
Draught beers: Greene King IPA, Abbot Ale
Average wine price by the glass: £4

Proprietor: Heston Blumenthal
Licensees: Susan and Andrew Proctor
Last orders for dinner: 9.30pm
Closed: Sunday evening
Closed for holidays: 25 December, 1 January
Main courses: from £14
Private dining: up to 25
Children welcome

BRAY, BERKSHIRE

Waterside Inn ★★★

Ferry Road, Bray, Berkshire SL6 2AT
Tel. 01628 620 691 Fax 01628 784 710
e-mail: reservations@waterside-inn.co.uk   **MAP 2** C3

ONCE inside this temple of superlative gastronomy, your table in the sophisticated, comfortable restaurant gives a vista of the River Thames, its mirror-smooth surface gently broken by a line of ducklings aiming at a pier that juts out from the terrace.

Lunch here is an experience, the pride of The Waterside being flaked duck set in a subtle jelly with a quail's egg and caviar, with crisp black radish. From the amuse-bouches, the self-confidence of the kitchen is obvious.

The Menu Exceptionnel, served in small portions, is faultless, with wonders such as pan-fried scallops, seaweed tartare, herb and marinated baby squid salad, and saffron flavoured vinaigrette.

An example of the fish courses is roasted fillet of monkfish flavoured with anchovy, baby artichoke and rocket salad.

From the meat dishes a good choice is loin of lamb with crisp parcels of risotto and carrot, slightly curry scented with a savoury jus.

Pâtisserie (in which Michel Roux won the Meuilleur Ouvrier de France years ago) is endlessly delicious, with the best pick being a dome of milk chocolate mousse flavoured with caramel and served with a mango and passion fruit sorbet.

Lunch is something of a gastronomic opera, finishing with supreme petits fours.

Their pride: Tronçonnette de homard poêlée minute au Porto blanc
Inexpensive wines: Chablis Etienne Defaix 2002, £37; Domaine de Triennes St. Auguste 2000, £30

> **Proprietors: Michel and Alain Roux**
> **Last orders for dinner: 10 pm**
> **Closed: Monday, Tuesday (open for dinner on Tuesday 1 June-31 August)**
> **Closed for holidays: 6 weeks from 26 December**
> **Set lunch: from £40**
> **Set dinner: from £89.50**
> **Private dining: 8-10**
> **Accommodation: 11 rooms**
> Limited wheelchair access

BRIDGE, KENT

White Horse Inn

GASTROPUB

53 High Street, Bridge, Canterbury, Kent CT4 5LA
Tel. 01227 830 249 Fax 01227 832 814
e-mail: whitehorsebridge@hotmail.com   **MAP 2** F3

SO FAMILY businesses still exist. And few can be more appealing than the Waltons' warmly comfortable, bustling affair in the heart of the Kentish countryside, little more than a Chaucerian trot from Canterbury. With twelve years as publican behind him, Alan Walton provides a warm welcome in the nicely pubby bar, with daughter Hannah serving brother Ben's appetising selection of home-cooked dishes (along with baguettes and ploughman's) throughout the cosy bars, a simple, elegant little dining-room hung with colourful works of modern art and a lush garden set well back from the main road.

So proud are they of the local suppliers and producers of the prime ingredients they put to such good use, a list of them takes up as much space as the menu itself. With fish and shellfish from Whitstable and Folkestone, meat and free-range poultry from Faversham and fruit and vegetables from nearby farms, they exercise uncompromising quality control to produce a shortish but regularly changing menu of 'Real British Food'.

This is not to say that influences from further afield do not creep into Ben Walton's delightfully varied selection. After a pre-starter of, perhaps, smoked salmon mousse, lime and coriander add zing to medallions of monkfish on red pepper dressing with fennel salad, for example. Other choices include goat's cheese ravioli with an olive and tomato salad and pistou, or a succulent breast of free-range chicken coated with tapenade and served with wild garlic risotto. Chunky steaks and braised lamb shanks are given a more traditional treatment and desserts are not to be ignored, especially the creamy lemon tart with rhubarb sorbet.

Speciality food: Local farm produce and seafood
Draught beers: Abbott Bitter, Greene King IPA
Average wine price by the glass: £3

Licensee: Alan Walton
Last orders for dinner: 9 pm
Closed: Sunday evening
Closed for holidays: 25 December and 1 January
Main courses: from £8.50
Private dining: 25-30
Beer garden
Children welcome

BRIGHTON, EAST SUSSEX

Due South

139 Kings Road Arches, Brighton, East Sussex BN1 2FN
Tel. 01273 821 218
e-mail: eat@duesouth.co.uk   **MAP 2** D5

ON THE lower promenade of Brighton's bustling seafront, below the faded Victorian grandeur of some of the big hotels, this little restaurant specialises in surprisingly imaginative treatment of fresh local produce, much of it organic.

Fish is greatly in evidence, of course, and is used to create richly flavoured stock for the excellent fish soup, which is satisfying enough to make a delicious, single-dish lunch. Indeed, all the items on the menu can be ordered singly at lunchtime.

The ambitious nature of the cooking shows through in pumpkin and sage ravioli, which are served with a creamy herb sauce, crisp, perfectly cooked baby vegetables and Parmesan, or else in a hot-pot of tender lamb that is bursting with flavour and very colourfully presented.

The dinner menu is based largely on the same dishes, perhaps more formally presented, though without detracting from the friendly, casual, bare-floorboards air of the place. The open-plan kitchen is on the lower level of the former fisherman's store, with most of the dining above – and out of doors when the weather is kind enough.

There are organic wines, too.

Their pride: Due South fish soup
Inexpensive wines: Curious Grape Flint Dry (England) 2003, £12.95; Tinto Crianza Clos de Torribas (Spain) 2001, £14.95

Proprietor: Robert Shenton
Last orders for dinner: 10 pm
Open every day
Private dining: up to 12
Al fresco dining
Wheelchair access

BRIGHTON, EAST SUSSEX

The Gingerman ★

21a Norfolk Place, Brighton, East Sussex BN1 2PD
Tel./Fax 01273 326 688
e-mail: info@gingermanrestaurants.com   **MAP 2** D5

A PRE-APPETISER of correct butternut squash soup with truffle oil and an individual home-baked loaf was a reassuring start, while waiting a very proper twenty minutes for an exemplary risotto to arrive – its texture and consistency just right, with the fine flavour of fresh chopped basil and elegantly shredded Parmesan.

Good alternatives might be hot game pâté en croûte with foie gras, or mussel soup with leek and saffron. Fresh fish from local boats is a draw each day, such as lemon sole served with tomato couscous, or fillet of sea bass with Provençal vegetable ravioli.

Roasted pheasant was tender and moist, with an exceptionally good flavour. Served carved in a pretty mound, with the breast meat predominating, on a bed of lentils with Madeira sauce, it was an intelligent treatment combining classical and modern styles well. A simpler staple is pork tenderloin accompanied by spinach and cauliflower purée.

Standards do not slip with the desserts. A plum pudding tasted freshly steamed and was richly flavoured, with the helping hand of a little port in the mix, the dish garnished with lightly poached fresh plums and clotted cream. There is also praline soufflé with honeycomb ice-cream, or bitter chocolate timbale, caramelised banana and banana ice-cream.

A short but super wine selection includes the exquisite Billecart-Salmon rosé champagne.

Their pride: Blackcurrant souffé with frozen yoghurt
Inexpensive wines: Los Espinos Sauvignon (Chile) 2004, £12.95; Malbec Santa Rosa 2003, £16

Proprietors: Ben and Pamela McKellar
Last orders for dinner: 9.30 pm
Closed: Monday
Closed for holidays: one week Christmas
Set lunch: from £12.95
Set dinner: from £22
Wheelchair access

BRIGHTON, EAST SUSSEX

The Greys

105 Southover Street, Brighton, East Sussex BN2 9UA
Tel. 01273 680 734
e-mail: chris@greyspub.com   **MAP 2** D5

TUCKED away in a steep, narrow thoroughfare in a corner of trendy Brighton is this emblem of the more avant-garde seaside hospitality. You will instantly feel at home among the mostly young crowd at this unassuming little bar-with-tables, where an infectious buzz will draw you into its natural warmth for some endearingly idiosyncratic food.

When 'Spats', who is as much the pub mascot as one-man-band in the kitchen, tells you that his oriental scallop dish is named after the Japanese head boy at his prep school, you get an inkling of the delightfully English eccentricity of both the cook and his offerings. And how many chefs design their cartoon place mats?

Widely travelled and steeped in French regional gastronomy, he has a very personal, concise list of French favourites, ranging from old-fashioned poule au pot to a 'northern' bouillabaisse, a hearty beef carbonnade or a real belter of lapin dijonnaise, all of which show an enduring passion for life's pleasures and a delight in sharing them with you.

Recipes and tips pour out of him and the straightforwardness and honesty of his creations, without the merest hint of garnish or hype, are a refreshing *retour aux sources* from a devoted artisan of the old school.

Among the limited starters even a slightly odd vegetarian terrine worked, its ingredients being heaped on a pile of home-made hummus. And make sure you save room for his Boodle's orange fool, served on a tiny, gold dessert plate.

Speciality food: French regional food with an English accent
Draught beers: Harveys Bitter, Timothy Taylor Landlord
Average wine price by the glass: £2.90

Licensees: Chris Beaumont and Gill Perkins
Last orders for dinner: 9 pm
Closed: Sun, Mon and Fri evenings for food
Set lunch: from £12.50
Set dinner: from £17
Beer garden
Children over 14 welcome
Wheelchair access

BRIGHTON, EAST SUSSEX

One Paston Place ★

1 Paston Place, Brighton, East Sussex BN2 1HA
Tel. 01273 606 933 Fax 01273 675 686
e-mail: info@onepastonplace.co.uk   **MAP 2** D5

THIS is a restaurant with a glorious history, which seems set to continue indefinitely if the creative Franco-Italian cooking of chef/patron Francesco Furriello is any guide.

The dining-room is simple but elegant, with its bare boards, plain white walls and expanses of gilt-framed mirrors to provide an impression of light and space. Service is an appropriate mix of formality and friendliness, the staff – led by Francesco's wife, Rachel – always ready to guide you enthusiastically through the highly original menus.

An eloquent evocation of two cultures is the constant theme and the results, skilfully embellished by striking presentation, are a real delight to both eye and palate.

The French dish of magret de canard might come with goat's cheese ravioli, a sweet garlic froth and honey. There is a cod 'strudel' with minted courgette tagliatelle, and veal noisette with a foie gras praline, quail's egg, potato ravioli and calvados sauce.

From the sea come lobster tortelli with veal broth; herb-crusted monkfish with parsley coulis; scallops in port jus with bitter cocoa and white truffle fondant; turbot and langoustine with cauliflower soufflé and Jerusalem artichoke chips.

Desserts are no less inventive, with the likes of sour cherry and kirsch iced soufflé partnered by mint ice-cream and spun sugar.

Their pride: Guinea fowl supreme filled with foie gras, served with artichoke stew and Norcia black truffle
Inexpensive wines Pinot Grigio Riserva Mezzacorona (Trentino) 2002, £19; Anjou Gamay 2003, £21

Proprietors: Francesco Furriello, Gusto Ltd.
Last orders for dinner: 9.30 pm
Closed: Sunday and Monday
Closed for holidays: 1 week August, 2 weeks January
Set lunch: from £16.95
Set dinner: from £32.50
Limited wheelchair access

BRISTOL, AVON

The Albion

Boyces Avenue, Clifton Village, Bristol, Avon BS8 4AA
Tel. 0117 973 3522
e-mail: info@thealbionclifton.co.uk   **MAP 1** E2

TUCKED away down a little cul de sac where parking is a hit or miss affair, this gastropub has only recently opened. Clifton, set aloft to the east of the city, is the district regarded as the ultimate in smart living in these parts. The university dominates the lower slopes and there are lots of trendy designer shops to browse before having lunch somewhere like The Albion.

Doors open on to an attractive frontage where customers make the most of sunny weather. The inside is deceptively spacious, with a large dining area upstairs for the evening and an attractive room for private functions. The pale green and burgundy walls and the stripped floors are very much in the gastropub style.

A range of menus, using locally sourced, organic ingredients, includes a brunch that offers such stalwarts as smoked haddock kedgeree, or drop scones, smoked bacon and maple syrup.

A typical lunch might start with pea and mint velouté with crème fraîche, or perhaps potted rabbit, pickles and toast. A good fish chowder served with a mild rouille and aged Parmesan comes with a choice of home-baked rye or 'overnight' bread.

You might continue with a twenty-eight-day Aberdeen Angus rib steak with chips and Béarnaise sauce, or baked duck egg with spinach and Somerset truffles. A creamy, buttery risotto of yellow courgettes, lemon and herbs shows just how to make the best of seasonal ingredients.

Speciality food: Bath Chaps
Draught beers: Butcombe, Codleigh Tawny Owl
Average wine price by the glass: £3.40

Licensee: Omi Partnership Ltd
Last orders for dinner: 10 pm
Closed: Sunday dinner and Monday lunch for food
Main courses: from £11
Private dining: up to 12
Beer garden
Children welcome until 7 pm
Wheelchair access

BRITWELL SALOME, OXFORDSHIRE

The Goose at Britwell Salome ★

Britwell Salome, Nr. Watlington, Oxfordshire OX49 5LG
Tel. 01491 612 304 Fax 01491 613 945

MAP 2 B2

THE GOOSE has two faces. At first glance, it is a simple pub with a pleasingly weather-worn sign outside and unpretentious but imaginatively excellent bar food. But it also has a restaurant of serious gastronomic ambition and merit.

In the bar, dishes range from from sandwiches such as steak and shallot with mustard mayonnaise (the bread home-made), or wild mushrooms on toast and poached egg, to cottage pie and beer-battered fish and chips, or Cape Malay chicken curry with fragrant rice. The skewered prawns 'mpumalanga' show a flourish of the exotic and hint at the imagination of the chef/proprietor, Michael North.

His skills are best shown in the restaurant at the rear, where Imogen Young presides with charm and watchfulness. A terrine of pork from a local farm has everything: rustic flavours boosted by a silky texture that comes from assured technique, the richness tempered by the clean, sharp taste of shredded sauerkraut.

Roasted saddle of Oxfordshire lamb is impeccable, light pink, with a splendid flavour, and served with oven-roasted fondant potato and creamed spinach. Fillet of Glenarm salmon with white wine sauce is a good option. For dessert, the Valrhona chocolate tart with crème fraîche is exceptional.

The wine list has 17 tempting selections by the glass, featuring a Chardonnay/Cataratto blend from Sicily and a 1999 Reserva Rioja. By the bottle, there are classic Italians such as Barolo Bussia from Prunotto and 2001 Tignanello from Antinori.

Speciality food: Apple tart, toffee pudding, praline ice-cream
Draught beers: Hook Norton, Stella Artois
Average wine price by the glass: £4

Licensees: Michael North and Imogen Young
Last orders for dinner: 9 pm
Closed: Sunday evening
Set lunch: from £15
Set dinner: from £15 Monday-Thursday
Private dining: 8-30
Beer garden
Children welcome
Wheelchair access

BROADHEMBURY, DEVON

Drewe Arms ★

GASTROPUB

**Broadhembury, Nr. Honiton, Devon EX14 3NF
Tel. 01404 841 267 Fax 01404 841 526**

MAP 1 D3

ONE of the West Country's hidden gems, this appealing village inn is in the heart of Broadhembury. Most of the village's thatched cottages are estate-owned, and fifteen years ago Swede Kerstin Burge and her English husband, Nigel, acquired a lease and set about creating a business that is now a place of pilgrimage for those wanting top-quality seafood. Five years ago their son Andrew took over the stoves, and the business.

A narrow snug with wooden pews by the bar is where the locals sit, but it is in the two adjacent dining-rooms that most of the culinary action takes place. These are delightful rooms, one with an inglenook fireplace and a wall of split logs, the other panelled and candlelit. In summer, relax in the garden, quaintly served through a window from the bar. Equally popular, but for different reasons, is the Cellar Bar (known as the dungeon), an additional dining area with wooden pews that used to be the wine cellar.

Blackboards proclaim the catch: griddled scallops with mango chutney, langoustines with rouille, crab thermidor or venison carpaccio among starters. Main courses include Dover sole with herb butter; turbot with hollandaise; whole crab; John Dory with anchovy and capers, or sea bream with orange and chilli. This may not be complex modern cooking, but the sheer quality of the ingredients, handled simply, leaves one eager to return.

Puddings are no less satisfying – try exquisite hazelnut parfait, made by someone in the village, or wonderful local cheeses that include Sharpham and Devon Blue. An impeccably chosen wine list with good tasting notes has an understandable bias towards whites.

Speciality food: Dover sole and seafood platters
Draught beers: Otter Bitter, Otter Ale
Average wine price by the glass: £3

Licensees: Andrew and Kerstin Burge
Last orders for dinner: 9.30 pm
Closed: Sun dinner
Closed for holidays: 25 Dec, 31 Dec & 1 Jan evenings
Set lunch: from £29
Set dinner: from £29
Private dining: 10-40
Beer garden
Children over 12 welcome

BROADWAY, WORCESTERSHIRE

Lygon Arms

Great Hall, Broadway, Worcestershire WR12 7DU
Tel. 01386 852 255 Fax 01386 858 611
e-mail: info@thelygonarms.co.uk   **MAP 3** E4

SOME country house hotels suffer the trauma of transformation to bring them kicking and screaming into the 21st century, others gradually fall apart in the wake of declining business and general neglect, and then there are those that manage to keep their heads proudly aloft as guardians of the national heritage.

Of the latter, this stately and rightfully celebrated pile has been at the forefront of Cotswold hospitality for almost half a millennium. Notwithstanding improvements to the hotel, time-travellers returning to the aptly named Great Hall would find that little has changed. The star-studded kitchen brigade have the difficult task of creating contemporary cuisine while respecting the style of the surroundings and the expectations of a cosmopolitan clientele.

This challenge is generally met with great confidence. One or two straightforward classics are kept on hand: fish soup with rouille, sautéd foie gras on toasted brioche, best end of lamb with its miniature shepherds' pie, fillet of beef with hollandaise and even a fillet of trout with toasted almonds. But their hearts are in more pioneering compilations in an effort to break free of the traditional mould. There is the startling, signature bortsch terrine with its shredded beef and onion pirags (miniature pasties), a salad of crayfish, cockle and celeriac with shellfish oil and lemon, or a supreme of guinea fowl with garlic fritters and tarragon.

A limited choice of desserts includes chocolate fondant, mango soufflé with mango, chilli and ginger ice-cream and an apple savarin which, unfortunately, was rather insipid.

Their pride: Bortsch terrine with shredded beef and onion pirags
Inexpensive wines: Trivento Viognier Viña Patagonia 2003, £21.50; Cabernet Sauvignon Sunnycliff (Australia) 2001, £21.50

Proprietor: Furlong Arms
Last orders for dinner: 9.30 pm
Open every day
Set lunch: from £15
Set dinner: from £39.50
Private dining: up to 100
Wheelchair access

BROCKENHURST, HAMPSHIRE

Le Poussin at Whitley Ridge ★

Beaulieu Road, Brockenhurst, Hampshire SO42 7QL
Tel. 01590 622 354 Fax 01590 622 856
e-mail: sales@lepoussin.co.uk   **MAP 2** A5

THIS former hunting lodge in the heart of the New Forest has lost none of its grand Georgian feel following renovations, and the splendour of the surroundings applies equally to the food.

Amuse-bouches of smoked salmon and chives, for instance, on the thinnest pastry base; chicken liver mousse enlivened by sweet chutney; the delicacy of the onion velouté, its light foam flavoured by sweet onion, served in an espresso cup.

Follow this with Isle of Wight lobster in one of three guises: a soft, delicate quennelle on barley, flaked in a pasta envelope on a tomato concassé, or lobster tail in tempura batter.

As alternatives, there could be saddle of hare, perfectly pink in small medallions; exquisitely moist steamed partridge with foie gras at its centre and wrapped in savoy cabbage, or else delicate charlotte of pheasant with a core of diced pheasant meat, the whole wrapped in paper-thin celeriac.

The à la carte menu offers four choices for each course. Starters might be roasted quail breast and its parfait, or cannelloni of smoked salmon with smoked salmon mousse, to be followed by roasted monkfish tail on the bone with the liver on toast, or fillet of Aberdeen Angus with ox tongue.

To finish, there is caramelised apple tart with calvados panna cotta, or chocolate fondant with Banyuls syrup.

Their pride: Quail foie gras and morel pie
Inexpensive wines: Syrah Domaine Coudoulet (France) 2000, £19.50; Pacific Rim dry Riesling (USA) 2003, £22.50

Proprietors: Alex and Caroline Aitken
Last orders for dinner: 9.30 pm
Open every day
Set lunch: from £15
Set dinner: from £35
Private dining: 6-40
Al fresco dining
Accommodation: 14 rooms and cottage
Wheelchair access

BROCKTON, SHROPSHIRE

The Feathers

GASTROPUB

Brockton, Much Wenlock, Shropshire TF13 6JR
Tel./Fax 01746 785 202

MAP 3 D3

DISCOVERING the car park full on arrival at 7.30 pm is always an encouraging sign. Then you step inside the entrance at the rear of the building, through a simple yard and summer room, into a whimsical interior of bare stone walls, statues, numerous candles and hessian-draped swags at the windows that lend a theatrical and Bohemian air – not always easy to pull off, but which works admirably here.

Specials written on a couple of boards offer an appealing choice of starters including a salad of baby artichokes, Parma ham and cannelini beans with a lemon dressing – a pleasing combination. Half a lobster seems excellent value at £14.95 and is popular.

So is the salmon and cod fishcake, the latter hearty, judiciously seasoned and with a tangy lemon butter sauce. Accompanying sauté potatoes are deliciously crisp and irresistible.

The à la carte menu features dishes such as hake goujons with herb mayonnaise or hoi sin duck, among the starters, and slow-cooked pork belly and black pudding with roasted apple and grain mustard sauce.

A warm chocolate fondant, vanilla ice-cream and nut brittle is worthy of a twelve-minute wait (customers are warned on the menu) and the blueberry compote or vanilla panna cotta with fresh raspberries are not easy to resist. The coffee is good and strong. The husband-and-wife team who own the restaurant moved from London and, judging by the comments from satisfied customers, they have clearly worked wonders.

Speciality food: Rib of beef for two
Draught beers: Hobsons, Secret Hop
Average wine price by the glass: £3

Licensees: Anna and Paul Kayiatou
Last orders for dinner: 9.30 pm (Sunday 9 pm)
Closed: Monday
Closed for holidays: 26 December
Main courses: from £8.95
Private dining: up to 25
Al fresco dining
Children welcome
Limited wheelchair access

BROUGHTON MILLS, CUMBRIA

Blacksmith's Arms

Broughton Mills, Broughton-in-Furness, Cumbria LA20 6AX
Tel. 01229 716 824
e-mail: blacksmithsarms@aol.com   **MAP 5** B3

AFTER a drive across the glorious Lakeland fells, take the narrow, twisting lane down to this hamlet in the inviting Lickle valley then ask yourself how it is that so many people could have heard of this hidden, ancient English inn where landlord Michael Lane has a job to keep pace at times behind his tiny bar.

Over the past 400-odd years, its flagstoned floors and jumble of rustic furnishings seem to have gathered a delightfully natural patina of hospitality. Family-friendly, with a children's menu and even a cupboard full of toys, the place oozes leisurely bonhomie.

And if by chance you have not eaten for a week, you have chosen the right place. Not only are the portions gargantuan, but the choice is also vast, with many blackboard specials in addition to the regular menu. It is the sort of solid, unpretentious country pub food – all produced with skill and enthusiasm – that fits the bill admirably in such warm and cordial surroundings.

The choice includes succulent gammon, steak and kidney with a pudding crust, braised fellside lamb with parsnip chips, sizzling steak platters and crunchy fat chips. More adventurous offerings feature crisply coated vegetable patties with sweet chilli sauce; piquant, juicy Cajun chicken with tomato and cucumber salsa, or duck breast with honey and lemon on a sweet potato purée. To follow are classic, well-made puddings in similar portions.

Despite the odd (and almost appropriate) rough edge here and there, you can but share in the enjoyment of a good job well done. But breathe in going up that narrow lane on your way out.

Speciality food: Traditional pub food with a modern twist
Draught beers: Cumberland Ale, Hawkshead bitter
Average wine price by the glass: £2.40

Licensees: Michael and Sophie Lane
Last orders for dinner: 9 pm
Closed: Monday lunch
Closed for holidays: 25 and 26 December (for food)
Main courses: from £6.95
Al fresco dining
Children welcome

BUCKMINSTER, LEICESTERSHIRE

Tollemache Arms

GASTROPUB

48 Main Street, Buckminster, Leicestershire NG33 5SA
Tel. 01476 860 007 Fax 01476 860 400
e-mail: enquiries@thetollemachearms.com   **MAP 4** B3

DESPITE its imposing, manorial-style frontage there is a chummy, pubby atmosphere at this extensively refurbished country inn. As the pints flow in the bar, the daily changing dinner menu (lighter lunches offer a more restricted choice) adds the required touch of class more befitting the surroundings, with a well-balanced assortment of interesting and sometimes original dishes, often with a Mediterranean slant, brought to your table in the dining section next door.

Salads abound among starters: chorizo with smoked mozzarella and avocado; smoked salmon with crème fraîche and caviar; crab and apple; a warm vegetable salad with courgette flowers stuffed with goat's cheese. You might otherwise go for a ballottine of foie gras or a perfectly cooked pair of local pigeon breasts and shallot Tatin.

Concisely described main courses might include sea bass with chorizo and an almost luminous basil mash, or suckling pig with rösti and caramelised apples, or fricassee of lobster. Nicely pink loin of lamb comes with Mediterranean vegetables, while for dessert, popular choices are apple and Stilton tart, the chocolate marquise with banana ice-cream, or apricot Tatin.

Fresh, honest flavours and hefty portions, but some investment in a little eye-catching interior décor would complement the well-prepared dishes, which deserve a brighter stage on which to show off their undoubted appeal.

Speciality food: Modern brasserie with a Mediterranean slant
Draught beers: Cooking Bitter, Timothy Taylor Landlord
Average wine price by the glass: £3

Licensee: Mark Gough
Last orders for dinner: 9 pm
Closed: Monday, no food Sunday evening
Set lunch: from £12
Main courses: from £12
Private dining: 10-20
Beer garden
Accommodation: 5 rooms
Children welcome

BUNBURY, CHESHIRE

Dysart Arms

`GASTROPUB`

Bowes Gate Road, Bunbury, Nr. Tarporley, Cheshire CW6 9PH
Tel. 01829 260 183 Fax 01829 261 286
e-mail: dysart.arms@brunningandprice.co.uk   **MAP 3** D2

ORIGINALLY a farm in the 1700s belonging to the Tollemache family, the Earls of Dysart whose coat of arms is still above the door, this building also housed an abattoir that supplied the local butcher in the 19th century.

Today, three small rooms lead off the bar and follow through to one large book-lined room at the far end. A pleasing mismatch of tables, chairs, pews, myriad spotlit pictures on the walls and rugs on tiled floors make it an ideal venue.

One menu serves for lunch and dinner. Starters might include a tartlet of smoked trout, broccoli and Shropshire blue cheese, or perhaps fried pigeon breast on potato cake with red onion jam and Cumberland sauce. Firm, meaty king prawns are generously portioned and come in a rustic sauce of mixed peppers, tomato and garlic, with garlic bread.

Main courses include Mediterranean fish casserole, confit of duck leg with wok-fried noodles and vegetables, or frittata. A home-made steak burger will come topped with smoked bacon and melted mozzarella with chips and tangy salsa. Vegetarians might opt for a baked omelette with potato, spinach and red pepper with salad and beetroot chutney or penne pasta with Mediterranean vegetables and chilli dressing.

Mango cheesecake and raspberry purée, apple and blackberry crumble tart, or waffles with a delicious honeycomb ice-cream might take your fancy. Alternatively, there is a good choice of cheese.

Speciality food: Lamb shoulder
Draught beers: Thwaites, East Gate
Average wine price by the glass: £2.50

Licensee: Darren Snell
Last orders for dinner: 9.30 pm
Open every day
Closed for holidays: 25 December
Main courses: from £7.95
Beer garden
Children under 10 welcome until 6 pm
Wheelchair access

BURFORD, OXFORDSHIRE

Jonathan's at The Angel ★

14 Witney Street, Burford, Oxfordshire OX18 4SN
Tel. 01993 822 714 Fax 01993 822 069
e-mail: jo@theangel-uk.com   **MAP 2** A2

THIS brasserie-with-rooms is run with great flair, although brasserie is rather too modest a description for a 16th-century inn where the cooking has real gastronomic merit, carried out with great imagination yet avoiding unnecessary fuss or complication.

The à la carte menu changes daily, but three dishes illustrate the chef's talent to the full.

First, the brûlée of wild trompette and chanterelle mushrooms with a Parmesan crisp and gossamer-light goat's cheese pastry parcel, accompanied by a wild rocket salad.

Then, something like expertly boned local partridge, the flavours fresh but well defined, jus lightened yet enriched with a de-glaze of Madeira and brandy, with the rissolé potatoes cooked in the partridge juices.

Last, but by no means least, these might be followed by a superb pear Tatin with caramel sauce and mascarpone in a brandy-snap basket decorated with a whole roasted pear.

There are also excellent set meals, including an inviting Mediterranean lunch with tapas and fresh linguine with sea crab and shellfish sauce.

The wine list has been expertly assembled from the best and most reasonably priced selections, particularly from Burgundy and Italy.

Their pride: Boneless saddle of wild rabbit, wrapped in smoked bacon, filled with walnut mousse
Inexpensive wines: Santa Rita Chardonnay (Chile) 2003, £13.75; Santa Rita Cabernet Sauvignon (Chile) 2003, £13.75

Proprietors: Jonathan and Josephine Lewis
Last orders for dinner: 9.30 pm
Closed: Sunday dinner, Monday
Closed for holidays: 17 January-11 February
Set lunch: from £14.50
Main courses: from £15.95
Private dining: up to 35
Al fresco dining
Accommodation: 3 deluxe rooms
Limited wheelchair access

BURFORD, OXFORDSHIRE

Lamb Inn

GASTROPUB

Sheep Street, Burford, Oxfordshire OX18 4LR
Tel. 01993 823 155 Fax 01993 822 228
e-mail: info@lambinn-burford.co.uk   **MAP 2** A2

JUST off Burford High Street, The Lamb is a timeless example of an English country inn and a magnet for discerning Americans touring the Cotswolds. One of its main charms is the fine balance of elegance and informality, creating a relaxed sense of well-being as soon as you cross the threshold. In the flag-stoned bar, the well-kept real ales draw hotel guests and locals alike. You will not feel like an outsider here.

The same menu is available in the bar, in the deep armchairs of the lounges, in the spacious walled garden and in the light, airy restaurant, where a fixed-price three-course dinner is also served.

Simplicity is the keynote. One of the most popular choices is the roast beef open sandwich with horse-radish potato salad, a meal in itself. Other sure options are the hearty ploughman's platters, especially the ham and blue cheese version.

Spinach and ricotta omelette with salad and chips makes a good supper dish, with other choices including lamb's liver with mashed potato or crab risotto. On Sundays there are traditional roasts.

For dessert, a great favorite for visiting Americans and local landowners and antique dealers is the strawberry Eton Mess and ice-cream made with clotted cream.

The dozen wines by the glass are as classy as the inn itself: from an aromatic Withies Hill New Zealand Sauvignon through a saline-crisp Durup Chablis to a rich and spicy Lehmann Shiraz, Barossa. The 15 en-suite bedrooms are full of character and comfort.

Speciality food: Open rare roast beef sandwich
Draught beers: Hook Norton, Brakspear
Average wine price by the glass: £3.85

Licensee: Gavin Thomson
Last orders for dinner: 9.30 pm
Open every day
Set dinner: from £32.50
Main courses: from £9.50
Beer garden
Accommodation: 15 rooms
Children welcome

BURLTON, SHROPSHIRE

Burlton Inn

GASTROPUB

Burlton, Nr. Shrewsbury, Shropshire SY4 5TB
Tel. 01939 270 284 Fax 01939 270 204
e-mail: reservations@burltoninn.co.uk   **MAP 3** D2

GUEST accommodation is tucked away behind the inn flanking the parking area. The rear entrance of the inn itself is approached through a sunny beer garden in which you are encouraged to eat.

A good selection of sandwiches has fillings, served in plain or green olive ciabatta, that include crispy bacon, melted Brie and cranberry sauce, rare beef, home-cooked ham, and minute-steak with fried red onions. There are wholemeal rolls or else jacket potatoes for those who want an alternative .

Three comprehensive menus ensure that most tastes and appetites are catered for. The steak and kidney pie is solidly packed with plenty of kidney and tender, succulent chunks of beef in a rich gravy, with the choice of either a puff pastry or shortcrust topping.

Other options include grilled fresh sardines served on a warm Greek salad of oven-roasted vegetables, or braised duck breast and leg served on a tartlet of parsnip purée with a bacon and red wine jus.

A Caesar salad starter with fresh anchovies and bacon has an authentic dressing and suitably whets the appetite, while lamb cutlets with a walnut and herb crust, from the specials menu, were succulent and flavoursome.

A sensibly priced Chilean Sauvignon is very quaffable and reflects the general reasonableness of the wine prices.

Speciality food: Steak and kidney pie
Draught beers: Shropshire Gold, Spring Whippet
Average wine price by the glass: £2.95

Licensee: Jerald Bean
Last orders for dinner: 9.30 pm
Open every day
Closed for holidays: Bank Holiday lunch, 24 December (evening), 26 December, 1 January
Main courses: from £8.95
Beer garden
Accommodation: 6 rooms
Children welcome
Wheelchair access

BURNHAM MARKET, NORFOLK

Hoste Arms

GASTROPUB

The Green, Burnham Market, Norfolk PE31 8HD
Tel. 01328 738 777 Fax 01328 730 103
e-mail: reception@hostearms.co.uk   **MAP 4** E2

WITH its chic clothes and shoe shops, Burnham Market, the most handsome and affluent of the seven Burnham villages on the north Norfolk coast, is now a destination for celebrities in search of serious retail therapy.

While catering for this market, the 18th-century, 37-bedroom Hoste Arms retains a fine pub atmosphere in the stone-floored front bar, where a log fire burns in winter and the spirit of Horatio Nelson hovers (he was a Saturday morning regular in the early 1800s).

Food is available in the period restaurant, two connecting rooms with fine old panelling set against modern furnishings.

The fish soup is genuinely aromatic and deeply flavoured, based on a proper shellfish stock and classically accompanied by rouille and croutons. Local fish from King's Lynn market is a mainstay of specials, anything from king prawns to sea bream and bass.

The fine Aberdeen Angus steak burger is served with good bacon and melted cheese. The big chips are nicely cooked.

Desserts range from fruit tarts and brûlées to a freshly-made, rich treacle pudding.

The wine list, extending to 300 bins of fine bottles, features as much from the southern hemisphere as from the classic vineyards of France, Spain and Italy.

Speciality food: Braised shoulder of pork with red wine dressing
Draught beers: Woodforde Wherry, Adnams
Average wine price by the glass: £5.75

Licensees: Emma Tagg, Paul Whittome and Sabrina Suttonland
Last orders for dinner: 9 pm
Open every day
Main courses: from £15
Private dining: up to 30
Al fresco dining
Accommodation: 37 rooms
Children welcome
Wheelchair access

BURTON BRADSTOCK, DORSET

Anchor Inn

GASTROPUB

High Street, Burton Bradstock, Dorset DT6 4QF
Tel. 01308 897 228

MAP 1 E4

AS YOU would expect from a location on the coast road east of Bridport, fish and all things nautical feature strongly throughout both the décor and menu at this listed, 350-year-old pub. The place may be a little faded in places, but all eyes are focused on the great platters of crustacea paraded from kitchen to table.

You have only to cast your eye over the myriad blackboards to feel confident that the time between ocean floor and plate must be no more than a matter of hours. Choices include hand-dived scallops from West Bay (which is just across the road), lobster Armoricaine or thermidor and, when they are available, grilled langoustines with garlic, white wine and butter sauce.

Fish platters and combinations such as sea bass and shellfish, red bream and red mullet, fresh cod and crab do not come cheap, but the choice is vast and the quality invariably high. Local trout, filled with a selection of shellfish, is steamed and served with a lobster and prawn sauce. Whole lemon sole is simply grilled and offered with a prawn and parsley butter. Fillet of brill is stuffed with local crab and accompanied by prawn rice.

Ten or so meat dishes, three or four vegetarian choices and a bar snack menu add to the mix, and then there is another menu for lunch as well, featuring such things as omelettes, jacket potatoes, baguettes and salads.

One is bewildered by the choice, with more than eighty items in total on various menus, but careful selection will be rewarded. A similar number of malt whiskies merits exploration, too.

Speciality food: Seafood
Draught beers: Ushers Best, Hobgoblin (Wychwood)
Average wine price by the glass: £2.95

Licensee: John R. Plunkett
Last orders for dinner: 8.30 pm
Open every day
Main courses: from £15.95
Al fresco dining
Accommodation: 2 rooms
Children welcome
Wheelchair access

BUXHALL, SUFFOLK

The Crown at Buxhall   `GASTROPUB`

Mill Road, Buxhall, Nr. Stowmarket, Suffolk IP14 3DW
Tel. 01449 736 521 Fax 01449 736 528
e-mail: trevor@buxhallcrown.fsnet.co.uk   **MAP 4** E4

THE ITALIAN espresso machine notwithstanding, it is hard to imagine a more quintessential example of the English country pub in all its traditional glory than this bustling little hostelry in the heart of the Suffolk countryside. Now crammed with polished tables since the food revolution took hold, it is still very much a drinker's rendezvous, with a good range of cask beers. The two small rooms, beams hung with dried hops and smoke-darkened walls covered with watercolours, bear witness to its origins and aeons of service to the business of hospitality.

The latter is still very much the name of the game, too, with young locals providing a pleasing, natural welcome and attentive but unfussy service. And if Trevor Golton's regularly changing blackboard menu evokes all the trappings of the gastronomic cook at work, the result retains an edge of bucolic charm totally in keeping with the time-worn setting.

While the inclusion of a degree of Latin influence may nowadays be considered *de rigueur* in, say, squid ink risotto with scallops, the use of basil and sun-blushed tomatoes to garnish a pan-fried sea trout, or herb-roasted chicken with pancetta and Parmesan potatoes, the general trend is rather more English. Aside from simple chargrills (steaks, fish, lamb kebabs), a perfectly cooked fillet of seabass on a rösti galette with saffron sauce is accorded honorary British status by the inclusion of fresh peas and buttered cabbage. The local suckling pig, meanwhile, has its pedigree appetisingly complicated with a sauce of chillies and calvados.

Thoroughly enjoyable, refined rusticity in cosy surroundings.

Speciality food: Modern British cookery
Draught beers: Woodforde Wherry, Tindall's Best Bitter
Average wine price by the glass: £3.20

Licensees: Trevor Golton and Cathy Clarke
Last orders for dinner: 9 pm
Closed: Sunday dinner, Monday
Main courses: from £8.95
Beer garden
Children welcome
Wheelchair access

CAMBRIDGE, CAMBRIDGESHIRE

Midsummer House ★★

Midsummer Common, Cambridge CB4 1HA
Tel. 01223 369 299 Fax 01223 302 672
email: reservations@midsummerhouse.co.uk   **MAP 4** D4

THE strikingly modern décor of this starkly elegant restaurant provides a well-engineered backdrop for the sort of stylish and impressive dishes you might find in glossy cookbooks.

The more 'mundane' offerings include ballottine of foie gras with apricots; seared scallops with celeriac, truffle and apple; sautéd turbot with cep risotto, or slow-roasted fillet of beef with shallot marmalade, celeriac purée and foie gras.

More pioneering creations go from navarin of Scottish lobster with roasted duck gizzards and girolle, through a confit of cod with kohlrabi purée and creamed snails, to braised monkfish with cumin and parsnip risotto and a pastille (a sort of tourte made of the north African equivalent of filo pastry) filled with oxtail.

Fine, fat langoustines interspersed with braised pork belly on a cod brandade, topped with crispy Parma ham, and the lightest of savoury cappuccinos, is a sheer delight. The stuffed pig's trotter is an impressive technical accomplishment, though some might prefer the more rugged chunkiness of the meat to the mousseline of veal sweetbreads and morels stuffed back into the skin and served on a rich reduction.

Desserts include a pistachio soufflé with chocolate sorbet, and walnut cheesecake with Devon Blue ice-cream and cannelloni.

Their pride: Cannelloni of red pepper, foie gras mousse with marinated green beans, Jamaican pepper
Inexpensive wines: Boca Vallina (Piedmont) 1996, £33; Domaine Bellvard's Gringet Savoie 2002, £33

Proprietor: Daniel Clifford
Last orders for dinner: 9.30 pm
Closed: Sunday and Monday all day, lunch Tuesday, Wednesday and Thursday
Closed for holidays: 2 weeks Christmas, 2 weeks August, 1 week Easter
Set lunch: from £26
Private dining: 8-20
Al fresco dining
Limited wheelchair access

CARTMEL, CUMBRIA

L'Enclume ★

Cartmel, Nr. Grange-over-Sands, Cumbria LA11 6PZ
Tel. 01539 536 362 Fax 01539 538 907
e-mail: info@lenclume.co.uk   **MAP 5** C4

THERE might be twenty courses on the gourmand menu that is presented to you, but in the end it is quality rather the quantity that counts at this quaint one-time forge.

The portions are tiny, the emphasis in the imaginative food being on texture and taste. Dishes such as roasted bass with calamint flavour and sweet nougatine, or duck with sour cherry, celery and a coffee bonbon, are merely the curtain-raisers for what turns out to be a gastronomic extravaganza.

Presentation is also an important part of this almost theatrical production, with myriad colours and garnishes and sometimes rather outlandish touches such as service from a test-tube.

The element of surprise is obviously something of an obsession here, but since the overall quality of the cooking is high and the talent and passion are obvious, you might as well just sit back amid the beams and whitewashed walls and relish the difference. Menus come in fourteen and eight courses, too.

Since it is obvious that this is not a place to do things by halves, there are more than 400 wines to choose from, many available by the glass.

Their pride: Cubism in foie gras (two cold, one hot) canteloupe and myrrh
Inexpensive wines: Pinot Gris Rockburn 2003, £38; Château Musar, Serge Hochar 1997, £26

Proprietors: Simon Rogan and Penny Tapsell
Last orders for dinner: 9.30 pm
Closed: Monday and Tuesday
Set lunch: from £25
Accommodation: 11 rooms
Wheelchair access

CASTLE DONNINGTON, DERBYSHIRE

Nag's Head

GASTROPUB

Hilltop, Castle Donnington, Derby, Derbyshire DE74 2PR
Tel. 01332 850 652 Fax 01332 812 741
e-mail: thenagsheadinn@tiscali.co.uk   **MAP 4** B3

THIS pub offers imaginative food, especially in the restaurant, where you can order home-made Thai fishcakes, ham jambalaya, steak and lamb in various guises, and venison and duck when available. Fresh fish is a speciality, and sandwiches and baguettes are offered in the bar at lunch.

The 'Early Bird' menu, served on weekday evenings, is particularly good value, offering two courses for £8.95. Seafood chowder was full of fresh cod in a creamy liquor, or there was a properly made prawn cocktail. Meat lasagne was skilfully prepared and filled with well-flavoured Bolognese sauce, and served with freshly made hot garlic bread.

Other options might be liver and bacon on a mustard mash and red wine gravy, or the speciality braised lamb shank with crushed new potatoes. For those who hanker after old-style pub food, try ham and eggs or Whitby scampi. A fine finish would be baby pineapple with mango ice-cream.

A short but intelligently selective wine list features very adequate wines by the glass, including South African Chenin Blanc and Australian Shiraz. Real ales, particularly the Banks Original, are well kept.

The service is attentive and well paced, yet the atmosphere is relaxed, making the place popular both with businessmen and with the locals. Accommodation is planned in the future and there is an attractive beer garden.

Speciality food: Braised lamb shank with crushed new potatoes
Draught beers: Marston Pedigree, Banks Original
Average wine price by the glass: £2.70

Licensees: Andy and Kylie Smith
Last orders for dinner: 9.30 pm
Open every day
Set lunch: from £8.95 (Monday-Friday)
Set dinner: from £8.95 (Monday-Friday)
Private dining: 20-45
Beer garden
Children welcome
Wheelchair access

CAUNTON, NOTTINGHAMSHIRE

Caunton Beck

GASTROPUB

Caunton, Nr. Newark, Nottinghamshire NG23 6AB
Tel. 01636 636 793 Fax 01636 636 828

MAP 4 B2

SYMPATHETICALLY restored, Caunton Beck dates back to a single 16th-century cottage and prides itself on being open from 8 am and serving food right through until midnight.

A set menu of two or three courses will offer soup of the day and perhaps grilled goat's cheese with baby beets and oranges as a starter. This could be followed by salmon, crème fraîche and capers, or a Barnsley chop with grain mustard mash.

Pigeon breast starter from the carte will not disappoint, yielding to the knife and having a subtle, gamey flavour. Intensely sweet sun-blushed tomatoes and dressed rocket salad make an ideal accompaniment.

Skewered chicken pieces as a starter, given an oriental touch with Thai seasoning and coriander, are irresistible, served with sour cream and lime.

Choose a main course of breast of chicken with mushroom and tarragon risotto with Taleggio, or roasted cod. While the latter might lack a crisp skin, the thick fillet will break into satisfying, creamy chunks and might be paired with flavoursome truffle crushed peas.

The ever-popular sticky toffee pudding could feature on the bar menu or, if preferred, chilled gin and elderflower jelly, which makes for a refreshing combination of flavours, neither ingredient stealing the limelight.

Speciality food: Sirloin steak with Café de Paris butter
Draught beers: Batemans XB, Black Sheep
Average wine price by the glass: £3.50

Licensees: Toby Hope and Julie Allwood
Last orders for dinner: 10 pm (Sunday 9.30 pm)
Open every day
Closed for holidays: 25 December
Set lunch: from £11
Al fresco dining
Children welcome
Wheelchair access

CAVENDISH, SUFFOLK

The George

GASTROPUB

The Green, Cavendish, Suffolk CO10 8BA
Tel. 01787 280 248 Fax 01787 281 703
e-mail: reservations@georgecavendish.co.uk   **MAP 4** D5

ON A prime corner of one of the most attractive village greens in England, this 600-year-old, timber-framed inn has recently been restored by new owners. You are still welcome to pop in for a pint and a snack, but the heart of the operation is now the fresh, well-prepared dishes from a varied, regularly changing menu, with blackboard specials adding further choice.

You can watch the kitchen team hard at work and, in 'modern British' style, imported influences abound. Try a Cantonese duck confit with Asian coleslaw; seared scallops with celeriac, chorizo and sherry dressing, or roast sea bass with peperonata, or Parma ham and mushroom risotto, Parmesan and white truffle.

There are also more home-spun creations such as asparagus with poached egg and hollandaise, Irish oysters or Scottish smoked salmon, roasted breast of chicken with fondant potato and morel sauce, or a chargrilled Scottish fillet with all the trimmings.

Innovative ideas, such as the pressed plum tomato 'cake' with a peppered goat's cheese cream, provide light, refreshing starters, followed by an accurately roasted rack of English lamb and some tasty, impressively garnished Mediterranean vegetables.

Nursery desserts, such as hot brioche bread and butter pudding, crème caramel, or the eternal sticky toffee pudding, are perhaps a better bet than a somewhat less successful bitter chocolate tart. Nice ideas overall from an enthusiastic young chef.

Speciality food: Modern British cooking
Draught beers: Nethergate Augustinian, Star Opramen
Average wine price by the glass: £3.50

Licensee: London and Edinburgh Inns
Last orders for dinner: 9.30 pm
Closed: Sunday dinner
Set lunch: from £10.95 (Monday-Friday)
Set dinner: from £10.95 (Monday-Friday)
Private dining: 10-60
Beer garden
Accommodation: 4 rooms
Children welcome

CERNE ABBAS, DORSET

Royal Oak

GASTROPUB

23 Long Street, Cerne Abbas, Dorset DT2 7JG
Tel. 01300 341 797

MAP 1 E3

BUILT from the ruins of the nearby Benedictine Abbey, all is cosy and full of character here, with remarkable collections of tea cups and ties hanging from beams, stone flagged floors and a jumble of memorabilia. Outside, there is a pleasant little patio garden at the rear.

Groups of walkers and tourists come to breathe in the history and atmosphere while supping the Royal Oak's own real ale, brewed by Dorchester brewer Hall & Woodhouse.

A huge menu attempts to be all things to all people, offering the likes of Caribbean duck, chicken Frascati, risotto Romano, moules marinière, chargrilled halloumi, chicken curry and chilli con carne. But if you look and choose carefully, there are some core dishes that feature good local ingredients.

Rabbit casserole; a wonderful pheasant and venison patty with Dorset Blue Vinny cheese; fresh Portland crab salad; baked Dorset pheasant breast filled with mushrooms and local Woolsery goat's cheese, and local game pie – these are among the most appealing examples, and one cannot help but wish the owners would have the courage to limit the menu to dishes of this kind.

Meanwhile, there are also pages of items for people on special diets and blackboards of daily specials, including sandwiches, open sandwiches and wraps.

Puddings are of the comfort food variety and a fairly pedestrian wine list offers nine by the glass.

Speciality food: Steak and Blue Vinny pie
Draught beers: Giant's Tipple, Badger Best Bitter
Average wine price by the glass: £2.95

Licensees: Tony and Christine Green
Last orders for dinner: 9 pm
Closed: 3-6 pm Monday to Friday
Set lunch: from £10
Main courses: from £9.95
Al fresco dining
Children welcome
Limited wheelchair access

CHADWICK END, WEST MIDLANDS

Orange Tree

GASTROPUB

Warwick Rd., Chadwick End, Nr. Solihull, W Midlands B93 0BN
Tel. 01564 785 364 Fax 01564 782 988

MAP 3 E3

ON THE Knowle to Warwick road, the Orange Tree is a typical modern gastropub. Inside it has the look and feel of a smart restaurant-brasserie. Enjoy a cocktail or a pint of well-kept real ale (Greene King) in the contemporary bar, all low-slung sofas with natural tiles and stonework.

The spacious dining area is also very stylish and comfortable, the colour of the walls and banquette cushions a shade of pistachio creating a cool atmosphere. In fine weather customers can eat in the pretty garden.

The food is mainstream modern, listed under headings: Sharing Plates (rustic bread and olive oil, pizette with garlic, rocket and Parmesan); Pastas and Grains (risotto of the day, pappardelle Bolognese). There are Grilled Meats and Fish (lamb chops, fillet steak burger, whole lobsters and lemon sole, swordfish) and Rotisserie and Stove (spit chicken, lemon and garlic confit). The choice of 'pizzas' includes spicy versions such as Thai chicken and one flavoured with chorizo and jalapeños.

Try, perhaps, little dishes such as chilli-crusted squid or onion and goat's cheese tart rather than the more substantial offerings such as suckling pig.

Desserts such as iced tiramisù parfait are imaginative and the espresso coffee is excellent. Above-average contemporary wines by the glass with notably fresh Chilean Sauvignon and a fruity Rioja Crianza. Also a good list of fine bottles, both classic and New World, with particular strengths in Spain and Italy.

Speciality food: Crispy duck salad
Draught beers: Greene King IPA, Greene King Abbot Ale
Average wine price by the glass: £2.95

Licensee: Gail Bishop
Last orders for dinner: 9.30 pm
Closed: Sunday evening
Closed for holidays: 25 and 26 Dec, 1 Jan
Main courses: from £12
Private dining: 8-14
Beer garden
Children welcome
Wheelchair access

CHAGFORD, DEVON

Gidleigh Park ★★

Chagford, Devon TQ13 8HH
Tel. 01647 432 367 Fax 01647 432 574
e-mail: gidleighpark@gidleigh.co.uk   MAP 1 C4

GIDLEIGH, which will be closed for refurbishment during the early months of 2006, still feels like a home, an impression that has always been strengthened by the handsome dining-rooms and by staff who are watchful and friendly yet never intrusive.

The food, however, is a world away from what we might think of as home cooking, rising at times to the status of art.

The range of starters alone gives an impressive clue as to the quality, beginning with lentil and foie gras soup, continuing through a raviolo of lobster with cabbage and girolles, a tartlet of quail and quail's egg with black truffles, and culminating in the magnificent terrine of lobster, red mullet, monkfish and scallops: a mosaic on a plate, the flavours fresh, rich and delicate.

Even the appetisers are in a class of their own, such as pumpkin soup finished with kirsch cream, which was as light as a feather and wonderful with pain de Morvan.

The cheeses offered are outstanding in their range and condition: Herefordshire goat's cheese, the nothern Italian Taleggio and the Burgundian Epoisses were exceptional. So was the hot apple tart with vanilla ice-cream, a justly popular dessert.

Gidleigh's cellar has always been one of the greatest in Britain. Where else will you find under one roof a run of vintages of Trimbach's Riesling Clos St. Hune, a superlative Alsace wine, or a range of Tuscan and Piedmont reds from the greatest growers?

Their pride: Roast best end and saddle of local lamb with fondant potato, tomato fondue, roast garlic and tapenade jus
Inexpensive wines: Au Bon Climat Santa Barbara (California) 2001, £30; Château Routas Côteaux Varois Agrippa 1998, £25

Proprietors: Andrew and Christina Brownsword
Last orders for dinner: 9 pm
Open every day
Set lunch: from £35
Set dinner: from £75
Al fresco dining for light lunches
Accommodation: 15 rooms
Wheelchair access

CHANNEL ISLANDS, JERSEY

Bohemia ★★

Green Street, St. Helier, Jersey JE2 4UH
Tel. 01534 880 588 Fax 01534 875 054
e-mail: bohemia@huggler.com   **MAP 1** E5

BEHIND a smart, popular bar, this little restaurant is both elegant and comfortable, and notable not only for the superior quality of the cooking but also for the ultra-friendly service by a young team whose members do everything they can to make your dinner as pleasurable as possible.

After an appetiser of, perhaps, herb-flavoured gnocchi in a crisp coating, an inspired combination of braised lamb's tongues and grilled scallops gives an idea of the exceptional nature of the starters. The tongues come in a Madeira wine emulsion and the dish is neatly garnished with a celeriac and watercress salad. Another successful blend is that of sweetcorn and crab velouté, the dish completed by buttered lobster and scallop ravioli.

As for main courses, poached chicken breast in Sauternes sauce is rich and full of flavour, and there are daily specials such as roast squab, which is cooked medium-rare and served in an intense red wine sauce.

The farmhouse cheeses are impressive in their range and quality. Desserts are equally noteworthy, with choices such as the sherry trifle flavoured with orange, or passion fruit crème brulée with coconut and peppered pineapple.

The wine list is a good balance of classic and New World, offering particularly fine selections from New Zealand and South Africa at reasonable prices.

Their pride: Warm salad of buttered Jersey lobster, white crab, baby fennel 'ceviche' and home-made macaroni
Inexpensive wines: Peter Lehman Grenache/Shiraz/Mourvedre (Australia) 2002, £22; Cairnbrae Sauvignon Blanc The Stones (New Zealand) 2003, £21

Proprietor: Lawrence Huggler
Last orders for dinner: 10 pm
Closed: Sunday for food
Set lunch: from £19.50
Set dinner: from £38
Private dining: up to 60
Al fresco dining
Accommodation: 36 rooms, 8 suites

CHANNEL ISLANDS, JERSEY

Jersey Pottery Garden Restaurant

Gorey Village, Jersey, Channel Islands JE3 9EP
Tel. 01534 850 850 Fax 01534 856 403
e-mail: admin@jerseypottery.com   **MAP 1** E5

A GARDEN is precisely what this restaurant feels like, with its spreading vines, flowers, shrubs and other greenery surrounding you in a bright, airy, conservatory-like room.

It is a place of pilgrimage for Sunday lunch, or brunch, as it is now called. This begins with a self-service table of seafood salad, local oysters, a terrine that might be foie gras and Parma ham, and it continues with beef, lamb, brill and so on.

You might finish with your choice from the range of British and French cheeses and then treat yourself with simple but tempting home-made desserts such as raspberry tarts and éclairs.

The lunch menu, which is available from Wednesday to Saturday, is rather more ambitious.

Starters could be crab risotto and seared scallops or tempura king prawns, followed main courses varying from grilled sea bass or lobster to confit de canard with black pudding and an excellent beef daube.

Among the wines on the list, two worth noting are a Château Fortia burgundy, vintage 2000, and a fine Châteauneuf from the Rhône, though there are also good Australian options.

Their pride: Plateau de fruits de mer
Inexpensive wines: Chardonnay Michel Laroche 2003, £12.95; Mersault Louis Jadot 1999, £42.50

Proprietors: Jones Family
Closed: Monday, dinner every day
Closed for holidays: October–Easter
Set lunch: from £15.95
Private dining: 20-300
Al fresco dining
Wheelchair access

CHANNEL ISLANDS, JERSEY

Longueville Manor ★

Longueville Rd, St. Saviour, Jersey, Channel Islands JE2 7WF
Tel. 01534 725 501 Fax 01534 731 613
e-mail: info@longuevillemanor.com   **MAP 1** E5

FISH is, not surprisingly, an important feature of the cuisine at what has long been one of Jersey's leading hotels. Locally caught sea bass, Dover sole, red mullet, scallops and crab are the main elements of the Taste of Jersey menu, their very freshness meaning that they require only the simplest of treatments.

In contrast, the carte and what is called the Menu Prestige follow very much the precepts of mainstream modern European cooking, presenting adventurous combinations of tastes and textures.

Thus John Dory is braised and served with a cassoulet of mixed beans and white pudding, while turbot is poached in red wine and accompanied by fennel and sauté scallops.

Similarly, beef carpaccio goes with ballottine of foie gras and a celeriac remoulade; beautifully cooked roast lamb and veal sweetbreads are served with lightly curried crab parcels.

Among some noteworthy and very tempting desserts, the best is probably hot passion fruit soufflé and raspberry sorbet, though it is not easy to ignore a model apple tarte Tatin – with Jersey cream, naturally – or a chocolate and orange pyramid and ice-cream flavoured with wattle seeds.

The wine list is well balanced in a variety of vintages of classics of Bordeaux and Burgundy, but Australia and New Zealand are also represented and there is a good choice of wines by the glass. Service is appropriately polished and professional.

Their pride: Grilled hand-dived Jersey scallops with baby leeks, sweet peas and Jabugo ham
Inexpensive wines: Baron Philippe De Rothschild Chardonnay 2003, £19; Wakefield Shiraz 2003, £23

Proprietor: Malcolm Lewis
Last orders for dinner: 9.30 pm
Open every day
Set lunch: from £12.50
Main courses: from £24
Private dining: up to 20
Al fresco dining
Accommodation: 30 rooms
Limited wheelchair access

CHANNEL ISLANDS, JERSEY

Suma's

**Gorey Hill, Gorey, St. Martin, Jersey JE3 6ET
Tel. 01534 853 291 Fax 01534 851 913**

MAP 1 E5

WHATEVER the weather, this smart and elegant restaurant with its bistro style gives you the surreal impression of summer with its blue furniture and colourful modern abstract paintings. From tables by the picture window, you may enjoy magnificent views of Gorey Harbour and Mont Orgueil Castle and there is a fine terrace for when it really is summer.

The cooking is full of bold flavours, based on fresh ingredients, particularly local fish. Scallops are deservedly a popular choice, especially when pan-fried with saffron potato, though whether they really need the trendy addition of black pudding is perhaps open to question.

Butternut squash soup with garlic and pine-nuts, accompanied by delicious cider bread, can be a fine autumn or winter starter, with to follow, perhaps, an excellent rump of lamb, particularly if you select a good bottle of red wine from the excellent list, which is full of discoveries.

Or, of course, you can stay with the superb fish – roast skate with fondant potato, courgettes, red and yellow peppers and tomato coulis, or fillet of brill with lasagne of crab, spring onion and green cabbage.

The service, which is quick and attentive, contributes to the sunny atmosphere.

Their pride: Grilled red mullet and pan-fried langoustine, crisp pineapple wafer on lightly scented Thai green curry tapioca with coco and shellfish cream
Inexpensive wines: Borgo Selene (Sicily) 2003, £9; Oveja Negra Chardonnay Viognier 2004, £12

**Proprietors: Malcolm Lewis and Sue Dufty
Last orders for dinner: 9.30 pm
Open every day
Closed for holidays: Christmas to mid-January
Set lunch: from £12.50
Set dinner: from £25
Al fresco dining**
Wheelchair access

CHEDWORTH, GLOUCESTERSHIRE

Hare and Hounds

GASTROPUB

Foss Cross, Chedworth, Gloucestershire GL54 4NN
Tel. 01285 720 288   Fax 01285 720 488

MAP 1 F1

RACING down the Fosse Way, you might dismiss this wayside inn and its 'Good Food' board as just another A-road pub going through the motions of satisfying passing trade. Pull into the car park, though, and find out what the promised good food means.

The comfort hits you first. Yes, the beams and flagstones are there, the fireplaces, exposed stone walls and solid furnishings, but there are also rows of books to add a genuine homely touch and friendly staff greet you with almost amateurish enthusiasm. There is nothing unprofessional about the choice of interesting dishes on the menu, though, with blackboard specials and a range of quicker snacks.

Stick to a simple prawn bisque, a plain steak or veal escalope with pasta if you must, but their real forte lies in innovations such as curried lamb samosa and lentils on Bombay potatoes, or fennel ravioli with beans and mozzarella in basil cream sauce topped with flaked Parmesan. And how about leeks, tarragon and apples as an original crust for a generous slice of fine, flaky halibut, or the combination of duck confit, chicken and pigeon breast in a kumquat jus?

To finish, try a creamy individual raspberry cheesecake on kiwi coulis from the short list of appetising desserts. The overall result is enjoyably more dinner party than dining out and, on their day, they can be up there with the best.

Speciality food: Modern British cooking
Draught beers: Arkells 2B, Arkells Summer Ale
Average wine price by the glass: £3.95

Licensees: Angela Howe and Gerry Ragosa
Last orders for dinner: 9.30 pm (Sunday 9 pm)
Open every day
Main courses: from £12.95
Private dining: 10-40
Beer garden
Accommodation: 10 rooms
Children welcome
Wheelchair access

CHELTENHAM, GLOUCESTERSHIRE

Le Champignon Sauvage ★★

24-28 Suffolk Road, Cheltenham, Gloucestershire GL50 2AQ
Tel. 01242 573 449 Fax 01242 254 365
e-mail: mail@lechampignonsauvage.co.uk   **MAP 1** E1

THE ATTENTION to detail here may be judged by the fact that no fewer than ten different varieties of pumpkin were tested to find the perfect purée intended to accompany a dish of scallops and squid. Nor does it end there. The choice of plate or dish on which items are presented is given as much care as everything else.

The emphasis is on flavour, with each component adding its own character to the overall effect. A starter might be terrine of guinea fowl, foie gras and shitake mushrooms, while main courses offer such delights as lamb with lavender, smoked garlic cream and artichoke hearts, or roasted monkfish tail with toasted barley jus.

A little pre-dessert of rose geranium cream, topped with tongue-tickling popcorn and damson sorbet, was great fun before a hot fig tart with burnt butter ice-cream. Other desserts included iced apple mousse with pressed caramelised apple and an apple and haw sorbet, and layered meringue with praline cream, chocolate and tonka bean ice-cream.

There is a good cheese tray and also an impressively varied array of petits fours. The wine list covers mainly France, with just a few entries from California, Australia and New Zealand. It has plenty to offer at under £30 and more than a few at less than £20. About 50 wines are available in half-bottles and some half-dozen by the glass.

Their pride: Pan-fried cock's kidneys and langoustines served with langoustine tortelloni and langoustine sauce
Inexpensive wines: Rully Blanc Premier Cru Jaqueson 2002, £25; Gigondas Domaine Saint Gayan Meffre 2001, £23

Proprietors: David and Helen Everitt-Matthias
Last orders for dinner: 9 pm
Closed: Sunday and Monday
Closed for holidays: 10 days Christmas, 3 weeks June
Set lunch: from £27
Set dinner: from £27
Limited wheelchair access

CHERINGTON, GLOUCESTERSHIRE

Trouble House ★

GASTROPUB

Cherington, Nr. Tetbury, Gloucestershire GL8 8SG
Tel. 01666 502206 Fax 01666 504508
e-mail: enquiries@troublehouse.co.uk   **MAP 1** E2

JUGGLING the personalities of the country pub and the serious restaurant is not easy, but here they carry it off with panache. The setting has all the necessary credentials – inviting, archetypical, whitewashed exterior, open fires and plain, scrubbed tables – and so does the food, chef/tenant Michael Bedford having served his time with the likes of Michel Blanc and Gary Rhodes.

His illustrious past is obvious in foie gras and apple terrine, smoked haddock and whisky risotto, roast duck breast and braised leg with apricots, prunes, apples and creamed potatoes, or the roasted veal sweetbreads with wild mushrooms and spinach.

Dishes such as these, however, happily rub shoulders with more traditional soups, pies and steaks on a nicely varied carte (which is also chalked up in the bar).

A starter of skewered scallops with bacon and a pea cappuccino showed real quality, in both the raw materials and their simple, effective treatment.

The pie that followed was perhaps not for the faint-hearted, but from the excellent, spongy crust, the fragrant power of its trapped ingredients – partridge and pheasant with foie gras and oodles of aromatic onions and garlic – escaped in one gloriously tantalising waft, given further power by a very gamey hare gravy. Swede mash and white haricot beans made for a rich garnish.

Speciality food: Hand-dived roasted scallops with South Lewney crayfish and crayfish cappuccino
Draught beers: Wadworth 6X, Henrys IPA
Average wine price by the glass: £5

Licensees: Michael and Sarah Bedford
Last orders for dinner: 9.30 pm
Closed: Sunday evening, Monday
Closed for holidays: 24 December-4 January
Main courses: from £16
Al fresco dining
Wheelchair access

CHESTER, CHESHIRE

Arkle Restaurant Chester Grosvenor

The Chester Grosvenor, Eastgate, Chester, Cheshire CH1 1LT
Tel. 01244 324 024 Fax 01244 313 246
e-mail: arkle@chestergrosvenor.com   **MAP 3** D1

IN THE heart of the city, this intimate yet formal hotel restaurant is softly lit and elegant and displays fine oil paintings of the great racehorse after which it is named. Now open only for dinner – the hotel's own bistro is a popular place for lunch – it offers a carte that is ambitious, sophisticated and entirely successful.

Fish is a feature of the cuisine, an excellent example being firm, moist monkfish with a wrapping of ham, which is served with a lobster bisque. As a starter, cod is accompanied by pork ravioli and sweet grape pickle.

Meat dishes that stand out among the main courses are saddle of roe-deer with Alsace cannelloni and flavoured with beer and chocolate malt, or suckling pig, which is served with a selection of other forms of pork.

The selection of cheeses is exceptional and desserts often display delightful originality, as in the William's pear baba steeped in caramel and balsamic vinegar and served with almond ice-cream.

The extensive wine list has been thoughtfully assembled and includes a range of good wines by the glass. As for service, the polish, focus and attention to detail of the staff are matched by their natural warmth and friendliness.

Their pride: Collection of local and Iberico pork miniatures
Inexpensive wines: Willandra Unoaked Chardonnay 2004, £20; Alejandro Fernandez Condado de Haza Ribero del Duero (Spain) 2002, £25.50

Proprietor: Duke of Westminster
Last orders for dinner: 9.30 pm
Closed: lunch every day, Sunday and Monday
Closed for holidays: 3 weeks January, 1 week August
Set dinner: from £55
Private dining: 10-50
Accommodation: 80 rooms
Wheelchair access

CHESTER, CHESHIRE

Old Harkers Arms

GASTROPUB

Russell Street, Chester, Cheshire CH3 5AL
Tel. 01244 344 525 Fax 01244 344 812
email: harkers.arms@brunningandprice.co.uk   **MAP 3** D1

IN THE restored warehouse area by the Shropshire canal that flows through Chester, this imaginatively resurrected pub, part of a small gastropub group, employs the successful formula of 'library bar and food-all-day'.

The menu follows the brasserie-style format. Twice-baked goat's cheese soufflé might be followed by an 8oz steak burger, fresh and accurately cooked, served with lightly melted mozzarella, fresh coleslaw and well-timed chips.

Braised lamb shank and whole grilled sea bass could be other options, and vegetarians are well looked after with the likes of butternut squash ravioli in white wine and rosemary sauce. There are good sandwiches, too, including Cumberland sausage on a bun with apple sauce.

Puddings are quite traditional, with an outstanding chocolate brownie in real hot chocolate sauce. The cheeseboard features oak smoked Cheshire and a variety of other regional cheeses, such as Staffordshire apple and mint.

Wines are skilfully chosen for variety, value and quality and there is a selection of more than 100 whiskies.

Speciality food: Salmon and smoked haddock fishcakes
Draught beers: Weetwood Oast House Gold, Thwaites
Average wine price by the glass: £2.50

Licensee: Paul Jeffrey
Last orders for dinner: Monday to Thursday 9.30pm,
Friday and Saturday 10pm, Sunday 9pm
Open every day
Closed for holidays: 25-26 December
Main courses: from £9.95
Children welcome until 5pm
Wheelchair access

CHIDDINGFOLD, SURREY

Swan Inn

GASTROPUB

Petworth Road, Chiddingfold, Surrey GU8 4TY
Tel. 01428 682 073 Fax 01428 683 259

MAP 2 C4

THE SWAN INN, an imposing red brick hostelry, is just south of the village green on the A283. It has an uncluttered, sophisticated interior, with a striking long bar, mellow wooden floors and well-spaced tables.

This is the epitome of a gastropub, where meals can be taken in the bar, dining-room or garden, and you can mix and match your choices from the bar and à la carte menus. The restaurant is more formal, but the service by a young team has the same friendly approach as in the bar. There is an attractive raised rear terrace where meals are served.

The carefully constructed menu is refreshed fortnightly and uses local seasonal ingredients where possible. For a light lunchtime snack there are sandwiches or ploughman's for consideration. Otherwise try the generous portion of liver pâté, with its smooth texture and thin coating of crushed black pepper, or fresh sardines with red onion and basil.

Main courses range from goat's cheese soufflé to duck confit or tender, accurately cooked sea bass and succulent scallops served with whole cooked garlic cloves, wild mushrooms and firm, fresh asparagus spears.

Puddings should not be overlooked – a smooth, light amaretto cheesecake with very good nougat ice-cream and fresh berries, perhaps, or white chocolate and bilberry brûlée. There is a large selection of French cheeses, such as Livarot and Reblochon, and 11 wines are offered by the glass.

Speciality food: Poached sea bass
Draught beers: Fullers London Pride, Hogs Back TEA
Average wine price by the glass: £3.50

Licensee: Daniel Hall
Last orders for dinner: 10pm
Open every day
Main courses: from £9.95
Private dining: 10-40
Beer garden
Accommodation: 11 en-suite rooms
Children welcome
Wheelchair access

CHIEVELEY, BERKSHIRE

Crab at Chieveley ★

GASTROPUB

Wantage Road, Chieveley, Newbury, Berkshire RG20 8UE
Tel. 01635 247 550 Fax 01635 247 440
e-mail: info@crabatchieveley.com   **MAP 2** B3

IF YOU are in the vicinity of Newbury, then this place is well worth a detour. It is on the B4494 north of the M4, near junction 13, but ask for directions when booking. Rolling countryside with long views is the setting for a substantial hostelry. It has a thatched roof, the pub sign hangs from an old oak tree and there is a large south-facing terrace where meals are served in summer. There is also a walled garden complete with fountain and palm trees. To one side is a smart bedroom complex.

Inside is an atmospheric bar area and snug with polished wooden tables and a ceiling hung with fishing nets. This theme continues into the restaurant, but here are rugs, white linen tablecloths and napkins, antique clocks and colourful models of fishing trawlers. Very good professional service flows throughout the meal.

The same menus are served in both areas, with seafood taking the central role. And very good it is, too – starters include large, grilled sardines in a light Pernod butter, smoked haddock risotto and soft-poached egg, Irish oysters or chunky fish soup with aïoli.

Irresistible main courses might be turbot fillet with fontina soufflé, or an impressive and generous dish of Cornish lobster, king scallops and tiger prawns in a subtle thermidor sauce. Carnivores can choose from Barbary duckling with pineapple and mango salsa, or Angus steak with goose-fat chips and Béarnaise sauce. There are indulgent puddings, such as citrus soup with coconut ice-cream, or maybe hot chocolate fondant in soft chocolate sponge casing. If you are planning to visit on Friday or Saturday evenings, book at least one week in advance.

Speciality food: Seafood
Draught beers: Fullers London Pride, San Miguel
Average wine price by the glass: £4.50

Licensee: David Barnard
Last orders for dinner: 9.30 pm (Fri and Sat 10 pm)
Open every day
Set lunch: from £16.95
Set dinner: from £16.95 (until 7 pm)
Private dining: 10-100
Al fresco dining
Beer garden
Accommodation: 10 rooms
Children welcome   Wheelchair access

CHILGROVE, WEST SUSSEX

White Horse

GASTROPUB

High Street, Chilgrove, Nr. Chichester, West Sussex PO18 9HX
Tel. 01243 535 219 Fax 01243 535 301
e-mail: info@whitehorsechilgrove.co.uk   **MAP 2** C4

A GLORIOUS location in the heart of the beautiful South Downs, close to Goodwood racecourse, is the setting for this attractive old coaching inn. Wisteria embellishes the white painted façade and the immaculate interior has been sympathetically modernised, retaining beams and fireplaces.

Meals are served in either the simply appointed bar area or in the more formal restaurant with gleaming glassware and crisp white linen tablecloths. Service is both friendly and efficient. If you feel like eating outdoors, you may do so in the raised garden with splendid views. Locals form the mainstay of the clientele and clearly enjoy the well-chosen menu dishes, including a short blackboard list of daily specials.

The menu features half-a-dozen light dishes – an excellent and popular idea, especially at lunchtime. To start, try the hand-dived scallops with king prawns, or the gazpacho, bursting with fresh yet piquant flavours, crisp crouton and diced raw vegetables.

Main courses feature slow-roasted Gressingham duck, seared calf's liver, organic Old Spot pork cutlet, or local Selsey crab and lobster. The oxtail ravioli with lentils and bacon in red wine sauce is an inventive and successful dish. Wild sea bass with hot lemon butter or lime hollandaise is another option.

Then try warm chocolate sponge fondant with orange ice-cream, citrus tart, or star fruit cheesecake. There are good wines from round the world and, in an annexe, eight en-suite bedrooms.

Speciality food: Seafood and game in season
Draught beers: Ballards, Heineken Export
Average wine price by the glass: £3.75

Licensee: Charles Burton
Last orders for dinner: 9.30 pm
Closed: Sunday evening, Monday
Main courses: from £9.95
Private dining: 12-50
Al fresco dining
Accommodation: 8 rooms
Children welcome
Wheelchair access

CHIPPING CAMPDEN, GLOUCESTERSHIRE

Noel Arms Oriental Restaurant `GASTROPUB`

High Street, Chipping Campden, Gloucestershire GL55 6AT
Tel. 01386 840 317 Fax 01386 841 136
e-mail: reception@noelarmshotel.com   **MAP 1** F1

SINGAPOREAN Loy Seng is keen to present a cross-section of South-east Asian dishes along with some nearer to home at this neat little High Street hotel. Two menus are offered and they can be mixed and matched by diners in the pretty courtyard, in the flagstoned conservatory or in an elegantly sparse dining-room.

Never short of ideas, the enthusiastic Mr. Loy runs an oriental food club, wine and whisky tastings and book nights, and he employs a multinational kitchen brigade to ensure the authenticity of each country's specialities.

Start with pre-dinner drinks – gin sling, perhaps, and some spiced anchovies – in the bustling, still pubby little bar, then go on to sample sour and spicy Thai prawn soup, a Vietnamese vegetarian roll or a Malaysian satay. These might be followed by Sri Lankan black curry, teriyaki beef, or Peking duck with all the trimmings. The set menus make life easier if you are undecided.

There is a vitality and a freshness of flavour that sets the oriental apart, as in crisp deep-fried squid laid on noodles with a few spicy vegetables, marinated Kung Po chicken exuding delicately vibrant spicing from its Szechuan peppercorns and red chilli, and a dessert of coconut soup with fresh fruit and coconut sorbet.

There is always the Cotswold menu if you want flavours that are more British. Try vegetable soup or grilled goat's cheese, followed by chicken and mushroom pie or even traditional cod and chips. You will be missing out on the cook's tour of Asia, but Mr. Loy's enthusiasm will still be there.

Speciality food: Oriental specialities
Draught beers: Hook Norton, Boddingtons
Average wine price by the glass: £3.50

Licensee: Loy Seng
Last orders for dinner: 9.30 pm
Open every day
Set lunch: from £22
Set dinner: from £22
Private dining: 12-30
Beer garden
Accommodation: 26 rooms
Children welcome

CHRISTCHURCH, DORSET

Ship in Distress

66 Stanpit, Christchurch, Dorset BH23 3NA
Tel. 01202 485 123 Fax 01202 483 997
e-mail: enquiries@theshipindistress.com   MAP 1 F4

A BRIGANTINE in heavy seas, with a large painted wooden fish slung underneath it, proudly announces this pub by the roadside. Inside, the bar is crammed with nautical artifacts such as a pirate statuette, a Titanic lifebelt and model sailing ships.

Meals are served in the bar as well as in the cottagey restaurant, which is on two levels and often full of well-informed locals, so it is wise to book. Seafood and home-made puddings are the main reasons for the pub's great popularity.

Patronne Sally Canning ensures that each table is well cared for and chats with her regular customers. Bar snacks are also taken seriously, with local Mudeford crab and smoked salmon sandwiches, fish and chips of either cod or skate wing with crispy beer batter and mushy peas, or tagliatelle with wild mushrooms, lemon and truffle oil. Breton-style fish soup is served with Gruyère croutons and rouille, and the tian of crab with sliced cucumber is as fresh as you will find anywhere.

For heartier appetites there are fruits de mer with shallot vinegar, mayonnaise and home-made bread, or pan-fried fillet of Cornish turbot with shallot mash, asparagus tips and wild mushrooms. Chargrilled fillet steak with peppercorn and mushroom sauce is a fine alternative to fish.

Desserts worth trying are the smooth-textured chocolate tart on a thin, crisp pastry base with a fruit compote, or steamed vanilla bean pudding with passion fruit, oranges and clotted cream.

Speciality food: Seafood
Draught beers: Ringwood Best, Adnams Broadside
Average wine price by the glass: £3.30

Licensee: Sally Canning
Last orders for dinner: 9 pm
Open every day
Closed for holidays: 25 December
Main courses: from £8.50
Private dining: 20-80
Al fresco dining
Children welcome
Wheelchair access

CLAVERING, ESSEX

Cricketers ★

GASTROPUB

Wicken Road, Clavering, Nr. Saffron Walden, Essex CB11 4QT
Tel. 01799 550 442 Fax 01799 550 882
e-mail: info@thecricketers.co.uk   **MAP 2** D1

NINE miles east of Buntingford and the greatly improved A10, cross the Hertfordshire/Essex border and you arrive at this 16th-century pub, where Trevor Oliver has plied his trade as landlord for thirty years, as well as fathering a chef called Jamie.

The bars sport old beams and the comfortable restaurant, with its horse brasses and halters, prints of cricketers and hunting packs, chintzy curtains and velveteen upholstered seating, takes you back to the 1950s.

Prices are quite high, but worth it. The menu is full of interest, taking in workable ideas from the Sub-continent – the juicy, spicy lamb patties with minted yoghurt are excellent – yet the dishes are never pretentious. The grilled pork chop served in a sage and cider sauce with lyonnaise-style diced potatoes is a good instance of imaginative simplicity.

Inviting alternatives range from fresh sardines cooked in garlic and parsley butter through to a warm salad of quail with honey mustard and soy dressing, as well as chargrilled peaches and Serrano ham on wild rocket and watercress dressed with fruity olive oil. Or go for a simple special such as fresh plaice and chips.

Puddings are just as tempting, the cool citrus tang of lime and lemon parfait or rice pudding with compote of Victoria plums.

Wines are fine and fairly priced, with a good Cinsault/Cabernet red blend from the Cape.

Speciality food: Carving trolley: roast ribs of beef
Draught beers: Adnams, Greene King IPA
Average wine price by the glass: £3

Licensee: Trevor Oliver
Last orders for dinner: 10 pm
Open every day
Closed for holidays: 25 and 26 December
Set lunch: from £23 (Sunday only)
Set dinner: from £21.50
Private dining: up to 25
Beer garden
Accommodation: 14 rooms
Children welcome   Wheelchair access

CLIPSHAM, RUTLAND

Olive Branch ★

GASTROPUB

Main Street, Clipsham, Rutland LE15 7SH
Tel. 01780 410 355 Fax 01780 410 000
e-mail: olive@work.gb.com   **MAP 4** C3

YOU WILL find the best of both worlds, restaurant and pub, at this delightful village inn. If the décor and ambience are essentially pubby, the quality of the food matches or beats that in many a more self-conscious dining-room.

English classic such as fish and chips, pork pie from Grasmere and sausages from Lincolnshire feature on the menu, but there are some wide-ranging variations on both Continental and eastern themes: duck confit served with white haricot beans, foie gras and peppercorn terrine; blanquette de veau, spring roll of crab with a Thai green curry dip.

And what flavours! A light, crisp tart containing perfectly grilled Mediterranean vegetables and creamy goat's cheese is given a dressing of balsamic vinegar with tomato and celery salt. Sea bass is crisply grilled, garnished with scallops and langoustine and vanilla bisque and served with excellent fennel rösti.

Desserts such as chocolate roulade are fittingly unpretentious and the young staff go about their work (to packed houses) with panache and enthusiasm.

Speciality food: Honey-roasted confit duck legs
Draught beers: Olive Branch Olive Oil, Grain Store BBB
Average wine price by the glass: £3.50

Licensee: Marcus Welford
Last orders for dinner: 9.30 pm
Open every day
Closed for holidays: 26 December, 1 January
Set lunch: from £13.50
Private dining: up to 30
Al fresco dining
Wheelchair access

COLERNE, WILTSHIRE

Lucknam Park The Park Restaurant ★

Colerne, Nr. Chippenham, Wiltshire SN14 8AZ
Tel. 01225 742 777 Fax 01225 743536
email: reservations@lucknampark.co.uk   **MAP 1** E2

IF YOU want opulence in all its elaborate glory, this is the place for you. The setting would be an ideal background for a television costume drama and service by the almost entirely French staff is designed for absolute comfort.

The cuisine is entirely in keeping with the luxurious surroundings. Ingredients of impeccable quality – organic salmon, Welsh lamb, Wiltshire rabbit, Brecon venison, local pork – are presented with great skill and flair, even though the garnishes are sometimes a surprise, like the beetroot Tatin and the boudin that accompanied perfectly roasted and correctly sauced venison.

The surprise, however, turns to delight with imaginative dishes such as a fricassee of scallops with snails, ceps and creamy turnip purée. Even more impressive is a sort of quartet of organic duck: parfait of foie gras, ballottine of leg, smoked breast and an accompanying consommé with the carcass.

Stars of the menu might include slow-roasted pork belly scented with Chinese five spice and served with baby onions and leeks and caramelised apple rings, or lasagne of crab, lobster and crevette with baby artichoke.

Desserts are notable for the range of Tatins, but particularly tempting is a lemon trio of tart, jelly in a shell and sorbet.

Prepare to be pampered.

Their pride: Scallops with turnip purée, fricassee of ceps and snails
Inexpensive wines: Vin de Pays des Côtes du Tarn 2003, £17.50; Vin de Pays D'Oc Merlot 2003, £17.50

Proprietor: Lucknam Park Hotel Ltd.
Last orders for dinner: 10 pm
Open every day
Set lunch: from £30
Set dinner: from £55
Private dining: up to 80
Al fresco dining
Accommodation: 41 rooms
Wheelchair access

COLSTON BASSETT, NOTTINGHAMSHIRE

Martins Arms Inn

GASTROPUB

School Lane, Colston Basset, Nottinghamshire NG12 3FD
Tel. 01949 813 61 Fax 01949 810 39

MAP 4 B3

THE Martins Arms dates from the 17th century, when it was a farm that then went on to brew its own beer. Records show that it took on the status of an inn about 1844. Not surprisingly, it has a wealth of period features – not least of which is an ornate carved fireplace in the bar – and its furnishings are appropriately traditional.

Local Stilton features strongly on the menu: in a ploughman's alongside Melton Mobray pork pie, or served with poached pear and croutons, in a ciabatta sandwich with sirloin steak and in the form of a potato cake served as a main course.

The bar menu has a good selection of sandwiches and a pretty comprehensive range of dishes.

Starters could include gravadlax with lemon blinis, fresh peas and crème fraîche or chicken galantine – a smooth and flavoursome terrine peppered with pistachio nuts and served with a delicate apple jelly.

'Duck two ways' (roasted and confit) with apple, wild mushrooms and fondant potato might appeal as a main course. Alternatively, try a delicious samphire and red pepper risotto, an ideal marriage with a succulent roasted fillet of cod.

Marshmallow ice-cream is served with poached rhubarb and rich shortbread – perhaps one of six desserts on offer, which can all be sampled in the assiette of Martins Arms puddings (for two).

Speciality food: Potato cake
Draught beers: Bass, Pedigree
Average wine price by the glass: £2.60

Licensee: Lyn Stafford Bryan
Last orders for dinner: 10 pm
Closed: Sunday evening (food)
Main courses: from £9.95
Private dining: up to 30
Al fresco dining
Children welcome in dining room
Wheelchair access

CORSCOMBE, DORSET

Fox Inn

GASTROPUB

Corscombe, Dorchester, Dorset DT2 0NS
Tel. 01935 891 330
e-mail: dine@fox-inn.co.uk

MAP 1 E3

SHARING a pint at the end of the slate-topped bar with locals, accountant-turned-publican Clive Webb is in his element. He is living a dream many would envy in his centuries-old thatched Dorset village inn with its stone flags, inglenook fireplaces and beams aplenty. A maze of rooms with their tables covered in blue gingham leads to a flower-filled conservatory with a communal table. Another room, hidden from view, contains an old Aga, a wooden sink and yet another inglenook fireplace. It makes you want to live there for ever.

The small menu might, according to the season, include a warm salad of pigeon breast and bacon; wild mushroom risotto; fillet of local estate venison with celeriac purée and game sauce, and 'Fox's Favourite', which is shreds of chicken in a creamy sauce of red pepper and celery, with a side-dish of sauté new potatoes, courgette, sugar snaps and carrot.

People seem to come from far and wide and they tend to go for the blackboard specials such as oxtail soup, gratin of crab and salmon, John Dory fillet with herb crust and beurre blanc, or duck leg confit with a cherry brandy sauce.

Puddings are all made at The Fox – how sad that many pubs need to state this – and include sublime meringues with clotted cream. A small but perfectly formed wine list is sourced exclusively from one of the region's top merchants.

There are four bedrooms, full of character, and there is a small garden across the lane bordering a stream.

Speciality food: Fish
Draught beers: Exmoor Ale, Butcombe Bitter
Average wine price by the glass: £2.90

Licensees: Clive Webb and Peter Rice
Last orders for dinner: 9 pm (Fri and Sat 9.30 pm)
Open every day
Closed for holidays: Christmas Day (for food)
Main courses: from £17
Private dining: 10-30
Beer garden
Accommodation: 4 rooms
Limited wheelchair access

CORTON DENHAM, SOMERSET

Queens Arms

GASTROPUB

Corton Denham, Somerset DT9 4LR
Tel. 01963 220 317
e-mail: relax@thequeens-arms.com   **MAP 1 E3**

REACHED down narrow, winding lanes between the A303 and Sherborne, the ancient village of Corton Denham lies in the lee of a lush, green, steep hill on the Dorset/Somerset border. In the most charming of settings, this 18th-century pub, with views over the handsome stone church, has undergone a transformation that has created what is now an appealing spot in which to enjoy some classy cooking.

There are two main dining areas: the sage green bar with rug-strewn stone-flagged floor and solid wooden furniture, and the terracotta red dining room.

Menus, amended weekly, might include Old English sausages with Montgomery Cheddar mash and red onion marmalade; coarse country terrine with granary toast and redcurrant sauce; an exquisite nectarine, walnut, blue cheese and shallot salad, or a crayfish sandwich on white farmhouse bread with mayonnaise and rocket.

The menus are small, offering only a handful of starters, main courses and puddings, with some sandwiches at lunch, but this is intelligent, robust cooking relying on quality ingredients and an unfussy approach.

On the bar, pork pies sit alongside marinated olives and pistachio nuts and there are fine local ales as well as a great selection of imported bottled beers and spirits. Rolls of butcher's paper hang from the walls as signs highlighting a wine special,

Speciality food: Corton Denham loin of lamb, rolled and stuffed with black pudding, bayleaf jus
Draught beers: Butcombe Bitter, Timothy Taylor Landlord
Average wine price by the glass: £3.45

Licensees: Rupert and Victoria Reeves
Last orders for dinner: 10 pm (Sunday 9.30 pm)
Open every day
Closed for holidays: 25 December (food)
Main courses: from £9.50
Private dining: 6-12
Beer garden
Accommodation: 5 rooms
Children welcome
Limited wheelchair access

COULTERSHAW BRIDGE, WEST SUSSEX

Badgers

GASTROPUB

**Coultershaw Bridge, Petworth, West Sussex GU28 0JF
Tel. 01798 342 651**

MAP 2 C4

A FORMER railway tavern, Badgers, on the A285 just south of Petworth, is today a white painted, sash-windowed inn sitting alongside the river Rother, with farmland beyond.

Outside, there is a pretty garden with weeping willows and an old lily pond to the side. The interior is divided into several rooms with well-spaced, solid old pine tables and comfortable chairs.

Daily specials are chalked up on various panels above the bar and the general menu content has a considerable fishy element.

Starters offer dishes such as fish tapas, filo pastry with chicken and cashew nut stir-fry, or spicy and tender squid in a sweet chilli and coriander sauce. There are also four salads and four pasta dishes.

For more substantial main dishes, try the roasted half-shoulder of lamb with garlic and rosemary, accurately cooked monkfish with pea and pancetta purée, or even one of the house specialities: zarzuela – a hearty casserole of fish, mussels, gambas and squid. Lobster salad or thermidor might also be available.

For pudding, sample the deeply filled Gascony apple tart, which is served warm and has a thin pastry crust. Alternatively, try the old favourite of treacle tart served with custard, or crème brulée, or marbled milk and dark chocolate torte.

The wine list includes six wines by the glass.

Speciality food: Zarzuela
Draught beers: Badgers Gold, Sussex Bitter
Average wine price by the glass: £3

**Licensees: Steve Pollard and Jules Arlette
Last orders for dinner: 9 pm
Closed: Sunday evening (October–March)
Closed for holidays: Bank Holiday Mondays
Main courses: from £6.95
Beer garden
Accommodation: 3 rooms**
Children over 5 welcome
Wheelchair access

CUCKFIELD, WEST SUSSEX

Ockenden Manor ★

Ockenden Lane, Cuckfield, West Sussex RH17 5LD
Tel. 01444 416 111 Fax 01444 415 549
e-mail: ockenden@hshotels.co.uk   **MAP 2** D4

AT DINNER in this civilised, 16th-century country house hotel, you can mix and match between two fixed-price menus, but perhaps the tasting menus at both dinner and lunch are a good way to explore the excellence of the cooking.

Nor is it simply the quality of the dishes. The attention given to even the smallest detail is impressive, as with the quenelle of tapenade and Parmesan, with croutons, which is offered as you begin to make your choices from the menu, or the appetiser of leek and potato broth with truffle oil that excites the palate.

Such care extends to the outstanding home-baked bread rolls (warm, crusty, judiciously salted) and the generous selection of petits fours, which might include a wonderful miniature lemon tart, its crunchy brulée top still warm.

Ingredients are, of course, first-class. Halibut from Scotland is topped with a perfect crust and is served with home-made fresh pasta and wild mushrooms in cep sauce – the whole dish designed to enhance the quality and freshness of the fish.

Portions are generous, with starters sometimes as substantial as main courses, as in the millefeuille of roasted sweetbreads, oxtail and celeriac. The wine list has some 200 bins, with informative notes at the top of each section. There are plenty of half-bottles and a dozen or so wines available by the glass.

Their pride: Whole scallops wrapped in smoked salmon, pea purée and haddock brandade fritters
Inexpensive wines: Deaking Estate Sauvignon Blanc 2003, £17.75; Laura Hartwig Merlot 2000, £21.50

Proprietors: The Goodman and Garminger families
Last orders for dinner: 9 pm
Open every day
Set lunch: from £13.95
Set dinner: from £46
Private dining: up to 75
Accommodation: 22 rooms
Limited wheelchair access

DANEHILL, EAST SUSSEX

Coach and Horses

GASTROPUB

School Lane, Danehill, East Sussex RH17 7JF
Tel. 01825 740 369
e-mail: coachandhorses@danehill.biz   **MAP 2** D4

WHAT WOULD the old Sussex character, with his smock and trug, have made of this, after trudging through the leafy lanes in the heart of his native county in search of a mug or two of cider and a chunk of bread and cheese? Pancetta risotto with shaved Parmesan? Slow-roasted tomatoes and asparagus on toasted brioche? Pan-fried halibut with white radish and ginger salad?

The smock may have given way to 'smart casual', but this collection of fairly Spartan rooms with bare boards, plain wooden furniture, dried hops and the odd artifact as token decor, remains very much a local watering-hole where the clientele spill out into the well-stocked gardens to browse on summer evenings. Host Ian Philpots has been in his element hereabouts for a good few years, happy in the knowledge that chef Chris Start is laying on an array of varied and interesting dishes often based on local produce.

Seasonal influence on the printed menu and blackboard extras is particularly marked and you are spoilt for choice between maybe a French-inspired lentil salad with nicely pink chicken livers, grilled sardines with tomato and olive dressing, or coq au vin.

Traditional favourites such as a watercress soup and home-made pasta with field mushrooms (vegetarian dishes abound) compete with inventive specials like crab and smoked haddock ravioli with buttered spinach. A finer and less doughy pasta would have made this a really star dish, but the strong flavours emanating from the rich filling were typical of the honest and imaginative fare, which more than occasionally touches on the really ambitious.

Speciality food: Local produce, especially lamb, game and fish
Draught beers: Harveys Sussex Best Bitter and Weltons Kid and Bard
Average wine price by the glass: £3

> **Licensees: Ian and Catherine Philpots**
> **Last orders for dinner: 9pm**
> **Closed: Sunday evening (for food)**
> **Closed for holidays: 25 Dec evg, 26 Dec, 1 Jan evg**
> **Main courses: from £9.25**
> **Private dining: up to 14**
> **Beer garden**
> Children welcome
> Wheelchair access

DARTMOUTH, DEVON

New Angel ★★

2 South Embankment, Dartmouth, Devon TQ6 9BH
Tel. 01803 839 425 Fax 01803 839 567
e-mail: reservations@thenewangel.co.uk   **MAP 1** D4

THE SETTING of the Angel, with its lovely views across the Dart estuary, has the beguiling atmosphere shared by all the fine waterside restaurants, but here the food is truly exceptional, which is not surprising when it comes from a chef as great as John Burton Race.

He became famous because of the inspired way in which he could combine intricate flavours into a perfectly balanced dish, but now his passion is simplicity – any supporting element on the plate is there essentially in a minor supporting role, subtly to enhance the centrepiece.

One of the greatest dishes of his new approach is the roasted monkfish with a ragout of local mussels in mussel liquor mixed with vermouth and white wine, a marriage of simple flavours which, together, turn into a masterpiece. Equally accomplished is a starter of ham hock and foie gras with piccalilli.

Daily specials might be simple yet sophisticated things such as black pudding tartlet with apple purée and beetroot syrup, beef in red wine with parsnip purée and fine beans, or lobster tortellini, with spinach and fennel.

There is a fine selection of cheeses from Devon and France, which features a truly excellent local ewe's cheese. The wine choice shows the same flair, with an eye to originality and value, and includes a good fruity red of the new Cabardes appellation near Carcassonne.

Their pride: Fillet of turbot, Exe mussels, cockles, clams, noodles and summer vegetables
Inexpensive wines: Vermentino Cala Silente 2003, £24; Vin de Pays de la Principauté d'Orange, 2000, £22

Proprietors: John and Kim Burton Race
Last orders for dinner: 10 pm
Closed: Sunday evening, Monday
Closed for holidays: January, 1st week September
Main courses: from £15
Limited wheelchair access

DEDHAM, ESSEX

Sun Inn ★

High Street, Dedham, Essex CO7 6DF
Tel. 01206 323 351
e-mail: info@thesuninndedham.com   **MAP 2** E1

AT THE heart of Dedham High Street, the Sun is a fine period inn run by owner and landlord Piers Baker, who previously ran a trio of highly successful gastropubs in London. He also owns the spice and vegetable shop next door, from where several of his exotic varieties find their way into his highly imaginative dishes.

A good example is the cavalo nero and potato soup, a delicious item based on Italian cabbage, enhanced by excellent Parmesan crostini. Another is the Tuscan sausage dish with an intriguing gratin of potato and kohlrabi.

Maybe start with a plate of tapas that include borlotti bean purée, sautéd chorizo with soft boiled egg and boquerones on toast with olive pesto.

Fashionable modern main courses in demand are well prepared: free-range chicken risotto with rosemary; warm octopus salad; grilled fillet of sea trout; grilled veal chop from naturally reared Holstein stock with pink fir apple potatoes; marinated roast lamb with shaved fennel, aubergine and peppers.

Puddings are equally interesting, especially white peaches with Pinot Noir and mascarpone, or lemon and lime tart with local Hadleigh ice-cream.

The wine list is a skilful trawl through growers in South Africa and Australia as well as the classic regions of France and Italy.

Speciality food: Modern British with Mediterranean influence
Draught beers: Crouchvale Brewers Gold, Adnams Broadside
Average wine price by the glass: £3.35

Licensee: Piers Baker
Last orders for dinner: 9.30 pm
Closed: Sunday evening
Closed for holidays: 25 and 26 December
Main courses: from £10
Private dining: up to 30
Beer garden
Accommodation: 4 rooms
Children welcome

DENHAM, BUCKINGHAMSHIRE

The Swan

`GASTROPUB`

Village Road, Denham, Buckinghamshire UB9 5BH
Tel. 01895 832 085 Fax 01895 835 516
e-mail: info@swaninndenham.co.uk   **MAP 2** C2

JUST off the busy A40, on the fringes of suburban metroland, take the sign to 'The village only' for this weathered brick, period pub in the picture-postcard Denham village.

The bar and eating area, welding together seamlessly, are rustic-smart with natural wood tables. The rear garden is delightful, ideal for an al fresco lunch.

The daily changing menu offers modern, quite imaginative brasserie cuisine without being over-elaborate or fussy. Gnocchi, made from champ potato, are successfully flavoured with fresh broad beans and melted Oxfordshire blue cheese. Or there is the perennially popular oak-smoked bacon on bubble and squeak as an alternative starter or a light meal in itself. Good to see the attractive simplicity of potted brown shrimps.

Local and naturally reared ingredients feature in the pan-roasted Chiltern lamb rump on minted couscous or in the chargrilled organic pork chop served with boulangère potatoes.

There is a good choice of fresh fish, maybe grilled sea bass fillets on salade niçoise, or crispy salmon fishcake on wilted spinach with sorrel cream sauce, or else smoked haddock on asparagus and blue cheese Boxty potato.

Above-average wines by the glass include a fine Grüner Veltlinger from Austria and an Omra Pinot Noir from Western Australia. If you are in the mood for the rich chocolate fondant, do try the Banyuls, the perfect sweet red wine for this dessert.

Speciality food: Oak-smoked bacon on bubble and squeak
Draught beers: Wadworth 6X, Oxford Bitter
Average wine price by the glass: £3.80

Licensees: David and Becky Salisbury
Last orders for dinner: 10 pm
Open every day
Closed for holidays: 25 and 26 December
Main courses: from £12
Private dining: up to 8
Beer garden
Children welcome before 7 pm
Wheelchair access

DODDISCOMBSLEIGH, DEVON

Nobody Inn ★

Doddiscombsleigh, Nr Exeter, Devon EX6 7PS
Tel. 01647 252 394 Fax 01647 252 978
e-mail: info@nobodyinn.co.uk   **MAP 1** D4

THE first glimpse of this inn's 16th-century exterior, with its crooked chimney, creates an expectation that is rewarded once inside. Low ceilings with solid, blackened beams, gleaming copper pans, polished wooden tables and a jumble of chairs and settles warm the soul as efficiently as the log fire in winter or the serried ranks of more than 240 whiskies behind the bar.

The walls, littered with certificates and awards, separate cosy rooms and corners where you can read the day's papers over a pint of local ale or enjoy some very fine cooking at keen prices.

The bar menu has much to ponder: duck liver pâté with tomato and apple chutney; gravadlax with smoked prawns and garlic mayonnaise; a sublime salad of smoked eel with crispy bacon and new potatoes, or the Nobody soup, served, one suspects, from a well-used stockpot.

Main courses are no less fulfilling: wild boar and apple sausages on cheese and garlic mashed potato; duck leg confit with roasted figs and balsamic vinegar, or monkfish, salmon and tiger prawns in a coconut broth. In the evening a separate menu has slightly more formal and ambitious choices.

Puddings are a catalogue of comfort, but it is the list of 40 or so cheeses that bewilder. On any given day there will be about 20 available from artisan producers from the surrounding counties. Try the unique Harbourne Blue if available. Like the items on the passionately compiled wine list of more than 800 bins, cheeses are available to buy over the counter or by mail order.

Speciality food: West Country cheese
Draught beers: Nobody Bitter (Branscombe), Otter Bitter
Average wine price by the glass: £2.70

Licensee: Nicholas Borst-Smith
Last orders for dinner: 9 pm (10 pm in bar)
Open every day
Closed for holidays: 25 and 26 December
Main courses: from £9.50
Private dining: 12-25 (Tuesday to Thursday only)
Beer garden
Accommodation: 7 rooms
Children over 14 welcome
Limited wheelchair access

DOWNTON, HAMPSHIRE

Royal Oak

GASTROPUB

Christchurch Road, Downton, Nr. Lymington, Hants SO41 OLA
Tel. 01590 642 297
e-mail: enquiries@oakdownton.freeuk.com   **MAP 2** A5

THE black painted woodwork of the Royal Oak stands out on the A337 midway between Christchurch and Lymington. Inside is a beamed, low-ceilinged bar area with tartan carpets, wheelback chairs and open fires.

The recently restored restaurant has large windows and plenty of space between the tables. There is also a terrace where during the summer, on Bank Holidays and Sunday evenings, a hog roast might be under way. Telephone to check availability if you would like to join in. There are sandwiches and ploughman's until 6pm, as well as children's meals.

The menu offers starters such as red onion and goat's cheese tart or pâté of the day, followed by salmon fishcakes and various steaks, but the main event is the daily blackboard choice.

You might start with Greek salad and feta cheese or else seared scallops with chilli and cucumber butter, and go on to veal cutlets with Taleggio and caper tomato sauce, or beef Wellington, or whole sea bass marinated in balsamic vinegar.

There is an oriental influence with, say, duck breast marinated in sweet chilli and teriyaki and served with egg noodles garnished with crunchy sliced capsicums, green beans and red onion.

Desserts should not be missed: try the mango cheesecake or strawberry brûlée. Fifteen wines are available by the glass. Willing and efficient service is provided by a young team dressed in black. It gets busy, so booking is recommended.

Speciality food: Lamb confit with flageolets and pork sausage
Draught beers: Gales HSB, Ringwood Bitter
Average wine price by the glass: £3.25

Licensee: Anthony Hughes Onslow
Last orders for dinner: 9pm (Fri and Sat 9.30pm)
Open every day
Main courses: from £6.90
Private dining: 50-80
Beer garden
Children welcome
Wheelchair access

DREWSTEIGNTON, DEVON

Drewe Arms

GASTROPUB

The Square, Drewsteignton, Exeter, Devon EX6 6QN
Tel. 01647 281 224 Fax 01647 281 179

MAP 1 C4

DRIVING along sleepy, narrow country lanes, following signs to Castle Drogo, one suddenly comes across this most atmospheric village square, with imposing church tower at one end, and next to it, the long thatched pub known to many as Aunt Mabel's. Mabel Mudge, affectionately dubbed 'Britain's oldest landlady', ran the pub for seventy-five years until her retirement, at the age of ninety-nine, in 1994.

Happily, the interior has remained pretty much unchanged for decades, save for the odd coat of paint here and there. There is no bar as such, more a room with a couple of small hatches and a collection of bottles and ales tapped from the cask.

There are many reminders of Mabel, not least her kitchen, which now serves as a lovely dining-room, complete with her old bespoke Rayburn stove. Food is solid and satisfying. Lunchtimes bring filled jacket potatoes, sandwiches and ploughman's, along with a few blackboard specials such as slow-braised lamb shank or a Ruby red steak pie.

Evenings tend to be more formal, with printed menus offering a wide range of competently prepared dishes that might include marinated sardines with a plum tomato and pesto salad, or pan-fried escalope of veal with mango and chilli.

Blackboard puddings such as seasonal berries cheesecake or rhubarb and ginger crumble strike the right note.

Speciality food: Lamb rump, rösti, prune and armagnac sauce
Draught beers: Otter Bitter, Butcombe Bitter
Average wine price by the glass: £3.15

Licensees: David and Lisa Jermey
Last orders for dinner: 9 pm
Open every day
Main courses: from £12
Private dining: 12-24
Beer garden
Accommodation: 2 rooms
Children welcome

EAST CHILTINGTON, EAST SUSSEX

Jolly Sportsman

GASTROPUB

Chapel Lane, East Chiltington, East Sussex BN7 3BA
Tel./Fax 01273 890 400
e-mail: info@thejollysportsman.com   **MAP 2** D4

WITH a car park full of vehicles the total value of which would be monumental, we are in the veritable buckle of the gentleman farmer/stockbroker belt, and Bruce Wass and his young team are there to give them what they want. Chalk boards cover the walls, advertising a huge array of wines, myriad malt whiskies and even 'champagne' from a nearby vineyard, while a row of barrels behind a somewhat token bar area offers a range of gravity-fed local bitters and guest ales.

Although the physical façade of the country pub is maintained, a sea of tables throughout the bar and dining areas, fresh and appealing in their simple attire, with prints and flowers for a splash of colour, indicates in no uncertain terms what the Jolly Sportsman is really about these days. Yet the atmosphere remains delightfully friendly and relaxed. You are here to enjoy yourself and nothing about the fine selection of interesting dishes from Richard Willis and David Phillips will detract from that.

A few tapas style pre-starters (cured lomo, guindillas and boquerones) is a clever idea to set the juices flowing. What follows is a European gastronomic constitution: Irish oysters, liver parfait with onion marmalade and brioche, risotto 'primavera', rabbit confit with black pudding, Cornish fish and a wealth of local produce like herbed Ditchling lamb with aubergines, asparagus and game in season. A courgette flower stuffed with goat's cheese, the whole vegetable deep-fried in a crisp light batter, is a test for any kitchen and it was carried off with aplomb, a typical insight into the care and imagination which makes your meal such an enjoyable occasion. Separate vegetarian menu, too.

Speciality food: Rabbit confit with black pudding and chickpeas
Draught beers: Dark Star Brewery Bitter, Itchen Valley Bitter
Average wine price by the glass: £2.70

Licensee: Bruce Wass
Last orders for dinner: 9 pm
Closed: Sunday evening, Monday
Closed for holidays: 24-26 December
Set lunch: from £12
Main courses: from £13.85
Private dining: 8-20
Beer garden
Children welcome
Wheelchair access

EAST COKER, SOMERSET

Helyar Arms ★

GASTROPUB

Moor Lane, East Coker, Nr. Yeovil, Somerset BA22 9JR
Tel. 01935 862 332 Fax 01935 864 129
e-mail: info@helyar.arms.co.uk   **MAP 1** E3

ONE of the prettiest Somerset villages, East Coker has several claims to fame. T.S. Eliot's family came from here and his ashes are interred in the local church. Explorer William Dampier, who discovered the western coast of Australia, was born here in 1651. Coker cloth, made from locally grown flax and used by the Royal Navy for more than 200 years, was woven by villagers until the late 19th century. The Helyar Arms dates back to 1468 and is allegedly named after Archdeacon Helyar, chaplain to Elizabeth I.

The inn makes good use of local produce: prime quality beef is reared by farmers in and around East Coker, bread is produced by an artisan baker using traditional methods, and Montgomery Cheddar, Dorset Blue Vinny and Somerset Brie make up the cheese board. Menus offer an appealing choice of dishes with pleasingly short descriptions. Spicy chicken won tons turn out to be crisp squares layered, rather than filled, with a tasty mixture of diced chicken, spring onion and mayonnaise.

Specials will invariably feature a fish dish, perhaps firm fillets of red mullet simply cooked and ideally matched with saffron mash and spinach. A well-balanced à la carte menu might include starters of grilled East Coker field mushrooms with black pudding, parsley and garlic bread, or venison terrine. Follow perhaps with baked honey and Guinness ham hock with watercress mash, or try the massive mixed grill.

What better way to finish than with an almond and plum tart: deliciously moist frangipane with sweet, juicy fruit accompanied by excellent vanilla ice-cream.

Speciality food: Lamb chops with garlic and rosemary potatoes
Draught beers: Butcombe, London Pride
Average wine price by the glass: £3.50

Licensee: Ian McKerracher
Last orders for dinner: 9.30 pm (Sunday 9 pm)
Open every day
Main courses: from £9
Private dining: up to 39
Beer garden
Accommodation: 6 rooms
Children welcome
Limited wheelchair access

EAST DEAN, WEST SUSSEX

Star and Garter

GASTROPUB

**East Dean, Nr. Chichester, West Sussex PO18 OJG
Tel. 01243 811 318**

MAP 2 C4

ALLOW yourself to be taken back in time in this 300-year-old brick and flint pub in a peaceful Downland village. The pine tables are generously spaced, and there is a terrace for dining outdoors. In summer there is often a shellfish bar displaying the choices.

All appetites are catered for, with an additional special bar menu at lunchtime providing a traditional range such as ham, egg and chips, liver and bacon or ploughman's.

For hearty eaters, fruits de mer come to the South Downs and while £75 may sound steep for the 'Garter Platter', the Selsey crab, whole lobster, hand carved smoked salmon, a dozen very large crevettes and prawns in their shells, will easily feed four. If you prefer, any of these constituents can be ordered individually.

There is plenty to choose from apart from the seafood, such as courgette and Parmesan soup or small asparagus, lightly grilled, tasting really fresh and tender. Then perhaps Thai chicken curry with saffron sauce or the memorable fillet of cod with crispy beer batter, which is served with excellent chips and a home-made tartare sauce.

Puddings range from refreshing fruit sorbets to the substantial bread and butter pudding with plump sultanas. There are some 11 wines by the glass – try the Malvasia Toro 2003 – or a bottle list leaning heavily towards white wines. There are three spacious and comfortabe en-suite bedrooms, one with a four-poster.

Speciality food: Seafood
Draught beers: Ballards Best, Arundel Gauntlet
Average wine price by the glass: £3.75

**Licensee: Oliver Ligterwood
Last orders for dinner: 10 pm (Fri and Sat 10.30 pm)
Open every day
Main courses: from £9.50
Private dining: 40-50
Beer garden
Accommodation: 3 rooms**
Children welcome
Wheelchair access

EAST END, HAMPSHIRE

East End Arms

GASTROPUB

**Lymington Road, East End, Nr. Lymington, Hants SO41 5SY
Tel. 01590 626 223**

MAP 2 B5

THE East End Arms, dating back to about 1780, belongs to John Illsley, bass player of Dire Straits, who lives nearby and bought it to ensure it continued its tradition as a haven for the locals. Indeed the saloon bar seems untouched by time or fashion.

The dining-room is hung with black and white photographs of rock, pop and screen stars from the Dire Straits era. Outside is a pretty and popular garden with hefty trestle tables and a giant parasol to combat showers. The place can be very busy; booking is advisable.

Previously a fishmonger, the chef certainly knows where to buy and how to cook his seafood. And 'Catch of the Day' could even bring turbot or lobster.

There is an intriguing and commendable element to the menu in that all first courses are the same price, as are the main courses and the puddings.

The theme running through the cooking is one of really fresh ingredients accurately handled and not over-complicated. Grilled Portobello mushrooms are filled with smoked haddock while the chicken pâté is accompanied by onion toast. The more substantial dishes include slow-roasted leg of lamb with coriander; fillet of bream that has a clear, super-fresh flavour and fine texture, and rib-eye steak.

Home-made desserts include lime tart, chocolate mousse and a bread and butter pudding with plump raisins and fresh cream.

Speciality food: Seafood
Draught beers: Ringwood Best, Archers Bitter
Average wine price by the glass: £3.25

**Licensee: John Illsley
Last orders for dinner: 9.30 pm
Open every day
Main courses: from £8 (lunch), £12 (dinner)
Beer garden**
Children welcome
Wheelchair access

EAST GRINSTEAD, WEST SUSSEX

Gravetye Manor

Nr. East Grinstead, West Sussex RH19 4LJ
Tel. 01342 810 567 Fax 01342 810 080
e-mail: info@gravetyemanor.co.uk   **MAP 2** D4

SET IN the rolling Sussex countryside, where pheasants, foxes and squirrels abound, Gravetye Manor offers excellent solid meals of manorial proportions, with roast meats and sturdy vegetables, but you will also find food that takes inspiration from the artistic tendency of modern gastronomy.

A periodically changing, varied selection of dishes on the set lunch and dinner menus reflects a passion for using the very best and freshest of first-rate ingredients, including local game, and for bringing out its innate qualities, whether through traditional or more exotic combinations.

The results can be a real delight, like the huge roasted scallops with coriander, caramelised garlic and a reduction based on Port and sesame, or sautéd red mullet and crab tempura, the turbot fillet with oxtail, or moist and tender duck breast which is glazed and served in its jus with roasted onions and rösti.

Meanwhile, the tradition of country-house eating is maintained with roasts as good as you will find anywhere and, of course, with monumental individual Yorkshire puddings

The smart, attentive and uncondescending service is a perfect complement to the surroundings

Their pride: Roasted Scottish scallops and langoustines with sea asparagus, tomato and basil butter
Inexpensive wines: Mâcon Lugny Les Genevièvres, Louis Latour 2002, £17; Condado de Haza Crianza 2001, £32

Proprietors: Andrew Russell and Mark Raffan
Last orders for dinner: 9.30 pm
Open every day
Set lunch: from £24
Set dinner: from £41
Private dining: 6-20
Accommodation: 18 rooms
Limited wheelchair access

EAST LAVANT, WEST SUSSEX

Royal Oak

GASTROPUB

**Pook Lane, East Lavant, Nr. Chichester, W Sussex PO18 0AX
Tel. 01243 527 434 Fax 01243 775 062
e-mail: ro@thesussexpub.co.uk**

MAP 2 C5

YOU just know it is going to be good the minute you cross the threshold as you are greeted by the efficiently cheerful serving staff. A welcoming hubbub comes from the bar and a happy hum radiates from delighted diners at their scrubbed tables. By the time your basket of excellent breads and the bowl of marinated olives arrive, you will be joining in.

Augmented by a few blackboard daily specials, the menu is a delightful mix of styles from just about every culinary horizon, from wood-roasted Spanish peppers, to chicken kebabs with tzatziki and peperonata dips, a highly recommended oriental duck with a ginger and honey dressing, a veal schnitzel with Parmesan potatoes, or loin of fresh, meaty monkfish with Bombay potatoes, fried pak choi and a delicate, creamy coconut and coriander sauce. If cross-culture cuisine holds the fort here, the home guard is well represented by soups, fish and fine, fat chips with mushy peas, or calf's liver with bubble and squeak.

Technical ability and unbridled imagination, along with attractive presentation, come together to produce consistently dependable delights with more than a touch of class, exuding well-defined savours from interesting combinations.

Even that often poorly produced dessert the profiterole with hot chocolate sauce is properly treated here, along with classic cousins such as apple Tatin, chocolate and orange tart and sticky toffee pudding, and this epitomises the care and skill on display. If you do not manage to back a winner at nearby Goodwood, it's odds-on you will be on one here.

Speciality food: Modern British cooking
Draught beers: King and Barnes Sussex Bitter, Badgers Bitter
Average wine price by the glass: £3.10

**Licensees: Lisa and Nick Sutherland
Last orders for dinner: 9.30 pm
Open every day
Main courses: from £11.50
Beer garden
Accommodation: 6 rooms**
Children welcome
Wheelchair access

EAST WITTON, NORTH YORKSHIRE

Blue Lion

GASTROPUB

East Witton, Nr. Leyburn, North Yorkshire DL8 4SN
Tel. 01969 624 273 Fax 01969 624 189
e-mail: enquiries@thebluelion.co.uk   **MAP 5** D4

THE grandfather clock stopped ticking at 11.38 but it seems as if nothing much has changed in this flagstoned bar for a couple of centuries or more. With its waiting staff in long white aprons, the entire place enjoys that delightfully lived-in look of the authentic country inn in this quiet corner of Wensleydale.

The blackboard menu can be enjoyed throughout, making use of the secluded garden in summer, the bar, or a more formal but equally homely dining-room, and the available choices appear to go on forever.

Enticing starters include baked goat's cheese on hazelnut brioche, breast of pigeon with roast fig and quince chutney, salads such as scallop with crispy bacon and grain mustard or black pudding with smoked bacon, shallots and a poached egg.

Copious main courses rely on fine ingredients simply treated and presented to bring out their natural qualities. Try pan-fried breast of chicken stuffed with blue Wensleydale cheese, or sautéd fillet of pork with crispy belly, black pudding and a honey and apple sauce, or a cassoulet of goose leg confit with Toulouse sausage.

There are fish dishes such as poached fillet of smoked haddock with leek and mushroom sauce, or monkfish wrapped in Parma ham with a tapenade sauce. And the varied puddings are also a sheer delight. This is traditional home cooking on a grand scale that complements the authenticity of the setting.

Speciality food: Traditional Anglo-French cooking
Draught beers: Black Sheep, Theakstons
Average wine price by the glass: £4.25

Licensee: Paul Klein
Last orders for dinner: 9.15 pm
Open every day
Closed for holidays: 25 December (food only)
Main courses: from £12.95
Private dining: 16-40
Beer garden
Accommodation: 12 rooms
Children welcome
Wheelchair access

EASTBOURNE, EAST SUSSEX

Mirabelle Restaurant Grand Hotel

King Edwards Parade, Eastbourne, East Sussex BN21 4EQ
Tel. 01323 412 345 Fax 01323 412 233

MAP 2 D5

RESOLUTELY old-fashioned, this imposing grande dame of Eastbourne hotels sets itself apart geographically and qualitatively at the far end of the promenade, its ornate frontage and marble-columned halls stoically defying the march of time.

Although the Mirabelle Restaurant was promoted as an almost autonomous operation some fifteen years ago, when the hotel was under the same ownership as its sister establishment in London, no effort was made to differentiate it, architecturally speaking, from the rest of the building and the columns, heavy drapes and patterned carpets seem now to belong to another era.

Service, too, is obviously intended to follow archaic lines, but the good humour of formally dressed yet casual young staff creates a more easygoing atmosphere in which to sample the food of chef Roser, once a celebrated member of the gastronomic jet-set.

While an enjoyable meal is still to be had here (and a three-course lunch for under £20 in surroundings like these has to be excellent value), there are flaws. Half of the superbly fresh, plump mussels, served in a rich cream sauce of red peppers, fennel and saffron, were practically unopened, for example.

Meat dishes, many from local sources, are well handled and the generous garnishes display powerful, natural flavours, but there is a certain lack of delicacy and finesse.

Their pride: Pike soufflé with langoustine sauce
Inexpensive wines: Chardonnay Baron Philippe de Rothschild Pays d'Oc £18; Merlot Baron Philippe de Rothschild Pays d'Oc £18

Proprietor: Elite Hotels
Last orders for dinner: 10 pm
Closed: Sunday and Monday
Closed for holidays: 2 weeks January
Set lunch: from £19
Set dinner: from £35
Private dining: up to 56
Accommodation: 152 rooms
Wheelchair access

EASTON GREY, WILTSHIRE

Whatley Manor The Dining Room ★

Easton Grey, Malmesbury, Wiltshire SN16 ORB
Tel. 01666 822 888 Fax 01666 826 120
e-mail reservations@whatleymanor.com   **MAP 1** E2

APPROACHED by a long tree-lined avenue, past manicured lawns and landscaped gardens, Whatley Manor is studied opulence.

The more formal dining-room is the stage for some complex, ambitious cooking. Open for dinner only, it offers a three-course, fixed-price menu from the carte and a tasting menu, both based on luxury ingredients which are often intricately combined.

The skill and panache of the cooking showed in two excellent amuse-bouches: beautifully flavoured breast of duck on a disc of celeriac, and light crisp samosas filled with mushroom duxelles.

Veal sweetbreads roasted, garnished with a poached quail's egg and the juices acidulated with caper, gherkin and parsley, were both impeccably executed and beautifully textured, though the wrapping of the sweetbreads in Parma ham was fussy and the quite strong flavour of the ham eclipsed that of the sweetbreads.

Less complex but more successful could be pan-fried foie gras with saucisse de Morteau, cauliflower purée and watercress salad.

For especially good main courses, go for the neatly titled Day Boat turbot roasted on the bone with langoustine tails and truffle Madeira essence, or roasted fillet of veal, tender, pink and subtly flavoured with porcini ravioli and rosemary foam.

An exceptional dessert features a chocolate soufflé and coffee ice-cream, iced granité and chocolate fondant.

Their pride: Breast of Anjou quail with Pedro Ximenaz sherry
Inexpensive wines: Chenin Blanc de Trafford (Stellenbosch) 2003, £32; Merlot Shaw and Smith (Adelaide Hills) 2003, £36

Proprietor: Christian Landolt
Last orders for dinner: 10 pm
Closed: Monday, Tuesday
Set dinner: from £60
Private dining: up to 28
Al fresco dining
Accommodation: 23 rooms
Wheelchair access

EMSWORTH, HAMPSHIRE

36 On The Quay ★

47 South Street, Emsworth, Hampshire PO10 7EG
Tel. 01243 375 592 Fax 01243 375 593

MAP 2 B5

DINING at water's edge is always relaxing and enjoyable, and perhaps nowhere more so than at this charming cottage, dating from the 17th century, which nestles on the fringe of Emsworth harbour.

It is all the more enjoyable when you sample the cooking of chef/proprietor Ramon Farthing, which concentrates on the main elements of the dishes, adding only restrained garnishes so as to allow free rein to the qualities of whatever they might be – veal, quail, duck, scallops, or locally caught fish such as brill.

The essential originality of Ramon's food is shown in its clever combinations, such as the apple and asparagus reduction that might accompany scallops. Notable, too, is that no aspect of a dish is treated with anything less than complete attention. For example, the so-called lasagne of calf's liver and spinach features miniature pancakes that are very carefully made wafer-thin.

What results from all this dedication is a series of appetisingly presented dishes of admirably uniform quality.

End your meal in style with one of the complex, mouth-watering desserts, among which even rhubarb, skilfully prepared, becomes something special.

Their pride: Pan-seared diver scallops with crisp organic pork belly on creamed parsnip with a warm vanilla dressing
Inexpensive wines: Red Bank Long Paddock Shiraz/Cabernet (Australia) 2002, £18.95; Boschenbal Chenin Blanc (South Africa) 2004, £17.95

Proprietors: Karen and Raymond Farthing
Last orders for dinner: 10 pm
Closed: Sunday and Monday
Closed for holidays: 3 weeks Jan, October half-term
Set lunch: from £17.95
Set dinner: from £42.95
Private dining: 8-12
Accommodation: 5 rooms
Wheelchair access

EMSWORTH, HAMPSHIRE

Fat Olives

30 South Street, Emsworth, Hampshire PO10 7EH
Tel. 01243 377 914
e-mail: info@fatolives.co.uk   **MAP 2** B5

NAMED after the Spanish queen olives served with aperitifs, Fat Olives is a no-nonsense, unpretentious establishment created from a 17th-century fisherman's cottage.

The menu is reserved in its descriptions, so when the dishes arrive, surprises are in store. Lightness and subtlety characterise all the cooking here, as in the partridge and wild venison from Balmoral that appear in season, but since the sea is only a few yards away, local seafood features strongly.

To begin with, the red mullet is a delight – perfectly cooked and accompanied by firmish risotto enhanced by tomato juice and just a touch of basil oil. The simply named fish stew is a revelation, with cod, haddock, brill and tiger prawns.

Yet the guinea fowl terrine should not be missed, marbled with breast meat and studded with firm peas and mint leaves, then encased in thin Serrano ham. Roast pheasant is a revelation, the breast meltingly tender, the confit of leg more fully flavoured and crisper in texture. It is served with a sublimely smooth and light bread sauce.

The baked chocolate mousse is nearer to a warm, gooey soufflé, with a marvellous thin crust, and complemented by Frangelica ice-cream. Plum and almond tart is a small roundel of light almond flavoured pastry, a central core of a whole plum giving a hint of sharpness to complement the lighter crème anglaise.

There is a small selection of thoughtfully chosen wines.

Their pride: Halibut, caraway crumb, confit fennel, orange sauce
Inexpensive wines: Sauvignon de Touraine Organic (Chile) 2003, £14; Bouchard Finlayson Blanc de Mer (South Africa) 2003, £18

Proprietors: Lawrence and Julia Murphy
Last orders for dinner: 9.15 pm
Closed: Sunday and Monday
Closed for holidays: 1 week Oct, 2 weeks Christmas
Set lunch: from £14.50
Main courses: from £12.50
Al fresco dining
Wheelchair access

EVERSHOT, DORSET

Acorn Inn

GASTROPUB

28 Fore Street, Evershot, Dorset DT2 0JW
Tel. 01935 83228 Fax 01935 83707
e-mail: stay@acorn-inn.co.uk   **MAP 1** E3

AT THIS 16th-century former coaching inn, immortalised as the Sow and Acorn in Thomas Hardy's *Tess of the d'Urbervilles*, two small dining-rooms promise a serious dining experience. Happily, much of what arrives lives up to expectations.

The focus on local produce, handled simply, pays off, with a well-balanced list of starters including grilled goat's cheese marinated in lime juice, sesame oil and chillies, or a delicious butterflied mackerel fillet topped with melted Parmesan on a bed of fresh tomato and red onion salsa. One nice touch is that a petit pain per person is freshly baked and delivered with salted butter curls.

Main courses include roasted breast of guinea fowl with a white wine, tarragon and green grape velouté, and a surprisingly tender schnitzel of English veal topped with witheringly crisp bacon and a terse salsa verde sitting on a creamy bed of mashed potato. A blackboard displays daily fish specials.

Some of the classic desserts offer an interesting twist on the norm, such as a ginger panna cotta with rhubarb compote.

A concise wine list contains several bottles priced at less than £20 and features wines from the owners' vineyards in South Africa.

Casual diners tend to be steered towards the public bar, where snacks include open sandwiches, salads, ploughman's, pies and burgers. A small terrace plus a beer garden provide fine-weather options.

Speciality food: Local produce
Draught beers: Draymans (Branscombe Vale), Nelson's Revenge
Average wine price by the glass: £4.50

Licensees: Todd Moffat, Sarah Dovey, Jonathan Raggett
Last orders for dinner: 9.30 pm
Open every day
Main courses: from £14.50
Private dining: 12-20
Beer garden
Accommodation: 10 rooms
Children welcome
Limited wheelchair access

EXETER, DEVON

Michael Caines at the Royal Clarence Hotel

Cathedral Yard, Exeter, Devon EX1 1HD
Tel. 01392 310 031 Fax 01392 310 032
e-mail: tables@michaelcaines.com   **MAP 1** D4

DESPITE some more modern shopfronts overlooking the green, a timeless appeal embraces the approach to the grand old lady of Exeter, the Royal Clarence Hotel, now owned by celebrated chef Michael Caines and business partner Andrew Brownsword.

There is little doubt the hotel's fortunes must have ebbed and flowed over the years, but since this eponymous restaurant, with frosted windows overlooking the cathedral, has opened, things can seldom have looked better. With a pedigree honed at Gidleigh Park, Michael Caines's vision for Exeter's smartest restaurant exudes quality and restrained style.

The dining-room is bright and designed along clean lines, with polished floor, modern art and lighting, and crisply laid tables which are separated by screens.

There is much to laud here with menus featuring perhaps a salad of quail with crispy belly pork and celeriac remoulade, or a ragout of peas, fennel and pine-nuts accompanying some extremely fine local lamb.

Desserts show equal panache, and the petits fours accompanying an excellent espresso were faultless.

Although most of the wines, apart from the house selections, are above £20, the fine list contains some real gems. Worth checking out, too, are the very good value fixed-price lunch and dinner menus.

Their pride: Fish
Inexpensive wines: Delibori Pinot Bianco/Pinot Grigio (Verona) 2004, £16.50; Sandford Shiraz-Cabernet (Victoria) 2002, £16.50

Proprietors: Michael Caines and Andrew Brownsword
Last orders for dinner: 10 pm
Closed: Sunday
Set lunch: from £12
Set dinner: from £22
Private dining: 10-80
Accommodation: 53 rooms
Wheelchair access

EXFORD, SOMERSET

Crown Hotel ★

GASTROPUB

Exmoor National Park, Exford, Somerset TA24 7PP
Tel. 01643 831 554 Fax 01643 831 665
e-mail: info@crownhotelexmoor.co.uk   **MAP 1** D3

IN ONE of West Somerset's prettiest villages, this 17th-century coaching inn is an ideal base for touring Exmoor National Park. The food in the welcoming, unspoilt bar with its hunting prints, belies the modest surroundings.

Seafood is a magnet here, a lot of it sourced from Falmouth. The sea bass is line-caught and has a proper firm texture.

The tian of crab, spanking fresh and served with dressed French leaves, is an excellent starter, and if you are in the mood for meat, the juicy grilled pork chop with a red wine jus is succulent, served with champ.

For a dessert with a difference, blood orange tart is exemplary, or there is passion fruit and pomegranate gratin or else banana and Bailey's parfait.

For lighter choices appealing to those who want a single dish, the offerings are just as good: moules marinière, dressed crab salad, marinated belly pork.

The more elegant and restful restaurant has more gastronomic pretensions, as in butternut squash and fennel seed risotto, baked courgette flowers with a ratatouille of tomato and pepper and marinated shin of Cornish beef.

The wines show a fine balance of good-value selections by the glass (South African Chenin Blanc, Australian Shiraz) with some aristocratic burgundies and clarets by the bottle.

Speciality food: Cornish pan-fried sea bass, bacon mash
Draught beers: Exmoor Ale, St. Austell
Average wine price by the glass: £3.50

Licensee: Hugo Jeune
Last orders for dinner: 9 pm
Open every day
Set dinner: from £32.50
Main courses: from £10
Private dining: up to 40
Beer garden
Accommodation: 17 rooms
Children welcome
Wheelchair access

FAIRFORD, GLOUCESTERSHIRE

Allium ★

1 London Street, Market Place, Fairford, Glos. GL7 4AH
Tel. 01285 712 200
e-mail: restaurant@allium.uk.net   **MAP 1** F2

JAMES GRAHAM is a fine, intelligent chef who believes that 'good food is small things correctly done'. Exceptional cooking is based on assured technique, and Allium's strength is that James and his wife, Erica, have brought the same kitchen team from the Wickham Vineyard restaurant in Hampshire to their new venture.

The restaurant is comfortable and elegant yet unpretentious, with a fine outlook through the bow window to the market-place. Erica is a natural at front-of-house, greeting customers warmly but unaffectedly. Gastronomic interest is high, but this is not a stuffy place and children are very welcome. The relaxed customers are here for the pleasures of the table. They will not be disappointed.

At lunchtime, pan-fried mackerel is impeccably fresh, garnished ideally with a subtly flavoured crêpe Parmentier, while pea and mint soup has beautifully defined flavours. A truly star dish is the slow-roasted belly of organic pork, moist yet crisp and finely accompanied by lyonnaise potatoes with leek and prunes. The faultless vanilla crème brûlée is memorable.

The set-price dinner moves to a higher gear with, say, langoustine bisque with its own ravioli, scallops with celeriac and apple and pan-fried turbot with a fricassee of vegetables and herb nage. Another great dish is assiette of suckling pig.

Service is kind, orchestrated by Erica with great aplomb, and she also has a great nose for quality and value in the finely selected wine list. Here you can drink very well for under £20 a bottle.

Their pride: Assiette of suckling pig
Inexpensive wines: Roero Arneis, Prunotto 2003, £23; St. Chinian, Domaine de Gabelas 2001, £19.50

Proprietors: James and Erica Graham
Last orders for dinner: 9 pm
Closed: Monday and Tuesday
Closed for holidays: 24-26 December; 2 weeks January
Set lunch: from £17.50
Set dinner: from £20
Children welcome
Wheelchair access

FAIRSTEAD, ESSEX

Square and Compasses

GASTROPUB

Fuller Street, Fairstead, Essex CM3 2BB
Tel. 01245 361 477
e-mail: enquiries@squareandcompasses.co.uk   **MAP 2** E2

YOU COULD be forgiven for thinking you were in part of the Natural History Museum at this low-ceilinged, little crossroads pub in a hidden corner of rural Essex, where myriad local wildlife sits stuffed and mounted amid a wealth of local memorabilia.

A word of warning: the portions served up by chef/patron Simon Daniel are huge – great groaning plates of colourful, fresh, appealing and interesting food with Asian influences often spicing up fine local fish and meats. Starters, large or small, such as prawns, potted shrimps, cod roe, Orkney herring, soup or deep-fried Brie, also act as bar snacks, while the dozen or so regularly changing main courses are chalked up over the bar.

There are vast vats of moules marinières; really spicy tiger prawns in coconut milk and chilli; a minted lamb steak of Desperate Dan proportions with rosemary potatoes; ginger and lemongrass chicken on an oriental stir-fry; 'traditional' beef Stroganoff with saffron and coriander; fillet of salmon with sweet basil pesto. All are tempting and full of punchy, no-nonsense flavours when the great plates are borne to your table.

Thinking of copping out with a plate of greenery? Forget it. Nothing prissy here either, with local pigeon breasts, bacon and croutons garnishing an enormous salad.

Cosy English puddings are on offer for the real trenchermen, but it takes a brave person to tackle a crumble, bread and butter pudding or a chocolate and raspberry truffle, good as they are, after such a feast.

Speciality food: Game in season
Draught beers: Ridleys Prospect, Ridleys IPA
Average wine price by the glass: £2.70

Licensee: Simon Daniel
Last orders for dinner: 9.30pm (Saturday 10pm)
Closed: Sunday evening, Monday except Bank Hols
Main courses: from £8.90
Private dining: 12-26
Beer garden
Children welcome
Wheelchair access

FARNBOROUGH, KENT

Chapter One ★

Farnborough Common, Locksbottom, Farnborough, Kent BR6 8NF
Tel. 01689 854 848 Fax 01689 858 439
e-mail: info@chaptersrestaurants.com   MAP 2 D3

THE OUTSIDE might be mock-Tudor, but inside all is modish modernity, including the French-influenced cuisine, in which the emphasis is on vivid but not aggressive flavours.

With this in mind, pan-fried black bream might come with a very tasty ragout of butter beans, girolles, cockles and squid in red wine, while delicate poached mallard could be given a lift by its confit of leg and raisin jus.

A boudin of sweetbreads and ham hock proves to be a successful combination, its excellent flavours developed by a garnish of caramelised apple with a raspberry and walnut salad.

Desserts come close to perfection, as, for example, in a lemon tart accompanied by a sorbet of crème fraîche and an amazingly light millefeuille of passion fruit.

The cellar is perfectly in tune with the kitchen, offering a good range of judiciously chosen bottles at very fair prices.

The restaurant obviously does very good business and can be quite full even at lunchtime on Saturdays, but the well-trained young staff provide swift, polished and always friendly service.

Their pride: Ravioli of lobster, cauliflower purée and lobster cognac sauce
Inexpensive wines: La Place Chardonnay Vin de Pays d'Oc 2003, £15.95; Baron Phillipe de Rothschild Merlot 2002, £18.50

Proprietor: Selective Restaurants Ltd
Last orders for dinner: Mon-Thurs 10 pm, Fri & Sat 11 pm, Sun 9.30 pm
Open every day
Closed for holidays: 1st week January
Set lunch: from £16.50
Set dinner: from £26.95
Private dining: 20-55
Al fresco dining
Limited wheelchair access

FARNDON, CHESHIRE

Farndon Arms

GASTROPUB

High Street, Farndon, Cheshire CH3 6PU
Tel. 01829 270 570
e-mail: info@farndonarms.com

MAP 3 D2

THOUGH just eight miles from Chester, Farndon is a peaceful Cheshire village with a delightful winding High Street leading down to the River Dee that divides England from Wales. The bluffs along the river bank are rich in the red sandstone that is the building material for Farndon's part-Saxon St. Chad's church.

The Farndon Arms is a fine blend of the main bar – with horse brasses and a pool table – and a comfortable, formal restaurant upstairs with Regency striped wallpapers, gilded mirrors and arrangements of fresh flowers.

Martin Bouchier owns and runs the inn, together with his parents. There is no concession to trendy gastropub décor or attitudes here, just fresh and wholesome food to suit all tastes.

In the bar, the hub of village life, traditional fare is to the fore: barbecued spare ribs; beer-battered cod, chips and mushy peas; well-hung rump steak; curry of the day or meat and potato pie are typical of the changing blackboard menus.

In the restaurant the dishes are more ambitious, based on good regional ingredients with an occasional foray into the exotic. Welsh rarebit with English grain mustard followed by seared loin of Black Country pork with black pudding are good choices. Then there is Chinese sea bass with stir-fry vegetables and pak choi.

The wine lists sports fine bottles, notably Chablis Vaillons (Fèvre) and Australian Old Vine Shiraz (Grant Burge). Immaculate housekeeping in the seven bedrooms and good breakfasts.

Speciality food: Halibut with buttered prawns
Draught beers: Adnams, Thwaites
Average wine price by the glass: £2.90

Licensee: Martin Bouchier
Last orders for dinner: 9.30 pm
Open every day
Closed for holidays: 26 December
Main courses: from £10
Private dining: 8-46
Al fresco dining
Accommodation: 7 en-suite rooms
Children welcome
Wheelchair access

FARNHAM, DORSET

Museum Inn ★　　　　　　　　　GASTROPUB

Farnham, Nr. Blandford Forum, Dorset DT11 8DE
Tel. 01725 516 261 Fax 01725 516 988
e-mail: enquiries@museuminn.co.uk　　　　　　**MAP 1** E3

EASILY found down a lane off the A354 Salisbury to Blandford
Forum road, the Museum Inn has, in few short years, achieved
almost legendary status in these parts. Built in the 17th century
by the splendidly-named General Augustus Lane Fox Pitt-Rivers,
the part-thatched inn offered accommodation to those visiting the
now defunct 'father of modern archaeology' museum nearby.

A new millennium brought new impetus and vision in the shape of
Vicky Elliot and partner Mark Stephenson, who renovated the
building and reopened in spring 2001. The result is both fresh and
homely: stone flags, pale yellow walls, good-sized wooden tables
and chairs, old prints and stuffed animals dominate the bar,
which leads to a small conservatory, the walls covered in hunting
trophies, and on to a little garden terrace.

There is also a lofty dining-room – perfect for parties and where
residents have breakfast – and a lounge full of books and freshly
cut flowers. Cooking is assured and of a uniformly high standard
and the brown paper menus are amended twice a day, usually
offering around eight starters and main courses (plus sandwiches
at lunchtime), half-a-dozen puddings and cheese.

The menu reads like a shopping list of enticing ingredients: Parma
ham; crostini; peppered smoked mackerel; avocado, Roquefort
cheese and so on. While not particularly of the region, produce is
often organic and of excellent quality. Pork belly has become
something of a signature and game appears in season. There is a
good cellar, too, with keenly-priced bin ends, helpful tasting notes
and plenty of half-bottles, magnums and vintage ports.

Speciality food: Slow-roasted belly pork
Draught beers: Ringwood Best Bitter, Hopback Summer Lightning
Average wine price by the glass: £3

Licensees: Vicky Elliott and Mark Stephenson
Last orders for dinner: 9.30 pm (Sunday 9 pm)
Open every day
Closed for holidays: 25 Dec, 31 Dec (evening only)
Main courses: from £14
Private dining: 12-32
Beer garden
Accommodation: 8 rooms
Children over 5 welcome
Wheelchair access

FARNHAM ROYAL, BUCKINGHASHIRE

King of Prussia ★

GASTROPUB

Blackpond Lane, Farnham Royal, Bucks SL2 3EG
Tel. 01753 643 006   Fax 01753 648 645
e-mail: info@tkop.co.uk   **MAP 2** C3

THE KING of Prussia, an old Victorian pub in a quiet, leafy lane, is a good place to enjoy lunch al fresco while the kids play safely. Inside, the bar has been sensitively modernised and the spacious, beamed dining-room is sometimes the setting for private dinners.

The draw here is the cooking of chef Andy Knight, who learned his craft with Phil Vickery, a partner in the pub, at the Castle Hotel restaurant in Taunton.

Though the bar and restaurant food have a no-nonsense style, with dishes such as dressed Cornish crab or chargrilled Barnsley chop, Knight's class at the stove shows through at every stage. Lightly textured asparagus and pecorino ravioli tossed in pesto reveals a love of Mediterranean flavours. Creamy chicken, leek and pea pie is transformed into something rather special, delicate, tender and full of flavour. The baked egg custard tart with green apple crumble ice-cream is a classic.

Other good choices are smoked mackerel mousse, whitebait with chilli, coriander and lime mayonnaise, and simply grilled lemon sole with parsley and brown shrimp butter. The British farmhouse cheeses are also of high quality.

Wines by the glass and bottle match the style of the cooking admirably. There is usually a full fruity Sauvignon from the southern hemisphere and rich, powerful Shiraz from Australia. The young staff are attentive and as welcoming to chance callers arriving late as to local regulars.

Speciality food: Baked egg custard tart, apple crumble ice-cream
Draught beers: Fullers London Pride, Shepherd Neame Spitfire
Average wine price by the glass: £3.75

Licensees: David Gibbs, Chris Boot, Phil Vickery
Last orders for dinner: 9.45pm
Closed: Sunday evening
Main courses: from £14
Private dining: up to 18
Beer garden
Children welcome
Wheelchair access

FAVERHSAM, KENT

Read's Restaurant ★

Macknade Manor, Canterbury Road, Faversham, Kent ME13 8XE
Tel. 01795 535344 Fax 01795 591200
e-mail: enquiries@reads.com   **MAP 2** E3

DESCRIBED quite simply as a restaurant with rooms, this is in fact a rather splendid Georgian mansion sitting in several acres of its own grounds, which include a huge walled garden that provides much of the produce for the kitchen.

In addition to the home-grown items, such as the tomatoes that go into an appetiser of tomato soup with basil oil, a great deal else on the menu is from local sources, including fish from the nearby Kent ports and game in season

On a constantly changing carte, main courses might include roast pork with black pudding and root vegetables or a duck breast and confit with foie gras and lentils. Sea bass might come with saffron potatoes and Mediterranean vegetables with olive oil.

Your starter could be a masterly terrine of chicken and foie gras with their own apple jelly, pickled wild mushrooms and granary toast, home-baked of course.

Order cheese, and a plate with halved grapes and an ivy leaf arranged to resemble a bunch of grapes will arrive in advance of a good, varied selection of British cheeses, with a knowledgeable waiter to help you choose.

A serious wine list is strong in offerings from Bordeaux and Burgundy, but Australia also makes a good showing. There are 80 'Best Buys', with nothing over £25, and about 50 half-bottles.

Their pride: New season's lamb, roasted pink, with Dauphinoise potatoes and lamb sweetbreads
Inexpensive wines: Louis Latour Chardonnay Vin du Pays Côteaux de l'Ardèche 2004, £16; Pinot Noir Akarua Gullies 2001, £24

Proprietors: David and Rona Pitchford
Last orders for dinner: 9 pm
Closed: Sunday and Monday
Set lunch: from £21
Set dinner: from £45
Private dining: 6-20
Al fresco dining
Accommodation: 6 rooms
Wheelchair access

FERNHURST, SURREY

King's Arms ★

GASTROPUB

**Midhurst Road, Fernhurst, Nr. Haslemere, Surrey GU27 3HA
Tel./Fax 01428 652 005**

MAP 2 C4

LOW CEILINGS, dark beams, the inglenook fireplace and the whitewashed walls are all part of the traditional country pub atmosphere here. There is pretty garden with trestle tables and views over farmland and forest and, for private parties, there is a separate barn with a spit for roasting, say, a whole hog.

Chef/patron Michael Hirst, previously of Green's restaurant in Mayfair, creates a changing menu of mainly English dishes with an enlightened approach. His raw materials include locally grown vegetables, meat from local butchers and fish from Portsmouth.

First courses include the now rare Scotch woodcock – scrambled egg on toast with anchovies, for the uninitiated – the mysterious 'soup of the moment', or asparagus with Parma ham and rocket.

To follow, plump Sussex pork chop is truly succulent and tender and even removed from the bone. Alternatively, the splendidly fresh and accurately grilled fillet of plaice with shallot and grape sauce is a real treat. There might also be duck confit or other fresh fish such as Dover sole off the bone and roasted monkfish. Accompanying sauces are light and subtle.

Among the puddings, banana fool is memorable for smoothness and delicacy, flavoured with a touch of chocolate. Otherwise try the pear and raspberry crumble, or settle for the selection of English cheeses.

Definitely worth a detour.

Speciality food: Rib-eye steak and game in season
Draught beers: Ringwood Fortyniner, Horsham Bitter
Average wine price by the glass: £3.25

**Licensees: Michael and Annabel Hirst
Last orders for dinner: 9.30 pm
Closed: Sunday dinner
Closed for holidays: 25 December
Main courses: from £11
Private dining: up to 60
Beer garden**
Children over 14 welcome after 7 pm
Limited wheelchair access

FERRENSBY, NORTH YORKSHIRE

General Tarleton ★

GASTROPUB

Boroughbridge Rd., Ferrensby, North Yorkshire HG5 0PZ
Tel. 01423 340 284 Fax 01423 340 288
e-mail: gti@generaltarleton.co.uk   MAP 5 D4

'GOAT'S cheese and tomato tart and a pint o' Black Sheep, love.' In that one, simple request is the whole ethos of the gastropub movement summed up. It also nicely explains the style of the 'G.T.', where an unequivocal orientation towards dining happily does not impinge on the relaxed, pubby image of the traditional roadside coaching inn.

There are various permutations attached to the choice of venue and their corresponding menus, as well as special promotions such as the weekday 'Passion for Yorkshire', Friday fish specials and an excellent-value Sunday lunch.

Whether you choose the bar, a conservatory-style courtyard area or the cosily formal restaurant, high standards prevail.

Home-made black pudding, glazed Whitby haddock, slow-braised Masham Dales lamb, or sumptuous pot-roasted Gloucester Old Spot on a parsnip mash with local baby vegetables, will keep the traditionalists more than happy in the bar/brasserie.

A touch more refinement and originality in the restaurant sees the same Old Spot given a tropical treatment as a starter with paw-paw and cashew salad; chilli, lime and palm sugar alongside Nidderdale salmon; leek ravioli with a carrot, ginger and lemon-grass broth; seabass with roasted fennel and ginger or chargrilled fillet of Birstwith beef with blue cheese polenta.

Impressive desserts include warm banana and walnut pudding, and a fine trio of rhubarb brûlée, crumble and compote.

Speciality food: Fish dishes and local produce
Draught beers: Black Sheep, Timothy Taylor Landlord
Average wine price by the glass: £2.45

Licensees: John and Claire Topham
Last orders for dinner: 9.15 pm
Open every day
Set lunch: from £9.95
Set dinner: from £23.95 (Monday-Thursday)
Private dining: up to 40
Beer garden
Accommodation: 14 rooms
Children welcome

FLETCHING, EAST SUSSEX

Griffin Inn

GASTROPUB

High Street, Fletching, East Sussex TN22 3SS
Tel. 01825 722 890 Fax 01825 722 810
e-mail: thegriffininn@hotmail.com   **MAP 2** D4

YOU might well wonder, at this celebrated inn in the half-timbered village High Street – it is said to be the oldest licensed premises in the county – where they all come from. The constant activity testifies to the enduring enthusiasm and natural hospitality of Bridget and Nigel Pullan, twenty-six years here and now joined by their son, James.

The griffin may be no more than the stuff of folklore, but there is nothing remotely mythical about the goods produced by the kitchen brigade, who present an impressive range of original and appetising restaurant food as well as bar snacks.

A bowl of Sicilian olive oil poured out on arrival gives a clue to the style in store and, with prosciutto, Parmesan, dried tomatoes, feta and aïoli much in evidence throughout, the treatment of some fine local ingredients (lamb and veal especially) is noticeably Mediterranean.

Pepper-smothered bruschetta with feta to start with, perhaps, or some local asparagus or a baby spinach, potato and Gorgonzola soup. Lamb, veal, guinea fowl or a fillet of beef may follow in a variety of original guises, or a chunky tail of monkfish wrapped in prosciutto with a creamy, pungent, warm basil aïoli – one of their signature dishes and worthy of the status.

Crumbles, tarts, brûlées and other homely desserts will end your meal in more familiar style and there are well-kept regular and guest beers to enjoy in the comfortably homely lounges and bars or out in the acre of wooded grounds

Speciality food: Sussex lamb
Draught beers: Harveys Sussex Bitter, King and Co. Bitter
Average wine price by the glass: £3.50

Licensees: Bridget, Nigel and James Pullan
Last orders for dinner: 9.30 pm
Open every day
Closed for holidays: 25 December
Private dining: 10-30
Beer garden
Accommodation: 8 rooms
Children welcome
Wheelchair access

FORTON, LANCASHIRE

Bay Horse Inn

GASTROPUB

Forton, Nr. Lancaster, Lancashire LA2 0HL
Tel./Fax 01524 791 204

MAP 5 C4

DARK furnishings, dried hops and sporting prints of this old coaching inn, along with open fires in winter and a convivial, family atmosphere, provide a comfortably welcoming stop on any journey.

The owners are proudly Lancastrian, as full of pride for their local produce as they are of their origins. Much play is made of these prime ingredients, where Morecambe Bay shrimps, Fleetwood haddock, five-week matured beef and lamb from the Bowland moors and celebrated Goosnargh poultry are put to excellent use across a varied menu.

If potted crab, soused herrings and a cracking Lune Valley ham hock and chicken terrine represent the old guard among the starters, with a rich, meaty, slow-cooked lamb shank, Lancashire hot-pot or a fish pie to follow, more contemporary styles are never far behind and still hotly in pursuit of a regional identity.

Baked goat's cheese on a salad of marinated olives and blush tomatoes is wrapped in Waberthwaite ham; grilled asparagus, saffron and truffles might be used to garnish a fillet of Lytham sea bass, with glazed figs, elderberry wine and honey to sweeten the Goosnargh duckling.

Tarts, warm puddings and plenty of chocolate to finish, well-kept real ales and a good choice of wines by the glass. A bucket of oats for the horses seems to be all that's missing.

Speciality food: Traditional dishes and local produce
Draught beers: Theakstons Black Sheep, Thwaites Lancashire Bomber
Average wine price by the glass: £3.10

Licensees: Brian and Craig Wilkinson
Last orders for dinner: 9.30 pm
Closed: Sunday evening (food), Monday
Set lunch: from £14.95 (Sunday)
Main courses: from £12.95
Beer garden
Children welcome
Wheelchair access

FOTHERINGHAY, CAMBRIDGESHIRE

The Falcon ★

GASTROPUB

Fotheringhay, Nr. Peterborough, Cambridgeshire PE8 5HZ
Tel. 01832 226 254 Fax 01832 226 046
e-mail: office@huntsbridge.co.uk   **MAP 4** C4

FOTHERINGHAY is probably best known for its association with Mary Queen of Scots, who ended her days here. An impressive church, built on the site of a former monastery, presides over this picturesque village of mellow stone houses and wide avenues.

The Falcon forms part of a group of four establishments that have built up a solid reputation for their food and service. However, it is not entirely given over to food: a snug tap bar hosts the village darts team, who appreciate well-kept ale.

Meals can be taken in the bar or in the airy conservatory with its comfortable wicker chairs. The Bargain Lunch Menu will have a choice of three starters and three main courses. Home-baked rosemary and sun-dried tomato bread is brought to the table with your starter.

A Caesar salad of crisp Romaine lettuce in a creamy dressing, with anchovies and plenty of Parmesan, should awaken the senses. Follow, perhaps, with breast of chicken, which could have a tasty forcemeat stuffing and accompaniments of roasted red onions and tomatoes and feta cheese.

Alternatively, choose chargrilled pavé of lamb from the carte with creamed cannellinni and garlic braised cavolo nero – a seldom seen vegetable, which is a shame since its distinct sweet flavour sets it apart from any other cabbage.

Puddings might include a caramelised lemon tart with raspberry vodka sorbet or vanilla panna cotta with blackberries.

Speciality food: Pavé of Cornish lamb
Draught beers: Adnams, IPA
Average wine price by the glass: £4.50

Licensee: Chris Isaac
Last orders for dinner: Monday to Friday 9.15pm, Saturday 9.30pm, Sunday 9pm
Open every day
Set lunch: from £12.50
Main courses: from £9.50
Private dining: 15-32
Al fresco dining
Wheelchair access

FRESSINGFIELD, SUFFOLK

Fox and Goose ★

Fressingfield, Suffolk IP21 5PB
Tel. 01379 586 247 Fax 01379 586 106
e-mail: foxandgoose@uk2.net   **MAP 4** E4

THE Fox and Goose has for many years provided the flat Suffolk countryside with a contour of gastronomic high ground. The young proprietor, Paul Yaxley, shows every sign of continuing to attract the faithful to this focal point of village life for many years to come. Paul's partner, Sarah, is at front of house, her smiling professionalism exuding the enthusiasm which is a trademark here, amply displayed in the fresh, imaginative food.

It is difficult to know quite where to start here when even the set lunch offers warm salad of duck confit; poached smoked haddock on crushed potatoes with honey, dill and mustard crème fraîche, or salmon and prawn fishcake, herb salad and butternut squash remoulade. Then perhaps a trio of fish with saffron mash and chervil sauce; pork fillet with peach and fennel chutney, or chicken breast marinated in cumin and oranges.

Scottish fish features regularly – fillet of monkfish, for example, with avocado, broad bean and sweetcorn risotto and a crab bisque. Lovers of red meat will enjoy beef fillet with foie gras and truffle butter, rösti, shallot purée and a brisket and boudin hash with thyme jus.

Impressive desserts, too, including an ethereal apricot mousse, chocolate mousse with a cappuccino parfait and lemon and basil tart with mango sorbet. Technical know-how, uncompromising flavours and the warmth and generosity of cuisine and service make a meal here a real delight. Lunchtime snacks are available, too, outside beside the duck pond in good weather.

Speciality food: Fillet of monkfish with avocado, broad bean and sweetcorn risotto and crab bisque
Draught beers: Adnams
Average wine price by the glass: £2.95

Proprietor: Paul Yaxley
Last orders for dinner: Tuesday to Friday 8.30 pm,
Saturday 9 pm, Sunday 8.15 pm
Closed: Monday
Closed for holidays: 2nd week January for 10 days
Set lunch: from £11.50
Main courses: from £12
Private dining: 16-30
Al fresco dining
Wheelchair access

FRILSHAM, BERKSHIRE

Pot Kiln

GASTROPUB

Frilsham, Yattendon, Berkshire RG18 0XX
Tel. 01635 201 366
email: info@potkiln.co.uk   **MAP 2** B3

THE exacting task of finding this gem is amply rewarded. Ignore the Frilsham sign, roughly a mile from Cromwellian Yattendon (take your camera), and your goal emerges some 400 yards on.

It has everything you hope for in a gastropub: hidden, yet with a peaceful view from the huge beer garden, surrounding a set of cosy dining-rooms with the instant appeal of warm simplicity. One hopes they will not be titivated in spite of rapid success (since May 2005).

Chef/patron Mike Robinson has worked in many simple country restaurants, promoted from the sink to the stove, in France and Switzerland. Homesickness for Berkshire finally reclaimed him and his wife Katie from Australia.

Game saturates the long menu (and blackboard) irrespective of season. Indeed, Mike shoots a good deal himself. Your feast of woodpigeon, wild rabbit, muntjak, venison, plus seasonal game, might be preceded by potted game – what else? – or by exquisite broccoli soup, and brought to a conclusion by a toothsome Eton Mess. If that is not a rare selection, what is? But beyond the very acceptable cooking standards (with highlights), civilised, natural informality is immediately evident. All these are what make a good gastropub.

The Robinsons' love of wine sticks out a mile from the wine list's comments, let alone the reasonable prices (the well kept Lérane Grenache/Syrah, Vin de Pays d'Oc 2004, is a steal at £12.50).

Speciality food: Local game
Draught beers: West Berkshire bitter, Pitsburger lager
Average wine price by the glass: £3.50

Licensee: Michael Robinson
Open every day
Set lunch: from £15 (Monday to Friday)
Main courses: from £14.50
Beer garden
Children welcome
Wheelchair access

FRITHSDEN, HERTFORDSHIRE

Alford Arms

GASTROPUB

**Frithsden, Nr. Hemel Hempstead, Hertfordshire HP1 3DD
Tel. 01442 864 480 Fax 01442 876 893
e-mail: info@alfordarmsfrithsden.co.uk**   **MAP 2** C2

IF THE village's absence from the maps and its hideaway setting on the edge of the Ashridge Forest might suggest a sense of secrecy or isolation, word has obviously got out. In spite of the location, or because of it, the Salisbury family's little gem does very nicely. Although scrubbed tables and bare boards present a somewhat basic interior layout, that does not deter the constant throng of diners and drinkers who provide a warm, exuberant ambience.

Local staff are great – attentive and easygoing – and the range of 'small plates' (as starters or lighter meals) alongside the main meals ensures an impressive choice.

Soups, potted shrimps, a gargantuan ham hock on black pudding mash, pan-fried cod on saffron boulangère potatoes, or salmon fishcakes on buttered cabbage, set the traditional scene. There is a touch of novelty about foie gras, ox tongue and chicken terrine, and classic hollandaise giving a lift to bubble and squeak with bacon, plus a touch of exotica from Thai chicken sausages on a sweet potato mash, or tender lamb parcels on caramelised sweet peppers with a broad bean jus.

Prime ingredients are allowed to display their natural qualities with the minimum of fuss. Save a corner if you can for one of the hearty desserts, such as a banana Tatin with hot butterscotch sauce, or a more unusual pistachio and cardamom tart.

Welcome to the warm heart of English hospitality. But remember, you still have to find your way out.

Speciality food: Traditional pub food
Draught beers: Flowers Original, Marston Pedigree
Average wine price by the glass: £3.25

Licensee: David Salisbury
Last orders for dinner: 10 pm
Open every day
Closed for holidays: 25 December (for food)
Main courses: from £10.25
Beer garden
Children welcome
Wheelchair access

FROGGATT, DERBYSHIRE

Chequers Inn ★

GASTROPUB

Froggatt Edge, Hope Valley, Derbyshire S32 3ZJ
Tel. 01433 630 231 Fax 01433 631 072
e-mail: info@chequers-froggatt.com **MAP 3** F1

FOR those who enjoy exploring the beautiful Peak District, this 16th-century inn offers an ideal base. Chatsworth is within easy reach and from the pub's elevated secret garden there are some fabulous views of hill country and woodland.

The food operation works informally but very comfortably at tables and settles in two bar-rooms blessed with exposed stone walls, Welsh dressers, a log-burning stove and pastoral prints to create an atmosphere in the best English pub tradition.

The food relies on good local suppliers, and fish comes in fresh every day from Grimsby. The chef's modern cuisine has flair and imagination, but sensibly combines flavours that work. After a satisfying home-made lentil soup made fruitier with a dash of tomato, fish is a favourite medium – grilled turbot, maybe, with grape velouté or pan-roasted sea bass with pak choi.

Calf's liver is accurately cooked to medium-rare pink perfection and set on a bed of finely flavoured bubble and squeak. Trencherman appetites will be met by lamb shank with red pepper and mint risotto, lighter ones by sandwiches, salads, or smoked haddock fishcakes, or else roast salmon and coriander brochettes.

A local speciality, Bakewell pudding, features among the desserts and there is a very good strawberry millefeuille. Good wines are well promoted with a notably fine Chablis, plus several quality choices in half-bottles. Owner Jonathan Tindall offers exemplary bar service – warmly welcoming, efficient and speedy. There are five comfortable bedrooms, one with a four-poster.

Speciality food: Grilled turbot with grape velouté
Draught beers: Charles Wells Bombardier, Greene King IPA
Average wine price by the glass: £3.70

Licensees: Jonathan and Joanne Tindall
Last orders for dinner: 9.15 pm
Open every day
Closed for holidays: 25 December
Main courses: from £9.95
Beer garden
Accommodation: 5 rooms
Children welcome
Limited wheelchair access

GATESHEAD, TYNE & WEAR

McCoys at the Baltic ★

South Shore Road, Gateshead, Tyne & Wear NE8 3BA
Tel. 0191 440 4949 Fax 0191 440 4950
e-mail: mccoys@balticmill.com   **MAP 5** D2

THIS is a classy setting, the long, airy dining-room, reminiscent of a luxury liner, opening before you as you step out of the glass lifts. Who else but those prodigies of Northern cookery, Tom and Eugene McCoy, would you expect to find running a restaurant on top of a contemporary arts centre? This is a smart operation from beginning to end, but the sophistication is kept in check by delightfully easygoing, professional staff and set menus that remain accessible in terms of both price and content.

Imaginative combinations abound in dishes such as cauliflower risotto with curry oil, cauliflower beignets and watercress; sweet potato, roast pepper and rosewater soup with a sweet potato wonton; black pudding and cep gnocchi, chilli jam and pancetta, or marinated pork fillet that comes with black pudding, belly pork, white bean purée, apple compote and sage and calvados jus.

If these descriptions sound daunting, what arrives displays almost disarming simplicity, many components appearing as no more than interesting garnishes to some fine ingredients without detracting from the qualities of the central element. Nicely crisp vegetables, a subtle onion purée, aubergine beignet and basil cream were served with seared fillet of firm, flaky cod after an assiette of duck with a wonderfully creamy liver mousse.

Presentation is surprisingly restrained, but contrasts of colour and texture are particularly evident in impressive desserts such as chilled coffee parfait, mousse and black cherry compote.

Their pride: Marinated pork fillet, French black pudding, belly pork, white bean purée, apple compote, sage and calvados jus
Inexpensive wines: Viognier Marsanne 2004, £15.75; Côtes du Ventoux 2003, £15.75

Proprietors: Tom and Eugene McCoy
Last orders for dinner: 9.30 pm
Closed: Sunday evening
Set lunch: from £16.95
Set dinner: from £30
Private dining: up to 20
Wheelchair access

GREAT GONERBY, LINCOLNSHIRE

Harry's Place ★

17 High Street, Great Gonerby, Nr. Grantham, Lincs. NG31 8JS
Tel. 01476 561780

MAP 4 C2

INSIDE this greenery-hung Georgian house, there are only three immaculately set antique dining tables, but each of them contains mementos of gastronomic dinners that bear witness to the skills and enthusiasm of chef/patron Harry Hallam and his wife Caroline.

Dishes are composed with intelligence and flair, the ingredients are excellent and there is an artful use of fresh herbs, such as the coriander and basil that flavour the sauce accompanying fillet of monkfish with lentils.

The menu offers just two options, one of them fish, the other meat or seasonal game. You might find Aberdeen Angus fillet with a Madeira and herb jus, or Scottish wild salmon, Gascony pork, king scallops.

After an appetiser such as a tomato, feta cheese and herb-topped pastry, still warm from the oven, your starter could be lightly seared foie gras with Cumberland sauce, watercress and grain mustard mayonnaise – a combination that works remarkably well.

There is a good selection of cheeses, and the desserts include a delicious cherry brandy jelly, with yoghurt and black pepper, and caramel mousse brûlée with summer fruits and berries.

Only about 20 wines are on the one-page list, though they are carefully selected and include two champagnes. Two reds, two whites, one of the champagnes and a dessert wine are available by the glass.

Their pride: Terrine of Orkney king scallops
Inexpensive wines: Luis Canas Rioja 2003, £20; Bodegas Rosado Navarra 2003, £26

Proprietors: Harry and Caroline Hallam
Last orders for dinner: 9 pm
Closed: Sunday, Monday
Closed for holidays: 1 week Christmas
Main courses: from £32
Private dining: 8-10
Limited wheelchair access

GREAT MILTON, OXFORDSHIRE

Le Manoir aux Quat'Saisons ★★

Church Road, Great Milton, Oxfordshire OX44 7PD
Tel. 01844 278 881 Fax 01844 278 847
e-mail: lemanoir@blanc.co.uk   **MAP 2** B2

THE immaculate state of the grounds surrounding this lovely manor house is an indication of the quest for perfection that marks every aspect of the food and the service within.

The cooking of Raymond Blanc, which achieved something like cult status as long ago as the late 1980s, remains iconic, its refinement and balanced complexity evident in foie gras and quince confit with a jelly of balsamic vinegar and Monbazillac.

A speciality of Le Manoir is roast mallard, served quite saignant in the popular French manner and also partnered by quince in a purée, along with a jus piquantly scented by redcurrant and juniper and cabbage robustly flavoured by the duck juices.

Desserts, especially those created by the pâtissier's art, have become a particular feature here, and with good reason. As an example, caramelised William's pear is baked in a thin brioche that is exceptionally fine, and served with a delicious ice-cream of cinnamon and vanilla.

The Manoir cellar is, of course, outstanding, covering in depth some of the great Bordeaux châteaux in several vintages. The prices are equally awe-inspiring, but for less than £7 you may enjoy a glass of a very good Chinon Vielles Vignes.

Their pride: Pan-fried Cornish sea bass, Scottish langoustine, Asian greens, star anise
Inexpensive wines: Bergerac Sec Château les Miaudoux 2003, £22; Marcillac Domaine du Cros 2002, £21

Proprietor: Raymond Blanc
Last orders for dinner: 9.30 pm
Open every day
Set lunch: from £45
Set dinner: from £95
Private dining: 10-55
Accommodation: 32 rooms
Wheelchair access

GREAT WHITTINGTON, NORTHUMBERLAND

Queen's Head *GASTROPUB*

Gt. Whittington, Nr. Corbridge, Northumberland NE19 2HP
Tel. 01434 672 267

MAP 5 D2

ONLY half an hour or so from Newcastle city centre, this quiet little backwater contains one of the most genteel of pub dining-rooms. Its unabashed chintziness might be too much for some, but its glass cabinets stuffed with porcelain and acres of bric-a-brac exude an almost tea-room charm, all perfectly in keeping with the village's well-manicured lawns and neatly kept stone cottages.

If time appears to have stood still within, the menu would not be out of place in any good modern restaurant, taking contemporary trends into account yet at the same time remaining faithful to the more traditional precepts.

Local produce predominates and regional influences abound with the likes of a fine black pudding deep-fried in the lightest of batters, or a rack of lamb from the nearby moors simply presented on fondant potato with roasted vegetables and a redcurrant and thyme glaze.

For Sunday lunch, the roasts offer something of an English gala event, while the kitchen's exuberant side shows in, say, sea bass with shellfish linguine and basil oil; breast of duck stuffed with baby spinach, potato rösti and balsamic vinegar and redcurrant glaze, or firm, flaky cod topped with a red pepper and pumpkin seed crust and served on a coarse-grained mustard beurre blanc.

Desserts such as bread and butter or sticky toffee puddings are perhaps better than the more adventurous mousse of dark and light chocolates. This is an accomplished performance by any standards, and in very relaxing surroundings.

Speciality food: Mediterranean-influenced modern British
Draught beers: Hambleton Bitter, Queen's Head
Average wine price by the glass: £3.50

Licensee: Ian Scott
Last orders for dinner: 8.45 pm
Closed: Sunday dinner, Monday
Set lunch: from £11.50
Main courses: from £9.95
Children welcome
Wheelchair access

GREAT WOLFORD, WARWICKSHIRE

Fox and Hounds

GASTROPUB

Great Wolford, Warwickshire CV36 5NQ
Tel. 01608 674 220 Fax 01608 674 160
e-mail: info@thefoxandhoundsinn.com   **MAP 3** F4

THE welcome at this quintessential little inn is as friendly as any you will find anywhere. Hidden in the heart of the Cotswolds, it has gleaming horse brasses everywhere, the beamed ceiling is hung with hop bines and the bar counter is replete with a row of real ale pumps.

In the winter, there is a glowing fire, while for those summer evenings, the patio is well equipped with wooden picnic tables and overhead heaters to keep off the chill.

An appetising array of dishes (plus a few standard snacks) is chalked up on the blackboard, showing some familiar favourites and more original offerings for what is very much a local clientele.

If pea and ham soup, chicken liver parfait and deep-fried Brie are not exactly ground-breaking, good as they no doubt are, then some grilled asparagus, marinated chicken on skewers or melting goat's cheese served on pickled vegetables provide promising starters, followed, perhaps, by duck breast with an olive oil mash, lamb chop with rosemary flavoured potatoes, monkfish tail wrapped in Parma ham, or an excellent juicy breast of guinea fowl with apricot stuffing and a thyme jus.

People of more adventurous tastes might be tempted by a Thai vegetable stir-fry or Asian salmon with ginger and spring onions, with Eton Mess, fruit parfait, or a banana Tatin to finish.

Enjoyable, comfort food in congenial surroundings with a smile on every face.

Speciality food: Modern British cooking
Draught beers: Bass, Hook Norton Bitter
Average wine price by the glass: £2.75

Licensees: Veronica and Paul Tomlinson
Last orders for dinner: 9 pm (weekends 9.30 pm)
Closed: Sunday evening (food), Monday
Closed for holidays: 1 week January
Main courses: from £9.50
Beer garden
Accommodation: 3 rooms
Children over 6 welcome

GUNTHORPE, NOTTINGHAMSHIRE

Tom Brown's Brasserie `GASTROPUB`

The Old Schoolhouse, Trentside, Gunthorpe, Notts NG14 7FB
Tel. 0115 966 3642 Fax 0115 966 4968
e-mail: info@tombrowns.co.uk   **MAP 4** B2

DESPITE a couple of big pubs nearby competing for his custom, Tom Brown is more than holding his own at this delightful little spot by the River Trent.

And it's not hard to see why – with a fresh, more contemporary, streamlined venue that retains the red brickwork and exposed beams, the name 'brasserie' applies most aptly to this collection of airy, sparsely decorated rooms, plus an outside decked area overlooking the river. Its appeal and ambience come largely from the constant throng of a cosmopolitan clientele.

It enjoys the successful formula of an accessible range of dishes in cheerful, buzzy surroundings. If the content is more restricted, sensibly priced menus for lunch and early evenings signify no loss of quality. You might find Thai fishcakes with mint and coconut mousseline; a Danish Blue cheesecake or a duck, spring onion and cucumber salad. Follow with pan-fried salmon fillet with Asian greens and a chilli and coriander pesto, or spiced meatballs of lamb with mint couscous, or else plainer medallions of sirloin steak with a classic Madeira jus and crisp pommes Pont Neuf.

More elaborate evening offerings still display many Asian and Mediterranean influences with pesto, mint, coconut, ginger and soy used to embellish some excellent local meat and fish. Diners with a sweet tooth will enjoy the Malteser ice-cream that goes with a hot chocolate pudding, or a refreshing white chocolate, pineapple and coconut praline iced parfait. This professionally-run operation maintains reassuringly even quality throughout.

Speciality food: Brasserie with a Mediterranean/Asian twist
Draught beers: Ruddles, Courage Directors
Average wine price by the glass: £3.25

Licensees: Adam and Robin Perkins
Last orders for dinner: 10 pm
Open every day
Set lunch: from £12.95
Set dinner: from £12.95 (early evening)
Private dining: 14-30
Beer garden
Children welcome
Wheelchair access

HADDENHAM, BUCKINGHAMSHIRE

Green Dragon ★

GASTROPUB

8 Churchway, Haddenham, Buckinghamshire HP17 8AA
Tel. 01844 291 403 Fax 01844 299 532
e-mail: paul@eatatthedragon.co.uk   **MAP 2** B2

TAKE IN the scene of Haddenham's Church End – the church is splendid – before walking over to the Green Dragon, everyone's idea of an idyllic local pub. In the walled garden, on immaculate lawns, you may dine in warm weather, perhaps with the owner's Schnauzer dog for company. Inside, the beamed bar is usually busy and animated, with no 'gastro-deco' touches such as scrubbed pine. One corner is lined with racks of good wine and there are tables placed near the copper-hooded fireplace, great for a winter dinner.

In contrast to the setting, the cooking is modern British, with the emphasis on fine seasonal produce prepared with precision and a light touch. Charred Wye Valley asparagus followed by braised shank of Buckinghamshire lamb would be typical choices. Exceptional value is found on Tuesday and Thursday evenings with the extremely popular Simply Dinner menu for £11.95. The place is packed on these nights with couples, their children and grandchildren.

Start with, say, the fine melding flavours of Gruyère, leek and spinach in a crisp tart, then on to lightly cooked, tender breast of guinea fowl with broad beans, sugar-snaps and lardons. Finish with the excellent cappuccino crème brûlée.

A fine option from the carte is fresh halibut done as fish and chips or with wild mushrooms and leeks in a light cream sauce. To drink, try Deuchars bitter from Dunbar, or a selection of 12 good wines by the glass and 50 by the bottle, rising to a mature Vosne Romanée Premier Cru for £55.

Speciality food: Modern British cooking
Draught beers: Deuchars, Wychert
Average wine price by the glass: £3.10

Licensees: Peter Moffat and Paul Berry
Last orders for dinner: 9.30 pm
Closed: Sunday evening
Closed for holidays: 25 December, 1 January
Set dinner: from £1l.95 (Tuesday and Thursday)
Main courses: from £11.95
Beer garden
Children over 7 welcome
Wheelchair access

HALFWAY, WEST SUSSEX

Halfway Bridge Inn

Halfway, Nr. Lodsworth, West Sussex GU28 9BP
Tel. 01798 861 281 Fax 01798 861 017

MAP 2 C4

MIDWAY between Petworth and Midhurst, this pub is close to the renowned Cowdray golf club. A Grade II listed building in local stone and brick, it consists of several interconnecting rooms which have recently been refurbished, though retaining the open fireplaces and cast iron cooking range. Newspapers are provided and there is a terrace for meals as well as a beer garden.

Food is a priority here, with a menu of imaginative variety, and with fish a particularly popular choice in the evenings. You might start with baked goat's cheese, smoked beetroot and chard, or crispy duck with beanshoots, ginger and honey dressing, or a crisp tomato and sweet red onion tart.

Among the main courses, there could be grilled Dover sole with a caper butter sauce, or oven baked turbot. Meat dishes include veal schnitzel with Parmesan potatoes and anchovy and black olive butter, or a Scottish rump beefburger with spicy salsa, cheese and bacon. Chunky chips are crisp and well seasoned.

Puddings to try might be crème brûlée with thin, crumbly peanut butter biscuits and a light zabaglione with honey tuile, or there are good cheeses. There are a dozen wines available by the glass, including champagne.

Accommodation is offered in six spacious, comfortable bedrooms in a large converted barn well away from the road.

Speciality food: Seafood (evenings)
Draught beers: Sussex Bitter, Cheriton Pots
Average wine price by the glass: £3.20

Licensee: Nick Sutherland
Last orders: 9.30 pm (Friday and Saturday 10 pm)
Open every day
Main courses: from £9
Private dining: 10-20
Beer garden
Accommodation: 6 rooms
Children welcome
Wheelchair access

HAMBLETON, RUTLAND

Finch's Arms

GASTROPUB

Oakham Road, Hambleton, Rutland LE15 8TL
Tel. 01572 756 575 Fax 01572 771 142
e-mail: enquiries@finchsarms.co.uk   **MAP 4** C3

THE interior of this 17th-century inn, with its mellow limestone and attractive slate roof, and overlooking Rutland Water, sets it apart from the rest.

Terracotta walls, beamed ceilings and an open fire in the bar make for a warm, traditional atmosphere. In contrast, modern textured paint, stone tables and wicker chairs in the Garden Room Restaurant lend something of a Mediterranean feel.

Sit by the window and look out on an attractive terrace with a vine-clad pergola and potted olive trees and let the eye wander over magnificent views of the lake.

Starters might include black pudding, Rutland and Cumberland sausages, or Stilton in various guises, reflecting regional tastes, while aubergine caviar gâteau or gambas a la plancha reinforce the Mediterranean theme.

While not as light and airy as a soufflé cooked once to order, a twice-baked Stilton soufflé has an acceptable consistency and manages to pack a punch.

A tender rack of lamb, cooked to your liking, may be accompanied by firm courgettes, mixed peppers and aubergine. Fillet of beef, similarly well handled might be paired with an intensely flavoured wild mushroom sauce.

Puddings follow the seasons and could offer such delights as grilled peach with cinnamon ice-cream.

Speciality food: Sea bass, new potatoes, black olives and fennel
Draught beers: Timothy Taylor Landlord, Greene King Abbott
Average wine price by the glass: £3.25

Licensee: Colin Crawford
Last orders for dinner: 9.30 pm
Open every day
Set lunch: from £9.95
Main courses: from £8.45
Private dining: 30-65
Beer garden
Accommodation: 6 rooms
Children welcome
Wheelchair access

HAMBLETON, RUTLAND

Hambleton Hall ★

Hambleton Village, Oakham, Rutland LE15 8TH
Tel. 01572 756 991 Fax 01572 724 721
e-mail: hotel@hambletonhall.com   **MAP 4** C3

THE kitchen garden of this fine country house hotel by Rutland Water makes its own contribution to the seasonal menus that draw much of their appeal from local produce, with a particular emphasis on game in season.

Main courses, especially when game is involved, might be treated quite straightforwardly – as in, say, grouse with all the usual accompaniments – or else given a the sort of novel twist shown by the prune an armagnac sauce that comes with hare Wellington and the foie gras raviolo and caper sauce partnering pigeon.

Fish dishes, too, can be intriguing. Poached fillet of sea bass is imaginatively served with tomato and caper couscous and light garlic sauce.

Starters might be fried foie gras with soused aubergine and plums or a surprising baked potato bouillon with cheese-filled tortellini. Everything from the bread rolls to the delicious petits fours is home made: they even smoke their own salmon.

The wine list contains plenty of celebrated names, particularly among the vineyards of Bordeaux and Burgundy, and there is a fine selection of dessert wines, five available by the glass.

Their pride: Essence of tomato with poached langoustines and tomato sorbet
Inexpensive wines: Vina Urbezo Carinena 2003, £18; Costières de Nîmes Château Mourgues du Gres, Les Galets Dorés 2004, £19

Proprietor: Timothy Hart
Last orders for dinner: 9.30 pm
Open every day
Set lunch: from £18.50
Set dinner: from £40
Private dining: up to 64
Al fresco dining: for light meals
Accommodation: 17 rooms
Wheelchair access

HAROME, NORTH YORKSHIRE

The Star ★★

GASTROPUB

Harome, Nr. Helmsley, North Yorkshire YO62 5SE
Tel. 01439 770 397 Fax 01439 771 833

MAP 5 D4

SINCE taking over this 14th-century thatched inn a decade or so ago, Andrew and Jacqueline Pern have created a little empire that is dedicated to good living. Their corner store is full of mostly home-grown delicacies and they even have their own butcher's shop supplied solely by a local producer.

The pub, heavily biased towards fine dining as it is, retains its character as a haven for those simply in search of a quiet pint and a quick sandwich. Even the latter takes on a new dimension, though, when home-made breads and buns are filled with the likes of coronation chicken, raisins, almonds and spices; Norfolk prawns, or seared steak with blue Wensleydale shavings.

A constant throng fills the tiny bar with its archetypical flagstones, beams, horse brasses and knick-knacks and fine old oak furnishings. Booking is a must for the next door dining-room, or get there early if you want a table in the peaceful garden.

Andrew's passion for food produces a range of sumptuous dishes based on the unequivocal use of the finest ingredients, handled with breathtaking skill and creativity. Try hot smoked salmon with marinated sardines and fresh Parmesan; locally smoked duck with fresh figs; Byland blue organic cheese, Buckler sorrel salad and roast hazelnut pesto. There is also a fabulous pasta dish of grouse breasts with fresh herbs, crispy pancetta and truffle cream.

Stunning desserts include chocolate brûlée, home-made ices and chocolate covered berries, lemon posset with a compote of local blackcurrants and treacle tart with orange blossom ice-cream.

Speciality food: Local produce
Draught beers: Black Sheep Special, Cropton Bitter
Average wine price by the glass: £4

Licensees: Jacqueline and Andrew Pern
Last orders for dinner: 9.30 pm (Sunday 6 pm)
Closed: Monday (for food)
Closed for holidays: 2 weeks January
Main courses: from £14.50
Private dining: 6-20
Beer garden
Accommodation: 11 rooms
Children welcome

HARPENDEN, HERTFORDSHIRE

The Fox at Harpenden   GASTROPUB

469 Luton Road, Kingsbourne Green, Harpenden, Herts AL5 3QE
Tel. 01582 713 817
e-mail: pubs@simon-king.co.uk   **MAP 2** C2

WHATEVER you do – book in advance! The entire local population seems to descend on this substantial but otherwise unassuming roadside pub not far from Luton Airport, spilling out of the smart lounge and dining areas on to the terraces and filling every seat.

So what's the attraction? Its clean, contemporary image, perhaps, or smart young staff in leather aprons, or maybe the apparently limitless array of beers, wines and assorted alcohols behind a glitzy bar that would not be out of place in the local disco? There is the food, of course, a competent young kitchen team providing a wide range of favourites with an occasional original twist, but based on a simple brasserie style and top-quality ingredients rather than overcomplicated extravaganzas.

The tersely worded and categorised menu sets the scene: the main components of each dish are separated by a '+' so we are offered Asparagus + Poached Egg + Prosciutto + Hollandaise, or Tomato + Shallot + Goats Cheese Tart Tatin (v. good + crisp + tasty); under 'Leaves' we might find Crispy Duck + Watercress + Mooli + Plum Sauce, or Chicken Liver + Pear + Blue Cheese.

Pizzas and pastas too, then more substantial, traditional main courses including perhaps spit roast gammon, grilled lobster or a succulent rump of top-quality lamb with minted pears and creamy dauphinoise potatoes. Daily specials include Pan-Fried Sea Bass + Tomato + Olives + Basil, and there are all the expected desserts. While ground-breaking innovation is evidently not their forte, they do what they do rather well – and with a style that obviously delights the locals.

Speciality food: Simple modern brasserie
Draught beers: Bass, Greene King IPA
Average wine price by the glass: £3.50

Licensee: Daniel Harries
Last orders for dinner: 9.30 pm (Sunday 7 pm)
Open every day
Main courses: from £8.95
Beer garden
Children welcome
Wheelchair access

HAYTOR VALE, DEVON

Rock Inn

GASTROPUB

Haytor Vale, Nr. Newton Abbot, Devon TQ13 9XP
Tel. 01364 661 305 Fax 01364 661 242
e-mail: enquiries@rock-inn.co.uk   **MAP 1** C4

YOU WILL know you're nearing this centuries-old inn, on the south-eastern fringe of Dartmoor, as the imposing rock formation from which it takes its name looms into view. Not surprisingly, the landmark features in pictures and photographs adorning the walls of the intimate jumble of rooms that invite with great warmth and traditional character.

The food is good comforting stuff, too, with half-a-dozen starters, main courses and puddings, all at fixed prices, available in the evening, and a slightly lighter menu, including a few sandwiches, plus a blackboard of specials, offered at lunchtime.

Home-made soup with a good wedge of crusty bread and curls of butter, warm goat's cheese on a bed of vine tomatoes with pesto and balsamic dressing, or a steaming plate of River Teign mussels in garlic butter make good starters or lighter bites.

In the evening, main courses could include pan-fried fillet of hake, rump of Devon lamb or roasted duck breast, while at lunch pork and honey sausages, seafood and herb fishcakes or steak and kidney pudding with a proper suet crust are the order of the day.

A well-stocked bar and cellar provide plenty of opportunity to wash it all down, and one could do worse than finish with a board of West Country cheeses.

In the same family for more than twenty years, the Rock Inn is built on firm foundations indeed.

Speciality food: River Teign mussels
Draught beers: Dartmoor Bitter, Old Speckled Hen
Average wine price by the glass: £3.55

Licensee: Christopher Hely-Hutchinson-Graves
Last orders for dinner: 8.30 pm winter, 9.30 pm summer
Closed: Sunday evening (January)
Closed for holidays: 25 and 26 December
Main courses: from £14.95
Private dining: 8-20
Beer garden
Accommodation: 9 rooms
Children welcome
Wheelchair access

HAYWARDS HEATH, WEST SUSSEX

Jeremy's at Borde Hill

Balcombe Road, Haywards Heath, West Sussex RH16 1XP
Tel. 01444 441 102 Fax 01444 441 355
e-mail: reservations@jeremysrestaurant.com　　**MAP 2** D4

CONVERTED stables in a beautiful parkland setting, five minutes' drive north of Haywards Heath, provide a highly individual place to eat, decorated with striking modern art.

During the summer, it is worth taking the opportunity to dine al fresco in splendid, south-facing gardens and sample a menu full of imagination.

Try, for instance, brandade of cod on crispy, thin toast – a treat served with aperitifs. Risotto with sweet, juicy mussels and tiny slivers of tender leek is especially successful in a delicate white wine sauce, while pan-fried calf's liver, thinly sliced and precisely cooked to personal taste, is enhanced by a lightly caramelised jus. Gratin Dauphinois excels in delicacy and lightness; slow-roasted free-range pork with a degree of fat, which helps the flavour and retains the moistness, is wonderfully tender.

Other dishes of particular merit include pan-fried squid on wild rice, calf's liver parfait to start and then roasted loin of Southdown lamb, or poached fillet of brill with mussel chowder.

William's pear sorbet stands out for finesse, while the poached pear, spiced with cinnamon, is a delight, coated in a rich, dark chocolate sauce and served with smooth yoghurt ice-cream. Or there is lemon posset with caramelised oranges and redcurrants.

A suitably varied wine list, with monthly recommendations, offers a very good selection of half-bottles and wines by the glass.

Their pride: Rye Bay scallops, leeks, ginger lime butter sauce
Inexpensive wines: Côtes de Gascogne Domaine de Millet 2004, £14; Gottim Bru Costers del Segre, Castel del Remei (Spain/Portugal) 2002, £19

Proprietors: Jeremy and Vera Ashpool
Last orders for dinner: 10 pm
Closed: Sunday evening, Monday
Closed for holidays: 1st week January
Set lunch: from £16.50
Al fresco dining
Wheelchair access

HENLEY-IN-ARDEN, WEST MIDLANDS

Edmunds Restaurant ★

64 High Street, Henley-in-Arden, West Midlands B95 5BX
Tel. 01564 795 666
e-mail: edmunds@watersbm.freeserve.co.uk   **MAP 3** E3

THERE is so much that attracts among the food on offer at this picturesque cottage restaurant with its small adjoining rooms and rather formal though inviting atmosphere.

The portions are quite manageable and prices are fair, which makes it possible to try several dishes. Choosing your main course can be a dithery process when you are confronted by the embarrassment of riches: tournedos of monkfish with Parma ham, oven-roasted tomatoes and basil cream; lamb shank, rump and sweetbreads; hake pot-au-feu; fillet and blade of beef with horse-radish cream

The starters are every bit as tempting, with perhaps the classic combination of flavours in a beautifully cooked smoked haddock risotto topped with poached egg. Vegetarians will be seduced by the confit of Romano peppers and goat's cheese, while for trencherman appetites there is the substantial pig's trotter with potato galette and roasted parsnip.

A good way to sample the range of excellent desserts is the grande assiette, or else you may make your choice between such delights as William's pear that comes poached, in parfait and in millefeuille, or rhubarb crumble served with apple sorbet.

The carefully selected wines, with good showings from Burgundy, Languedoc and northern Spain, are reasonably priced.

Their pride: Roasted rack of lamb, pistachio fondant, vanilla and parsnip purée, rich burgundy jus
Inexpensive wines: Stimson Estate Merlot (USA) 2001, £14; Kintu Sauvignon Blanc (Chile) 2004, £12.75

Proprietors: Andy and Beverley Waters
Last orders for dinner: 9.45 pm
Closed: Sunday and Monday, Saturday lunch
Closed for holidays: 4 weeks throughout the year
Set lunch: from £5 per course
Set dinner: from £25.50

HENLEY-ON-THAMES, OXFORDSHIRE

Three Tuns Food House   GASTROPUB

5 Market Place, Henley-on-Thames, Oxfordshire RG9 2AA
Tel. 01491 573 260
e-mail: thefoodhouse@btconnect.com   **MAP 2** B3

AT FIRST sight, this little old pub in the market-place seems an unlikely spot in which to look for good food. Henley's town gallows once stood on this site but, fear not, the warmest of welcomes awaits you in the endearingly plain front bar.

You order your food from an intriguing menu of modern British cooking, then move into the bijou dining-room, the old joists and boards now painted white. At the half-dozen or so tables, your neighbours are likely to be serious eaters, but the atmosphere is relaxed, with peals of laughter from people having a good time.

Typical starters could be roast butternut soup with new season's garlic, or griddled English asparagus and vegetable salad. Fresh fish options range from pan-fried squid and salsa verde to John Dory, mash and fresh morels. For the carnivore, there could be Scottish rib-eye with sauté potatoes and vine tomatoes.

Sunday lunch is deservedly popular: the roast poulet noir platter, featuring sweet potato with ginger, broad beans, green beans, Parmesan, roast potatoes and onion, is a feast full of splendid flavours. If you have room for pudding, try the exceptional tiramisù with coffee granita, or glazed lime tart with a strawberry and jelly shot. The coffee is very superior espresso.

As this is a brewery-tied house, the range of wines is a little short, but both the Australian Shiraz from Peter Lehmann and the Shiraz from Bruce Guigan are very drinkable. There are plans to expand the list.

Speciality food: Modern British cooking
Draught beers: Brakspear, Kronenbourg
Average wine price by the glass: £3.75

Licensee: Kieron Daniels
Last orders for dinner: 10 pm
Open every day
Main courses: from £14
Private dining: 10-30
Beer garden
Children welcome
Wheelchair access

HERTFORD, HERTFORDSHIRE

Hillside ★

GASTROPUB

Port Hill, Benged, Hertford, Hertfordshire SG14 3EP
Tel. 01992 554 556 Fax 01992 583 709

MAP 2 D2

THIS bijou gastropub (no more than 30 covers) is a real find, serving food of star quality.

The lunch menu is a deft range of superior brasserie dishes such as 'The Hillside' veal burger with beef tomato, flat mushroom and real chips, with options such as a great beetroot gazpacho, or the faultless pan-fried grey mullet with samphire and saffron risotto.

Dinner might start with pressed terrine of duck confit, foie gras and red wine shallots, or smoked mackerel rillette and pickled cucumber, going on to new season's Welsh lamb, cooked pink, with sweetbreads, fennel and butter beans.

An alternative could be a dish of wild rabbit, the leg as a confit, the saddle wrapped in Parma ham, and the accompaniment a chickpea and chorizo stew. In the game season, the house prides itself on its roast grouse with savoy cabbage and truffled roast potatoes.

Among the desserts, the tarte Tatin is exceptional.

The selective wine list is a compilation of classic and avant-garde, the reds ranging from a Lalande de Pomerol 2000 (great vintage) to the single vineyard Clos de la Siète Malbec from Mendoza, Argentina. The whites include a first-rate Pouilly Fuissé La Roche.

Speciality food: Pan-fried skate wing with saffron and samphire
Draught beers: Hoegaarden, Löwenbrau
Average wine price by the glass: £3.50

Proprietor: Barry Hilton
Last orders for dinner: 9.30 pm
Closed: Sunday dinner
Main courses: £15
Children welcome during day
Wheelchair access

HETTON, NORTH YORKSHIRE

The Angel

GASTROPUB

Hetton, Nr. Skipton, North Yorkshire BD23 6LT
Tel. 01756 730 263 Fax 01756 730 363
e-mail: info@angelhetton.co.uk   **MAP 5** D4

JUST another quiet little foodie pub tucked away in a sleepy village in the wilds of North Yorkshire? Not quite: the village itself may be dozing contentedly in perfect rural tranquillity, but down in the High Street, something is stirring.

Their core pub and restaurant business aside, Bruce Elsworth and Luc Daguzan run their own newspaper, nearby lodgings, charity events and a retail wine *cave*. You can also be married here, and small weddings are in great demand. In their relaxed, elegant collection of bars and dining-rooms, plus a heated terrace, smart staff in waistcoats and long aprons, armed with an impressive wine list, give the impression of a chic Parisian brasserie.

Not only will you find Gloucester Old Spot pork loin, Newby Hall Aberdeen Angus beef, Goosnargh duck or Bishop Monkton whole hog sausages, but also a culinary style and presentation that owe more than a little to European influences.

Clean, classic and unfussy, with the main (generously portioned) element offset by flavoursome, well-balanced accompaniments such as crisp spring rolls, cumin carrots and crunchy pak choi on perfectly cooked duck breast, professional expertise is proudly displayed across a shortish menu doubled by blackboard specials, usually fresh seafood specialities.

Excellent desserts, including a refreshing Granny Smith frozen parfait alongside Yorkshire rhubarb cheesecake and an impressive cherry and chocolate trio.

Speciality food: Seafood specialities and local produce
Draught beers: Black Sheep, Timothy Taylor Landlord
Average wine price by the glass: £3.50

Licensee: Bruce Elsworth
Last orders for dinner: 9.30pm summer, 9pm winter
Open every day
Closed for holidays: 1 week January
Set lunch: from £9.25
Set dinner: from £16.50
Private dining: 10-40
Al fresco dining
Accommodation: 5 rooms
Children welcome   Wheelchair access

HIGH ONGAR, ESSEX

The Wheatsheaf ★

GASTROPUB

**King Street, High Ongar, Nr. Blackmore, Essex CM5 9NS
Tel. 01277 822 220 Fax 01277 822 441**

MAP 2 D2

THIS jewel can be found half-a-mile past the village of Ongar on the A414 Chelmsford road, by a small garage and car forecourt. Turn right into King Street (a rural lane) and the pub is about two minutes' drive.

Inside, The Wheatsheaf still has the charm of a country pub, with civilised lighting and comfort. The tables in the bay window are especially comfortable with cushioned banquettes.

The cooking here has real class, with no short-cuts. The excellent chicken spring rolls are beautifully spiced with what tasted like ginger and lemongrass and the fresh prawn Thai red curry, which is judiciously flavoured with coconut and accompanied by perfect jasmine rice and home-made pastes, is outstanding.

The fig and almond tart is also exceptional, the medley of sweet fruit and nut flavours exactly right, the pastry thin and crisp.

Back to British, and fishcakes are much in demand, as is local game in season, and other surefire winners are rack of lamb with couscous salad and grilled Mediterranean vegetables, or seared scallops with chilli, coriander and lime sambal.

Traditional preferences are not forgotten, either, with such old favourites as calf's liver with bubble and squeak or baked fillet of cod with mash and a crispy cheese and bacon topping.

The pouring wines are chosen with great care, the Andes Cabernet Sauvignon being especially satisfying.

Speciality food: Seasonal British with oriental touches
Draught beers: Greene King IPA, Kronenbourg
Average wine price by the glass: £3.50

**Licensees: Brendan Daly and Annette Stuart-Box
Last orders for dinner: 8.45 pm (Fri and Sat 9.30 pm)
Closed: Sunday evening, Monday
Closed for holidays: 2 weeks after Christmas, 1 week
June, 1 week November
Set lunch: from £8.95
Main courses: from £12.95
Private dining: 6-14
Al fresco dining**
Children welcome before 7 pm   Wheelchair access

HIGHCLERE, BERKSHIRE

Yew Tree

GASTROPUB

Hollington Cross, Andover Road, Highclere, Berks RG20 9SE
Tel. 01635 253 360 Fax 01635 255 035
e-mail: gareth.mcainsh@theyewtree.net   **MAP 2** B3

THE enfant terrible of cutting-edge cuisine is a country publican now, and in case there was any doubt as to the instigator of this recently acquired venture, Marco-Pierre White's name is writ large on the whitewashed front of the old inn. If his presence in the heart of rural Berkshire seems at odds with his flamboyant and at times petulant past, nowhere could be more sedately relaxing than the cottagey interior of this 17th-century roadside eating house. White's fame has gone before him, so booking is strongly recommended both for lunch and dinner.

Resolutely and proudly British in style, pea and ham soup, Welsh rarebit, excellent potted prawns, sausages, colcannon, fish and chips and even shepherd's pie all appear on the eclectic menu. The specials carry the master's unmistakable signature as prime mover behind the house style, with crayfish risotto, sage-crusted calf's liver with cauliflower purée and immaculate confit of lamb with creamy flageolet beans being typical examples.

Even such foreign imports are offered without pomp or pageantry, relying on traditional values rather than ornamentation to impress, as with the use of mousseline, tartare and Béarnaise sauces for example.

There is a simple choice of tried and trusted desserts, too, such as a 'Wally Ladd' sherry trifle which was creamy if a touch stodgy. The odd shortcoming like this will no doubt be ironed out in time and Marco's pub, with its cheerfully attentive staff, must surely be set for a bright future.

Speciality food: Inventive British cooking
Draught beers: Fullers London Pride, Timothy Taylor Landlord
Average wine price by the glass: £2.45

Licensee: Gareth McAinsh
Last orders for dinner: 9.30 pm
Closed: Sunday evening (food only)
Main courses: from £9.75
Beer garden
Accommodation: 6 rooms
Children welcome
Wheelchair access

HIGHER BURWARDSLEY, CHESHIRE

Pheasant Inn ★

GASTROPUB

Higher Burwardsley, Tattenhall, Cheshire CH3 9PF
Tel. 01829 770 434 Fax 01829 771 097
e-mail: info@thepheasantinn.co.uk   **MAP 3** D2

SET on a ridge at Higher Burwardsley, the Pheasant probably has the finest view of any inn in Cheshire. There is a glorious panoramic sweep westwards over farmland to the Welsh hills and the first peaks of Snowdonia, and north as far as Liverpool.

This is a smart, fashionable place, and a favourite of the Cheshire fast set in more senses than the purely automotive – though a Ferrari 330 was clearing its throat in the car park. It is a country inn with ten very comfortable bedrooms, but the Pheasant also exudes a quasi-metropolitan atmosphere, and the elegantly dressed staff could just as well be in Chelsea or the Rive Gauche.

Informality is the keynote round the bar and in the lovely garden. Only tables of more than six people can be booked and there is not really a formal restaurant. The food is sensibly conceived and very good with the odd nod to fashion: sizzling monkfish and tiger prawns in sweet chilli jam, for example, or teriyaki salmon on Thai noodles. But the thrust of the menu is imaginatively traditional.

Light bites range from Morecambe Bay shrimps on Welsh rarebit (unusual but successful) to hot beef sandwich with Dijon mustard on toasted bread. The cod in beer batter is first-rate, as are the freshly cooked chips. Start with gravadlax, perhaps, and end with apple and blackberry crumble or the very superior Cheshire Farm ice-creams.

Excellent real ales are from the local Weetwood Brewery. Eight wines by the glass are chosen with flair, including a very good Vouvray demi-sec – perfect with the spicier dishes.

Speciality food: Monkfish and tiger prawns in sweet chilli jam
Draught beers: Weetwood Best, Weetwood Eastgate
Average wine price by the glass: £3.40

Licensee: Andrew Nelson
Last orders for dinner: 9 pm (Sunday 8.30 pm)
Open every day
Closed for holidays: 25 December (evening)
Main courses: from £10
Private dining: 10-20
Beer garden
Accommodation: 12 rooms
Children welcome during day
Wheelchair access

HOGSNASTON, DERBYSHIRE

Red Lion

GASTROPUB

Main Street, Hogsnaston, Derbyshire DE6 1PR
Tel. 01335 370 396
e-mail: info@lionrouge.com   **MAP 3** F2

JUST to the north-east of Ashbourne, this is a substantial village pub with a beautifully proportioned main bar. Lunchtime snacks are sensibly kept to filled baguettes and ciabatta sandwiches, but dinner is another story.

After something like an exemplary soup of butternut squash, choosing the main course can be difficult, since every one of the eight dishes looks worth trying for their promising combination of flavours. It is clear that a talented chef is at work here.

Loin of lamb with apricot and hazelnut stuffing is memorable, the meat light pink, moist, sweet-flavoured and tender, the edges roasted crisp, the garnish a redcurrant reduction and creamy dauphinoise potatoes.

Other dishes show the same calibre, be they chargrilled venison with caramelised pears and juniper jus, or else fillet of bream with walnut gremolata.

Options for vegetarians include penne with courgettes, walnuts and pecorino and, particularly appetising, wild mushroom and roasted pepper millefeuille with whole grain mustard sauce.

For dessert, the pear tart with vanilla ice cream is first-rate. This is starred restaurant-style cooking in a relaxed pub environment. The wine selection does full justice to the food.

Speciality food: Loin of lamb, apricot and hazelnut stuffing
Draught beers: Marston Pedigree, Marston Burton Bitter
Average wine price by the glass: £2.95

Licensee: Jason Waterall
Last orders for dinner: 9.30 pm
Open every day
Main courses: from £7.95
Private dining: 16-18
Al fresco dining
Accommodation: 3 rooms
Children welcome
Wheelchair access

HORNDON-ON-THE-HILL, ESSEX

Bell Inn ★

GASTROPUB

High Road, Horndon-on-the-Hill, Essex SS17 8LD
Tel. 01375 642 463 Fax 01375 361 611
e-mail: info@bell-inn.co.uk   **MAP 2** E3

THE BELL has been welcoming travellers for more than 500 years and it has probably never been in better hands. John and Christine Vereker have achieved exactly the right balance between fine dining and family pub, with excellent draught beers and friendly buzz. Much of the Tudor fabric of the interior has been retained, especially in the long, narrow dining-room, where beams and gleaming copper pots and pans give something of the feel of a medieval great hall in miniature.

Chef Stuart Fay comes up with a constantly evolving, eclectic selection of favourites and surprises, his own creations often echoing Gallic themes but with a twist to every tale and subtlety and interest apparent on every plate.

While Stuart is not averse to putting excellent local produce to simple good use in, say, a dish of asparagus with hollandaise sauce, a hearty roast or lamb chump with black pudding mash and a redcurrant jus, he carries off more ambitious collations with equal aplomb.

There is a twice-baked dolcelatte soufflé, or a deliciously light haddock brandade served with clam chowder and tempura shallot rings. Grilled whiting comes with herb and lemon crust on spinach, mussel and saffron velouté, while a dish of confit, braised and roast duck with savoy cabbage and marmalade of red onion is expertly handled. Even side-vegetables are spot-on and desserts display real class, with offerings like chocolate truffle torte or pavlova of plum and apple under a spun sugar dome.

Speciality food: Eclectic cuisine
Draught beers: Bass, Greene King IPA
Average wine price by the glass: £3

Licensees: John and Christine Vereker
Last orders for dinner: 9.45 pm
Open every day
Closed for holidays: Bank Holidays
Main courses: from £10.50
Private dining: 15-22
Beer garden
Accommodation: 15 rooms
Children welcome
Wheelchair access

HORRINGER, SUFFOLK

The Beehive

GASTROPUB

**Horringer, Nr. Bury St. Edmunds, Suffolk IP29 5SN
Tel. 01284 735 260 Fax 01638 730 416**

MAP 4 D4

IT IS a joy to see two dedicated professionals still so obviously enjoying their chosen metier after twenty years at this flint-built, 200-year-old roadside inn. Di and Gary impart genuine bonhomie to both customers and staff and the warmest of welcomes awaits regulars and passers-by alike.

The Beehive is all unpretentiousness, from the plain, polished tables to the black-and-white photos evoking scenes of rural life. The meals and generous snacks are so fresh that you need to keep your eye on the blackboards because the choice can change several times during one service.

What emerge from the kitchen are well-made compositions that offer honest, uncluttered delight. Cured herrings, fish soup, a meaty pâté, an overflowing goblet of crayfish tails or tasty bruschettas of goat's cheese and roast olives are just the thing to get you going.

Follow these with roast pork with a sage rösti, duck confit, liver and mash with a balsamic jus, or try a fish dish such as the fillet of sea bass with pesto, or a moist, accurately chargrilled tuna steak on a crisp salade niçoise. There are even some old favourites such as steak and kidney pie and home-made sausages.

If you want more, there is butterscotch raisin tart, or chocolate bread and butter pudding or a lemon posset – and if the damask napkins (a recent addition) seem more restaurant than pub, the easygoing atmosphere and cosy surroundings allay any doubts.

Speciality food: Local produce with a Mediterranean slant
Draught beers: Greene King IPA, Speckled Hen Bitter
Average wine price by the glass: £2.95

**Licensees: Di and Gary Kingshott
Last orders for dinner: 9.30 pm
Closed: Sunday dinner (food only)
Closed for holidays: 25 and 26 December
Main courses: from £8.95
Beer garden**
Children welcome

HOUGHTON CONQUEST, BEDFORDSHIRE

Knife & Cleaver

The Grove, Houghton Conquest, Bedfordshire MK45 3LA
Tel. 01234 740 387 Fax 01234 740 900
e-mail: info@theknifeandcleaver.com   **MAP 4** C5

ON the Bedford–Ampthill road, opposite the 16th-century village church, this is a smart pub-cum-restaurant with a pretty garden, dovecot and white wrought-iron tables for al fresco eating.

The front bar, which has a decent range of bar snacks and lighter fish options such as fresh sardines, is traditional and intimate, with an attractive panelled nook round a fireplace flanked by neat piles of logs for a winter fire.

Seafood is the speciality of the main restaurant. Start with deep-fried whitebait, crisp and not too oily, with a good gremolata dressing (parsley, lemon, garlic and olive oil), or maybe seared scallops with a St. Agur and boudin blanc risotto.

The rack of Welsh lamb, cooked pink, is a fine choice, tender and well flavoured, served beyond the predictable with aubergine crisps and couscous. Alternative main courses include classic fish dishes such as large, plump grilled Dover sole, John Dory and 'organic' Scottish salmon.

Puddings include a home-made chocolate marquise and the cheeses, both British and Continental, are in good condition.

Wine is taken seriously: a good range by the glass, impeccably kept under nitrogen, includes Pouilly Fuissé and well-aged Rioja, and by the bottle there can be specials such as the rarely seen Mercurey premier cru from Aubert de Villaine.

Speciality food: Grilled sea bass fillets with vignotte cheese and tomato and mustard sauce
Draught beers: Batemans XB, Fullers London Pride
Average wine price by the glass: £3.40

Licensee: David Loom
Last orders for dinner: 9.30 pm
Closed: Saturday lunch (restaurant), Sunday evening
Closed for holidays: 3 days at Christmas
Set lunch: from £12.95
Set dinner: from £22
Private dining: 10-12
Beer garden
Accommodation: 9 rooms
Children welcome   Wheelchair access

HUDDERSFIELD, WEST YORKSHIRE

Weaver's Shed

Knowl Road, Golcar, Huddersfield, W Yorkshire HD7 4AN
Tel. 01484 654 284 Fax 01484 650 980
e-mail: info@weaversshed.co.uk   **MAP 5** D5

IT IS only a little more than thirty years since this former cotton mill reverberated with the sound of the looms, and some of the atmosphere of that time has been retained, from the weaving shed itself to the mill owner's quarters, now a comfortable and spacious lounge area littered with coffee-table cookery books, its walls adorned by and menus of the great and good.

The short set menus and the carte promise natural, sometimes organic ingredients, many from the place's own gardens. These are found in the risotto of caramelised pumpkin, home-cured salmon with cauliflower cream and duck with red cabbage.

On the other hand, some of the dishes and their presentation have little to do with the announced earthy approach. The current fashion for mixing sweet and savoury pops up in a sugary finish to a wild mushroom tart with truffle scented mascarpone, while caramelisation is a much employed technique.

As for presentation, rough-hewn sheets of home-made crispbread come in slits cut into local stone and the fat chips are served in newspaper in a flower pot.

The most successful dishes are probably the straightforward ones, like the tender breast of Goosnargh duck plainly garnished with red cabbage and potato. The wine list is particularly interesting for its selection of some less well-known French country wines.

Their pride: Chargrilled fillet of Worsbrough red deer with Lincolnshire Poacher potato gratin and sautéd wild greens
Inexpensive wines: Petit Pinotage Forrester's Winery (South Africa) 2004, £13.95; Côtes de St. Mont Les Vignes Retrouvées 2002, £13.95

Proprietors: Stephen and Tracy Jackson
Last orders for dinner: 9 pm
Closed: Sunday and Monday
Closed for holidays: Christmas–New Year
Set lunch: from £11.50
Main courses: from £13.95
Private dining: up to 16
Accommodation: 5 rooms
Limited wheelchair access

HUNGERFORD, BERKSHIRE

Hare Restaurant ★

GASTROPUB

Hare & Hounds, Lambourn Woodlands, Hungerford RG17 7SD
Tel. 01488 71386 Fax 01488 71186
e-mail: cuisine@theharerestaurant.com   **MAP 2** A3

JUST a mile and a half from the M4, this handsome pub has three intimate and very comfortable rooms, one in crimson, the others with exposed beams, grouped round the bar, in which you can enjoy some impressively serious cuisine.

Menus genuinely do follow the seasons and feature such finely balanced flavours as crayfish ravioli and roast fillet of beef, and roast chestnuts and red cabbage to complement braised rabbit.

Lentils and caramelised apple are juxtapopsed with foie gras, a striking combination of rich savoury elements, and among the fish choices, a combination of oyster and cucumber in ravioli makes a deliciously light accompaniment for poached fillet of turbot.

There is no shortage of ideas either when it comes to desserts. Caramelised banana is used in a beautifully baked tarte Tatin with a banana bavarois and brown bread ice-cream, while kirsch jelly and griottines partner cherry parfait.

The wines are intelligently selected and balanced, with well-priced bottles from Bordeaux, Sicily and New Zealand. There is a range of champagne, including a demi-sec cuvée from Piper-Heidsieck that goes well with fruit-based desserts.

Speciality food: Braised pork belly with langoustines, onion compote and parsley potato foam
Draught beers: Wadworth 6X
Average wine price by the glass: £3.75

Licensees: Helen Windridge and Paul Whitford
Last orders for dinner: 9.30 pm
Closed: Sunday dinner, Monday
Set lunch: from £17
Main courses: from £18
Private dining: 10-22
Al fresco dining
Wheelchair access

HUNTINGDON, CAMBRIDGESHIRE

Old Bridge Hotel ★

1 High Street, Huntingdon, Cambridgeshire PE29 3TQ
Tel. 01480 424 300 Fax 01480 411 017
e-mail: oldbridge@huntsbridge.co.uk   **MAP 4** C4

IDEALLY situated overlooking the River Ouse, this delightful hotel has seen many changes over the years and today it is probably the jewel in the crown of four establishments run by the Huntsbridge group. Small undoubtedly equates with good.

The smart dining-room is open on Friday and Sunday nights for formal dining, but The Terrace restaurant should fit most needs. A charming loggia for semi-al fresco eating leads off the main restaurant.

Starters and main courses on the dinner menu are unashamedly Italianate in style. Vitello tonnato – veal with tuna, caper and anchovy mayonnaise – or a crab risotto with Prosecco and marscapone could feature as starters. This risotto is irresistible, moist and creamy, with sufficient crab to register but not stifle the other ingredients.

A British Saddleback pork chop marinated with lemon, rosemary and garlic, is made really delicious by the addition of buttery girolles, borlotti beans and spinach with lemon oil. Puddings might include sticky toffee, apricot soufflé with peach roasted in honey and rosemary, or marinated pineapple with five spice ice-cream. Wafer thin slices of sweet pineapple work particularly well with this unusually flavoured ice-cream.

Savoury-lovers will find something to their taste among a good selection of cheeses.

Speciality food: Verdura Mista – aubergine with tomato sauce, spinach and pine-nuts
Draught beers: Adnams, Hobson's Choice (City of Cambridge)
Average wine price by the glass: £4.50

Licensees: John Hoskins, Nina Beamond, Paul Richardson
Last orders for dinner: 10 pm
Open every day
Set lunch: from £13.50
Main courses: from £10.50
Private dining: up to 60
Al fresco dining
Accommodation: 24 rooms
Children welcome
Wheelchair access

HURLEY, BERKSHIRE

Black Boys Inn ★★

 GASTROPUB

Henley Road, Hurley, Berkshire SL6 5NQ
Tel. 01628 824 212
e-mail: info@blackboysinn.co.uk   **MAP 2** C3

THE name of this pub dates from the 17th century when slavery was at its height, but so sensitive is the name now that most signs have been changed to depict a black Labrador. The place has been sympathetically renovated and incorporates eight bedrooms. On the ground floor there is one large room with a bar, stripped wooden floors and wood-burning stove.

Big, fat, juicy olives with delicious, home-made warm bread, and served with excellent olive oil and balsamic vinegar dip, can be enjoyed while perusing the menu.

Starters might include rillette of duck flavoured with hazelnuts and pistachio, or perhaps fresh Salcombe crab with pink ginger and grapefruit jelly. There is a delicate anise flavour of caramelised fennel to offset lightly grilled goat's cheese.

Main courses include game pot-roasted with red cabbage, salsify and rowanberry gravy. Poached chicken breast is lifted by a flavoursome girolle and truffle bouillon. A medley of carrot, savoy cabbage and two types of beans with buttery mashed potato proves especially good as an accompaniment.

Fresh fish is delivered from Newlyn. Pastrami is prepared on the premises and smoked in nearby Henley.

For dessert, choose from a good cross-section of puddings such as French apple tart with vanilla ice-cream and calvados, plum and grape pancake with brandy cream, or Chocolate Nemesis.

Speciality food: Seasonal produce
Draught beers: Brakspear, Fosters
Average wine price by the glass: £4

Licensees: Helen and Adrian Bannister
Last orders for dinner: 9 pm
Open every day
Closed for holidays: 2 weeks at Christmas
Main courses: from £9.95
Beer garden
Accommodation: 8 rooms
Children over 12 welcome
Wheelchair access

ILFRACOMBE, DEVON

The Quay ★

11 The Quay, Ilfracombe, Devon EX34 9EQ
Tel. 01271 868 090 Fax 01271 865 599
e-mail: quayrestaurant@btconnect.com   **MAP 1** C3

THIS amazing modern restaurant has been designed with virgin white décor, arched ceilings and lovely views over the harbour from its two rooms. The walls are lined with the work of Damian Hirst, who happens to own the restaurant, which offers splendid modern cuisine.

The results on the plate are stunning, with memorably defined flavours and delicate textures – best illustrated in a seared fillet of sea trout, perfectly cooked, firm, bathed in a luxurious sauce, beurre blanc-style, and faultlessly partnered by clams, garden herbs, samphire, champ and spinach.

Preface this with exceptional Lundy dressed crab and elegant strips of marinated cucumber, or a salad of woodland mushrooms and globe artichoke.

These dishes come from the exceptional value £18.50 four-course set lunch, which includes a cheese course of Red Shield, a strong cow's milk Somerset cheese, as well as very fine desserts such as Valrhona bitter chocolate tart or lemon and yoghurt mousse.

On the six-course tasting menu, selected wines matched with each couse, the roast fillet of veal, with gratin potatoes and etuvé of leeks and rosemary, catches the eye. The emphasis is on lengthy several-course meals for gastronomes not in a hurry.

The wine list is intelligently selective. Old Vines Saint-Chinian from Languedoc and exceptional Sauvignon from the Western Cape do the cooking full justice.

Their pride: Seared fillet of sea trout with clams and samphire
Inexpensive wines: Vergelegen Sauvignon Blanc (Cape) 2004, £21.50; Saint-Chinian Domaine des Terres Falmet 2001, £17.50

Proprietors: Damian Hirst and Simon Browne
Last orders for dinner: 9.30 pm
Closed: Sunday evening, Monday and Tuesday
Closed for holidays: 25 December
Set lunch: from £18.50
Main courses: from £20
Private dining: 12-14

ILKLEY, WEST YORKSHIRE

Box Tree ★★

Church Street, Ilkley, West Yorkshire LS29 9DR
Tel. 01943 608 484 Fax 01943 607 186
e-mail: info@theboxtree.co.uk **MAP 5** D4

THIS pretty, English doll's house cottage at one end of Ilkley High Street is unique. With old oak settles in cosy rooms and open fires, it evokes country house majesty in miniature. The welcome, too, from new owner Rena Gueller and her team, is as warm as you will find, followed by attentive service that pampers without ever becoming oppressive. If the menus are short, what arrives is nothing short of grandiose.

With dishes of 'refined rusticity' such as sardine fillets in a warm citrus marinade, roasted calf's liver with summer cabbage and country bacon, a herb-roasted cannon of lamb with cocos beans, chillies and Morteau sausage, Simon Gueller makes it look simple, but the exquisite balance of tastes and textures he coaxes from the very finest of raw materials makes for a dazzling display throughout.

Excellent Gressingham duck comes with a straightforward red wine jus and roasted vegetables, the Muscat grapes and wood-roasted almonds providing contrasts of taste and texture and an ideal foil for the beautifully tender, pink breast of meat. More superb contrasts, too, in a passion fruit soufflé, the sweetness of which is wonderfully 'cut' by a refreshing pineapple sorbet, with a rich banana milkshake completing the complementary trio.

One might question the true worth of a sweet melon jelly with a tangerine mousse as a pre-starter, and chocolates might be more appropriate than what amount to post-desserts with the coffee, but that is a question of style rather than quality.

Their pride: Hand-dived scallops, celeriac purée with truffles
Inexpensive wines: Sauvignon Blanc Eradus (New Zealand) 2003, £25.25; Merlot Weinert (Argentina) 1999, £25.50

Proprietor: Rena Gueller
Last orders for dinner: 9.30 pm
Closed: Monday
Closed for holidays: 1st week January
Set lunch: from £18
Set dinner: from £28
Private dining: 8-14
Wheelchair access

ILMINGTON, WARWICKSHIRE

Howard Arms

GASTROPUB

Lower Green, Ilmington, Warwickshire CV36 4LT
Tel./Fax 01608 682 226
e-mail: info@howardarms.com   MAP 3 E4

THOSE in urgent need of sustenance should prepare themselves before setting foot inside this square Cotswold stone hostelry on the green: Save room for pudding! You could even be excused for starting with the apple, pear and gooseberry flapjack crumble or the chocolate mousse cake with ginger ice-cream, before moving on to a summer pudding bursting with hedgerow fruit as a main course and finishing your meal with either the sticky almond cake or 'Mrs. G's toffee meringue'.

This may sound as if the flagstoned pub is straightforwardly English, but the menu has instant appeal and variety with some terminology and a few of the ingredients hailing from further afield. For example, try the trout rillettes, deep-fried haloumi cheese, chicken with mascarpone and prosciutto or a supreme and confit leg of guinea fowl in a kind of bortsch of beetroot, red onions and soured cream. These outside influences are used to create a personalised style around homespun culinary ideology.

A tomato tarte Tatin dusted with Parmesan is a nice idea, even if the pastry was a little chewy. Braised lamb with mint and spices has added zest, while sea bass with brown shrimp risotto comes with a parsley-based pesto, and a tempting waft of tangy mustard escapes from the crisp, flaky crust of a hefty beef and ale pie.

This is all served by immensely likeable young men in long aprons who understand your plight perfectly and will no doubt provide a doggy truck to take home any unfinished platefuls. The nursery puds are a must, though.

Speciality food: Inventive British cooking
Draught beers: Everards Tiger, North Cotswold Genesis
Average wine price by the glass: £2.95

Licensees: Martin Devereux, Rob Greenstock
Last orders for dinner: 9 pm (Sunday 8.30 pm)
Open every day
Main courses: from £9.50
Beer garden
Accommodation: 3 rooms
Children welcome
Wheelchair access

ISLE OF WIGHT, YARMOUTH

The George ★

Quay Street, Yarmouth, Isle of Wight PO41 0PE
Tel. 01983 760 331 Fax 01983 760 425
e-mail: res@thegeorge.co.uk   **MAP 2** B5

OVERLOOKING the yachting harbour, this 17th-century former town house has retained all of its character – from fine entrance hall to a dining-room with maroon walls, heavy drapes, soft light, very comfortable chairs and elegantly set tables evocative of a gentleman's club in St James's.

Aperitifs are accompanied by finely chopped smoked salmon on a crisp base, with olives. Then a chicken liver mousseline, served with style in an eggshell, delivers high aspirations for following courses. Foie gras crème brûlée astonishes with its thin crust of caramelised sugar on a smooth parfait with a sweet cherry purée, tiny croutons and crushed pistachios – a real highlight. Turbot, perhaps a touch dry from roasting but delicate nevertheless, is served with the tiniest girolles, the crispest of little onion rings and a fine saffron sauce.

Alternative first courses are langoustine and pig's trotter lasagne and ox tongue tortellini with chicken confit. Followed maybe by roasted veal sweetbread with pork belly, sauce Maltaise, or Bresse chicken with truffle and cabbage sauce.

The hot chocolate fondant is not to be missed – crack the shell and the dark molten chocolate oozes out. A tuile of orange and Grand Marnier tastes distinctly of zesty orange and liqueur, while a hot cinnamon doughnut is soft and delicate. The final surprise is a parsnip panna cotta served in a glass and flavoured with vanilla – it has ethereal qualities.

Their pride: Roast lobster, courgette flower filled with lobster mousse on pineapple tapioca
Inexpensive wines: Muscadet de Sèvre et Maine sur Donatien Bahuaud 2002, £14.75; Bardolino Monte del Frà 2003, £14.75

Proprietors: Jeremy Willcock and John Illsley
Last orders for dinner: 9.30 pm
Closed: Sunday and Monday
Closed for holidays: 25 December
Set dinner: from £46.50
Private dining: 8-30
Accommodation: 15 rooms
Wheelchair access

ITTERINGHAM, NORFOLK

Walpole Arms

GASTROPUB

**The Common, Itteringham, Nr. Norwich, Norfolk NR11 7AR
Tel. 01263 587 258 Fax 01263 587 074
e-mail: goodfood@thewalpolearms.co.uk**   **MAP 4** E3

DEEP in the Norfolk countryside, the popular Walpole has large blackboards announcing a wide range of gastro-brasserie fare, everything clearly cooked to order and based on good, fresh ingredients.

The timbered restaurant in a barn-like extension has the same menu as the bar, £1.50 added to prices for waitress service, though it is worth noting that the prices are very reasonable for a gastropub.

Fresh and wholesome fish soup is presented with rouille, croutons and shredded Cantal cheese. For starters there are samphire with butter, lemon and black pepper, or squid cooked in its own ink. The main course might be confit of duck or perhaps a special such as dogfish. Rib-eye steak is perfectly cooked to a medium rare order and comes with oxtail jus and herb-flavoured polenta.

Puddings are as nicely varied: summer berry soup with crème fraîche, peach tarte Tatin and double strawberry ice-cream with brandy-snap.

For a quick snack, try something like the Walpole Ploughman's, which features Isle of Mull Cheddar.

Wines are promoted with flair. Each month there is a special of two fine wines at lower prices – like the Sancerre taste-alike, a fresh domaine-bottled Quincy that would be ideal with black bream, a popular fish choice here.

Speciality food: Warm pigeon salad, capers and soft egg
Draught beers: Woodforde Wherry, Adnams
Average wine price by the glass: £3.40

**Licensees: Christian Hodginson and Richard Bryan
Last orders for dinner: 9 pm winter, 9.30 pm summer
Closed: Sunday evening
Closed for holidays: 25 December
Main courses: from £9
Private dining: up to 35
Beer garden**
Children welcome
Wheelchair access

KEYSTON, CAMBRIDGESHIRE

The Pheasant ★

GASTROPUB

Keyston, Huntingdon, Cambridgeshire PE18 0RE
Tel. 01832 710 241 Fax 01832 710 340
e-mail: office@huntsbridge.com   **MAP 4** C4

THIS thatched inn, run by the same family for forty years, forms part of an association of chefs who use their expertise to the full in four establishments. Featuring all the traditional trappings of a period property, The Pheasant offers three eating areas and a comfortable bar with rustic-style furniture and open fireplaces.

There is plenty of choice for vegetarians: buffalo mozzarella with courgettes marinated in chilli, lemon and mint with Morello single estate olive oil, or perhaps a special of tiropitakia, which is parcels of deep-fried filo pastry filled with mozzarella, Parmesan and fontina cheese with spring onion and dill.

Whole baked sea bass with citrus braised fennel might make an appearance on the 'Cornish fish of the day' board if you're lucky, while for carnivores, the slow-cooked shank of Cornish lamb, served with caramelised onion and spinach, fried garlic and Parmesan polenta, should fit the bill.

Otherwise, one of the specials could be rump of Aberdeenshire beef - thick, succulent slices of pink meat with a superb flavour, accompanied by shredded savoy cabbage and pancetta with sautéd potatoes.

To follow, try apricot and almond tart with Devonshire cream, or chocolate and hazelnut truffle cake with crème fraîche.

It is worth drawing attention to the acclaimed wine list created by John Hoskins, the restaurant world's first Master of Wine.

Speciality food: Cornish fish
Draught beers: Adnams, City of Cambridge Bitter
Average wine price by the glass: £4.50

Licensees: John Hoskins and Jonathon Dargue
Last orders for dinner: 9.30 pm
Open every day
Closed for holidays: 25-26 December, 1 January
Main courses: from £8.95
Private dining: 20-30
Al fresco dining
Children welcome
Limited wheelchair access

KINGHAM, OXFORDSHIRE

Tollgate Inn

GASTROPUB

Church Street, Kingham, Oxfordshire OX7 6YA
Tel. 01608 658 389 Fax 01608 659 467
e-mail: info@thetollgate.com   **MAP 2** A2

THE Tollgate is a fine Cotswold inn at the centre of this handsome village, much favoured by the owners of second homes because it is easily accessible from London. Paul and Anne Smith took over the inn in the spring of 2005, and they have sensitively given the bar and the restaurant a modern touch without losing the period character. They are drawing in the locals to sup the beautifully kept 'Hooky' real ale while also catering for couples and families touring the Cotswolds.

The food is the real focus here. The chef is Vietnamese and a light touch and precise cooking are evident in such things as crisp chestnut and mushroom parcels with a piquant tomato and chilli dip, and Thai marinated chicken stir-fry, which is a good main course, the chicken tender and flavoursome and accompanied by pak choi and Chinese cucumber.

There are also plenty of European options such as pasta, risotto, and meat pies. The daily changing blackboard might offer carrot and coriander soup, salad of chorizo and Spanish Blush tomatoes, and from North Africa, fillet of pork tagine with tabbouleh. You might find a 'bouillabaisse' of sorts on the board, consisting of, say, salmon, hake, prawns, sea bass and mussels.

A carefully chosen wine list includes notably fresh and aromatic true Beaujolais and there is a good showing from Spain and the southern hemisphere. Paul and Anne are naturally good hosts, and there are nine comfortable bedrooms, all en-suite, both at the inn and in an annexe.

Speciality food: European and Asian cuisine
Draught beers: Hook Norton, Stella Artois
Average wine price by the glass: £3

Licensees: Paul and Anne Smith
Last orders for dinner: 9 pm
Closed: Monday
Main courses: from £12
Beer garden
Accommodation: 9 rooms
Children welcome
Wheelchair access

KIRK DEIGHTON, NORTH YORKSHIRE

Bay Horse

GASTROPUB

Main Street, Kirk Deighton, Nr. Wetherby, N Yorks LS22 4DZ
Tel. 01937 580 058 Fax 01937 582 443

MAP 5 D4

THERE IS A distinctly 'foodie' accent at this little village hostelry, but they are keen to retain its innate character as a drinkers' pub, and the lively discussion and ribald laughter coming from the bar bear happy testimony to the success of their policy. Everything has been judged about right, really, from the authenticity of the interior with its copper-topped tables, wheelback chairs, sporting prints and dried hops, to the natural hospitality of young staff and a menu rich in variety.

Provenance is all-important, too, from the free-range organic eggs to pasture-grazed local beef and daily arrivals of fish direct from independent Scarborough fishermen. The prime ingredients are carefully prepared to get the best out of their natural appeal and flavour, judiciously perfumed sauces and accompaniments adding just the right edge.

There are traditional English favourites such as home-made black pudding, prize-winning 'bangers' with onion gravy, battered fresh cod and chips and well-aged steaks. Gressingham duck with a Wakefield rhubarb sauce, tempura prawns, Thai fishcakes or a succulent fillet of halibut with a fruity pesto and nicely al dente asparagus add to the diversity of treats in store. Desserts are equally tempting. And if you just want a snack, there are huge sandwiches made with country bread.

A reasonably priced evening menu is available for early diners: 'The kind of food we like to serve to our friends and families,' promises the menu. So bring a friend and join the family!

Speciality food: Traditional English cookery
Draught beers: John Smith Bitter, Cumberland Ale
Average wine price by the glass: £2.85

Licensee: Karl Mainey
Last orders for dinner: 9.30 pm
Closed: no food on Sunday evening and Monday lunch
Closed for holidays: 26 & 27 December & 1 January
Set lunch: £12.95
Set dinner: £12.95 (until 7 pm)
Beer garden
Children welcome

KNOSSINGTON, LEICESTERSHIRE

Fox and Hounds ★

GASTROPUB

6 Somerby Road, Knossington, Leicestershire LE15 8LY
Tel. 01664 454 676 Fax 01664 454 031

MAP 4 B3

THE rear of the property boasts a floodlit pétanque pitch. This is a popular game with locals, so you may find parking a little restricted on evenings when games are in full swing.

Flanked by tables and chairs, the pub entrance leads into an unfussy room where a plain, painted wooden bar with an alloy counter takes centre stage. Scrubbed pine tables, tiled floors and open fires make this equally inviting for both drinker and diner. A smaller dining-room leads off the bar.

A two-course set lunch menu offers good value, such as a soup or bruschetta with various toppings followed by grilled loin of pork with sauté potatoes or mixed fish, fishcakes and baby spinach. Vegetarians who may feel that they get short shrift when it comes to eating out will have no such gripe here.

The dinner menu has a Mediterranean slant. Choose griddled, marinated aubergine with feta and herbs or buffalo mozzarella with red pepper sauce and basil. A thin, crisp tartlet filled with braised, sweet tomatoes might come topped with fresh anchovy fillets and soft boiled quail's eggs surrounded by dressed rocket.

Lightly spiced tomatoes and crunchy chickpeas may accompany pink and succulent roast rump of lamb. If the chef has been on one of his frequent forays to Norfolk, samphire might feature with pan-fried fillet of cod, say, or salmon.

Puddings such as apricot tiramisù with strawberry salsa will follow the seasons.

Speciality food: Rib of beef for two
Draught beers: Marston Pedigree, Adnams
Average wine price by the glass: £3.25

Licensees: Brian Baker and Clare Ellis
Last orders for dinner: 9.30 pm
Closed: Monday (food)
Set lunch: from £9.95
Main courses: from £10.25
Private dining: 12-18
Al fresco dining
Children welcome
Wheelchair access

KNOWSTONE, DEVON

Mason's Arms ★

GASTROPUB

Knowstone, South Molton, Devon EX36 4RY
Tel. 01398 341 231

MAP 1 C3

IT cannot be long before this 13th-century thatched pub, with its buttermilk exterior and rolling rural views, is known countrywide as a small but perfectly formed temple of gastronomy.

It is extraordinary to think that the youthful Mark Dodson, who spent 18 years at the Waterside Inn at Bray, more than half that time as head chef, would be content doing twenty-four covers with only one other in the kitchen, but content he is. He and his wife Sarah, who runs front-of-house, wanted a lifestyle change.

The bar oozes character with its stone flags, polished wooden counter and blackened inglenook fireplace complete with bread oven, and is a good place to sup on a pint while nibbling roasted Spanish almonds and perusing the day's menu.

This is confident, mature, nothing-to-prove cooking, where the simple is elevated to the exceptional.

The dining-room, its green walls hung with commemorative plates, does not distract from the artistry on the plate in front of you. Witness a wild mushroom risotto, small in stature but rich in texture and intriguing flavours; a yielding roulade of pork belly with braised red cabbage, the carefully turned potatoes and caramelised shallots showing the same slow, patient preparation and cooking as the main ingredient, and a sublime warm fig tart, faultlessly executed, with a sweet onion jam.

The wine list is compiled with equal skill and contains some gems.

Speciality food: Salad of crab
Draught beers: Cotleigh Tawny
Average wine price by the glass: £3.50

Licensees: Mark and Sarah Dodson
Last orders for dinner: 9.30 pm
Closed: Sunday evening, Monday
Closed for holidays: 2 weeks January
Main courses: from £15
Beer garden
Children welcome

LAPWORTH, WARWICKSHIRE

The Boot

GASTROPUB

Old Warwick Road, Lapworth, Nr. Knowle, Warks B94 6JU
Tel. 01564 782 464 Fax 01564 784 989

MAP 3 E3

EMPHASISING good food while retaining the characteristics of a pub and not discouraging the drinking fraternity is often a difficult balance to achieve. An attractive bar area with tables means no one is marginalised, and the plaster walls and quirky caricatures with subtle lighting downstairs make for a relaxed atmosphere.

Upstairs there is a more airy feel in the dining area, with light coloured painted tables and chairs that are far enough apart to discourage any ear-wigging.

The standard menu is unshowy and well balanced, with starters that include a robust game terrine; whisky and honey cured salmon blinis; oriental duck salad, and pumpkin, goat's cheese and pine-nut lasagne.

The specials are mainly fish, which is accurately cooked, or calf's liver served with truly crisp bacon and onions, and well-executed chargrilled rib-eye steak did not disappoint.

A selection of puddings features seasonal fruit and caters both for people with room to spare and those looking for something lighter to finish their meal.

The wine list is made up of some 50 sensibly priced wines from top producers round the globe, such as Brampton Sauvignon from the Cape and Italian Corvina Alpha Zeta, which represent good value. A congenial manager and his young team provide friendly and attentive service.

Speciality food: Bubble and squeak, smoked bacon and poached egg with hollandaise
Draught beers: Old Speckled Hen, Tetley
Average wine price by the glass: £3

Licensee: James Elliot
Last orders for dinner: 10 pm
Open every day
Closed for holidays: 1 January
Main courses: from £11
Private dining: 15-18
Al fresco dining
Children welcome
Wheelchair access

LEAFIELD, OXFORDSHIRE

Navy Oak

GASTROPUB

110 Lower End, Leafield, Nr. Witney, Oxon OX29 9QQ
Tel. 01993 878 496
e-mail: thenavyoak@aol.com **MAP 2** B2

LEAFIELD (originally named Field Town) sits amid the triangle formed by the towns of Witney, Burford and Charlbury. In this largely unspoilt village featuring the distinctive Cotswold stone, Morris dancing was big in the mid-19th century. It fell into rapid decline in the latter half of the century, apparently because of 'the unwillingness of young men to participate in a cultural form regarded as rowdy, uncouth and lacking social respectability.'

The Navy Oak is on the outskirts of the village, a locale possibly to its disadvantage when the hub of any such rural community tends to be round its green. However, the enthusiasm and skills of the owner/chef and his wife certainly deserve recognition. A set two-course lunch for £12 that includes a glass of house red or white wine is excellent value.

Typical dishes from this menu would be Thai fishcakes with an agreeable chilli sauce as a starter, followed by a succulent leg of lamb steak, cooked to your liking, served with a tomato concassé and flavoursome jus and accompanied by crisp, roasted new potatoes and perhaps spinach and crunchy French beans. Alternatively, the à la carte menu offers starters such as courgette and marjoram soup, or salad of black pudding and bacon with mustard dressing, followed possibly by grilled tranche of brill with spinach, tomato and herb oil, or pan-fried saddle of venison with corned beef croquette and red wine sauce.

A moist spotted dick with a good fruity content could be a little more generous with the crème anglaise, but it is a pleasing finish to a well-executed meal.

Speciality food: Fish tagine and local produce
Draught beers: Hook Norton, Brakspear
Average wine price by the glass: £4

Licensees: Alastair and Sarah Ward
Last orders for dinner: 9.30 pm
Closed: Monday
Set lunch: from £12
Main courses: from £10.50
Private dining: up to 25
Al fresco dining
Children welcome
Wheelchair access

LEEDS, WEST YORKSHIRE

Anthony's ★

19 Boar Lane, Leeds, West Yorkshire LS1 6EA
Tel. 0113 245 5922
e-mail: reservations@anthonysrestaurant.co.uk   **MAP 5** D4

DURING the short time since its opening, this stylishly modern restaurant has become very much the place to go in Leeds, attracting customers from all over the North of England. From the light ground-floor bar you go downstairs to the restaurant, but the feeling of being in a basement is cleverly banished by curving walls and shapes.

The overall effect is minimalist but a warm, welcoming ambience is created by stained wooden floors, rich-brown leather chairs and cream tablecloths.

And then, of course, there is the cooking, which is certainly impressive and sometimes strikingly different. Roasted loin of venison, tender and rich in flavour, comes with venison carpaccio and foie gras, and is served on what might look like couscous but is in fact Peruvian quinoa grains, which are finer in texture as well as taste.

Appetisers can show similar innovative tendencies: dough flavoured with black beans baked around mashed potato and vanilla, pine-yeast added to pear velouté. The desserts, too, are created with imagination. Try the apple and mascarpone mousse with ravioli of pumpkin.

The wines are good and sensibly priced and there is one page devoted to specialist beers, including Belgian Deus champagne beer, which is made and matured in the same perfectionist way as a champagne in Epernay or Reims. This is a place to watch.

Their pride: Risotto of white onion, Parmesan air
Inexpensive wines: Viognier Dela Frères Vin de Pays d'Oc 2003, £14.95; Santa Rita Sauvignon Blanc (Chile) 2004, £13.95

Proprietor: Anthony Flinn
Last orders for dinner: Tuesday-Thursday 9.30 pm, Friday and Saturday 10 pm
Closed: Sunday and Monday
Closed for holidays: Bank Holidays, first week Sept
Set lunch: from £18.95
Main courses: from £22.95
Wheelchair access

LEEDS, WEST YORKSHIRE

Pool Court at 42

44 The Calls, Leeds, West Yorkshire LS2 7EW
Tel. 0113 244 4242 Fax 0113 234 3332
e-mail: info@poolcourt.com   **MAP 5** D4

POOL COURT moved to its riverside location a decade ago and occupies a prime position in the heart of this former industrial site, the revamping of which has helped to breathe new life into the old centre of Leeds. There is a deck overlooking the River Aire where drinks or lunch may be served.

It is a small, restrained and elegant setting for a selection of uncomplicated dishes designed to please rather than to show off the chef's art.

Foie gras is a suitably popular starter, as is the dish of lobster and scallops with leeks and dill. Scottish beef and seasonal game give a flavour of the home-sourced meats that are used, the beef being richly garnished with ox tongue ragout and caramelised shallots.

Not that contemporary cooking styles are ignored, with such things as a black pudding beignet (in chip-shop batter) and a crunchy breadcrumb coating on well-cooked sweetbreads.

The desserts, on the other hand, are unashamedly conservative, featuring spotted dick, rice pudding, crumble and trifle.

Pool Court is part of a small catering complex that also includes a brasserie and a bar.

Their pride: Risotto of spring carrots, langoustines, delicately curried almonds
Inexpensive wines: Cousiño Macul Chardonnay (Chile) 2003, £15.80; Los Vascos Cabernet Sauvignon (Chile) 2002, £17.95

Proprietor: Michael Gill
Last orders for dinner: 9 pm
Closed: Sunday
Closed for holidays: 25 and 26 December
Set dinner: from £39.50
Private dining: 25-36
Al fresco dining: lunch only
Wheelchair access

LEVINGTON, SUFFOLK

The Ship Inn

GASTROPUB

Church Lane, Levington, Suffolk IP10 0LQ
Tel. 01473 659 573

MAP 4 E5

SEEKING a site for his new venture, chef/proprietor Mark Johnson traipsed around 200-odd properties before settling on this little gem. And who can blame him? Tunnel-like lanes lead you to the hidden village of Levington, meandering parallel to the Orwell where, beyond the yachts rocking peacefully at anchor, the mighty container depot cranes at the distant mouth of the river occasionally appear through gaps in the hedgerows.

There's even a glimpse of the water from one of the cosy bar areas, with its wood-burning stove, and Mark is keen to retain the intrinsic atmosphere of this endearing thatched pub, where scrubbed tables and nautical paraphernalia abound and local youngsters serve with cheery aptitude.

Traditional English food is announced, but while this is certainly true of slow-roasted shank of lamb, plainer grills – including fine local fish – and cosy desserts, the tendency is noticeably towards more imaginative fare. Greek salad, home-cured gravadlax, tiger prawns with chilli and excellent taramasalata might start you off, to be followed by varied and stunningly presented brochettes of chicken and prawns marinated in coriander and yoghurt, or pork tenderloin with chorizo, or veal cutlet with brandy cream.

A classy dish of scallops with hollandaise sauce, perfectly cooked asparagus and crisp, buttery vegetables and new potatoes would not have been out of place on the finest restaurant table.

Tables cannot be booked, so be prepared to wait at busy times. You'll find it's well worth the trip off the beaten track.

Speciality food: Traditional English/Modern European
Draught beers: Adnams Bitter, Greene King IPA
Average wine price by the glass: £3.40

Licensees: Mark and Stella Johnson
Last orders for dinner: 9.30 pm
Closed: Sunday dinner
Closed for holidays: 25 and 26 December, 1 January
Main courses: from £9.95
Beer garden
Children welcome in garden
Wheelchair access

LEYBURN, NORTH YORKSHIRE

The Sandpiper ★

`GASTROPUB`

Market Square, Leyburn, North Yorkshire DL8 5AT
Tel. 01969 622 206 Fax 01969 625 367

MAP 5 D4

THIS ivy-clad stone inn, well-placed in the attractive market square, has a cosy little bar, a simply laid out dining-room and a sunny front terrace in which to enjoy a range of traditional and international food specialities.

Superb meat, poultry and vegetables are mostly sourced within a twenty-mile radius of the town, and from them come striking depths of flavour, the often rustic appeal of heartily portioned dishes belying the professionalism behind their conception.

A starter like ham hock terrine is particularly smooth, meaty and well seasoned here, and given a worthy accompaniment of wild mushroom dressing. The fishcakes, Caesar salad and warm goat's cheese are familiar favourites, but smoked mackerel and salmon rillettes, or lamb kofta with mint and coriander dressing, provide welcome alternatives.

Main courses are nicely varied. Moroccan spiced chicken with couscous, fillet of pork wrapped in Parma ham and served with roasted peppers, or beef fillet with leeks and black bacon sit alongside roasted salmon on a smoked haddock and leek risotto, or a medley of fish and prawns with saffron and capers. A rather unassuming plate of braised beef with root vegetables is made rich by a proper meat jus base.

Particularly well-made desserts include a mouth-watering terrine of three chocolates and a refreshingly different duo of glazed lemon and lemon pudding.

Speciality food: Pork wrapped in Parma ham
Draught beers: Black Sheep, Copper Dragon
Average wine price by the glass: £2.85

Licensee: Jonathon Harrison
Last orders for dinner: 9 pm (weekends 9.30 pm)
Closed: Monday
Closed for holidays 2 weeks January
Main courses: from £9.25
Beer garden
Accommodation: 3 rooms
Children welcome

LICKFOLD, WEST SUSSEX

Lickfold Inn

GASTROPUB

Lickfold, Nr. Petworth, West Sussex GU28 9EY
Tel. 01798 861 285
e-mail: thelickfoldinn@aol.com **MAP 2** C4

SET IN a country lane close to the little river Lod, the Lickfold Inn is a handsome, 15th-century part timbered, part brick free house. It stands in solitary splendour, with lanterns and abundant floral displays decorating the façade. Rugs, a huge inglenook, sofas, Windsor chairs and a substantial oak counter all add to the cosy atmosphere in the bar. The dining area has carved wooden settles and a fine brick floor, with a terrace outdoors where meals are served, and a further area which is a beer garden.

This is a well-tended establishment where the Hickey family ensure their customers are looked after. They also take pride in their food. The main menu is changed every six weeks and there are daily specials – you might be lucky and find lobster.

Game is served in season, venison coming from a local estate, and seafood is becoming ever more popular. First courses could be saffron cream moules marinières, lightly battered tender squid with aïoli, or gazpacho with home-made bread. Then perhaps wild boar sausages with red onion gravy, the popular Lickfold burger with salsa, or cornfed chicken wrapped in crispy bacon and served with mozzarella and a dressed salad.

Space permitting, there could be chocolate and almond torte or a crème brûlée packed with passion fruit and mango.

An ideal aperitif is the locally made Gospel Green vintage cider, served by the glass from champagne bottles. There are eight wines by the glass.

Speciality food: Fillet of sea bass with chilli herb crust
Draught beers: Hogs Back T.E.A., Horsham Best Bitter
Average wine price by the glass: £3.25

Licensees: Hickey Family
Last orders for dinner: 9.30 pm
Closed: Mon (not Bank Hols), Sun evening (food only)
Closed for holidays: 25 and 26 December
Main courses: from £9.95
Private dining: 15-40
Beer garden
Children welcome
Wheelchair access

LIDGATE, SUFFOLK

The Star ★

GASTROPUB

The Street, Lidgate, Nr. Newmarket, Suffolk CB8 9PP
Tel./Fax 01638 500 275

MAP 4 D4

SOUTH from Newmarket, on the B1063 Clare Road, you will find this pretty period pub with a difference.

People often sit in the attractive front garden eating steaming bowls of paella. The bars are a jumble of delightful rooms which include a tiny restaurant where you sit with other customers, the atmosphere joyful and thoroughly pleasurable.

The Mediterranean influences of the Catalan owner are evident in the vivid flavours of a real paella Valenciana, in tender baby squid brushed with olive oil and garlic – and supremely in the Spanish roast shoulder of lamb cooked with white wine and onions.

The flavours of Spain also dominate favourites such as ham and melon, pimentos and Spanish meatballs.

Seafood is obviously a chosen medium, too, in Mediterranean fish soup, cod in garlic mousseline and monkfish in various guises.

A delightful English influence creeps into the puddings – with the treacle tart being especially good, rich and with crisp pastry and a spicy element.

There is an unusual Valdepeñas blanco by the glass – clean and a good foil to the baby squid – and a fruit-driven Tempranillo, plus some well-aged reds by the bottle from Rioja, Ribero del Duero, Navarra and Penedes.

Speciality food: Mediterranean with English influence
Draught beers: Abbot, Greene King IPA
Average wine price by the glass: £3

Licensee: Maria Teresa Axon
Last orders for dinner: 10 pm
Closed: Sunday evening (food)
Closed for holidays: 25 and 26 December
Set lunch: from £12.50
Main courses: from £15.50
Private dining: up to 20
Beer garden
Children welcome
Limited wheelchair access

LIFTON, DEVON

Arundell Arms ★

GASTROPUB

Lifton, Devon PL16 0AA
Tel. 01566 784 666 Fax 01566 784 494
e-mail: reservations@arundellarms.com   **MAP 1** C4

IN THE early 1960s, Anne Voss-Bark bought this old fishing hotel with twenty miles of rights on the River Tamar. Today, she is still here, razor-sharp, ensuring that classical standards in the hotel and the kitchen are high – staff and management are unfailingly courteous – yet all the while giving help and financial support to her chefs who have gone on to start their own ventures.

Nowadays, bar food is an important part of the business and the Arundell is a model of what a country hotel bar should offer: an excellence belying simple and appetising starters such as roasted tomato and sweet pepper soup, given a lift by nutmeg cream, or maybe a summer vegetable risotto, or slowly cooked confit of duck. Look out for fritters of hake with chips and salad.

The grilled sirloin steak excels, the beef coming from one of the South-West's finest butchers. In the elegant restaurant – with spoon-back Victorian chairs, wall inserts of classical scenes and a discreet chandelier – the quality of produce from local suppliers is even more evident. The Cornish scallops could not be fresher, with a ragout of clams, lemon and parsley; the medium rare roasted fillet of Devon beef is outstanding, enriched by a fine port sauce.

The chef's dedication to his craft is shown in champagne jelly with wild strawberry ice-cream – a pudding of delicious subtlety.

The range of really excellent house wines has more age and character than most: try the Romanian Pinot Noir, a revelation of natural richness and maturing complex flavours.

Speciality food: Roast fillet of Devon beef, baby vegetables, port wine sauce
Draught beers: John Smith, Carlsberg
Average wine price by the glass: £3.75

Licensee: Anne Voss-Bark
Last orders for dinner: 9.30 pm
Open every day
Set dinner: from £35
Private dining: 20-70 (winter)
Accommodation: 21 rooms
Children welcome
Wheelchair access

LITTLE BARROW, CHESHIRE

Foxcote Inn ★ `GASTROPUB`

Station Lane, Little Barrow, Nr. Chester, Cheshire CH3 7JN
Tel. 01244 301 343 Fax 01244 303 287

MAP 3 D1

FIVE miles east of Chester (on the B5132 that runs from the A51 to the A56) this pub is famed locally, and with good reason, for very fresh fish and seafood.

Have a drink at the cosy, mellow bar, where the food orders are also taken, then head for the simple but airy restaurant.

The choice of fish relies heavily on the blackboard. The quality of the ingredients, their undoubted freshness, and the accuracy of the cooking yield all the right tastes and textures.

A tempura of king prawns comes through with flying colours, the tempura crisp and light, perfectly timed, the prawns juicy. Roasted halibut was equally good, the fish cutting into bite-sized slices, firm yet tender. Other choices could be grilled sardines with lemon butter, crispy breaded whitebait and fillet of haddock. Lobster thermidor is a perennial favourite.

For people who prefer to eat meat, meanwhile, there could be a joint, perhaps braised lamb on the bone.

The desserts are appetising and original. One of the best is the delicious bowl of marinated cherries with red wine syrup and vanilla ice-cream.

The wines, too, are excellent, especially the Picpoul de Pinet from Languedoc and a textbook Sancerre, either of which is ideal for the type of food.

Speciality food: Baked lobster thermidor
Draught beers: Boddingtons, John Smith
Average wine price by the glass: £3.80

Licensee: Leigh Parry
Last orders for dinner: 9.30 pm
Closed: Sunday evening
Closed for holidays: 25 and 26 December (evening)
Set lunch: from £7.95
Set dinner: from £13.95 (Monday to Thursday)
Al fresco dining
Children welcome
Wheelchair access

LITTLE BEDWYN, WILTSHIRE

The Harrow at Little Bedwyn ★

Little Bedwyn, Marlborough, Wiltshire SN8 3JP
Tel. 01672 870 871
e-mail: bookings@harrowinn.co.uk   **MAP 1** F2

THE last thing you would expect to find in a quiet village by the Kennet and Avon canal is a true gem of a converted pub with a restaurant having an outstanding wine list which also happens to be keenly priced. For instance, you can savour Krug and Dom Perignon (1996) along with other notable wines and rare sherries by the glass.

Outside, the garden terrace is a delightful setting for a summer al fresco lunch. Inside is a bar and several cosy rooms, a centrally located wood-burner, ceiling fans and vases of fresh flowers. Tables are spread with crisp white linen and napkins.

The menu is renewed each day and the first surprise might be a gossamer light chilled cauliflower foam with thinly sliced locally picked truffle. Choose from starters of, say, a grilled fillet of baby red mullet with salade niçoise or the more extravagant lightly grilled foie gras with lightly seared scallop, savoury black pudding and vintage sherry reduction.

Main courses include Aberdeen Angus fillet, hung for twenty-eight days and served with horse-radish blini, or perhaps a fillet of Northumberland venison and bashed neeps, or line-caught turbot with a memorable wild mushroom accompaniment.

The second surprise might be a passion fruit jelly served in a tiny glass. Cinnamony bread and butter pudding and a glass of dark, chilled Pedro Ximinez sherry make a fine finishing combination, though you might prefer the lemon tart.

Speciality food: Grilled foie gras, black pudding, seared scallop
Draught beers: Fullers London Pride, Butts
Average wine price by the glass: £6

Licensee: Roger and Sue Jones
Last orders for dinner: 9 pm
Closed: Sunday-Tuesday evening
Closed for holidays: 2 weeks Christmas, 2 weeks Aug
Set lunch: from £25
Set dinner: from £30
Al fresco dining
Children welcome
Wheelchair access

LIVERPOOL, MERSEYSIDE

60 Hope Street

60 Hope Street, Liverpool, Merseyside L1 9BZ
Tel: 0151 707 6060 Fax 0151 707 6016
e-mail: info@60hopestreet.com   **MAP 5** C5

A POPULAR meeting-place close to Liverpool's Roman Catholic cathedral, and on the quieter extremity of the city's lively night life quarter, this restaurant is in a terraced town house, the other floors of which offer a bistro and bar.

Here, it is rather like eating in an empty art gallery, with its plain white décor and bare boards. The house style is clean and slick, with black-clad youngsters providing capable service. Exactly the right culinary chord is struck for this kind of operation, with sparsely garnished dishes in a classical mould, restraint and straightforward good taste being the order of the day.

Technical accomplishment is particularly marked in light rabbit ballottine with a simple salad of grated carrots in thyme dressing, and in excellent loin of tender Kendal lamb topping out a stack of model pommes Anna, and creamed spinach in a meaty ragout jus.

Original touches make furtive appearances, like the herb spätzle, pine-nut and honey dressing on roast breast of Goosnargh duck, or a deep-fried jam sandwich with ice-cream. But in general, the conventional prevails, based on the widespread use of prime local ingredients.

The honest flavours and reassuring technique are a very welcome surprise in such upbeat surroundings.

Their pride: Roast breast of Goosnargh duck, wild mushrooms, broad beans, confit duck and herb spätzle
Inexpensive wines: Brushwood Semillon Chardonnay (South Australia) 2004, £13.95; Bottle Tree Cabernet Merlot (Australia) 2003, £13.95

Proprietors: Colin and Gary Manning
Last orders for dinner: 10.30 pm
Closed: Sunday
Closed for holidays: 25 December, 1 January
Set lunch: from £12.95
Set dinner: from £12.95 (before 7 pm)
Private dining: up to 30

LIVERPOOL, MERSEYSIDE

London Carriage Works

40 Hope Street, Liverpool, Merseyside L1 9DA
Tel. 0151 705 2222 Fax 0151 709 2454

MAP 5 C5

GONE is the sepia image of industrialisation to be replaced by the phoenix of revitalisation. If Liverpool's cathedral was a forerunner of this new lease of life, the nearby converted Carriage Works is a particularly poignant example of urban rehabilitation.

Cool it most certainly is: the open-plan ground floor is split by stylish glass partitions between a trendy coffee shop and brasserie and the more formal restaurant. Simply decorated behind its picture windows, the bare boards and intentionally sparse interior acquire greater intimacy of an evening, and the smart, willing staff display an admirable blend of chatty bonhomie and easygoing professionalism.

One would naturally imagine the food to be fashionably up to date and the use of regional ingredients is impressive throughout an interesting range of innovative dishes on set lunch and dinner menus: pressed carrot terrine with orange and cumin; fillet of sea bass with fondant turnip, bulgar wheat, black olive purée and scallop and langoustine sauce; pheasant stuffed with haggis, and the famous Welsh Black beef; Scottish halibut or Cornish John Dory.

One wonders if such prime raw materials really need the host of complex garnishes that often accompany them. But the upbeat environment presumably requires a new-wave approach – and they are certainly giving it their best shot.

Their pride: Spring lamb with roasted garlic mash, caramelised onion and kidney tart, loin with purple kale and confit shoulder wrapped in spring cabbage
Inexpensive wines: Les Fleurs d'Alsace Hugel 2003, £17.95; La Remonta Malbec Mendoza 2003, £20

Proprietor: Paul Askew
Last orders for dinner: 10 pm
Closed: Saturday lunch, Sunday dinner
Set lunch: from £19
Set dinner: from £35
Private dining: 4-60
Accommodation: 48 rooms
Wheelchair access

LIVERPOOL, MERSEYSIDE

Simply Heathcotes

Beetham Plaza, 25 The Strand, Liverpool, Merseyside L2 0XL
Tel. 0151 236 3536 Fax 0151 236 3534
e-mail: liverpool@simplyheathcotes.co.uk   **MAP 5** C5

BETWEEN Liverpool's celebrated dockland and the city's office blocks, this particular link in Paul Heathcote's ever-lengthening chain comes as something of a pleasant surprise. Although it is a bit like eating in a goldfish bowl – a few soft furnishings would break up the grey marble and the stark furnishings – it's that sort of contemporary, buzzy place. The young staff do their best to soften the impact.

Yet what they serve here epitomises the gastropub in its culinary style. The list is long and comprehensive, even complemented by blackboard specials, with frequent use made of regional products.

'Simply' Heathcotes is a misnomer when well turned-out dishes such as marinated lamb chump with tabbouleh and pomegranate dressing, or succulent herb-roasted Goosnargh chicken with a faultless, creamy white wine sauce and buttered leeks, appear alongside a spiced chicken liver salad, goat's cheese and chive risotto, or potted ham with tarragon and green peppercorns.

But in true pub fashion, local favourites such as fish pie, sausages or Whitby cod in beer batter provide the treats expected of a brasserie-like operation such as this with no loss of face. Even an often-maligned and mistreated fishcake actually tasted of its key component – and little touches such as the excellent bread demonstrate the care and commitment that is applied to what might easily be taken for a run-of-the-mill bistro.

Their pride: Home-made black pudding with a herb crumpet
Inexpensive wines: Bottle Tree Semillon Chardonnay 2004, £16.95; Mill Cabernet Merlot, Cowra 2003, £19

Proprietor: Paul Heathcote
Last orders for dinner: Mon-Fri 10 pm, Sat 11pm, Sun 9pm
Open every day
Closed for holidays: Bank Holidays
Set lunch: from £14.50 (Sunday only)
Main courses: from £9
Private dining: 6-40
Al fresco dining
Wheelchair access

LLANFAIR WATERDINE, SHROPSHIRE

The Waterdine ★★

GASTROPUB

Llanfair Waterdine, Knighton, Shropshire LD7 ITU
Tel. 01547 528 214

MAP 3 D3

THE setting of The Waterdine is about as bucolic as they come, surrounded by hills and with a stream running through its garden. This area of Shropshire near the Welsh border, a stone's throw from Offa's Dyke, is a walker's paradise, but another good reason for visiting is the serious kitchen at this gastropub with rooms.

It is not often that every dish on a menu has instant appeal and deciding what to choose requires serious deliberation. This is the case here, perhaps in one of the two small sitting-rooms, or else in the garden when the weather is fine.

Starters might include Cornish scallops on creamed leeks with scallop and vermouth sauce, or artichoke hollandaise. Bayonne ham is served in a generous portion and comes with a pungent remoulade.

A thick fillet of John Dory had a crisp skin and was served with samphire and crab couscous. It tasted as good as it looked, the crab and couscous making a superb combination that went well with the John Dory. Roast duck with dauphinoise potatoes, broad beans and wild mushroom sauce is another option.

Those with a sweet tooth might want to try brioche and ginger pudding with crème fraîche, or else hazelnut cheese cake with chocolate sauce.

Meat comes from local organic farmers and game is also sourced locally. Fish is delivered every day from Newtown in Cornwall.

Speciality food: Local organic produce
Draught beers: Shropshire Lad, Old Sam
Average wine price by the glass: £2.25

Licensees: Ken and Isabel Adams
Last orders for dinner: 9 pm
Closed: Sunday evening, Monday
Main courses: from £12
Private dining: 10-16
Beer garden
Accommodation: 3 rooms
Children welcome (over 8 years in evening)
Wheelchair access

LONGRIDGE, LANCASHIRE

The Longridge Restaurant

104-106 Higher Road, Longridge, Lancashire PR3 3SY
Tel. 01772 784 969 Fax 01772 785 713
e-mail: longridge@heathcotes.co.uk   **MAP 5** C4

DESPITE its pristine smartness, this is a friendly and relaxed sort of place ideal for a family meal that includes the children and where you can attend special events and cookery classes.

Blackboards announce the 'specials' that complement an already extensive, seasonally changing menu based on ingredients that are often produced organically – locally reared meat and fowl, Scottish fish, shrimps from Morecambe Bay and even vegetables that are grown exclusively for the restaurant.

The cooking is essentially British and the choices offered include some of the old favourites such as steak and kidney pie, fat chips and good, straightforward pumpkin soup. At the same time, there is a range of dishes of greater complexity that sometimes mixes the traditional with a more modern approach.

One example of this is the extensive use of black pudding, which seems to be enjoying a new lease of life as one of the staples of modern British cuisine. Here it is home-made and appears in a variety of guises.

There might be the occasional lapse of finesse, but the subtle flavouring and appetising presentation bear witness to the strong commitment of the kitchen.

Their pride: Black pudding
Inexpensive wines: Brampton Sauvignon Blanc (South Africa) 2003, £21.50; Rioja Crianza Sierra Cantabria (Spain) 1998, £26.75

Proprietor: Paul Heathcote
Last orders for dinner: 10 pm
Closed: Monday
Closed for holidays: 1 January
Set lunch: from £14
Set dinner: from £25
Private dining: 8-18
Wheelchair access

LOW LAITHE, NORTH YORKSHIRE

Dusty Miller

**Low Laithe, Summerbridge, Nr. Harrogate, N Yorks HG3 4BU
Tel. 01423 780 837 Fax 01423 780 065**

MAP 5 D4

THIS little roadside restaurant of no more than a dozen or so tables has a delightfully homespun atmosphere and the food it offers is appropriately unpretentious. There are two small lounges with a very homely feel and just a dozen or so damask-covered tables in the tiny dining-room.

Apart from the 'proprietor's menu', there are five or six starters and main courses, nicely simple things such as melon with Parma ham, duck liver pâté, roasts, braised lamb shank and fillet steak, along with good local produce like smoked fish or Whitby crab.

An excellent starter would be the brown prawns in a light cream sauce with some chopped chive and you might follow that with the crisp-roasted duck, which has a certain affinity to Peking duck in style (though without the five spice or pancakes) and comes out superbly moist and tender.

Add some sage, some apple purée and the proper British gravy, then put it all together with a separate plate of beautifully cooked vegetables and you have a dish that cannot be faulted for pure traditional virtue.

A juicy, rich and nicely caramelised apple tarte Tatin provides a fitting end to an unfussy but highly accomplished meal.

Their pride: Crisp roast duckling
Inexpensive wines: Riesling D'Alsace Domaine Trapet 2002, £28; Chablis William Fèvre 2003, £17.90

**Proprietors: Brian and Elizabeth Dennison
Last orders for dinner: 11 pm
Closed: Sunday and Monday
Closed for holidays: Christmas, first week July
Set dinner: from £24.90
Private dining: up to 14**
Wheelchair access

LOWICK, NORTHAMPTONSHIRE

Snooty Fox ★

GASTROPUB

Main Street, Lowick, Northamptonshire NN14 3BH
Tel. 01832 733 434 Fax 01832 733 931

MAP 4 C4

AN ENORMOUS car park at the rear almost filled to capacity on a Monday night is impressive in anyone's books. The fact that the majority of these customers were dining is even more remarkable and is testament to the skills of the kitchen brigade here.

From a menu refreshingly short and succinct, Mersea oysters can be had with red wine and shallot dressing, or grilled in their shells with garlic and Parmesan. Superior Serrano ham, cut to a decent thickness, comes in a generous portion with slivers of sweet red pepper and dressed, peppery rocket.

Main courses could feature three fresh fish dishes, which might include skate wing with caper berries, or fish in beer batter with fat chips and mushy peas. But the pièce de résistance has to be the superb beef on offer. Customers are encouraged to select their steak from cuts of sirloin, rump, rib-eye and fillet, which has been properly hung for up to forty days. The flavour and texture of any of these cuts (sourced from the Orkneys) will be superb.

Accompanying fat chips are crisp on the surface and deliciously floury inside. Rocket and Parmesan salad or mixed vegetables, perhaps wilted spinach and crunchy French beans, make fine side-dishes.

A good selection of artisan cheeses to follow for savoury-lovers, or possibly a lemon polenta cake. Deliciously moist and tangy, this might come with raspberries and crème fraîche. Great service throughout.

Speciality food: Steaks
Draught beers: IPA, Ale Fresco
Average wine price by the glass: £3.50

Licensee: Clive Dickson
Last orders for dinner: 9.30 pm
Open every day
Set lunch: from £9.95
Main courses: from £9.50
Private dining: up to 50
Beer garden
Children welcome
Wheelchair access

LUDLOW, SHROPSHIRE

Hibiscus ★★★

17 Corve Street, Ludlow, Shropshire SY8 1DA
Tel. 01584 872 325 Fax 01584 874 024

MAP 3 D3

PAST the famous timbered Feathers Hotel at the top of the town, go down Corve Street, the main thoroughfare northwards, and in a tall house with an elegant sign you will find the restaurant, its low-key exterior belying the great gastronomic pleasures within.

In the two delightful dining-rooms, service confidently takes a perfect line between friendliness and watchful professionalism. The pace of the meal is ideal – you never feel the need to ask for anything, it just arrives at the right moment.

The cuisine of Claude Bosi, a Lyonnais in his early thirties who has established himself as one of the great cooking talents in Britain, is highly intelligent and thoughtful, his understanding of marrying flavours and textures masterly and truly exciting.

This was shown to brilliant effect in a pre-appetiser of a warm velouté of savoy cabbage with coconut milk, deep-flavoured yet refined, followed by marvellous fricassee of pumpkin with toasted pumpkin seeds, blue cheese ice-cream and velouté of pumpkin.

Saddle of Cornish lamb, pink and cut like a T-bone, was enhanced by a crisp strip of lamb fat and a classic choux farci, the stuffing composed of the lamb leg flesh, foie gras and apricot. For lovers of unusual fish dishes, the eel cooked in truffle juice, confit of pineapple and roasted globe artichoke is a signature dish. And to finish, apple tart with the crispest puff pastry is served with another wonderful flavour combination, salted butter caramel and Puy lentil ice-cream.

Their pride: Savoury ice-cream of foie gras, warm emulsion of brioche balsamic vinegar caramel
Inexpensive wines: Petaluma Clare Valley Riesling (Australia), 2004, £26; Bourgogne Vielles Vignes Darviot-Perrin 1999, £34

> **Proprietor: Claire and Claude Bosi**
> **Last orders for dinner: 9.30 pm**
> **Closed: Sunday and Monday**
> **Closed for holidays: 3 weeks January, 1 week August**
> **Set lunch: from £19.50**
> **Set dinner: from £45**
> Limited wheelchair access

LUDLOW, SHROPSHIRE

Mr. Underhill's ★

Dinham Weir, Ludlow, Shropshire SY8 1EH
Tel./Fax 01584 874 431

MAP 3 D3

WHAT better place from which to explore the attractive, historic town of Ludlow than this charming little restaurant, which also offers accommodation, where unflustered relaxation and warm, matter-of-fact hospitality are the order of the day.

A no-choice menu of six courses, changing daily, is always full of interest, neither plain nor outlandish and created to appeal to most tastes. They will check before you arrive for anything you might not like.

There is a frank cleanliness of execution and presentation throughout, beginning perhaps with butternut squash velouté enlived by pickled cauliflower and continuing with halibut fillet flavoured with lime and coconut.

The garnishing is minimal, as in the threads of crisp, lightly spiced vegetables that accompany Périgord duck, which comes with nothing else but creamy mashed potato with cardamom.

One nice surprise is the pre-dessert of white chocolate ice-cream, which is paired with chilli syrup and prepares the way for such tempting confections as Italian-style bread and butter pudding

There are some uncommon selections on the nicely varied wine list.

Their pride: Foie gras custard and sweetcorn cream, sesame glaze
Inexpensive wines: Collection Mourat-Fiefs Vendéens 2004, £18; Brolettino Lugana Ca'Dei Frati 2003, £24

Proprietors: Chris and Judy Bradley
Last orders for dinner: 8.15 pm
Closed: Monday and Tuesday
Closed for holidays: 3 weeks winter
Set dinner: from £40
Al fresco dining
Accommodation: 9 rooms

LUDLOW, SHROPSHIRE

Unicorn Inn

Corve Street, Ludlow, Shropshire SY8 1DU
Tel. 01584 873 555 Fax 01584 876 268

MAP 3 D3

THE River Corve runs at the rear of this inn and there is a small seating area right by the water's edge where you are welcome to eat. The period property with a beamed bar area, oak panelling, an original fireplace and pine tables dotted about, has a pleasant atmosphere.

Menus have been carefully thought out and the kitchen is more than able. Dishes are clearly written on strategically placed blackboards. Several fish choices include a Seafood Medley for two, priced at just under £35, which might be sea bass, red mullet, giant crevettes, mussels, whitebait and the 'fish of the day' served with sauté potatoes.

A good starter is crispy whitebait with a light garlic mayonnaise and, if you stay with fish, you might follow with firm fillets of red mullet and well-executed tagliatelle nero with puttanesca sauce.

For meat-eaters, an alternative for two is the Châteaubriand with peppercorn sauce, while an interesting culinary note is struck by duck khoresh (an Iranian stew) with basmati rice.

Unusually, there are some five vegetarian options, including herb crusted aubergine with vegetable risotto and mixed vegetarian tempura with stuffed mushroom and tomato served on aromatic rice.

The most expensive wine on a fairly comprehensive list is from New Zealand, Whitehaven Estate Pinot Noir at £20.95.

Speciality food: Duck khoresh
Draught beers: Hancocks HB, Robinsons Unicorn
Average wine price by the glass: £2.50

Licensees: Michael and Rita Knox
Last orders for dinner: 9.15 pm
Open every day
Closed for holidays: 25 December
Main courses: from £7.25
Private dining: up to 40
Beer garden
Children welcome
Wheelchair access

LYDFORD, DEVON

Dartmoor Inn at Lydford ★ GASTROPUB

**Moorside, Lydford, Devon EX20 4AY
Tel. 01822 820 221 Fax 01822 820 494
e-mail: info@dartmoorinn.co.uk**   **MAP 1** C4

ON the A386 Okehampton to Tavistock road, this white painted inn on the fringes of the village stands in the lee of Dartmoor. Here, nine years ago, Philip and Karen Burgess were among the first in the gastropub movement, Philip having started at L'Ecu de France in London in the 1970s, and still a consultant there.

The exuberantly colourful pictures and murals of artist/designer Karen enliven the bar, where her sure decorative touch is much in evidence in the powder blue panelled walls of the side eating area beside the bar and in the restaurant.

Patrick plays to the strengths of the South-West – superb local ingredients – and is passionate about Devon Ruby beef, the meat beautifully marbled and the fillet making the perfect mignon tournedos, the flavour superb and positive and the meat tender.

Fish from Looe, in Cornwall, is peerless, as in the casserole of sea fish with saffron and sweet potato. Dinner – à la carte – offers quite modish dishes in the modern idiom such as lightly seared carpaccio of beef fillet with Parmesan and grain mustard or else pan-fried hake with basil mash, or Aylesbury duck cooked pink with roasted squash.

But do leave room for West Country cheeses with oatcakes and some innovative puddings such as raspberry and red wine jelly with rose scented custard.

Speciality food: Devon Ruby beef
Draught beers: Otter Ale, Dartmoor best
Average wine price by the glass: £3.50

**Licensees: Karen and Philip Burgess
Last orders for dinner: 9.30 pm
Closed: Sunday evening, Monday
Set lunch: from £13.50
Set dinner: from £25
Private dining: up to 20
Beer garden
Accommodation: 3 rooms**
Wheelchair access

LYMINGTON, HAMPSHIRE

Fisherman's Rest

GASTROPUB

All Saints Road, Lymington, Hampshire SO41 8FD
Tel. 01590 678 931 Fax 01590 678 650

MAP 2 A5

HUNGRY yachtsmen can walk here from their moorings in Lymington harbour, guided by a ship's figurehead on the rooftop. The nautical theme continues with lobster pots, ships' navigation lanterns and bells, and the freshly painted exterior is decorated with hanging baskets.

The operation is run by a well-organised and friendly team who create a convivial atmosphere in this quiet corner at the southern end of Lymington. Weekday lunchtimes feature a well-chosen menu of two courses for just £8.50, amazing value. There are also lighter dishes of toasted ciabatta with bacon, Brie and mushrooms or home-made salmon fishcakes, or crispy duck with five spice sauce, or potted crab with smoked salmon.

More substantial offerings include such things as home-made steak and Guinness pie and lamb cutlets. Seek out the blackboard for 'catch of the day' – you might find locally caught plaice cooked so the skin just starts to bubble. Fresh vegetables are just as carefully treated.

Evenings bring further, more elaborate choices among lobster thermidor, local skate wing or escalope of veal. If you are still not defeated, try the well-made rhubarb crumble or banoffi pie. Wherever possible, local suppliers are used for fish and meat as well as for vegetables, wine and draught beers.

Ten wines by the glass, seven different half-bottles, including champagne, and the full bottles on the list are all keenly priced.

Speciality food: Seafood
Draught beers: Ringwood Best, Gales Best
Average wine price by the glass: £3

Licensees: Michael and Deana Stevens
Last orders for dinner: 9.30 pm (Sunday 9 pm)
Open every day
Set lunch: from £8.50
Main courses: from £9.25
Private dining: up to 40
Al fresco dining
Children welcome
Limited wheelchair access

356

MADINGLEY, CAMBRIDGESHIRE

Three Horseshoes ★

High Street, Madingley, Cambridge CB3 8AB
Tel. 01954 210 221 Fax 01954 212 043

MAP 4 D4

TURN the clock back some 30 years and you would find that The Three Horseshoes at Madingley was one of only a handful of places in the Cambridge area worthy of mention when it came to good food. Today there is plenty of competition, but this pub has withstood the test of time.

Eat in the bar or in the more sedate confines of the conservatory, which overlooks a lush green lawn.

Fruity olive oil features on all tables – the perfect accompaniment to the excellent focaccia bread on offer. As an appetiser, this will lead on to the a carte with a strong Italian influence. Pancetta, porcini, crostini and bruschetta with specialised olive oils appear liberally in all the dishes.

A spiedino (skewer) of fresh mackerel takes on new life when served with crushed potatoes, crispy pancetta and capers with green bean salad. Other starters, such as risotto of vongole, brown shrimps, cockles, dill and pecorino, continue the theme.

A main course of yellow fin tuna with gremolata – a colourful melange of parsley, garlic and lemon – comes with sweet vine tomatoes, spinach and sauté potatoes. Castelluccio lentils cooked with Swiss chard, cottechino sausage and anchovy might accompany a tender breast of chicken.

Desserts include affogato – vanilla ice-cream with hot espresso poured over – Chocolate Nemesis and caramelised lemon tart with seasonal fruit.

Speciality food: Mozzarella and tomato salad
Draught beers: Adnams; Guest ales – often City of Cambridge
Average wine price by the glass: £4

Licensees: John Hoskins and Richard Stokes
Last orders for dinner: 9 pm (Saturday 9.30 pm)
Open every day
Closed for holidays: 31 December-2 January
Main courses: from £13.50
Beer garden
Children welcome
Limited wheelchair access

MANCHESTER

The Bridge ★

58 Bridge Street, Deansgate, Manchester M3 3BW
Tel. 0161 834 0242 Fax 0161 832 3370

MAP 5 C5

THIS is almost certainly the best food pub in central Manchester, and priced most reasonably. Top-quality produce comes mainly from within a 70-mile radius and game features strongly on the menu, a favourite dish being wood pigeon breast with baby peas, dry-cured bacon and black pudding.

Reading through the menu, it is clear that the kitchen team have a real feeling for food, imaginative but never pretentious, and the assured skills to make for an exceptional pub dinner.

A lovely starter is the Morecambe Bay shrimp pastry, beautifully flavoured brown shrimps in very light puff pastry set on a bed of spinach and Chat Moss herbs, moistened with a little shellfish stock and shrimp cooking liquor.

Almost as good is the quite complex three-bone rack of local lamb, of exceptional flavours, savoury yet sweet, served with roast garlic and jus, the dish finished with broad beans and herb mashed potato. A fine fish option is poached plaice with a delicate lobster and vegetable cream sauce.

Desserts include a faultlessly made Manchester tart, shredded fresh coconut and jam on a gossamer-light pastry. Cheeses are as interesting as the rest of the carte, with a pronounced local emphasis: Kidderton goat's cheese and Burland Green organic 'Brie', both from Cheshire, as well as Kirkham's Lancashire.

An excellent wine list features less common choices by the glass.

Speciality food: Morecambe Bay brown shrimp pastry with Chat Moss herbs
Draught beers: Old Speckled Hen, Pendle Witch
Average wine price by the glass: £3

> **Licensee: Robert Owen Brown**
> **Last orders for dinner: 10 pm**
> **Open every day**
> **Main courses: from £10**
> **Private dining: up to 50**
> Children welcome
> Wheelchair access

MANCHESTER

Establishment ★

43-45 Spring Gardens, Manchester M2 2BG
Tel. 0161 839 6300 Fax 0161 839 6353
e-mail: info@establishmentrestaurant.com   **MAP 5** C5

THERE is evidence all round you that this large restaurant is in a building that used to be a bank – marble walls, stately columns, ornate stucco mouldings and twin cupolas. It has been recently transformed with the addition of some strikingly modern features including swathes of violet and expanses of glass and the food it offers is equally contemporary.

From a base of carefully sought out, high-quality ingredients come interesting dishes such as a tart of smoked haddock with peppered tangerines, Parmesan risotto and basil ice-cream, or else venison garnished with a beignet of bitter chocolate.

At the same time, there are a lot of tables to fill, so rather more conventional choices are plentiful – terrines and soups, smoked salmon (which is carved at the table), pan-fried sea bass and braised beef.

Whatever your taste, the raw materials will be excellent. Scallops come from the Skye, fish from Cornwall, seasonal game from Cumbria.

Nor is anything ever bland, as is demonstrated by touches like the rich tapenade with anchovy that brings to life a straightforward fish starter and the rich meat jus, which have more pungent flavours than most you will find, sometimes benefitting from the strong aroma of wild mushrooms.

Their pride: Slow-roasted rare Scottish beef fillet
Inexpensive wines: Bottle Tree Chardonnay (Australia) 2003, £14.50; Bottle Tree Cabernet Merlot (Australia) 2002, £14.50

Proprietors: Carl Lewis and Tim Molloy
Last orders for dinner: 10 pm
Closed: Sunday and Monday
Closed for holidays: Christmas
Set lunch: from £17.50
Set dinner: from £45
Wheelchair access

MANCHESTER

Second Floor at Harvey Nichols

21 New Cathedral Street, Manchester M1 1AD
Tel. 0161 828 8899/8 Fax 0161 828 8815
e-mail: secondfloorreservations@harveynichols.com   **MAP 5** C5

NOT MANY restaurants can boast a Big Wheel outside their picture windows or that you have the opportunity to buy a pair of socks on the same premises.

Some people might say that you cannot have a serious restaurant in a department store, but the the chances are that plenty of restaurants would love to serve as many glasses of champagne as they do here, even at lunchtime.

Yes, the setting may be unconventional, but the food really is very good. Mediterranean and Asian influences are at work in dishes like terrine of red peppers with feta, stuffed onion with a lemon and herb tabbouleh, and duck rillettes with a plum sauce and Asian salad, which complement classics such as oxtail soup, seared scallops or chicken and tarragon blanquette.

The high standards in the kitchen are evident in a perfectly cooked fillet steak with shin of beef ravioli and girolles, or else in a creamy and deliciously light butternut squash risotto.

One minor grumble might be a general lack of 'punch' in dishes that could benefit from a touch more seasoning.

Service is attentive and highly professional, and there is a definite buzz that comes from enjoying your meal with a view of the busy city centre.

Their pride: Three styles of strawberries and cream
Inexpensive wines: Harvey Nichols Bourgogne Blanc 2002, £17.50; Madfish Shiraz (Australia) 2002, £20

Proprietor: Harvey Nichols Group
Last orders for dinner: 10.30 pm
Closed: Sunday 6 pm, Monday 7 pm
Closed for holidays: 25 & 26 December, Easter Sunday
Main courses: from £15
Wheelchair access

MANCHESTER

Mr. Thomas's Chop House `GASTROPUB`

52 Cross Street, Manchester M2 7AR
Tel. 0161 832 2245 Fax 0161 839 0042

MAP 5 C5

IN THE centre of Manchester, close to department stores and big banks, this Victorian gastropub has been intelligently adapted to 21st-century lunchtime needs.

The cooking is competent rather than stylish, and while retaining a strong emphasis on traditional dishes with a Lancastrian slant, there is the odd nod towards modern trends, as in saffron and smoked haddock risotto.

Start with half-a-dozen Irish oysters on crushed ice, or maybe the popular corned beef hash cake. For the more ambitious, try the guinea fowl, bacon and shallot terrine or the Garstang salad based on the eponymous Lancashire cheese and garnished with mixed leaves, caramelised walnuts and a balsamic dressing.

The old faithfuls are the best main choices here: the pot-roasted shoulder of lamb, the pan-fried Lancastrian calf's liver and Mr. Thomas's home-made steak and kidney pudding.

The piscivorous can opt for good-looking traditional fish and chips or the seared fillets of line-caught seabass on champ potato.

For afters, there are puddings rarely seen nowadays, such as the vanilla blancmange with fresh raspberries, and the selection of local Lancastrian cheeses is laudable.

The wine list is intelligently selective and serious. By the glass, try the perfumed Viña Esmeralda from Spain as a white aperitif, or if you're feeling expansive, the top-flight rosé champagne.

Speciality food: Traditional English food
Draught beers: Black Sheep, Boddingtons
Average wine price by the glass: £4

Licensees: Steven Pilling and Roger Ward
Last orders for dinner: 9 pm
Closed: Sunday evening
Closed for holidays: 24 Dec (evening), 25 and 26 Dec
Main courses: from £11.95
Beer garden
Children welcome before 7pm
Wheelchair access

MANCHESTER

The Ox

---

71 Liverpool Road, Castlefield, Manchester M3 4NQ
Tel. 0161 839 7740 Fax 0161 839 7760
e-mail: theox@baabar.co.uk   **MAP 5** C5

OFF the far end of Deansgate, in the renovated Castlefield district, this is a bright and justly popular gastropub opposite the Museum of Science and Industry. The Ox is a buzzy place, rich red being the dominant colour as if symbolic of the energy and vitality of the young crowd who come here from all walks of life.

The food is competently prepared, everything fresh and cooked to order. Start with fresh tomato soup, ripe yet subtly flavoured and with crème fraîche; alternatively, flash-fried salt and pepper squid with a coriander, spring onion and chilli salad is a winner for those who like strong, spicy flavours, or there are Scottish mussels and clams in a garlic-infused ragout.

Chicken piri piri is innovative with patatas bravas, chorizo and leaf spinach. Oven-roasted breast of Barbary duck, a regular special, is enhanced by wok-fried vegetables accurately timed.

Herb crusted loin of Welsh lamb with boulangère potatoes is also much in demand, as is whole grilled sea bream with citrus fruit scented pasta ribbons.

Good puddings could include bitter chocolate torte or apricot crème brûlée.

Very potable wines by the glass, such as a fruit-driven blend of Australian Chardonnay and Colombard and, to go with the lamb, a superior Chianti Ruffino from the Selvapiani estate near Florence.

Speciality food: Chicken piri piri
Draught beers: Deuchars, Timothy Taylor
Average wine price by the glass: £3

Licensee: Nick Bayne
Last orders for dinner: 9.45 pm
Open every day
Set lunch: from £11.95 (Sunday)
Main courses: from £10
Private dining: up to 70
Al fresco dining
Accommodation: 7 rooms
Children welcome
Wheelchair access

MARLDON, DEVON

Church House Inn GASTROPUB

Village Road, Marldon, Nr. Paignton, Devon TQ3 1SL
Tel. 01803 558 279

MAP 1 D4

TRAVEL a couple of miles out of Paignton and the South Devon Riviera, down a winding lane to the church, and there appears this tall period inn, painted white, with fine Gothic windows giving views across to the village cricket pitch – a very English scene.

At lunchtime, an extensive specials board offers laudably fresh and well-prepared dishes such as excellent, properly seasoned carrot and ginger soup in a huge generous plate, or maybe a home-made coarse pork and apple pâté.

There are king prawns to start with, pan-fried in lemon and chilli batter, and a smoked fish platter. At Sunday lunch, the sirloin of quality beef comes medium rare and full of flavour with well-risen Yorkshire pudding. Finish with a commendable crème brûlée or fine ice-creams made with Devon double cream.

Dinner moves up an imaginative gear to offer choices such as smoked salmon roulade with a Nordic dressing, smoked haddock chowder or collops of monkfish with salsa verde, followed perhaps by shoulder of lamb, the jus flavoured with mint. For vegetarians, perhaps a baked Italian flan with peperonata and mozzarella.

The house pouring wines are excellent and well priced. There is a creamy Michel Laroche Languedoc Chardonnay and a well-aged Rioja Crianza. Service in the restaurant is at once professional yet informal and conversational, creating a warm, inviting ambience.

Speciality food: Braised shoulder of lamb, mint jus
Draught beers: Greene King IPA, Dartmoor Ale
Average wine price by the glass: £2.40

Licensee: Julian Cook
Last orders for dinner: 9.30 pm
Open every day
Closed for holidays: 25 December
Main courses: from £13.50
Private dining: up to 36
Beer garden
Children welcome
Wheelchair access

MARLOW, BUCKINGHAMSHIRE

Hand and Flowers ★

GASTROPUB

West Street, Marlow, Buckinghamshire SL7 2BP
Tel./Fax 01628 482 277

MAP 2 C3

THERE is a particular category of up-market eating house where the staff, in jeans and long aprons, may address a table of women with a 'Hi guys, what can I get you?'. This breezy front-of-house style in the cottagey interior of Beth and Tom Kerridge's recent acquisition results in a wave of contentment.

Nothing is too much trouble and you are instantly put at ease from the first cheery smile to the final 'ciao', the entire team apparently enjoying the place as much as you do. Tom and his wife, with a wealth of top-flight experience behind them, aim to please, the menu offering interest without extravagance and a simplicity of style that belies the technique behind their creation.

A straightforward potted Dorset crab to start, perhaps, or a glazed smoked haddock omelette; a plum tomato tart with whipped goat's cheese – packed with natural flavour on a pastry base of crispy lightness, warm tomatoes and their cream cheese topping delightfully perked up with a classic shallot dressing.

Main courses afford respectfully innovative treatment to fish and locally raised meat. A fillet of sea trout is given a touch of class with foie gras ravioli and cauliflower purée. A honey-roast spring chicken and Parmesan risotto are lightly bathed in a truly classic morel sauce, while rump of lamb is garnished with pickled and puréed aubergine, saffron couscous and sauce vierge.

No stinting on the desserts, either: dark cherry and chocolate torte or a pistachio cheesecake might feature alongside a truly sublime individual lemon and passion fruit tart.

Speciality food: Modern British cooking
Draught beers Greene King IPA, Abbott Ale
Average wine price by the glass: £4

> **Licensees: Beth and Tom Kerridge**
> **Last orders for dinner: 9.30 pm**
> **Closed: Sunday evening, Monday**
> **Closed for holidays: 1st week January**
> **Main courses: from £14**
> **Beer garden**
> Children welcome

MARLOW, BUCKINGHAMSHIRE

Royal Oak

GASTROPUB

Frieth Road, Bovingdon Green, Marlow, Bucks SL7 2JF
Tel. 01628 488 611   Fax 01628 478 680
e-mail: info@royaloakmarlow.co.uk   **MAP 2** C3

FROM Marlow it is a three-mile drive through the wooded Chiltern hills to this country pub where regulars of all ages meet. Most of the natural wood tables around the bar have views of the garden where one may dine in fine weather. Licensee and manager Trasna Rice Giff can take full credit for drawing the crowds to this smoothly run, imaginative food operation.

There are daily specials at lunch and dinner but otherwise the menu does not change. At midday you might go for fresh leek and potato soup or the popular and competently prepared smoked haddock on spinach and potato pancake, served with fresh sorrel cream sauce.

Dinner might bring slow-cooked Chiltern lamb shoulder on braised lentils, or seared Marlow pigeon breast with black pudding, both dishes using local ingredients. Grilled sea bass with crushed new potatoes is a lighter option, and there is always something for vegetarians. A variety of tempting puddings includes an apple, cinnamon and blueberry strudel.

The real ales, notably Brakspear, are finely kept and Trasna takes a great interest in the wine list. The selection by the glass ranges from a first-rate Austrian Grüner Veltlinger to a fine Sicilian Nero d'Avola Riserva. There is excellent, keenly priced premier cru champagne, too.

Speciality Food: Modern British cooking
Draught Beers: Brakspear, Fullers
Average wine price by the glass: £4

Licensee: Trasna Rice Giff
Last orders for dinner: 10 pm
Open every day
Closed for holidays: Boxing Day
Main courses: from £11.50
Beer garden
Children welcome
Wheelchair access

MARSTON MONTGOMERY, DERBYSHIRE

Bramhall's at The Crown Inn ★

Rigg Lane, Marston Montgomery, Ashbourne, Derbys DE6 2FF
Tel. 01889 590 541
e-mail: info@bramhall.co.uk   **MAP 3** E2

THE Crown Inn is a handsome, genuine pub that strikes a good balance between a traditional bar atmosphere, with excellent draught beers, and a sensitively integrated brasserie.

The food is a model of the mainstream modern, fresh European style, with Mediterranean flavours to the fore and even touches from the East. Specials are consistently fine, as in a terrine of poussin and smoked chicken, and soups are both inventive and successful – cream of parsnip and bramley apple, for example.

Fresh fish of the day is always worth ordering, ranging from John Dory and sea bass to zander and bream in various forms.

Fowl and meat choices are imaginative without being outlandish: the roasted rack of Derbyshire lamb comes juicy, pink and flavoursome, accompanied by chilli and ginger couscous; breast of Barbary duck is partnered by roast sweet potato and creamed spinach. Back to fish again, and délice of salmon is served with chive risotto.

For something simpler, the steaks are well hung and the vine tomatoes nicely ripe.

Desserts laudably reflect what is fresh and seasonal: raspberry cheesecake and red fruit coulis, perhaps, or a summer berry brioche pudding with mint crème fraîche.

Try one of four intriguing dessert wines by the glass, including a Vidal ice wine from Canada. There are eight house selections.

Speciality food: Roasted rack of lamb, chilli and ginger couscous
Draught beers: Bass, Marston Pedigree
Average wine price by the glass: £3

Licensees: Timothy and Tracey Bramhall
Last orders for dinner: 9 pm (Fri and Sat 9.30 pm)
Closed: Sunday evening,
Closed for holidays: 25 December, 1 January
Set lunch: from £9.95
Main courses: from £12.50
Beer garden
Accommodation: 7 rooms
Children welcome
Wheelchair access

MILL BANK, WEST YORKSHIRE

The Millbank ★

GASTROPUB

Mill Bank, Nr. Sowerby Bridge, West Yorkshire HX6 3DY
Tel. 01422 825 588
e-mail: themillbank@yahoo.co.uk   **MAP 5** D5

BEAMS and oak settles have been replaced with contemporary pinks and mauves in this country pub, but even so, there is still a certain pubbiness, especially in summer when you can enjoy a simple sandwich with your pint in the steeply banked gardens overlooking the valley below.

The revamped interior implies a modern approach to the food, but simple steaks and even local sausages are also available. The extensive selection of inventive but carefully compiled dishes offers cutting-edge cuisine without histrionic excesses. A smoked chicken croquette lightly fried with chorizo, avocado, olive oil, garlic and a hint of chilli makes an appealing opener, while fillets of black bream on a light and beautifully perfumed basil mash, offset by the gentle tang of tomato and lemon, can be enjoyed as a starter or main course.

Poached halibut with Jersey Royals, asparagus, mussels, saffron and cream is a dish that exudes fine, clear-cut flavours while an ambitious trio of duck – the succulent breast wrapped in cabbage, a roasted leg and a wrapped parcel of confit – is carried off with real aplomb, given just the right accompaniment with a spiced honey jus.

Desserts include banana fritter with banana and rum fool and hot caramel sauce, but there are those who simply will not want to miss the oozing chocolate fondant with raisin purée and vanilla ice-cream, and who could blame them? Great food with informal service and a relaxing setting – book early for the conservatory.

Speciality food: Modern British cooking
Draught beers: Tetley Bitter, Timothy Taylor Landlord
Average wine price by the glass: £2.20

Licensee: Joe McNally
Last orders for dinner: 9.30 pm
Closed: Monday lunch
Closed for holidays: 2 weeks Oct, 2 weeks Jan
Set lunch: from £11.95
Set dinner: from £11.95 (Monday-Thursday)
Private dining: 10-24
Beer garden
Children welcome

MILTON ERNEST, BEDFORDSHIRE

Strawberry Tree ★

3 Radwell Road, Milton Ernest, Nr. Bedford MK44 1RY
Tel./Fax 01234 823 633
e-mail: strawberrytree_restaurant@yahoo.co.uk   **MAP 4** C4

TWENTY years ago, when this 17th-century cottage began its career in hospitality, it offered only afternoon teas, but John and Wendy Bona, with the help of their self-taught chef sons, Jason and Andrew, have developed it into a serious restaurant where the cooking is as immaculate as the surroundings.

The starting point is simply first-rate ingredients that are often locally produced, such as vegetables from a neighbour's garden and organic eggs from the next village. Gloucester Old Spot pig is among the rare-breed meats used, perhaps a chop with savoy cabbage, apple purée and sage and onion gnocchi.

Other offerings might include home-made tortellini stuffed with wild mushrooms and served on a bed of wilted spinach with a Puy lentil sauce finished with truffle oil, and pan-fried cod with king prawns and home-made noodles and a ginger sauce.

One outstanding dish is rack of lamb, roasted evenly pink, with the tender braised shank neatly wrapped in a cabbage leaf on a bed of potato purée.

Excellent desserts include white chocolate and lime parfait with a mascarpone sorbet and passion fruit, or yoghurt panna cotta with almond meringue and blueberry sauce.

The short wine list majors on France and includes good tasting notes for each offering. There is a small range of half-bottles and there are house and dessert wines available by the glass.

Their pride: Pot-roasted pork, hot-pot potato cake, apple purée
Inexpensive wines: Chardonnay Château Los Boldos (Chile) 2003, £16.20; Bordeaux Château Fantin 2001, £18.90

Proprietor: John Bona
Last orders for dinner: 8.30 pm
Closed: Sunday, Monday, Tuesday
Closed for holidays: 2 weeks winter, 2 weeks summer
Set dinner: from £25
Private dining: up to 10
Wheelchair access

MITTON, LANCASHIRE

Three Fishes ★★

GASTROPUB

Mitton Road, Mitton, Nr. Whalley, Lancashire BB7 9PQ
Tel. 01254 826 888 Fax 01254 826 026

MAP 5 C4

FOUNDED more than four hundred years ago, The Three Fishes has been completely refurbished by new owners Nigel Haworth and Craig Bancroft, who also own the starred Northcote Manor nearby, to create a 21st-century look, with an airy dining space serving 130 covers, while retaining the values of a traditional English pub.

It aims to serve the finest produce of Lancashire and the North-West and thirty-three regional producers are treated like heroes, their pictures on the walls, several dishes named after them and a listing of all of them on a map at the back of each menu.

The results are stunning. The freshness of the ingredients, the accuracy of the cooking and the well-balanced sauces combine to create cuisine that gives the impression of a starred restaurant rather than a pub.

Morecambe Bay shrimps are served with blade mace butter sauce and toasted muffin. Cauliflower tempura is lightly fried and comes with a deliciously light curry sauce. Lancashire hot-pot, made with local lamb, is cooked to perfection, mixed with red cabbage and topped with a delicious, slightly crispy potato crust.

A signature dish is Three Fishes Pie – fish baked with mashed potato and sprinkled with Mrs. Kirkham's Lancashire cheese.

There is an additional menu of seasonal alternatives and there are children's menus. There is only partial waitress service. Every table has a number and the food order is given at the bar.

Speciality food: Three Fishes Pie
Draught beers: Warsteiner, König Ludwig
Average wine price by the glass: £3.50

Licensees: Craig Bancroft and Nigel Haworth
Last orders for dinner: Monday to Thursday 9 pm, Friday and Saturday 9.30 pm, Sunday 8.30pm
Open every day
Main courses: from £7.50
Al fresco dining
Wheelchair access

MONK'S ELEIGH, SUFFOLK

Swan Inn ★

GASTROPUB

The Street, Monks Eleigh, Suffolk IP7 7AU
Tel: 01449 741 391
e-mail: carol@monkseleigh.com   **MAP 4** E5

EVERYTHING is as spick and span inside the Ramsbottoms' village eatery as the flower-filled gardens of the thatched houses lining the High Street on which it stands. Very much an integral part of village life (they even organise film nights), it has been simply modernised to create a comfortable, relaxing environment in which to enjoy Nigel's specialities chalked up in the bar where his wife, Carol, provides a cheery welcome.

The simplicity of the surroundings is echoed in food that delights with its raw, natural appeal and unadulterated flavours. Roasted peppers stuffed with goat's cheese on bruschetta are a deserved hit. Among other starters might be smoked prawns with lemon mayonnaise, asparagus with balsamic dressing, or spicy Thai pork with red chillies.

Chargrills feature strongly among the main courses – steaks, chicken and fish, either plain or sauced and garnished with crispy rösti, fat chips, garlicky aubergine compote with cherry tomatoes and basil, or a creamy mash. There may be an assortment of fresh fish such as fillet of salmon with a heavenly scented pesto, a slice of roast cod with more traditional parsley sauce, or else pan-fried sea bass with orange and beetroot salad.

Interrupt your dreams of Tuscan vineyards and Greek islands to order a huge, but truly divine white chocolate cheesecake and passion fruit coulis (unless tempted by the rich chocolate loaf with its accompanying chocolate sauce) and then prepare yourself for the English weather. Delightful.

Speciality food: Anglo-Mediterranean cuisine
Draught beers: Adnams Best Bitter, Adnams Broadside
Average wine price by the glass: £2.90

Licensees: Carol and Nigel Ramsbottom
Last orders for diner: 9.30 pm
Closed: Monday, Tuesday (except Bank Holidays)
Closed for holidays: 25 and 26 December, 1 January
Main courses: from £9
Private dining: 12-40
Beer garden
Children welcome

MORSTON, NORFOLK

Morston Hall ★

**Morston, Holt, Norfolk NR25 7AA
Tel. 01263 741 041 Fax 01263 740 419
e-mail: reception@morstonhall.com**   **MAP 4** E3

EVERYTHING about this country house hotel is well judged so as to provide satisfaction, from the fixed dinner-hour and no-choice menu to the composition of dishes and the size of the portions. And if there is something on the carte that you don't particularly like, chef/patron Galton Blackiston's kitchen team will provide an alternative.

The key to Galton's cooking is simplicity, together with his use of first-rate ingredients, often from local sources. That, however, does not mean the food is dull.

An exemplary fish course of griddled sole with beurre noisette and capers is typical of the approach, as is sliced duck breast simply presented with savoy cabbage, celeriac and mashed potato.

An appetiser such as puff pastry topped with onion marmalade and melting Brie comes with an aperitif, then a second one – it might be partridge consommé – when you reach your table.

Your meal could start with creamily sauced Parma ham, wild mushrooms and Parmesan with tagliatelle, and end delightfully with hot prune and armagnac soufflé. Good cafetière coffee and a selection of home-made petits fours offer a nice finishing touch.

Galton Blackiston runs popular midweek cookery demonstrations and residential courses.

Their pride: Lasagne of Morston lobster
Inexpensive wines: Viré Clessé Trenel fils 2003, £18; Graves de Vayres Château Bel-Air, Philippe Serey-Eiffel 1999, £18

**Proprietors: Tracy and Galton Blackiston
Last orders for dinner: 7.30 pm for 8 pm
Open every day
Closed for holidays: January
Set lunch: from £29
Set dinner: from £43
Accommodation: 7 rooms**
Wheelchair access

MOULSFORD-ON-THAMES, OXFORDSHIRE

Boat House, Beetle & Wedge ┃ *GASTROPUB*

Ferry Lane, Moulsford-on-Thames, Oxfordshire OX10 9JF
Tel. 01491 651 381 Fax 01491 651 376

MAP 2 B3

THE conservatory of this gastropub, part of the charming Beetle & Wedge Hotel, has a magical setting overlooking the Thames. Little surprise that the author Jerome K. Jerome chose to live here, the nearness of the river no doubt inspiring him to write *Three Men in a Boat*.

Following a change of ownership, the cooking turns out to be very sound, ingredients fresh, no short-cuts taken – as illustrated in a proper Mediterranean fish soup that has a good deep taste of shellfish stock, is aromatic and rich, the accompaniments of rouille and Gruyère as they should be.

Oak smoked cod's roe pâté with toast looks a fine option, or there is a half-pint of prawns with herb mayonnaise, or else crispy duck and salade frisée. As for main courses, if you are not in a meat-eating mood, try panaché of halibut, salmon, Dover sole and sea bass with a chive risotto.

The large charcoal grill is the heart of the operation, producing whole fresh sardines with grainy mustard sauce; well-flavoured and moist lamb steak served with flageolet beans and rosemary jus; rump steak with Béarnaise sauce, and so on. For lovers of game, escalope of venison with chestnuts, creamed cabbage and port wine sauce is a dish that calls for one of the well-priced Rhônes on an absorbing wine list.

The rich chocolate and orange pudding is a good choice and there is a correct crème brûlée, plus superior ice-creams and sorbets.

Speciality food: Crispy duck and salade frisée
Draught beers: Wadworth 6X, Stella Artois
Average wine price by the glass: £4

Licensees: Stephanie Hicks and Warren Musk
Last orders for dinner: 9.45 pm
Open every day
Main courses: from £16.50
Private dining: up to 50
Al fresco dining
Accommodation: 6 rooms
Children welcome
Wheelchair access

NETHER ALDERLEY, CHESHIRE

Wizard

Macclesfield Road, Nether Alderley, Cheshire SK10 4UB
Tel. 01625 584 000

MAP 3 E1

IN AN area that bears a strong similarity to the leafier suburbs of broker-belt Surrey and parts of the Thames Valley, enormous mansions lurk behind wide tree-lined avenues and trendy 4x4s surround fashionable shops in the nearby towns.

Despite its reputation for quality food, The Wizard is exceptionally low-key; one gets the impression that it really does not need to shout its wares too loudly. Situated about a mile from Alderley Edge, this period property has plenty of parking space at the rear. Totally in keeping with its surroundings, the interior is furnished with antiques, paintings and subdued wall lights.

The chef believes fresh ingredients should speak for themselves, as in a starter of chicken satay served with plain basmati rice and cucumber and yoghurt dipping sauce. Succulent pieces of chicken with subtle spices and the nutty flavour of the basmati awaken the taste-buds.

Pursuing this theme, a fillet of fresh, wild sea bass as a main course will be accurately cooked with a very crisp skin and might be accompanied by plain, griddled asparagus with a just a hint of balsamic. Potatoes and vegetables are an optional extra. Other main courses could feature roast rack of English lamb with whole-grain mustard mash and rosemary jus, or wild mushroom risotto, Parmesan and truffle cream.

You can splurge on puddings such as wicked chocolate marquise with delicious coffee ice-cream and crème anglaise. Attentive service is guaranteed.

Their pride: Local produce
Inexpensive wines: Brampton Sauvignon (South Africa) 2004, £18; Lark Hill Pinot Noir (Australia) 2001, £28

Proprietor: Martin Ainscough
Last orders for dinner: 9.30 pm
Closed: Sunday evening, Monday
Closed for holidays: Christmas-New Year
Set lunch: from £18.95
Main courses: from £10
Private dining: up to 40
Al fresco dining
Limited wheelchair access

NETTLEBED, OXFORDSHIRE

White Hart

High Street, Nettlebed, Nr. Henley-on-Thames, Oxon RG9 5DD
Tel. 01491 641 245 Fax 01491 649 018
e-mail: info@whitehartnettlebed.com   **MAP 2** B2

WITHIN easy reach of both the M4 and M40, The White Hart is well-placed for a variety of activities – from visits to National Trust houses to excellent golfing and river and countryside walks.

The interior has been given a contemporary make-over with chocolate brown tables, modern prints and a light, welcoming bar with a log fire in winter.

A set lunch is offered from Monday to Thursday, otherwise the menus change seasonally and an interesting selection of daily specials will ring the changes for regular customers.

Small, flavoursome mussels in a tasty tomato, garlic and herb broth is a good choice, perhaps followed by succulent braised belly of pork with a delicious Chinese salad including pak choi and bean sprouts with spicy jus.

Other options on the bistro menu might include starters of fried crab cake with tomato salsa and coriander oil, or Parma ham with celeriac salad.

Main courses might include such delights as the local beef with Dauphinoise potatoes or fillet of sole, poached egg, tomato and butter sauce.

Puddings could feature apple crumble with cinnamon ice-cream, sticky toffee pudding, or poached pear with chocolate tart and crème anglaise.

Speciality food: Local produce
Draught beers: Brakspear, Fosters
Average wine price by the glass: £3.50

Licensee: Jean-Christophe Roumignac
Last orders for dinner: 9.30 pm (Fri and Sat 10 pm)
Open every day
Set lunch: from £9.95 (Monday-Thursday)
Set dinner: from £9.95 (Monday-Thursday)
Private dining: 10-80
Beer garden
Accommodation: 12 rooms
Children welcome
Wheelchair access

NEW MILTON, HAMPSHIRE

Chewton Glen ★★

Christchurch Road, New Milton, Hampshire BH25 6QS
Tel. 01425 275 341 Fax 01425 272 310
e-mail: reservations@chewtonglen.com   **MAP 2** A5

THIS 18th-century Palladian mansion exudes both peaceful and genteel grandeur, the dining-room named after Frederick Marryat, who wrote *Children of the New Forest* here.

For soufflé-lovers, the double-baked Emmental version is an essential choice, with thin cheese-crusted surface and celestially light textured centre, a flavour of pinpoint accuracy, the fondue sauce smooth and delicate.

The simply named Nage of Monkfish, Scallops and Langoustine belies the treat in store: tender monkfish cooked with supreme accuracy, plump scallops and shelled langoustine tails in a fine Noilly Prat sauce, with a distinct taste of the sea.

The warm apple filo pastry Tatin transcends all expectations. Grape-sized balls of caramelised apple infused with cinnamon are placed in a basket of crispy filo pastry and adorned with crushed toasted almonds. Leaf-thin crystallised apple slices accompany, with vanilla ice-cream.

Other dishes include terrine of local game or chicken consommé to start, perhaps followed by cannon of Hampshire lamb, breast of Quantock duck or chargrilled or sautéd Dover sole.

To finish, choices could be warm ginger gâteau, citrus fruit trifle or bread and butter pudding.

The wine list stands out for the quality and range of some of the finest wines in the world. Vintage ports date back to 1945.

Their pride: Fillet of Scottish beef with ceps, salsify and spinach
Inexpensive wines: Tokay d'Alsace Pinot Gris 2002, £21; Merlot Robert Skalli (France) 2003, £21.50

Proprietors: Martin and Brigitte Skan
Last orders for dinner: 9.30 pm
Open every day
Set lunch: from £22.50
Set dinner: from £59.50
Private dining: up to 140
Al fresco dining
Accommodation: 58 rooms
Wheelchair access

NEWARK, NOTTINGHAMSHIRE

Café Bleu ★

14 Castle Gate, Newark, Nottinghamshire NG24 1BG
Tel. 01636 610 141 Fax 01636 705 149
e-mail: info@cafebleu.co.uk   **MAP 4** B2

THIS smart brasserie in the heart of historic Newark prides itself on its warm, Gallic welcome and relaxed setting. Try pre-dinner drinks in the garden before returning to the smart interior with its colourful canvasses and halogen lighting, to enjoy a range of modern classics on the frequently changing menus.

Excellently conceived, beautifully balanced and cleanly executed compilations, often seafood-based, offer interest and originality throughout a consistent display of technical acumen.

Traditional standards are well represented in a simple and simply delicious celeriac soup, albeit with crisp scallop and tarragon tortellini, or melt-in-the-mouth braised beef with baby vegetables and salsa verde, or unadulterated roast chicken, a perfect potato fondant and just its roasting juices for company.

But it is hard not to be tempted by more inventive monkfish with a crisp, light Indian tempura coating and candied aubergine, or a pressed terrine of smoked haddock with toasted hazelnut salad, or roast Cornish cod with celeriac and crab remoulade.

The passion and expertise never flag, right through to deliciously different desserts such as bitter chocolate pudding with Horlicks ice-cream, or assiette of raspberries including trifle, jelly and raspberry ripple. Enjoy, too, a selection from the generously priced wine list.

Their pride: Braised blade of beef, confit garlic and salsa verde
Inexpensive wines: Valle Dorado Chardonnay (Chile) 2004, £12.95; Saddle Creek Shiraz Cabernet (Australia) 2003, £13.50

Proprietor: Café Bleu Ltd.
Last orders for dinner: 9.30 pm
Closed: Sunday evening
Main courses: from £9.95
Al fresco dining
Wheelchair access

NEWBURY, BERKSHIRE

Wine Press Restaurant

Donnington Valley Hotel, Old Oxford Road, Newbury RG14 3AG
Tel. 01635 551 199 Fax 01635 551 123
e-mail: general@donningtonvalley.co.uk   **MAP 2** B3

PART of the Donnington business and leisure complex that includes a hotel and a golf course, this aptly named restaurant is owned by Sir Peter Michael, whose other enterprises include the Vineyard at Stockcross and a Californian wine estate. Off the main hotel foyer, the restaurant is comfortable, attractive and informal, the young front-of-house team both alert and friendly.

Dinner menus feature price bands covering two or three courses, though there are supplements for the likes of lobster, Dover sole and fillet of beef.

Starters might be ham hock terrine with chutney, a Californian salad with mozzarella, or artichoke soup with pan-fried ceps and truffle oil. Move on to calf's liver with bacon, buttered mash, spinach and black pudding, or honey glazed belly of pork with Puy lentil casserole, or else an excellent fillet of halibut, very fresh, with crushed new potatoes and chives.

As for dessert, the lemon trio might be the one to go for among a list that sometimes seems a little odd, featuring cherry beer and marshmallow or peanut butter and coconut.

Carefully selected cheeses include an excellent Touraine chèvre that would go well with one of the fine Sauvignon blancs from the fairly priced wine list, which is a serious compilation of the best growers' wines worldwide, including those from Sir Peter's own Sonoma vineyards.

Their pride: Loin shoulder of lamb, spinach and potato
Inexpensive wines: Little Chardonnay Reserve, Hunter Valley (Australia) 2000, £26.50; Rosenblum Cellars Zinfandel, Napa Valley (California) 2003, £19.50

Proprietor: Sir Peter Michael
Last orders for dinner: 10 pm
Open every day
Set lunch: from £13
Set dinner: from £19.50
Private dining: up to 120
Al fresco dining
Accommodation: 58 rooms
Wheelchair access

NEWCASTLE UPON TYNE, TYNE & WEAR

Fisherman's Lodge ★

Deep Dene House, Jesmond, Newcastle upon Tyne NE7 TBQ
Tel. 0191 281 3281 Fax 0191 281 6410
e-mail: enquiries@fishermanslodge.co.uk   **MAP 5** D2

FISH IS very much the speciality at this Victorian villa in a sylvan setting still within the limits of the city. That is hardly surprising, given that daily deliveries arrive from North Shields, just down the road, but there are supplementary supplies, too, such as Cornish lobster and Skye scallops.

Lovers of meat are by no means ignored, however, since there are abundant sources of beef and lamb in Northumberland, as well as game, of course.

These fine ingredients are handled with skill and imagination, which shines through in a signature dish such as pan-fried sea bass with saffron mash and bouillabaisse sauce, presenting a wonderful and well-judged combination of flavours.

There is a satisfying set lunch that might feature a starter of salmon and coriander fishcakes with Thai dressing, a main course of duck confit with polenta, and a dessert of banana flavoured bread and butter pudding with crème anglaise.

It is at dinner, though, when desserts come into their own, with chocolate and orange ganache torte and crushed strawberry and champagne shortcake catching the eye.

Ask the sommelier for advice on what you might choose from the excellent wine list, strong in all departments, from admirable selections by the glass to the heights of Bienvenu Batard Montrachet, Leflaive 1999 and a true rarity, Dom Pérignon Oenothèque 1959.

Their pride: Ravioli of lobster with shellfish vinaigrette
Inexpensive wines: Pinot Grigio Mezzacorona 2002, £17.95; Rioja Conde de Valdemar 2001, £23.95

Proprietor: Tom Maxfield
Last orders for dinner: 10.30 pm
Closed: Sunday
Closed for holidays: Bank holidays
Set lunch: from £22
Private dining: 6-40
Al fresco dining
Wheelchair access

NEWCASTLE UPON TYNE, TYNE & WEAR

King Neptune

34 Stowell Street, Newcastle Upon Tyne, Tyne & Wear NE1 4XQ
Tel. 0191 261 6657

MAP 5 D2

A HUGE ornamental gateway facing United's space-age stadium proudly announces the entrance to Newcastle's Chinatown, with the celebrated brewery just round the corner. Neon signs of what seem like thousands of restaurants invite and cajole, but Peggy Wong's constantly bustling, two-storey restaurant appears to have the edge on its competitors in turnover alone.

The warm, attentive service is led by Peggy herself and prepares you for treats in store, which never fail to justify the restaurant's reputation. All the dishes are infused with partner Jackie Law's authentic interpretation of regional Chinese cookery. These range from deep-fried strips of beef in Cantonese sauce and pungently spiced Szechuan chicken stir-fry with black pepper, to aromatic crispy duck and hot-plate dishes brought sizzling to your table. There is a choice for vegetarians, such as a stir-fry of vegetables in a spicy satay sauce, or Singapore vegetarian vermicelli.

Fish features heavily, too, with king prawns, scallop, squid and Northumberland crab well represented alongside, maybe, an excellent stir-fry of monkfish with green peppers and black bean sauce. And if you really can't decide, there are no fewer than six 'banquets' to make your life easier.

This is something of a party place, especially for members of the local Chinese community. The powerful flavours, skilled handling of fresh market produce and a bubbly atmosphere transport you briefly away from Tyneside and the Premier League.

Their pride: Aromatic crispy duck
Inexpensive wines: Whistling Duck Semillon Chardonnay (Australia) 2003/04, £16; Ruitersvlei Pinotage (South Africa) 2004, £16

Proprietor: Peggy Wong
Last orders for dinner: 10.45 pm
Open every day
Set lunch: from £8
Set dinner: from £13
Private dining: 20-50

NEWCASTLE UPON TYNE, TYNE & WEAR

Treacle Moon

**5-7 The Side, Quayside, Newcastle Upon Tyne NE1 3JE
Tel. 0191 232 5537   Fax 0191 221 1745**

MAP 5 D2

OCCUPYING a prime position in Newcastle's now quite fashionable quayside area, this restaurant is just a few yards from the river, its deep purple interior an extension of the night sky and its black-clad waiters like shadows in the gloom.

In such a contemporary setting, it is hardly surprising that the concise, set-price menu draws on modern cookery styles, although there are more traditional dishes such as the chargrilled sirloin of Angus beef with Pont Neuf potatoes, or roast best end of Northumbrian lamb.

The essential ingredients of designer cuisine are all to hand. Salads predominate among the starters, with baked goat's cheese, watercress, pear and pesto, or an Asian salad with charred king prawns, sweet chilli and sesame alongside a ham and foie gras terrine (with crispy black pudding), or a velouté of artichokes with girolles.

Main courses are more impressive and appetisingly presented and might include a caramelised breast of Gressingham duck with sweet potato, shitake mushrooms, honey and five spice, or fillet of hake generously accompanied by three plump scallops and creamy risotto.

There follows a rather limited selection of desserts which includes panna cotta, roasted pineapple and chocolate tart with raspberry ice-cream.

Their pride: Fillet of hake with chervil mascarpone, scallop and baby vegetable risotto.
Inexpensive wines: Cabernet Sauvignon Les Templiers, £14.50; Chardonnay Les Templiers, £14.50

**Proprietors: Tom and Jocelyn Maxfield
Last orders for dinner: 10.30 pm
Closed: lunchtime, Sunday
Closed for holidays: Bank Holidays
Set dinner: from £30**

NEWTON LONGVILLE, BUCKINGHAMSHIRE

Crooked Billet

2 Westbrook End, Newton Longville, Nr. Milton Keynes MK17 0DF
Tel. **01908 373 936** Fax **01908 631 979**
e-mail: **emma@thebillet.co.uk**   **MAP 2** C1

IT IS a little odd to find this ancient, thatched coaching inn sitting in the middle of a housing estate, but the potential clientele is on the doorstep – and lucky clientele for having the Crooked Billet on theirs. Large and impeccably kept gardens provide an attractive frontier between the inn and its surroundings.

Inside you are propelled into a polished operation within pristine, olde worlde confines. Delicate little amuse-bouches are brought to the table with your pre-dinner drink, and a tasting menu – in a pub? Of course you can just pop in for a pint, but the stylish fare is the *raison d'être* here, from lunchtime snacks, sandwiches and light meals to more sophisticated offerings.

Imported influences abound – crispy duck with hoi sin, sea bass with chorizo, home-made mezze, cassoulet or duck confit and foie gras terrine. Otherwise there are corned beef hash, calf's liver, sausage, kidney and onion, or crispy belly of pork with apple and black pudding.

Seafood is particularly well represented – scallops with spinach and caviar, salmon and smoked salmon fishcakes, or swordfish in the most discreet of curried sauces with king prawns on a creamy risotto base. Vegetarians might enjoy the tempura vegetables.

There is rather less choice among the home-made desserts, but they are augmented by fresh fruit, including apricots with a glass of armagnac. But after the hefty portions and rich flavours that went before, this is just right. They really do set out to please.

Speciality food: Modern English cooking
Draught beers: Abbott Ale, Greene King IPA
Average wine price by the glass: £2.85

Licensee: Emma Gilchrist
Last orders for dinner: 9.30 pm
Closed: Sunday evening and Monday lunch (for food)
Set dinner: Tasting menu £45
Beer garden
Children welcome
Wheelchair access

NORTON, SHROPSHIRE

Hundred House Hotel

GASTROPUB

Norton, Nr. Shifnal, Shropshire TF11 9EE
Tel. 01952 730 353 Fax 01952 730 355
e-mail: reservations@hundredhouse.co.uk   **MAP 3** E3

FOOD and garden lovers alike have a treat in store here – at the rear of the property is an intriguing herb and flower garden that is really something special. Almost at every turn some engaging horticultural or stone feature delights the eye, and herb cuttings can be bought and the money left in an honesty box.

The main building abounds with original features, ranging from oak-panelled walls and red-tiled floors to the fireplace inlaid with ivory in one of the side rooms. Dried flowers hanging from the ceiling give an unashamedly snug feel. Fresh herbs feature on each table and diners are invited to use them for drinks or food.

An à la carte menu offers an appealing selection of dishes. Seared scallops on pea purée with crispy pancetta, and three bruschetta – red pepper, smoked aubergine and caponata – with a chickpea, melon and crème fraîche salad, are two starters from a choice of six, possibly followed by roast rack of lamb with savoury lentils, roast peppers and rosemary jus, or grilled Gloucester Old Spot pork chop with mustard sauce, special sausage and apple chutney.

Spicy tomato and lentil soup on the specials menu is subtly spiced and flavoursome. A main course of baked cod with rosemary and lemon crust is cooked to perfection and deftly set off with a chive sauce.

The summer pudding looks exquisite with its garnish of mixed berries, cherries and flowers.

Speciality food: Asparagus and wild mushroom risotto
Draught beers: Heritage Bitter, Sadlers Bitter
Average wine price by the glass: £3.30

Licensee: Henry Phillips
Last orders for dinner: 9.30 pm
Open every day
Main courses: from £10.95
Private dining: 6-90
Beer garden
Accommodation: 10 rooms
Children welcome
Wheelchair access

NORWICH, NORFOLK

Adlard's

79 Upper St. Giles Street, Norwich, Norfolk NR2 1AB
Tel. 01603 633 522 Fax 07092 011 486
e-mail: info@adlards.co.uk   **MAP 4** E3

AN INTIMATE and friendly sort of place, Adlard's offers cooking that might on occasion feature challenging combinations, such as sea bass with pied de cochon sausage, but which never strays into the realm of the bizarre.

Presentation is precise and the attention to detail is awesome, as in the quail dish that comes with goat's cheese, truffle fritters and a quail's egg, or else halibut poached in claret with ravioli of crab and pickled beetroot, or yet roast partridge with petit pain de foie and bread sauce, bacon and red cabbage.

Even starters are often multi-faceted, as in lobster canneloni that sits on thin slices of minted potato salad and is accompanied by smoked eel and soused cauliflower.

Desserts show a similar spirit of invention. Poached pineapple is presented with caramel panna cotta and chilli and lime syrup, while coffee cream in puff pastry has chocolate and cardamom sorbet in a brandy-snap basket. There is also a good selection of British and French cheeses.

An extensive wine list is well described and offers more than 50 half-bottles. There is a 'fine wine cellar reserve' section and those bottles are kept in a cellar away from the restaurant, so they have to be ordered in advance.

Their pride: Scallops with crisp pork belly, pea purée and pea shoot salad
Inexpensive wines: Ovega Negra 2004, £15.50; Forest Estate Pinot Noir (New Zealand) 2003, £23.50

Proprietor: David Adlard
Last orders for dinner: 10.30 pm
Closed: Sunday and Monday
Closed for holidays: 25 December and 1 January
Set lunch: from £21
Main courses: from £19
Limited wheelchair access

NORWICH, NORFOLK

1up at the Mad Moose Arms ★ GASTROPUB

2 Warwick Street, Norwich, Norfolk NR2 3LD
Tel. 01603 627 687

MAP 4 E3

ASK exact directions to get to the Mad Moose Arms. Off Unthank Road, on the crest of a modest Edwardian residential street, at first sight it looks like a conventional pub. But then you glance up at the blackboard to note some imaginative-looking bar snacks and, more important, a sketched pointing hand to the upstairs restaurant.

Having worked your way through the innards of the pub by the kitchen entrance, fire escape and the stairs, you are at '1up'. This text-speak title is apt for a simple but comfortable room in which some of the best modern food in Norwich is served – classically rich chicken liver parfait and toasted brioche, with a nice modern twist of saffron pickled courgettes, for a start. Or try the confit of Barbary duck with celeriac remoulade and capers.

Fish is delivered every day, so you might find pan-fried organic salmon with a Cromer crab and baby spinach tartlet, or else the excellent fillet of sea bream roasted in its skin and served with saffron butter potatoes and the famous Stiffkey samphire from the north Norfolk coast.

Meat-eaters can feast on Gressingham duck breast and fondant potato or rump of English lamb with creamed haricot beans.

For dessert try the upside-down pear and almond sponge with cinnamon and plum ice cream – a delicious medley of flavours.

The wine list offers a fine 2004 Sancerre (available in half-bottles) for the fish maybe and an Australian Semillon with dessert.

Speciality food: Fillet of sea bream and saffron butter potatoes
Draught beers: Mad Moose Ale (Wolf Brewery), Greene King
Average wine price by the glass: £4.50

Licensee: Henry Watt
Last orders for dinner: 10 pm
Closed: Lunchtimes (except Sunday), Sunday evening
Main courses: from £12.95
Private dining: 30–50
Children welcome

NOTTINGHAM, NOTTINGHAMSHIRE

Benton's Brasserie ★

GASTROPUB

34-38 Heathcoat Street, Nottingham NG1 3AA
Tel. 0115 959 9800 Fax 0115 941 5039
e-mail: bentons.brasserie@btconnect.com   **MAP 4** B2

ON THE edge of the city's fashionable lace market, Benton's has the look and feel of a smart brasserie and there's a buzzy vitality about it. The room is light and airy, the tables set with freshly laundered white tablecloths and elegant tulip glasses. One part is on a raised level, which nicely varies the shape of the dining area.

The cooking is excellent, drawing all the right flavours from fine ingredients, yet the menu is fairly priced. Soup of the day could be a classy tomato and basil, the balance of herb and tomato exactly right. The pastry and harmonious medley of flavours is also laudable in a delicious sweet pepper, Brie and courgette tart, a fine alternative starter.

Braised lamb, from Nottingham's premier butcher, Owen Taylor, sweet and tasting like first-rate shoulder, is exceptional, enhanced by a splendid red wine gravy and an innovative mashed potato mixed with spinach and wild mushroom. And for the piscivorous, there is always fresh fish such as pan-fried sea bass and citrus dressing, or mussels with creamed leeks. Vegetarians are catered for with a leek, cauliflower and smoked cheese roulade.

Puddings retain gastronomic interest in a good home-made and naturally textured white chocolate and strawberry cheese, other interesting choices being roasted pineapple and vanilla ice-cream, or rhubarb crumble tart.

Good wines feature a rich Ravenswood Zinfandel from Sonoma County, ideal with roasted duck breast, another staple of the menu.

Speciality food: Herb salmon and crab cakes, plum tomato chutney
Draught beers: Theakstons, Becks
Average wine price by the glass: £3.40

Licensee: Fiona Huckerby
Last orders for dinner: 10 pm
Open every day
Set dinner: from £10.50
Main courses: from £13.95
Children welcome
Wheelchair access

NOTTINGHAM, NOTTINGHAMSHIRE

Hart's ★

1 Standard Court, Park Row, Nottingham NG1 6GN
Tel. 0115 911 0666 Fax 0115 911 0611
e-mail: ask@hartsnottingham.co.uk   **MAP 4** B2

IN A GATED court off Maid Marion Way, this stylish restaurant is very much part of the thrusting, modern, fashionable Nottingham, popular with the theatregoers of the Playhouse and the rising generation of local business executives.

The room is suitably contemporary with its fabrics in the colours of the Mediterranean enlivening white walls and columns. The central service section is topped with a huge bowl of lilies and its shelves are stocked with fine brandies and other digestifs.

Mediterranean-style décor is matched by the strong flavours of the food, which sometimes comes in unusual combinations, such as the use of chorizo and yellow peppers to accompany squid. In fact, this proves to be an excellent match.

Other confident, well-prepared dishes include fried foie gras with roasted peaches and sherry vinegar sauce and monkfish with clam and saffron risotto.

Among the desserts, a dark chocolate trifle with mixed berries stands out.

The wines are carefully selected to complement the nature of the food, with good choices from Spain, Italy and South America.

Their pride: Roast chump of local lamb with fried sweetbreads, broad beans and asparagus
Inexpensive wines: Azumbre Verdejo Rueda 2003, £16.50; Château Le Thou Sauvian 1999, £14

Proprietor: Tim Hart
Last orders for dinner: 10.30 pm (Sunday 9 pm)
Open every day
Closed for holidays: 26 December and 1 January
Set lunch: from £12.95
Set dinner: from £15.95 (Sunday only)
Private dining: up to 110
Al fresco dining
Accommodation: 32 rooms
Wheelchair access

NOTTINGHAM, NOTTINGHAMSHIRE

Restaurant Sat Bains ★

Trent Side, Lenton Lane, Nottingham NG7 2SA
Tel. 0115 986 6566 Fax 0115 986 0343
e-mail: info@restaurantsatbains.net   **MAP 4** B2

LIKE a light at the end of a gloomy tunnel, this totally refurbished and revamped restaurant with rooms appears as a welcoming haven in a suburban industrial zone. Factories and warehouses are forgotten as you are taken in hand by a professional team in surroundings where there is little in the way of soft furnishings to relieve the austere red brickwork and flagstones. The focus is on the Sat Bains dining experience, best enjoyed in the attractive conservatory.

The daily changing set, surprise and dégustation menus are object lessons in delicacy and classically inspired artistry. Two first courses epitomise the mixture of traditional and contemporary approaches: the finest of rabbit terrines with a carrot purée and salad, on the one hand, and a single, fat scallop with the more assertive and original accompaniment of peanut brittle, fennel, kohlrabi and apple on the other.

More delicacy follows, perhaps Cornish brill, deliciously offset by sweet and sour chicory, or melting slices of salt marsh lamb with its own perfectly cooked offal in a simple jus with goat's cheese.

Variations of texture play a vital role, too, particularly in the more unusual combinations such as the organic salmon with fennel and vanilla, or the spiced scallop with 'textures of cauliflower', even extending to some similarly ground-breaking desserts such as passion fruit with yoghurt, toffee and liquorice, wild blackberries with olive oil sorbet or a chocolate mousse with further 'textures', this time of banana and pistachio.

Their pride: Roasted scallop with Indian spices and 'textures of cauliflower'
Inexpensive wines: Côtes du Rhône Château Mont Redon Blanc 2003, £22; Montepulciano 2002, £25

Proprietor: Sat Bains
Last orders for dinner: 9.30 pm
Closed: lunchtime, Sunday and Monday
Closed for holidays: 2 weeks Aug, 2 weeks Jan
Set dinner: from £55
Private dinning: 10-30
Accommodation: 8 rooms

NOTTINGHAM, NOTTINGHAMSHIRE

World Service

Newdigate House, Castle Gate, Nottingham NG1 6AF
Tel. 0115 847 5587 Fax 0115 847 5584
e-mail: enquiries@worldservicerestaurant.com **MAP 4** B2

WITH High Street shops on one side and the celebrated castle on the other, the old world and the new convene at this stylishly elegant refurbishment of the city's ex-servicemen's club with its attractive walled garden – the site (legend has it) of Britain's first planting of celery, brought from distant lands by early travellers.

Colourful batiks and Eastern artifacts now mingle with military inscriptions on the wood panelling, the hushed colonial feel of the spacious lounge area a far cry from the bustle of the consumer paradise outside. Not surprisingly, the varied carte presents a gastronomic tour in which home-grown and imported flavours and compilations come together in an explosion of fresh, alluring flavours and classy presentation.

Starters might be roasted tomato and red pepper soup with coriander and cumin scones; rich, creamy, chicken liver parfait, or a half-lobster with curried mango salad. Main courses include a nicely perfumed Thai steamed chicken breast with cashews, roasted mango and pak choi; bream baked with a tomato crust, thyme-scented potatoes and a Provençal dressing, and roasted rump of veal with smoked almond pesto.

Though tried and trusted crème brûlée and panna cotta feature among desserts, you might be tempted by toasted marshmallow with tropical fruit and a sesame brittle, or a blackcurrant crumble soufflé with apple sorbet.

Their pride: Thai steamed chicken breast with cashew nuts, roasted mango, jasmine rice and steamed bok choi
Inexpensive wines: Pinot Blanc Klevener Reserve Hunawihr 2003, £16.75; Boland Shiraz Paarl 2003, £15

Proprietors: Ashley Walters, Philip Morgan and Chris Elson
Last orders for dinner: 10 pm
Open every day
Closed for holidays: 25 and 26 December
Set lunch: from £11.50
Main courses: from £13.50
Private dining: 14-32
Al fresco dining
Wheelchair access

OAKSEY, WILTSHIRE

The Wheatsheaf

GASTROPUB

Wheatsheaf Lane, Oaksey, Wiltshire SN16 9TB
Tel. 01666 577 348

MAP 1 F2

THE NEW chef/proprietor here, Tony Robson-Burrell, is intent on putting this sleepy little Cotswold village and its only pub firmly on the gastronomic map. Tucked away just off of the main street, the uncluttered, cosy bar resounds to the lively banter of local topers. Dine here for the atmosphere, in the rear dining-room for peace and quiet, or in the garden if the weather allows.

Tony's four starters, four main courses and three desserts, plus British and French cheeses, offer just enough variety at prices weighted to tempt new customers. Caution is the name of the game and classic Caesar salad, pea soup with mint oil and goat's cheese or fine, meaty Old Spot rillettes might provide your starter.

Along with the roasts, steaks and casseroles, a desire to push out the culinary boundaries is also evident in such things as confit of duck leg with choucroute, pan-roasted salmon with chorizo mash, spinach and leeks, or risotto of wild mushrooms with truffle oil. Building the range and diversity slowly makes sense, especially when the technical know-how is so evidently on hand.

The cooking of fine ingredients is well judged – especially the pink roast beef – and even simple, fresh vegetables are nicely handled as is that old standby, sticky toffee pudding, which remained notably light despite its gooeyness.

Ice-creams are a more refreshing alternative and there are appetising bar snacks for those who just want a quick bite. The attentive young staff add to the friendly, easygoing atmosphere.

Speciality food: Modern British cooking
Draught beers: Bath Ales Gem, Fullers London Pride
Average wine price by the glass: £3.25

Licensee: Tony Robson-Burrell
Last orders for dinner: 9.30 pm
Closed: Monday for food
Main courses: from £11.95
Beer garden
Children welcome
Wheelchair access

OCKLEY, SURREY

Bryce's at the Old Schoolhouse `GASTROPUB`

Stane Street, Ockley, Surrey RH5 5TH
Tel. 01306 627 430 Fax 01306 628 274
e-mail: bryces.fish@virgin.net

MAP 2 C4

THIS white painted, gabled building was once a boarding school for boys and the restaurant is in what used to be the gymnasium. Parasols decorate the tables outside and hanging baskets add colour. Inside there are several cottagey rooms with blackened beams, fireplaces and a cosy bar with about a dozen well-chosen single malt whiskies and a bustling atmosphere.

The cheerful team provide a warm welcome and attentive service throughout. Seafood is the *raison d'être* here, with shellfish from Cornwall and wet fish from Billingsgate. Starters include a dish of richly flavoured roasted salmon with sliced fresh asparagus and a thin flaky pastry, or Loch Fyne scallops served with spinach and hollandaise sauce.

The blackboard daily specials might feature Dover sole, sea bass or lemon sole. If available, go for the mixed grill of seafood, with impeccably fresh monkfish, cod, hake, tuna, salmon and mussels in the shell, the dish served with al dente vegetables. There is also a printed menu with even more choice – including red mullet and gilthead bream. Carnivores, meanwhile, might prefer seared calf's liver or rib-eye steak.

Those with a sweet tooth should try raspberry and kiwi fruit crème brûlée, quenelles of chocolate and aniseed mousse, or the steamed orange and stem ginger pudding.

As for wines, there are an impressive eight white, two rosé and six reds offered by the glass, in addition, of course, to those that are available by the bottle.

Speciality food: Seafood
Draught beers: Sussex Bitter, Fullers London Pride
Average wine price by the glass: £3.25

Licensee: Bill Bryce
Last orders for dinner: 9.30 pm
Closed: Sun evening November, January & Februrary
Closed for holidays: 25 and 26 Dec, 1 and 2 Jan
Set lunch: from £22
Set dinner: from £22
Private dining: 40-60
Al fresco dining
Children welcome
Wheelchair access

OMBERSLEY, WORCESTERSHIRE

Venture Inn

Main Road, Ombersley, Worcestershire WR9 0EW
Tel./Fax 01905 620 552

MAP 3 E3

FACED with this black and white Elizabethan façade, you could be forgiven for thinking you were about to enter an olde worlde tea shoppe. However, any such association will disappear the moment you step inside. There is an inglenook and there are beams, but contemporary music playing softly in the background and large sofas in the small bar/sitting-room dispel notions of tweedom.

Pale yellow walls, creamy napery and a plaid carpet in the dining-room further allay such fears. The room will seat about thirty, so it is advisable to book.

As for the food on offer, an attractively presented salmon terrine with tiny diced vegetables in light aspic has a delicate touch. Other starters include mixed mushroom soup with truffle oil, and smoked salmon with mixed leaf salad.

It is difficult to make a decision when faced with a choice of hake (larded with bacon), plaice fillets with salmon risotto, from the specials, or poussin with a thyme jus from the main menu.

The accompaniments are thoughtful. Strips of courgette, carrot and parsnip in a light, tempura-style batter make a welcome change from the usual round of plain, unadorned vegetables, while a potato galette mops up sauce admirably.

Indulge in a rich chocolate tart ideally offset by an intensely flavoured orange ice-cream.

Their pride: Pan-roasted lamb's sweetbreads, buttered noodles, peas and mint
Inexpensive wines: Concha y Toro Sauvignon (Chile) 2004, £14; Côtes du Rhône Château du Grand Moulas 2003, £15

Proprietor: Toby Fletcher
Last orders for dinner: 9.30 pm
Closed: Sunday dinner, Monday
Closed for holidays: 2 weeks in February, 2 weeks in August, Christmas
Set lunch: from £17.95
Set dinner: from £31.50
Wheelchair access

ORFORD, SUFFOLK

Trinity at The Crown and Castle

Orford, Woodbridge, Suffolk IP12 2LJ
Tel. 01394 450 205
e-mail: info@crownandcastle.co.uk   **MAP 4** F5

ORFORD is a tranquil, attractive place and you could be forgiven for imagining that the sort of local hostelry that lies in the heart of such a sleepy little village would be redolent of mothballs and mulligatawny, bombazine and old money.

What a welcome surprise, then, to discover that the experienced owners have transformed this hotel into a stylish, elegant venue with more than its fair share of quirkiness. Max Dougal's eclectic, daily changing dishes (under wife Ruth's guiding hand) are, like the personal service, more smart brasserie than formal restaurant.

Starters tend towards simplicity, with local smoked eel and trout on potato and beetroot salad, marinated feta with water-melon and toasted seeds; crayfish, cucumber and dill cocktail, or beef carpaccio with 'Harry's Bar dressing' and some tangy shaved Parmesan.

Inventive main courses could include seared Orford sea bass with a warm salade niçoise; Vietnamese-style beef, bean-sprouts, pak choi stir fry, or a scrumptious 'Ruddy fish stew' with a shellfish broth, bursting with freshness and strong, natural flavours. The marriage of flavours in duck confit with curried peas was rather less successful, with the pancetta tending to dominate.

Rich and original desserts include hot, bitter chocolate mousse, lemon meringue ice-cream sundae, or a light and well-executed warm pecan nut and Bourbon tart, to end a dining experience that never lacks style or interest.

Their pride: Local skate wing, nut brown butter, capers and brown shrimps
Inexpensive wines: Stormy Cape (Stellenbosch) 2004, £12.50; Alta Vista Cosecha (Argentina) 2003, £14.50

Proprietors: Ruth and David Watson
Last orders for dinner: 9.30pm (Sat, Bank Hols 10pm)
Closed: 25 and 26 December, 3 days at New Year
Set lunch: from £14.50
Main courses: from £11.50
Private dining: 6-10
Al fresco dining
Accommodation: 18 rooms
Children welcome
Wheelchair access

OSMOTHERLEY, NORTH YORKSHIRE

Golden Lion

GASTROPUB

**6 West End, Osmotherley, Nr. Northallerton, N Yorks DL6 3AA
Tel. 01609 883 526 Fax 01609 884 000**

MAP 5 D3

PERCHED right on the edge of the magnificent Cleveland Hills, part of the North Yorkshire National Park, this quiet little village of solid, stone-built houses is a haven for walkers. What better place to head for after a hard day on the moors than Christie Connelly's lively little corner pub?

With your head still full of images of the majestic countryside, the cosily workaday interior will not steal any thunder from Mother Nature, but good draught beers, a wide range of snacks and full meals in pure pub tradition will help to prolong the pleasure.

The choice is vast, from fresh mussels, crab and sardines to soups, vegetarian dishes such as spicy lentil burgers or a tasty, if slightly heavy, goat's cheese and red pepper terrine. Or try pasta and risotto (creamy lemon with caramelised onion, for example), spare-ribs, salads, grilled meat, fish and burgers.

You will find almost every pub dish you have ever heard of here, from chicken Kiev to cod and chips, calf's liver and onions, rack of lamb and, inevitably, a particularly hearty and well-made steak and kidney pudding.

There are also predictably comforting desserts to choose from – the warm apple, prune and walnut cake was light and luscious. If the owner's two-year stay in the Mediterranean has left its mark in such offerings as spaghetti vongole, bresaola with fresh Parmesan and pan-fried pork with Parma ham, sage and marsala sauce, in general the accent remains stoically British with good honest flavours, no-nonsense presentation and generous portions.

Speciality food: Traditional pub food with a Mediterranean slant
Draught beers: Hambleton Ale, Timothy Taylor Landlord
Average wine price by the glass: £2.50

Licensee: Christie Connelly
Last orders for dinner: 9.15 pm
Open every day
Closed for holidays: 25 December
Main courses: from £7.50
Private dining: 10-50
Beer garden
Children welcome

PADSTOW, CORNWALL

Seafood Restaurant

Riverside, Padstow, Cornwall PL28 8BY
Tel. 01841 532 700 Fax 01841 532 942
e-mail: reservations@rickstein.com

MAP 1 B4

RICK STEIN is not only a worthy icon among TV chefs, but is now also a 'brand', with a Padstow operation that extends to a deli, a pâtisserie and a fish and chip shop.

It is satisfying to note that the staple dishes that have helped to establish the reputation of his original venture, the Seafood Restaurant, during what is now almost a quarter of a century, are as good as ever.

Roasted tronçon of turbot with hollandaise sauce, one of Rick's signature dishes, is still the simplest and probably the best way of treating this great fish, rather than anything more elaborate.

The plateau of fruits de mer is faultless, and to these classics there have been added intriguing ideas such as a ginger and chilli massala stuffing that turns mackerel into something special.

Of course, there is another special quality about the Seafood Restaurant, and that is the wine list.

Rick Stein has an ineffable nose for a fine wine, and he has found some splendid bottles, not only in Burgundy and the other French regions but also in Australia. In addition, there is a splendid range of house wines by the glass.

Their pride: The 'Fruits de Mer'
Inexpensive wines: Sauvignon de Haut Poitou 2004, £18.50; Muscadet Château de Cleray 2003, £20

Proprietors: Rick and Jill Stein
Last orders for dinner: 10 pm
Open every day
Closed for holidays: 25 and 26 December, 1 May
Set lunch: from £65
Set dinner: from £65
Accommodation: 14 rooms and 6-room annex
Wheelchair access

PADSTOW, CORNWALL

St. Petroc's Bistro ★

4 New Street Padstow, Cornwall PL28 8EA
Tel. 01841 532 700 Fax 01841 533 455
e-mail: reservations@rickstein.com   **MAP 1** B4

THIS is the other Padstow restaurant of Rick Stein, of Seafood Restaurant and TV fame, and it hums with good cheer among a mix of locals and visitors. A fine yet informal sitting-room with comfortable sofas leads to the bistro, sympathetically modern with pine tables and chairs and boldly coloured paintings. Style without pretension would sum it up.

Here, Rick's celebrated cooking style flourishes, bursting, of course, with the fresh flavours of the sea. The fish soup, a meal in itself, has whole pieces of sea bass, mackerel, cod and squid and comes with delicious white or granary bread. Or there are breaded goujons of plaice with tartare sauce.

As good an unadulterated fish dish as you could hope for is the wing of skate au poivre with capers and Béarnaise sauce, served with perfect thin-cut chips and leaf spinach, but as an attractive alternative you could try the underrated gurnard, pan-fried with sage and garlic butter.

Apart from fish, you will find chicken liver parfait as a starter, and to follow chargrilled rib-eye of beef or rabbit with tarragon sauce, both of which are superb. Sticky toffee pudding is a fine dessert.

The wines are chosen with flair and an eye for value. There are good branded Stein blends from Australia, the reds ideal with steak, while the Haut-Poitou Sauvignon and Gamay admirably suit the fish dishes.

Their pride: Hot Toulouse sausage, tomato, caper and shallot salad
Inexpensive wines: Rick Stein Seafood White 2004, £18.50; Château de Sours Rosé 2004, £20.50

Proprietors: Rick and Jill Stein
Last orders for dinner: 10 pm
Open every day
Closed for holidays: 25 and 26 December, 1 May
Main courses: from £12.95
Al fresco dining
Accommodation: 10 rooms
Wheelchair access

PARTRIDGE GREEN, WEST SUSSEX

Green Man Inn

GASTROPUB

Church Road, Partridge Green, West Sussex RH13 8JT
Tel. 01403 710 250 Fax 01403 713 212
e-mail: info@thegreenman.org

MAP 2 C4

MANY a pub owner would envy the bubbly, welcoming atmosphere at this unassuming little red brick hostelry on the edge of a quiet Sussex village. Neither tap-room rustic nor commuter-belt classy, this really is a venue for all seasons and every occasion. With their tempting set lunch, appetisers or tapas to accompany your drink, a full-blown menu and daily specials, you can relax in anticipation, the candlelight and scrubbed tables providing the background to impromptu gatherings and more grandiose celebrations.

The choice and style of the dishes perfectly complement the straightforwardness and no dish is ever more complicated than it need be to present its main ingredients in the best possible light. The more fastidious might prefer a little extra refinement, but the technique here is all about honesty and well-defined flavours.

Although imported, mostly Mediterranean influences have crept in with the likes of deep-fried haloumi cheese with a tomato and chilli jam, chargrilled vegetables with herb couscous or a breast of duck with honey and oriental spices, the underlying trend remains stoically English and above all stylishly uncomplicated, as in smoked haddock, cream and Parmesan on bubble and squeak.

Grilled asparagus is perked up with a few shavings of Parmesan, a fine chump of lamb requires nothing more than some juicy red cabbage and gratin Dauphinois to produce a comforting blueprint of sheer and unpretentious delight. One could perhaps look for a lighter touch here and there, although a chunky chocolate and hazelnut marquise did have a certain earthy charm. Enjoy!

Speciality food: Modern British cooking
Draught beers: Harveys Bitter
Average wine price by the glass: £2.35

Licensee: Will Thornton
Last orders for dinner: 9.30 pm
Closed: Sunday evening, Monday
Closed for holidays: 1 week Christmas
Set lunch: from £14.95
Main courses: from £8.95
Private dining: 10-20
Beer garden
Children welcome

PETER TAVY, DEVON

Peter Tavy Inn

GASTROPUB

Peter Tavy, Nr. Tavistock, Devon PL19 9NN
Tel. 01822 810 348 Fax 01822 810 835

MAP 1 C4

WITH its slate floors, beams and numerous nooks and crannies, this splendidly rustic old inn is rightly known for its robustly flavoured food. The female chef has the skill to take a steak pie and give it a modern touch of Stilton in the pie crust, which, with slow-cooked, tender beef and rich gravy, makes for an excellent main dish.

However, before that, try the very fresh crevettes with a delicate lemon mayonnaise, goat's cheese and pancetta salad or a tart of avocado, mozzarella and sun-dried tomato. Pink bream from Brixham comes with a successful pesto dressing, as does the swordfish with lemon butter.

The general thrust of these dishes from a changing blackboard is in the modern gastro style, from lamb shank with a mint and gooseberry jus to duck breast, stir-fry vegetables and oyster sauce, the latter better than you will find in many a Chinese restaurant.

Puddings are certainly acceptable, if not quite at the same level, with tiramisù or meringue and fresh fruits – probably the best are the ice-creams made with Devon double cream.

Wines by the glass and bottle are above-average, the Chilean Cabernet Sauvignon full of grown-up wine flavours and ideal with the steak and Stilton pie.

The real ales are very local and well kept.

Speciality food: Steak and Stilton pie
Draught beers: Princetown Jail Ale, Sharps Doom Bar
Average wine price by the glass: £3

Licensees: Jo and Chris Wordingham
Last orders for dinner: 9 pm
Open every day
Closed for holidays: 25 and 31 December
Main courses: from £7.95
Private dining: up to 40
Beer garden
Children welcome
Wheelchair access

PETERSFIELD, HAMPSHIRE

JSW ★

1 Heath Road, Petersfield, Hampshire GU31 4JE
Tel. 01730 262 030

MAP 2 B4

THIS little town-centre restaurant has a solid reputation, with well-earned accolades pouring in as regularly as customers. You must book, even midweek, to delight in the simple but polished fare since a maximum of twenty-two diners can be accommodated at any one time.

Simplicity is the keyword, but neither this nor the limited-choice menu – four starters, four main courses and three desserts – in any way detracts from unpretentiously sophisticated cooking using the finest ingredients, including many from the Parisian market of Rungis and line-caught fish from the Solent.

There are some excellent home-made breads, too, and wonderful parsnip chips with your aperitif. And do let yourself be tempted by the tasting menu.

Most dishes are represented in condensed form, with delightfully undaunting portions which pour out a wealth of contrasting but complementary flavours and textures.

The sauces are light but aromatic while the cooking of the main ingredients is spot-on, though desserts could perhaps benefit from a touch more imagination.

The wine list takes you through more than 700 bins, which include startling arrays of Alsatian, Austrian, Australian and North American crus.

Their pride: Fricassee of sole with ceps and asparagus
Inexpensive wines: Stringy Bark Semillon/Chardonnay (Australia) 2004, £16.50; Terrazzo Alto Malbec (Argentina) 2003, £17

Proprietor: Jake Watkins
Last orders for dinner: 9.30 pm
Closed: Sunday and Monday
Closed for holidays: 2 weeks summer, 2 weeks Jan
Set lunch: from £22.50
Set dinner: from £33.50

PLUCKLEY, KENT

Dering Arms

GASTROPUB

Station Road, Pluckley, Kent TN27 0RR
Tel. 01233 840 371 Fax 01233 840 498
e-mail: jim@deringarms.com   **MAP 2** E4

YOU could be forgiven for being wary of the somewhat sinister façade of this 19th-century hunting lodge, especially if you knew that there was a resident poltergeist who was likely to upturn the odd glass during your stay. But fear not, once through the door, beyond the leaded lights and stone mullions, there is a warm, family atmosphere accentuated by rustic furnishings and period artifacts.

There is also a certain dependable rusticity about the menus, which are augmented by blackboard specials where fish and seafood are particular favourites.

Pan-fried herring roes, oysters, prawns, Sussex smokies (smoked mackerel in a creamy sauce) provide natural, uncomplicated starters along with a tasty, if not terribly authentic, fish soup, and there is an evenly distributed selection of 'surf and turf' to follow.

The treatment given to a variety of fresh fish and meat dishes tends to follow classical lines – skate wing with capers and beurre noisette, tuna steak with garlic and lemon butter, black-peppered steak or duck confit with bubble and squeak.

The fresh turbot needed absolutely nothing more than its tangy crayfish butter to produce an appealing main course, especially with some super-crisp chips.

An enticing range of desserts was let down by a disappointing tarte Tatin, though perhaps this was the fault of the resident phantom.

Speciality food: Seafood
Draught beers: Goachers Dering Ale, Goachers Gold Star
Average wine price by the glass: £2.95

Licensee: James Buss
Last orders for dinner: 9.30 pm
Closed: Sunday evening, no food Monday
Closed for holidays: 25-27 December, 1 January
Main courses: from £9.45
Private dining: 30-70
Beer garden
Accommodation: 3 rooms
Children welcome

PLUSH, DORSET

Brace of Pheasants

GASTROPUB

Plush, Nr. Dorchester, Dorset DT2 7RQ
Tel. 01300 348 357

MAP 1 E3

SET IN glorious Dorset countryside, this idyllic pub is easily reached in a few minutes from the main A35 and from Dorchester. Or if you would prefer a leisurely chug down country lanes from Sturminster, that is an Arcadian delight.

The menus here, which change daily, display a sophistication that is almost metropolitan, with starters such as roasted quail with spiced pear, tomato and raspberry, and it is good to see such well-executed specials as eggs Benedict with smoked salmon.

Where the real strength of the cooking lies, though, is in the fresh fish, which might be the local Chesil Beach mackerel with minted couscous, or smoked haddock with samphire and hollandaise sauce. There is also local game in season and that familiar staple, calf's liver and bacon, with mash and rosemary jus.

Desserts do not lack imagination with offerings such as Jamaican ginger and butter pudding, for example, or lemon and lime crème brûlée, and the densely rich coffee and cognac tiramisù.

The bar and the charming flower-filled dining-room, which serves the same menu, both have all the rustic charm you would expect in a Dorset village.

There are excellent real ales, as well as elderflower wine and a wine list that includes a couple of vintages of Château Musar, the claret of the Levant.

Speciality food: Game and fish
Draught beers: Ringwood, Butcomb
Average wine price by the glass: £2.75

Licensees: Toby and Suzie Albu
Last orders for dinner: 9.30 pm
Closed: Monday
Closed for holidays: 25 December, I January
Main courses: from £13.50
Private dining: 6-24
Beer garden
Children welcome
Wheelchair access

PORT GAVERNE, CORNWALL

Port Gaverne Hotel

Port Gaverne, Port Isaac, Cornwall PL29 3SQ
Tel. 01208 880 244 Fax 01208 880 151

MAP 1 B4

ON A raised hillside overlooking a delightful cove just up the coast from Port Isaac, this old hostelry is as much a pub as a hotel. The front bar, which with its glimpses of boats moored on the beach, protected by a bluff from the Atlantic breakers, has the feel, unmistakably Cornish, of a smuggler's haunt and is the best place to eat the home-made crab soup or the conventional run of pub dishes, such as smoked mackerel pâté or a ploughman's served with Cornish cheeses like yarg and the soft St. Endellion.

Here, too, you may enjoy substantial main courses, which might be seafood pie, smoked haddock and spring onion fishcakes, or ham, egg and chips.

The more formal restaurant seems determined to be something of an evocation of the 1950s, and there are few surprises on the set-price dinner menu, though the food is very competently handled by the kitchen.

You might start with smoked salmon and cucumber and dill relish, going on, perhaps, to whole lemon sole with buttered prawns. Or you might prefer meat, with a good claret from the decent wine list. The sirloin steak is well hung and the peppercorn sauce is spicy without being fiery.

Then is also Port Isaac lobster – not surprisingly a speciality here, which is as a salad, grilled or thermidor.

Speciality food: Port Isaac lobster thermidor
Draught beers: Sharp, St. Austell
Average wine price by the glass: £2.90

Licensee: Graham Sylvester
Last orders for dinner: 9 pm
Open every day
Set dinner: from £25
Main courses: from £11.50
Beer garden
Accommodation: 14 rooms
Children welcome in dining room

PRESTON BAGOT, WARWICKSHIRE

The Crabmill ★

Preston Bagot, Claverdon, Warwickshire B95 5EE
Tel. 01926 843 342 Fax 01926 843 989
e-mail: thecrabmill@aol.com   **MAP 3** E3

FIVE minutes' drive from Henley-in-Arden in the village of Preston Bagot, The Crabmill combines tradition, modern comfort, great service and very good cooking. Outside, this is a white painted old pub with weathered timbers, but contemporary restoration inside creates an elegance that does not detract from its period character, flagstones in the main bar contrasting with modern but lived-in leather chairs and sofas in the delightful lounge bar, which offers a soothing view of the finely kept garden.

The staff take their lead from hands-on general manager, Sarah Robinson, and they make you feel instantly at ease, giving the impression that nothing is too much trouble.

Fresh ingredients and accurate cooking result in fine textures and really positive flavours, especially in sauces. Specials of the day can give the most satisfaction, as, for instance, the smoked duck strips with gnocchi in a fine porcini mushroom velouté with Parmesan, followed by moist tranches of oven-roasted loin of pork on the bone, the skin crisp and crackling-like.

From the main menu, popular choices include a starter of crab, basil and ginger pancakes and, to follow, confit duck with pickled plums or roast halibut with parsley and shallot rösti.

For dessert, the chocolate brownies served in a rich chocolate sauce, accompanied by vanilla ice-cream in a light brandy-snap basket, are a treat. The espresso coffee is excellent. Notable Abbot Ale is on draught and a very user-friendly, skilfully chosen wine list gives punchy, one-line taste descriptions

Speciality food: Crab, basil and ginger pancake
Draught beers: Abbot Ale, Tetley Ale
Average wine price by the glass: £3.50

Licensee: Sarah Robinson
Last orders for dinner: 9.30 pm
Closed: Sunday evening
Closed for holidays: 25 December
Main courses: from £13
Private dining: 16-25
Beer garden
Children welcome
Wheelchair access

RAMSGILL-IN-NIDDERDALE, NORTH YORKSHIRE

Yorke Arms ★★

Ramsgill-in-Nidderdale, Nr. Harrogate, N Yorks HG3 5RL
Tel. 01423 755 243 Fax 01423 755 330
e-mail: enquiries@yorke-arms.co.uk   **MAP 5** D4

THE setting is idyllic and unspoilt, human habitation amounting to no more than a cluster of stone houses round the village green, where the only evidence of any urgency is the peat-brown stream rushing down from the moors to help fill the nearby Gouthwaite reservoir.

It may seem surprising to find a restaurant of this calibre in what you might well think of as the back of beyond, but with a wealth of local ingredients – the moorland lambs and the abundant game are just two sources – why not?

Many of the trappings of the village inn have been retained, such as polished bitumen on the flagstoned floors and the time-worn furniture in the bar. You can drop in for a serious bar snack, too, for this is serious hill-walking country.

But if you settle down to lunch or dinner, the rustic setting gives way to a range of inventive, contemporary and creative dishes that will surprise and delight you.

A starter of lobster ravioli, with gossamer-thin pasta and a rich filling, comes with foamy shellfish broth and crunchy, tender young fennel. Faultless. Mallard, saddle of hare and the grouse in season lose none of their appeal for being more simply treated and solidly garnished with perhaps black pudding and cabbage. Modern trends return in some attractively presented desserts combining lightness with depth of flavour.

Speciality food: Yorkshire potted beef, ham hock and foie gras terrine
Draught beers: Black Sheep, Theakson
Average wine price by the glass: £3.50

Licensees: Gerald and Frances Atkins
Last orders for dinner: 9 pm
Open every day
Closed for holidays: 25 December
Set lunch: from £21.50
Main courses: from £20
Private dining: up to 10
Al fresco dining
Accommodation: 13 rooms
Wheelchair access

REDMILE, LEICESTERSHIRE

Peacock Inn   `GASTROPUB`

Church Corner, Main Street, Redmile, Leics NG13 OGA
Tel. 01949 842 554 Fax 01949 843 746
e-mail: reservations@thepeacockinnredmile.co.uk   **MAP 4** B3

ONLY a mile and a half from Belvoir Castle, this soft honey-stone Grade II listed building opposite the church has its name boldly emblazoned in white on its roof and is therefore difficult to miss.

And that is just fine, because it has much to offer. Meals or drinks can be taken outside at the front, where an attractive, gravelled space with navy parasols will allow you to watch the world go by. Alternatively, try the decked seating area leading off the garden room at the rear. Inside, there is a snug bar with a wood-burning stove, another informal eating-room leading off it, while the main dining-room lies off the hall.

Open sandwiches served on foccacia, ciabatta or baguette offer an appealing choice of toppings such as roasted Mediterranean vegetables or minute steak with sautéd onions and mushrooms. The bar menu is fairly extensive, ranging from salads such as niçoise, Greek feta and seafood, to more substantial dishes encompassing tagliatelle carbonara, Lincolnshire sausages on mustard mash, or albondigas – spicy Spanish lamb meatballs that might be served with tabbouleh and spiced yoghurt. Fishcakes are always popular, served on wilted spinach with a tasty chive sauce, as either a starter or a main course.

Main courses from the carte could include a couple of fish dishes such as a rolled plaice fillet with smoked salmon and lobster velouté, or baked bream. Huge profiteroles filled with vanilla ice-cream to follow if you are feeling brave. Choose from a good range of coffees, or herbal and fruit teas, while you appreciate a level of service that is pleasant and efficient throughout.

Speciality food: Smoked haddock and salmon fishcakes
Draught beers: Timothy Taylor Landlord, London Pride
Average wine price by the glass: £3.05

Licensees: Mark Attewell and Andrew Mackley
Last orders for dinner: 9.30 pm
Open every day
Closed for holidays: 25 December evening
Main courses: from £6.50
Private dining: 10-24
Beer garden
Accommodation: 10 rooms
Children welcome
Wheelchair access

REED, HERTFORDSHIRE

The Cabinet ★

GASTROPUB

High Street, Reed, Royston, Hertfordshire SG8 8AH
Tel. 01763 848 366 Fax 01763 849407

MAP 2 D1

FOUR miles south of Royston, off the A10, the 16th-century Cabinet offers cooking of serious gastronomic interest. It is a place where excellent ingredients (the beef dry-aged for thirty days), which are locally supplied where possible, are transformed into dishes of real flavour and finesse with often silky textures such as you would find at a good London address.

The class, potential and style of the cuisine is illustrated in a text-book chicken liver parfait, the richness nicely checked by the brisk freshness of a fine bean and walnut salad.

Even more stunning is bitter chocolate marquis of memorably persistent flavours, perfectly partnered by home-made raspberry sorbet.

For excellent beef flavours there is the modestly named onglet (skirt steak) of splendid aged flavour and rightly offered only rare to keep it tender.

All these fine dishes come from the menu for the reasonably priced set lunch.

The carte continues in superior brasserie style with pan-fried red mullet, assiette of new season's lamb, calf's liver and Suffolk sweet-cure bacon, or fillet of Galloway beef.

There is also an exceptional wine list with particularly good house claret by the glass and some very fine grand cru Chablis from Domaine Laroche for a special occasion.

Speciality food: Bitter chocolate marquis with raspberry sorbet
Draught beers: Ruddles County, Greene King IPA
Average wine price by the glass: £3.75

Licensee: Dawn Abrams
Last orders for dinner: 9 pm
Open every day
Closed for holidays: 1 January
Set lunch: from £11.95
Main courses: from £13.75
Private dining: 8-12
Beer garden
Children welcome at lunch only
Wheelchair access

RIDGEWAY, SOUTH YORKSHIRE

Old Vicarage ★

Ridgeway, Nr. Sheffield, South Yorkshire S12 3XW
Tel. 0114 247 5814
e-mail: eat@theoldvicarage.co.uk   **MAP 3** F1

THIS could only be an old vicarage, with its echoes of *Wuthering Heights* or *Middlemarch,* square-set, Victorian and discreet, in a quiet rural corner yet only a mile or so from the tramways and urban sprawl of Sheffield.

It is the sort of place where you might expect to be served tea and scones, or perhaps a traditional roast for Sunday lunch, but what you actually find is a varied selection of dishes influenced by not only Mediterranean but also oriental influences.

An appropriately clerical fillet of beef, for example, comes not simply with parsnips but with polenta, glazed onions, girolles and tarragon potato. Equally traditional rack of lamb is given a herb crust and served with a compote of strawberries and mint.

Starters such as lime seared scallop appetiser, or lemon, basil and goat's cheese tortellini, and desserts like an apple medley of crème brûlée, sorbet and a tart are interesting and distinctive, completing a very well-balanced meal.

Service is relaxed and charming, the dining-room quite simply decorated and delightfully airy.

Their pride: Crisp roasted fillet of sea bass on potato galette, Whitby crab salad and mango, peas and asparagus with minted Muscat sabayon
Inexpensive wines: Menetou-Salon Pinot Noir (France) 2002, £25; Dehesa la Granja Alejandro Fernández 2000, £27

Proprietor: Tessa Bramley
Last orders for dinner: 9.45 pm
Closed: Sunday and Monday
Closed for holidays: 2 weeks end July/early August, 26 December-6 January
Set lunch: from £30
Set dinner: from £49
Private dining: 10-50
Al fresco dining
Wheelchair access

RIPLEY, NORTH YORKSHIRE

Boar's Head

Ripley, Nr. Harrogate, North Yorkshire HG3 3AY
Tel. 01423 771 888 Fax 01423 771 509
e-mail: reservations@boarsheadripley.co.uk   **MAP 5** D4

THIS stylish county hotel beside the castle is named after a boar that had the effrontery to run down Edward III while he was out hunting in the 14th century. One Thomas Ingleby saved the day and the king and probably provided supper. The Ingleby family reopened the inn in the 1970s after a forebear had banned the sale of alcohol in the village for more than half a century.

You are welcomed by professional staff in the comfortable lounges and in the classically decorated dining-room, where the lunchtime menu is really something of a steal in these august surroundings.

The varied evening selection maintains a certain conservatism but still exhibits real flair in, say, a layered tower of Parmesan and sesame seed wafers with Stilton and port mousse, a brochette of wood pigeon with diver scallops in a sweet and sour salsa, or a duo of lemon sole and bitter-sweet smoked salmon with razor clams, garlic butter, spinach and pine-nuts.

This lightness of touch and purity of flavour is also particularly noticeable in, for example, a light terrine of haddock and crab, or a perfectly cooked breast of moist farm chicken with fennel, which is offset by a raspberry infused jus.

Fruit from the estate gardens features in a multi-element dessert of rhubarb cappuccino, rhubarb and vanilla and rhubarb sorbet, with richer chocolate concoctions for those who cannot resist.

Their pride: Grilled breast of Gressingham duck with Earl Grey tabbouleh, baby fennel and raspberry vinegar
Inexpensive wines: Côtes du Ventoux, Cuvée Terrasses 2001, £15.95; Sauvignon de Touraine 2002, £15.95

Proprietors: Sir Thomas and Lady Ingleby
Last orders for dinner: 9 pm
Open every day
Set lunch: from £15
Set dinner: from £30
Accommodation: 25 rooms
Wheelchair access

RIPLEY, SURREY

Drake's Restaurant ★

The Clock House, High Street, Ripley, Surrey GU23 6AQ
Tel. 01483 224 777 Fax 01483 222 940

MAP 2 C3

THE ground floor of this fine-looking Georgian house has been opened up to create a spacious, comfortable restaurant with a tasteful décor in shades of green. During the summer the patio of the delightful garden to the rear is truly the perfect setting for pre-dinner drinks.

Clear, true flavours are at the heart of a menu that changes with the seasons. For example, a wild mushroom casserole topped by a perfectly poached egg and exemplary Béarnaise sauce is just bursting with flavour. Other starters range from a salmon and herb terrine with celery mayonnaise and pickled cucumber to roasted langoustines with plump, langoustine-filled ravioli and quenelles of seafood jelly.

Typical of the well-judged main courses are roasted turbot with pea purée, braised chicory, crushed potato and red wine sauce, and saddle of lamb cooked in a coriander and mint crumb.

Desserts might include a banana parfait rolled in praline, with a pineapple sorbet and caramel sauce, or a winning combination of coffee bavarois, macerated figs and a fruity apricot sorbet.

The wine list, which offers about 65 bins but is gradually being expanded, is predominately French, with just a handful from Spain and Italy and some New World representation.

Prices start at a gentle £14 for the house wine and up to half the list is priced at under £30. There are about a dozen wines by the glass and some half-bottles.

Their pride: Carpaccio of aromatic duck with roast langoustine
Inexpensive wines: Riesling Trocken Dr. Bürklin-Wolf 2003, £20.50; Domaine Daniel Dugois Troussean 1999, £24.50

Proprietors: Steve and Serina Drake
Last orders for dinner: 9.30 pm
Closed: Sunday, Monday, Saturday lunch
Closed for holidays: Christmas, 2 weeks August
Set lunch: from £18
Set dinner: from £33.50
Private dining: up to 10

ROMALDKIRK, CO. DURHAM

Rose and Crown

GASTROPUB

Romaldkirk, Nr. Barnard Castle, Co. Durham DL12 9EB
Tel. 01833 650 213 Fax 01833 650 828
e-mail: hotel@rose-and-crown.co.uk   **MAP 5** D3

THIS 18th-century coaching inn set in a gloriously unspoilt corner of rural Teesdale is an absolute gem. The walls are covered with certificates of culinary excellence and sporting prints, and there are huge bouquets of fresh flowers everywhere. Potted geraniums sit on the outside tables. A choice of snacks and meals can be enjoyed here when the weather allows, or otherwise in the bar-brasserie.

In the evening, a more formal set menu, which changes every day, is offererd in the pretty little dining-room. Simplicity is the watchword, with dishes almost devoid of garnishing, but the encyclopaedic repertoire exhibits both flair and unwavering technique.

Starters might include cheese fritters or the lightest of smoked haddock soufflés, farmhouse ham with figs, or chicken liver pâté, before the soup course with, say, a deliciously different cream of courgettes and sweet pear.

Local game features regularly according to the season – pan-fried pigeon breasts with a tartlet of creamed parsnip and a juniper berry sauce, perhaps, or tender, pink loin of local lamb with braised kidneys in a woodland mushroom casserole. There is always a vegetarian choice and fish such as fillet of sea bass with lemon butter sauce.

Homely tarts, fudge cake, home-made ice-creams and traditional desserts finish things off as you soak up the atmosphere of this living museum of hospitality.

Speciality food: Modern British cookery
Draught beers: Theakstons, Black Sheep
Average wine price by the glass: £3.05

Licensees: Christopher and Alison Davy
Last orders for dinner: 9 pm
Open every day
Closed for holidays: 1 week Christmas
Set dinner: from £26
Beer garden
Accommodation: 12 rooms
Children welcome
Wheelchair access

ROTHERFIELD PEPPARD, BERKSHIRE

The Greyhound ★

**Gallowstree Road, Rotherfield Peppard, Berkshire RG9 5HT
Tel. 01189 722 227 Fax 01189 242 975**

MAP 2 B3

SET in a pretty rural Berkshire village between Henley and Sonning, and once the site for hanging robbers and footpads, The Greyhound is the first country venture for Antony Worrall Thompson.

It is a real pub with beams and well-kept real ale. The décor of the main restaurant is a warm, rich red – the arched ceiling eye-catching – and there is a cushioned area by the bay windows near the bar counter. The patio and garden are ideal for al fresco meals, and service is smooth and professional.

The thrust of the operation is very much the grill-restaurant formula. Beef dry-aged for thirty-five days ensures exceptional steaks; the home-reared suckling pig is excellent, also well aged and with more succulence and flavour than most. Starters include welcome classics such as well-wrought eggs Florentine, or tender and most accurately cooked chilli salt squid.

A starter house speciality called Ménage à Trois – the name of Antony's first restaurant – is three hot cheese pastry parcels of leek and Roquefort, Camembert and cranberry, spinach and Boursin. Courgettes grown on Antony's smallholding are used to present a fine dish of courgette flowers stuffed with three cheeses and basil, fried in a light tempura batter.

Premium Irish and English cheeses are a feature, along with good puddings such as home-made fruit crumbles, cheesecakes and chocolate brownies. Wines of the world are well selected, with fine choices from Languedoc, the Cape and Australasia.

Speciality food: Salmon and smoked haddock fishcakes
Draught beers: Fullers London Pride, Fullers Discovery
Average wine price by the glass: £3.65

**Licensees: Antony Worrall Thompson and David Willy
Last orders for dinner: Monday to Thursday 9.30 pm,
Friday-Sunday 10.30 pm
Open every day
Main courses: from £15
Private dining: up to 30
Beer garden**
Children welcome
Wheelchair access

ROWDE, WILTSHIRE

George and Dragon ★

High Sreet, Rowde, Nr. Devizes, Wiltshire SN10 2AN
Tel. 01380 723 053
e-mail: thegandd@tiscali.co.uk   **MAP 1** E2

A WELCOMING bar in this 15th-century inn features a large inglenook and a snug spot for a casual meal, while a more formal room leading off the bar will seat about two dozen customers.

The chef, previously at Soho House, London, features a few meat dishes on the à la carte menu, for example a sirloin steak with Béarnaise sauce or slow-roasted belly pork with Chinese spiced braised cabbage. A fixed lunch menu might offer spicy meatballs, meaty and seasoned well, paired with a subtle garlic mayonnaise.

However, this is predominantly a fish restaurant, with fresh fish delivered four or five times a week from St. Mawes, Cornwall. On any one day you might find lobster, John Dory, bream, skate wing, monkfish, scallops and moules written up on boards above the bar.

Fishcakes, ever popular, do not usually come up to expectations. Here, happily, they do, made with chunky pieces of salmon and white fish enhanced by spring onion and dill, they are full of flavour, as is the accompanying tartare sauce.

Nothing more than truly ripe plum tomato and onion salad is needed to accompany sea bream cooked to perfection with a crisp skin.

Caramelised citrus fruits with crème chantilly might be one of the pudding options, or maybe a fruit crumble of juicy plums topped with a crunchy crumb and a thick dollop of clotted cream.

Speciality food: Halibut with asparagus and hollandaise
Draught beers: Butcombe, Guinness
Average wine price by the glass: £3.80

Licensees: Christopher Day, Philip and Michelle Hale
Last orders for dinner: 10 pm
Closed: Sunday evening (food), Monday
Closed for holidays: Bank Holidays
Set lunch: from £13
Main courses: from £12
Al fresco dining
Children welcome
Wheelchair access

ROWSLEY, DERBYSHIRE

The Peacock at Rowsley `GASTROPUB`

**Bakewell Road, Rowsley, Nr. Matlock, Derbyshire DE4 2EB
Tel. 01629 733 518 Fax 01629 732 671
e-mail: reception@thepeacockatrowsley.com**   **MAP 3** F2

A FINE 17th-century building in Peak District stone, once the dower house on the local aristocratic estate, The Peacock is owned by Lord Edward Manners and it now makes a comfortable inn of understated class and style. In the intimate bar, with stone walls and Bruegel reproduction mural, there is a snack menu offering a good range of sandwiches, home-made soup of the day, fresh scampi in lemonade batter or haddock in beer batter with mushy peas and chips. The real ales are well kept.

Across the hall is the elegant restaurant with mullioned windows overlooking the pretty garden, the fine tables and chairs the work of the famous Yorkshire furniture maker Mousey Thompson. The cooking is sound in the modern European style and relies on fresh local ingredients as far as possible – the Castle Gate roast beef at Sunday lunch being a particular winner.

Dinner brings more modish choices such as monkfish saffron risotto, or halibut with celeriac and mashed potatoes, confit of belly pork with a cinnamon sauce, and cannon of local lamb served with roast potatoes and redcurrant jus.

Desserts are a strength, as in a compote of berries with sabayon glaze or pineapple tarte Tatin. Wines by the glass and bottle are interesting and superior, the choice from the Rhône strong in a Viognier de Drôme and an exceptional organic village wine from Perrin.

There are 16 handsome en-suite bedrooms as well as a limited number of rods for fishing on the Derwent.

Speciality food: Modern European cooking
Draught beers: Bakewell Best, Abbot Ale
Average wine price by the glass: £3.25

**Licensee: Ian Mackenzie
Last orders: 9.30 pm (Sunday 8.30 pm)
Open every day
Set lunch: from £16.50
Main courses: from £21.95
Private dining: 12-20
Al fresco dining: lunchtime
Accommodation: 16 rooms**
Children welcome at lunchtime
Limited wheelchair access

ROYDHOUSE, WEST YORKSHIRE

Three Acres ★

GASTROPUB

Roydhouse, Nr. Huddersfield, West Yorkshire HD8 8LR
Tel. 01484 602 606 Fax 01484 608 411
e-mail: 3acres@globalnet.co.uk **MAP 5** D5

WHAT'S in a name? Although this turn-of-the-century drover's inn set in the Pennine countryside is easily spotted by its '3' sign, its full name is the Three Acres Inn 'The Grocer'. This is because its main entrance is via a smart delicatessen whose speciality foods include a wonderful cheese counter, breads, chutneys and oils.

The melodious strains of Cole Porter, provided by a live band in the latter half of the week, gently permeate the dining areas. Menus from well-known restaurants are randomly displayed on dark green walls; heavy brocade curtains and crisp white napery on the tables complete the scene.

Starters range from traditionally English potted shrimps and omelette Arnold Bennett, to hot and sour pork and prawn soup, or crispy vegetable samosa with lentil dhal and coriander cream.

Main courses are more grounded in English cuisine with some Mediterranean and oriental flourishes. Tender Gressingham duck with an exceptionally crisp skin, served with a sage and onion stuffing and a tart apple purée, will not disappoint. Black pudding is made on the premises and features alongside a Gloucester Old Spot pork chop with a compote of apples. Seafood lovers will be delighted with the oyster bar, whose tempting array includes rock oysters, fruits de mer platter and lobster cocktail.

Puddings are beautifully presented – a delicate crème brûlée with diced mango and mint looks stunning on a square glass plate with a vivid, green-lined red border. Friendly, super-efficient staff are there when you need them, but never intrusive.

Speciality food: Local produce
Draught beers: Timothy Taylor Landlord, Black Sheep
Average wine price by the glass: £3.75

Licensees: Neil Truelove and Brian Orme
Last orders for dinner: 9.45 pm
Open every day
Closed: 1 week Christmas
Main courses: from £13.95
Private dining: up to 20
Beer garden
Accommodation: 20 rooms
Children welcome
Limited wheelchair access

SALT, STAFFORDSHIRE

Holly Bush Inn

GASTROPUB

Salt, Stafford, Staffordshire ST18 0BX
Tel. 01889 508 234 Fax 01889 508 058
e-mail: geoff@hollybushinn.co.uk   **MAP 3** E2

THE licensing of public houses originated during the time of Charles II and the Holly Bush, with several accolades under its belt, is reputed to be the second licensed pub in the country, though its origins are claimed to reach as far back as 1190.

The area has a rich history – one of the battles of the English civil war was fought at nearby Hopton Heath and the A51 lying north of Salt was the main 18th-century coaching route from London to Liverpool.

Moving on a few centuries, a packed car park and limited parking space on the road attest to the popularity of this inn.

A comprehensive laminated menu will offer starters such as green shelled mussels with a blue cheese and garlic sauce, pan-fried calf's liver, or watercress, potato and bacon salad, the ingredients of the trio working well together but perhaps better served with the addition of a dressing.

Main courses by way of steak and kidney pudding, Greek lamb and grilled pork chops with cheese and beer are all trencherman stuff. Greek lamb, an enormous hunk of shoulder, falls off the bone and has a distinct cinnamon flavour. The Greek-style salad features salad leaves, red/yellow/green peppers, spring onions, radish and Cape gooseberries along with tomato, cucumber and feta cheese.

For dessert, choose from chocolate mousse, sticky toffee pudding and steamed treacle sponge, or opt for award-winning cheeses.

Speciality food: Steak and kidney pudding
Draught beers: Adnams, Pedigree
Average wine price by the glass: £2.25

Licensee: Geoff Holland
Last orders for dinner: 9.30 pm
Open every day
Main courses: from £6.25
Beer garden
Children welcome
Wheelchair access

SAPPERTON, GLOUCESTERSHIRE

The Bell at Sapperton

GASTROPUB

Sapperton, Nr. Cirencester, Gloucestershire GL7 6LE
Tel. **01285 760 298**
e-mail: **thebell@sapperton66.freeserve.co.uk**   **MAP 1** E1

HOW many pubs have a parking space reserved 'For Horses Only', equipped with gleaming galvanised buckets of water? The proud owners do things rather well at their picturesque inn, its tidy lawns bordered with lavender, while indoors you find candlelight and fresh flowers.

The sophisticated ambience may seem more Pimm's than pints, but bare boards and scrubbed tables create a pleasantly rustic atmosphere, and the smart young staff are relaxed and friendly. A comprehensive menu and blackboard specials offer stylishly eclectic Anglo-Continental dishes.

Starters might include truffle and Parmesan risotto, marinated scallops or seared foie gras on brioche with port and redcurrant jelly. Some of the main courses are ambitiously complex, such as organic salmon filled with spinach and salmon mousseline on a salad of buffalo mozzarella; breast of chicken with couscous, feta, green olive and olive oil dressing, or tenderloin of Old Spot pork with black pudding, celeriac fritters and honey and mustard cream.

These more exotic offerings may make calf's liver with bacon and shallots, beer-battered fish and chips or their own burgers look decidedly plain. But the quality of the locally sourced ingredients guarantees enjoyment of the plainer items where well-defined, natural flavours are allowed to emerge unencumbered.

Overall, a dining experience in which the professionalism shines dazzlingly through.

Speciality food: Modern British cooking
Draught beers: Hook Norton Bitter, Old Spot Bitter
Average wine price by the glass: £4

Licensees: Paul Davidson and Pat LeJeune
Last orders for dinner: 9.30 pm
Open every day
Closed for holidays: 25 December for food
Main courses: from £11.50
Private dining: 8-12
Beer garden
Children over 10 welcome
Wheelchair access

SAWLEY, LANCASHIRE

Spread Eagle

GASTROPUB

Sawley, Nr. Clitheroe, Lancashire BB7 4NH
Tel. 01200 441 202 Fax 01200 441 973
e-mail: ncw@the-spreadeagle.co.uk　　　　　　**MAP 5** C4

AS IF the peaceful setting beside the river Ribble was not enough to bring in the customers, with the main dining-room's picture windows overlooking water meadows, the go-ahead owners of this solid, whitewashed, 17th-century coaching inn are intent on making an already popular venue a centre of the gastro-social scene through a series of promotional initiatives.

Celebrity evenings, special events and – the latest award-winning scheme – Blind Dining, where the choice is left entirely to the chef for a previously arranged budget, all help to keep things ticking over, together with an attractively priced lunch and special prices for early-evening weekday diners.

If the velour, floral carpets, sensible place mats and the clientele denote homely, traditional tendencies, echoed to a certain extent by the menu, there are also invention and originality that beguile rather than surprise.

They have reinvented Lancashire hot-pot, with layers of buttered potato, braised neck of Swaledale lamb and black pudding. From further afield might hail a pressed terrine of plum tomatoes and sweet peppers with mozzarella and basil; pan-fried fillet of sea bass with globe artichoke, soy, ginger, sesame and coriander, or grilled breast of duck with poached pineapple, spring onions and anise.

Enjoyably homely desserts complete the impression of consistent reliability.

Speciality food: Braised neck of lamb with layered buttered potato, onions and black pudding
Draught beers: Sawleys Drunken Duck, Amstel
Average wine price by the glass: £3.20

Proprietors: Ysanne and Nigel Williams
Last orders for dinner: 8.45 pm
Closed: Sunday dinner, Monday
Closed for holidays: 1 week in January
Set lunch: from £9.95 (Tuesday to Friday)
Set dinner: from £10.75 (until 7 pm excluding weekends)
Private dining: 10-100
Wheelchair access

SEAHAM, CO. DURHAM

Seaham Hall The White Room ★

Lord Byron's Walk, Seaham, Co. Durham SR7 7AG
Tel. 0191 516 1400   Fax 0191 516 1410
e-mail: reservations@seaham-hall.com   **MAP 5** D3

JUST outside this North Sea port, the manicured grounds pave the way for the contemporary designs awaiting you in a cool, elegant environment that has been transformed since Lord Byron took his marriage vows here. The White Room is the setting for meals as design-conscious as the surroundings in which they are served.

You may think such luxury comes with an outrageous price tag, but think again: the set lunch of what amounts to eight courses is just £22. Two pre-starters might be gilding the lily, but the rocket and ginger 'cappuccino' and a delicate celeriac and duck mousse alone show the tasteful creativity one can expect throughout. Delicate nuance and startling finesse need not mean insipidity and even a light, rich jus infused with thyme and used to sauce a pair of pink, tender wood pigeon breasts, along with some crisp, colourful summer vegetables, packed a deliciously natural punch.

The main evening menu makes use of local ingredients. Flowering courgette with crab, cauliflower purée and a shellfish vinaigrette, or roast scallops with a sauce vierge, tomato sorbet and tomato soda are seasonal starters. To follow, try some local lamb and its sweetbreads, tongue with a rosemary jus, or pan-fried sea bass with crushed potatoes and a bouillabaisse sauce.

To finish on a high note, there is prune and armagnac soufflé or caramelised lemon tart with yoghurt ice-cream. This is all very impressive stuff and you may even wax poetic.

Their pride: Roast lamb rump, braised tongue and sweetbreads, onion purée and rosemary jus
Inexpensive wines: Sauvignon Blanc (Boschendahl) 2003, £22; Santa Christina, Marchesi Antinori (Italy) 2003, £18.50

Proprietors: Tom and Jocelyn Maxfield
Last orders for dinner: 10 pm
Open every day
Set lunch: from £22
Main courses: from £18
Accommodation: 19 rooms
Wheelchair access

SEASALTER, KENT

The Sportsman

GASTROPUB

Faversham Road, Seasalter, Whitstable, Kent CT5 4BP
Tel. 01227 273 370
e-mail: thesportsman1@gmail.com   **MAP 2** E3

THERE IS something enigmatic about this square-set outpost of
rurality on the edge of holiday-land. A rather plain main bar has
something of the feel of a colonial club, with ceiling fans and bare
boards, and no attempt appears to have been made to exploit a
potentially attractive conservatory. Yet it all fits somehow, the
bohemian feel of the place enhanced by an air of bonhomie under
the guiding hand of landlord Philip Harris – with, as you might
expect, nothing remotely twee about brother Stephen's robust,
down-to-earth offerings, chalked up on a single board so that, at
busy times, crowds throng to make their choices.

After generally simple starters – rock oysters and hot chorizo,
asparagus soup and soft-boiled egg, Serrano ham with artichokes
and Parmesan, for example, all served with delicious home-made
breads – the chef gives full flight to his prowess and imagination
in a daily changing selection of main courses based on excellent
local ingredients (especially fish).

Try crispy duck with smoked chilli salsa and soured cream; grilled
gurnard with bouillabaisse sauce; thornback ray with brown
butter, cockles and sherry dressing, or plainly roasted farm
chicken with morels and roasting juices and lamb with mint
sauce, served pink.

If honest and unequivocal flavourings are Stephen Harris's
undoubted hallmarks, note, too, the details – the perfectly cooked
asparagus garnish and al dente broad beans, the lightness of a
creamy mash, the airy homeliness of almond and raspberry tart.

Speciality food: Local produce and fish
Draught beers: Shepherd Neame Masterbrew, Early Bird (seasonal)
Average wine price by the glass: £2.95

Licensees: Philip and Stephen Harris
Last orders for dinner: 9 pm
Closed: Sunday evening and Monday (for food)
Main courses: from £12.95
Conservatory dining
Beer garden
Children welcome

SELLACK, HEREFORDSHIRE

Lough Pool Inn

GASTROPUB

Sellack, Ross-on-Wye, Herefordshire HR9 6LX
Tel. 01989 730 236
e-mail: david@loughpool.co.uk   **MAP 3** D4

THE well-balanced selection of starters at this cosy bar includes cabbage, potato and chorizo broth, jellied pork and organic chard terrine, or grilled, marinated squash which, served sliced and with a delicious, smoky flavour, comes with dressed local salad leaves and generous, grainy curls of Parmesan.

Choosing a main course from the à la carte menu will cause much deliberation, given such toothsome dishes as Cornish brill roasted on the bone with chips, crushed peas and covered in Béarnaise sauce, or slow-cooked belly of pork.

Resembling a giant noisette, this cut of pork might lack a crisp rind, but the tender flesh falls apart on the plate and the flavour is good. Accompanied by sliced red apple with a sweet, spiced sauce, this is a truly pleasing dish.

There are also daily specials, while the pudding menu offers a selection of organic ice-creams, with mouth-watering flavours such as damson, prune and armagnac, as well as treacle toffee and lemon curd. Alternatively, try dark chocolate mousse with white chocolate ice-cream

British farmhouse cheeses are also on offer, and coffee comes with the chef's own chocolate truffles.

Speciality food: Brixham cod in cider batter
Draught beers: Wye Valley, Brecon Red Dragon
Average wine price by the glass: £3.25

Licensees: David Birch and Janice Birch
Last orders for dinner: 9 pm
Open every day
Main courses: from £10
Private dining: 10-30
Beer garden
Children welcome
Wheelchair access

SHEPTON MALLET, SOMERSET

Charlton House ★

Charlton Road, Shepton Mallet, Somerset BA4 4PR
Tel. 01749 342 00 Fax 01749 346 362
e-mail: enquiry@charltonhouse.com   **MAP 1** E3

WELCOME – and they do welcome you here – to what must be one of the prettiest conservatory dining-rooms in England. It is worth booking early to ensure a table in this gloriously sunny and airy, stone-tiled room, which is more an extension of the garden than the house. White ceiling drapes reflect crisp damask napery and brocades and velvets give an almost Renaissance feel to the cleverly conceived interior. Despite the age and style of this Mendip country house, Roger Saul, its design-conscious owner, is keen to instil a feeling of subdued modernity.

These delightfully comfortable and restful surroundings form a perfect backdrop to the new chef's creative efforts with dishes that are imaginative, not over-complicated and worth including in your choices.

There is, for instance, lamb of continuously guaranteed quality (it comes from a farm owned by the proprietor of the hotel), its loin roasted and coupled with slow-braised shoulder with celeriac purée. Another one for meat lovers is cannon of pork, hot-smoked belly, caramelised onions and a confit of potatoes and beans. Understandably well liked is roast fillet of turbot with a sauce made of clams and parsley.

Equally diverse are desserts, perhaps the best example being the chocolate pot de crème served with a tequila and grapefruit ice, an innovative delicacy if you like tequila. Also alcohol based is a sharp lemon mousse with a sorbet made of gin and tonic – an excellent idea after a rich main course.

Their pride: Roast loin of Sharpham lamb, slow-braised shoulder, celeriac purée, pea and mint mash
Inexpensive wines: Frascati Fontana Candida 2003, £18; Saint-Chinian Terres Rouges 2001, £22

Proprietor: Roger Saul
Last orders for dinner: 9.30 pm
Open every day
Set lunch: from £24
Set dinner: from £49.50
Private dining: 8-60
Accommodation: 25 rooms
Wheelchair access

SHINFIELD, BERKSHIRE

L'Ortolan ★

Church Lane, Shinfield, Reading, Berkshire RG2 9BY
Tel. 01189 888 500 Fax 01189 889 338
e-mail: info@lortolan.com

MAP 2 B3

FIVE minutes from the M4, this well-known restaurant housed in a Grade II listed Georgian vicarage has recently had its interior modernised in rather Art Deco style, all brown and beige shades, to provide an elegantly attractive setting for its modern European cuisine.

Lunchtime might feature an amuse-bouche of something like tapenade with goat's cheese and an imaginative starter such as scallops and cauliflower purée and beignets with a touch of caviar.

The main course choices could be braised shoulder of lamb, roast best end, kidneys and sweetbreads, or else turbot with ceps and morels.

There will be a daily special which, depending on the season, might feature woodcock in sherry sauce with fondant potato and Brussels sprouts.

Among the excellent desserts you will be tempted by rhubarb charlotte and champagne mousse or perhaps the pavé of white chocolate.

The extensive, thoughtfully compiled wine list is very fairly priced. The surroundings are comfortable, with the tables given plenty of space, and service is both attentive and swift.

Their pride: Chocolate tasting plate
Inexpensive wines: Riesling Pallise Estate Martinborough (New Zealand) 2004, £25; Chianti Classico Brolio 2003, £26

Proprietor: NewFee Ltd.
Last orders for dinner: Tuesday to Thursday 9.30 pm, Friday and Saturday 10.30 pm
Closed: Sunday and Monday
Closed for holidays: 26 December-4 January
Set lunch: from £18
Set dinner: from £55
Private dining: 8-42
Wheelchair access

SHUTTLEWORTH, LANCASHIRE

Fisherman's Retreat ★

GASTROPUB

Bye Road, Shuttleworth, Nr. Ramsbottom, Lancs BL0 0HH
Tel. 01706 825 314 Fax 01706 821 518
e-mail: mail@fishermansretreat.com   **MAP 5** C5

SET on a ridge in the hills overlooking the Twine Valley nature park, the bar and restaurant of the Fisherman's Rest has the air of a pinewood mountain cabin with splendid views, the townships below looking very much as they might in a Lowry painting.

The pub itself is home to traditional Lancastrian cooking that relies totally on local ingredients scrupulously selected. The real Lancashire black pudding, made in the Rossendale Valley, is as good an example as you will ever eat, served perfectly with home-made English mustard and a salad of shredded carrot and cherry tomatoes.

Fresh cod and haddock is deep fried in beer batter and the chips are to die for, the mushy peas exceptional.

Beef is selected with the greatest care and dry-aged for at least four weeks. The steaks here are famous in east Lancashire and the same high-quality meat is used for the home-made chilli beef, mince and onion suet pudding, spicy meatballs and steak and ale shortcrust pie.

There are specials such as fillet of pork with wok-fried vegetables, and even on occasion wacky options such as crocodile steak, to be followed by apricot crumble.

There are several beautifully kept real ales. The Timothy Taylor goes down beautifully with both black pudding and battered cod. Note, too, a fine collection of 50 malt whiskies.

Speciality food: Real Lancashire black pudding
Draught beers: Timothy Taylor, Black Cat Mild
Average wine price by the glass: £2.50

Licensee: Hervey Magnall
Last orders for dinner: 9 pm
Open every day
Main courses: from £10
Private dining: up to 50
Al fresco dining
Children welcome
Wheelchair access

SLAPTON, DEVON

Tower Inn

GASTROPUB

Church Road, Slapton, Kingsbridge, Devon TQ7 2PN
Tel. 01548 580 216
e-mail: towerinn@slapton.org   **MAP 1** D4

THIS historic 14th-century inn stands adjacent to the imposing ruined tower of the chantry of St. Mary, about two miles inland from Slapton Sands, an area now forever associated with the influx of American troops who used the beaches to practice for the D-Day landings in 1944.

Originally built as cottages to house the men working on the chantry, it seems likely hospitality has been dispensed here since 1347.

The interior is much as you would expect: rough-hewn stone bar and log fireplace, old beams and pillars, rustic wooden tables and chairs and hop bines framing blackboards with the day's specials.

Laminated menus offer familiar favourites – home-made soup, deep-fried Camembert, sausages with wholegrain mustard mash, smoked haddock fishcake and sandwiches at lunch. There are slightly more adventurous dishes in the evening, such as lemon and tarragon roasted sea bass, medallions of pork tenderloin and fillet steak tournedos Rossini.

Puddings offer plenty of comfort, with such treats as treacle orange tart, ice-creams in a brandy-snap basket and exotic fruit salad as examples.

A garden menu is aimed at summer holidaymakers looking for early supper. Children have their own, above average, menu and a carpeted separate dining-room, but the garden in the shadow of the tower must be one of the nicest spots in which to relax.

Speciality food: Lemon and tarragon roasted whole sea bass
Draught beers: Adnams Bitter, Tanglefoot (Badger)
Average wine price by the glass: £2.50

Licensees: Andrew and Annette Hammett
Last orders for dinner: 9 pm
Closed: Monday (November–March)
Closed for holidays: 2 weeks January
Main courses: from £12
Beer garden
Accommodation: 3 rooms
Children welcome (over 14 in the bar)
Limited wheelchair access

ST. ERVAN, CORNWALL

St. Ervan Manor ★

The Old Rectory, St Ervan, Nr. Padstow, Cornwall PL27 7TA
Tel. 01841 540 255
e-mail: info@stervanmanor.co.uk **MAP 1** B4

HIDDEN among the timeless country lanes of North Cornwall is this restored early Victorian rectory and its beautiful garden, with a light and airy restaurant decorated in elegant powder blue. Although it opened recently, the cuisine is already exceptional, thanks to enlightened new owners Lorraine and Alan Clarke, who combine perfectionism and a natural way with people.

They had the vision to bring Nathan Outlaw, the lauded chef at The Black Pig, Rock, to lead the kitchen and he has blossomed. While still modern and creative, he has shed some of his more outlandish combinations and his cooking is impeccable.

Open for dinner only, Wednesday to Saturday, there are just two faultlessly executed six-course tasting menus (£45 and £65), which change often, both displaying blends of flavours that are imaginative and successful.

A watercress soup, rich with great taste definition, is enhanced by a charcoal crumbed quail's egg; fine cured salmon is matched with a delicate beetroot risotto and horse-radish foam; John Dory is cooked with pinpoint accuracy, accompanied by mushrooms in sherry vinegar; pork belly is light and crisp, served with an onion purée. Both the Sauternes jelly with vanilla cream and the peach tart are truly memorable.

The wine list is still in evolution. It has excellent German Riesling and keenly priced claret from improved areas such as Côtes de Castillon, as well as some classic bottles from around the world. Alan and Lorraine really cosset their guests at front of house.

Their pride: Cornish lobster risotto with tarragon and orange
Inexpensive wines: Hermann Dönnhoff Riesling 2002, £22; Falesco Vitiano 2002, £17

Proprietors: Lorraine, Allan and Jonathan Clarke
Last orders for dinner: 9 pm
Closed: lunchtime, Monday and Tuesday
Closed for holidays: 8-31 January, 19-27 December
Set dinner: from £45
Private dining: 6-12
Accommodation: 5 rooms, 1 luxury suite
Wheelchair access

ST. IVES, CORNWALL

Alba ★

Old Lifeboat House, The Wharf, St. Ives, Cornwall TR26 1LF
Tel. 01736 797 222 Fax 01736 798 937

MAP 1 A5

RIGHT by the harbour, Alba is a gastronomic godsend in quaint old St. Ives with its jumble of narrow lanes, galleries and trinket shops. This bijou restaurant – it seats thirty – is full of light, with views of the harbour through the plate-glass windows.

The cooking is bold yet elegant in a modern style with noticeable Mediterranean and Asian influences, using the freshest local ingredients, particularly fish. The set-price menus are selective but of stimulating interest, and they whet the appetite with their mini-gastro-tour of the world's cuisines.

Start with Provençal fish soup, rouille, Parmesan and croutons, or a warm salad of chicken breast with coconut milk, vermicelli and pak choi. Otherwise try the fresh fillets of mackerel with tomato, cucumber, lime and coriander salsa, or the Cornish crab risotto, or a visually exquisite and delicately flavoured nage of scallops, mussels and vegetables flavoured with star anise.

If you are particularly hungry, there is cassoulet of gurnard with chorizo, pancetta and haricots blanc, or prime organic pork chop served with a warm potato and spinach salad.

Skill shines through the desserts, too: in light, rich caramelised prune pudding with home-made armagnac ice-cream, or crème brûlée taster with wild strawberry, vanilla and English rose. An intelligently selective yet wide-ranging wine list features the great Tilly's Vineyard white from Henschke (Barossa). The service is informal but effective.

Their pride: Scallop, mussel and green vegetable nage
Inexpensive wines: Henschke Tilly's Vineyard, Barossa, 2000, £21.50; Rioja Reserva Viña Alberdi 1998, £15.95

Proprietors: Julia Stevens and Grant Nethercott
Last orders for dinner: 10 pm
Closed: Limited opening November-March
Closed for holidays: 25 December
Main courses: from £12.95
Private dining: 25-40
Wheelchair access

ST. MAWES, CORNWALL

Rising Sun ★

GASTROPUB

The Square, St Mawes, Cornwall TR2 5DJ
Tel. 01326 270 233 Fax 01326 270 198
e-mail: info@risingsunstmawes.com   **MAP 1** B5

WITH its crowds and the fashionable yachtsmen, the Rising Sun, overlooking St Mawes harbour, is an ideal pub, restaurant and inn, maintaining its Cornish character in the flagstoned bar.

The cooking, under the aegis of chef/partner Ann Long, is quite exceptional, both in the bar and in the restaurant. The bar menu is inviting and imaginative, triggering the taste-buds, but at the same time eschewing trendy options.

Always available is the fish soup, deliciously flavoured with orange and saffron; the Cornish crab sandwiches are first rate; there is a good choice of superior salads (try the scallop and bacon version), plus mouth-watering daily blackboard specials such as the hot smokies crumble.

The elegant, airy and light-filled brasserie restaurant, which offers a fine vista of the quayside and is very different from the cramped dining-room of old at the back, is open only for dinner, and this is where the kitchen really comes into its own.

Fruit and nut bread, baked fresh every day, was splendid with an olive compote. A perfect lobster and asparagus risotto arrived after a proper twenty-minute wait, set in a Parmesan basket. To follow, steak and venison pudding was excellent, the tender meat gently cooked with red wine in a suet case.

The finale, rhubarb tiramisù, was a medley of richly sweet yet acidulous flavours, a dessert both unusual and successful.

Speciality food: Fillet steak with sherry and cream sauce
Draught beers: St. Austell Tribute, St. Austell Tinners
Average wine price by the glass: £3

Licensee: John Milson
Last orders for dinner: 9 pm
Open every day
Set dinner: from £27
Al fresco dining
Accommodation: 8 rooms
Children welcome at lunchtime
Wheelchair access

ST. MAWES, CORNWALL

Victory Inn ★

GASTROPUB

Victory Hill, St. Mawes, Nr.Truro, Cornwall TR2 5PQ
Tel. 01326 270 324 Fax 01326 270 238

MAP 1 B5

UP THE narrow Victory Steps leading from St. Mawes harbour, this old inn has changed little with the years. The Victory has always served excellent Cornish crab sandwiches and continues to do so, made with very fresh granary bread and garnished with rocket. But nothing stands still, and the reach of the menu in the long white bar or the bright upstairs restaurant is now much more imaginative and impressively realised.

Start with a first-rate cream of watercress and potato soup, rich yet refined, or smoked Charlestown fish with horse-radish crème fraîche. Fish is very much the strong suit at the Victory Inn, as in faultless roasted whole plaice with anchovy and caper butter or Thai baked sea bass, soy and coriander dressing, or pan-fried hake, white bean and chorizo stew.

Vegetarians may choose the aubergine bake, roasted red pepper and Cornish yarg cheese, while for meat-eaters there is peppered rib-eye steak and Béarnaise sauce. The Cornish early potatoes are particularly good, especially with the fish dishes.

Local emphasis is evident in Boddington Farm strawberries and Roddas clotted cream. Both the summer pudding and the white chocolate with rhubarb are fine desserts.

The place is always busy during the season, with a good mix of locals, young and more elderly couples happily co-existing in the bar. Service is charming and swift. Excellent local Sharps Doom Bar bitter.

Speciality food: Local fish and shellfish
Draught beers: Sharps Doom Bar, Adnams Broadside
Average wine price by the glass: £3.30

Licensee: Ross Andrew
Last orders for dinner: summer 9.30 pm, winter 9 pm
Open every day
Main courses: from £13
Private dining: 6-24
Al fresco dining
Accommodation: 2 rooms
Children welcome
Wheelchair access

ST. MAWGAN, CORNWALL

Falcon Inn

St. Mawgan, Newquay, Cornwall TR8 4EP
Tel. 01637 860 225 Fax 01637 860 884

MAP 1 B4

THREE miles or so inland from the windswept Atlantic beaches of Newquay Bay, St. Mawgan is a jewel of a village nestling in a tree-covered dell, with an ancient church and this fine old inn. Such surroundings make the inn's patio and garden great places to eat on a sunny day.

Inside, the bars are mellow and traditional, a word that seems to be the order of the day at lunchtime, when good sandwiches, including crab and carved ham off the bone, are available.

The lunch fish pie is solidly satisfying, full of good tasty fish like haddock and salmon – and not too much potato. Specials are backed by a full range of staples: battered cod and hand-cut chips; chilli con carne; steak and ale pie; grilled shellfish and big steaks well hung and accurately cooked.

At dinner there is monkfish with basmati rice, or grilled fillet of hake with champ potato and basil pesto, and even the puddings rise above the ordinary, with the likes of a scrumptious brandy and orange treacle tart.

There are three fine real ales – Tinners, Tribute and HSD – from the St. Austell Brewery, and choice wines by the glass and bottle from the southern hemisphere as well as the classic regions of Europe.

Speciality food: Grilled fillet of hake, champ potato, basil pesto
Draught beers: St. Austell Tinners, St. Austell Tribute
Average wine price by the glass: £3

Licensee: Andy Marshall
Last orders for dinner: summer 9.30 pm, winter 9 pm
Open every day
Closed for holidays: 25 December
Set lunch: from £7.95
Set dinner: from £7.95
Beer garden
Accommodation: 3 rooms
Children welcome
Wheelchair access

ST. MERRYN, CORNWALL

Ripley's ★

St. Merryn, Padstow, Cornwall PL28 8NQ
Tel. 01841 520 179 Fax 01841 521 641
e-mail: chefripley@aol.com

MAP 1 B4

A SERIOUS and imaginative approach to cooking combines with a friendly and relaxed attitude at this appealing village restaurant a couple of miles west of Padstow. Here you will enjoy an unhurried meal in the hands of competent and personable enthusiasts.

The menu will usually contain four starters and four main dishes, often featuring local, line-caught fish that might well arrive in the baskets of amateur fishermen. There is a real touch of class about a roasted fillet of cod under a fine brioche crust set off by velouté of smoked haddock.

The quality of the kitchen manifests itself throughout, even in more conservative offerings such as sautéd scallops with saffron potatoes and leeks, game terrine, braised cheek of beef, or a duck breast with foie gras sauce.

There is the odd surprise, like the warm salad of tea-smoked mackerel with satsumas and dates, or sea bass fillet with parsnip purée, garlic confit and cumin scented vegetables.

Desserts are generally simple but light and effective, like the fine apple crumble that comes, naturally, with Cornish clotted cream.

A varied wine list offers no particularly outstanding crus but a wealth of reasonably priced bottles

Their pride: Fillet of beef on the bone with bone-marrow butter and Bordelaise sauce
Inexpensive wines: Sauvignon de Touraine Château de la Presle 2004, £13.95; La Serre Merlot Vin de Pays D'Oc 2003, £12.95

Proprietor: Paul Ripley
Last orders for dinner: 9.30 pm
Closed: Sunday and Monday
Closed for holidays: last 2 weeks of January and first 2 weeks of February
Main courses: from £15.50
Limited wheelchair access

STADDLEBRIDGE, NORTH YORKSHIRE

McCoys Bistro ★

The Cleveland Tontine, Staddlebridge, North Yorks DL6 3JB
Tel. 01609 882 671 Fax 01609 882 660
e-mail: enquiries@mccoysatthetontine.co.uk   **MAP 5** D3

THIS handsome stone inn has become almost legendary for its warm, relaxed hospitality, thanks to the flair and professionalism of the McCoy brothers who own and run it. You can stay in one of the six comfortable rooms and lunch in the conservatory, but the bistro itself is the real attraction for those who love good food.

Fish arrives daily from the harbour at Whitby, so you are bound to find something fresh and delicious. Roasted cod fillet, served with mashed potato and polenta, was of superb quality, but there might also be sea bass with pak choi and noodles or halibut with gnocchi, wild mushrooms and smoked bacon.

Not that the meat dishes are to be overlooked. Regulars favour the beef Wellington with brandy sauce au poivre, or the rack of lamb under a herb crust, which is served with a tranche from the shoulder. There are good brasserie-style dishes, too, such as the flavoursome black pudding accompanied by sauce Gribiche, onion marmalade and celeriac remoulade.

Desserts follow a path from the refectory – ginger sponge and custard, sticky toffee pudding – to the elegant dining-room, as in lemon tart with meringue topping and lime syrup.

The wines from an independent local shipper are excellent, with especially good selections from the Rhône and northern Spain. Service by a young team is infectiously charming as they take their lead from the top.

Their pride: Venison Wellington
Inexpensive wines: Sauvignon Blanc 2003, £14.95; Côtes de Ventoux 2003, £14.95

Proprietors: Tom and Eugene McCoy
Last orders for dinner: 9.30 pm
Open every day
Closed for holidays: 25 & 26 December, 1 January
Set lunch: from £12.95
Main courses: from £16.95
Private dining: 12-50
Accommodation: 6 rooms
Limited wheelchair access

STAFFORD, STAFFORDSHIRE

The Swan ★

GASTROPUB

46 Greengate Street, Stafford, Staffordshire ST16 2JA
Tel. 01785 258 142 Fax 01785 223 372
e-mail: info@theswanstafford.co.uk   **MAP 3** E2

THE Swan has been sensitively modernised, with the heart of the place now being a brasserie, its tables set on two levels. The carte, however, is rather more imaginative than in your average brasserie, but sensibly disciplined and not outlandish. Starters include smokehouse salmon with horse-radish blinis and caper vinaigrette, and new potato salad with truffle cream.

Fresh fish is a strong feature, with innovative twists – roast sea bass with tapenade and fennel confit, say, or pavé of cod with pea purée. Poultry and meat, such as breast of duck with caramelised pear and summer cabbage or the signature rack of lamb with basil jus and Dauphinoise potatoes, show the same deft touch in flavour combination. Vegetarians are catered for imaginatively in basil roulade with Stilton and beetroot caviar.

On the exceptionally good-value set-price lunch menu (£8.95 for three courses) was a most refreshing clear broth with real depth of ham-bone stock flavours, strips of ham, butter beans and broad beans, all enhanced by a glass of Oppenheimer Kabinett from the Rhine.

Lamb kebabs were perfectly cooked and you might finish with a light pancake of compote of summer berries and real espresso. Full marks for quality and value.

The wine list has a good range of choices by the glass and rises in the bottle selection to very fine vintage champagne.

Speciality food: Rack of lamb and Provençal tomato with basil infused jus
Draught beers: Marston Pedigree, Boddingtons
Average wine price by the glass: £4

Licensee: Chris Lewis
Last orders for dinner: 10 pm
Open every day
Closed for holidays: 25 December
Set lunch: from £6
Set dinner: from £10
Beer garden
Accommodation: 31 rooms
Children welcome
Wheelchair access

STAMFORD, LINCOLNSHIRE

The George ★   **GASTROPUB**

St. Martins, Stamford, Lincolnshire PE9 2LB
Tel. 01780 750 750 Fax 01780 750 701
e-mail: reservations@georgehotelstamford.com   **MAP 4** C3

THIS 16th-century coaching inn, with a wealth of period features and a rich history, is in a league of its own. Even before looking at the menu, you are spoilt for choice when it comes to deciding where to eat.

An oak-panelled restaurant leads off the imposing hallway and offers a fairly formal venue for a light lunch or dinner. Across the hall, the warm and inviting York Bar is available for quick snacks and excellent cask ale. Alternatively, there is the refurbished Garden Lounge or, weather permitting, the delightful courtyard garden. Bookings are advisable for dinner, when a dress code applies.

You might well find guests queuing for lunch at 2 pm, such is the popularity of this cobblestoned haven. In the Garden Lounge, the tables, surrounded by imposing ivy-clad walls, are interspersed with tubs containing various fruit trees set amidst vibrant flowers.

The menu is an appetising selection of dishes, many of which can be either a starter or a main course. They might include fragrant Thai mussels, beef satay or Gruyère cheese fritters. Choose the home-ground beef burger with chilli jam and proper chips, or maybe indulge in the Brittany platter of seafood. Linguine vongole is just one of four pasta dishes on offer

Desserts will engage both the eye and palate, encompassing many tarts, pancakes, puddings, sorbets and ice-creams, before you linger over coffee and cantuccini biscuits in the lounge with its enormous fireplace

Speciality food: Fish and chips
Draught beers: London Pride, Adnams
Average wine price by the glass: £3.20

Licensee: Chris Pitman
Last orders for dinner: 10 pm
Open every day
Set lunch: from £17.50 (weekdays)
Main courses: from £15.95
Private dining: up to 80
Al fresco dining
Accommodation: 47 rooms
Children welcome
Wheelchair access

STATHERN, LEICESTERSHIRE

Red Lion Inn ★

GASTROPUB

**Red Lion Street, [Stathern], Leicestershire LE14 4HS
Tel. 01949 860 868 Fax 01949 861 579**

MAP 4 B3

DISPLAYED on a dresser at the rear this quirky period inn, allegedly where the death warrant of King Charles I was signed, are various pickles, chutneys, vinaigrettes and oils for sale, and a blackboard informs customers that picnic hampers can be ordered and dinner parties can be catered for.

The lunch and dinner menus are similar and could offer such enticements as smoked salmon, toasted brioche with poached egg and hollandaise sauce, or gnocchi with a tasty smoked cheese sauce, prosciutto, sweet cherry tomatoes and watercress.

Small, whole loaves of home-baked bread are brought to the table on a board, which is a welcome touch.

Halibut saltimbocca, pan-fried calf's liver, or roasted breast of guinea fowl could appear as main courses. One of the staples is Lincolnshire pork sausages – meaty and well seasoned, served with ultra-smooth mashed potato and a robust onion gravy. Alternatively, choose from the set lunch menu. which will offer good value, possibly a soup or moules marinères to start, followed by home-made lamb sausages or pan-fried salmon salad.

Some puddings are definitely worth waiting for: apricot tarte Tatin with ginger ice-cream, or hot chocolate pudding with vanilla ice-cream and chocolate sauce. There is a good selection of cheeses including local Stilton, Mull of Kintyre Cheddar and smoked Lancashire.

Speciality food: Sausages and mash
Draught beers: Olive Oil, Hop Head
Average wine price by the glass: £3

**Licensee: Ben Jones
Last orders for dinner: 9.30 pm
Closed: Sunday evening
Closed for holidays: 1 January
Set lunch: from £12.25
Main courses: from £9.50
Private dining: up to 25
Beer garden**
Children welcome
Limited wheelchair access

STEDHAM, WEST SUSSEX

Hamilton Arms

GASTROPUB

School Lane, Stedham, Nr. Midhurst, W Sussex GU29 ONZ
Tel. 01730 812 555   Fax 01730 817 459
e-mail: hamiltonarms@hotmail.com   **MAP 2** C4

DRIVING past the Hamilton Arms (just off the A272 west of
Midhurst) you would be unaware of the Thai treasure within. This
well-established pub serves English and Thai bar meals, but the
real action is in the restaurant, which offers a generous choice of
authentic Thai dishes, including a vegetarian menu.

The bar feels like a private house with strong oriental overtones,
heavily carved wooden tables sitting alongside conventional
English furniture. The restaurant is a series of interconnecting
rooms with comfortable chairs, which creates a very relaxed
atmosphere, and service here is by Thai waitresses. The sunny,
south-facing terrace with a leafy view provides al fresco dining in
the summer.

You may choose to start with khanom cheeb (dim-sum), a soft,
delicate ravioli-style coating filled with minced pork, chilli spicing
and served with soya sauce, or else tod man pla, which is cod with
green beans and curry paste, deep-fried.

Beware of the fresh green chillies in the stir-fried pork: they are
searingly hot. The red chilli paste of gaeng ped gai chicken is
milder. Do not miss the excellent crispy prawn crackers served
with a fine peanut sauce, and leave room for the pudding of Thai
egg custard – a fragrant combination of ground rice, coconut milk
and palm sugar.

A sensibly priced wine list offers a varied choice. Try one of the
Thai wines from the floating vineyards of Monsoon Valley, where
the grapes are picked from boats at sunrise.

Speciality food: Thai
Draught beers: Fullers London Pride, Ballards
Average wine price by the glass: £2.60

Licensee: Suhail Hussain
Last orders for dinner: 10.30 pm (Sunday 9.30 pm)
Closed: Monday (except Bank Hols)
Closed for holidays: 10 days from 1 Jan
Set dinner: from £19.50
Main courses: from £5.90
Private dining: 10-20
Beer garden
Children welcome
Wheelchair access

STOCKBRIDGE, HAMPSHIRE

The Greyhound ★

31 High Street, Stockbridge, Hampshire SO20 6EY
Tel. 01264 810 833 Fax 01264 352 965

MAP 2 B4

AT THE eastern end of the old market town of Stockbridge, the Greyhound's brick frontage and leaded windows hide a spacious, elegant interior. The polished wooden bar gleams with bottles, including some impressive armagnacs, and photographs of local scenes add to the atmosphere.

An old butcher's block placed alongside the bar serves as a desk and there are dark beams and old pine tables. The young team provide friendly, relaxed and accomplished service. The chef hails from South Africa and before she settled here she worked in London's Aurora and Criterion restaurants. No surprise, then, that the modern, predominantly English menu is both creative and very successful.

To begin, why not savour the delicate, crisply coated, sautéd chicken livers with a smooth Béarnaise sauce, or the precisely cooked risotto with avocado and spicy chorizo – bold in concept and powerful in spice. A more traditional choice might be the eggs Benedict with Wiltshire ham, or fresh fish, which comes from Cornwall and the Devon coast. The black bream, with its crisp skin, couscous flavoured with saffron and lemon and peeled broad beans, is a worthy option.

When game is not in season, try roasted guinea fowl with sherry vinaigrette or fillet of Scottish beef with smoked bacon dumplings and consommé.

High standards continue to impress with puddings – tarte Tatin with soft, caramelised bananas and thin pastry and excellent banoffi ice-cream, or warm chocolate fondant with fresh mint being among them.

Speciality food: Greyhound fishcake, chive beurre blanc
Draught beers: George Gale's HSB, Butcombe Bitter
Average wine price by the glass: £3.50

Licensee: Tim Fiducia
Last orders: Mon-Thurs 9 pm, Fri-Sat 9.30 pm
Closed Sunday evening
Closed for holidays: 25 and 26 December, 1 January
Main courses: from £12
Private dining: 10-58
Beer garden
Children welcome
Wheelchair access

STOCKCROSS, BERKSHIRE

Vineyard at Stockcross ★

Stockcross, Newbury, Berkshire RG20 8JU
Tel. 01635 528 770 Fax 01635 528 398
e-mail: general@the-vineyard.co.uk   **MAP 2** B3

THIS extravagantly Californian styled split-level restaurant is a comfortable and agreeable place for an unhurried meal, with its ambience of Art Deco, its well-spaced tables and its abundance of natural light.

The cooking is as luxurious and bold as the surroundings, often based on what is called a scientific approach, with unusual flavour combinations such as that in a starter of roast squab served with black treacle and celeriac.

Another imaginative dish is roast John Dory matched with smoked confit of pork belly, garlic soubise and Jerez sauce. Alternatively, chicken might come with a shallot tart and truffled egg, breast of duck with endive and garbure cannelloni.

Excellent desserts give unalloyed pleasure, as in tarte fine of pear with almond ice-cream, and the chocolate fondant with raspberry granita.

This kitchen has great technical skill and the centrepieces such as the squab, John Dory and pear tart are excellent. To appreciate its work fully, though, be prepared for some combinations that might seem to be rather experimental.

The wine list must be one of the best in the country, with model coverage internationally of the finest wines (particularly fine Piedmont classics) always chosen with a keen eye to value as well as quality.

Their pride: Organic salmon 'mi-cuit', spiced lentils, confit foie gras
Inexpensive wines: Domaine de la Terre Rouge Sentinel Oak Village 1998, £25; Soave Classico Monte Tenda Tedeschi 2003, £17

Proprietor: Sir Peter Michael
Last orders for dinner: 9.30 pm
Open every day
Set lunch: from £22
Set dinner: from £29
Private dining: up to 120
Al fresco dining
Accommodation: 49 rooms
Wheelchair access

STOKE-BY-NAYLAND, SUFFOLK

The Crown

GASTROPUB

Stoke-by-Nayland, Suffolk CO6 4SE
Tel. 01206 262 001 Fax 01206 264 026
e-mail: crown.eoinns@btopenworld.com   **MAP 4** E5

DETRACTORS might be inclined to decry this 1530 inn as being something of a gastro-Disneyland. It's true that on entering, faced by a pristine interior (featuring low ceilings and the odd original exposed beam), with its nicely spaced, polished tables, a smart, state-of-the-art bar area and modern kitchens open to public scrutiny, one does get the feeling of entering the British Pub section of a theme park.

There is also the air of a well-oiled machine, constantly in full swing, which ensures slick service and reliably enjoyable fare. In catering for such large numbers, they do tend to err on the side of caution, with soups, terrines, a classic Caesar salad or even a prawn cocktail (with particularly juicy prawns, it has to be said) to start, some of which are available as larger portions to provide a main course.

Main courses tend to offer greater variety. Gloucester Old Spot sausages, Suffolk hot-pot, calf's liver with onion gravy and black pudding, or beer-battered haddock will suit the traditionalists, but then there is caramelised Gressingham duck, or spinach, walnut and goat's cheese crumble, or tender, herb-crusted pork fillet with potato and spinach gratin – not to mention the fresh local fish chalked up as 'Catch of the Day'.

Desserts seem to conform to typically English tastes, with such classics as golden syrup pudding and custard.

Chef Paul Wharrier is obviously a capable professional, but it would be good to see him spread his creative wings.

Speciality food: Modern British cookery
Draught beers: Greene King IPA, Adnams Best Bitter
Average wine price by the glass: £2.80

Licensee: Richard Sunderland
Last orders for dinner: 9.30 pm (Sunday 9 pm)
Closed: 25 and 26 December
Main courses: from £8.95
Beer garden
Children welcome
Wheelchair access

STOKE HOLY CROSS, NORFOLK

Wildebeest Arms ★

82-86 Norwich Road, Stoke Holy Cross, Norfolk NR14 8QJ
Tel. 01508 492 497 Fax 01508 494 353
e-mail: mail@animalinns.co.uk   **MAP 4** E3

FOUR miles south of Norwich in a peaceful village off the A140 Ipswich road, the Wildebeest Arms is very much a restaurant in a pub – but it's one with a true pub ethos: a welcoming bar, good Adnams beer and an informal atmosphere for a relaxed meal. Add to this accomplished cooking and a shrewd sense of value for money and you have a surefire formula for success.

Laudably, there are reasonably priced set menus alongside the carte: they regularly do 40 covers for lunch midweek and are always full at dinner – is there a moral lesson here for some extravagantly priced gastropubs?

The eating area is smart-rustic, the cooking modern European and imaginative but without pretension. An exemplary lunch from the set-price menu might feature home-baked bread and roasted vine tomato soup (the tomato taste beautifully defined), then maybe a proper baked chicken Kiev, the breast tender and well-flavoured, the hot garlic butter as it should be, finely spiced and seasoned with fresh coriander and black pepper and accompanied by parsley purée potato and wild rocket. Or go for the fillet of salmon, olive oil crushed potatoes and buttered samphire.

Puddings include a Chocolate Nemesis flavoured with caramelised orange and topped with mascarpone. For the calorie-conscious, there is lemon panna cotta with lemon coulis.

Wines by the glass include a textbook Sauvignon and with the dessert try the nutty sweet, but not cloying, Dinderello from the Veneto.

Speciality food: Cumin and yoghurt marinated lamb chump
Draught beers: Adnams, John Smith
Average wine price by the glass: £3.25

Licensee: Henry Watt
Last orders for dinner: 9.30pm
Open every day
Closed for holidays: 25 and 26 December
Set lunch: from £11.95
Set dinner: from £15
Main courses: from £13
Al fresco dining
Children welcome
Wheelchair access

STOKE ROW, OXFORDSHIRE

Crooked Billet ★

GASTROPUB

Newlands Lane, Stoke Row, Nr. Henley-on-Thames, Oxon RG9 5PU
Tel. 01491 681 048 Fax 01491 682 231

MAP 2 B3

THERE IS an almost Dickensian feel about this unmodernised old inn, with its labyrinth of cosily lived-in dining and drinking areas inviting carefree relaxation. The rusting front end of a Morris Minor sits amid the shaded, slightly skew-whiff tables outside on what is definitely more field than lawn. And just to maintain a bit of entente cordiale there is a similarly dilapidated black Citroën in what passes for the car park, providing more than a hint of what lies in store *à table*.

Just deciding could well leave you asking for extra supplies of your chosen aperitif from the delightful staff because the available choice is huge, as are the portions. On Sundays the additional lunch menu (offering excellent value) complicates things even further, making it all the more surprising and impressive that the cooking throughout such a varied range of dishes is of such a high standard.

Stay classily plain if you like, but the real interest lies in the often French-inspired favourites that draw on traditional influences. Dishes are sometimes highly convoluted but sensibly concocted blends of the very best available ingredients. Country-style braised rabbit, for example, or chicken breast stuffed with goat's cheese and baked in pancetta; sea bass with sautéd garlic shrimps; fricassee of lamb's sweetbreads, and venison fillet with haggis.

Steamed puddings, tarts and crumbles to finish. No showing off, nothing outlandish and if it all looks so reassuringly appetising on paper, the results are nothing short of splendid examples of how it can be done.

Speciality food: Anglo-French traditional cooking
Draught beers: Brakspear Bitter, Guinness
Average wine price by the glass: £3.50

Licensee: Paul Clerehugh
Last orders for dinner: 10 pm
Open every day
Closed for holidays: 25 December
Set lunch: from £12.95
Main courses: from £14
Private dining: 10-60
Beer garden
Children welcome
Wheelchair access

STOW-ON-THE-WOLD, GLOUCESTERSHIRE

King's Arms

GASTROPUB

**Market Square, Stow-on-the-Wold, Gloucestershire GL54 1AF
Tel. 01451 830 364 Fax 01451 830 602**

MAP 1 F1

THE MAIN square of this historic Cotswold market town has always been dominated by the King's Arms. Yet the dark wood bar and the upstairs dining-room are now more than ever the place where everyone eats at lunchtime. There are tourists, but also the local wine merchant and the estate agent who helps the landlords rear and prepare for table their own Gloucester Old Spot pigs.

A large chop of this well-flavoured pork, served with fennel mashed potato, is one of the house's special dishes, along with fresh fish from Cornwall. There is an attractive first-floor dining-room overlooking the Market Square.

Excellent ingredients, from the fine Daylesford organic bread to spanking fresh lemon sole and home-cured beef fillet, skilled cooking and – above all – good value for money. The sea trout, Béarnaise, bacon and green salad costs £11 and a very generous glass of one of 10 fine house wines just £2.50 (try the Fransschoek Chenin Blanc from the Cape or the Mendozan Merlot from the foothills of the Andes).

Even the best claret, Château Patache d'Aux Médoc, is only £27 a bottle. The St. Austell real ale makes a great pint and the garden rhubarb and oatmeal crumble is a wonderful pudding. No wonder the bar is packed by 12.30 pm. You might have to wait for a table, so either read the papers or, better still, book if you can. It is equally busy in the evening.

Speciality food: Old Spot pork
Draught beers: St. Austell, Greene King
Average wine price by the glass: £2.50

Licensee: David Burr
Last orders for dinner: 9.30 pm (Sat 10 pm, Sun 9 pm)
Open every day
Main courses: from £7 (lunch), £13.50 (dinner)
Accommodation: 10 rooms
Children welcome

STOW-ON-THE-WOLD, GLOUCESTERSHIRE

Old Butchers' ★

GASTROPUB

**Park Street, Stow-on-the-Wold, Gloucestershire GL54 1AG
Tel. 01451 831 700 Fax 01451 831 118
e-mail: info@theoldbutchers.com**   **MAP 1** F1

PETER and Louise Robinson moved here in July 2005, down the road from the King's Arms. In this old butcher's shop converted into a gastropub, they are making a great success of it – natural Cotswold stone walls hung with stags' heads and antlers, a bright, well-lit bar counter where regulars sup the splendid Czech draught Star Opramen beer. A blackboard also displays a fine range of premium European beers, notably Belgian.

The daily-changing menu is in the best British and European modern style, with a liking for vivid Mediterranean flavours. Start with brandade de morue or a whole globe artichoke vinaigrette. The steak tartare is top-quality beef properly mixed with capers and gherkins, and quite first-rate. Local grilled Gloucester Old Spot pork chop features among the main courses, which range from rare-grilled tuna and slow-cooked tomato sauce to a succulent and maturely flavoured saddle of lamb, cut as a tournedos and nicely served with spiced aubergine and faultless sauté potatoes. In season, there is roast grouse with game chips.

For lighter appetites there could be courgette and pea risotto or, for trenchermen, grilled sirloin steak with horse-radish and lovage butter. It is worth waiting fifteen minutes for chocolate fondant, or try the ricotta and blueberry pancake.

Excellent, reasonably priced wines by the glass and bottle offer house selections such as the Gascon St. Mont rosé – great with steak tartare – and Norton Merlot from Argentina. Service is fast, warm-hearted, accurate and efficient.

Speciality food: Roast saddle of lamb with spiced aubergine
Draught beers: Star Opramen
Average wine price by the glass: £3

**Licensees: Peter and Louise Robinson
Last orders for dinner: 9.30 pm
Open every day
Closed for holidays: 1 week May, 1 week October
Main courses: from £12
Al fresco dining**
Children welcome
Wheelchair access

STRETE, DEVON

Kings Arms ★

 GASTROPUB

Dartmouth Road, Strete, Devon TQ6 0RW
Tel. 01803 770 377
e-mail: info@kingsarms-dartmouth.co.uk   **MAP 1** D4

STANDING on the cliff-hugging coastal road south of Dartmouth, this once decrepit village pub, distinguished by its handsome Victorian iron lace balcony, has had a change of fortune.

Now, as you sit in the upstairs dining area with its limed wood panelling and crisply laid tables looking out over the very pretty beer garden and the sweep of Start Bay, you could almost be in the Mediterranean.

A meal here is a leisurely affair, but there is much to savour. A bowl of marinated olives, another of balsamic vinegar with olive oil float, accompany home-made bread and an unsalted butter block on a slate dish.

Starters might be steamed Devon mussels, grilled sardines or perhaps seared local scallops, sweet, firm, burstingly fresh, with a silky minted pea purée and crisp wafers of grilled pancetta. Main courses include whole Start Bay crab, or pan-fried halibut on an aubergine and spring onion ragout, or the sublime fillets of grilled sea bream with exquisite braised baby fennel and an intense orange and thyme reduction.

This is wonderful cooking: accurate, assured, done with love and reverence, showing great respect for the ingredients.

Desserts are no less enticing, with white chocolate panna cotta, glazed poached pear in Monbazillac, or the creamiest crème brûlée scented with lavender and honey.

Speciality food: Roast cod and chorizo stew
Draught beers: Adnams Bitter, Otter Ale
Average wine price by the glass: £3.25

Licensees: Robert Dawson and Virginia Heath
Last orders for dinner: 9 pm
Closed: Monday (October-March)
Closed for holidays: Last two weeks January
Set lunch: from £10 (winter)
Main courses: from £16
Beer garden
Children welcome
Wheelchair access

STRETTON, LEICESTERSHIRE

Jackson Stops Inn ★   **GASTROPUB**

Rookery Road, Stretton, Oakham, Leicestershire LE15 7RA
Tel. 01780 410 237
e-mail: james@jacksonstops-inn.fsnet.co.uk   **MAP 4** C3

MANY houses in this pretty village, with its dry stone walling and limestone buildings so characteristic of the region, formed part of an estate before being sold off and the pub derives its name from the estate agent who handled the sales.

A former barn – with echoes in the old farming implements on the walls – it is in the same mellow stone and has attractive mullioned windows and a grassy area at the front set with solid tables and chairs.

The entrance, flanked by bay trees, leads into a snug bar with a selection of daily specials and sandwiches written on boards. A deceptively small interior unfolds to offer three dining-rooms.

The à la carte menu might include starters such as spiced lamb fillets, braised Puy lentils with yoghurt dressing, or chicken liver and garlic pâté which, served with lightly toasted brioche and tangy chutney, has a silky-smooth texture and an impressive depth of flavour.

Fish main courses might feature naturally smoked haddock with leek risotto and poached egg, or roasted halibut with saffron potatoes and spinach. Alternatively, pan-fried calf's liver will melt in the mouth. Braised lettuce, potatoes, glazed shallots and a crisp rasher of bacon complete the dish.

Desserts include apple tarte Tatin with vanilla ice-cream, or you might like to try an egg custard tart, ideally contrasted with firm rhubarb and rhubarb vodka in a shot-glass.

Speciality food: Seared scallops, black pudding mash, garlic sauce
Draught beers: Oakham JHB, Timothy Taylor Landlord
Average wine price by the glass: £3.15

Licensee: James Trevor
Last orders for dinner: 10 pm
Closed: Sunday evening, Monday
Closed for holidays: 27 December for 8 days
Main courses: from £7.50
Private dining: 10-20
Beer garden
Children welcome
Wheelchair access

STUCKTON, HAMPSHIRE

Three Lions ★

Stuckton, Nr. Fordingbridge, Hampshire SP6 2HF
Tel. 01425 652 489 Fax 01425 656 144
e-mail: the3lions@btinternet.com   **MAP 2** A4

THE spectacular New Forest National Park is the peaceful setting for a gastronomic cornucopia. Inside this red brick building all is pristine with open fireplaces and salmon pink walls. A family-run establishment with a friendly approach, this feels like a French auberge – indeed, it does call itself a restaurant with rooms. Chef/owner Mike Womersley performed culinary artistry at Lucknam Park before taking command here some ten years ago.

Locally sourced fish and game in season are on the changing blackboard menu, and accuracy and finesse are evident in delights such as pan-fried scallops and shrimps with fresh chives and dill. Other first courses might be foie gras, ceps and brioche; home-made gravadlax, or galette of smoked haddock.

For main courses there may be free-range pork and crackling; roast quail and wild mushrooms, or thinly sliced duck breast with fresh cherries and light jus. Or you might prefer wild turbot with saffron sauce, with thinly sliced Dauphinoise potatoes and lightly poached beetroot among the vegetables.

The patron is renowned for his soft-centred hot chocolate pudding (allow fifteen minutes for preparation), or else try the super smooth lemon posset with crème caramel and crisp tuile. Fresh strawberry gratin is another temptation in season.

Wines are taken seriously and there is a good selection of half-bottles. Seven comfortable and well-equipped bedrooms complete the picture.

Speciality food: Hot chocolate pudding
Draught beer: Ringwood, Warsteiner
Average wine price by the glass: £2.75

Proprietors: Mike and Jayne Womersley
Last orders for dinner: 9.30 pm
Closed: Sunday dinner, Monday
Closed for holidays: last 2 weeks Jan, 1st week Feb
Set lunch: from £16.75
Private dining: 10-60
Al fresco dining
Accommodation: 7 rooms
Wheelchair access

SULGRAVE, NORTHAMPTONSHIRE

Star Inn ★

GASTROPUB

Manor Road, Sulgrave, Nr. Banbury, Northants OX17 2SA
Tel. 01295 760 389 Fax 01295 760 991

MAP 4 B5

IN A lovely Northamptonshire village close to the stately Sulgrave Manor, The Star is a quintessential country pub, with a good deal of charm, where the food is first-class, simple and traditional in snacks and lighter things while quietly imaginative at dinner.

It is reassuring to see soup, terrines and sandwiches as the thrust of the lunchtime bar snacks. The watercress soup is exceptional, the flavour of the cress well defined, not watery, and beautifully seasoned, finished with a touch of cream.

No less striking is a delicious sandwich of hot roast loin of pork spread with a little home-made apple sauce between two slices of lightly grilled rustic bread. Alternatives at lunch might be terrines of wild boar or chicken liver, or else battered cod and chips.

Dinner moves into higher gear with, perhaps, scallops in a sweet chilli dipping sauce, fishcakes of smoked haddock with lime and ginger mayonnaise, and, the great speciality here, rib of beef for two with Béarnaise sauce.

Excellent desserts include panettone bread and butter pudding and, in season, fresh local strawberries served with home-made meringues of exemplary texture.

Speciality food: Deep-fried scallops with chilli dip
Draught beers: Hook Norton, Adnams
Average wine price by the glass: £2.50

Licensees: Jamie and Charlotte King
Last orders for dinner: 9 pm
Closed: Sunday evening, Monday
Closed for holidays: 2 days Christmas
Main courses: from £10
Private dining: 16-20
Beer garden
Accommodation: 3 rooms
Children welcome
Wheelchair access

TAPLOW, BERKSHIRE

Waldo's at Cliveden ★

Cliveden Estate, Taplow, Berkshire SL8 0JF
Tel. 01628 668 561 Fax 01628 661 837
e-mail: reservations@clivedenhouse.co.uk   **MAP 2** C3

DANIEL GALMICHE had very big shoes to fill when he succeeded
the very talented Mark Dodson as head chef at Waldo's in 2005.
He is making a very respectable showing, even if his cooking does
not yet quite scale the heights Dodson effortlessly attained. The
approach to the menu is in the same classical, disciplined moulds
– that is, not too many competing flavours.

Ingredients are first-class and saucing well wrought, exemplified
by poached lobster with wild mushrooms and herb sabayon.
Modern touches are evident in other starters such as terrine of
Périgord duck foie gras interestingly matched with a compote of
apricot and chilli.

Another convincing combination is Scottish monkfish roasted on
the bone and pleasingly balanced by the gentle flavours of a
ragout of vegetables, the 'meaty' fish quite rightly finished with
guinea fowl jus.

Perhaps the best dish of all is cornfed Anjou pigeon, tender and
of subtle richness, served simply with sautéd potatoes, spinach
and a reduction of the juices with sherry vinegar. Nor are classic
traditions ignored in the Aberdeen Angus beef fillet accompanied
by rösti and bordelaise sauce.

Desserts are well up to standard and the wine list is a collection
of the world's greatest bottles at prices as rarefied as the palatial
Cliveden itself, though there is good and relatively affordable
drinking among Beaujolais crus and crisp whites from Trentino.

Their pride: Sautéd Cornish langoustines caramelised cauliflower purée
Inexpensive wines: Pinot Grigio Cru Vorberg (Trentino) 2003,
£37; Morgon Domaine Marcel Lapierre 2003/4, £36

Proprietor: Von Essen Hotels
Last orders for dinner: 9.30 pm
Closed: Sunday and Monday
Closed for holidays: 2 weeks Christmas, 2 weeks Aug
Set dinner: from £65
Accommodation: 39 rooms

TAUNTON, SOMERSET

Castle Hotel ★

**Castle Green, Taunton, Somerset TA1 1NF
Tel. 01823 272 671 Fax 01823 336 066
e-mail: reception@the-castle-hotel.com**   **MAP 1** D3

THIS is a delightful hotel restaurant with excellent service and cooking that is confidently grown-up. The prix fixe menus offer very good value, but in order to enjoy to the full the quality of the food, it would probably be advisable to choose from the carte.

Seafood is something of a speciality here, beginning with perhaps mussels and linguine with a little seafood salad as an amuse-bouche and continuing with the likes of warm crab cake flavoured with chervil and dill and accompanied by marinated baby carrots and purple cauliflower.

Otherwise, there is superb, succulent braised lamb with yellow and green courgettes, leeks, cabbage and pommes rissolées that are infused with lamb stock.

The bitter chocolate tart with poached William's pear and Chantilly cream is a first-rate dessert, but it is only one among a variety of sweet temptations.

The wine list is unusual for its selection of some particularly good sherries, but it is also strong across the whole range, with notably good selections from Burgundy and the Rhône.

Decorated in something like a classical French provincial style, the dining-room features ornate gilded mirrors and paintings by local artists, against a background of opulent crimson.

Their pride: Celebration of British beef
Inexpensive wines: Chardonnay Domaine Montrose 2003, £19; Old Vine Grenache 2002, £19

**Proprietor: Kit Chapman
Last orders for dinner: 9.30 pm
Closed: Sunday dinner
Set lunch: from £38
Set dinner: from £38
Private dining: 12–70
Al fresco dining
Accommodation: 44 rooms**
Wheelchair access

447

TAVISTOCK, DEVON

Horn of Plenty ★

Gulworthy, Tavistock, Devon PL19 8JD
Tel./Fax 01822 832 528
e-mail: enquiries@thehornofplenty.co.uk   MAP 1 C4

PERCHED above the Tamar valley that separates Devon and Cornwall, this lived-in country house offers spectacular views of the hills on the Cornish side, the tall chimney of an old tin mine silhouetted against the sky as a reminder of times past.

The cooking here goes from strength to strength, innovative and lively but so well thought out in terms of which flavours really work together that there is no sense that the customer is ever a guinea-pig in a culinary laboratory, as can happen in some other restaurants.

The set lunch is excellent value for money, but those who know the place are inclined to opt for the full table d'hôte because of the inevitable delights it contains.

You might start with an appetiser of salmon tartare and a tartlet of ewe's cheese then go on to scallops with mushroom ravioli and watercress sauce. Grilled brill comes with tempura king prawns and there is also an oriental touch in duck salad with a mango, spring onion and ginger dressing.

Caramelised apple pancakes with cider ice-cream form a dessert that really caresses the palate.

The wine list is notable not only for the excellence and originality of the selection but also for its reasonable pricing. Service by an all-female team immediately puts you at ease.

Their pride: Sautéd sea bass on sweet potato blinis with a light courgette and curry-flavoured cream
Inexpensive wines: Viura Chardonnay, Castillo de Montblanc 2003, £14; Merlot Libertad 2004, £14

Proprietors: Paul Roston and Peter Gorton
Last orders for dinner: 9.30 pm
Closed: Monday lunch
Closed for holidays: 24-26 December
Set lunch: from £25
Set dinner: from £42
Private dining: up to 12
Al fresco dining at lunch
Accommodation: 10 rooms
Wheelchair access

THORNBURY, GLOUCESTERSHIRE

Thornbury Castle

Castle Street, Thornbury, Gloucestershire BS35 1HH
Tel. 01454 281 182 Fax 01454 416 188
e-mail: info@thornburycastle.co.uk   **MAP 1** E2

TECHNICALLY speaking, this is not a castle but a fortified house, its castellation having cost the poor old Duke of Buckingham his head. Yet in spite of its grand façade and historical associations, Thornbury is really a rather homely and relaxing sort of place that appeals as much to locals as to tourists.

A practised reception and service team maintain service that is at once professional and unpretentious as you settle in among the traditional trappings of manorial life. Traditional, that is, apart from the omnipresent background music, which seems rather inappropriate in such surroundings.

The kitchen works hard to match the food to the environment, with dishes which, while they owe more than a little to what one might call 'nouvelle' trends, are nevertheless based on the more conventional principles of conception and preparation.

The short, continually changing menus make no bones about it, describing what is on offer in concise, no-nonsense terms: seared scallops, sautéd chanterelles, lentils and bacon; pan-fried wild sea bass with cocotte potatoes, artichokes, vanilla cappuccino; roast loin of Gloucestershire Old Spot, red onion tart, creamed savoy cabbage, red wine jus... What you see is what you get.

An exception is the perhaps presumptuously entitled 'Study in West Country Lamb', though it is an interesting idea to serve loin and cutlet with a slice of sweetbread and a rustic garnish of creamed potatoes and mushy peas.

Their pride: Loin of Gloucestershire Old Spot, shallot and sage tart
Inexpensive wines: Thornbury Castle Müller-Thürgau (England) £18; Premier Côtes de Bordeaux Château Anniche 2001, £19.50

Proprietor: Andrew Davis
Last orders for dinner: 9.30 pm (Friday and Saturday 10 pm
Open every day
Set lunch: from £22.50
Set dinner: from £42.50
Private dining: up to 30
Al fresco dining if pre-booked
Accommodation: 25 rooms
Wheelchair access

THORPE LANGTON, LEICESTERSHIRE

Bakers Arms

GASTROPUB

Main Street, Thorpe Langton, Leicestershire LE16 7TS
Tel. 01858 545 201

MAP 4 B3

LIMITED opening times make this inn a popular venue in the evening and at weekends. Chocolate-box pretty from the outside, with a thatched roof and hanging baskets, its interior offers a more quirky character. There are beams and a large open fire, but an inner arched window screens off a charming area housing a table for eight. A tiny room by the entrance provides a snug retreat, while rugs, cushioned nooks and crannies and lighted candles combine to create an inviting atmosphere.

Although printed menus would be preferable to the blackboards situated some distance from the tables, you will find the starters might feature a goat's cheese tartlet with roasted peppers and pesto dressing, or a salad of crevettes, asparagus and soft-boiled eggs. Try ogen melon paired with cassis sorbet and garnished with seasonal berries – a truly refreshing appetiser, particularly before a robust meat dish.

Main courses such as fillet steak with creamed runner beans, bacon and onion, or breast of lamb with mango and ginger salsa, are attractively presented and substantial. Gratin Dauphinois and crunchy vegetables might come with the main course. Thursday nights are given over to fish, with at least four varieties on offer. Sea bass with a cheesy, polenta crust could appear as a main course, served on rocket with asparagus spears.

Delicious vanilla ice-cream accompanies a sticky toffee pudding or crêpes in an orange liqueur. Deft cooking and good service are provided by the owner and her young team.

Speciality food: Scallops with Clonakilty black pudding
Draught beers: Bakers Dozen, Guinness
Average wine price by the glass: £3.50

Licensee: Kate Hubbard
Last orders for dinner: 9.30 pm
Closed: Sunday evening, Monday, lunchtime Tuesday to Friday
Main courses: from £11.25
Al fresco dining
Children over 12 welcome
Limited wheelchair access

TILLINGTON, WEST SUSSEX

Horse Guards Inn

GASTROPUB

Upperton Road, Tillington, Nr. Petworth, W Sussex GU28 9AF
Tel. 01798 342 332 Fax 01798 345 126
e-mail: thehorseguardsinn@hotmail.co.uk   **MAP 2** C4

THE PRETTY stone and cream painted village pub is opposite the beautiful church, overlooking the South Downs. Inside, the rustic bar has a wooden floor, dark beams and chintz curtains. There are several dining areas, all with scrubbed wooden tables and open fireplaces for the winter months.

Locals mix with visitors here to enjoy the imaginative dishes. Service throughout is welcoming and friendly. Book one of the two tables in the galleried window to get the best of the long views to the Downs. There is an attractive garden at the rear, where meals are served in good weather. Chef/patron Andrew Margolis sources locally produced meat and vegetables where possible – some of which are organic.

Home-made chicken liver and pistachio pâté with toasted brioche and pear chutney may start your meal, or caramelised onion tart with a thin, crisp pastry filled with sliced onion and decorated with rocket and red chard. Grilled asparagus is available in season.

Main courses include truffled mushroom macaroni cheese, poached smoked haddock with spring onion mash and poached egg, or the popular tender calf's liver cooked just pink, with streaky bacon and a tower of thinly sliced Dauphinoise potatoes.

For pudding there may be apple, pear and hazelnut crumble, sticky toffee with butterscotch sauce, or white chocolate tart made with shaved white chocolate and locally grown strawberries in season. There are also three Sussex cheeses: Olde Sussex, Scrumpy Sussex and Tillington goat's cheese.

Speciality food: Crispy Goodwood pork belly
Draught beers: Gales Best, Youngs Bitter
Average wine price by the glass: £2.95

Licensee: Andrew Margolis
Last orders for dinner: 9.30 pm (Fri and Sat 10 pm)
Open every day
Main courses: from £7.75
Private dining: 10-25
Beer garden
Accommodation: 3 rooms
Children welcome
Wheelchair access

TITLEY, HEREFORDSHIRE

Stagg Inn

Titley, Nr. Kington, Herefordshire HR5 3RL
Tel. 01544 230 221 Fax 01544 231 390
e-mail: reservations@thestagg.co.uk   **MAP 3** D4

LOCALLY born owners Nicola and Steve Reynolds are intent on maintaining the many period features of this neat little crossroads inn, with its open fires and beams, and also to exploit to the full the produce of their region, much of it from organic farms and most of the meat arriving from within the county.

Natural flair is evident in Steve's pigeon breast on braised Puy lentils and smoked bacon, or fillet of sea bass with mushroom duxelle and herb oil, and there is real style in well-cooked meats sauced with meaty reductions.

Straightforward soups, terrines, roasts and steaks reflect the rural surroundings and vegetarians are not overlooked, with a separate menu offering the likes of a crisply encased blue cheese, pear and walnut tart.

Home-made ice creams and sorbets are full of natural flavour and the classy caramelised lemon tart, which has a nice fruity tang, is top-notch. You can also choose from an award-winning range of regional cheeses.

Nicola is a chatty and amiable host and both food and atmosphere retain their charmingly unrushed, bucolic feel with more than the occasional touch of urban chic. Light bar meals are also served and accommodation is available.

Speciality food: Pedro Ximenes sherry cheesecake
Draught beers: Reverend James, Hobsons
Average wine price by the glass: £3

Licensee: Steve and Nicola Reynolds
Last orders for dinner: 9.30 pm
Closed: Mon and Sun evening (except Bank Holiday)
Closed for holidays: 25 and 26 December, 1 January,
May Day, 2 weeks November
Main courses: from £12.50
Private dining: 16-30
Al fresco dining
Accommodation: 3 rooms
Limited wheelchair access

TOTLEY, SOUTH YORKSHIRE

The Cricket

GASTROPUB

Penny Lane, Totley, Sheffield, South Yorkshire S17 3AZ
Tel. 01142 365 256 Fax 01142 356 582

MAP 5 D5

APTLY named, this pub, set on the Derbyshire-Yorkshire borders just a few miles from the centre of Sheffield, backs on to edge of a cricket pitch and cricket memorabilia features strongly inside.

For sandwiches, choose from a selection including their Cricket Club, comprised of feather steak, roast chicken, bacon, red onion marmalade, Cheddar and mayonnaise. There is also a Vegetarian Club sandwich of roast peppers, aubergine, tomatoes, mixed leaves, Brie and mayonnaise.

Staying with salads and light bites, you might be tempted by a three-cheese omelette or Posh Fish & Chips with 'Yorkshire caviar' (mushy peas). Scrambled eggs, so often reduced to a rubbery, tasteless mass, come in soft, creamy curds enhanced by dill and judicious seasoning, with moist slivers of pale smoked salmon, all on toasted brioche.

The choice of main courses is short but pleasing. Try confit of Barbary duck leg served with champ potatoes and a rosemary jus, or maybe seafood black pasta with firm, meaty king prawns and tasty mussels. Chilli, lemon zest and garlic admirably round off this dish .

Side-orders such as rocket and Parmesan salad, sautéd potatoes with chorizo and wilted rocket and parsnip crisps make a change from the usual offerings. Puddings might include Bailey's bread and butter pudding with vanilla ice-cream, or home-made rice pudding with poached fruit.

Speciality food: Fish and chips
Draught beers: Stones, Black Sheep
Average wine price by the glass: £3.10

Licensee: Fabrice Limon
Last orders for dinner: 10 pm
Closed: Monday (for food)
Main courses: from £6.95
Private dining: up to 34
Beer garden
Children welcome
Wheelchair access

453

TUNBRIDGE WELLS, KENT

Thackeray's ★

85 London Road, Tunbridge Wells, Kent TN1 1EA
Tel. 01892 511 921 Fax 01892 527 561
e-mail: reservations@thackeraysrestaurant.co.uk   **MAP 2** D4

THINK of Royal Tunbridge Wells and it is hard to escape its image as a bastion of the Establishment in all its slightly dotty glory, a place where change is naturally resisted and nothing is allowed to become brash or abrasive.

It was in this apparent bastion of conservatism, however, that the chef Richard Phillips, after stints with Marco-Pierre White among others, took over the oldest house – one-time home of the great writer for whom the restaurant is named – in order to indulge in a little innovation.

As if deferring to the watch-dogs of the local cultural heritage, he kept the main dining-room stylishly simple, with bare boards and minimum decoration, and for a time his newly installed kitchen brigade also devoted much of their efforts towards reassuring a wary clientele of their good intentions before allowing creativity to take flight.

The attention to quality and detail has paid off, however, so that now, some five years on, Thackeray's can offer such delicacies as roasted scallops with pan-fried black pudding, or a fillet of sea bass with a liquorice infused risotto.

This is inventive, metropolitan-style cooking which is notable for its artistic finesse and subtlety of touch, exemplified by a dessert of warm chocolate and mint fondant with white chocolate ice-cream – a fitting finale.

Their pride: Trio of foie gras with apricot and walnut bread
Inexpensive wines: La Croix Vin de Pays de l'Aude 2003, £12.95; Bourgogne Beau-Monde 2002, £22.

Proprietors: Richard Phillips, Paul Smith
Last orders for dinner: 10.30 pm
Closed: Sunday dinner, Monday
Set lunch: from £12.95
Set dinner: from £55
Private dining: 8-16
Al fresco dining
Wheelchair access

ULLINGSWICK, HEREFORDSHIRE

Three Crowns Inn

GASTROPUB

Ullingswick, Herefordshire HR1 3JQ
Tel. 01432 820 279 Fax 01432 820 991
e-mail: info@threecrownsinn.com   **MAP 3** D4

YOU might spot the owner of this inn working in the garden, the produce of which will no doubt feature later on your plate. It is a place where food is taken seriously.

Typical dishes on the bar menu could include baked local duck egg with Parma ham and 'soldiers'; smoked haddock with Welsh rarebit, leeks and bubble and squeak, or 'Mr Legge's' Cumberland sausages with smoked garlic mash.

A no-nonsense lunch/dinner menu offers six starters all priced at £6 and six main courses at £14.25. For starters, choose from crisp oriental pork belly with hot mustard dressing, or grilled crottin goat's cheese, lightly browned and served with sliced beetroot, mixed leaves and walnuts with an agreeable dressing.

Main courses have a good cross-section of meat and fish dishes. Glazed breast of Magetts Farm duck with cassis sauce and Camargue rice might appeal, or grilled sea bass with samphire, which is taken to greater heights through the addition of crayfish and shredded savoy cabbage. The further addition of tagliatelle seems almost superfluous.

On the pudding menu, a Chocolate Nemesis would satisfy the most serious chocoholic – a dense, rich confection well matched with fresh cherries and a refreshing pistachio ice-cream. Lighter, more seasonal desserts might include raspberry and Chartreuse Vacherin or vanilla ice-cream with grilled Amaretto apricots.

Speciality food: Local cheese and chard soufflés
Draught beers: Hobsons, Butty Bach
Average wine price by the glass: £4

Licensees: Brent Castle and Rachel Baker
Last orders for dinner: 9-9.30 pm
Closed: Monday
Closed for holidays: 2 weeks from 24 December
Main courses: £8.95
Private dining: 20-80
Beer garden
Accommodation: 1 room
Children welcome
Wheelchair access

ULLSWATER, CUMBRIA

Sharrow Bay ★

Howtown, Ullswater, Cumbria CA10 2LZ
Tel. 01768 486 301 Fax 01768 486 349
e-mail: info@sharrowbay.co.uk   **MAP 5** C3

IN SPITE of its obvious smartness, this model of gracious living is completely unstuffy and relaxed, the sort of place in which you feel instantly and contentedly at one with the world. Ever since it became a country house hotel, Sharrow Bay has been a byword for service that offers the perfect balance of formality and warm hospitality.

Many 'traditional' touches have been thankfully maintained since a change of ownership: lunch is at one, dinner at eight; the array of desserts is temptingly displayed for inspection on the way to your table.

The dinner menu, including your little pre-starter served with drinks in one of the lounges or the garden room, runs to seven thoroughly enjoyable and mostly uncomplicated courses – no swishes of sauce or gimmicky compilations, garnishes delivered with restraint when they are used at all.

Rustic terrines are much in evidence among the starters and what follow them tend to be delicious roasts and grilled fish. Good, honest flavours are what count.

It says much about the classical nature of the food here that among the most daring items on the menu are an aubergine caviar to accompany sea bass and the inclusion of mozzarella and figs in an avocado salad.

Their pride: Best end of lamb with black olive and herb crust served with braised shoulder and seasonal vegetables
Inexpensive wines: Menetou-Salon Clos des Blanchais (France) 2004, £22.50; Valpolicella Classico Allegrini (Veneto) 2004, £23.50

Proprietor: Andrew Davis
Last orders for dinner: 9 pm
Open every day
Set lunch: from £30
Set dinner: from £49.75
Private dining: up to 40
Al fresco dining: light meals
Accommodation: 24 rooms
Wheelchair access

Lords of the Manor

Upper Slaughter, Nr. Bourton-on-the-Water, Glos GL54 2JD
Tel. 01451 820 243 Fax 01451 820 696
e-mail: enquiries@lordsofthemanor.com   **MAP 1** F1

BUILT of honey-coloured Cotswold stone, this former rectory dates from the 17th century and is set in parkland, with its own lake, the surroundings seen at their best in the summer from the charming terrace.

There is a menu for the bar and the terrace, with perhaps salmon fishcakes, Caesar salad or duck confit, and a short lunch menu offering the likes of braised lamb and seared salmon with herb risotto. It is dinner that brings a sense of culinary adventure.

You will be surprised at the sometimes brilliant addition of ices and sorbets to such things as blue cheese panna cotta (celery and apple), fried foie gras (tamarind) and tuna carpaccio (fennel).

The other surprise is how well some unexpected combinations really work, as with braised pork belly and roast scallops. More traditional tastes are not overlooked, however, so that menu choices might include saddle of venison with braised red cabbage and salsify, brill with chive crushed potatoes and fillet of beef with beetroot confit.

Desserts range from roast fig with honeycomb to an accomplished hot caramel soufflé.

There is a very good selection of English and French farmhouse cheeses, and toasted apricot and walnut bread to go with them.

Their pride: Dry-roasted peanut risotto with seared scallop and coriander relish
Inexpensive wines: Cabernet Sauvignon Réserve Jean Léon 2001, £32; Chardonnay Kim Crawford 2003, £28

Proprietor: Empire Ventures
Last orders for dinner: 9.30 pm (Fri and Sat 10 pm)
Closed: Monday lunch
Set lunch: from £21.50
Set dinner: from £49
Private dining: up to 50
Accommodation: 27 rooms
Limited wheelchair access

WALTON, WEST YORKSHIRE

Fox and Hounds

GASTROPUB

Hall Park Road, Walton, Nr. Wetherby, W Yorks LS23 7DQ
Tel. 01937 842 192 Fax 01937 845 811

MAP 5 D4

OWNER Karl Manley can often be seen working in the kitchen of his thriving village hostelry, and his presence both here and at his nearby sister pub is typical of his hands-on approach. He seems to have the formula just right, the cottagey furnishings, warm colours and bubbly atmosphere complementing a serious attitude towards some gloriously varied, fresh, inventive food. Most of the dishes are written on blackboards, with regular fixtures on the printed carte and good value in the set menus.

There is something for everyone, with excellent Thai fishcakes, home-made gnocchi, a goat's cheese risotto with basil, tempura prawns or asparagus rösti, as well as a Wensleydale tart, steak and ale pie, home-made black pudding, good old-fashioned bangers or fish and chunky, home-made chips.

Fresh fish features particularly on the daily changing blackboard specials and after Whitby crab, moules marinières or Scottish scallops, how about a juicy monkfish tail wrapped in bacon, grilled lemon sole, or sea bass given a Mediterranean look with a tangy pesto and charred peppers? Carnivores may opt for a duck confit, calf's liver or a breast of farm chicken on wild mushrooms.

Even a snack becomes a full meal here, with the rough-hewn granary bread making trenchermen's sandwiches. Desserts follow fairly traditional lines – crumbles, sticky toffee pudding and crème brûlée with a chocolate base. All the wines are available by the glass. A thoroughly enjoyable meal in expert hands.

Speciality food: Modern British cookery
Draught beers: John Smiths Cask, Deuchars IPA
Average wine price by the glass: £2.85

Licensee: Karl Manley
Last orders for dinner: 9 pm
Closed: Sunday dinner (food only)
Set lunch: £12.95
Set dinner: £12.95 (until 7 pm)
Beer garden
Children welcome
Wheelchair access

WARE, HERTFORDSHIRE

Jacoby's

GASTROPUB

15 West Street, Ware, Hertfordshire SG12 9EE
Tel. 01920 469 181 Fax 01920 469 182
e-mail: info@jacobys.co.uk   **MAP 2** D2

JUST off the High Street, this 16th-century building has been an inn, a bakery and a bicycle shop. Restored to its old timbered splendour, Jacoby's is now a smart pub-brasserie that combines period features with a modern bar, a contemporary bistro and a beamed dining-room upstairs.

The bar does have a pubby feel, while in the bistro, the casual mood is typical of this prosperous part of Hertfordshire. The food in both bar and bistro comes from the carte.

At lunchtime there are options such as open steak sandwiches or steamed mussels in red Thai curry and coconut broth. In the evening there are seven starters and ten main courses, all in the modern Mediterranean style with interesting Asian influences.

Begin with Parma ham with ricotta stuffed figs and rocket salad, or the successful combination of sardine escabèche with Roma tomato and basil tart. Grills predominate in main courses, as in seared tuna steak with Shanghai noodles, or the cleanly flavoured Moroccan grilled chicken with yoghurt and vegetable couscous. Asia appears in the Chinese duck strudel with roasted breast. All these dishes are most competently handled.

There are the usual brasserie desserts, such as Vacherin of fresh fruits, and to drink, the Stella Artois is well kept, and the good wines by the glass and bottle are fairly priced: try a glass of the Pantelleria sweet wine with dessert.

Speciality food: European with Asian influence
Draught beers: Stella Artois, Carlsberg
Average wine price by the glass: £2.95

Licensees: Paul Linkson and Jacqueline Linkson
Last orders for dinner: 9.30 pm
Closed: Monday
Closed for holidays: 1 week at Christmas
Main courses: from £13
Private dining: 14-70
Al fresco dining at lunch
Children welcome
Limited wheelchair access

WARHAM, NORFOLK

Three Horseshoes

The Street, Warham All Saints, Norfolk NR23 1NL
Tel. 01328 710 547

MAP 4 E2

THIS well-known flintstone pub on Warham's village green has always done business on very much its own terms: no chips, no credit cards, no bookings, last orders in the bar for lunch and supper sharp at 1.45 pm and 8.30 pm. The warren of rooms surrounding the bar offers nostalgic delight, little changed, one imagines, since the early 1900s: gas lighting, stone floors and stuffed pheasants, old cigarette cards and food adverts such as 'Salmon tea served here'.

It is deservedly popular because the traditional but appetising food is cooked to order, with an emphasis on local ingredients, often from recipes you will not find elsewhere: Norfolk potted pork cheese made from strips of pork in a pork jelly and served with a Norfolk chutney, or marinated local herring fillet soused in cider vinegar. The specials from the board are the dishes to go for: chicken and leeks in a suet pudding and the garlic lamb are full of flavour, while game and shellfish are regularly featured.

Lighter options range from Warham crab soup and Stilton and walnut cream pâté, to Mr. Pork Sausage Roll, which uses excellent sausage from Howell's of Wells. The home-made puddings relive school lunches, but here they are prepared properly, particularly the ginger sponge with real custard.

The pub's Woodforde beers are not pumped from the cellar, but instead are drawn straight from the cask in the bar, which makes for an even better pint. Decent Cabernet, Shiraz, Muscadet and Chardonnay are available for a very reasonable £2.95.

Speciality food: Norfolk potted pork cheese
Draught beers: Woodforde Wherry, Woodforde Bitter
Average wine price by the glass: £2.95

Licensee: Ian Salmon
Last orders for dinner: 8.30 pm
Open every day
Closed for holidays: 25 December
Main courses: from £6.80
Beer garden
Children welcome
Wheelchair access

WELLS-NEXT-THE-SEA, NORFOLK

Crown Hotel

GASTROPUB

The Buttlands, Wells-Next-The-Sea, Norfolk NR23 1EX
Tel. 01328 710 209 Fax 01328 711 432
e-mail: reception@thecrownhotelwells.co.uk   **MAP 4** E2

ON THE elegant, elongated 'square' of Wells stands The Crown, a traditional inn brought into the 21st century with an all-day brasserie menu served round the bar and, at dinner, in a more formal, softly-lit restaurant.

In the latter, there is obvious gastronomic ambition in a typical dinner. An appetiser of seafood tartlet comes in very light pastry; crisp Thai crab cakes are based on fresh, largely white crab meat enhanced by spices, notably ginger; beef fillet of fine quality is cooked very accurately to medium-rare order, and served on rösti potato with horse-radish cream, though the beetroot relish could be thought fussy.

The brasserie bar menu goes for trendy, myriad flavours, as in Chris's Black Slate – salmon belly, grilled chorizo, marinated chicken wings, crab spring roll, smoked chicken and peanut salad, which might be too many flavours for some.

Happily, the chef calms down a little in such appetising dishes as goujons of haddock in beer batter and hand-cut sweet potato chips, or roast cod on watercress mash with chive butter sauce. In the bar at lunchtime there is a generous Crown club sandwich or a toasted minute-steak version.

Puddings in both the bar and the restaurant can be thoroughly recommended, especially an iced summer fruit parfait and the strawberry Eton Mess. The good, varied wines on the list are well annotated.

Speciality food: Chris's Black Slate
Draught beers: Foxs Branthill Best
Average wine price by the glass: £3.65

Licensee: Chris Coubrough
Last orders for dinner: 9 pm
Open every day
Set dinner: from £24.95
Main courses: from £10.25
Private dining: up to 60
Beer garden
Accommodation: 12 rooms
Children welcome
Wheelchair access

Welwyn, Hertfordshire
Auberge du Lac

Just before the Guide went to press, chef Jean-Christophe Novelli announced that he had left the Auberge du Lac and that he would be pursuing other ventures in 2006

WEST BAY, DORSET

West Bay

GASTROPUB

Station Road, West Bay, Bridport, Dorset DT6 4EW
Tel: 01308 422 157 Fax 01308 459 717

MAP 1 E4

STANDING between fine pebble dunes, this unassuming inn is one of the most successful food pubs for many miles. Licensees John Ford and Karen Trimby became tenants six years ago, and they have built a business many would envy. The thick stone walls and old beams testify to a long history, but the decoration inside is very much up to date.

The small, wooden-floored bar area near the entrance keeps shrinking as the popularity of the cooking and also the dining area have grown. Snacks such as baguettes, sandwiches, ploughman's and salads and a handful of hot dishes are available in the bar at lunchtimes only, but most people head for the dining area or the pretty garden outside.

Blackboards list a daily menu, but the separate board detailing a dozen or so fish and shellfish dishes has become the West Bay's popular signature.

Cooking and presentation are admirably straightforward: whole lemon sole with prawn and lemongrass butter, cod fillets with pesto butter in beer batter, or turbot fillets with clams, scallops and salsa verde. A 'posh fish pie' consists of cod, salmon, sea bass and scallops. The hot crab medley (half a crab, scallops, prawns and mussels) is about as complicated as it gets, and a lobster platter with all manner of good things needs to be booked (and budgeted for) in advance.

Wines, supplied by the brewery, cover most continents. Booking is advised in the evenings.

Speciality food: Seafood platters/hot crab medley
Draught beers: Palmers IPA, Palmers Copper Ale
Average wine price by the glass: £2.75

Licensees: John Ford and Karen Trimby
Last orders for dinner: 9.15 pm
Closed: Sunday evening
Main courses: from £15
Beer garden
Accommodation: 4 rooms
Children welcome
Limited wheelchair access

WHITBY, NORTH YORKSHIRE

Green's

13 Bridge Street, Whitby, North Yorkshire YO22 4BG
Tel. 01947 600 284
e-mail: info@greensofwhitby.com   **MAP 5** E3

SET in the central harbour area of a fishing port that harvests some of the best seafood in Britain, you will find Green's across the swing bridge into the old town and there you can choose from a menu of fish chalked up on the blackboard.

Given good weather, there is usually a fine pick from the deep: sole, sea bass, turbot, John Dory, plaice, cod, sea bream and exceptional little lobsters. There is also fine Yorkshire beef from Radfords of Sleights, whose meat makes for excellent steaks and Sunday roasts.

The cooking is not particularly subtle, but it is not meant to be. The attraction is the freshness of the fish and meat, honestly cooked.

Soft-shell crab cooked with garlic and butter was a good, richly flavoured starter, balanced by a fresh wild rocket salad. Whitby halibut, roasted slowly in the oven with tomato and flavoured with basil, was the best dish, the fish very fresh, juicy and thick-cut, though perhaps the red cabbage was too strongly flavoured an accompaniment.

Good desserts range from banana and toffee crème brûlée to chocolate mousse with maple and pecan biscuits, or warm pear and frangipane tart with home-made vanilla ice-cream.

The wine list features excellent bottles at extremely reasonable prices, particularly from Australia and New Zealand.

Their pride: Ragout of turbot, queen scallops and vegetables
Inexpensive wines: Riesling Waipara Hills (New Zealand) 2003, £19; Rioja Vega Crianza 2000, £16.50

Proprietors: Rob and Emma Green
Last orders for dinner: 9.30 pm
Closed: Lunchtime Monday to Thursday
Closed for holidays: 25-26 December, 1 January
Main courses: from £14

WHITEWELL, LANCASHIRE

The Inn at Whitewell

GASTROPUB

Whitewell, Nr. Clitheroe, Lancashire BB7 3AT
Tel. 01200 448 222 Fax 01200 448 298
e-mail: reception@innatwhitewell.com   **MAP 5** C4

FROM its humble 16th-century beginnings as a hunters' cottage, this imposing, gable-fronted stone edifice has grown to the point where it appears to go on forever. Now it offers almost manorial bars and dining-rooms decorated with sporting prints and suitably furnished with antique chairs round well-spaced tables.

From the more formal restaurant and Orangery rooms, the tranquil rear views across the river to the rolling fields beyond are shared by many of the delightfully appointed, recently added bedrooms.

The traditional, almost earthy style is reflected in food that prides itself on its honest simplicity for the most part. The occasional dash of spirited originality creeps on to the specials board or the more elaborate evening restaurant menu in the form of a grilled belly of pork with vanilla mash, ginger and soy, or chicken and pistachio ravioli with asparagus and a morel cream.

Such exotica apart, the enjoyment lies in well-sourced reliable favourites such as the smoked fish from Norfolk, old-fashioned Cumberland sausages (supplied by the same maker for many years), fish pie, lamb from the adjacent moors, hefty fillet steaks and Goosnargh poultry.

Apart from the odd touch of balsamic vinegar and pesto here and there, this is proudly dependable English inn food that really flies the flag – generously portioned and packed with honest flavours that delight as much as the impressive surroundings and friendly, easygoing staff.

Speciality food: Fish pie
Draught beers: Sawley Tempted, Copper Dragon
Average wine price by the glass: £2.90

Licensee: Charles Bowman
Last orders for dinner: 9.30 pm
Open every day
Main courses: from £8.50 (lunch), £15 (dinner)
Private dining: up to 20
Beer garden
Accommodation: 23 rooms
Children welcome
Limited wheelchair access

WHITLEY, WILTSHIRE

Pear Tree ★

GASTROPUB

Top Lane, Whitley, Wiltshire SN12 8QX
Tel. 01225 709 131

MAP 1 E2

IF YOU have ever fancied the idea of hot air ballooning, now is your chance. Flights sometimes take off from a field behind the Pear Tree. You could spend the morning soaring over the Wiltshire countryside, Stonehenge, Salisbury cathedral and the Great Western Railway before landing to crown the experience with a memorable meal.

Word of mouth and high standards have ensured a constant stream of customers over several years. In attractive landscaped gardens, this period property offers great comfort and ambience. Dusty pink walls display various artifacts with no obvious theme, but somehow it all pulls together.

It sounds like an oxymoron, but the fixed lunch menu is flexible. You can either stick to it or choose starters and main courses from the carte at no extra cost. Starters such as courgette and Parmesan soup, or rissole of rare-breed white pork with a fried egg, caper and parsley mayonnaise might feature on the set lunch. Slices of deep-fried avocado – crisp on the surface, retaining flavour and texture – are particularly toothsome when combined with pancetta and grilled courgette as a starter salad.

Maybe roasted hake with mixed leaf and polenta crouton salad might appeal as a main course, or pork shoulder. The latter comes with a meaty jus, apple sauce and seasonal vegetables.

A delicious, home-made praline ice-cream is served with langue de chat biscuits. Alternatively, try the banana ice-cream with caramelised fig tart. Exceptionally good service.

Speciality food: Local produce
Draught beers: Local guest ales, Wadworth 6X
Average wine price by the glass: £4.75

Licensee: Martin Still
Last orders for dinner: 9.30pm (Fri and Sat 9.45pm)
Open every day
Closed for holidays: 25 December, 1 January
Set lunch: from £13.50
Main courses: from £11.50
Private dining: up to 50
Al fresco dining
Accommodation: 8 rooms
Children welcome   Wheelchair access

WINCHCOMBE, GLOUCESTERSHIRE

5 North Street

5 North Street, Winchcombe, Gloucestershire GL54 5LH
Tel. 01242 604 566 Fax 01242 603 788
e-mail: marcusashenford@yahoo.co.uk   **MAP 1** F1

THE GOOD folk of Winchcombe are certainly lucky to have No. 5 on their doorstep. This delightful little dolls' house tea-room of a restaurant has a cosy, welcoming feel despite culinary aspirations that go way beyond the intimate, cottagey setting.

Marcus Ashenford certainly pulls out all the stops to both please and surprise guests. When his wife, Kate, arrives with a plate of cheese and rhubarb Welsh rarebits to accompany your drinks, you know that things are not quite what they seem, even if a solidly traditional base remains the underlying trend of the cooking.

Just about every item on the short, varied menus is given a twist, so that smoked haddock with spinach might be embellished with duck egg and truffle, a fillet of sea bass is laid on wilted pak choi flavoured with black beans, and, though local game is still graced with bread sauce, when combined they form an intriguing basis for a choucroute.

The moist fillet of salmon was accurately cooked and served on a kaleidoscope of colourful ingredients such as peppers, a balsamic reduction and basil oil. Beautifully tender braised beef with its accompanying slice of tongue was served with mashed potato and cabbage, and a rich, meaty and well-reduced jus.

There are nice touches throughout, such as the two excellent home-made breads baked as one, and ambitious assiettes of desserts, the passion fruit mousse and its fellow sorbet better than the hot chocolate fondant and white chocolate dip.

Their pride: Red mullet, foie gras, cauliflower purée, orange dressing
Inexpensive wines: Alamos Chardonnay (Argentina) 2004, £15; Saint-Chinian Terres Rouge 2001, £17.50

Proprietors: Marcus and Kate Ashenford
Last orders for dinner: 9 pm
Closed: Sunday dinner, Monday, Tuesday lunch
Closed for holidays: 2 weeks January, 1 week August
Set lunch: from £17.50
Set dinner: from £25
Private dining: up to 24
Wheelchair access

WINCHESTER, HAMPSHIRE

Chesil Rectory ★

1 Chesil Street, Winchester, Hampshire SO23 0HU
Tel. 01962 851 555 Fax 01962 869 704

MAP 2 B4

THIS ancient timber-framed building was at one time scheduled for demolition, but it survived to become a smartly informal restaurant offering seriously good food from a chef who gained his spurs at, among other places, the Dorchester.

The rule of the house is to use only the very finest ingredients, with the result that many of the raw materials – duck, rabbit, beef and game in season – are ordered directly from the best markets.

There is a wide-ranging choice of main courses on the evening menu, mostly garnished quite simply with potato in all its various forms. The basis of many of the dishes is appropriate jus that will be strong in rich, natural flavours, while at the same time more aromatic ingredients, such as wild mushrooms, are added in ways that allow them full, flavoursome expression.

At lunchtime, the menus tend to revolve round a rather simpler approach, but that does not detract in any way from the wholly admirable quality of the cooking.

The welcome is warm and the service attentive, though always maintaining the homely feel of the place.

Their pride: Pan-roasted turbot with a bisque of white port, Devon cock crab and asparagus
Inexpensive wines: Unoaked Chardonnay Evans & Tate (Australia) 2003, £20; Corbières Château Veredus 2001, £24

Proprietors: Carl and Anna Reeve
Last orders for dinner: Tuesday to Thursday 8.30 pm, Friday and Saturday 9.30 pm
Closed: Sunday and Monday
Closed for holidays: First two weeks August, 2 weeks Christmas
Set lunch: from £25
Set dinner: from £40
Private dining: up to 14

WINCHESTER, HAMPSHIRE

Wykeham Arms

75 Kingsgate Street, Winchester, Hampshire SO23 9PE
Tel. 01962 853 834 Fax 01962 854 411

MAP 2 B4

THE 250-year-old Wykeham Arms, with its fourteen bedrooms, wood panelling, open fires and old school desks from Winchester College, is crammed with memorabilia and an atmosphere that is all its own.

It offers a light lunchtime menu, supplemented by what appears on the blackboard, which might include a sandwich of the day, cream of mushroom soup or chargrilled lamb on skewers with honeyed tzatziki.

Among particularly notable lunch dishes are the combination of wild mushroom risotto with rocket and truffle oil, and confit of duck, with its tender meat slipping effortlessly off the bone. If fish is your preference, you might find whole lemon sole available.

On Sundays you will be offered very good set lunches of two or three courses.

Evenings bring a more elaborate menu, with first courses such as beef stir-fry with pak choi noodles, or crab cakes with avocado salsa. Popular main courses are roast rack of Hampshire Downs lamb with redcurrant jus, or oven-baked fillet of halibut.

Temptation levels remain high on the pudding front: the smooth and rich cappuccino mousse with shaved fresh coconut and crushed pistachios is a highlight, but the apple and redcurrant crumble is also a strong contender.

As many as 20 wines are served by the glass.

Speciality food: Wykeham pie
Draught beers: Gales Best, Gales HSB
Average wine price by the glass: £3.50

Licensees: Kate and Peter Miller
Last orders for dinner: 8.45 pm
Closed: Sunday evening
Closed for holidays: 25 December
Set lunch: from £14.50 (Sunday only)
Main courses: from £5.95 (lunch), £10.85 (dinner)
Private dining: up to 8
Beer garden
Accommodation: 14 rooms
Children over 14 years welcome   Wheelchair access

WINDERMERE, CUMBRIA

Gilpin Lodge ★★

Crook Road, Nr. Windermere, Cumbria LA23 3NE
Tel. 01539 488 818 Fax 01539 488 058
e-mail: hotel@gilpinlodge.com   **MAP 5** C3

NESTLING alongside Windermere's golf club, amid the fells and
dry stone walls of some of the Lake District's finest walking
country between Kendal and the lake itself, this romantic and
discreetly situated country hotel has just about everything.

With 20 acres of formal gardens and wilder woodland, it is hard
to imagine a more agreeable place for pampered seclusion. Relax
with a drink and excellent nibbles on the terrace, if the weather
allows, or in comfortable lounges offering warm colours, fresh
flowers, glistening copper and acres of soft furnishings.

A five-course dining menu that changes daily offers a panorama
of taste and texture, subtlety and creative originality. Harmonious
blending allows the qualities of each ingredient to be exploited to
the full across a range of dishes that excite but never shock.

Breast of Anjou pigeon comes with Scottish girolles, choucroute
and a beetroot jus, while other choices include minestrone of
hand-dived scallops; a delicately balanced tian of crab and skate
with the lightest of cucumber veloutés; roasted fillet of pork with
black pudding ravioli, or even roasted halibut with leeks and a
fricassee of lobster.

After a gamut of British and Irish cheeses, an iced banana parfait,
chocolate marquise with a passion fruit sorbet, or a heavenly and
richly flavoured apricot soufflé with chocolate sorbet, will finish
things off in style.

Their pride: Swaledale lamb, hot-pot vegetables, fondant potato
Inexpensive wines: Viognier Domaine de Sarret 2003, £19.75;
Cabernet Sauvignon/Merlot Chameleon Jordan (Stellenbosch)
2003, £21.50

Proprietors: The Cunliffe Family
Last orders for dinner: 9.15 pm
Open every day
Set lunch: from £20
Set dinner: from £42.50
Private dining: 6–30
Al fresco dining at lunch
Accommodation: 14 rooms
Wheelchair access

WINDERMERE, CUMBRIA

Holbeck Ghyll ★

Holbeck Lane, Windermere, Cumbria LA3 1LU
Tel. 01539 432 375 Fax 01539 434 743
e-mail: stay@holbeckghyll.com   **MAP 5** C3

THE charmingly attentive staff at this former hunting lodge among the wild mountain scenery of the Lake District treat you less as customers, more as favoured guests at a country house gathering.

In the panelled dining-room, the food served is also reassuringly civilised, full of interest but never outlandish and always refined without being fussy. Flavours are strong and uncompromising, with aromatic jus and rich sauces

If the underlying trend is towards the classics, the fine, often local ingredients are handled in a way that is intelligently modern. Celeriac and balsamic vinegar, for example, are added to a dish of roasted scallops, while beef is given truffled potatoes and wild mushrooms.

Other choices might be lamb from the moors with rosemary and shallots, or brill with soused vegetables, asparagus and white bean foam.

The desserts, too, are taken from among the classics, including date pudding and, of course, crème brûlée.

Their pride: Breast and confit leg of Périgord duckling choucroute, smoked bacon and foie gras cassoulet
Inexpensive wines: Grand Ardèche Louis Latour 2001, £19.50; Puerta Vieja Crianza Rioja 2000, £19.50

Proprietors: David and Patricia Nicholson
Last orders for dinner: 9.30 pm
Open every day
Set lunch: from £22.50
Set dinner: from £45
Private dining: up to 35
Al fresco dining
Accommodation: 21 rooms
Wheelchair access

WINDERMERE, CUMBRIA

Jericho's

Birch Street, Windermere, Cumbria LA23 1EG
Tel./Fax 015394 42522
e-mail: enquiries@jerichos.co.uk   **MAP 5** C3

SIMPLE enjoyment but with more than a touch of class, that is the best way of summing up a meal at Jericho's.

The menu is just three courses, comprising four starters, five main dishes and three desserts – no pre-starters, pre-desserts or anything of that sort – and the result is sheer, unpretentious pleasure.

The freshest of ingredients, in generous portions, are combined to express themselves naturally through straightforward preparation and spot-on seasoning: pan-fried black pudding on spiced chick-pea and butter bean casserole, for example; Thai green risotto with balsamic reduction; sea bass with coriander and, caviar and tomato basil reduction.

Sauces are colourful and drizzled in rather nouvelle style, but the overall effect is not at all pretentious or fussy.

Note, too, the permanent presence of a vegetarian starter and main course on the list, as well as prime fillet of Scottish beef.

The wine list is cleverly arranged to help non-experts make the right choice to accompany their dishes and there is a good range of reasonably priced bottles.

Their pride: Shellfish risotto
Inexpensive wines: Las Condes Merlot (Chile) £13; Paul Mas Sauvignon Blanc £13

Proprietors: Chris and Jo Blaydes
Last orders for dinner: 9.30 pm
Closed: Monday from April to December, Sunday and Monday from January to March
Closed for holidays: 4 weeks November-March (can vary)
Main courses: from £14.50
Private dining: 16-36

WINDERMERE, CUMBRIA

The Samling ★

Ambleside Road, Windermere, Cumbria LA23 1LR
Tel. 01539 431 922 Fax 01539 430 400
e-mail: info@thesamling.com   **MAP 5** C3

STYLE comes to Windermere where you might least expect it, in a discreet country retreat peeping almost surreptitiously through immaculate gardens towards the lake. A little dining-room, where heavy glassware, stainless steel cutlery and slate presentation plates bestow an almost Scandinavian feel, offers an exciting modern approach to eating.

The food is excellent, displaying total refinement and a continual exploration of flavours and textures that can sometimes produce stunning combinations

Amuse-bouches include vegetable spring roll and mini-canapés of foie gras and salmon, to be followed, perhaps, by water-melon soup. As a starter, two small langoustines come with a delicious avocado croquette, marrying superbly with a tangy lime jelly and a perfectly cut red pepper and cucumber relish – overall a truly wonderful collation.

Main-course choices might feature a miniature shepherd's pie, glazed Châteaubriand and cutlet of lamb with a plain meat jus, and you could follow this with a pre-dessert of caramelised pineapple on yoghurt with a refreshing granité topping. Among the desserts themselves, fig Tatin was first-rate, its fruit well caramelised, and partnered by a really outstanding goat's cheese ice-cream nicely set off with aged balsamic.

A good range of nibbles comes with the coffee, in particular a heavenly miniature lemon meringue tart

Their pride: Roast supreme of guinea fowl, lentil purée, smoked bacon and tarragon cream sauce
Inexpensive wines: Terre Rouge Enigma 2001, £24; Chenin Blanc Old Vines 2003, £29

Proprietor: Tom Maxfield
Last orders for dinner: 9.30 pm
Open every day
Set lunch: from £48
Set dinner: from £48
Private dining: 6-24
Al fresco dining
Accommodation: 11 rooms

WINGHAM, KENT

Dog Inn

Canterbury Road, Wingham, Kent CT3 1BB
Tel. 01227 720 339 Fax 01227 720 339
e-mail: thedoginn@netbreeze.co.uk   **MAP 2** F3

IN ADDITION to being able to eat, drink and sleep in the heart of this archetypical Kentish village, you can also get married at The Dog. It is licensed for civil weddings, which take place, almost Vegas-style (when the English weather allows), under a little gazebo in the back garden.

Richard and Sherry Martin's recent acquisition, with rough beams and oak-panelled bars, as well as an appealing little conservatory room, combines comfort and a certain rusticity in which to enjoy Richard's comprehensive selection of home-made restaurant meals and bar snacks, along with a pint or two of decent draught, including regular guest beers.

A nicely varied selection of starters offers appetising combinations such as a salad of king scallop with ginger and bacon, lemon dressing and fennel shavings; potted tiger-tail prawns with smoked salmon and brill; salt and chilli squid with aged balsamic vinegar and aïoli. Main courses tend towards greater conformity, with down-to-earth Scottish steaks, juicy, herb crusted rack of Romney Marsh lamb (pity about the rather heavy rosemary jus), baked lemon sole with thyme and lemon butter, or beer-battered haddock with pea and mint purée.

Local fish is a particular favourite here and simpler dishes perhaps work best, but leave some room for a rich, chocolatey roulade made with cream liqueur, or a fresh strawberry mini-charlotte. It's fairly early days still, and the young staff could perhaps relax a little more into their jobs, but then, aren't you always nervous on the big occasion?

Speciality food: Scottish steaks and local fish.
Draught beers: Greene King IPA, Courage Best Bitter.
Average wine price by the glass: £3.25.

Licensees: Sherry and Richard Martin
Last orders for dinner: 10.30pm
Open every day
Main courses: from £8.95
Private dining: up to 50
Beer garden
Accommodation: 9 rooms
Children welcome

WINTERBOURNE, BERKSHIRE

Winterbourne Arms

Winterbourne, Nr. Newbury, Berkshire RG20 8BB
Tel. 01635 248 200 Fax 01635 248 824
e-mail: winterbournearms@tiscali.co.uk   **MAP 2** B3

IN A village four miles north of Newbury, the Winterbourne Arms is a long-fronted building, in keeping with its history. During its 300 years, parts have been a bakery a shop and a 'local', but only as recently as the 1980s has the whole become a pub.

The lovingly preserved bread ovens (no longer functioning) are at one end of the bar, which can be sectioned off for private dinners. The remainder of the bar is mellow, with attractive old brickwork.

Lunchtime offers a good range of sandwiches and ploughman's and, while the menu has few surprises or imaginative flights of fancy, the cooking is careful and competent, with no short-cuts.

Classics appear among the starters, as in eggs Benedict, the egg accurately poached, the hollandaise well married, and the place is obviously demanding in the freshness and quality of fish and meat.

A T-bone steak exhibited well-hung and marbled fat flavours and was properly cooked medium rare. Hamburgers are home made, and accompanied by a tomato salsa relish that is a cut above the average. Among desserts, blackberry and apple crumble is a very good choice.

There is a good selection of wines by the glass, including some attractive Argentinian reds.

Speciality food: Contemporary European/British
Draught beers: Ramsbury Gold, Good Old Boy (West Berkshire Brewery)
Average wine price by the glass: £3.40

Licensee: Frank Adams
Last orders for dinner: 10 pm
Open every day
Main courses: from £9.95
Private dining: up to 20
Beer garden
Children welcome
Wheelchair access

475

WINTERINGHAM, LINCOLNSHIRE

Winteringham Fields ★★

Winteringham, Lincolnshire DN15 9PF
Tel 01724 733096 Fax 01724 733898
e-mail: wintfields@aol.com

MAP 5 E5

AMONG the fields of north Lincolnshire, Winteringham village is at first sight a tranquil backwater, but it is actually close to the mighty Humber Bridge and its links to the motorway network of the North-East. This revered restaurant takes its name precisely from the location, the ease of access drawing customers from nearby Scunthorpe to Leeds and beyond.

The restaurant is extremely comfortable, even luxurious, with marble floors, a handsome pine dresser, large lamps and bronze busts, but it remains cosy and intimate.
.
The superb amuse-bouches, such as the crispest fritter of hare and rabbit and a croûte of root vegetables with chervil, served with minted yoghurt and apple, are the shape of great things to come. A fricassee of wild salmon, beautifully fresh with a hint of dill, comes with an exquisitely herbed salmon rillette, then there is a magnificent tranche of saddle of lamb, pink, warmed through, served with a farce of lightly cooked lamb's kidneys.

Another meal might start with cannelloni of pike and crayfish, consommé of crayfish and chilli, followed by a great speciality, potato crushed halibut with a warm salad of truffle and foie gras. The cheeseboard is outstanding for range and quality with as many as 35 cheeses to choose from.

Desserts are dazzling: a fine bread and butter pudding made from malted apricot bread and served with vanilla pod ice-cream; liquorice soufflé with orange powder and liquorice ice-cream, or a range of home-made sorbets.

Their pride: Pastilla of local rabbit, Moroccan spices, lemon jelly
Inexpensive wines: Alsace Pinot Blanc 2003, £22; Sonsierra Rioja 2003, £22

Proprietors: Colin and Rebecca McGurren
Last orders for dinner: 9.30 pm
Closed: Sunday and Monday
Closed for holidays: 2 weeks Christmas, last week March, first 10 days August
Set lunch: from £33
Set dinner: from £40
Private dining: up to 10
Accommodation: 10 rooms
Wheelchair access

WOBURN, BUCKINGHAMSHIRE

The Birch

GASTROPUB

20 Newport Road, Woburn, Buckinghamshire MK17 9HX
Tel. 01525 290 295 Fax 01525 290 899
e-mail: ctaverns@aol.com   **MAP 4** C5

IT may be unusual these days to transform what was an Indian restaurant into a smart gastropub, but it has paid dividends at this roadside inn, a short distance from Woburn's attractive town centre, with booking a must even in midweek.

Arranged on several levels along clean, contemporary lines, with colourful artworks and Venetian blinds on the conservatory-style structure, the almost outdoor appeal of the surroundings makes this an ideal venue for every occasion.

Pop into the semi-open-plan kitchen and select your meat or fish if you just want a simple grilled steak, plain seafood or a hearty chunk of game in season, such as the meaty and accurately cooked venison.

There are Mediterranean-Asian influences evident in tuna, crab and lime fishcakes; wild mushroom, smoked bacon and Parmesan salad with fresh pesto; fillet of trout steamed with ginger and lemongrass, or aubergine and mozzarella paupiettes served on couscous. Home-spun favourites appear, too – the likes of roasts, burgers and Cumberland sausage – but an osso bucco of pork with honey and cider, breast of chicken with apple and walnut filo parcels, and monkfish poached in lemon oil, show the occasional spark of genuine originality.

Creamy pana cotta, crème brûlée or the chilled lime and tequila soufflé are good desserts.

Speciality food: Modern classics and griddled meats and fish
Draught beers: Fullers London Pride, Stella Artois
Average wine price by the glass: £2.35

Licensee: Mark Campbell
Last orders for dinner: 10 pm (Sunday 5 pm)
Open every day
Closed for holidays: 25 and 26 December, 1 January
Main courses: from £8.95
Al fresco dining
Children welcome
Wheelchair access

WOODSTOCK, OXFORDSHIRE

Feathers Hotel

Market Street, Woodstock, Oxfordshire OX20 1SX
Tel. 01993 812 291 Fax 01993 813 158
e-mail: enquiries@feathers.co.uk   **MAP 2** B2

IN THIS Cotswold town, where hotels and pubs appear to be out-numbered only by art galleries, it is reassuring to see the owners investing in a quality-driven refurbishment of this hotel formed out of six town houses. There is a restful elegance throughout the public areas, with a delightfully secluded walled garden equipped with heated parasols for cooler evenings under the stars.

The wood-panelled restaurant is warm and intimate with fresh flowers and comfortable chairs providing a welcoming setting for concise but appetising menus evoking traditional styles with a contemporary twist. Some of the items are almost audaciously simple – soft boiled duck egg with potato 'soldiers', chicken livers on toast, or roasted Cornish halibut with peas 'à la française', but then brevity and simplicity form the house style.

The lighter lunch menu offers an exercise in economy of both method and content, but crispy-skinned bream with a creamy seafood risotto is an ideal main course after a goat's cheese salad, a tangy lemon posset and sweet pesto rounding things off nicely.

A more elaborate and adventurous evening dinner menu offers seared scallops with celeriac and white truffle oil; spiced balsamic vinegar and soy-roasted duck breast, or the speciality dish of 'twelve-hour' shoulder of lamb with rosemary sorbet.

You will still have room for finely crafted desserts without feeling you are overdoing things. An enjoyable display of restraint and consistency, served by affable and attentive staff.

Their pride: Twelve-hour shoulder of lamb with rosemary sorbet
Inexpensive wines: Chenin Blanc Boland Cellars (South Africa) 2004, £17.90; Rioja Joven Criadores 2003, £17.95

Proprietors: Bespoke Hotels
Last orders for dinner: 9.30 pm
Closed: Sunday evening, Monday
Set lunch: from £19
Set dinner: from £25
Private dining: 10-30
Al fresco dining
Accommodation: 20 rooms
Wheelchair access

WRIGHTINGTON, LANCASHIRE

Mulberry Tree

GASTROPUB

Wrightington Bar, Nr. Wigan, Lancashire WN6 9SE
Tel./Fax 01257 451 400

MAP 5 C5

THESE cavernous, ivy-clad premises that variously served as a wheelwright's, brewery and latterly a pub, have been transformed into a haven of quiet, select enjoyment. Delightfully light and airy behind leaded windows, it impresses immediately because of the spotlessness of every surface, ornament and fitting. Gleaming copper utensils, framed menus and accolades jostle for space below the light oak beams while heavy soft furnishings lend a luxurious note.

A comprehensive menu and blackboard specials offer plenty to satisfy the demands of a cosmopolitan clientele. Not that the choice is devoid of superior, often locally sourced ingredients, or evidence of the flair and technique into their preparation. Oysters, caviar, lobster and foie gras are on hand along with fillet of Scottish beef under a basil crust, roast lamb with a rosemary, honey and lavender scented jus, and plump, tender Goosnargh duckling with bramble and blackcurrant sauce.

The bar menu, in particular, adopts a more earthily traditional approach, with battered cod and chips, chargrills, Cumberland sausage and hearty lunchtime sandwiches providing more honest, homely treats.

Champagne jelly, summer pudding, panna cotta and chocolate fondant present a fitting end to what can amount to anything from a simple meal to a true banquet.

There is a reassuring feeling of consistency and class about the constantly flowering Mulberry.

Speciality food: Modern British eclectic brasserie food
Draught beers: Boddingtons, Tetleys
Average wine price by the glass: £3.75

Licensee: Mark Prescott
Last orders for dinner: 9 pm (Friday and Saturday 10 pm)
Open every day
Closed for holidays: 26 December, 1 January
Main courses: from £10.95
Beer garden
Children welcome
Wheelchair access

YATTENDON, BERKSHIRE

Royal Oak

GASTROPUB

The Square, Yattendon, Berkshire RG18 OUG
Tel. 01635 201 325 Fax 01635 201 926
e-mail: info@royaloakyattendon.com   **MAP 2** B3

THIS large, very handsome pub dominates the tiny, enchanting, genuinely Cromwellian village of Yattendon. Under one or two of its landlords many years ago, Yattendon acquired gastronomic fame that has not lived on, but it may have started on the long and arduous road back to culinary glory. The future is up to chef William Boyle, who hails from the team of the man who ran the kitchens of the Waterside Inn, Bray, for sixteen years.

The interior does not let down the impressive façade. A friendly and lively small bar opens on to the dining areas, which are an incongruous mixture of homely informality and the well-honed skill conspicuously reflected in the accomplished way the tables are laid and the swift and friendly service is conducted. The menu is the same (and so are prices) in the formal restaurant at the far end of the building, where the sophistication would be worthy of London's St. James's Street.

A superb terrine of foie gras, properly accompanied by good brioche, supports the hope of the chef's future achievements here (with a half-bottle of Alsatian Gewürtztraminer René Nuré 2002 at £16, it's a marriage made in heaven). Praiseworthy, too, are his ice-creams and sorbets, all home made.

The menu (plus blackboard) is long and interesting: one good sequence might be salade niçoise or a skate wing followed by slow-roasted belly of pork (or, for vegetarians, suitably garnished, home made tagliatelle) and roasted figs and brown sugar parfait with port wine syrup. You could have all this in the garden, or just a pre-prandial glass of local brew.

Speciality food: Game
Draught beers: West Berks Good Old Boy, Wadsworth 6X
Average wine price by the glass: £3.50

Licensee: William Boyle
Last orders for dinner: 10 pm
Open every day
Closed for holidays: 1 January
Set lunch: from £12 (Monday-Friday)
Main courses: from £15
Private dining: up to 12
Beer garden
Accommodation: 5 rooms
Children welcome   Limited wheelchair access

YORK, NORTH YORKSHIRE

Melton's Restaurant ★

7 Scarcroft Road, York YO23 1ND
Tel. 01904 634 341 Fax 01904 635 115
e-mail: greatfood@meltonsrestaurant.co.uk   **MAP 5** D4

HERE the setting may be seem to be that of one of any number of simple, sympathetic neighbourhood restaurants, but that is merely the impression you have before you taste the food. There is real gastronomic interest on the menu at Melton's, where absolutely everything is cooked to order.

Set lunches and the early dinner menu are based on excellent, bistro-style dishes such as blue cheese gnocchi with walnuts and, perhaps, confit of duck or fish kebab with warm vegetable pickle. To experience the best of the cooking, though, you must follow the carte, which changes every month.

As a starter, you might find fried duck egg with ceps on toast, then move on to fresh-caught cod, or roasted thighs of cornfed chicken in tarragon sauce, accompanied by fresh pasta and spinach, or else rack of lamb with a herb crust and parsnip purée.

The kitchen is justly proud of its desserts, which might leave you with a choice between caramelised plum and almond frangipane with vanilla ice-cream or blackberry fool served with apple sorbet in a tuile basket.

The excellent house wines come from Sicily, while the realistically priced list runs the gamut of the classics, with particularly good dessert wines.

Their pride: Saddle of Yorkshire lamb with aubergine and red pepper, Dauphinoise potatoes and rosemary jus
Inexpensive wines: Les Yeuses Sauvignon Blanc 2004, £13.50; Préférence Merlot 2004, £13.50

Proprietors: Michael and Lucy Hjort
Last orders for dinner: 10 pm
Closed: Sunday, Monday lunch
Closed for holidays: 3 weeks Christmas, 1st week Aug
Set lunch: from £19
Main courses: from £13.50
Private dining: 14–18
Al fresco dining
Limited wheelchair access

YORK, NORTH YORKSHIRE

Rish ★

7 Fossgate, York YO1 9TA
Tel. 01904 622 688 Fax 01904 671 931
e-mail: rishrestaurant@aol.com   **MAP 5** D4

IN the heart of the city, up from the Foss bridge, this modern restaurant has an unobtrusive, simple and elegant design, and the cooking shows great class and a real awareness of congenial flavour combinations that excite the palate.

A pre-starter of carrot and ginger velouté has beautifully defined flavours, the perfect appetiser. Mosaic terrines are subtly flavoured beyond their obvious prettiness, ringing the changes from duck liver, pigeon, ham hock and foie gras to a special made of lobster, salmon and leeks garnished with an intriguing lobster rouille mayonnaise. Another fine starter is duo of rabbit – confit leg and seared loin – with white pudding.

Eight typical main courses offer a choice of balance and variety: roasted Barbary duck breast, vanilla mash and figs, maybe, or roasted sea bream, pommes ecrasées, caper sauce vierge. 'Le Fleuron' guinea fowl breast, cooked en papillotte (foil), keeps all its succulence and cooking juices, enhanced by a red wine jus and an impeccable risotto of Parmesan and lemon.

Desserts show an equally well-judged balance of the innovative and the classic, as in a tonka bean panna cotta with blackcurrant foam contrasting with a very light chocolate tart and Drambuie ice-cream. Or if you are still in good shape, with your partner try the assiette of four desserts.

Wines are selected with an eye for quality and value, notably the unusual J. Lohr's Wildflower, California's answer to Beaujolais.

Their pride: Rump of Yorkshire Dales lamb, Niçoise vegetables
Inexpensive wines: Côtes du Rhône Laurent Brusset 2003, £18.50; Sauvignon Blanc Giesen Estate (Marlborough) 2004, £20.50

Proprietors: Sam and Maria Abu Rish
Last orders for dinner: 9.30 pm (Fri and Sat 10 pm)
Closed: Sunday, Monday
Closed for holidays: 3 days Christmas, 3 days Jan
Set lunch: from £15
Main courses: from £17.90
Private dining: up to 60
Children welcome
Wheelchair access

Scotland

ABERDEEN, ABERDEENSHIRE

Silver Darling

Pocra Quay, North Pier, Aberdeen, Aberdeenshire AB11 5DQ
Tel. 01224 576 229 Fax 01224 588 119

MAP 6 E3

FISHERMEN and merchant seamen are said to fix their sights on The Silver Darling between the lights of the harbour entrance. The place has been a feature of this quiet corner of the busy port for two decades now, tucked behind the harbourmaster's office.

Given these surroundings, it is not surprising that, apart from a foie gras starter and the meat of the day, Didier Dejean's menus are all to do with seafood – except for the silver darling herself, because there is no sign of the herring, the fish upon which the fortunes of Aberdeen once depended. Perhaps the boom ushered in by North Sea oil leaves no taste for such humble fare.

Instead, the menus read more like recipe books: Cocktail de Crabe avec Salade de Ratte et Ciboulette, Coulis de Betterave Acidule et Julienne de Rave Croquante. Will the plates be large enough to hold so many ingredients?

Lemon-grass marinated grilled langoustines on a red curry, apple and pak choi salad with coconut milk and ginger is another of the compilations, and steamed sea bass with a courgette chartreuse, red onions, tomatoes and young spinach shoots with a warm salad and purple basil vinaigrette.

Such treament of what is probably Britain's freshest fish seems rather exaggerated, especially when the raw materials are so well handled. An excellent fillet of gilt-head bream seemed to look on as a bit of a bystander while caramelised carrots and chicory, chanterelles and orange veal jus competed with each other.

Their pride: Grilled blue fin tuna, crushed ginger and ratte citrus, rocket salad and ginger emulsion
Inexpensive wines: La Combe de Grinou Bergerac white 2004, £18.50; Rully Premier Cru Olivier le Flaive 2003, £29.50

Proprietors: Didier Dejean and Karen Murray
Last orders for dinner: 9.30 pm
Closed: Sunday, Saturday lunch
Closed for holidays: Christmas-New Year
Main courses: from £10.50 (lunch), £19.50 (dinner)
Private dining: 6-8 in bar
Limited wheelchair access

ACHILTIBUIE, ROSS-SHIRE

Summer Isles Hotel ★

Achiltibuie, By Ullapool, Ross-shire IV26 2YG
Tel. 01854 622 282 Fax 01854 622 251
e-mail: info@summerisleshotel.co.uk   **MAP 6** C2

A COLLECTION of higgledy-piggledy shacks and bungalows makes up this village too far off the beaten track for commercial tourism. Overlooking the breathtakingly beautiful sound with its beaches, creeks and islands, it feels like the edge of the world.

The Irvines set up shop here more than thirty years ago and their son, Mark, continues in much the same vein. Home comforts more in the style of an exclusive B&B than grand hotel attract a flow of summer visitors who come to do nothing much except eat and drink, between the odd spot of walking.

In addition to the daily changing table d'hôte menu, the vast cellar, wherein lie some truly exceptional vintages, is worthy of many a more illustrious establishment. If lunch is a strikingly simple affair, intended as a no-frills showcase for the local seafood and Achiltibuie's smokehouse (oysters, crab, langoustines, lobster and salmon), the evening menu runs the gamut of regional produce.

A filo parcel of langoustine tails with tamarind sauce, perhaps, or lamb, beef and venison – the latter roasted with pancetta and juniper – from the surrounding hills and glens. Or there is halibut, locally smoked haddock, organic Shetland salmon and, of course, the fabulous array of shellfish. Who needs elaborate preparation and presentation?

Finish with a fine summer pudding of red berries from the sweet trolley and retire to the comfortable little lounge in a reflective and satisfied mood as the sun goes down over the water.

Their pride: Local seafood
Inexpensive wines: Mâcon Uchizy Domaine Talmard 2002, £16.50; Fronsac Château La Vieille Croix 1999, £18.40

Proprietors: Mark and Gerry Irvine
Last orders for dinner: 8 pm
Open every day
Closed for holidays: Mid October - end March
Set dinner: from £47
Accommodation: 12 rooms
Wheelchair access

AIRD UIG, ISLE OF LEWIS

Bonaventure

Aird Uig, Isle of Lewis HS2 9JA
Tel. 01851 672 474
e-mail: jo@bonaventurelewis.co.uk   **MAP 6** B1

ENDLESS miles of open skies and barren moorland, passing turf cutters, and countless lochs (often full of water lilies) lead to the front door of what was a clifftop RAF base during the Cold War.

Since those days, of course, the tourists have moved in, but Bonaventure does not just tick over during the summer and close for the rest of the year. With a bit of help from the awe-inspiring countryside around it, the Breton owners have worked wonders in transforming this once forlorn military outpost.

The Auld Alliance lives on in an eclectic menu of Franco-Scottish dishes, where even Cajun venison makes an appearance among the starters, in honour of the original Bonaventure in Quebec, alongside toasted goat's cheese and Stornoway black pudding, monkfish with garlic crumbs and even a popular haggis crêpe with sweet red chilli.

The French influence comes more to the fore in the saucing of main courses, with, say, cranberry, mushroom and red wine on the perfectly judged Barbary duck, honey and rum on the loin of local lamb and a mild curry and lime leaves to spice up scallops.

Home-made ice-creams, plus a deliciously rich, creamy toffee, accompany expertly handled desserts such as the warm banana sponge or lemon crêpe.

This place is just made for quiet, informal enjoyment, with the local larder providing most ingredients and Breton savoir-faire putting them to excellent use.

Their pride: Haggis crêpe with sweet chilli sauce
Inexpensive wines: Vouvray Ph. De Sivray 2002, £16.25; Côtes du Rhône Lysis 2001/2, £15.50

Proprietors: Richard and Jo Leperoux
Last orders for dinner: 9 pm
Closed: lunchtime, Sun dinner, Mon for non-residents
Closed for holidays: February
Set dinner: £26.95
Accommodation: 5 rooms
Wheelchair access

AUCHTERARDER, PERTHSHIRE

Andrew Fairlie at Gleneagles ★★

**The Gleneagles Hotel, Auchterarder, Perthshire PH3 1NF
Tel. 01764 694 267 Fax 01764 694 163
e-mail: andrew.fairlie@gleneagles.com**   **MAP 6** D4

TO THE maxim that there are those who seek celebrity status and those who have it thrust upon them one could add, 'and those who earn it through sheer dedication and hard work'. Mix this with equal measures of technical know-how and artistic flair and the recipe for success is complete.

Perhaps, though, 'celebrity' is not quite the right term in Andrew Fairlie's case, for it is difficult to imagine a more discreet, soft-spoken ambassador for the cause of excellence. And despite the opulence of the legendary monolith in which he has set up shop, his little corner of it is not a place of brash ostentation.

The menu, set out rather like a fine art brochure, merely hints at what is to come rather than divulging the whole story. Chou farci of crab, langoustine cappuccino; potato and truffle gnocchi, wild mushrooms and Parmesan; assiette de porc Gascony, jus rôti; textures of chocolate – the descriptions do not give much away. It is only when you see the 'pictures' themselves that the breadth of their content becomes evident.

Combinations of marked, wholly natural individual perfumes and savours tend to creep up on your senses, as in the hint of vanilla in creamed parsnip or else a few drops of lemon or truffle oil to help bring out the intrinsic qualities of superb raw materials.

The staff deserve a special mention and obviously share their mentor's passion for good living. Without a dress code, feel free to come as you are – perhaps at the end of a hard day's driving, chipping and putting – and simply enjoy the experience.

Their pride: Home-smoked lobster with herb and lime butter sauce
Inexpensive wines: Pinot Blanc Barriques Domaine Ostertag 2002, £26; Salice Salentino Cantine due Palme 2001, £25

**Proprietor: Andrew Fairlie
Last orders for dinner: 10 pm
Closed: Sunday
Closed for holidays: 3 weeks January
Set dinner: from £60**
Wheelchair access

BALLACHULISH, ARGYLL

Ballachulish House ★

Ballachulish, Argyll PH49 4JX
Tel. 01855 811 266 Fax 01855 811 498
e-mail: mclaughlins@btconnect.com   MAP 6 C3

IF YOU are looking for the real Scotland – perhaps a glimpse into a bygone age in the form of a laird's lodge, complete with plain polished tables, tartans and a piper – venture no further than the shores of Loch Linnhe, not far from Glencoe. There you will receive the warmest of Scottish welcomes from Marie McLaughlin as she opens the door to 17th-century Ballachulish House, a place she loves to share with her guests.

But don't be deceived by the old-fashioned gentility of the setting. Ballachulish House is steadily acquiring a reputation as a gastronomic institution. Husband and wife team Allan and Eileen Donald produce set menus (they offer a main course choice only in the evening) that feature local raw materials and testify to their skills, honed at Inverlochy Castle, Gleneagles and elsewhere.

Their ability to bring the best out of high-quality ingredients in dishes of simplicity and finesse is amply demonstrated by the five-course dinner menu. The traditional heartiness of the spring onion risotto with butternut squash and seared scallops, roasted saddle and braised shoulder of lamb, or fillet of Mallaig turbot with lobster, is tempered by a light touch that achieves a harmonious balance complemented by attractive presentation.

The pride the Donalds take in their work is evident even in a straightforward Jerusalem artichoke cappuccino, or the tender house-smoked duck with a light liver parfait and onion confit.

Their pride: Roast turbot with Loch Linnhe langoustines
Inexpensive wines: Cranswick Smith Shiraz/Merlot (Australia) 2003, £20.75; Old Vines Chenin Blanc (South Africa) 2003, £19.95

Proprietor: Marie McLaughlin
Last orders for dinner: 7.30 pm
Open every day
Closed for holidays: 2 weeks January
Set lunch: from £21.50
Set dinner: from £44
Private dining: 10-32
Accommodation: 8 rooms
Wheelchair access

BALLATER, ABERDEENSHIRE

Darroch Learg Hotel & Restaurant

Braemar Road, Ballater, Aberdeenshire AB35 5UX
Tel. 01339 755 443 Fax 01339 755 252
e-mail: info@darrochlearg.co.uk   **MAP 6** D3

ISOLATED, healthy and, more importantly, appetite-inducing walks around Deeside and the slopes of Craigendarroch are a must when spending time in this gloriously unspoilt corner of the Highlands, before adjourning to the 'oak wood on a sunny hill-side', as its name translates, a former private residence with a personal feel still much in evidence.

You are immediately cosseted by its traditional, understated style, heavy armchairs and comfortable sofas round the drawing room fire in winter, colourful soft furnishings, bookshelves full of tomes of local interest and even a pile of board games in one corner. The ideal setting in which to peruse a short but adequately varied, regularly changing menu that follows seasonal availability and makes the most of the local produce and west coast seafood.

Highland beef, moorland lamb, Deeside hare, pigeon and local sea trout are afforded respect in their treatment throughout a range of traditionally-inspired dishes which still manage to display the odd twist of ingenuity.

Roasted calf's sweetbreads make an appetising starter, served on purée of Jerusalem artichoke with a mushroom tuile, pungently perfumed tortellini of Arbroath smokie and scallops in Sauternes sauce with curry oil, before a juicy breast of guinea fowl with broad beans and morels or fillet of beef with an oxtail and wild mushroom jus.

Desserts include classic tarts or a refreshing iced tiramisù terrine.

Their pride: Fillet of Highland beef with horse-radish risotto, caramelised root vegetable and oxtail sauce
Inexpensive wines: Old Vines Chenin Blanc (South Africa) 1998/99, £19; Château Jonqueyres (France) 2001, £21

Proprietors: Nigel and Fiona Franks
Last orders for dinner: 9 pm
Open every day
Closed for holidays: Christmas, 3 weeks January
Set lunch: from £22 (Sunday)
Set dinner: from £38
Accommodation: 17 rooms
Wheelchair access

BALQUHIDDER, PERTHSHIRE

Monachyle Mhor ★

Balquhidder, Perthshire FK19 8PQ
Tel. 01877 384 622 Fax 01877 384 305
e-mail: info@monachylemhor.com   **MAP 6** C4

TWENTY-ODD years ago the Lewises fell in love with Monachyle Mhor and, despite being occasionally cut off by snow or landslides, they find such natural hazards are a small price to pay for waking up each morning in the midst of a gloriously unspoilt wilderness spreading out round two neighbouring lochs. Visitors to the hotel, too, have the opportunity to enjoy the magnificent spectacle from the conservatory dining-room.

No doubt inspired by the landscape, Tom Lewis is never at a loss for ideas of what to do with the determinedly local produce. The seasonally changing menu is limited: one soup, three or four starters and three main courses. The choice will usually include fish, which might be baked fillet of turbot with roasted tomato and ginger chutney, or else seared skate wing with the interesting accompaniment of a rich meat jus, celeriac and capers.

Meat – especially the local lamb – is handled with equal aplomb, accompanied by such things as confit of sweet potato and seared kidneys, while the almost obligatory smoked salmon might come with a salsa of beetroot and lime and marinated leeks. Even after such a long tenure, Tom has lost none of his passion and the style of his cooking has certainly developed with the times.

The content and presentation of such elaborate dishes are impressive, and are obviously appreciated by the clientele even in such a traditional setting. It is interesting to note that stylishly modern desserts featuring several elements are more successful than the conservative, nutty crumble that is also on offer.

Their pride: Glen Almond rabbit rillette with loin of rabbit, apple, red chicory and Mizuna salad
Inexpensive wines: Vendimia Excepcional Con Class (Spain) 2002, £13; Corbières Château de Cabriac 2001, £15

Proprietor: Tom Lewis
Last orders for dinner: 8.45pm (Sunday 8.30pm)
Open every day
Closed for holidays: January-February
Set lunch: from £25
Set dinner: from £39
Private dining: up to 14
Al fresco dining
Accommodation: 11 rooms
Wheelchair access

BOWMORE, ISLE OF ISLAY

Harbour Inn

GASTROPUB

The Square, Bowmore, Isle of Islay PA43 7JR
Tel. 01496 810 330 Fax 01496 810 990
e-mail: info@harbour-inn.com   **MAP 6** B4

AFTER a guided tour of one of Islay's celebrated distilleries, why not join the locals in the tiny snug bar for a wee dram before lunch or dinner in this old inn, just a few steps from the quayside?

Renovated a few years ago, it retains a family atmosphere amid the elegant charm of bright, well-kept public areas, their wide bay windows looking out over the sea.

The lobster pots stacked up on the harbour wall give an indication of the delights you can expect in the neat little dining-room (book early for a window seat) and the remarkable range, especially in the evening, offers an impressive epicurean tour of the island's larder, from Loch Gruinart oysters, Loch Etive mussels, Lagavulin scallops, halibut, monkfish, Islay beef and lamb and Dunlossit pork.

Small really is beautiful, with the outstanding natural quality of produce farmed on a miniature scale, or brought ashore by the local fleet of tiny boats, needing little enhancement.

A dash of cream sauce or a beurre blanc here, a light tomato and basil coulis there, the interest and variety that is brought to bear never becomes extravagant or showy and, while crab soufflé, seafood chowder, or a chicken and walnut terrine are on hand to demonstrate the chef's capabilities, visitors might well want to stick to the natural approach for a real taste of the local treasures.

Chocolate terrine, iced cranachan (Scots for trifle) parfait and lemon brûlée to finish – along with maybe a peaty malt.

Speciality food: Local seafood
Draught beers: Bellhaven Best, Bellhaven Export
Average wine price by the glass: £3.15

Licensees: Neil and Carol Scott
Last orders for dinner: 9 pm
Open every day
Closed for holidays: 25 and 26 December
Main courses: from £7.95 (lunch), £17.25 (dinner)
Beer garden
Accommodation: 7 rooms
Children welcome

CAWDOR, NAIRNSHIRE

Cawdor Tavern

GASTROPUB

Cawdor, Nairnshire IV12 5XP
Tel. 01667 404 777
e-mail: cawdortavern@btopenworld.com   **MAP 6** D2

THIS old building, once the joiners' workshop of the nearby castle and now the unofficial headquarters of the village bowling club, is a staunch defender of Scots values. Eat on the terrace if weather permits, but this being north of the Border you are more likely to find yourself in the cosily formal dining-room with Highland prints, oak settles and a bubbly, family atmosphere.

You are in for a real taste of Scotland brought gingerly up to date, with its roots still firmly embedded in Hibernian turf. Haggis and black and white puddings abound in many forms and the use of local ingredients is proudly predominant.

Continental influences make timorous appearances with the likes of bruschetta, risotto, or Parmesan gnocchi. More likely to warm the cockles of your heart and set the bagpipes ringing in your ears are home-made haggis dumplings in a whisky cream sauce; a tiered terrine of black and white puddings and haggis; superbly succulent beef collops on a haggis mousseline (a pity about the rather overpowering 'jus'); Scottish steaks; Morayshire pork with a mustard and heather honey sauce, or chicken breast 'Culloden' stuffed with – you've guessed it – haggis.

Despite inevitable heartiness, they manage to instill finesse and panache through the use of these traditional ingredients without spoiling their intrinsic values.

It all adds up to a thoroughly satisfying experience in which the welcome – even for the English – is warm and inviting.

Speciality food: Scottish
Draught beers: Stagg Bitter, Tradewinds
Average wine price by the glass: £2.95

Licensee: Norman Sinclair
Last orders for dinner: 9 pm
Open every day
Closed for holidays: 25 December, 1 January
Main courses: from £9.95
Beer garden
Children welcome
Wheelchair access

COLBOST, ISLE OF SKYE

Three Chimneys ★

Colbost, Nr. Dunvegan, Isle of Skye IV55 8ZT
Tel. 01470 511 258 Fax 01470 511 358
e-mail: eatandstay@threechimneys.co.uk   **MAP 6** B2

IMAGINE going to your bank manager with the idea of taking a remote cottage in this island paradise and turning it into a viable restaurant-with-rooms, adding that you have no experience in the hospitality business. Imagine, too, twenty years later, someone phoning a fortnight ahead for a table on a Monday evening in the middle of November to be told that there is just one left.

Over the years the accolades and customers have poured in and Shirley and Eddie Spear now find themselves leading lights of the burgeoning Scottish restaurant scene.

This success story is entirely the result of a dogged belief in their project and of Shirley's skills in the kitchen. Her creed is simple: 'I take all this fabulous food from nature's local larder and do nothing with it.' Technical skill, flair and inspiration make it all work and all are apparent throughout a meal here.

Seafood is limitless – diver scallops, oysters, lobster, crab, turbot, halibut, prawns and salmon – while poultry, wildfowl, meats and game are all to hand. There are even local supplies of organic salad and every kind of vegetable.

The style is not French, or particularly nouvelle or classical, but straightforward assemblages of complementary ingredients just pointed up with a touch of sherry sauce here, a gamey gravy there, or the likes of a light lemon and olive oil vinaigrette used to sauce the main-course warm salad of duck with scallops. Unpretentious and homely are the order of the day.

Their pride: Roast saddle of wild rabbit and hare
Inexpensive wines: Domaine de Laballe de Terroirs Landais (France) 2004, £17.95; Lopez Cristobal, Ribera del Duero (Spain) 2003, £21.75

Proprietors: Eddie and Shirley Spear
Last orders for dinner: 9.30 pm
Closed: Sunday lunch; lunch during winter
Closed for holidays: 1 week Dec, 3 weeks Jan
Set lunch: from £18.50
Set dinner: from £45
Al fresco dining
Accommodation: 6 rooms
Wheelchair access

CRINAN, ARGYLL

Crinan Hotel, Panthers Arms `GASTROPUB`

Crinan, By Loch Gilphead, Argyll PA31 8SR
Tel. 01546 830 261 Fax 01546 830 292
e-mail: nryan@crinanhotel.com   **MAP 6** C4

CAN there be anywhere better for a pre-dinner drink on a warm summer's evening than this tranquil little terrace, watching the day draw to a close as the sun goes down over the loch and the distant hills of Mull? The Crinan Hotel and its neat little bar is the undisputed focal point of this tiny, lochside village, offering a warmly hospitable haven.

Flamboyant proprietor Nick Ryan, rarely seen without a bow tie, has been at the helm for nearly four decades and is fully intent on maintaining the traditional, slightly quirky values that have been the hallmark of his extended watch. A maritime theme runs through the comfortable public areas, with elegant panelling in the bar and stunning views from the main dining-room.

It is no surprise that the surrounding waters provide the main theme of the restricted bar selection and on the more formal, daily changing restaurant menu. In the latter, Loch Fyne scallops, langoustine bisque, Loch Crinan prawns and line-caught halibut sit alongside rabbit and foie gras terrine, wood pigeon with braised fennel, and fillet of Buccleuch beef.

You can turn a snack into a full meal of no lesser quality in the bar, with such things as steamed mussels, Arbroath smokies, steaks, splendid sausages and enjoyably original dishes such as scallop tart with bacon and goat's cheese cream.

The Crinan Hotel is something of a gem in a landscape that is a national treasure.

Speciality food: Local seafood
Draught beers: Bellhaven Best, Tennents Velvet
Average wine price by the glass: £3.75

Licensee: Nick Ryan
Last orders for dinner: 8.30 pm
Open every day
Closed for holidays: Christmas to end January
Main courses: from £9.95
Private dining: 20-60
Beer garden
Accommodation: 20 rooms
Children welcome
Wheelchair access

CRINAN, ARGYLL

Crinan Hotel, Westward Restaurant

Crinan Hotel, Loch Gilphead, Argyll PA31 8SR
Tel. 01546 830 261 Fax 01546 830 292
e-mail: nryan@crinanhotel.com   **MAP 6** C4

DASH and spirit are the words that perhaps best sum up the atmosphere of a meal here. They seem to serve four courses in record time. The results, however, are thoroughly enjoyable

The menu is short: five starters, soup, three main courses and a couple of desserts, but within the limitations there are interesting and innovative ideas.

Roasted Loch Fyne scallops, risotto of Shetland crab, pan-fried sea bass or local lamb are straightforward enough, but the more imaginative side of the cooking shows itself in the likes of sautéd oysters on duck-fat potatoes with pickled carrot and spiced chips, which is a splendid miscellany of flavours and textures worthy of many a more illustrious setting.

Tomato and sage soup, baked in the oven under a featherlight pie-crust, was as fruity as it can be and the loin of nicely pink and tender Barbreck lamb, with its rather tasty aubergine caviar and an over-crisp rösti, was a more than respectable main course.

They warn you that the bitter chocolate saveur will take as long as eight minutes, then, after cinnamon parfait with caramelised roasted fruits and a plum granité, you are already on your way back to the lounge for coffee.

Their pride: Whole Loch Crinan jumbo prawns
Inexpensive wines: Viura/Chardonnay Castillo de Montblanc (Spain) 2003, £19.50; Merlot Les Souches Vin de Pays d'Oc 2003, £19.50

Proprietor: Nicholas Ryan
Last orders for dinner: 9 pm
Open every day
Closed for holidays: Christmas and New Year
Set dinner: from £45
Main courses: from £10.95
Private dining: 10-20
Al fresco dining
Accommodation: 20 rooms
Wheelchair access

CROSSMICHAEL, DUMFRIES & GALLOWAY

Plumed Horse ★

Crossmichael, Nr. Castle Douglas, Dumfries & Galloway DG7 3AU
Tel. 01556 670 333
e-mail: plumedhorse@aol.com   **MAP 6** D5

THE journey to this smart, serious restaurant in a sleepy village in the wilds of southern Scotland is always worth it. There is real talent at work behind the door marked 'Danger – Men Cooking'.

From solidly classical foundations, evident in fine mousselines, moist, meaty terrines and knowledgeable handling of local meats and fish, chef/patron Tony Borthwick has developed a style that is highly individual.

Single dishes often comprise two or more elements that involve differing cookery styles in tandem. Good examples are celeriac and chive soup with smoked haddock ravioli; partridge that is poached and roasted; pan-fried fillet of Aberdeen Angus beef accompanied by slow-braised shoulder, and fillet of salmon with a white chocolate and Parmesan crust that is served with a boudin of langoustines.

There are more interesting combinations of flavour, too, in the crisp, colourful vegetables that abound in the garnishes of these imaginative compilations.

It must have required almost missionary zeal to start a restautant like this in such a remote setting, but, some six years and a host of accolades later, people are beating a path to Tony's two little dining-rooms, where the welcome is warm, the atmosphere is relaxed and the service delightfully affable.

Their pride: Foie gras trifle, Banyuls raisins
Inexpensive wines: Sancerre Domaine de la Grand Maison 2003, £26; Gigondas J. Vidal-Fleury 1998, £25

Proprietor: Tony Borthwick
Last orders for dinner: 8pm (9pm if busy)
Closed: Sunday dinner, Monday
Closed for holidays: 2 weeks Jan, 2 weeks Sept
Set lunch: from £21
Main courses: from £19
Private dining: 8-24
Wheelchair access

DALRY, NORTH AYRSHIRE

Braidwoods ★

Drumastle Mill Cottage, Dalry, North Ayrshire KA2 44LN
Tel. 01294 833 544 Fax 01294 833 553
e-mail: kandnbraidwood@braidwoods.co.uk   **MAP 6** C4

THIS whitewashed cottage set among rolling hills is a haven of calm cordiality where you feel instantly at ease, its popularity the result in no small measure of the warm welcome offered by Nicola and Keith Braidwood and the general easygoing atmosphere.

And then, of course, there is the food, straightforward and yet deftly prepared, the unassuming nature of the dishes on Keith's daily set menus showing no sign of the careful thought that goes into their conception and execution.

A traditional liver pâté becomes something rich and rare with the addition of a little foie gras, a toasted sultana brioche and an accompaniment of gooseberry chutney. Similarly, a creamy soup of pumpkin and squash is transformed by means of the Parmesan and truffle oil used to set it off.

As is only to be expected, local crab, scallops and fish are regular features, but in their cases, too, the excellence of the ingredients stimulates the imagination, so that grilled halibut, for example, is served with a risotto of smoked salmon and roasted fennel.

As for meat dishes, Scottish lamb comes with a rosemary jus but also with ratatouille, while tender fillet of pork is given a stuffing of black pudding, and the game in season is handled with restraint and respect.

Among desserts, the most delicate bread pudding, which is served with custard and home-made ice-cream, is highly recommended.

Their pride: Roast best end of Ayrshire lamb with neck fillet stew
Inexpensive wines: Viognier Domaine Galetis 2003, £18.95; Carmenere Santa Ema (Chile) 2003, £17.95

Proprietors: Nicola and Keith Braidwood
Last orders for dinner: 9pm
Closed: Sunday, Monday, Tuesday lunch (open lunch Sunday October-April)
Closed for holidays: 25 & 26 December, 3 weeks Jan, 2 weeks Sept
Set lunch: from £17
Set dinner: from £33
Wheelchair access

DUNKELD, PERTHSHIRE

Kinnaird ★

Kinnaird Estate, by Dunkeld, Perthshire PH8 0LB
Tel. 01796 482 440 Fax 01796 482 289
e-mail: enquiry@kinnairdestate.com   **MAP 6** D3

KINNAIRD is an apparently thriving, living and working Scottish estate of the old school. Despite its grandeur, the opulence of the heavy drapes, its big open fireplaces and the family trophies and heirlooms, the owner, Constance Ward, has managed to maintain an invitingly accessible appeal in what is still very much a family home.

For residents, especially, it is the sort of place to relax over a game of snooker or backgammon, tinkle on the baby grand piano or simply enjoy an unhurried chat away from it all. It is a place, above all, to be enjoyed and nowhere more than *à table*, most particularly from the bay window overlooking the Tay valley.

This cool, refined setting provides the perfect background for a comprehensive compendium of gastronomic themes featuring scallops, halibut, sea bass, duckling, game in season. Lunch tends to be a straightforward affair and it was nice to see the humble pig respected with a perfectly crispy-skinned, tender belly and hearty braised cheek on a bed of spinach with al dente crosnes (Chinese artichokes).

There are, however, bursts of bravado, too, so don't be surprised to find stuffed rabbit with cardamom and chorizo, organic duckling with Szechuan pepper, roasted squash and beetroot, or braised pig's head with crispy ears, among more mundane but equally well-executed terrines, roasted fish, crumbles and even a sticky toffee pudding.

Their pride: Saddle of mountain hare, stuffed savoy cabbage cooked with coconut, beetroot and chutney sauce
Inexpensive wines: Chablis Joseph Drouhin 2003, £21; Pinotage Winemakers Reserve Babich Hawkes Bay 2000, £21

Proprietor: Constance Ward
Last orders for dinner: 9.30 pm
Open every day
Set lunch: from £21
Set dinner: from £50
Private dining: up to 20
Accommodation: 9 rooms
Wheelchair access

DUNNING, PERTHSHIRE

Kirkstyle Inn

Kirkstyle Square, Dunning, Perthshire PH2 0RR
Tel. 01764 684 248 Fax 01764 684 695

MAP 6 D4

THE great and good, when they are not gracing the lush fairways of nearby Gleneagles (or putting the world to rights within the hallowed portals of its hotel), could do worse than to drop down a notch or two for a bit of local colour in this square-set, village centre inn.

Something of an epitome of the genre, acting as community focal point and tourist attraction, the dining-room attracts groups of Americans in search of a genuine taste of Scotland. No one is a stranger in the lively front bar, while the quieter dining-room at the rear offers the perfect setting for a comprehensive selection of well-executed food on both menu and blackboard – though you can eat among the drinkers if ambience is what you are after.

Scottishness abounds, with a range of supper dishes, copious snacks and pub favourites such as steak and ale pie or roast pork fillet with haggis and black pudding, but there is also a more eclectic selection with many influences, characterised by maybe roasted goat's cheese, tempura battered prawns with a garlic dip, or Cajun chicken.

Solid reliability is perhaps more prevalent than originality, but even a humble liver pâté is light, creamy and full of flavour and a generous portion of fillet of local venison was beautifully tender.

A fairly standard choice of nursery desserts, including raspberry cranachan, reminds us once again that we are north of the Border.

Speciality food: Fresh fish and local game in season
Draught beers: 70 Shilling Bitter, Deuchars IPA
Average wine price by the glass: £2.20

Licensees: Michael and Susan Lee
Last orders for dinner: 9 pm
Open every day
Main courses: from £6.95
Beer garden
Children welcome
Wheelchair access

EDINBURGH

King's Wark

36 The Shore, Leith, Edinburgh, Midlothian EH6 6QU
Tel. 0131 554 9260

MAP 6 D4

THIS Grade A listed building, once James I's private residence and armoury and later a Black Plague hospital, naturally evokes an historical atmopsphere well beyond the capabilities of even the most creative interior designer.

Full marks, too, for the refreshing honesty and vitality that comes from the impossibly small kitchen.

Fish plays an all-important role. Steamed mussels and clams or the house seafood plate are popular starters, along with peppered tuna with a mango, ginger and basil salad. Even sardines are given a terrific lift with pink peppercorn and lemon hollandaise.

More seafood might include a plain, pan-fried fillet of fine sea bass with a few scallops and chorizo in a tangy lime vinaigrette, or cod with smoked paprika feta and almond pesto

Roast duck breast with lentils and a sherry dressing, or medallions of venison with roast artichoke and a raspberry and mint coulis, are on offer for the carnivores. The much simpler desserts appear to be something of an afterthought.

What you see is very much what you get – scrumptious, candid flavours providing the very essence of the enjoyment.

Cooks such as these should be Grade A listed, too.

Speciality food: Contemporary Scottish fish dishes
Draught beers: Deuchars IPA, Caledonian 80 Shilling
Average wine price by the glass: £2.90

Licensee: Nick Donald
Last orders for dinner: 9.45 pm
Open every day
Closed for holidays: 25-26 December, 1 January
Main courses: from £6.50
Children welcome

EDINBURGH

Martin Wishart ★★

54 The Shore, Leith, Edinburgh EH6 6RA
Tel. 0131 553 3557 Fax 0131 467 7091
e-mail: info@martin-wishart.co.uk   **MAP 6** D4

MARTIN WISHART brings his artistic talent to Edinburgh's modest Rive Gauche in the largely revamped port area, with its galleries, buzzing nightlife and its lively, cosmopolitan feel. Very much on display to the world, the 'shop' front of his smart, businesslike dining-room overlooks the Water of Leith.

The style here is intentionally formal as you settle down to enjoy the master's latest works. And from the first amuse-bouche to the last bite of a heavenly dessert, you sometimes wonder if these dishes are meant to be eaten or framed. The aromas and colours of each one creep over your senses in unison before getting to work on the palate.

There is evidence of constant research into new combinations and experimentation and a great deal of time must be spent at the planning and 'interior designing' stage, illustrating the passion for an excellence that relies on solid, well-founded values.

The lobster tortellini simply exploded with richly perfumed flavours from the finest of velvety fillings, a contrast of textures provided by the lone slice of brioche-coated pig's trotter, before a traditionally styled roast fillet of the most tender veal imaginable, its braised oxtail and wild mushroom garnish redolent of powerful meat juices.

An almond and plum tart of intricacy, precision and real depth of natural flavour brought this exhibition of sophisticated talent to a suitable climax.

Their pride: Lobster and smoked haddock soufflé, lobster cappuccino
Inexpensive wines: Pernand Vergelesses (France) 2003, £34; Coudoulet de Beaucastel 2001, £35

Proprietor: Martin Wishart
Last orders for dinner: 10 pm
Closed: Sunday and Monday
Closed for holidays: Christmas, 1 January, 1 week Feb
Set lunch: from £22.50
Set dinner: from £50
Wheelchair access

No. 3

3 Royal Terrace, Edinburgh EH7 5AB
Tel./Fax 0131 477 4747

MAP 6 D4

A SHORT, brisk walk from the bustle of Prince's Street, there is a peace and tranquillity about this elegant, elevated, colonnaded crescent overlooking tranquil gardens that detach it physically and metaphorically from the hubbub below.

The high-ceilinged main dining-room, dominated by more columns framing the bar area and huge chandeliers, lend quite an opulent note to a setting of contemporary sophistication.

The menu is a model of restrained classicism, designed to appeal to a wide clientele among whom prime Scottish steaks in various cuts and guises, simply grilled and served with a variety of sauces and excellent, hand-cut chips, are a particular favourite.

There is more than a hint of native showcasing in the Shetland mussels; a deliciously traditional cullen skink; a filo pastry parcel of haggis; Scottish salmon, of course (given a new twist here with the addition of a pineapple salsa), or local fish such as the pan-fried sea bass with rösti and a mustard and Parmesan sauce. Smoked chicken and butternut squash risotto was well executed.

A thoroughly enjoyable dish of roast duck breast with cannelloni beans would have been immeasurably improved by a garnish more creative than the somewhat unnecessary Toulouse sausage, good as it was, and a few new potatoes.

Their pride: Prime Scottish steaks
Inexpensive wines: Sauvignon Blanc Montana Timara NV (New Zealand) 2003, £16.95; Rioja Viña Alcorta NV (Spain) 2002, £18.95

Proprietor: Nigel Cameron Hogg
Last orders for dinner: 10 pm
Open every day
Set lunch: from £13.95
Set dinner: from £13.95 (until 7.30 pm)
Private dining: 10-40

EDINBURGH

Number One ★

The Balmoral Hotel, 1 Princes Street, Edinburgh EH2 2EQ
Tel. 0131 557 6727 Fax 0131 557 3747
e-mail: numberone@thebalmoralhotel.com   **MAP 6** D4

WITH an address as prestigious as this, the reputation of a restaurant cannot fail to be constantly in play. But the proficiency and dedication of the talented team at the famous Balmoral Hotel, a mere haggis's throw from the Scott Monument, ensures that their good name is never tarnished.

There is a 'society' feel about surroundings that are surprisingly spacious and airy. Clean lines and tints of beige and gold add to the classy environment, with half-moon seating round circular tables worthy of a glitzy Hollywood movie. Smooth, professional, but engagingly affable service is exactly what is required of the setting, as is the stylish and innovative food.

Turbot, scallops, langoustines, game, beef and lamb vie with Anjou pigeon and French rabbit for a place among top ingredients. All are put to excellent use on a continually evolving, extensive menu that spoils you for choice and titillates with its descriptions. There are scallops with white truffle risotto and croustillant wafer; white crab meat layered with pasta, avocado and vine tomato with mango jelly; halibut with smoked brandade beignets, red wine sauce and pancetta foam; roast beef fillet with curried oxtail, spinach and lie de vin sauce.

The results certainly match expectations. A well-integrated and loyal team produce dishes that show not only solid, traditional dependability but also ingenuity and imagination, entirely without gimmickry. This is impressive stuff in both quality and variety. A tasting menu helps people who just cannot make up their minds.

Their pride: Poached Scottish lobster, baby artichokes, saffron cocotte with shellfish sauce
Inexpensive wines: Olivier Leflaive Les Sétilles Burgundy Blanc 2003, £26; Santa Ema Maipo Valley Merlot Reserve 2002, £27.50

Proprietor: Sir Rocco Forte
Last orders for dinner: 10 pm
Open every day
Closed for holidays: 2 weeks in January
Set lunch: from £18.95
Main courses: from £25
Accommodation: 186 rooms
Wheelchair access

ELIE, FIFE

Sangster's ★

51 High Street, Elie, Fife KY9 1BZ
Tel./Fax 01333 331 001
e-mail: bruce@sangsters.co.uk   **MAP 6** E4

MORE THAN thirty years at the forefront of a demanding industry have not dampened Bruce Sangster's enthusiasm, which in fact seems stronger than ever now that he has his own restaurant. How considerate of him to treat his clients to the culmination of a career's work rather than oblige them to follow his learning curve!

And 'treat' is the word at this neat little town-centre hostelry only a few yards from unspoilt, sandy beaches. Like the simply laid-out interior under the auspices of Jacquie Sangster, nothing is out of place, nothing jars during a meal of remarkably even quality and apparently effortless endeavour. Concise but varied menus change constantly and follow seasonal and local availability, with often a touch of some unusual spice or other exotica to give added colour to top-quality ingredients.

For example, Isle of Mull scallops might come with bang bang noodles and chilli, while roasted cumin squash and aubergine caviar add a certain excitement to breast of guinea fowl. A superb piece of firm, tender halibut with basil pesto oozed raw, fresh savour, with crisply fried, tempura-battered onion rings providing a well-judged additional texture.

A dessert of brioche and sultana brûlée was perhaps slightly less successful, but there will always be minor hiccups in a constant search for new ideas and perfection. The intimate surroundings and the husband and wife influence help to create a hospitable atmosphere with the stamp of true professionalism. Generous pricing tops an already scrumptious cake.

Their pride: Slow-braised noisette of lamb
Inexpensive wines: Kanu Sauvignon Blanc (South Africa) 2004, £19.25; Villa Antinori Rosso Marchesi Antinori 2001, £22

Proprietors: Bruce and Jacqueline Sangster
Last orders for dinner: 9.30 pm
Closed: Lunch Monday, Tuesday and Saturday, dinner Sunday
Closed for holidays: 3 weeks Jan, 1 week Nov
Set lunch: from £16.75
Set dinner: from £25
Wheelchair access

FORT WILLIAM, HIGHLANDS

Inverlochy Castle ★

Torlundy, Fort William, Highlands PH33 6SN
Tel. 01397 702 177 Fax 01397 702 953
e-mail: bookings@inverlochy.co.uk   **MAP 6** C3

QUEEN VICTORIA 'never saw a lovelier or more romantic spot' and dear old Lord Abinger really did have it made in terms of the setting chosen for his stately seat. In the shelter of Ben Nevis and surrounded by some of Scotland's wildest and most spectacular scenery, this Victorian castle, transformed from a private home into a hotel some thirty years ago, epitomises gracious living on an almost operatic scale.

The huge choice of fine, locally produced ingredients gives the kitchen a head start, and these are handled with evident ability that combines a modern approach with respect for the traditional values.

A touch of Mediterranean sun comes with roasted Skye scallops and a tomato and smoked mozzarella salad, or sautéd cannon of lamb with green olive tapenade, or yet pan-fried monkfish tail with fennel rösti and chorizo sausage.

A terrine of home-smoked salmon is given a new twist with its garnish of vegetable tempura and wasabi, while the rather more conventional roast pigeon is enhanced by vanilla scented risotto. Plainer items include poached veal fillet with carrot purée and grilled turbot with salsify and foie gras.

It is worth noting that the dessert selection at lunchtime comes second to what is available in the evening, and dinner generally is a grander and more vibrant occasion.

Their pride: Home-smoked marinated tuna, crushed avocado, cucumber sorbet and curry mayonnaise
Inexpensive wines: Bordeaux Sauvignon Blanc Château du Cros 2002, £30; De Wetshof Chardonnay 2003, £30

Proprietor: Inverlochy Castle Limited
Last orders for dinner: 9 pm
Open every day
Closed for holidays: 8 January–4 February
Set lunch: from £23.50
Set dinner: from £52.50
Private dining: up to 20
Accommodation: 18 rooms

GAIRLOCH, ROSS-SHIRE

The Old Inn

GASTROPUB

Flowerdale, Gairloch, Ross-shire IV21 2BD
Tel. 01445 712 006 Fax 01445 714 445
e-mail: info@theoldinn.net   **MAP 6** C2

FOR nearly three hundred years, sailors have been mooring their boats and crossing the road to the welcoming warmth of this aptly named inn with the Isle of Skye in the distance and the majestic Torridon Mountains behind.

The rustic little bar resounds nightly to tales of wind and tide, walks and climbs. The town also calls itself the whale-watching capital of the UK, so you might well hear stories of sightings, too, but you will have to make do with somewhat smaller specimens on the varied menu.

Often landed no more than a hundred yards or so from the kitchen door, fish is the obvious choice here and daily specials might include whole plaice, plainly treated with some garlic or lemon butter, or monkfish tail wrapped in pancetta, alongside the regular presence of homely beer-battered haddock with fat chips, a rustic fish pie, or a more adventurous, colourful dish of scallops on beetroot mash with light saffron cream.

So far as dedicated meat-eaters are concerned, the game season is probably the best time to come.

Starters are more limited, though they might include breast of pigeon and duck from the hotel's own smokehouse, while desserts offer a range of markedly Scottish delicacies such as cloutie dumpling, chocolate and orange bread and butter pudding, or a rich and satisfying Ecclefechan butter tart with walnuts and raisins.

Speciality food: Local fish and game
Draught beers: Red Cuillin, Abbot Ale
Average wine price by the glass: £3

Licensees: Alastair and Ute Pearson
Last orders for dinner: 10 pm
Open every day
Closed for holidays: 2 weeks in January
Main courses: from £6.75
Private dining: 10-25
Beer garden
Accommodation: 17 rooms
Children welcome
Wheelchair access

GATEHOUSE OF FLEET, DUMFRIES & GALLOWAY

Masonic Arms

GASTROPUB

10 Ann Street, Gatehouse of Fleet, Dumfries & Galloway DG7 2HU
Tel. 01557 814 335 Fax 01557 814 037
e-mail: info@themasonic-arms.co.uk **MAP 6** D5

JUST off the square, this little town-centre hostelry, with its own real ale made by a local brewery, provides a glorious setting for lunch or dinner. People who like to take their children out for a meal will particularly enjoy the walled garden, with its overtones of *Alice in Wonderland,* when the weather allows.

The success of the Masonic Arms lies in maintaining a tried and tested formula for less adventurous clients while tempting the more audacious with often Asian-inspired offerings.

Galloway beef features strongly, either as a range of steaks or as a good Sunday roast offering an alternative to the native lamb. The local butcher's specialities – game sausages and haggis, which are served in a 'tattie scone tower' with Drambuie sauce – provide strong regional flavours alongside local seafood such as the loch scallops or a generous duet of firm, moist salmon and halibut in a light lobster sauce. All come with excellent vegetables and home-made bread.

Other offerings range from a honey roast duck with spring onion and chilli stir-fry to baked red snapper with Japanese five spice, or even pungent Kashmiri chicken.

Dessert could be a date and walnut pudding, or a rich, light chocolate truffle torte nicely presented amidst plenty of drizzled accompanying sauces, or baked Alaska.

Speciality food: Scottish brasserie with an oriental twist
Draught beers: Deuchars IPA, Masonic Boom
Average wine price by the glass: £2.10

Licensees: Chris and Sue Walker
Last orders for dinner: 8.45pm
Open every day
Closed for holidays: 2 weeks Nov, 4 days Christmas
Set lunch: from £12.95 (Sunday only)
Main courses: from £7.50
Beer garden
Children welcome
Wheelchair access

GLASGOW

Ubiquitous Chips

12 Ashton Lane, Glasgow G12 8SJ
Tel. 0141 334 5007 Fax 0141 337 1302
e-mail: mail@ubiquitouschip.co.uk   **MAP 6** D4

'THE CHIP', as it is affectionately known, has been a fixture of the metropolitan scene for 30 years or more and there is no sign of any imminent change.

Its appeal is especially evident in the evening, when strings of lights illuminate a forest of greenery under its central, covered courtyard area, bringing a hint of Mediterranean climes – and a constant throng of animated diners – to this cornerstone of Glasgow's West End.

The Chip's continuing success is due in no small measure to the startlingly eclectic and often original offerings in an astonishingly varied range of dishes

Take, for instance, Scottish salmon brandade in 80 Shilling beer batter; Scrabster ling on clapshot (a Scottish version of champ that has Swede mixed with the potatoes) with roast pepper and crispy seaweed; a light prawn and fish sausage redolent of fresh coriander attractively presented on green apple mayonnaise; Perthshire pig's cheek with wild mushroom sauce and truffled potato omelette.

There is also a surprisingly effective dish of leg of tender local mutton stuffed and garnished with west coast mussels.

To finish, you might try one of a wide selection of Scottish cheeses, oatmeal ice-cream, or a simpler but equally enjoyable peach and frangelica tart, the light, crisp pastry evidence enough of the solid technique constantly buttressing the novel ideas.

Their pride: Smitton's Farm mutton stuffed with mussels
Inexpensive wines: Salice Salentino Riserva 2002, £23.80; Marques de Riscal Blanco Rueda 2003, £18.95

Proprietor: Ronnie Clydesdale
Last orders for dinner: 11 pm
Open every day
Closed for holidays: 25 December, 1 January
Set lunch: from £22.80
Set dinner: from £33.80
Private dining: 20-70
Wheelchair access

GULLANE, EAST LOTHIAN

La Potinière

Main Street, Gullane, East Lothian EH31 2AA
Tel./Fax 01620 843 214

MAP 6 E4

WITH its gentle, unobtrusive style, the La Potinière, which is something of a local landmark in East Lothian gastronomic circles, could well be taken for one of ye olde tea shoppes upon first encounter, but surprises are in store.

Although there are only six tables and twenty covers, everything here is refreshingly effective. Concise, straightforward menus give a hint of exotic interest in the house favourite, Thai coconut soup with Scottish scallops, or prawns with fruit and avocado salad and curry ginger mayonnaise. Overall, though, the food tends to rely understandably on tried and tested formulas in deference to a faithful local clientele.

Soups and savoury tarts feature regularly among the limited choices, followed, perhaps, by a duet of roasted and braised meats garnished à l'ancienne, with a rich jus and some seasonal vegetables, as an alternative to a popular fish dish such as steamed halibut filled with salmon mousse and served on creamy mussel stew infused with saffron and dill.

Tiny plates do not really do justice to the presentation of the food, but details such as really excellent soda bread and home-made chocolates are indicative of the care and dedication that is applied throughout.

Set in the golfer's paradise of Gullane – with three championship courses – this unassuming, cottagey watering-hole makes a very delightful and charming nineteenth hole.

Their pride: Thai coconut soup with west coast scallops
Inexpensive wines: Alella Classico (Spain) 2003, £16; La Rareza Reserve (Argentina) 2003, £16

Proprietors: Mary Runciman and Keith Marley
Last orders for dinner: 8.30 pm
Closed: Monday and Tuesday
Closed for holidays: 25-26 December, Bank Holidays
Set lunch: from £16.50
Set dinner: from £36.50
Private dining: 10-28
Wheelchair access

HOWGATE, MIDLOTHIAN

The Howgate

GASTROPUB

Howgate, Penicuik, Midlothian EH26 8PY
Tel. 01968 670 000 Fax 0870 751 7547

MAP 6 D4

AFTER something of a chequered past as a riding stables, a pub and a cheese-making dairy, The Howgate appears at last to have found its true vocation.

The tartan carpet and monogrammed napkins may present an aura of the chic corporate venture, but in practice this is the sort of place in which to relax.

Meat-lovers are in for a real treat, with three-week matured Scottish steaks very much the house forte and served plain or sauced with some brilliant (unpeeled) crispy, home-cut chips. However, the extensive menu also offers a nicely varied selection of more inventive specialities for the less conventional.

They even make a version of Brie nearby and this is served in filo parcels. With a light plum sauce, it makes for an original starter alongside more prosaic steamed mussels, fishcakes, or a touch of home-grown tradition in the cullen skink or tasty haggis with a leek and garlic sauce.

If the range of grills really is not your thing, you might be find the more pubby beef, ale and mushroom pie more tempting, or the breast of chicken stuffed with more of that local cheese. And there is plenty of choice for vegetarians.

Save some room for one of the well-made desserts, though. Banana bread and butter pudding with banoffi ice cream, or a wickedly good rhubarb and white chocolate crème brûlée, provide welcome new twists on tried and trusted themes.

Speciality food: Matured Scottish steaks
Draught beers: Belhaven Best, Tennents Lager
Average wine price by the glass: £3.75

Licensee: Nigel Hogg
Last orders for dinner: 9.30 pm
Open every day
Main courses: from £7.95
Private dining: 10-50
Beer garden
Children welcome
Wheelchair access

INVERNESS, INVERNESS-SHIRE

Abstract Glenmoriston Town House Hotel

20 Ness Bank, Inverness IV2 4SF
Tel. 01463 223 777 Fax 01463 712 378
e-mail: reception@glenmoristontownhouse.com   **MAP 6** D2

IT must be slightly galling for a young French cook who seemed intent on setting alight the restaurant scene in Scotland with his startling talents to be corrected in no uncertain terms by a Scottish chef. It was no ordinary chef, however, and Gordon Ramsay certainly appears to have helped Loïc Lefebvre find the missing ingredient in his recipe for success.

Verbose descriptions and at times jumbled concoctions have been replaced by neat, concise and comprehensible presentations of the dishes' main elements: scallops with leek and potato risotto, meat jus and summer truffle; roast pigeon on girolles salad with a chickpea caviar; fillet of red mullet with fennel compote and crispy belly pork; Scottish lamb with sweet pepper confit, coconut and curry sauce; slow-cooked John Dory with oyster and citrus tartare and coriander oil.

An adventurous and colourful dish of fresh crab 'three ways' is accompanied by a cold cauliflower cream base and a lemony couscous, and overall the content and presentation have been streamlined to allow more harmonious development of character in the individual dishes.

Distinctive flavours readily emerge from the rather more studiously engineered compilations and it is notable that deft, technical touches, exemplified by a perfectly simple tartlet of red berries on a yoghurt filling, have replaced extravagant showiness.

Their pride: Salmon 'three ways': tartare with pineapple granité, smoked with spices and 'tataki'
Inexpensive wines: Columbia Winery Pinot Gris (USA) 1999, £18.50; Côtes du Rhône Domaine du Vieux Chêne 2000, £18

Proprietor: Barry Larsen
Last orders for dinner: 10 pm
Closed: Monday
Set lunch: from £14
Set dinner: from £34
Private dining: 6-16
Al fresco dining
Accommodation: 30 rooms
Wheelchair access

KILBERRY, ARGYLL

Kilberry Inn

GASTROPUB

Kilberry, By Tarbert, Argyll PA29 6YD
Tel./Fax 01880 770 223
e-mail: relax@kilberryinn.com   **MAP 6** C4

WITH a bird sanctuary as its near neighbour and the beautifully wild wastes of the Isle of Jura beckoning across the loch, the noise and stress of modern life will be no more than a distant memory at this remote little settlement tucked away in a hidden corner of Scotland's west coast.

The stags' heads and other tawdry trappings of former times have given way to elegant banquettes and colourful works of art on the rugged stone walls.

Whether you are dropping in for a light lunchtime bite (creamy green pea soup, for example) or the full dinner menu, seafood, often brought by local fishermen, is a particular favourite – from fat herrings grilled with Arran mustard to crispy grilled mackerel, or sautéd scallops with a honey and orange dressing, and crab cakes with a tangy tomato and chilli jam.

The eclectic style runs throughout, from starkly plain to admirably creative, with more than a hint of the Mediterranean alongside home-grown favourites.

Piedmontese roast peppers laced with fine olive oil; cod roasted with chorizo, tomatoes and Tio Pepe, or a slow-baked salmon niçoise cohabit easily with a homely cottage pie with braised red cabbage, simple steaks, or a hearty dish of rich, tender beef cooked in Scottish ale. To finish, try chocolate truffle cake with Orkney ice-cream, a refreshing sundae of local red berries, or light and authentic Tunisian orange and almond cake.

Speciality food: Scottish brasserie with a Mediterranean touch
Draught beers: Tennents Velvet, Stella Artois
Average wine price by the glass: £3

Licensees: Clare Johnson and David Wilson
Last orders for dinner: 9 pm
Closed for holidays: Monday; 1 January – early March
Main courses: from £6.50
Private dining: up to 12
Beer garden
Accommodation: 3 rooms
Children welcome

LINLITHGOW, WEST LOTHIAN

Champany Inn ★

Linlithgow, West Lothian EH49 7LU
Tel. 01506 834 532 Fax 01506 834 302
e-mail: reception@champany.com   **MAP 6** D4

THIS former pub dating from the 16th century is now all about meat. The clients are confirmed carnivores and one can easily see why. For this is no ordinary steakhouse, and the simplicity of style belies the care and unseen preparation that goes into making meals this good.

Carefully selected Aberdeen Angus meats are hung on the bone in chill-rooms for at least three weeks before being set upon by the in-house butcher. The result is the most magnificent red meat you will ever taste. Succulent, tender, with just the right amount of 'bite', and a full, almost gamey, flavour, this is connoisseurs' gourmandising with portions that are not for the faint-hearted.

Sirloin, rib-eye, entrecôte, fillet and the daunting porterhouse – all the cuts are there on display for inspection. There is probably no need to stray from the plain, chargrill treatment they are given on the specially designed kitchen range, but among the sauces on offer a punchy black pepper cream can add real zest to perfectly marinated and cooked meat.

You can also select lobster or start with some oysters, scallops or home-smoked salmon before attacking the meat. If you can face a dessert, there is crisply crusted bread and butter pudding.

The circular dining-room, housed in the original mill-room with its pointed roof, gives the impression of eating in a sort of medieval wigwam. Come armed with an enormous appetite.

Their pride: Hot smoked salmon
Inexpensive wines: Champany Own Label White £16.50; Champany Own Label Red £17.50

Proprietors: Clive and Anne Davidson
Last orders for dinner: 10 pm
Closed: Saturday lunch, Sunday
Closed for holidays: 25 & 26 December, 1 & 2 January
Set lunch: from £16.75
Main courses: from £29.50
Al fresco dining: lunch only
Accommodation: 16 rooms
Wheelchair access

MELROSE, SCOTTISH BORDERS

Townhouse Hotel

Market Square, Melrose, Scottish Borders TD6 9PQ
Tel. 01896 822 645 Fax 01896 823 474
e-mail: enquiries@thetownhousemelrose.co.uk   **MAP 6** E5

POPULAR with walkers, golfers and tourists, there is a traditional feel about the pretty town of Melrose, in Scotland's lush, rolling Border country. Victorian architecture and geranium-bedecked windowsills add an air of time-worn gentility to the busy High Street, into which the Henderson family, who already own a more traditional hostelry across the road, are hoping to inject some contemporary colour with their latest venture.

Behind its modest frontage, the interior seems to go on forever. Clean, stylish lines and up-to-date furniture and fittings in the public areas have replaced a run-down lounge and four-ale bar. The brasserie operation's well-balanced menu covers two dining-rooms – one simple, the other more formal. There is also a sunny conservatory ideal for the lighter lunchtime selection, and a rear terrace for the summer.

You really can eat your way across culinary frontiers here, helped by eye-catching presentation from a kitchen brigade determined to impress. Escabèche of sardines with roasted baby tomatoes, aubergine roulade with basil mascarpone cheese and a timbale of couscous, or breast of chicken with pancetta, boudin noir and a whisky jus are typical of the compilations you can expect.

And their technical dexterity is amply displayed in the pressed game terrine packed with succulent meats, or a fine fillet of sea bass with smoked haddock mousse under a creamy chive aïoli. Simpler salads and steaks, along with hearty desserts, complete the central theme of the new operation, which must provide a breath of fresh air for local gastronomes.

Their pride: Scottish fusion food
Inexpensive wines: Mâcon Lugny Louis Jadot 2004, £16.95; Bellingham Pinotage (South Africa) 2003, £14.95

Proprietors: Henderson Family in partnership with Burts Hotel
Last orders for dinner: 9 pm
Open every day
Closed for holidays: 26 December
Main courses: from £8.25
Private dining: 20-60
Al fresco dining
Accommodation: 11 rooms

NETHERLEY, ABERDEENSHIRE

Lairhillock Inn Crynock Restaurant `GASTROPUB`

Netherley, Nr. Stonehaven, Aberdeenshire AB39 3QS
Tel. 01569 730 220 Fax 01569 731 175
e-mail: lairhillock@breathemail.net   **MAP 6** E3

A BURNT-OUT barn attached to this two-hundred-year-old inn, set in rolling countryside in the outer reaches of Aberdeen, has been turned into a brasserie with an Austrian chef. It may not be Montmartre, but you can see the aim: to break down the divide between the more down-to-earth bar food (of which there is a wide choice) and what was, until recently, strictly formal eating.

The easygoing atmosphere, with a pianist tinkling away, friendly welcome and the relaxed, chattering, family groups eating by candlelight, are a far cry from classical dining. Colourful works by local artists break up the otherwise sombre interior, gleaming copper and pewter and dark furnishings providing an almost manorial setting. Simpler snacks and meals tend to be popular with families in the brighter, more airy conservatory with its splendid views over the beautiful rolling countryside.

Hermann Schmid has some fine, simply treated local produce including venison, wood pigeon, salmon and, naturally, Aberdeen Angus steaks, with the occasional Mediterranean import.

It is a pity there is not greater emphasis on his native and Scottish cross-culture ideas: the smoked haddock and leek strudel, plainly and amply served with a mixed salad, was carried off with great assurance. They might well consider adding more of these tastily inventive ideas.

No Austrian pastries, either, among desserts that adhere to strictly classical lines.

Speciality food: Scottish brasserie
Draught beers: Timothy Taylor Landlord, Lairs Isle of Skye
Average wine price by the glass: £2.65

Licensee: Roger Thorne
Last orders for dinner: 9.30 pm
Closed: Lunchtimes (except Sunday), Tuesday
Closed for holidays: 25 and 26 Dec, 1 and 2 Jan
Set dinner: from £18.75
Private dining: 10-25
Children welcome
Wheelchair access

Peat Inn

Peat Inn, By Cupar, Fife KY15 5LH
Tel. 01334 840 206 Fax 01334 840 530
e-mail: reception@thepeatinn.co.uk   **MAP 6** E4

DAVID WILSON has been at the helm of this endearing country
inn for a third of a century and he can look back with pride on an
impressive achievement that is marked by his indelible stamp of
proficiency and perseverance.

The style of the cooking – and particularly its presentation – is as
stoically conventional as the inn's interior is comfy-country. But
just as vibrant yellow fabrics add a contemporary touch to the
lounge, so the advance guard of culinary revolution occasionally
manages to creep under the wire.

However the kitchen's style may evolve, the accent at present is
on hearty fare, with lusciously natural flavours untainted by fussy
garnishes.

Local crab with coriander and lime, or fillet of cod on chorizo with
a julienne of pigeon breast on spiced pork, seem to veer off at a
tangent from roasted scallops on a potato, leek, bacon and pea
purée, or fillet of beef in Madeira sauce with shallots, or cassoulet
of lamb, pork and duck.

There was a slight imbalance, perhaps, in offering a confit duck
leg on a bed of lentils to precede cod on lobster and herb risotto,
but both were deliciously honest and enjoyable – the cod tender
and moist under a well-seared skin.

Good old-fashioned chocolate and caramel flavours are strong
among the desserts.

Their pride: Cassoulet of lamb, pork and duck, flagelot beans
Inexpensive wines: Costières de Nimes Château Grande
Cassagne 2002, £18; Côtes du Rhône Cuvée Syrah, Jean Lionnet
Domaine de Rochepertuis 1998, £20

Proprietors: David and Patricia Wilson
Last orders for dinner: 9.30 pm
Closed: Sunday and Monday
Closed for holidays: 25 December, 1 January
Set lunch: from £22
Set dinner: from £32
Private dining: up to 24
Accommodation: 8 rooms
Wheelchair access

PORTPATRICK, DUMFRIES & GALLOWAY

Knockinaam Lodge

Portpatrick, Dumfries & Galloway DG9 9AD
Tel. 01776 810 471 Fax 01776 810 435
e-mail: reservations@knockinaamlodge.com   **MAP 6** C5

NESTLING in a hollow in this glorious, rolling countryside with the sea pounding nearby and the pretty little port of Portpatrick a short drive away, this impressive laird's hunting lodge offers a family-run environment with none of the snootiness of many country houses.

Their attitude is perhaps summed up by the mounted stag's head in the club-like panelled bar (with its huge range of malt whiskies) which proudly sports a pair of sunglasses.

A daily changing, no-choice set menu quite neatly combines neo-classical trends with traditional values throughout five appealing courses which put local fish (do not be surprised if this is your main course) and meat to excellent use.

Much of the descriptive terminology of contemporary cuisine is apparent, with the emulsions, savoury 'cappuccinos' and the reductions implying cutting-edge craftsmanship from the kitchen. The overall impression is of an impassioned enthusiastic team.

Local wild mushrooms might perfume a creamy velouté starter; a firm, moist fillet of brill is eloquently offset by a crisp potato crust, and tender, well-judged Galloway lamb is simply presented with a light, rosemary scented jus.

Their pride: Baked native sea scallop, with a julienne of root vegetables, champagne butter sauce, herbs and pastry crust
Inexpensive wines: Château Puyframabe 2000, £23; Mâcon Uchizy 2004, £23;

Proprietor: David Ibbotson
Last orders for dinner: 9 pm
Open every day
Set lunch: from £35
Set dinner: from £45
Private dining: 10-20
Al fresco dining at lunch
Accommodation: 9 rooms
Limited wheelchair access

SORN, AYRSHIRE

Sorn Inn ★

GASTROPUB

35 Main Street, Sorn, Ayrshire KA5 6HU
Tel. 01290 551 305 Fax 01290 553 470
e-mail: craig@sorninn.com   **MAP 6** C5

CHEF/PATRON Craig Grant, after stints at Langan's Brasserie and Rookery Hall, finally has a place of his own and the enthusiasm for his venture is much in evidence. Leading from the tastefully elegant little formal dining-room, the kitchen with its ever-open door seems to invite everyone to share in his creative passion.

And that is exactly what they do, through well-balanced lunch and dinner menus in which just the right touch of creative flair adds welcome zest to traditionally based, though beautifully executed, compilations using fine fish and other local ingredients. Simpler food and blackboard specials are on offer in bar next door.

If the generously priced, less diverse lunch menu adopts a more conservative approach, the quality of even its straightforward but for once appropriately named 'parfait' of chicken livers, or the deliciously tender navarin of confit lamb with some crisp, neatly turned vegetables, give ample indication of the technical aptitude of Craig and his team.

In the evening, imagination really comes more into play with the likes of an innovative assiette of rillette, smoked and boudin Gressingham duck, or the lasagne of crab and red snapper with gazpacho ginger foam.

Impressive desserts include a fine, rich, crisply crusted chocolate tart.

Speciality food: Scottish beef and local fish
Draught beers: McEwans 60 Shilling, John Smiths Bitter
Average wine price by the glass: £3.25

Licensee: Craig Grant
Last orders for dinner: 9 pm
Closed: Monday
Set lunch: from £12.95
Set dinner: from £20.50
Private dining: 10-16
Accommodation: 4 rooms
Children welcome
Wheelchair access

STEIN, ISLE OF SKYE

Stein Inn

GASTROPUB

McCleod's Terrace, Stein, Waternish, Isle of Skye IV55 8GA
Tel. 01470 592 362

MAP 6 B2

THE setting cannot have changed much in the 300 or more years of this inn's existence, and while it might have been tempting to turn such a gem into something a bit smart, this is pure pub, where locals and visitors gather to chat over a glass of single malt whisky, nearly a hundred examples of which line the bar.

It is all as rustic and cosy as you could wish for and meals are enjoyed against the hubbub of the bar or in a slightly 'bunk-house' dining-room, or else right down at the water's edge when wind and rain allow.

Perhaps surprisingly, given the location, seafood does not figure all that strongly, though langoustines and prawns from the loch are popular choices and the beautifully plump, sweet mussels steamed in cider and sage are a particular treat, with perhaps salmon in tarragon and vermouth sauce or breaded haddock to follow.

A homely style and honest simplicity come before any notions of pretence or showiness, and one gets the feeling that the range of salads, steaks and specials such as beef Stroganoff are more accessories to the tippling and tourism than the main raison d'être for a visit here.

Fruit pies and crumbles to finish are typical of the unpretentious approach, and as you gaze out over the sea to the hills and islands beyond it is hard to not to imagine escaping to a place like Stein.

Speciality food: Traditional pub food
Draught beers: Red Cuillin, Deuchars IPA
Average wine price by the glass: £2.50

Licensees: Angus and Teresa McGhie
Last orders for dinner: 9.30 pm
Open every day
Closed for holidays: 25 December, 1 January
Main courses: from £6
Al fresco dining
Accommodation: 5 rooms
Children welcome
Wheelchair access

STORNOWAY, ISLE OF LEWIS

Digby Chick

**28 Point Street, Stornoway, Isle of Lewis HS1 2XG
Tel. 01851 700 026**

MAP 6 B1

BUSY shopping centre restaurants are not usually noted for their contribution to gastronomic initiative and flair, but the Digby Chick (named after a Canadian kipper) is full of surprises.

From the little bar to a colourful, stylish dining-room, the place seems permanently full even on weekday lunchtimes – and little wonder, with prices that defy all logic and no stinting on quality.

Innovation and interest are injected into the most down-to-earth ingredients. Take, for instance, a refreshing fan of melon, with a balsamic strawberry compote, graced with the presence of a home-made Irn Bru sorbet; or pan-fried herring on assorted leaves with red pepper and basil butter; or breast of chicken brought to life with sweetcorn fritters and Cajun spiced bacon risotto.

The list goes on with the likes of smoked haddock, grain mustard mash and Cheddar sauce, and a succulent, crispy-skinned belly of pork dusted with paprika and impressively served with a Stroganoff cream and deep-fried sweet potato chips.

Prices gradually rise throughout the day, the early evening choice merging into a full à la carte dinner menu with still more novel creations such as haggis spring roll or breast of guinea fowl stuffed with almond mousse, and giant portions of iced raspberry and lemon curd meringue, or gingernut and lime cheesecake, to finish.

Their pride: Pan-fried halibut with baby leeks and crab and parsley cream
Inexpensive wines: Sauvignon Blanc Torreon de Paredes (Chile), £12.50; Crianza Vegeval (Spain), £12.50

**Proprietors: Marianne and James McKenzie
Last orders for dinner: 8.45 pm
Closed: Sunday
Closed for holidays: 2 weeks November
Set lunch: from £7.95
Set dinner: from £13.95 (early evening)
Private dining: 10-20**
Wheelchair access

STRACHUR, ARGYLL

Creggans Inn

GASTROPUB

Strachur, Argyll PA27 8BX
Tel. 01369 860 279 Fax: 01369 860 637
e-mail: info@creggans-inn.co.uk   **MAP 6** C4

THE very idea, as a restaurateur, of being able to look out of your front door, across the loch, to the green, rolling hills beyond and know that the source of just about all your fine ingredients is more or less within sight, must be reassuring to say the least.

Especially when you know the producers and growers: fishermen who provide seafood such as oysters and mussels (served with a Guinness and pepper cream, they are unbeatable); the female diver who brings scallops to be served in a filo horn with saffron sauce; the butcher who provides not only local lamb, beef and haggis, but also some cracking venison sausages to go with the mustard mash, as well as a grower who drops all manner of greenery at your back door, direct from the garden.

Everything, it seems, is just on the doorstep and such produce requires little enhancement, although that does not stop the chef giving rein to his creative instincts for the main dining-room with the likes of leek, caraway seed and tomato tarte Tatin, or breast of chicken infused with foie gras, brioche and truffle oil .

Well-executed favourites such as cullen skink or steak and ale pie, steaks and battered fish and chips, or a more cross-culture breast of chicken with haggis sauce on the more restricted lunch menu are served in the plain but comfortable collection of rooms behind the rustic and drolly named McPhunn's Bar.

Family-run, with families in mind, there is a touch of class here that disdains to be chic.

Speciality food: Local seafood and game
Draught beers: Deuchars IPA, Timothy Taylor Landlord
Average wine price by the glass: £3.20

Licensee: Alex Robertson
Last orders for dinner: 8.45 pm
Open every day
Closed for holidays: 25 and 26 December
Set dinner: from £32
Main courses: from £6.50 (lunch)
Beer garden
Accommodation: 14 rooms
Children over 10 welcome in restaurant

TAYVALLICH, ARGYLL

Tayvallich Inn

Tayvallich, By Lochgilphead, Argyll PA31 8PL
Tel. 01546 870 282 Fax 01546 870 330

MAP 6 C4

THERE is a real air of thriving, workaday authenticity about the beautiful little harbour of Tayvallich, with the constant to-ing and fro-ing of enthusiastic yachtsmen and working fishermen landing their catches at the pier head.

Not surprising, then, to discover that there is a nautical feel throughout the panelled bar and dining-room of this former bus garage at the end of the bay.

The same menu and daily specials can be enjoyed inside or out on the decking, with only the access road to the tiny village between you and the water's edge.

The family were born and bred here, but the son left to tour the world before returning to take the reins of the family business. He brought back a few ideas from his travels, such as the deep-fried feta, the garlic and ginger used to spice up some superb loch prawns, and delicious grilled squid a la plancha with tomato salsa.

The daily catch from local fisherfolk is advertised on the board outside and, from the steamed mussels to fresh oysters, scallops and lobster (roasted with tarragon butter), the treatment of these prime ingredients tends rightly to follow uncomplicated lines, with even a fine, meaty black bream simply oven-baked under a light herb crust, surrounded by a few roasted vegetables.

Meat-eaters will be more than content with speciality sausages or a steak and ale pie, and there toothsome puddings like a rich chocolate truffle tart.

Speciality food: Local fish
Draught beers: Loch Fyne Dark Ale, Loch Fyne Pale Ale
Average wine price by the glass: £3.15

Licensee: Roddy Anderson
Last orders for dinner: 9 pm
Closed: Monday between November and March
Main courses: from £7.95
Beer garden
Children welcome

TROON, AYRSHIRE

Apple Inn

89 Portland Street, Troon, Ayrshire KA10 6QU
Tel./Fax 01292 318 819

MAP 6 C5

THERE is little wonder that this hybrid pub/café/brasserie/bar, with its vast, eclectic menu (plus blackboard specials) and cheery unpretentiousness has been such an instant hit in the celebrated seaside golfing town.

Gone are the old pub carpets and dark woodwork, to be replaced by tiling and colourful prints providing a fresh, bistro setting beyond the little bar area.

More importantly, there is a range of dishes to suit all tastes, from light bites to full meals, and the technical know-how of the kitchen brigade is certainly more than capable of rising to the occasion when required.

While a multi-cultural theme prevails, from sticky beef on Thai noodles to teriyaki salmon, Toulouse sausage, Cajun beef and sole tempura, local traditions are not entirely overlooked. The plainer pan-fried scallops, beautifully plump Scottish mussels (served marinière or more exotically with coconut and lemon grass), or a moist, tender breast of chicken stuffed with haggis, are certainly not outclassed by their imported rivals.

One of the additional touches is the nicely original dish of accompanying vegetables, which consists of cabbage, snow peas and butter beans.

Desserts also go off at a welcome tangent, with banoffi crumble, chocolate fondant with lime coulis, or well-executed lemon tart with blueberry crème fraîche ice-cream.

Speciality food: Scottish brasserie with a Mediterranean twist
Draught beers: McEwans 70 Shilling, Guinness
Average wine price by the glass: £3.15

Licensees: Kirsty MacLeod and Allan Low
Last orders for dinner: 9.30 pm (Sunday 9 pm)
Open every day
Closed for holidays: 25 and 26 December, 1 January
Main courses: from £7.50
Children welcome
Wheelchair access

Wales

BEAUMARIS, ANGLESEY

Ye Olde Bull's Head Inn   `GASTROPUB`

Castle Street, Beaumaris, Anglesey LL58 8AP
Tel. 01248 810 329 Fax 01248 811 294
e-mail: info@bullsheadinn.co.uk   **MAP 3** C1

ONCE a garrison town where Cromwell's troops were billeted, this seaside spot remains remarkably unspoilt. The rear entrance of this 17th-century inn features what is designated as the oldest hinged door in the country by the *Guinness Book of Records*.

While the main bar and residents' sitting-room are traditionally furnished, the rear brasserie is far more contemporary. A light, airy room – with large windows that are open in the summer – it has tongue-and-groove walls and fishy pictures.

Upstairs, a recently refurbished room, The Loft Restaurant, is more formal and open only in the evenings and on high days and holidays. A fixed menu here offers a well-balanced choice that might include starters such as velouté of leek and potato, seared scallops and truffle cappuccino or a terrine of confit duck with smoked foie gras.

Aside from supremely fresh fish, the chef makes use of other local ingredients such as Anglesey Welsh Black beef. This could feature as a main course accompanied by fondant potatoes and oxtail boudin with a Madeira sauce.

Downstairs, the menu ranges from a charcuterie selection, grilled gravadlax and various salads and sandwiches through to burgers and main courses such as local prize-winning pork and herb sausages with garlic mash and Provençal sauce.

Desserts include white chocolate and apricot ice-cream and lighter options such as panna cotta with fruit salad or sorbet.

Speciality food: Fish
Draught beers: Hancocks, Bass
Average wine price by the glass: £2.85

Licensees: David Robertson and Keith Rothwell
Last orders for dinner: 9 pm
Open every day
Closed: 25 and 26 December, 1 January (evening)
Main courses: from £7.95
Private dining: up to 14
Accommodation: 13 rooms
Children welcome
Wheelchair access

525

CAPEL DEWI, DYFED

Y Polyn ★

GASTROPUB

Capel Dewi, Nr. Nantgaredig, Carmarthen, Dyfed SA32 7LH
Tel. 01267 290 000
e-mail: ypolyn@hotmail.com   **MAP 3** B4

YOU would be lucky just to stumble across this pub, slightly off the beaten track along a winding, narrow lane, its presence only discreetly revealed by a little brown tourist sign at the roadside.

But to miss it would be a pity, because food is taken seriously here, as witness the montage of menus from some of the very best restaurants that greets you and the many cookery books on display in the eating area.

Menus are pleasingly short – six starters and six main courses on the lunch menu, for example. Starters might include mackerel escabèche, Carmarthen ham with peach and feta salad, or else a traditional fish soup of satisfying depth and with just a hint of aniseed.

To follow, pork chops with pea mash and apple and cider sauce might take your fancy, or perhaps a thick tranche of baked hake ideally accompanied by tangy pickled lemon, onion and bayleaf confit.

Finish with Y Polyn honey and almond ice-cream or a delicious apricot frangipane tart – melt-in-the-mouth pastry, moist almond filling and plump, juicy fruit – that could grace a smart pâtisserie.

As if this were not enough to whet the appetite, guest chefs such as Sean Hill occasionally make an appearance

Speciality food: Y Polyn Fish Pie
Draught beers: Tomos Watkins OSB, Tomos Watkins cwrw hâf
Average wine price by the glass: £3

Licensee: Mark Manson
Last orders for dinner: 9.30 pm
Closed: Monday
Set dinner: from £25.50
Main courses: from £8.50
Beer garden
Children welcome
Wheelchair access

CARDIFF

Le Gallois ★

6-10 Romilly Crescent, Canton, Cardiff CF11 9NR
Tel. 029 20 34 1264 Fax 029 2023 7911
e-mail: info@legallois-ycymro.com   **MAP 3** D5

THE cooking at this smart Franco-Welsh bistro is of a high order, shown impressively in the aromatic, deep, stock-led flavoured fish soup, which is as good as any you will find, robust yet still refined and served with first-rate rouille and excellent shredded cheese that tasted like Gruyère.

Alternative starters might be wild mushroom and truffle risotto or roast pigeon on toast with fricassee of livers.

Among the main courses, rump of veal was properly thick and perfectly cooked, faint pink enough to bring out all the flavour, accompanied by well-trimmed strips of tender sweetbreads and root vegetables moistened by a finely textured Madeira sauce.

Alternatively, there might be glazed Goosnargh duck breast with spinach, baby navets and rosemary duck jus, or a signature dish of herb-crusted cannon of lamb. Grilled lemon sole, served with Pont Neuf potatoes and split pea purée, is particularly good.

A delicious dessert is prune and armagnac soufflé, perfectly risen, the mix of soft prune textures with fine definition of flavour brought out well by the brandy.

The wines are expertly chosen by Francis Dupuy, brother-in-law of the Welsh chef, Padrig Jones. The list includes some excellent champagne and burgundy. Service is tireless and always friendly in a setting notable for its sense of space and light, thanks to its two levels and décor in white and cream.

Their pride: Pot-roasted pig, honey and clove pot sauce, truffle potato purée and baby vegetables
Inexpensive wines: Côtes de Gascogne 2003, £14.95; Costières de Nimes 2000, £14.95

Proprietors: Jones and Dupuy Families
Last orders for dinner: 10.30 pm
Closed: Sunday, Monday
Closed for holidays: 1 week Christmas, Last week Aug
Set lunch: from £17.95
Set dinner: from £30
Wheelchair access

CRICKHOWELL, POWYS

Bear Hotel

GASTROPUB

Crickhowell, Powys NP8 1AY
Tel. 01873 810 408 Fax 01873 811 696
e-mail: bearhotel@aol.com   **MAP 3** D4

DRINKS and bar meals at this popular 15th-century coaching inn can be enjoyed outside in either an attractive courtyard or the tranquil and secluded rear garden. Inside, a snug room and a more formal dining-room afford a quiet, sedate ambience.

The extensive bar menu offers sixteen main courses – and they do not include Welsh Black beef steaks or specials – and covers a broad spectrum from starters such as Thai prawn cakes with a chilli dip or chicken liver parfait with toasted brioche through to such hearty dishes as a half-duck confit or home-made faggots in onion gravy.

From the restaurant menu, a meaty and robust ham hock terrine with foie gras was accompanied by prune with vanilla chutney and toasted fruit loaf, which might be a little excessive for some palates.

Overall, strong flavours prevail: moist chicken supreme on a smoked bacon rösti, tasty in its own right, is served with girolle mushrooms and pungent vegetables; trio of lamb comes with a delicious butternut fondant and the same selection of vegetables.

For dessert, choose from bread and butter pudding (the house speciality) or sticky toffee or, as a lighter option, poached pear and lemon délice.

There is also an unusual selection of petits fours which includes a toffee lolly with sherbet.

Speciality food: Trio of Brecon lamb
Draught beers: Rev. James, Bass
Average wine price by the glass: £4

Licensee: Judy Hindmarsh
Last orders for dinner: 9.30 pm
Closed: Sunday and Monday evening
Main courses: from £12.25
Private dining: 8-60
Beer garden
Accommodation: 35 rooms
Children over 7 welcome in restaurant
Wheelchair access

CRICKHOWELL, POWYS

Nantyffin Cider Mill Inn `GASTROPUB`

Brecon Road, Crickhowell, Powys NP8 1SG
Tel. 01873 810 775 Fax 01873 810 775
e-mail: info@cidermill.co.uk   **MAP 3** D4

THIS pink painted, 16th-century drovers' inn, at the foot of the Black Mountains between Crickhowell and the market town of Brecon, is extremely popular with holidaymakers and locals alike, so booking is advisable.

There is a blackboard menu, but this is both inconveniently placed and somewhat difficult to read, making the printed list of daily specials more accessible. These might include starters such as Black Mountain oak-smoked salmon with potato salad, or baked Welsh goat's cheese crouton, or seared scallops with crispy bacon, broad beans and rocket in a subtle basil dressing.

Portions are hearty, as in main courses like home-reared lamb shank with herb mash, or goujons of sole that are in fact two large fillets served with very fat chips and a pea purée flavoured with truffle.

If you can still find room for dessert, try sticky toffee pudding, the Belgian milk chocolate torte with dark chocolate sauce, or else the lighter affogato al caffe, which is vanilla ice-cream with espresso poured over it. Welsh cheeses and home-made chutney are also on offer.

Speciality food: Confit of lamb
Draught beers: IPA, Rhymney
Average wine price by the glass: £3.50

Licensees: Glyn & Jessica Bridgeman & Sean Gerrard
Last orders for dinner: 9.30 pm
Closed: Monday
Closed for holidays: 25 December, 1 week January
Set lunch: from £10
Private dining: 8-20
Beer garden
Children welcome
Wheelchair access

EGLWYSFACH, POWYS

Ynyshir Hall ★★

Eglwysfach, Nr. Machynlleth, Powys SL20 8TA
Tel. 01654 781 209 Fax 01654 781 366
e-mail: info@ynyshir-hall.co.uk   **MAP 3** C3

QUEEN VICTORIA is said to have upgraded and restocked the magnificent gardens at this secluded former shooting lodge she once owned on the beautiful Dovey estuary. Today, Ynyshir Hall remains very much a family home, and Rob and Joan Reen's active and enthusiastic presence is a testament to their concern for the twenty or so guests their dining-room holds.

Add to this the flair and skill of chef Adam Simmonds and you are in for a gastronomic experience full of surprise and delight. Unexpected associations of tastes abound: roasted quail, parsnips, cranberry and coffee oil; seared scallops, apple jelly and mustard ice-cream; chocolate soufflé with fennel ice-cream and Ricard sorbet. Such combinations make langoustine risotto with ceps and truffle, or a fillet of John Dory with watercress purée, figs and red wine, seem almost mundane.

Combining bitter-sweet rhubarb with spiced lentils to garnish two tiny fillets of red mullet is a masterstroke, while an organic pork fillet with a lightly sauced oyster, parsnip purée, confit cabbage and onion ice-cream, is a cornucopia of fascinating contrasts.

You might well want to just sit back and admire a dessert such as Adam's liquorice parfait before tasting it. If the main element is exquisitely creamy, with none of the expected assertiveness of its chief ingredient, when garnished and laced with a slice of confit pineapple, coconut and tea jelly, the dish offers extraordinary mouthfuls of joy and discovery.

Their pride: Red Mullet with spiced lentils, melon purée, foie gras
Inexpensive wines: Côté Tariquet Chardonnay Sauvignon 2003, £19; St. Bernard Merlot 2004, £19

Proprietors: Rob and Joan Reen
Last orders for dinner: 8.45 pm
Open every day
Closed for holidays: 3 January – 31 January
Set lunch: from £29.50
Set dinner: from £55
Private dining: up to 14
Al fresco dining
Accommodation: 9 rooms
Wheelchair access

FELIN FACH, POWYS

Felin Fach Griffin ★

Felin Fach, Brecon, Powys LD3 0UB
Tel. 01874 620 111 Fax 01874 620 120
e-mail: enquiries@eatdrinksleep.ltd.uk   **MAP 3** C4

THE 'Eat, Drink, Sleep' signage with its quirky logo quickly grabs the attention of the idle passer-by or those on a more serious quest for somewhere to eat and/or stay that will offer something different and memorable. Inside this converted farmhouse, large, squishy sofas in the bar area afford a peek through a raised fireplace into the main dining-room, which successfully juxtaposes the old with the new.

To begin a relaxed, unhurried meal, an appetiser such as fennel and parsley broth will sharpen the taste buds admirably. The menu offers a range of carefully selected dishes, including local produce that is the owners' pride. Your starter could be smoked salmon from the Black Mountains with cucumber and crème fraîche, or quail on a skewer with risotto of girolles.

The choice of main courses might feature Welsh rib-eye steak, with Béarnaise sauce and chips, or well-prepared duck breast with sour cherries.

Among the desserts, crème brûlée with elderflower syrup stands out, and there is an impressive array of Welsh cheeses, including Perl Wen and Pant Mawr Preseli, served with home-made soda bread.

If you want to stay, the luxurious accommodation and the prospect of an excellent breakfast will ensure that you sleep like the figure depicted in the logo.

Speciality food: Local produce
Draught beers: Tomos Watkins OSB and Tomos Watkins cwrw hâf (during summer)
Average wine price by the glass: £3.75

Licensees: Charles and Edmund Inkin
Last orders for dinner: 9.30 pm
Closed: Monday lunch
Main courses: from £8.95
Private dining: up to 20
Al fresco dining
Accommodation: 7 rooms
Children welcome
Wheelchair access

LLANDENNY, MONMOUTHSHIRE

Raglan Arms

GASTROPUB

Llandenny, Nr. Usk, Monmouthshire NP15 1DL
Tel. 01291 690 800 Fax 01291 690 155
e-mail: raglanarms@virgin.net   **MAP 3** D5

LOCATED near the Monmouth to Abergavenny road and not far
from the M4, this pub is conveniently placed for those wishing to
break their journey but avoid the slightly less than appealing
pubs/restaurants invariably to be found on arterial roads.

This establishment should be placed firmly on the map, setting
the benchmark for any aspiring restaurateur setting up in the
area.

Built in the vernacular red stone and wisteria clad, the Raglan has
a raised decked area leading off the dining conservatory at the
rear, with solid tables and chairs surrounded by attractive foliage.
There is also a separate beer garden.

Deep terracotta painted walls in the bar and large leather sofas
make for a relaxed, warm atmosphere. Magazines and current
food guides are on hand.

Both the carte and the bar food are written up on boards. Tapas,
marinated Scottish beef, rocket and Parmesan and Mediterranean
prawns in a sweet chilli dressing are just some of the starters
available from a carefully selected menu.

Fish is delivered daily from Cardiff central market. Tender calf's
liver served with champ is very satisfying with its accompanying
rich onion gravy.

An iced summer parfait with a pronounced strawberry flavour hit
the spot followed by good, strong coffee.

Speciality food: Saddle of Welsh salt marsh lamb
Draught beers: Wye Valley Real Ale, Gem
Average wine price by the glass: £2.40

Licensees: Andrew and Irene Davis
Last orders for dinner: 9 pm
Closed: Sunday evening, Monday
Main courses: from £10
Private dining: up to 25
Beer garden
Children welcome
Wheelchair access

LLANDEWI SKIRRID, MONMOUTHSHIRE

Walnut Tree ★

GASTROPUB

Llandewi Skirrid, Abergavenny, Monmouthshire NP7 8AW
Tel. 01873 852 797 Fax 01873 859 764

MAP 3 D4

SET back a little from the road, this attractive period property, between Monmouth and Abergavenny, has tables immediately in front of it for al fresco dining, offering far-reaching views towards the Brecon Beacons and the Sugar Loaf Mountain. Pore over the menu in the snug bar with its panelled walls, flagstone floor and comfortable armchairs.

An appetiser, perhaps gazpacho in high summer, is brought to the table with a cheesy crouton. The menu has an Italian bias and features a range of antipasti dishes as well as salads and starters.

The starters could be fillet of red mullet with pistachio, guacamole and vanilla, or home-cured bresaola. The majority of the pasta and gnocchi dishes can be taken as a starter or as a main course.

Deliciously light, roasted gnocchi with asparagus, fennel and dried, baby tomatoes will not disappoint.

As many fish dishes as meat appear on the main course and might include pan-fried fillet of sea bass with broad beans and samphire risotto, or roasted cod with Swiss chard, sweet potatoes and a lightly curried mussel sauce. Roast chicken breast, flattened out, tender and flavoursome with crisp, sautéd potatoes, might be accompanied by grilled corn on the cob.

Seasonal puddings could include a raspberry soufflé with local clotted cream, undoubtedly worth the twenty-minute wait. A pear tart tastes freshly cooked – sweet sliced fruit with cheesy pastry that is ideally matched by rich almond ice-cream.

Speciality food: Local produce
Draught beers: Peroni, Speckled Hen
Average wine price by the glass: £3.50

Proprietor: Francesco Mattioli
Last orders for dinner: 9.30 pm
Closed: Sunday dinner, Monday
Main courses: from £15
Private dining: 10-22
Al fresco dining
Wheelchair access

LLANDRILLO, DENBIGHSHIRE

Tyddyn Llan ★ ★

Llandrillo, Nr. Corwen, Denbighshire LL21 OST
Tel. 01490 440 264 Fax 01490 440 414
e-mail: tyddynllan@compuserve.com   **MAP 3** C2

THE descriptions of the dishes (best seen at dinner) are spare and simple but their tastes in the mouth are often superb, signalling that they have been created by a masterly hand at this most civilised of restaurants in the shadow of the Berwyn Mountains.

You will travel far before you encounter a better dish of griddled scallops with vegetable relish and rocket. Beautifully sweet and tender, with the lightest touch of griddling colour, the scallops took centre stage, as they should, and were ideally supported by the simplicity of the accompaniments.

Alternative starters might be grilled red mullet, aubergine purée, chilli and garlic oil, or terrine of foie gras, confit of duck and Carmarthen ham.

Equally flawless execution is demonstrated in the main courses, among which is breast of Gressingham duck roasted just right to a warm, light pink and served in six generous slices along with a delicious potato pancake and a moistening of cider and apples.

If you want to stay with fish, the fillet of turbot, leek risotto and red wine sauce is another attractive choice, which you could try with one of the fine Pinot Noirs from the excellent wine list.

British farmhouse cheeses in prime condition precede some fine desserts, the prune and almond tart served with mascarpone ice-cream being a model of its kind. Otherwise, after such a feast, pana cotta with poached rhubarb would be a refreshing finale.

Their pride: Grilled scallops, vegetable relish and rocket
Inexpensive wines: Duck Pond Pinot Gris 2003, £21.50; Pata Negra Gran Reserva 1997, £19

Proprietors: Susan and Bryan Webb
Last orders for dinner: 9.30 pm
Closed: lunch Monday-Thursday
Closed for holidays: 2 weeks January
Set lunch: from £19.50
Set dinner: from £32.50
Private dining: up to 40
Al fresco dining
Accommodation: 13 rooms
Wheelchair access

LLANDUDNO, CONWY

Bodysgallen Hall

Llandudno, Conwy LL30 1RS
Tel. 01492 584 466 Fax 01492 582 519
e-mail: info@bodysgallen.com   **MAP 3** C1

CONWY mussels, Welsh lamb and the famous Welsh Black beef, as well as fruit from the estate's own orchards, feature regularly throughout an eclectic menu at this grand, 17th-century country house now protected by the National Trust.

In keeping with the classical style of the surroundings, there is a strongly traditional slant to much of the menu, including such things as ballottines, game terrines, fillet of sea bass with leek and lobster and slow-cooked shoulder of lamb.

However, creativity is also evident in, for example, warm goat's cheese mousse with cider caramel; roasted veal with pak choi, cassis and thyme, and roast loin of lamb with lemon and garlic and a sweetbread sausage.

At lunchtime, a shorter carte offers simpler fare which is none the less still thoroughly enjoyable, as well as being very reasonably priced.

A deliciously creamy goat's cheese fondant exhibited none of the sharpness often associated with its main ingredient while at the same time retaining its innate character.

As a main course, slow-cooked shoulder of lamb was succulence personified in its archly orthodox red wine jus served with a less than adventurous accompaniment of mash and a few (albeit crisply cooked) mangetout and baby carrots.

Their pride: Roasted loin of Welsh lamb with faggot and red wine sauce
Inexpensive wines: Premières Côtes de Bordeaux Château Lezongars 2000, £21.50; Tempero Verdejo-Viura Rueda 2003, £14.50

Proprietor: Historic House Hotels Ltd.
Last orders for dinner: 9.30 pm
Open every day
Set lunch: from £17.50
Set dinner: from £38
Private dining: 12-45
Accommodation: 35 rooms
Wheelchair access

LLANFRYNACH, POWYS

White Swan ★

GASTROPUB

Llanfrynach, Brecon, Powys LD3 7BZ
Tel. 01874 665 276 Fax 01874 665 362

MAP 3 C4

IN ITS distant past the White Swan played host to a brewery and then, in the 1950s, a general store. More recently, the interior has been opened out to accommodate a comfortable bar area on two levels and a spacious dining-room.

Daily specials on a board in the bar might offer such enticements as tender strips of sesame crumbed chicken with orange, ginger and coriander dip (delicious), or scallops, black pudding and asparagus, the sweet, firm nuggets losing none of their delicacy.

While several pubs take advantage of local lamb and beef, the White Swan goes further on its à la carte menu, featuring local wild boar and venison – the loin of boar topped with apple and onion confit wrapped in puff pastry, while a haunch of Brecon venison is stuffed with a peppered raspberry mousse.

Bacon and chive mash, a pleasing sop for a shallot, thyme and red wine sauce, might accompany chargrilled rib-eye of Welsh beef. The flavour of the local beef really should be savoured.

Puddings such as gooseberry crumble tart with crème anglaise and vanilla ice-cream are satisfying, or there is a lighter fruit soup with balsamic syrup ice-cream.

Welsh cheeses are served with home-made digestive biscuits and red onion marmalade.

Speciality food: Welsh lamb
Draught beers: Hancocks HB, Breconshire County Ale
Average wine price by the glass: £2.50

Licensee: Stephen Way
Last orders for dinner: 9.30 pm
Closed: Monday and Tuesday
Closed for holidays: 25 and 26 December, 1 January
Main courses: from £9.95
Private dining: up to 40
Beer garden
Children welcome
Wheelchair access

LLANSANFFRAID GLAN CONWY, CONWY

Old Rectory Country House ★

Llansanffraid Glan Conwy, Conwy LL28 5LF
Tel. 01492 580 611 Fax 01492 584 555
e-mail: info@oldrectorycountryhouse.co.uk   **MAP 3** C1

FOUR well-balanced courses here terminate with a triumphant dish of varied desserts which might include a heavenly – and for once not too sweet - chocolate fondant, an ethereal, fruit-based mousse and a refreshing, home-made honey ice-cream.

The lack of choice implies a certain restraint in the selection of dishes, but these are admirably compiled to include just the right amount of interest and variety while remaining within reach of even the most conservative palate.

A dash of almost fluorescent basil oil will give colour and tang to a firm, meaty fillet of brill laid on sweet potato. Braised oxtail will provide an unrivalled jus (and a few strands of meat) to sauce a seared fillet of Welsh Black beef of stunning pedigree, the lightest of pastry baskets alongside it containing some lightly sautéd wild mushrooms perfumed with a generous touch of truffle.

The portions are generous but they retain a pleasing lightness of touch unencumbered by over-garnishing or faddish presentation and the fish starter (depending on availability) and meat main course formula involves such delights as seared monkfish with a vanilla risotto, rack of lamb with an olive and anchovy crust, or a breast of Gressingham duck with savoy cabbage, black-eyed beans and port fig jam.

A well-priced wine list has plenty of interest and a good number of half-bottles. The overall impression in intimate surroundings is of attending a private dinner party.

Their pride: Welsh mountain lamb with anchovy and olive crust
Inexpensive wines: Givry Premier Cru Gerard Mouton 2002, £19.90; Picpoul de Pinet (Languedoc) 2004, £15.90

Proprietors: Michael and Wendy Vaughan
Last orders for dinner: 8 pm (one sitting)
Closed: Sunday, Monday (except Bank Holidays)
Closed for holidays: 15 December-15 January
Set dinner: from £39.50
Accommodation: 6 rooms

NANTYDERRY, MONMOUTHSHIRE

The Foxhunter ★

Nantyderry, Nr. Abergavenny, Monmouthshire NP7 9DN
Tel. 01873 881 101 Fax 01873 881 377
e-mail: info@thefoxhunter.com   **MAP 3** D5

THIS pub was named for the great show-jumper on which Harry Llewellyn (a local man) famously won the only British gold medal at the 1952 Olympics.

Situated in a pretty, unspoilt village, and once a stationmaster's house, then tea-rooms, the listed building has received a pleasing make-over – Welsh flagstones and wood-burning stove in the bar, wooden floor in the dining-room, where country prints share wall space with modern paintings.

The set lunch menu is refreshingly short – just two starters, two main, two puddings. Delicious foccaccia with green peppers is brought to the table when you are seated. The Caesar salad, so often let down by a bogus dressing, is especially good, subtle anchovy and mustard flavours in a creamy dressing and plenty of Parmesan.

Savour Old Spot gammon steak, succulent and not too salty, with a crunchy bean salad. Other popular choices include sewin (the local term for sea trout) teamed with samphire, if you're lucky, and roast suckling pig with artichokes and crisp potatoes.

Desserts will not disappoint. Cherry and almond sponge and St. Emilion of chocolate with mint ice-cream are just two among a mouth-watering selection.

Speciality food: Chargrilled squid, chilli jam and crème fraîche
Draught beers: Speckled Hen, Brains SA
Average wine price by the glass: £2.50

Licensee: Lisa Tebbutt
Last orders for dinner: 9.30 pm
Closed: Sunday and Monday
Closed for holidays: Christmas, 2 weeks February
Set lunch: from £17
Main courses: from £12.95
Private dining: 10-50
Al fresco dining
Children welcome
Wheelchair access

PONTDOLGOCH, POWYS

The Talkhouse ★

GASTROPUB

Pontdolgoch, Nr. Caersws, Powys SY17 5JE
Tel. 01686 688 919 Fax 01686 689 134
e-mail: info@talkhouse.co.uk   **MAP 3** C3

ANYONE arriving in this part of Wales will gaze in wonder at the stunning scenery, but will also wonder why finding a good pub or restaurant in the area is so difficult. The Talkhouse goes some way towards redressing the balance. It also manages the difficult task of keeping the local drinkers happy without compromising the needs of diners.

A comfortable sitting-room for diners and residents sits happily alongside the cosy bar, with its log fire and traditional coaching inn atmosphere. Laura Ashley wallpaper and furnishings – it was just a couple of miles down the road that the creation of her empire began – feature here and in the pleasant dining-room ,which looks out on a pretty, enclosed garden.

The owners pride themselves on their use of local ingredients and handle them in superior fashion, as in a mushroom risotto starter, from the well-balanced choice of dishes on the bar blackboard, which was rich, creamy and not overcooked. Local Welsh lamb, which, of course, has an excellent flavour, is served suitably pink. Other main courses include Gressingham duck with bubble and squeak and fillet of Welsh beef with horse-radish rösti.

Be warned, though – the portions are gargantuan. Even a dessert of delicious greengage and damson fool, containing whole bits of fruit, almost makes a meal in itself.

Accommodation is limited but luxurious.

Speciality food: Local produce
Average wine price by the glass: £3.25

Licensees: Stephen and Jacky Garratt
Last orders for dinner: 9 pm
Closed: Sunday evening, Monday
Closed for holidays: 2 weeks January
Main courses: from £12.95
Private dining: 16-24
Al fresco dining
Accommodation: 3 rooms
Children over 14 welcome
Limited wheelchair access

PWLLHELI, GWYNEDD

Plas Bodegroes ★

Nefyn Road, Pwllheli, Gwynedd LL53 5TH
Tel. 01758 612 363 Fax 01758 701 247
e-mail: gunna@bodegroes.co.uk   **MAP 3** B2

TIES with the beautiful North Wales peninsula brought Christopher Chown – who originally intended to become an accountant – and his wife, Gunna, to their discreet, 18th-century house in the woods, which now also offers a dozen rooms.

In the kitchen, nouvelle tendencies are brushed aside in favour of strong, uncompromising flavours and the pronounced seasoning of Mediterranean and Asian influences.

There is a refreshing vigour about dishes that are presented in all their authentic simplicity, and a mouth-watering honesty about the likes of chicken, chorizo and tarragon terrine with red onion marmalade; lamb's liver with cannelini bean and garlic casserole; fillet of sea bass with crab, ginger and spinach with a crab sauce, or roasted tenderloin of pork with braised cheek and tongue.

After a delightful pre-starter of home-cured bresaola, the seafood ragout that accompanied fillet of nicely grilled red mullet was sheer Mediterranean bliss, packed with raw, natural flavour and enhanced by a rich pesto with plenty of bite.

Then on to Greece or Lebanon for juicy chunks of lamb, kidneys and kofta on a branch of rosemary, a dish of pure simplicity. An aromatic garlic cream and al dente courgettes provided a fitting accompaniment, along with crunchy mangetout and baby maize, before a straightforward apple and rhubarb compote between crisp, light cinnamon wafers on an elderflower custard.

Their pride: Chargrilled monkfish and asparagus with chorizo and lemon
Inexpensive wines: Picpoul de Pinet Beauvignac 2004, £15; Vitiano Falesco (Italy) 2003, £19.50

Proprietors: Chris and Gunna Chown
Last orders for dinner: 9 pm
Closed: Sunday, Monday
Closed for holidays: Mid November-Mid March
Set lunch: from £17.50
Set dinner: from £40
Private dining: 12-16
Accommodation: 11 rooms
Limited wheelchair access

ROSSETT, CLWYD

Churton's Wine & Food Bar ★

Machine House, Chester Road, Rossett, Nr. Wrexham LL12 0HW
Tel. 01244 570 163 Fax 01244 570 099

MAP 3 D2

THIS atmospheric wine and food bar is the best, most relaxed place to eat and drink in the Wrexham area. Converted from a machine-house by Nick Churton sixteen years ago, the mellow bar and vaulted nooks and alcoves ooze character. You could be in the cellar of a traditional wine merchant, which is appropriate since Nick's family were Liverpool's leading wine-shippers.

He still runs a wholesale wine business and imports directly his own champagne, excellent New Zealand Sauvignon and Côtes du Roussillon, all available by the glass. In no way does food play second fiddle to the wine, though. Local fresh produce is the base for some very good cooking, while fresh deliveries of maybe sea bass, king scallops and Morecambe Bay potted shrimps arrive every day.

Care in preparation and finely defined flavours are the keynotes of a home-made cream of mushroom soup and also of the main course, slices of tender and richly flavoured lamb (which has first been marinated), ideally accompanied by faultless boulangère potatoes and mangetout.

To finish, a rich but light chocolate mousse served with fresh, ripe raspberries. What more could one ask?

There are particularly fine burgundies and ports on the serious wine list.

Their pride: Morecambe Bay potted shrimps
Inexpensive wines: Viña Carmen Reserve Carmenère 2002, £17.50; Churton's Sauvignon Blanc (Marlborough) 2004, £16

Proprietor: Nicholas Churton
Last orders for dinner: 10 pm
Closed: Saturday lunch, Sunday
Closed for holidays: 24 December–1st week January
Main courses: from £8.95
Al fresco dining
Wheelchair access

SYCHDYN, FLINTSHIRE

Glasfryn

GASTROPUB

Raikes Lane, Sychdyn, Nr. Mold, Flintshire CH7 6LR
Tel. 01352 750 500 Fax 01352 751 923
e-mail: glasfryn@brunningandprice.co.uk   **MAP 3** D1

SET on a hillside next door to Mold's theatre, this pub overlooks the North Wales market town and the Flintshire countryside. The theatre has made quite a name for itself since Terry Hands, ex-Royal Shakespeare Company, became its director, so customers of the pub are a mix of theatregoers, holidaymakers and locals.

Food is served continuously from 12 noon to 9.30 pm. Standards of food are sound across the board, though sandwiches and lighter things such as Welsh rarebit or roast beef and horse-radish on white bloomer are among the best choices. So is a traditional roast like tender and sweet-flavoured braised shoulder of Welsh lamb.

A superior ploughman's is offered with what might be called broadly local cheeses such as Welsh Brie, Mrs Kirkham's Lancashire and Aldridge's Tournegus.

Other options range from whole grilled lemon sole and haddock and salmon fishcakes to grilled calf's liver with bacon and sweet onions.

Puddings are acceptable, the cherry and almond tart perhaps a touch heavy though the fruit and nut flavours are quite positive.

Unusually, Royal Tokaji Aszu is offered as a dessert wine at a very fair £10.95 for a small bottle (½ litre), which is quite enough for four people. The range of dry whites and reds by the glass comes from across the northern and southern hemispheres. Real ales are well kept and served at correct cellar temperature.

Speciality food: Steak burger, mozzarella, bacon and chips
Draught beers: Timothy Taylor Landlord, Flowers Original
Average wine price by the glass: £2.40

Licensee: James Meakin
Last orders for dinner: 9.30 pm
Open every day
Closed for holidays: 25 and 26 December
Main courses: from £11
Beer garden
Children under 14 welcome before 7 pm
Wheelchair access

WHITEBROOK, MONMOUTHSHIRE

The Crown at Whitebrook ★

Whitebrook, Nr. Monmouth, Monmouthshire NP25 4TX
Tel. 01600 860 254 Fax 01600 860 607
e-mail: infor@crownatwhitebrook.co.uk   **MAP 3** D5

THIS stunning restaurant in a hamlet, well off the beaten track and bordering the Forest of Dean, is set amidst ancient trees with a river flowing below.

The food is exceptional, starting with a selection of hors d'oeuvres which might include venison koftas, salmon roulade and chicken skewers with a cauliflower and cumin broth.

Every dish is a work of art. For instance, an amuse-bouche such as minced, crispy belly of pork will be brought to the table in a porcelain Chinese spoon.

For starters you might opt for a crab and basil muffin, which is deliciously moist, with an intense crab flavour, and accompanied by chilled tomato sabayon. Alternatively, a white asparagus and broad bean mousse is delicate and beautifully paired with a lemon and truffle dressing.

Cleanse the palate with a jasmine and apple granité, then go on to main courses such as chargrilled wild boar, thinly sliced and cooked to perfection, which might come with tiny, fresh girolles, glazed parsnip and a judiciously seasoned thyme velouté. Another option could be pot-roasted quail with port and sage and warm foie gras crème.

Among exquisite desserts, you might try blood orange and lemon Verdemer trifle with ginger crisps.

Their pride: Pot-roasted quail with port and sage
Inexpensive wines: Meinklang Pinot Noir (Austria) 2003, £19; Xarello Classico (Spain) 2004, £13.50

Proprietor: Oliver Bleckmann
Last orders for dinner: 9.30 pm
Closed: Sunday dinner, Monday
Closed for holidays: 23 December-2 January
Set lunch: from £20
Set dinner: from £37.50
Private dining: up to 12
Al fresco dining
Accommodation: 8 rooms
Wheelchair access with notice

Northern Ireland

BELFAST

Aldens

229 Upper Newtownards Road, Ballyhackamore, Belfast BT4 3JF
Tel. 028 9065 0079 Fax 028 9065 0032
e-mail: info@aldensrestaurant.com   **MAP 6** B6

ULSTERMAN Jonathan Davis and his partner Cath Gradwell offer honest, generous fare in this relaxed, smart little no-nonsense restaurant that is well worth the drive or bus ride out to its bustling Belfast suburb.

The formal setting, which relies on subdued contrasts rather than extravagance in its colour scheme, suits lunching businessmen as much as it does courting couples or girls' nights out, but still reflects a serious approach to cooking.

The wide range of largely predictable but nicely varied dishes is the work of Cath Gradwell, who arrived on holiday from Bolton seven years ago and fell in love with bubbly Belfast.

While she might rely largely on trusted favourites such as her cream of celeriac soup with blue cheese croutons, or chicken Caesar salad, steaks and popular fish dishes, there is a touch of innovation in risotto with chorizo and chilli, roasted butternut squash with ceps and goat's cheese fritters, and the impressively presented medallions of tender pork interlaced with thin slices of fried aubergine and fresh spinach in a rich, creamy paprika sauce.

Pan-fried scallops were spot-on and given a nicely contrasting edge of crisply fried angel hair topping creamed leeks spiked with saffron.

Prices are extremely reasonable, without any loss of quality.

Their pride: Crème brûlée
Inexpensive wines: Cheverny Sauvignon Blanc Domaine de Salvard (France) 2003, £14.75; Côtes du Rhône Domaine de Durban 2001, £14.95

Proprietor: Jonathan Davis
Last orders for dinner: 10 pm (Friday & Saturday 11 pm)
Closed: Sunday
Closed for holidays: Bank Holidays
Set dinner: from £17.95
Main courses: from £8
Wheelchair access

BELFAST

Restaurant Michael Deane

36-40 Howard Street, Belfast BT1 6PF
Tel. 028 90331 134 Fax 028 90560 001
e-mail: michael@deanesbelfast.com   **MAP 6** B6

A LEADING light of the Belfast restaurant scene – with the core of his enterprise a brasserie in the style of a Victorian gentlemen's club – Michael Deane is very much hands-on at this city-centre dining-room, where he is proud to retain a decidedly Irish edge to the contemporary influences of a short carte and tasting menu.

Clonakilty black pudding is served with roasted local scallops, scallion crushed potatoes with Irish lamb, native lobster in the sauce accompanying local salmon and cod-stuffed pepper. These are all fine ingredients whose qualities speak for themselves and require straightforward, respectful treatment.

On the other hand, fine, meaty monkfish is wrapped in chunky Irish bacon, which runs the risk of overwhelming the delicate flavours of the seafood and its accompanying bean and parsley broth.

A dessert of rich chocolate roulade and its accompanying mousse was very nicely offset by a fruity black cherry compote.

Guests are very close to the preparation of the meal and, if they want to, can watch Michael Deane and his chef as they go about their duties just beyond the serving hatch.

Their pride: Roasted scallops with black pudding and cauliflower
Inexpensive wines: La Cajole Sauvignon Blanc 2002, £19; Zilzie Shiraz 2001, £19

Proprietor: Michael Deane
Last orders for dinner: 9.30 pm
Closed: lunchtime, Sunday; Mon and Tues (except for private parties)
Closed for holidays: 25-26 December, 1 week July
Main courses: from £35 (2 courses)
Private dining: up to 40

BELFAST

Roscoff ★

7-11 Linenhall Street, Belfast BT2 8AA
Tel. 028 90311 150 Fax 028 90311 151

MAP 6 B6

THE jewel in the crown of TV chef Paul Rankin's multifarious chain of catering outlets is this smart restaurant along the lines of a stylish brasserie. Chic but relaxed, it proclaims itself as devoutly Gallic, with the odd transalpine hint. Dishes have clearly defined, full flavours without much need for modern contrivance. Onion soup, foie gras parfait, duck confit, salmon with a mustard crust, loin of lamb, sirloin of beef with Béarnaise sauce – these old friends jostle the more authentically regional offerings such as seafood bourride, goat's cheese and celeriac tart and slow-roasted shoulder of wild boar with salsify.

The more adventurous customer is catered for with the likes of Roquefort soufflé with pears and walnuts, or butternut squash tortellini with sage butter, or that new-wave favourite scallops with black pudding, accompanied here by leeks.

Generous Irish portions of the best quality ingredients are deftly handled throughout a meal of pleasing regularity and, if there is an underlying simplicity in the approach, that does not detract in any way from the enjoyment of, for instance, veal sweetbreads, perfectly cooked and laid on a bed of nicely nutty lentils with some crispy pancetta for added bite.

A langoustine gratin starter with tomato and basil was bursting with natural flavours and founded on a rich seafood cream with fennel, while a dessert of hazelnuts in attractively rough-cut millefeuille wafers containing plump and still firm roasted plums was a real winner.

Their pride: Crispy duck confit, summer bean cassoulet, Swiss chard
Inexpensive wines: Falasco Garganega Catina val Pantena (Italy) 2003, £16.25; Beaujolais Villages Celliers des Samsons 2004, £18.95

Proprietors: Paul and Jeanne Rankin
Last orders for dinner: Monday-Thursday 10.15 pm, Friday and Saturday 11.15 pm
Closed: Sunday, lunch Saturday
Closed for holidays: 12 July, 25-26 Dec, 1 Jan
Set lunch: from £15.25
Set dinner: from £21.50
Wheelchair access

BUSHMILLS, CO. ANTRIM

Distillers Arms

GASTROPUB

140 Main Street, Bushmills, Co. Antrim BT57 8QE
Tel. 028 2073 1044 Fax 028 2073 2843
e-mail: simon@distillersarms.com   **MAP 6** B5

APART possibly from a guided tour and tasting at the celebrated old whiskey distillery, what could be better than to head for this welcoming hostelry after a trip to the nearby Giant's Causeway?

Extensive refurbishment over the years has created a spacious, airy interior almost along the lines of an Alpine chalet, with acres of pine for the ceiling, floor and simple furnishings, and exposed stonework adding a suitably rustic touch.

Collapse on to well-worn Chesterfields in the bar area with a plate or two of tapas perhaps (including local oysters) to accompany your pre-meal drink while you peruse lunch and dinner menus with no surprises, apart, perhaps, from Asian-influenced scallops won-ton and a Thai green seafood curry, or a breast of duck with rhubarb, kumquat and lemongrass confit.

Excellent local produce ranges from aged Irish beef with chunky chips to fresh lobster, roasted fillets of cod or monkfish and whole sea bass. A richly flavoured (if a touch thin) seafood chowder, with giant prawns and off-cuts of smoked fish, perfumes an enjoyable hotch-potch of root vegetables. In winter, tender beef braised in Guinness, and served in a hollowed-out wheaten loaf provides the ideal warmer.

A deftly accomplished touch is displayed in some impressive desserts such as the rich, light chocolate tart with a chocolate and cardamom sauce, and alternatives such as panna cotta, crème brûlée or mango and passion fruit parfait.

Speciality food: Modern Irish cuisine
Draught beers: Hoegaarden, Bass
Average wine price by the glass: £2.85

Licensee: Simon Clarke
Last orders for dinner: 9 pm
Closed: Monday and Tuesday (during winter)
Main courses: from £10
Private dining: 12-30
Al fresco dining
Children welcome
Wheelchair access

DONAGHADEE, CO. DOWN

Grace Neill's

GASTROPUB

33 High Street, Donaghadee, Co. Down BT21 0AH
Tel. 028 9188 4595 Fax 028 9188 9631
e-mail: info@graceneills.com   **MAP 6** C6

IF THE claim to be Ireland's oldest inn is good enough for Mr. Guinness and his record book, it's obviously good enough for the teeming Americans and Japanese who flock to take photographs amid the beams and collection of antique bottles. In truth, most of the building dates from Victorian times, and today the ghost of the indomitable Grace Neill continues to play the odd trick.

And if the smart, formal restaurant could be called Ireland's newest, the high-ceilinged Library Bar, with wall-to-wall designer books and nautical pictures, nicely bridges the gap between the two eras. A trapdoor leads from there to a tunnel once used by smugglers to bring contraband from the nearby harbour.

Today, the fish in which the place specialises might not use the same route, but most of it is landed from local boats. Traditional pub standards combine excellently with well-made classics that would not be out of place in a smart city dining-room.

But plump mussels; simple grilled plaice; prawn, saffron and chive risotto, or the particularly enjoyable medallions of monkfish with a chorizo cream, crispy pak choi and spiced basmati – all add real class to the customary grills, salads and home-made burgers.

Impressive desserts range from homely steamed ginger pudding to a spot-on crème brûlée with summer berries. It is nice to know that an institution such as this can be remembered as much for its food as for its history.

Speciality food: Local seafood
Draught beers: Guinness, Tennants
Average wine price by the glass: £2.85

Licensee: Grace Neill's Ltd.
Last orders for dinner: Monday-Thursday 9 pm, Friday and Saturday 9.30 pm, Sunday 8 pm
Open every day
Closed for holidays: 25 December, 12 July
Main courses: from £10
Beer garden
Children welcome
Wheelchair access

DUNDRUM, CO. DOWN

Buck's Head

GASTROPUB

77 Main Street, Dundrum, Co. Down BT33 0LU
Tel. 028 4375 1868 Fax 028 4481 1033
e-mail: buckshead1@aol.com   **MAP 6** B6

NOTHING in the record books reveals whether Irish entertainer and songwriter Percy French stopped off in Dundrum, but 'the Mountains of Mourne sweep down to the sea' nearby and he may well have been inspired to compose his verses after a meal at Michael and Alison Crothers' neat little roadside hostelry.

And from the mountains and, especially, the sea come the main ingredients for their enjoyable menus and dinner specialities. That culinary miracle, Irish soda bread, is never far away, used to accompany local oysters (oven-baked or plain), Mourne lamb shank, organic Irish salmon or County Down beef.

Outside influences, often of Asian origin, are skilfully handled, too, from a potently spiced duck salad with pineapple and cracked pepper, to bang-bang chicken salad, Thai mussels (they come from Dundrum) in coconut milk, ginger and chilli, and even Asian chicken with tomato tortilla and Greek salad. Or how about some Kilkeel smoked salmon with Szechuan pickled cucumber?

Their selection of homely desserts is fairly standard, and surely they can do better than a rather dull almond cake that would have benefited enormously from a soaking in some sort of syrup.

Attractive but unfussy presentation matches the squeaky-clean surroundings as black-clad staff serve smilingly in the welcoming bar, in the elegant, wood-panelled dining-room with landscapes by local artists, or out in the pretty little beer garden when the weather allows. Attractive, appetising and unpretentious – it almost makes you want to break into song.

Speciality food: Fresh local seafood
Draught beers: Bass, Erdinger
Average wine price by the glass: £3

> **Licensees: Michael and Alison Crothers**
> **Last orders for dinner: 9.30 pm**
> **Closed: Monday (October-April)**
> **Set dinner: from £21.50**
> **Main courses: from £7.90**
> **Beer garden**
> Children welcome
> Wheelchair access

GILFORD, CO. DOWN

Oriel ★★

2 Bridge Street, Gilford BT63 6HF
Tel. 028 3883 1543 Fax 028 3883 1180
e-mail: info@orielrestaurant.com   **MAP 6** B6

AT THIS little whitewashed corner house a short walk from the town centre, accolades have been fulsome for its brand of modern Irish cooking with strong French influences. Anjou rabbit and pigeon, Bresse chicken and wild mushrooms are flown from France to supplement the best local seafood, the wonderful Fermanagh black pig and Scottish beef, and often organic fruit and vegetables. With these raw materials, culinary imagination and expertise run riot in a comprehensive carte of seasonally inspired offerings full of interest and originality.

Even an often dull carpaccio takes on a new dimension with the addition of foie gras shavings, wild rocket, pickled baby girolles and horseradish aïoli. And a humble risotto is revitalised with local crab, leeks, roasted langoustines and a shellfish cappuccino.

A dish of Fermanagh black pig – braised cheek, confit belly and smoked fillet – with shallot jam, foie gras and reduced jus is put together along fairly traditional lines, as is roasted breast of Gressingham duck with confit leg. It is the stunning presentation that enhances the classical style.

Each garnishing element has its place – like perfectly crisp rösti used to give a welcome crunch to ravioli of Fermanagh ham on celeriac purée, or the delicately tempura battered langoustines topping sublimely grilled sea bass.

As we went to press, the restaurant announced it would move to new premises in 2006.

Their pride: Noisette of Cooley mountain lamb, Clonakilty black pudding, pommes Anna, petits pois à la française, sauce foie gras
Inexpensive wines: Château Haut Roudier 2002, £14.95; Fleur du Cap Chardonnay 2003, £14.95

Proprietor: Barry Smyth
Last orders for dinner: 9.30 pm
Closed: Monday-Wednesday
Closed for holidays: 1 week July, 1 week January
Set lunch: from £15.95
Set dinner: from £15.95
Private dining: 8-14
Wheelchair access

HILLSBOROUGH, CO. DOWN

The Plough

GASTROPUB

3 The Square, Hillsborough, Co. Down BT26 6AG
Tel. 028 9268 2985 Fax 028 9268 2472

MAP 6 B6

THIS warren of dining-rooms and bars, full of antique farming paraphernalia, cosy nooks and crannies with gnarled old beams, and served by cheerfully welcoming staff, certainly seems like a pub, but maybe 'travel agency' would be a more appropriate sign to hang over the door.

For what lies within is a confusion of tastes and culinary styles that launch a world food cruise through sometimes indecipherable menu descriptions. After nibbles – eastern breads, onion bhajis and dips, perhaps – how about black sesame-crusted tuna with samphire, mooli and mizuma salad and zesty lime ponzu dressing for starters?

And even when the ingredients are recognisable – as in crostini of chilli-fried quail's eggs with asparagus, truffle oil and boar bacon rashers, or slow-roasted lamb with sesame sauce, green chilli and lemongrass, beans and curry oil infused couscous – you wonder where some of the ideas originated. The quality of individual ingredients becomes diluted with so much competition on one plate, but what arrives is an enjoyable miscellany of flavours and textures.

Boston fishcakes garnished with meaty Donegal crab and a sweet and sour Asian salad make a cracking starter, and if the seared liver with crispy wild boar, cauliflower gratin and balsamic sage butter amounted to little more than liver and bacon, it was none the worse for that. By comparison, desserts are traditional and the bistro menu is augmented by simpler steaks, home-made burgers and generous and original sandwiches.

Speciality food: Fusion food and seafood specialities
Draught beers: Stella Artois, Guinness
Average wine price by the glass: £3.25

> **Licensee: Richard Patterson**
> **Last orders for dinner: 9.30 pm**
> **Open every day**
> **Closed for holidays: 25 December**
> **Main courses: from £7.50 (bistro), £10.50 (restaurant)**
> **Al fresco dining**
> Children welcome in bistro
> Wheelchair access

Recommend a Restaurant or Gastropub

If you think you have found a restaurant or a gastropub of outstanding quality and worthy of being included in a future Egon Ronay's Guide, then we would like to know about it. Simply fill in the details below, telling us why you believe the place is so special, then cut out the page along the dotted line on the left, and post it to:

Egon Ronay's 2006 Guide
37 Walton Street
London SW3 2HT

RESTAURANT/GASTROPUB NAME

....

ADDRESS

....

....

....

REASONS FOR RECOMMENDATION

YOUR NAME..

YOUR ADDRESS ....

....

....

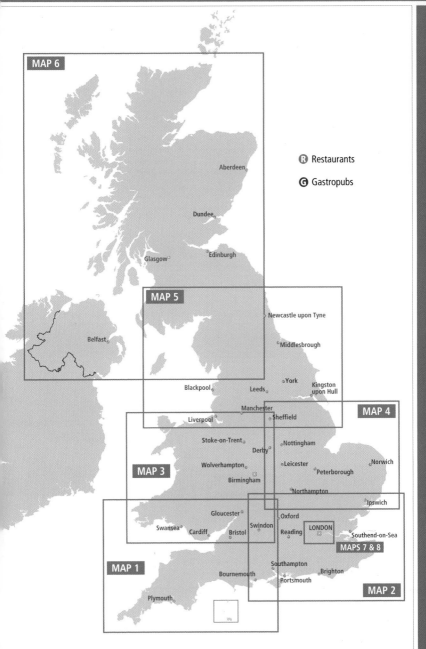

MAP 6

Aberdeen

Dundee

Glasgow
Edinburgh

R Restaurants

G Gastropubs

MAP 5

Belfast

Newcastle upon Tyne

Middlesbrough

York
Kingston
upon Hull

Blackpool   Leeds

Manchester   MAP 4

Liverpool   Sheffield

Stoke-on-Trent
Derby   Nottingham

Wolverhampton   Leicester   Norwich

MAP 3   Birmingham   Peterborough

Northampton

Gloucester   Ipswich

Oxford

Swansea   Cardiff   Swindon   LONDON
Bristol   Reading   Southend-on-Sea

MAPS 7 & 8

MAP 1   Southampton   Brighton

Bournemouth   Portsmouth

Plymouth   MAP 2

Maps prepared by European Map Graphics Ltd.

MAP 1 - SOUTH WEST

	A	B	C
1			
2			
3			Ilfracombe ® Knowstone © DEVON
4		Port Gaverne © Padstow St. Merryn ® ® ® St. Ervan St. Mawgan © CORNWALL	Drewsteignton ® Lifton © Lydford © Chagford © Haytor Vale © Tavistock ® © Peter Tavy PLYMOUTH
5	St. Ives ®	St. Mawes ©	

MAP 2 - SOUTH EAST

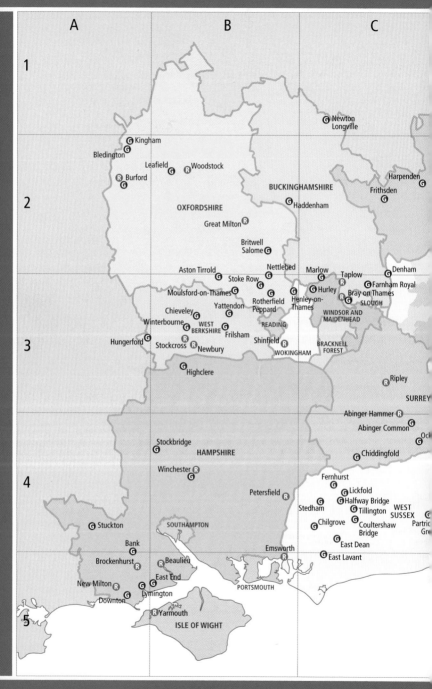

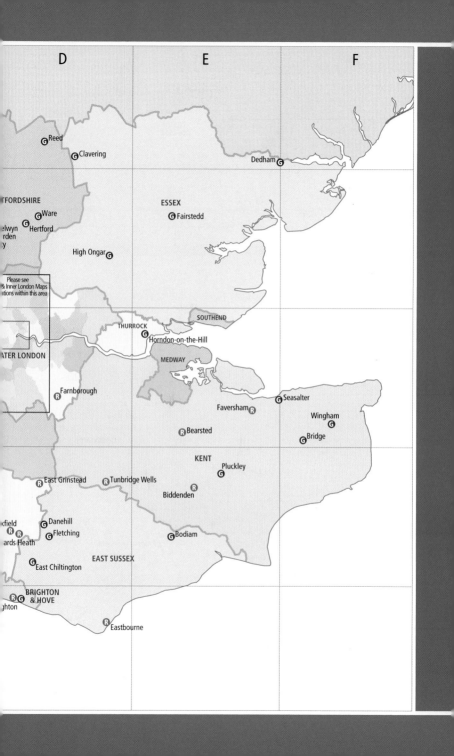

D   E   F

Ⓖ Reed
Ⓖ Clavering
Dedham Ⓖ

HERTFORDSHIRE

ESSEX
Ⓖ Fairstedd

Ⓖ Ware
Ⓖ Hertford
Welwyn
rden
y

High Ongar Ⓖ

Please see
& Inner London Maps
ations within this area

THURROCK
Ⓖ
Horndon-on-the-Hill

SOUTHEND

GREATER LONDON

MEDWAY

Ⓖ Seasalter

Faversham Ⓡ

Wingham
Ⓖ

Ⓡ Farnborough

Ⓡ Bearsted

Ⓖ Bridge

KENT
Pluckley
Ⓖ

Ⓡ East Grinstead   Ⓡ Tunbridge Wells
Biddenden
Ⓡ

xfield
Ⓡ Ⓡ   Ⓖ Danehill
ards Heath   Ⓖ Fletching

Ⓖ Bodiam

EAST SUSSEX
Ⓖ
East Chiltington

BRIGHTON
Ⓡ Ⓖ **& HOVE**
ghton

Ⓡ Eastbourne

MAP 3 - WALES AND WEST MIDLANDS

	A	B	C
1		ISLE OF ANGLESEY · Beaumaris Ⓖ	Llandudno Ⓡ · Llansanffraid Glan Conwy Ⓡ · CONWY · DEN
2		Pwllheli Ⓡ · GWYNEDD	Llandrillo Ⓡ
3		Eglwysfach Ⓡ · CEREDIGION	Pontdol Ⓖ · WALE · POW
4		PEMBROKESHIRE · CARMARTHENSHIRE · Capel Dewi Ⓖ	Felin Fa · Llanfryn
5		SWANSEA · NEATH PORT TALBOT · BRIDGEND	RHONI CYN TAF · VALE GLAMO · M

MAP 4 - EAST MIDLANDS

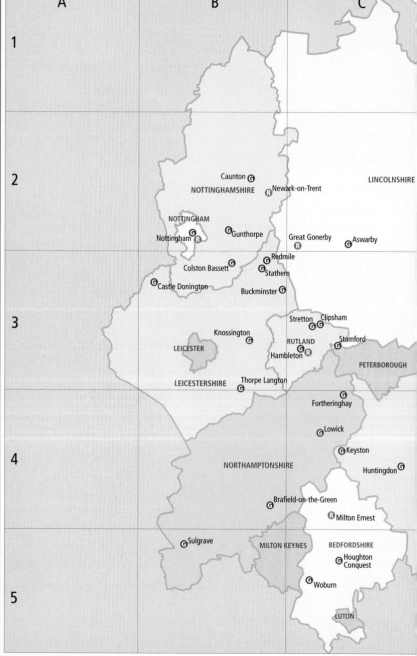

MAP 5 - NORTH

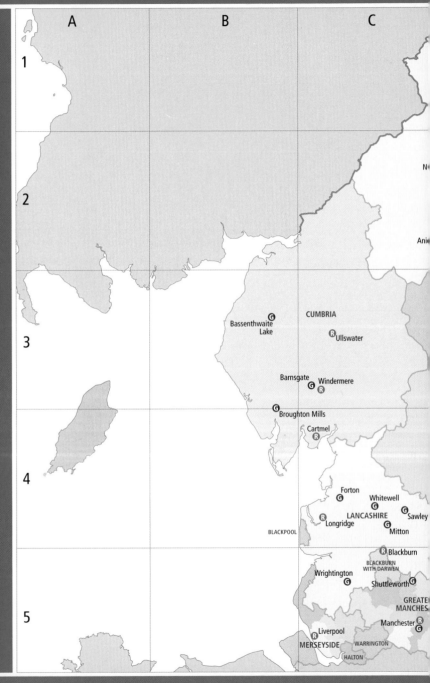

MAP 6 - SCOTLAND & N. IRELAND

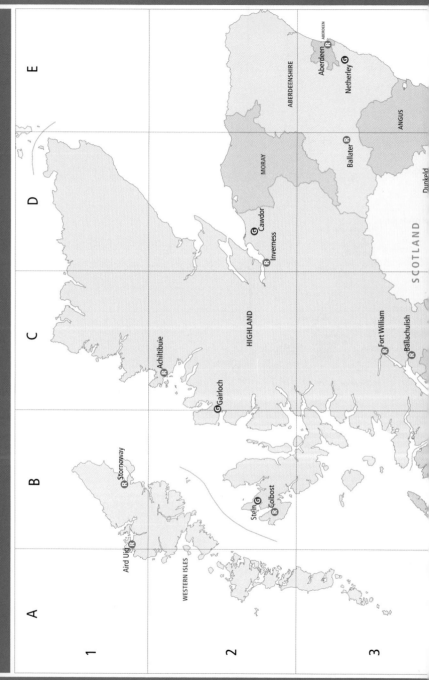

MAP 7 - CENTRAL LONDON

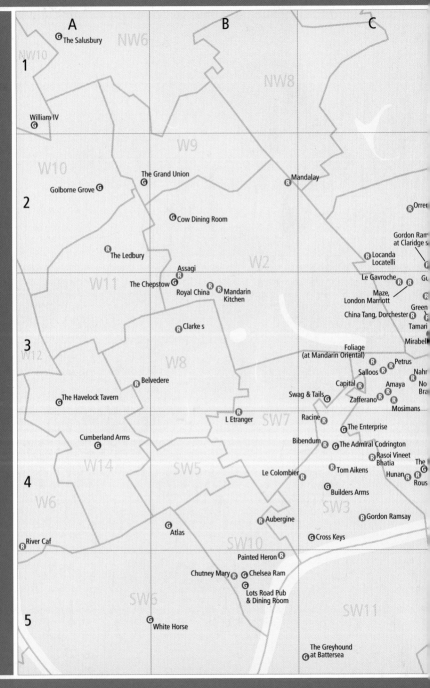

A   B   C

NW6

NW10

1   NW8

William IV

W9

W10

W8

The Grand Union   Mandalay

Golborne Grove

2   Orret

Cow Dining Room

Gordon Ram
at Claridge s

The Ledbury   Locanda
Locatelli

Assagi   W2   Le Gavroche   Gu

The Chepstow   Maze,
Royal China   Mandarin   London Marriott
Kitchen   China Tang, Dorchester   Green

Clarke s   Tamari

Mirabel

3   Foliage
W12   (at Mandarin Oriental)
W8   Salloos   Petrus

Belvedere   Capital   Amaya   Nahr
No
The Havelock Tavern   Swag & Tails   Bra
Zafferano

Mosimans

L Etranger   Racine

Cumberland Arms   The Enterprise

Bibendum   The Admiral Codrington

W14   SW5   Rasoi Vineet   The
Bhatia

Le Colombier   Tom Aikens   Rous

4   Hunan
W6   Builders Arms   SW3

Gordon Ramsay

Atlas   Aubergine
SW10

River Caf   Cross Keys

Painted Heron

Chutney Mary   Chelsea Ram

Lots Road Pub   SW11
& Dining Room

SW6   SW7

5   White Horse

The Greyhound
at Battersea